MACROECONOMICS

 With Study Guide CD-ROM

MACROECONOMICS

 With Study Guide CD-ROM

Jagdish Handa

McGill University, Canada

 **World Scientific**

NEW JERSEY · LONDON · SINGAPORE · BEIJING · SHANGHAI · HONG KONG · TAIPEI · CHENNAI

Published by

World Scientific Publishing Co. Pte. Ltd.

5 Toh Tuck Link, Singapore 596224

USA office: 27 Warren Street, Suite 401-402, Hackensack, NJ 07601

UK office: 57 Shelton Street, Covent Garden, London WC2H 9HE

British Library Cataloguing-in-Publication Data

A catalogue record for this book is available from the British Library.

MACROECONOMICS
(With Study Guide CD-ROM)

ISBN-13 978-981-4289-44-3
ISBN-10 981-4289-44-2

Typeset by Stallion Press
Email: enquiries@stallionpress.com

Printed in Singapore by World Scientific Printers.

To Sushma,
And our sons: Sunny and Rish,
And our delightful grandchildren: Riley, Aerin, Devyn and Logan

Contents

Part III Topics in Open Economy Macroeconomics 373

12. The Foreign Exchange Market, IMF, and Globalization 375

Preface

The state of macroeconomics

"What went wrong with economics? And how the discipline should change to avoid the mistakes of the past"

was on the cover page, and

"Where it went wrong — and how the crisis (of 2007–2009) is changing it"

was the lead article of the venerable *The Economist* in its 18–24 July 2009 issue. Among the subheadings of the related article were *"Rational fools"* and *"Blindsided and divided"*. [*The Economist*, 18 to 24 July 2009, front page and pages 11 to 12.]

On the state of research and teaching of macroeconomics

Some of the opinions from prominent economists quoted by *The Economist* were:

"The past thirty years of macroeconomics training at American and British Universities were a 'costly waste of time'".

"Mr. (Paul) Krugman feared that most macroeconomics of the past thirty years was 'spectacularly useless at best and positively harmful at worst' . . . 'We are living through a 'Dark Age of macroeconomics', in which the wisdom of the ancients has been lost'".

"Mr. (Willem) Buiter argues that a training in modern macroeconomics was a 'severe' handicap at the onset of the financial crisis . . .".

"The mainstream macroeconomics embodied in DSGE (Dynamic Stochastic General Equilibrium Models) was a poor guide to the origins of the financial crisis" . . . "According to David Colander, . . . macroeconomics is often the least popular class . . . . Mr. Colander asked a group of Chicago students. "Did you do the dynamic stochastic general equilibrium model?' 'We learnt a lot of junk like that,' one replied." [Above quotes taken from *The Economist*, 18 to 24 July 2009, pages 11–12 and 65–67; material in parentheses added.]

"The unfortunate uselessness of most state of the art monetary economics. . . . (research) since the 1970s has been motivated by the internal logic, intellectual sunk capital and aesthetic puzzles . . . rather than by a powerful desire to understand how the economy works; let alone how the economy works during times of stress and financial instability" (Willem Buiter, quoted in *The Hindu*, Business Line, 18 March 2009; material in parentheses added).[1]

The Economist has not been the only magazine to express such views. The last two years have witnessed a cacophony of similar views in serious journals, in newspapers, and magazines, on the radio, TV, and the Internet. Among others have been:

'The emperor has no clothes'.

And we might add:

'Economists are no better than astrologers and soothsayers. But the public and the country suffer far more from their views'.

---

[1] http://www.blonnet.com/2009/03/18/stories/2009031850070900.htm.

But then, what justifies another macroeconomics textbook?

In view of all the doubts and dismal opinions of the dismal science[2] held by the public and economists about the validity and relevance of macroeconomics and its teaching, it must be a wonder that one not only admits to teaching macroeconomics but even dares to write another textbook on the subject. We do so because of our strong belief that macroeconomics and its policy prescriptions are both relevant and need to be learnt to understand what has been happening in recent years, while recognising that the subject and its presentation do need to be changed. Further, there is a glaring lacuna in macroeconomics in that it does not incorporate an adequate analysis of the role of credit in the economy. It is also unfortunate that the teaching of macroeconomics in recent decades has dropped the analysis of disequilibrium and the scope of policies relevant to disequilibrium.

The reformulation of macroeconomics

Macroeconomics is not only one of the pillars of economics, it is probably the most relevant and exciting part of economics for most people, since it deals with the economy and its impact on their job prospects and personal portfolios, as well as explaining the analysis behind the economic and business headlines in newspapers and periodicals. Macroeconomics is rich in theories, but not all are equally good at explaining the stylized facts. This book teaches the students the differences between their assumptions and implications and the use of stylized facts to discriminate among them.

What the quotes above on the sorry state of macroeconomics clearly indicate is that the exposition of macroeconomics needs to be revised, perhaps drastically. As a starting point, its theories have to be tested by their concordance with facts and, if they prove to be invalid (i.e., useless for explaining the economic reality that we live in), they need to be rejected or revised. The revision of theories has to start with the empirical validity of their assumptions, and move on to testing the validity of their implications and predictions. This book undertakes these tasks, and makes the relevance of the established theories to the related stylized facts of the economy a central part of its exposition.

While the general equilibrium assumption can be useful in learning about the healthy state and good times of the macroeconomy, its dominance in macroeconomics to the exclusion of disequilibrium analysis has been central to the recent failure of macroeconomics and its teaching. It should be now beyond dispute that economies do sometimes go into disequilibrium and stay in it. The causes of potential disequilibrium and its analysis have been missing from most macroeconomics textbooks for some decades, and need to be reinstated. Chapter 9 of this book does so.

What also seems to be indicated by the proclaimed sorry state of macroeconomics is that divisions within its schools have been overdone to the detriment of the validity of macroeconomics.[3] The presentation of and emphasis on these divisions needs to be reduced. If any observation can be explained by several theories (from different schools), we should integrate all of them for a fuller explanation of the observation. Why care from which school the various components originated? This implies downplaying the schools in macroeconomics,

---

[2] 'The dismal science' was the name given to economics by the social reformer Thomas Carlyle in the mid-19th century. The name stuck, and justly so in many ways.

[3] "The fault lies not with economics, but with economists. The problem is that economists became overconfident in their preferred models...". "They forgot that there were many other models that led in radically different directions. Hubris creates blind spots. If anything needs fixing, it is the sociology of the profession". (Quotes taken from an article by Dani Rubrik, in *The Hindu*, New Delhi, 14 March 2009).

and looking directly at the relevant theories. This book adopts this approach (see especially Chapter 8) and subsequently collects the main theories of macroeconomics into the classical and Keynesian paradigms and confines the presentation of these two paradigms into one chapter. Its approach is: learn the relevant theories first (in Chapters 1 to 10), independent of their origins, and then learn the paradigms (set out in Chapter 11) and, to satisfy one's intellectual curiosity, find out in which paradigm they originated.

The emphasis in macroeconomic textbooks has for some decades drifted toward the presentation of long-run equilibrium and growth theories, to the detriment of short-run and disequilibrium analysis. Such an orientation is justified for studying the changes in the standards of living over long periods. It is less justified from the perspective of understanding the economic world that we constantly experience. This book redresses this trend, and brings the presentation of the short-term economics to the early parts of the book.

Understanding the economic crisis of 2007–2010 requires revision of macroeconomics to address the glaring omission of credit in current macroeconomic modelling.[4] This crisis also firmly establishes the non-neutrality of both money and credit in the short run. This book incorporates the relevant analysis of credit (see Chapter 16) and implies its non-neutrality, as well as the non-neutrality of money and financial institutions, in the modern economy (Chapters 8 and 9).[5] Even in the context of very long-term growth, this book distinguishes between the neutrality of money and the non-neutrality of the economy's financial structure (Chapter 15).

More specifically on this book

This book presents the current state of knowledge of macroeconomics relevant to elementary and intermediate undergraduate courses. The goal of the book is to provide students with adequate knowledge to: (i) understand the stylized macroeconomic facts, (ii) to learn the rich variety of economic theories and the differences in their implications, (iii) to use the theories to explain the stylized facts, and (iv) to understand the major differences between the developed economies and the developing ones.

This book brings to its treatment of macroeconomics a fresh perspective on the coverage of macroeconomic theories and their validity. Economics is a social science, whose objective is to explain economic reality. This perspective focuses on the ability or inability of the existing theories to explain the established stylized macroeconomic facts, especially on the relationship between monetary and fiscal policies and output and employment. The relevant stylized facts have been established over several decades by intuition and empirical studies, though few macroeconomics textbooks pay adequate attention to them. The recent (2007 to 2010) economic crisis and recession in many economies provide a rich topical confirmation of many of these stylized facts.

Among the stylized facts of macroeconomics is that related to the behavior of the central bank in its pursuit of monetary policy. The general assumption of most macroeconomics books is that the central bank controls and operates on the money supply as the primary monetary policy tool, so that the appropriate assumption for the exposition of macroeconomics is that the money supply is held exogenous. This assumption leads to the IS-LM model for the determination of aggregate demand. This assumption and the resulting IS-LM model are quite unrealistic for many countries, especially developed ones, whose central banks have claimed at least since the mid-1990s that they operate on interest rates as their primary monetary policy tool. This claim changes the exposition of short-run macroeconomics to one in which the interest rate is held exogenous. Few

---

[4]For virtually all textbooks, financial institutions providing credit do not exist, so that a credit collapse can have no impact on output and employment in the economy. The extent to which banks are envisaged is as creators of money, but not as providers of credit.

[5]In many macroeconomic models, finance is a veil, as is money, so that a credit collapse has no impact on output.

textbooks set out this exposition. This book does so, and calls the resulting short-run macroeconomic model of aggregate demand the IS-IRT model. However, for completeness and to allow instructors a choice between the IS-LM and IS-IRT expositions, this book presents both these models.

Major features of this book

Among the highlights of this book are:

- Rigorous economic analysis and intuitive insights.
- Stylized macroeconomics facts, which are used to discuss the validity and usefulness of theories.
- Treatment of open economy macroeconomics early in the book and throughout the book. Open economy material is integrated into the macroeconomic analysis from the very beginning (Chapters 3 and 5). This treatment is supplemented by Chapters 12 and 13, which include coverage of many topics such as the foreign exchange market, persistence of deficits and surpluses in the balance of payment even when the exchange rate is floating, the J curve, Globalization, Dollarization and Currency Boards, the Gold Standard, and the IMF (including discussion of whether the IMF should evolve into the world's central bank).
- As an illustration of the use of stylized facts to select among theories and/or modify them, this book (Chapters 3 and 13) questions the validity of Purchasing Power Parity on the basis of the stylized facts on price differences across economies, and does not assume PPP in setting up its macroeconomic models. Similarly, Chapters 3 and 13 question some of the unrealistic implications of the Interest Rate Parity theory and modify the Interest Rate Parity condition to allow for deviations of interest rates among countries.
- A fundamental stylized fact relates to how central banks seek to control or influence output and employment through their monetary policies: do they act in such a way that macroeconomic theory can build its model on an exogenously given money supply (leading to the IS-LM model of aggregate demand) or do they act in such a way that macroeconomic theory can build its model on an exogenously given interest rate (leading to the IS-IRT model, which is explained in Chapter 5 of this book (and almost never in other macroeconomic textbooks). This is a factual question on which many central banks, especially in developed economies, claim that they directly operate on interest rates, not the money supply, in the economy. This monetary policy procedure renders the traditional IS-LM model of aggregate demand irrelevant for many economies, though it is still the mainstay of most macroeconomics textbooks. This book also examines the conditions under which the central bank would prefer to use interest rate targeting or monetary targeting, and vice versa.
- The assumption that the central bank uses the interest rate, rather than the money supply, as its primary monetary policy instrument for controlling aggregate demand is central to the currently popular Taylor Rule and the New Keynesian economics. However, the relevant analysis (called the IS-IRT one in this book, with IRT standing for 'interest rate targeting' as against 'monetary targeting' that leads to the IS-LM analysis) is not set out in almost all other undergraduate and even most graduate, books on macroeconomics. This book presents in Chapter 5 the relevant macroeconomic analysis for the case in which the central bank primarily sets the interest rate.
- For completeness, this book provides both the IS-IRT (Chapter 5) and IS-LM (Chapter 6) models of aggregate demand for the open economy. The instructor is thus provided with the choice of doing only the analysis relevant to their particular country and its central bank's monetary policy, or doing both.

- This book separates the analysis of the long run (Chapter 7), the analysis of the short-run based on errors in expectations, adjustment costs of changing prices, employment, the capital stock and output (Chapter 8), and disequilibrium (Chapter 9). A major argument differentiating this book from others is that the economy can be out of both long-run and short-run equilibrium — and therefore, in disequilibrium. Chapter 9 shows that the implications of disequilibrium for monetary and fiscal policies can differ considerably from those of long run and short run equilibrium.

- The treatment of short-run deviations of output from the long-run one is explained in Chapter 8 as arising from many causes. These include errors in expectations (due to the costs of acquiring adequate information and deriving its implications for the revision in expectations), and the adjustment costs of changing prices (as in the menu cost theory). But they also include the adjustment costs of changing employment (leading to labor hoarding and Okun's rule), the physical capital stock and output. All these occur in the short-run and collectively determine the short-run output and employment.

- The analysis of disequilibrium and the likely behaviour of firms and households and the policies relevant to disequilibrium have often been neglected in many macroeconomics textbooks published over the last three decades. This book devotes a whole chapter (Chapter 9) to this analysis. The relevance of this chapter to the economic crises and fluctuations in output and employment, as during 2007–2010, should not be ignored.

- On the basis of the stylized facts established from earlier studies — and reinforced by the recession of 2007–2010 — one has to reject the relevance and validity of the long-run equilibrium and short-run equilibrium theories to the explanation of many of the stylized facts. The disequilibrium analysis, especially of demand-deficient conditions, presented in Chapter 9 of this book is more appropriate.

- This book provides an explicit analysis of credit as distinct from bonds, and the impact of a credit crisis on the other sectors of the economy. This material is especially relevant to understanding the causes of many downturns in the economy, and to the study of financial and economic crises. Such analysis is missing from most other macroeconomics textbooks but is vital to understanding the Asian Crises of the mid-1990s and the worldwide one during 2007–2010.

- This book discusses (in Chapter 11) the heritage and evolution of theories of the major schools of thought in macroeconomics. It organizes them into the classical and Keynesian *paradigms*, and explains why it is desirable to study both. The exposition of the theories is followed by a comparison of the predictions of the theories with the stylized macroeconomics facts to decide on the validity and relative usefulness of the various theories.

- This book divides its presentation of the analysis of economic growth into two chapters. Chapter 14 focuses on the Solow/neoclassical model of growth, without technical change and with exogenous technical changes. An important topic treated in this chapter is the historical experience of growth epochs, starting with the Malthusian theory for agricultural societies and ending with the modern and post-modern stages of growth of already industrialized societies. Chapter 15 sets out the endogenous growth theories. It also studies the relationship between the growth of output on the one hand and, on the other hand, money supply growth, the inflation rate and the development of the financial structure of the economy.

- The ups and downs of business cycles are very important to the average person and to firms. Contrary to a belief prevalent in the 1980s and 1990s, cyclical fluctuations have not been eliminated or sufficiently moderated. Chapter 16 explains their causes and the evolution of their stages. It also explores the relationship between financial developments and crises and economic crises. Further, it provides an explicit treatment of how a credit crisis can cause adverse shifts in both aggregate supply and aggregate demand in the economy. This exposition helps students to explain why the credit crisis of 2007 in the USA developed into an economic one in 2008 and how the stimulatory monetary and fiscal policies were able to shorten its duration and decrease its intensity.

The book also innovates in its presentation in several ways. These include:

- **Fact Sheets**: Each chapter has Fact Sheets to provide graphs on the major points relevant to the chapter. These Fact Sheets use data from: the USA, the world's largest economy; Canada, a developed small economy; and several developing economies, which include Thailand, Malaysia, China, and India.
- **Boxes**: There are three types of boxes (Boxes, Extended Analysis Boxes, and Mathematical Boxes) in each chapter. These boxes dig deeper into the analysis or the relevant facts, so that they extend the material beyond that in the text. Extended Analysis boxes provide advanced material and are meant to give the instructor the choice between whether to omit them or cover them. Mathematical boxes provide the students with the knowledge relevant to the economic theories presented in the chapter.
- **Review of material**: Besides bulleted Conclusions, each chapter has at its end Key Concepts and Summary of Critical Conclusions, which facilitates the student's review their knowledge of the material of the chapter.
- **Questions**: The book divides the questions at the end of each chapter into Review and Discussion Questions, and Technical and Advanced Questions. Less mathematically oriented courses can omit the Technical Questions.
- **Technical Questions**: The technical questions at the end of each chapter require knowledge of high school algebra and the ability to solve linear equations, but do not require any university level mathematical courses and specifically do not require knowledge of calculus. While the technical questions and their solutions can be omitted from courses using only verbal arguments, intuition, and diagrams, they do illustrate and deepen the knowledge of the theories and their implications presented in the chapter.
- **Calculus**: While the book, especially its Mathematical boxes and Technical Questions, rely on knowledge of high school mathematics, they do not require a prior knowledge of calculus (or teach it).

Coverage of the Textbook Over Two Semesters

This book consists of 16 chapters, which are meant to be covered over two semesters, so that each chapter would take on average about two weeks to cover. Instructors can choose the pattern of coverage of the chapters according to:

- Chapters 1 to 9 are designed to provide a very good one-semester introductory course in macroeconomics, with the major emphasis on short-run economics. If desired, these chapters can be supplemented by Chapter 16 on business cycles and economic crises. If this beginning course is followed by an intermediate macroeconomics course, the latter would cover the more advanced Chapters 10 to 16.
- If the desired focus of the first course is more on growth, the appropriate chapters for it would be Chapters 1 to 3 and 14 to 16, along with some additional chapters selected by the instructor.

Study Guide

The book comes with a Study Guide on an enclosed CD. Each chapter of the Study Guide provides an introduction to the main topics in the chapter, followed by answers to the Review and Discussion questions, as well as the Technical and Advanced questions, at the end of the chapter.

Acknowledgments

I am indebted to several generations of students who used my macroeconomics course notes. Their comments helped me refine the material in this book. I am especially indebted to several teaching and research assistants over the years for writing or revising the answers in the Study Guide.

I especially wish to acknowledge the assistance of Oana Ciobanu with the Fact Sheets in the chapters, and of Marc Jean Baraghid with the final version of the Study Guide.

Prof. Jagdish Handa
McGill University, Montreal, Canada
Jagdish.handa@mcgill.ca

About the Author

The author is Professor of Economics at McGill University, Montreal, Canada, and has taught Macroeconomics for more than 40 years.

Prof. Handa has published several books and numerous articles in journals, many of them related to macroeconomics and monetary economics. Among his related textbooks is *Monetary Economics* (first edition, 2000; second edition, 2008), which provides a comprehensive treatment of monetary theory and policy at an advanced level.

Glossary of Symbols

B	nominal balance of payments
B^c	nominal balance of payments on current account
B^k	nominal balance of payments on capital account
c	consumption expenditures
c_0	autonomous consumption
$D^\$$	demand for our currency ($) in foreign exchange markets
e	aggregate expenditures (in real terms)
FR	foreign exchange reserves
g	government expenditures on commodities
i	(planned/desired/*ex ante*) investment expenditures
i^u	unintended investment
i_0	autonomous investment
i^a	actual investment ($\equiv i + i^u$)
K	real capital stock
L	labor force
LR	long run
M	money
M0	monetary base
M1	narrow definition of money ($=$ currency $+$ demand deposits)
M2	broad definition of money ($=$ M1 $+$ savings deposits)
n	employment (labor employed)
NR	net inflows of funds to the country for interest and dividend payments ($=$ IR $-$ OR)
NT	net inflows of funds to the country from unilateral transfers ($=$ IT $-$ OT)
OR (IR)	outflows (inflows) of funds to the country for interest and dividend payments
OT (IT)	outflows (inflows) of funds from the country due to unilateral transfers
r	real rate of interest
r^T	target real rate of interest set by the central bank
R	nominal/market rate of interest
P	price level (i.e., consumer price index or GDP deflator)
P^F	foreign price level
$S^\$$	supply of our currency ($) in foreign exchange markets
s	(private) saving
s^n	national saving ($\equiv s + t - g$)
SR	short run

t net taxes paid (government's tax revenues less government transfers to the public)
t_0 autonomous net taxes paid
u actual rate of unemployment
U level of unemployment
u^n natural (i.e., long-run equilibrium) rate of unemployment
u^* short-run equilibrium rate of unemployment
$u^* - u^n$ deviation of short-run equilibrium unemployment rate from the natural one
$u - u^*$ unemployment rate due to disequilibrium (i.e., deviation of actual unemployment rate from the short-run equilibrium one)
x_c real amount of exports of commodities in domestic commodity units
X_c nominal value of exports of commodities in domestic currency units
y aggregate quantity of commodities (also often referred to as real output/national income)
Y nominal value of output ($=$ nominal national income $= Py$)
y^d aggregate real demand for commodities
y^s aggregate real supply of commodities
y^f full-employment (i.e., long-run equilibrium) real output/income
y^* short-run equilibrium level of real output/income
z_c/ρ^r real amount of imports of commodities in domestic commodity units
Z_c nominal value of imports of commodities in domestic currency units
π [pi] rate of inflation ($\equiv P''$)
π^e expected inflation rate ($\equiv P''^e$)
ρ ['rho'] nominal exchange rate ($=$ amount of a foreign currency required to purchase one unit of the domestic currency, denoted as £/$)
ρ^r real exchange rate ($=$ amount (i.e., number of units) of foreign commodities required to purchase one unit of the domestic commodity)

The small letter symbol indicates the real value of the variable while the capital one indicates its nominal (dollar) value. One exception to this rule is the use of K to designate the real value of the physical capital stock.

The superscript d on a variable indicates its demand and the superscript s will indicate its supply. The variable symbol without either of these superscripts indicates its actual value. If there exists equilibrium, the actual value is the equilibrium one, i.e., one at which the demand and supply for that variable are equal. Thus, n^d is the demand for labor and n^s is its supply, while n is actual employment.

Symbols Used in Growth Theory Chapters 14 and 15

K real amount of capital
k real capital–labor ratio
L labor force ($=$ employment)
n growth rate of labor force
η rate of growth in the efficiency of workers
S total real saving
s saving per capita ($= S/L$))
σ average propensity to save (APS) out of output ($= S/Y$)
Y real value of output ($=$ real income $= Py$)
y output per capita ($= Y/L$)

Useful Mathematical Symbols and Formulae for Economics

∂ [di] change in the following symbol, holding all other things, i.e., other exogenous variables, the same (e.g., $\partial y/\partial i$ means change in y for a *very small* change in i, *ceteris paribus*). ∂ is a mathematical symbol pronounced as 'di', so that $\partial y/\partial i$ is pronounced as 'di y di i').

Δ [delta] change in the following symbol, holding all other things, i.e., other exogenous variables, the same. Δy is pronounced as 'delta y'.

$\equiv$ identity (that is always true) or identical to

$=$ equilibrium condition or equal to

$'$ change in (the preceding variable)

$''$ rate of change (growth) in (the preceding variable)

Superscripts

d demand for (the preceding variable)

e expected value

F foreign (e.g., P^F is foreign price level)

s supply of (the preceding variable)

Special use of subscripts

y_d disposable real national income

Greek Letters Used

α alpha

β beta

γ gamma

ρ rho

σ sigma

η eta

θ theta

∂ di

Δ delta

Designation of the change in a variable

Economics often focuses on the *change in a variable caused by a change in another variable*, if all other variables were to be held constant. The Latin phrase used for 'holding all other things (variables) constant' is *ceteris paribus*. The most appropriate symbol (borrowed from calculus) for a change (which need not be 'small') in y caused by a 'very small' change in x, *ceteris paribus*, is $\partial y/\partial x$. ∂ is a Greek symbol, which is pronounced as 'di'. The term $\partial y/\partial x$ is pronounced as 'di y, di x' and is often spoken as 'the derivative of y with respect of x'. Using this symbolism is much more convenient than writing the longer form 'change in y for a very small change in x, all other things held constant'. Therefore, we will often use this symbol, though without invoking the use of calculus for any derivation connected with it. That is,

$$\partial y/\partial x = \text{a change in } y \text{ for a very small change in } x, \text{ with other things being held constant.}$$

Designation of the rate of change (growth rate) in a variable

Economics often examines the effect of *a change in a variable over time*. The symbol for the change in a variable y over time is $\partial y/\partial t$. We will usually use the even shorter symbol y' for it. For period analysis, y'_t will equal $(y_{t+1} - y_t)$, or Δy_t (where Δ is a Greek symbol pronounced as capital delta), where the subscript t stand for the time period and Δ stands for 'change in'. However, for continuous time analysis, the appropriate symbol is $\partial y/\partial t$. That is,

$$y'_t = (y_{t+1} - y_t) = \partial y/\partial t$$

where $y'_t \ (= \partial y/\partial t)$ means the change in y for a very small change in t.

The *rate of growth (or change) of the variable y over time* will be designated as y''. It is obtained by dividing y'_t by y_t, so that:

$$y''_t = (y_{t+1} - y_t)/y_t = \frac{\partial y}{\partial t} \cdot \frac{1}{y}$$

In continuous time analysis, the rate of growth is also often designated by a dot placed over the variable symbol. However, our usual usage for the rate of growth (over time) will be y''.

If output y grows at the rate 5% per period, it is often written as 0.05. Conversely, writing the growth rate 0.05 in percentage terms requires multiplying it by 100, which gives 5%.

Useful mathematical formulae on growth rates to remember

If

$$z = xy$$

then,

$$z'' = x'' + y''$$

That is, if a variable is a multiple of two other variables, its growth rate is the sum of the growth rates of the two component variables.

If

$$z = x/z$$

then,

$$y'' = x'' - z''$$

That is, if a variable is a ratio of two other variables, its growth rate equals the difference between the growth rates of the numerator and the denominator.

Splitting the growth rate of nominal (value of) output into real output growth and inflation

An example of the preceding formulae occurs from the definition of nominal output Y (which is the dollar value of the quantity produced) as equal to the price level multiplied by real output y (which is the physical amount of the quantity produced). That is, $Y \equiv Py$. The symbol $\equiv$ indicates an identity, while $=$ indicates an equilibrium. From $Y \equiv Py$, we derive $Y'' \equiv P'' + y''$. Since P'' is the rate of change of the price level, which is the definition of the rate of inflation, for which our symbol will be π, we can write:

$$Y'' \equiv y'' + \pi$$

This equation asserts that the growth rate of the nominal (dollar) value of the commodities produced in the economy equals the growth rate of their real value (i.e., the quantity produced) plus the rate of inflation.

From the preceding discussion, we can derive the following formula:
If

$$x \equiv y/z$$

then,

$$x'' \equiv y'' - z''$$

That is, if a variable is a ratio of two other variables, its growth rate is the difference between the growth rates of the numerator and the growth rate of the denominator. Therefore, since $y \equiv Y/P$, we have:

$$y'' \equiv Y'' - P''$$

$$\equiv Y'' - \pi$$

Hence, the real output growth rate is the growth rate of its nominal value *less* the inflation rate.

PART I
Introduction to Macroeconomics

CHAPTER 1
Output, Unemployment, and the Basic Concepts

Macroeconomics studies the functioning of the economy at the aggregative level. It encompasses the study of the economy when it is performing at its optimal level as well as when it has deviations from this level. In both cases, macroeconomics examines whether the economy's performance can be improved through the use of monetary, fiscal, and other governmental policies.

The fundamental questions of macroeconomics concern the levels of output and its rate of growth, unemployment and inflation in the economy, and changes in them. Their determination is studied in the contexts of the short run and the long run.

Economics is a science. It builds theories to explain the real-world, real-time observations on its variables of interest and subjects the predictions of its theories to statistical tests through the use of econometrics.

1.1 Introduction to Macroeconomics

Macroeconomics is the study of the functioning of the economy at the macro or aggregative level. Its main variables of interest are:

- output and the standard of living,
- unemployment,
- the price level and inflation,
- interest rates and the money supply,
- balance of payments and exchange rates,
- the impact of government expenditures, taxes, and deficits on the economy, and
- the central bank's policies on money supply and interest rates and their impact on the economy.

A proper study of these topics involves the study of numerous other variables. Among these are wages, consumption, saving and investment, exports and imports, capital flows between countries, labor demand and supply, money demand and supply, etc.

1.1.1 The nature of macroeconomic analysis

A general study of the whole economy can be formulated in two distinct ways:

i. As a *general equilibrium microeconomic model.*
   This formulation includes a separate specification of the market for each good, as in microeconomic analysis. Such a system is a very detailed one, studying as it does the separate demand, supply, and price of each good in the economy. It is, however, quite cumbersome for macroeconomic purposes where the objective is to focus on a few macroeconomic variables only.

ii. As a *macroeconomic model*.

Such a model aggregates the very large number of goods in the economy into a small number of categories. This formulation reduces the number of goods and their markets to be studied to a manageable level. Obviously, the degree of aggregation used must depend upon the intended use of the resulting model or framework.

The classification of goods in macroeconomics

Short-run macroeconomics normally classifies all goods in the economy into five categories.

1. commodities (commonly known as 'goods and services'),
2. money (i.e., currency and demand deposits),
3. bonds (i.e., non-monetary financial assets, so that the term 'bonds' in macroeconomics includes equities),
4. labour,
5. foreign exchange (mainly foreign currencies and gold).

Closed economy versus open economy analysis

For heuristic reasons, macroeconomics is often first presented in closed economy models that are later extended to the open economy. *A closed economy* is one that does not have international trade in commodities or capital flows with other countries. *An open economy* is one that has such linkages. These linkages imply an additional degree of complication of analysis, so that one needs to master the closed economy models to better understand the open economy ones.

The closed economy macroeconomic models analyze the markets for four goods: commodities, money, bonds, and labor, and assume that there is no trade in these between the domestic economy and foreign ones. The open economy models of macroeconomics assume that there is trade in the above four goods between the domestic and foreign economies. They also include the analysis of the market for foreign exchange.

Short-run macroeconomic theories, growth theories and business cycle theories

The main focus of the *short-run macroeconomic theories* is on the impact of shocks to the macro economy and the effects of fiscal, monetary, and other policies on aggregate output, unemployment, and the other variables of interest mentioned above. The main focus of *growth theories* is on the long-run evolution of the total output of the economy and of the standard of living. The main focus of *business cycle theories* is on the variations in output and unemployment, inflation and interest rates over the business cycle.

1.2 The Classification of Economic Agents and Markets in Short-Run Macroeconomic Models

Macroeconomics treats labor as an input in the production of commodities, whose purchase for consumption or investment is transacted with money as a medium of exchange/payments. Labor is provided by workers/households who receive wages as payment for the work. Households receive not only wages but also interest and profits from their ownership of physical capital (including land and housing). The sum of these receipts constitutes national income. The demands for domestic and imported commodities (including physical capital), bonds (non-monetary financial assets), and money depend on national income (which is generated by production) and national wealth.

The basic classification of economic units in the economy is into:

- Households, which supply labor as workers and are the owners of capital. They receive wages and profits (or interest) from their ownership of capital, and decide on consumption, saving, and money and bond holdings.
- Firms, which engage in the production of output by hiring labor (and any other inputs) to use with their capital. They incur investment to change their capital stock, and issue bonds (including equities) to finance their investment. Financial institutions, such as banks, are firms under this classification. Firms are assumed to maximize profits.
- While non-government organizations (NGOs)[1] usually do not attempt to maximize profits, macroeconomic analysis, for simplification, does not include their separate analysis and just lumps them in the category of firms.
- The government ('the fiscal authority'), which decides on the government expenditures and taxes. It finances its fiscal deficits by raising funds in the financial markets by selling bonds to the public. It uses fiscal surpluses to buy back some of its (outstanding) bonds from the public. In contrast with firms, it is not assumed to be a profit-maximizer.
- The central bank ('the monetary authority'), which decides on the money supply and interest rates.
- Foreign economies, which trade in commodities (as exports and imports) and bonds (which result in financial capital flows between the foreign and the domestic economies). These flows of commodities and financial capital are captured in the balance of payments. The amount of foreign currencies, foreign bonds, and gold held by the country are the major part of its foreign exchange reserves and the exchange rate is the rate of exchange between the domestic currency and foreign ones.

As mentioned earlier, there are five distinct, composite goods in macroeconomic analysis: commodities (including physical capital), bonds, money, labor, and foreign exchange. Their 'markets' are referred to as markets or sectors, the two terms being used interchangeably. Therefore, the macroeconomic model has five markets:

1. the commodity (or product) market,
2. the money market,
3. the financial (i.e., bonds, and equities) market,
4. the production-employment sector composed of the labor market and the production function, and
5. the foreign exchange market, whose analysis captures payment flows occurring due to the country's economic exchanges with the rest of the world.

The specification of each market requires (i) its demand function, (ii) its supply function, and (iii) an equilibrium condition.

Only the first four markets are studied for the closed economy — that is, an economy that does not have commodity or capital flows with other countries. Virtually all countries now have an open economy — that is, an economy with exchanges of goods with other economies. The common procedure in macroeconomics is to first build models for the closed economy and then to modify them to capture the open economy elements.

---

[1] NGOs are private organizations that produce goods and services but are not profit maximizing. Examples of NGOs are the Salvation Army, Oxfam, and other charitable organizations.

Box 1.1: The Analytical Devices of the Short-Run Versus Long-Run Analysis

Macroeconomics separates the forces that operate on economic variables into long-run ones and short-run ones. The *long run* is an *analytical* (not chronological) *period* during which all variables are free to change and there are no adjustment costs. The *short run* is an *analytical* (again, not chronological) *period* during which some variables are fixed in value and/or there are costs to adjusting them. The main differences between the short-run and the long-run analysis are: the long run allows changes in the physical capital stock, population, and technology, while the short run holds them constant (fixed).

The analytical distinction between the long run and short run is used to distinguish between economic forces that mainly operate over longer periods and those that operate mainly over shorter periods. The analytical device of the long run is especially useful for the analysis of the growth of output and standards of living over long periods. The analytical device of the short run is especially useful for the analysis of several variables of topical interest: differences in the actual rate of output from its long-run potential, unemployment, interest rates, inflation, balance of payments, exchange rates, etc. The short-run analysis constitutes the greater part of the theories in macroeconomics. Most of the chapters of this book present the short-run theories.

Real Time Concepts: The Short Term and the Long Term

The corresponding *chronological* concepts in *real time* are the long term and the short term. The short term is sometimes used to cover a period as short as the current quarter and sometimes a period as long as the business cycle, which can run for about ten years. The long term is taken to cover a period of several years.

The correspondence between the long term and the long run is vague and ambiguous, as is that between the short run and the short term. In general, the long run embodies economic forces that operate all the time, even during the short term. Similarly, the short run incorporates economic forces that operate not only in the short term but will also be in evidence in the economy over long chronological periods since a long chronological period incorporates a sequence of short runs.

Business cycles occur in real time. Their explanation incorporates both short-run and long-run forces.

1.3 Introduction to AD-AS Analysis

The dominant concern of macroeconomics is with the determination of the economy's *marketed* output — defined so as to include that provided by firms, government, and non-government organizations (NGOs) — as well as the rate of inflation. Their analysis is encapsulated in the AD-AS diagram, in which the demand for all the (*marketed*) commodities in the economy is represented by the concept of aggregate demand (AD) and the supply of all (*marketed*) commodities is represented by aggregate supply (AS). In the AD-AS diagram with the price level P on the vertical axis and the quantity of commodities y on the horizontal one, the AD curve is downward sloping, just as in the case of the demand for a single commodity.

The aggregate supply behavior of the economy is somewhat different from that of the supply of a single commodity: macroeconomic analysis implies that the AS curve for the economy is upward sloping in the short run but vertical in the long run.

1.3.1 The supply of commodities

The long-run (equilibrium) aggregate supply of commodities

Long-run output is that level of the output that would be produced in the economy if all its labor, capital, and other factors of production were 'fully employed' in production with the technology available at the time in the economy. Economics interprets the term '*fully employed*' in a special way. *It is to be interpreted as the level of output — and employment — that can be sustained by the economy over the long run with its current supplies of the factors of production and its current technology — given its current economic, political, and social structures as well as the wishes of the owners of the factors of production.* To illustrate the last point, the full employment of labor does not mean that the workers are working 24 hours a day, 7 days a week, since workers will choose to work a smaller number of hours. After all, they need to sleep and have time for leisure also. Similarly, factories and offices are rarely used at night but can still be 'fully employed' for macroeconomics analysis if they are in use for the time that their owners consider to be optimal. Therefore, the full employment of the factors of production is to be interpreted as the levels of employment that their owners wish to maintain over long periods. The level of full-employment (i.e., the long-run equilibrium) output is also loosely referred to as the '*potential output*', meaning by this 'the capability to produce sustainable output over long periods', of the economy.

As shown later in this book, macroeconomic theory establishes that the full-employment output — determined by the existing level of technology and the full employment of the factors of production — is independent of the price level in the long run. Therefore, if we were to draw the 'curve' for full-employment output in a diagram with the price level on the vertical axis and output on the horizontal one, this curve would be a vertical line at the level of output equal to the full-employment one. The associated full-employment curve is designated as the long-run aggregate supply of commodities and is labeled as the LRAS curve. It is vertical, as shown in Figure 1.1.

This book designates the full-employment output by the symbol y^f, which is to be read as 'full-employment output'. Its determination is specified more explicitly in Chapter 6.

The short-run aggregate supply of commodities

The short-run equilibrium level of output can differ from its long-run equilibrium level y^f because of mistaken expectations about future demand and prices and/or because of the costs of adjusting prices, output and employment to meet fluctuations in demand or supply. These reasons are explored in Chapters 7 and 8. Basically, an increase — especially an unanticipated increase — in demand leads profit-maximizing firms to accommodate some part of it by increasing their output by:

- increasing the work effort of existing employees and using the existing capital stock more intensively and
- increasing employment in the form of overtime and by hiring additional workers, and buying types of equipment that are more easily variable.

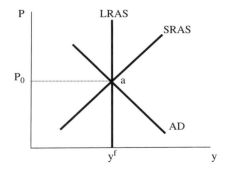

Figure 1.1

Note that a firm's profit-maximizing short-term response to an increase in demand is likely to include both increases in prices and output and is likely to depend on the relative costs of changing them. Hence, the short-run aggregate supply (SRAS) curve is likely to indicate an increase in the output of commodities at a higher price level — i.e., to have a positive slope, as shown in Figure 1.1.

1.3.2 The components of aggregate demand

The aggregate demand (AD) for commodities results from expenditures on commodities. It is composed of:

- consumption expenditures by households,
- investment expenditures by firms,
- expenditures on commodities by the government,
- the value of net exports (i.e., exports minus imports), which is foreigners' expenditures on our commodities less our expenditures on theirs.

The sum of all these types of expenditures constitutes AD. Aggregate demand decreases as prices rise and commodities become more expensive, so that the AD curve in Figure 1.1 is downward sloping. The detailed specification of aggregate demand is presented in Chapters 4 and 5.

1.3.3 The diagrammatic AD-AS analysis

Figure 1.1 shows the aggregate demand and supply curves. This figure has the *quantity* of commodities, designated as y, on the horizontal axis, with the price level, designated as P, being on the vertical one. Aggregate demand is shown in these figures by the curves marked AD, which shows the quantities demanded at various prices. This curve slopes downwards, thereby showing that the aggregate demand for commodities falls as the price level rises. The long-run aggregate supply of commodities is shown by the curve marked LRAS (for long-run aggregate supply), and the short-run supply of commodities is shown by the curve marked SRAS. The LRAS curve is drawn at the full-employment output y^f.

The economy is in short-run equilibrium at the intersection of the AD and SRAS curves. It is in long-run (full-employment) equilibrium at the intersection of the AD and LRAS curves. It is in disequilibrium if it is at neither of these points. Figure 1.1 shows that full-employment equilibrium exists in the economy at the point a, with $y = y^f$. But if the three curves intersect at different points, as in Figure 1.2a, the economy for the current short run will be in equilibrium at the intersection of the AD and SRAS curves. This is shown by the point b in Figure 1.2a. At this point, the economy's output will be y_1, higher than the economy's long-run productive capacity shown by y^f. Since the economy at the point b is not at its long-run equilibrium, economic forces will move the economy away from the point b toward the long-run equilibrium at the point c.

Macroeconomics focuses on the determination of the equilibrium values of the major macroeconomic variables, the shifts or shocks that change them, and the forces that tend to return — or not to return — the economy to equilibrium.

The possibility of disequilibrium in the economy

The commodity and labor markets do not always respond so fast to shifts in aggregate demand or supply that we can take them to reach the equilibrium position instantly. Following any such shift, the achievement of the price level and output to its new equilibrium takes time and involves lags, with changes in output and

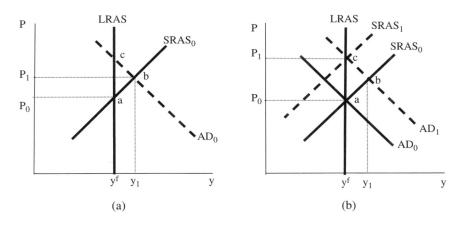

Figure 1.2

prices occurring in this period. During this adjustment period, the economy is said to be in disequilibrium. The analysis of disequilibrium levels of output and employment is presented in Chapter 8.

The actual aggregate supply of commodities

Therefore, there are two potential sources of differences between the actual output of the economy and its full-employment level. These are:

1. Short-run equilibrium deviations: these occur in response to shifts in aggregate demand, if the economy moves along the SRAS curve and away from the LRAS curve.
2. Disequilibrium deviations: these occur if shifts in aggregate demand or supply move the economy away, for some time, from even the short-run equilibrium position of the economy.

The long-run aggregate supply of output will be designated as LRAS (or y^f). The short-run aggregate supply will be designated as SRAS. Actual output will be denoted by the symbol y.

The impact of an increase in aggregate demand

To see how a point such as b in Figure 1.2b can come about, assume that the economy had the initial curves as AD_0, $SRAS_0$, and LRAS, so that it was in full-employment equilibrium at the point a in Figure 1.2b. Now, suppose that a sudden spurt of investment by firms increases their demand for commodities for investment purposes. This shifts the AD curve from AD_0 to AD_1, causing the economy to move temporarily to the point b. At b, since the level of output is higher than the economy's long-run capacity at y^f, it cannot be sustained on a continuing basis. Workers will begin to push for higher wages and profit-maximizing firms will also want to take advantage of the high demand to increase their prices and profits. Hence, the excess demand pressure (i.e., demand > y^f) will cause a sufficient increase in prices to force the economy to gradually adjust from the point b to the point c. As the price level rises, the quantity demanded adjusts (i.e., falls) along AD_1 to match the long-run supply. Further, as nominal wages rise to match the increase in prices and other adjustments occur, the SRAS curve will shift up to $SRAS_1$. Eventually, through the adjustments in prices and wages, full-employment equilibrium will be restored in the economy at the point c.

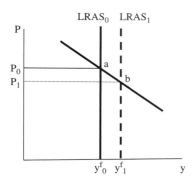

Figure 1.3

Compare points a and c: both have the same level of output but prices are higher at c than at a. Therefore, the effects of the increase in demand were: output increased for some time but then fell back to its full-employment level while the price level initially increased by less than its long-run increase.

The impact of an increase in the long-run productive capacity of the economy

A similar analysis to the above one can be performed for increases in aggregate supply. Increases in the aggregate supply can come about through increases in the supply of the factors of production and/or their productivity through technical change. Suppose one of these occurs and increases the quantity supplied at any given price level. This is shown by the shift of the LRAS curve from $LRAS_0$ to $LRAS_1$ in Figure 1.3. Given the aggregate demand curve as AD_0, the new long-run equilibrium is at the point b. Hence, the increase in supply has the long-run effect of increasing full-employment output from y_0^f to y_1^f while lowering the price level from P_0 to P_1.

The stability of equilibrium

An equilibrium is said to be stable if a deviation from it sets up forces that cause the market to return to equilibrium. We illustrate this in the context of Figure 1.3. The commodity market was initially in equilibrium at the point a (P_0, y_0^f), with aggregate demand equal to aggregate supply y_0^f. With the increase in supply to $LRAS_1$, the equilibrium shifts to the point b. What forces would move the economy from a to b? Suppose that supply has become y_1^f while demand is still at y_0^f. Since demand is less than supply, the price level will fall. It will keep on falling as long as supply exceeds demand, i.e., until the price level falls to P_1, so that the market adjustment of the price level will take the economy to the new equilibrium at b.

Since a similar argument can be used for any other divergence between demand and supply in this diagram, any equilibrium position in this diagram will be stable. The stability of the short-run equilibrium with the AD and SRAS curves can be shown in a similar manner, but is left to the students.

1.4 The Relationship between Output, Employment, and Unemployment in the Economy

The relationship between output and employment is specified by the production function:

$$y = f(n, K),$$

(1)

where

n = employment and
K = (physical) capital stock.

This production function assumes that for the modern economy, the main factors of production are labor and capital. There are obviously other factors of production such as land, but these are considered to be of minor significance and ignored in the usual analysis. Capital is allowed to vary in growth theory but kept constant in short-run macroeconomics. Therefore, the production function used in the short-run analysis is simplified to:

$$y = f(n) \tag{2}$$

This relationship is shown in Figure 1.4 by the 'output curve' marked y. In this diagram, the horizontal axis shows employment n and the vertical axis shows output y. Output and employment are positively related but output increases less than proportionately with employment. This means that the marginal product of labor — that is, the increase in output for a unit increase in labor — is positive but diminishing as the number of workers increases with the given capital stock.

The labor force

The labor force can be defined in one of two ways as:

1. The number of workers willing to work at a given market wage, irrespective of their skills, abilities, and other characteristics and, therefore, irrespective of their productivity.
2. The number of workers already employed plus those looking for a job at a given market wage, irrespective of their skills, abilities, and other characteristics and, therefore, irrespective of their productivity.

For practical, empirical purposes, the labor force is often simply defined as the number of persons in a specific age group, such as between 15 and 65 years.

Unemployment

Unemployment is defined as the labor force less the number of workers actually employed. Hence,

$$U = L - n,$$

where

U = the level of unemployment and
L = the labor force.

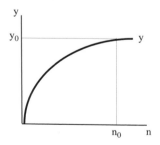

Figure 1.4

The unemployment *rate u* is:

$$u = U/L = 1 - n/L. \tag{3}$$

An unemployment rate can be written as either 0.05 or 5%, with the latter expressing it in percentage terms.

The '*natural rate of unemployment*' u^{n} is defined as the rate of unemployment that exists when the economy is at full employment. It is the long-run rate of unemployment. Hence,

$$u^{\mathrm{n}} = u^{\mathrm{f}} = U^{\mathrm{f}}/L = 1 - n^{\mathrm{f}}/L, \tag{4}$$

where

u^{f} = the 'full-employment rate of unemployment' ($\equiv u^{\mathrm{n}}$),
u^{n} = the natural rate of unemployment ($\equiv u^{\mathrm{f}}$), and
n^{f} = the full-employment (long-run equilibrium) level of employment.

Note that

- The natural rate of unemployment is not a constant. It can be altered by changes in technology or in labor supply behavior.
- The actual unemployment rate often differs from the natural one. This occurs whenever actual output is different from the full-employment one.

The determination of the natural rate of unemployment and the deviations from it are among the most important topics studied in macroeconomics.

1.5 Measures of National Output and Expenditures

National output is often measured by statistical measures such as GDP, GNP, and related variables. Their definitions are as follows.

1.5.1 Gross domestic product (GDP)

GDP is the statistical measure of the amount of *commodities* — our name for what are commonly called as 'goods and services' — produced in the *domestic* economy during a *specific* period *and* (a) intended for sale in the market or (b) provided by agencies, including the government and non-government organizations (NGOs), through production involving the payment of factors of production, even though a (full market-determined) price is not necessarily charged to the buyers or users of the resulting products.[2] *The nominal value of GDP* is the sum, in current prices, of the value of the commodities in (a) and the payments to the factors of production — which constitute their cost of production — in (b).

GDP differs from all goods produced in the economy in the period in question because:

- It does not include commodities that are excluded by (a) and (b) above. These include the great deal of production that goes on in the home. Therefore, GDP does not include most home and leisure activities.
- It does not include economic activities that result from *unpaid* volunteer work and goods and services for which there is no charge.

---

[2]Examples of such products are free education in government schools, partly subsidized education in universities, and activities of service organizations such as the YMCA.

- It does not include items that are not commodities (including services). Among the excluded items are notes and coins, and financial instruments such as bonds (remember, their definition in macroeconomics includes equities shares corporations).

GDP is calculated for each period, such as a quarter or a year. The GDP for a given period does not include items that were produced in earlier periods. Therefore, old (meaning, produced in some earlier period) paintings, old houses, and old refrigerators are not part of the current GDP, though the services they render in the current period are.

Fact Sheet 1.1: Global Trends in GDP Per Capita, 1950–2003

This Fact Sheet shows that different groups of countries have seen quite varied patterns of growth of GDP per capita over the past 50 years. In 1950, western Europe and its offshoots (the United States, Canada, Australia, and New Zealand) already had much higher GDP per capita than other countries. Since 1950, they have diverged further from the rest of the world. Though aggregate production in Asia has surpassed that of many European countries, their high population has limited growth in their GDP per capita. In Africa, GDP per capita has seen very little growth since 1950. Countries that were formerly part of the USSR saw a substantial fall in GDP per capita after 1990 due to difficult transitions to the market-oriented economy, but are already on the road to recovery.

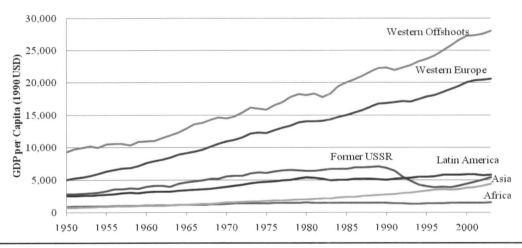

1.5.2 Gross national product (GNP)

GNP measures the gross national income of the residents of the country. This income accrues in the form of wages, profits, and rents. Most of it results from the production of output by factors of production owned by the residents and located within the country. However, the residents may also derive income from other countries through their investments abroad. Such foreign income is not part of the country's GDP. Conversely, some of the income from the production of goods included in the country's GDP may accrue to residents of other countries because of their ownership of capital and labor used in the domestic economy. Therefore, GDP needs to be adjusted for these flows of income to arrive at GNP.

For many countries, the net flow of income — that is, the inflow of income to residents less the outflow to non-residents — is very small as a proportion of GDP and is usually ignored in macroeconomic modelling. GDP is, therefore, normally used as the appropriate proxy for both domestic output and national income.[3]

1.5.3 Net domestic product (NDP) and net national product (NNP)

NDP equals GDP less the depreciation of capital used in its production. 'Net' stands for 'net of the depreciation of the economy's capital during the relevant period'.

Similarly, NNP is GNP less the allowance for depreciation.

Fact Sheet 1.2: Comparing GDP and GNP, 1965–2004

The following graph plots the ratio of GDP to GNP for a selected number of countries. For many countries the differences between GDP and GNP are insignificant. For the United States, the ratio of GDP to GNP is consistently close to 1. In others, where foreign owned companies produce a considerable share of aggregate product, GNP can differ substantially from GDP. In the following graph, Canada and to a larger extent Malaysia are examples of countries where GNP is less than GDP, because foreigners have invested more in those economies than residents of these countries have invested abroad, so that more of their output is used to make dividends and interest payments to foreigners than their residents receive from abroad. Notice the sudden jump in the GDP to GNP ratio in China during the last half of the early 1990s, i.e., after the market economy reforms put in place led to the jump in China's inflows of foreign investments.

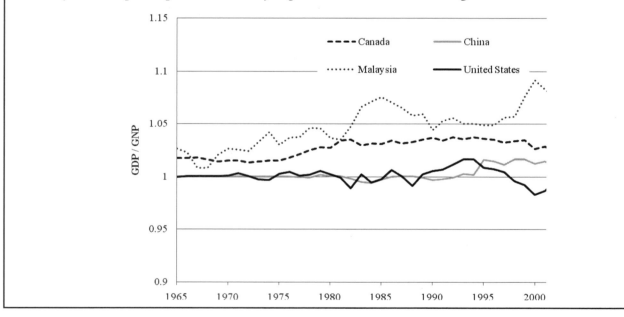

1.5.4 Measuring GDP

Nominal GDP is (roughly) the value of currently produced goods and services at current prices. The common methods of compiling the statistics on it lead to three concepts of GDP. They are:

---

[3]GNP can be significantly lower than GDP for countries that have significant foreign ownership of its assets and foreign workers, without a corresponding ownership by it of foreign assets and its workers working abroad.

1. 'GDP at market prices',
2. 'GDP by value added', and
3. 'GDP at factor cost'.

GDP at market prices is the most direct method of measuring GDP. This method sums:

- The expenditures on the various commodities included in GDP and marketed by firms. These expenditures are at market prices and include any indirect taxes, such as sales taxes, which are charged on the purchase of commodities. The taxes collected by the firms are remitted to the government. The remainder is used to pay wages, interest, and rents, with the residual becoming profits.
- The cost of production of the commodities included in GDP and provided by government organizations (GOs) and non-government organizations (NGOs).

GDP by value added sums the *value added* by the firms, government and NGOs in production. The value added to the economy by these production units is the increase in the value of GDP by their activities. For a firm, its value added equals its sales revenue minus (i) the cost of (raw materials and intermediate) inputs, other than labor, purchased from other firms and (ii) sales taxes paid by it. For the government and NGOs, which do not sell their output at market prices and/or are not supposed to have profits, value added is calculated as the sum of the payments to factors of production. Note that value added by the various economic units does not include the amount of indirect taxes forwarded by the firms to the government. Compared with the calculation of GDP at market prices, this method avoids the potential for miscalculating GDP because of 'double counting', which is explained later.

GDP at factor cost is calculated on the basis of the factor incomes paid in the production of commodities plus the profits of firms, which are assumed to be a cost of production by private profit-maximizing firms. Since profits are included as a cost, the total payment to the factors of production is identical with the amount collected by firms from purchasers — i.e., total expenditures on commodities — less the indirect taxes that are collected from purchasers but directly remitted to the government and, therefore, not paid to inputs. Therefore, indirect taxes are not part of GDP at factor cost and represent the difference between GDP at market prices and GDP at factor cost. Compared with the calculation of GDP at market prices, this method avoids the potential for miscalculating GDP because of double counting.

Note that the amount of indirect taxes collected by the government is only included in GDP at market prices, but not in GDP at factor cost or by value added.

The calculation of value added by an economic unit is illustrated later by an example.

The calculation of GDP and double counting

In calculating GDP at market prices, care has to be taken not to double-count (i.e., count twice) expenditures on raw materials and intermediate goods that go into the production of other goods. Double counting arises because the revenues of firms that produce raw materials and intermediate goods occur through sales to other (finished-goods producing) firms and become part of the costs and sales revenues of the latter. If the sales revenues of both types of firms are added together in calculating GDP at market prices, the sales revenue of the former types of firms will be counted twice: once as the sales revenue of firms producing raw materials and/or intermediate goods and once as part of the sales revenues of firms producing finished goods.[4] Such double counting has to be avoided in the calculation of GDP at market prices.

---

[4]This problem does not arise for the 'in-house' production of intermediate goods within the same firm.

The problem of double counting and how it can be avoided is illustrated by the following example. Note that in this illustration, we simplify by setting the production by the government and NGOs to zero.

An illustration of the three methods of calculating GDP

Assume that firm A produces 200 bales of fabric. It sells 150 bales for $1,000 to firm B to be made into clothes and sells 50 bales directly to consumers as fabric for $750. Most of the clothes made from the 150 bales are sold for $5,000. The rest of the clothes (unsold clothes), worth $200 at market prices, become an addition to inventories. The fabric-producing firm A had bought raw cotton for $600. The wages paid by both firms total $4,000 and rents are $500. There are no indirect taxes, such as sales taxes, though there may be income or corporate taxes. Assume that these are the only transactions related to GDP for the year.

(a) The calculation of GDP at market prices

Under this method, GDP consists of the commodities sold to the final purchasers and unsold goods. These are the 50 bales sold for $750 to consumers, the clothes sold for $5,000 and unsold production worth $200, so that the nominal value of GDP would be $5,950.

The above calculation of GDP does not include the 150 bales sold for $1,000 as an intermediate good to other firms. The reason is that these bales are indirectly included in the clothes made from them, so that including both would represent double counting of these bales, once as fabric and then as part of the clothes made from them. To avoid double counting, GDP at market prices only includes the values of the final goods and unsold or unused intermediate goods — with the latter constituting the value of the changes in their inventories.

(b) The calculation of GDP by value added

First, note that the fabric-producing firm A had bought raw cotton for $600. The value-added calculation for GDP is as follows:

Value of basic raw materials	$600
Value added by firm A ($= \$1,000 + \$750 - \$600$)	$1,150
Value added by firm B ($= \$5,000 + \$200 - \$1000$)	$4,200
GDP at market prices by the value-added method	$5,950

(c) Calculating GDP at factor prices

This method sums the labor incomes paid, rents paid, and interest and profits paid by each of the firms, and also arrives at the same number ($5,950). The wages paid by both firms totaled $4,000 and rents were $500. Since the firms' revenue is $5,950,[5] their profits equal $1,450 and are treated as a factor cost of production. Note that the calculation of profits is done in a manner that ensures that the GDP at factor cost always equal the GDP at market prices.

Therefore, in the absence of indirect taxes, the nominal value of GDP at market prices is the same under each of the three methods. If there are indirect taxes, GDP at market prices is higher than GDP by value-added or at factor prices by the amount of indirect tax revenues. However, the actual calculations usually involve

---

[5]Note that unsold products are evaluated at market prices and included as part of this revenue.

statistical errors in the collection and computation of data, so that the estimate of these is used to bring about the equality of the numbers derived for GDP under the three methods.

Cautions on the use of GDP data

Some types of production and transactions that should be part of GDP under its economic definition are not included in the usual calculations of GDP or are included more or less approximately since it is difficult to collect accurate data on them. The most important of these are (i) illegal (black market) activities and (ii) legal activities but with underground transactions. Examples of the former are the growing and processing of illegal drugs. Examples of the latter are home repairs by casual workers who are paid informally without a receipt so as to evade the payment of sales taxes by the homeowner on the transaction, as well as the payment of income taxes by the recipient. Small shopkeepers, farmers, and restaurants sometimes follow such practices to avoid or reduce their tax payments. The payments in many of these transactions are in currency.[6]

Further, the actual calculation of GDP is elaborate and costly. It is done better in some countries than in others. Even in countries that do it very well, the data collected for GDP is not likely to accurately reflect some items that fall within the definition of GDP. Therefore, the calculated GDP data always suffers from errors and omissions. To adjust for these, the reported GDP data often includes estimates for such errors and omissions. As a result, the reported amounts are often revised for some years after the initial data is released.

Further, although the three methods of measuring GDP are supposed to yield identical data, they never do. To address this problem, a 'statistical discrepancy' item is added or subtracted to present consistent estimates for the three methods.

Box 1.2: GDP per capita as a Measure of the Standard of Living

Simply put, GDP, or rather its approximation GNP, is the sum of incomes in the economy. Therefore, one way of measuring the standard of living in a country is by dividing its real GDP by its population — that is, by GDP per capita — since this reflects the average income levels in the economy. We can break GDP per capita into three components in the following manner.

$$\text{Standard of living} = \frac{y}{Pop} = \frac{y}{n} \cdot \frac{n}{L} \cdot \frac{L}{Pop},$$

where n is employment, L is the labor force, and Pop is population. y/n is labor productivity, n/L is the 'employment rate' — which is the converse of the unemployment rate,[7] since a lower value of n/L means that a smaller proportion of the labor force is employed and, therefore, indicates a higher unemployment rate — and L/Pop is the labor force participation rate. Therefore, the standard of living rises with labor productivity, the employment rate and the participation rate. It declines as the unemployment rate increases. In the short and medium term, changes in all three factors can be significant. Over long periods, the most important determinant of the standard of living is the growth of labor productivity. Its growth is studied in Chapters 14 and 15 on growth theory.

---

[6]Therefore, some economists use an exceptionally high usage of currency as an indicator of unreported transactions and production. They use the excess usage of currency to estimate the levels of unreported production and sales and add these amounts to the reported levels of production to compute GDP.

[7]The unemployment rate equals $(L - n)/L$.

GDP as a Measure of Welfare

Increases in GDP (and GDP per capita) often do not accurately reflect increases in society's (family's) welfare. While this welfare normally depends to a considerable extent on the availability of commodities included in GDP (i.e., provided by the market or government), there are also many other elements that also contribute to the quality of life. Among these are 'production activities' in the home[8] — whose value, if quantified at market prices, would be very high as a percentage of the market-based GDP — and leisure activities. GDP also does not encompass the quality of the environment — e.g., air, water, forests, etc.

If the increase in GDP comes about *without* a decrease in home production, leisure, and the environmental quality, the increase in GDP per capita can be more readily accepted as an increase in society's welfare. Examples of such beneficial improvements include the information technology (IT) revolution, which increased productivity (because of more capital per worker or technical change) and increased GDP per capita — without necessarily higher labor force participation rates, without a reduction in leisure and without the deterioration in the environment.

However, in other cases, the increase in GDP per capita could be due to a higher labor force participation rate, longer working hours, and decreases in leisure — all of which tend to increase stress levels in the home and decrease the availability of parental time for children — or increases in pollution. In these cases, the change in social and the family's welfare has to be adjusted for these additional costs. An increase in the labor force participation rate increases GDP per capita but reduces leisure time, so that the net increase in welfare is less than that indicated by the increase in GDP per capita. Similarly, the increase in production at the cost of more pollution increases welfare less than the GDP increase.

Another side of the picture is also to be noted. As factor incomes rise, the demand for leisure tends to increase, so that more holidays tend to be taken. In this case, all other things remaining the same, the family's welfare increases by the increase in its income and the increase in its leisure, so that the increase in the family's income, as indicated by GDP per capita, does not fully indicate the increase in the family's welfare. Further, higher incomes usually increase the demand for a better environment, and allow the society to 'purchase' cleaner air by legislating anti-pollution requirements or by using home air and water purifiers.

1.6   Measuring the Price Level and the Rate of Inflation

1.6.1   Measures of the price level

The economy's price level can be defined as the average price of the commodities sold in the economy. The data on the price level is usually in the form of an index. These indices assign a base figure of 100 for the price level in a designated (base) year.

Several measures are used to represent the price level. The most commonly used measures are the GDP deflator, the consumer price index (CPI), and the industrial product price index (IPPI).

---

[8]Examples of this are: home-cooked meals, care of children, personal interaction, etc.

The GDP deflator

This index provides the average price level for all the commodities included in the economy's GDP. Note that the GDP deflator includes the prices of both consumer goods and capital goods (i.e., those goods which are sold to other firms for investment purposes). The GDP deflator is the more appropriate measure of the price level relevant to the GDP. Note also that the GDP deflator is a price index — which measures the change in the economy's price level over time — while an index of GDP (or the GDP index) is a quantity index — which measures the amount of the quantities that are produced.

The consumer price index (CPI)

This index measures the average price of a 'basket' of commodities purchased by the economy's consumers. The CPI includes only the prices of consumer goods and is more relevant for deriving the impact of inflation on the real value of consumer incomes.

Other indices similar to the CPI can be also constructed for specific groups, such as for students and pensioners, which would use as quantity weights the particular set of commodities bought by the specified group. Note that the GDP deflator includes both capital and consumer goods, while the CPI excludes capital goods.

The industrial product price index (IPPI)

This index measures the average price of industrial products produced in the economy during the designated period. It includes the prices of many commodities — such as raw materials and intermediate (i.e., semi-finished) goods used in further production — which are not directly purchased by consumers. It excludes the prices of other commodities — such as services — that are not industrial products, so that it differs from both the GDP deflator and the CPI. In particular, as compared with the CPI and the GDP deflator, it measures the prices of commodities at an earlier stage of production and distribution than at the final retail stage to consumers. This index includes the output of semi-finished commodities in its weights.

There are also many other types of price indices. Among these could be a 'students' price index', which would measure the changes in the average prices of goods and services bought by students, and a 'pensioners' index', which would measure the changes in the average prices of goods and services bought by pensioners. In general, these different price indices would not show identical changes in any given year since they incorporate different weights and different methods of computation. The selection among them has to be relevant to their usage. Therefore, if the purpose is to proxy the cost of living of consumers, the CPI is the most appropriate one. But if the purpose is to find real GDP from nominal GDP, the GDP deflator is the most appropriate one. Since an increase in the prices of producer goods increases the costs of production of goods at the retail level and leads to an increase in the retail prices, the IPPI is useful as a *leading (i.e., occurring before) indicator* of changes in both the GDP deflator and the CPI.

The GDP deflator is the more appropriate proxy for the theoretical concept of the price level for the economy as a whole.

1.6.2 The inflation rate

The inflation rate is the rate of change in the price level. If the price level increases by 5%, we can specify the inflation rate as being 5% or as 0.05. In practice, barring unusual periods such as those of wars and severe economic depressions, the price level rises in most years. Consequently, a graph of the price level over a long period has an upward slope. However, the inflation rate tends to fluctuate a great deal. The inflation rate tends to be positive and especially high during wars, when government expenditures are mostly financed by increasing the money supply. It can be negative, i.e., prices fall, in the deflation following some wars and in some recessions. The biggest declines in the price level in peacetime occurred during the Great Depression of the 1930s. Fact Sheet 1.3 provides an illustration of the CPI and the inflation rate based on it for Canada.

The central banks of many of the developed economies now follow 'inflation targeting,' which is a policy of keeping the inflation rate to a low level. To illustrate, since the 1990s, the Bank of Canada has tried to attain the average inflation rate of 2%, with fluctuations in inflation kept between 1% and 3%.

Fact Sheet 1.3: Inflation in Canada, 1915–2007

This Fact Sheet illustrates movements in the inflation rate that can occur in a country. This illustration is taken from Canada's experience. Over the last century, the price level in Canada has had an upward trend. However, the inflation rate has followed a more cyclical pattern. Periods including World War I, World War II, the Korean War, and the two oil crises of 1973–1975 and 1980–1981 saw substantial price increases and therefore sharp spikes in inflation. Deflation (i.e., negative inflation rate) occurred in post-WWI period as well as during the Great Depression.

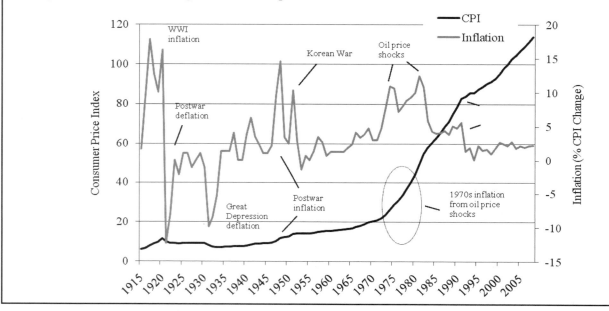

For each of the preceding measures of the price level, there is a corresponding measure of inflation.

1.6.3 Core inflation

The prices of some of the goods in the economy are very volatile and fluctuate a great deal, so that increases are sooner or later offset by declines, and vice versa. Among such goods are food[9] and energy

---

[9] Food prices tend to be sensitive to weather and seasonal influences. An exceptionally rainy season or a drought can cause such prices to rise very significantly, and then be offset some weeks or months later as supplies come in from other areas.

prices.[10] A measure that excludes their prices from the price index and focuses on the more stable prices of the other commodities is that of 'core inflation'. Core inflation is thus meant to be a measure of price changes that, having occurred, are likely to persist for several years. Core inflation measures can be prepared for the CPI, GDP deflator and other price indices.[11]

Mathematical Box 1.1: Calculation of the Price Index and Growth Rates

The construction of a price index: an illustration

Suppose that we are given information on the quantities bought and the prices of the commodities A and B for 3 years 0, 1, 2 and we need to construct a price index for all the three commodities. The information on prices and quantities is given in Table 1.1, where $q_{i,0}$ refers to the commodity i bought in year t, $t = 0, 1, 2$, and $p_{i,t}$ specifies its price in year t.

Table 1.1

commodity	$q_{i,0}$	$p_{i,0}$	$p_{i,1}$	$p_{i,2}$
A	200	10	10	5
B	50	20	30	30
C	10	30	40	40

To construct a price index for the specific basket of commodities that contains the three commodities in the amounts bought in year 0 and specified in column 2, we first calculate the expenditures on the three commodities for each of the three years. These are shown in the next table.

Table 1.2

commodity	$q_{i,0}$	$p_{i,0} \, q_{i,0}$	$p_{i,1} \, q_{i,0}$	$p_{i,2} \, q_{i,0}$
A	200	2000	2000	1000
B	50	1000	1500	1500
C	10	300	400	400
Total expenditures		3300	3900	2900

Suppose we now want to set the price index for total expenditures on the designated basket of commodities bought in year 0 at 100. Then, the price index for year 1 would be calculated as $(3900/3300)100 = 118.19$ and the price index would for year 2 will be $(2900/3300)100 = 87.88$. The price index and the rate of inflation calculated from the price index is:

Table 1.3

Year	Expend.	Price index	Rate of inflation
0	3300	100	$[(118.19 - 100)/100]100 = 18.19$
1	3900	$= (3900/3300)100 = 118.19$	$[(87.88 - 118.19)/118.19]100 = -25.65$
2	2900	$= (2900/3300)100 = 87.88$	

---

[10] Energy prices are sensitive to weather conditions such as exceptionally cold weather, to manipulation by the international oil cartel, OPEC, and to its ability to stabilize overall oil supply levels by enforcing production quotas on its members.

[11] Core inflation measures are especially useful for the formulation of monetary policy since the central bank needs to know which price increases are likely to persist and which are likely to be reversed later.

Mathematical Box 1.1: (*Continued*)

Differences between Laspeyres and Paasche indices

Note that the quantities bought are held fixed at the level bought in a designated year. In the above example, this was done for the year 0. The year selected for this purpose is called the base year. The index calculated with a past base year for quantities is called a *Laspeyres index*.

However, the quantities bought tend to change over time. Some price indices, therefore, use the basket of commodities bought in the current year. If the last year (year 2 in the above table) were to be the current year, the quantities bought in that year would be used to calculate expenditures for that and all previous years. These are likely to be different from the ones in the base year. The index calculated with the basket of commodities bought in the current year as the standard basket is called a *Paasche index*.

There are, therefore, two types of price indices:

i *The Laspeyres (base-period weights) index*:

This type of index uses base period quantities as weights in constructing the price index.

The disadvantage of a Laspeyres index with base period quantity weights is that as time passes, new commodities come into existence and new versions and qualities of base period commodities emerge. Since these were not available in the base period, their prices are not incorporated in the index, so that the index becomes increasingly inappropriate over time. Examples of a Paasche index are the CPI (which uses the amounts of the commodities bought for consumption in the economy during the base year) and the IPPI (which uses the amounts of the industrial commodities produced in the economy during the base year).

ii *The Paasche (or current-period weights) index*:

This type of index uses the current-period quantities as weights in constructing the price index.

In this case, the bundle of commodities used in calculating the index consists of commodities consumed (or produced) in the current (not in the base) period. Therefore, a Paasche index uses *current-period quantity* weights. The advantage of a Paasche index over the Laspeyres one is that it can take account of the new products and the improved versions of older products, which did not exist in the base period.

The GDP deflator is often constructed as a Paasche index and uses for its weights the amounts of the commodities included in the current year's GDP.

Also note that the price index for each year is relative to a given year, which is often the base year (i.e., year 0 in the above example), with the value of the index in that year set at 100.

Separating the rate of growth of nominal income into the real growth rate and the inflation rate

Table 1.3 showed the calculation of total expenditures for our numerical example. These expenditures can be treated as nominal GDP, which is Y in our usual symbols. Suppose that we wish to find the growth rate of real GDP, i.e., which is y" in our usual symbols. To do so, we first need to derive the expenditures on each commodity for each year by multiplying the actual (not base year ones) quantities bought/produced in each year by the prices in that year and then obtaining total

Mathematical Box 1.1: (*Continued*)

expenditures for each year by summing over the expenditures on each commodity. This is done in Table 1.4.

Table 1.4

comm.	$q_{i,0}$	$p_{i,0}$	$p_{i,0} q_{i,0}$	$q_{i,1}$	$p_{i,1}$	$q_{i,1} p_{i,1}$	$q_{i,2}$	$p_{i,2}$	$q_{i,2} p_{i,2}$
A	200	10	2000	220	10	2200	220	5	1100
B	50	20	1000	55	30	1650	55	30	1650
C	10	30	300	11	40	440	11	40	440
Total exp.			3300			4290			3190

The last row in Table 1.4 shows the value of Y for each year. We next use this data and that on the price level P calculated in Table 1.2 to derive the value of y, which equals Y/P, for each year and then derive its change y' and its growth rate y''. These calculations are shown in Table 1.5. Note that the relevant formulas are: $y'_t = y_{t+1} - y_t$ and $y''_t = y'_t/y_t$.

Table 1.5

Year	Y	P	$y = Y/P$	y'	y''
0	3300	100	33	$= 36.33 - 33 = 3.30$	$= (3.30/33)100 = 10\%$
1	4290	118.19	36.30	$= 36.30 - 36.30 = 0$	$= (0/36.33)100 = 0\%$
2	3190	87.88	36.30		

A comparison of the quantities in Table 1.4 shows that there was a 10% increase in the quantity of each commodity from year 0 to year 1, but there was no change in them from year 1 to year 2. This is confirmed by the derived growth rate y'' of total output in Table 1.5. Note that we cannot derive the growth rate of output in year 2 since we do not have the data for year 3.

The growth rate of real output can also be calculated from the formula $y'' = Y'' - P''$. This calculation is presented in Table 1.6.

Table 1.6

Year	Y	Y''	P	P''	y''
0	3300	$= (4290 - 3300)/3300 = 0.3$	100	$= (118.19 - 100)/100 = 0.18$	0.12
1	4290	$= (3190 - 4290)/4290 = -0.26$	118.19	$= (87.88 - 118.19)/87.88 = -0.26$	0
2	3190		87.88		

The calculation of y'' in Table 1.6 yields 0.12 (12%) while its calculation in Table 1.5 was 10%, which, in fact, is the correct value, as we can see from the increase in the quantities of the individual commodities in Table 1.4. The reason for this difference is that the formula $y'' = Y'' - P''$ is only correct for 'very small changes' in magnitudes but introduces an approximation error for large changes. In our illustration, the change in magnitudes was 10%, which is not a very small change. For analytical purposes, the formula is very convenient and is the one to be used. However, when working with data that embodies large changes, the calculations should be done as in Table 1.5.

1.6.4 Deriving the rate of inflation from a price index

The rate of inflation during a period is the rate of change in the price level during the period. The rate of inflation during a period t is, therefore, given by:

$$P_t'' = \pi_t = \frac{P_{t+1} - P_t}{P_t},$$

where P'' is our symbol for the rate of change in P, so that P'' and π are synonyms for the rate of inflation. P_t is the price level at the beginning of period t and P_{t+1} is the price level at the beginning of period $t + 1$. Suppose the former is 100 and the latter is 105, we have:

$$P_t'' = \pi_t = \frac{105 - 100}{100} = 0.05.$$

The rate of inflation is more familiarly expressed in percentage terms, so that, for this example, π_t will equal 5% (0.05×100).

The inflation rate is usually reported on an annualized basis. Suppose the length of the period is one year and we want to calculate the inflation rate for the year 2000. The calculation will be as follows:

$$\pi_{2000} = \frac{P \text{ on Dec. 31, 2000} - P \text{ on Jan. 1, 2000}}{P \text{ on Jan. 1, 2000}}.$$

But suppose the data was reported on a quarterly basis. To annualize the rate, the procedure is:

$$\pi_{2000:Q1} = \frac{P \text{ on Mar. 31, 2000} - P \text{ on Jan. 1, 2000}}{P \text{ on Jan. 1, 2000}} \cdot 4,$$

where we have multiplied by 4 since there are 4 quarters in the year.[12]

Box 1.3: Mathematical Formulae to Learn

Although this box presents mathematical formulae, they are essential for economic analysis and must be learnt. The following derivations are also included in the section on Useful Mathematical Formulae for Economics on page xliii of this book. Since they are being utilized for the first time in this book, their derivation is repeated here.

For the nominal value of GDP, designated as Y, the definition of the change in Y, designated as Y' ($\equiv \Delta Y$) is:

$$Y_t' = Y_{t+1} - Y_t,$$

where the subscript refers to the time period, so that Y_t' is the change in Y during period t. The definition of Y'' — that is, the rate of change (growth rate) of Y — is:

$$Y_t'' = Y_t'/Y_t = (Y_{t+1} - Y_t)/Y_t.$$

Nominal GDP equals the price level multiplied by real GDP. Omitting the subscripts, $Y = Py$. Note that the change in Y is decomposed into the changes in P and y in the following manner:

$$Y' = P' \cdot y + y' \cdot P.$$

Dividing the left side by Y and the right side by Py, we get the growth rate (rate of change) of Y as:

$$Y'' = Y'/Y = P' \cdot y/Py + y' \cdot P/Py$$
$$= P'/P + y'/y = P'' + y''.$$

---

[12]This formula is an approximation to the correct one, which requires compounding of the growth rate.

Box 1.3: (*Continued*)

Note that P'' is the rate of change of the price level, i.e., the 'inflation rate', and y'' is the rate of growth of real GDP. This is an example of a very useful formula: *if a variable is a multiple of two other variables, its growth rate is the sum of the growth rates of the two variables.*

The above derivation implies another useful formula. Since $y = Y/P$, we have:

$$y'' = Y'' - P''.$$

This is an example of another useful formula: *if a variable is a ratio of two other variables, its growth rate is the difference between the growth rates of the variable in the numerator and the variable in the denominator.*

Fact Sheet 1.4: Measures of Inflation for the USA, 1960–2007

As the indicator for the change in price levels, inflation measures vary depending on the basket of goods used in its calculation. Inflation measures derived from the CPI and GDP deflator tend to follow the same general pattern but can also vary considerably. The following graph illustrates the differences in inflation measures. During the 1973 and 1979 energy crises, consumption goods experienced a large increase in prices as a result of the increased cost of crude oil. This is captured in a spike in CPI inflation much larger than that depicted by the GDP deflator, which is based on a much larger group of goods and only those that are domestically produced.

Nowadays, the preferred measure of core inflation for the Federal Reserve System of the USA is the PCE (Personal Consumption Expenditure) Index. It provides a better index for long-term inflation as it does not reflect prices of goods that can experience temporary price shocks such as energy or food. Notice that the PCE Index is less volatile than either inflation based on the GDP deflator or on the CPI.

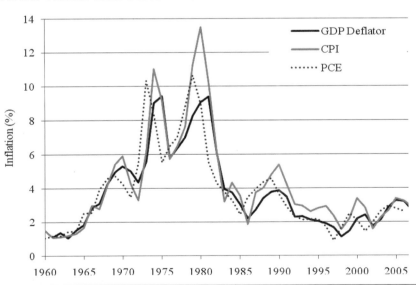

1.6.5 Disinflation versus deflation

'*Inflation*' is the rate of increase in the price level. '*Disinflation*' is a decrease in the rate of inflation, so that the inflation rate falls, though still remaining positive. By comparison, the term '*deflation*' can be used to refer to a deflation/decline in the level of economic activity or, in some cases, a negative inflation rate, which would be a persistent decline in the price level.

Economists and policymakers usually prefer a low rate of inflation. For example, the central bank of Canada has set its desired/target rate of core inflation at 2%. If the actual rate goes above, especially substantially above, this level, the Bank of Canada pursues contractionary monetary policies to cause a disinflation to lower the inflation rate to the target inflation rate. Therefore, disinflation is often viewed as a desirable squeezing out of inflationary pressures from the economy.

Economists and policymakers are usually wary of deflation that produces a negative inflation rate, since it is associated with significant and persistent declines in economic activity, so that output is falling and unemployment is rising over several quarters and years.

1.7 Nominal Versus Real Output

The data on GDP and its related variables has to be collected in the form of the dollar value of its various components. This dollar value of GDP is known as the nominal value of GDP. The corresponding real values of GDP is obtained by dividing the nominal GDP by its price index, which measures the price changes of its component commodities and was designated above as the GDP deflator.

Our symbol for nominal national output is Y and that for its real value is y. The relationship among Y, P, and y for a given period is:

$$Y = Py \quad \text{or} \quad y = Y/P.$$

In terms of the rate of change of the variables,

$$Y'' = P'' + y'' = \pi + y'',$$

so that nominal income grows by the rate of inflation plus the growth of real output.

Alternatively, we have:

$$y'' = Y'' - \pi.$$

This formula is useful for calculating the growth rate of real output.

The data for GDP is collected in nominal (dollar) terms, so that it needs to be deflated by the price level to find the real GDP and its growth rate. The procedure is as follows:

$$\text{Real GDP in } t = \frac{\text{Dollar value of GDP in } t}{\text{Price level in } t}.$$

To calculate the growth rate of real GDP for a given year t, the procedure is:

Real GDP growth rate in t = nominal GDP growth rate in t − rate of inflation in t.

That is, for each year, the real GDP growth rate is calculated by subtracting the rate of inflation from the nominal GDP growth rate.

1.8 The Economic Relationship between Real Output and Inflation

The AD-AS analysis presented in this chapter implies both a short-run and a long-run relationship between real output and the inflation rate. In the long run, output is independent of the price level and, therefore, of the rate of inflation. However, in the short run, increases in aggregate demand can increase the price level and cause inflation while also increasing real output. Figure 1.5 shows the short-run relationship by the curve

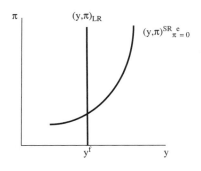

Figure 1.5

marked $(y, \pi)^{SR}$ and the long-run one by the curve marked $(y, \pi)^{LR}$. There is a separate short-run AD curve for each expected rate of inflation, so that the curve marked $(y, \pi)^{SR}_{\pi^e=0}$ is drawn for a zero expected inflation rate.

Note that, in terms of output increases, there is no benefit in the long run from having inflation but there can be some benefit in the short run. Chapters 8 and 10 will examine the precise causes and limitations of this benefit.

1.9 The Nature of Economic Relationships

There are three types of relationships among economic variables. These are:

1. *Identities.* These arise because of definitional concordance between economic variables or because of mathematical and linguistic relationships. An identity always holds no matter what the nature of the economy.
2. *Behavioral relationships.* These reflect economic behavior and are the result of choices made by economic agents. Examples of these are the aggregate demand and aggregate supply relationships or curves in the preceding analysis.
3. *Equilibrium conditions.* The equilibrium condition for a particular market is that the demand equals the supply in that market. In addition, *general equilibrium* in the macroeconomy specifies the requirement that demand equals supply in *all* the markets of the economy. There is no presumption that equilibrium will always exist in all markets or that it will always exist in any given market. If equilibrium does not exist — that is, when demand does not equal supply — in a market, the market is said to be in *disequilibrium*.

Box 1.4: Definition of Equilibrium

Equilibrium is that state in a market when the demand and supply in it are equal, so that, at the equilibrium price, the buyers can buy as much as they want and the sellers can sell as much as they want. Such a market is said to 'clear' at the equilibrium price. For the macroeconomic model as a whole, the clearance of all markets in the economy is referred to as 'general equilibrium'.

Equilibrium conditions versus identities

Equilibrium conditions differ from identities. The latter are meant to apply under all conditions, irrespective of the nature of the economy. The former hold only sometimes — i.e., when the economy is in equilibrium — but do not apply in disequilibrium. For example, the equality of the demand and supply in the market for a product (apples) represents an equilibrium condition. Since the demand for a product (apples) does not sometimes equals it supply, the equality of demand and supply is not an identity.

Box 1.4: (*Continued*)

Equilibrium versus disequilibrium

When the demand for a good does not equal its supply, there is said to be *disequilibrium* in the market for that good. For the macroeconomic model, we can have equilibrium in some markets while there is disequilibrium in other markets. For example, at a particular point in time, the demand and supply of commodities may be equal while those for labor may not be equal. In this case, the commodity market will be in equilibrium while the labor market will not be in equilibrium, even though it may be moving toward equilibrium. Therefore, in this case, *general* equilibrium will not exist in the economy.

Stable versus unstable equilibrium

It is always important not only to know the condition for equilibrium in any given market but also to know the forces that exist — or are needed — in disequilibrium to bring about changes (in price, the quantity demanded and/or the quantity supplied) in the market. Further, we need to know if this movement will be toward equilibrium or away from it. In the former case, the equilibrium is said to be *stable*. In the latter case, it is *unstable*.

   Even in the case of a stable equilibrium, movement from a disequilibrium situation to the equilibrium one usually takes time, which could mean a few days, a few quarters, or a few years. For example, estimates show that the impact of a change in the interest rate by the central bank continues to have effects on nominal GDP for more than six quarters. In this case, we say that a *lag* exists in the impact of a change in the interest rate on nominal GDP. Lags in the economy are common and important if we want to explain the performance of economies in real time. Economists try to measure the length of such lags.

1.10   Exogenous and Endogenous Variables and the Concept of Shocks in Macroeconomics

The AD-AS model included the three basic elements of an economic model, which are:

1. Endogenous variables
   These are variables whose values are determined within the model.
2. Exogenous variables
   These are variables whole values are not determined within the model but are specified to it. As such, they are said to be 'exogenous' or 'given' to the model. However, it is expected that they will change over time or be changed by the modeller. One purpose of the model is to examine the impact of such changes on the endogenous variables. Exogenous variables can be:

   - *Policy variables*, whose values are determined by a policymaker. They are not determined within the model itself. Examples of policy variables are the money supply, which is at the discretion of the central bank, and government deficits, which are at the discretion of the government.
   - *Non-policy exogenous variables.*

3. Parameters
   These are the elements of the model that are specified as constants and as such are not expected to change. Therefore, they are also known as the constants of the model. They usually appear as coefficients attached

to variables. However, they are sometimes changed to investigate the impact of such changes on the endogenous variables.

1.10.1 An illustration

Suppose our model solely explains consumption expenditures and specifies that consumption expenditures c depend on disposable national income y_d which equals national income y less taxes paid t. Let us assume that this relationship is of the form:

$$c = a + b(y - t).$$

Here, c is an endogenous variable (explained by the model), y is an exogenous (not explained by the model) non-policy variable, t is an exogenous policy variable determined by the government, and a and b are parameters.

1.10.2 Shocks

A *shock* can be defined in a broad sense as a shift in the value of an exogenous variable or parameter. Such a change may be anticipated or unanticipated. However, in some ways, the notion of a shock is more appropriate for an unanticipated shift than for an anticipated shift and some economists use this term in this narrower sense.

1.10.3 Multipliers

A major purpose of macroeconomic modelling is to study the impact of changes in the policy variables or the non-policy exogenous variables on the endogenous variables. This impact is often captured through the notion of 'multipliers'. *A multiplier indicates the change in an endogenous variable for a unit change in an exogenous variable.* For example, if the endogenous variables are nominal income Y and real income y, while the policy variable is the money supply M, the relevant multipliers are designated as: $(\partial Y / \partial M)$[13] and $(\partial y / \partial M)$. Here, the interpretation of $(\partial Y / \partial M)$ is 'the change in Y for a very small change in M', with 'all other variables being held constant'. The symbol ∂ is a Greek letter pronounced as 'di' and designates '*a small change*' in the *following variable, when all other variables are held constant*. $(\partial y / \partial M)$ is pronounced as 'di y di M'.

Our earlier analysis of the long-run real output in the economy implied that changes in aggregate demand do not affect real output in the long run, so that we have for the long-run $(\partial y / \partial AD)^{LR} = 0$. Our earlier analysis also showed that in the short run, $(\partial y / \partial AD)$ was not zero along the short-run SRAS curve, so that $(\partial y / \partial AD)^{SR} > 0$. Hence, the values of the economic multipliers can differ between the short run and the long run. The long-run and the short-run multipliers are analytical ones, without a precise chronological correspondence in real time. These analytical multipliers have to be distinguished from the chronological or real-time multipliers.

In terms of chronological time, with data on a quarterly basis, the *impact multiplier* is the value of the multiplier during the first quarter after a shock. If the data are on an annual basis, the impact multiplier is the value of the multiplier during the first year after the shock. If there exist lags in the effects of the shock, the impact multiplier would be less than the short-run and the long-run multipliers. This is a common occurrence for the policy and other multipliers in macroeconomics. Therefore, in assessing the impact of any policy on

---

[13]To reiterate, this expression is a short form for 'the change in Y for a small change in M, other things remaining the same'.

the real-time economy, we not only need to know the analytical multipliers but also have knowledge of the impact multipliers and the likely lags — or, at least, possess some intuition on them.

1.11 Growth Theory

Economics studies the *very long-run* growth of real output and standards of living under the heading of growth theory. The focus of this theory is on the analytical forces contributing to growth over long periods.

Our earlier discussion, in the AD-AS analysis, of the long-run AS curve shows that the long-run growth of output will mainly depend on the growth of the labor force and physical capital, and improvements in technology. Growth theory analyses their role and importance, as well as the contribution of other forces to growth. Growth theories are covered in Chapters 14 and 15.

1.11.1 Growth of the standard of living

We argued earlier that a rough measure of the standard of living is output per capita. Using this measure, the standard of living *in the long run* would equal the full-employment output divided by the population. We can, therefore, express the long-run standard of living as:

$$\text{long-run standard of living} = \frac{y^{\text{f}}}{Pop} = \frac{y^{\text{f}}}{n^{\text{f}}} \cdot \frac{n^{\text{f}}}{L} \cdot \frac{L}{Pop},$$

where n^{f} is the full-employment level of employment, L is the labor force, and Pop is population. Therefore, in the long run, the growth rate of the standard of living is the sum of the growth rates of its three components. In symbols, the above equation implies that the growth rate of the standard of living is given by:

$$\left(\frac{y^{\text{f}}}{Pop}\right)'' = \left(\frac{y^{\text{f}}}{n^{\text{f}}}\right)'' + \left(\frac{n^{\text{f}}}{L}\right)'' + \left(\frac{L}{Pop}\right)'',$$

where $''$ indicates the growth rate of the ratio in the preceding bracket. Of these ratios, n^{f}/L cannot grow indefinitely and neither can L/Pop, though both can increase (or decline) over some periods. Therefore, the long-run growth of living standards can only result from the growth rate of $y^{\text{f}}/n^{\text{f}}$, which is long-run output per worker or labor productivity. This increase in labor productivity occurs because of improvements in the techniques of production (technical change) and increases in the amount of capital per worker. As Chapters 14 and 15 on growth theory indicate, empirical estimates show that the major part of the long-term increases in living standards has been due to technical change, i.e., changes in the methods of production, such as those which occurred in the Industrial Revolution or have been occurring in recent decades in what may be called the Computer and Internet Revolution. The 'carriers' or embodiment of this technical change have been human and physical capital.

1.12 Business Cycle Theories

Real output does not always increase at a constant growth rate. It grows faster in some years than in other years; it may even decline in some years. Overall, there is a cyclical pattern with some years of rising output, followed by some years of falling output, which are followed by rising output, and so on. Since output has a long-term rising trend — that is, it increases over long periods — the deviation of output around this trend is used to specify the cyclical behavior of output.

Since the unemployment rate is negatively related to real output, the fluctuations in unemployment follow an opposite pattern to that in output and are said to be *counter-cyclical*.

Business cycles are defined as short-term fluctuations in real output and its related variables such as unemployment. These fluctuations are called cycles since they are somewhat periodic, with a *downturn* following a *peak* and an *upturn* following a *trough*. In Canada, the typical business cycle in output has an upturn that lasts several years while the downturn is usually milder and lasts at most a couple of years. Other popular terms associated with business cycles are booms and recessions. The economy is said to be in a *boom* if its output is above its long-run potential level or above its average level over the business cycle. This happens toward the top of an upturn and the early parts of the downturn. The economy is said to be in a *recession* if its output is below its long-run potential level or below its average level over the business cycle. This happens toward the bottom of a downturn and the early part of the upturn.

The internal structure of the economy is a significant factor in producing its cyclical activity. Some economies may have an internal mechanism that produces fluctuations while others need periodic shocks to do so. In the latter case, the economy must respond to shocks through fluctuations in its performance. A real-world economy may possess both these characteristics.

The preceding AD-AS analysis — with the SRAS curve rather than the LRAS one — implies that the changes in output can come about because of shifts in either aggregate demand or in aggregate supply. This leads to two radically extreme types of business cycles theories. They are:

1. Business cycle fluctuations in output are mainly caused by shocks originating in aggregate supply.
2. Business cycle fluctuations in output are mainly caused by shocks originating in aggregate demand.

Intuitively, as our earlier basic treatment of the AD-AS model shows, both demand and supply shocks can cause changes in output and unemployment. In practice, both are likely to occur and lead to or contribute to the actual business cycles experienced in the economy. This is spelled out in Chapter 16 on business cycles.

Business cycle theories study the determinants of the real-time, real-world cyclical fluctuations in output and other economic variables. Therefore, the concern of business cycle theories is with *chronological*, rather than analytical, periods during which both shifts in both AD and AS routinely occur. Business cycle theories attempt to sift through the relative importance of these AD and AS shifts. Some theories claim that the main sources of real-world fluctuations lie in real-time shocks to aggregate demand while others claim that the main sources of fluctuations lie in real-time shocks to aggregate supply. An extreme version of the latter asserts that only shocks originating from the supply side of the economy can cause business cycles. The theories that explain business cycles in this manner are called *real business cycle models*. They form a subset of business cycle theories. However, as pointed out above, shifts in both aggregate demand and supply do occur frequently and each can cause fluctuations in economic activity, so that there are two broad sources of business cycles. Their analysis is pursued in Chapter 16.

Fact Sheet 1.5: Booms and Recessions in the USA Since 1960

Economic fluctuations are a persistent pattern of output variations in every industrialized economy. This Fact Sheet illustrates such fluctuations for the USA. These economic fluctuations are composed of booms, recessions, and the turning points of troughs and peaks.

Recessions are prolonged non-positive growth periods in GDP. In the United States, the dates of recessions are officially announced by the National Bureau of Economic Research (NBER), which is a think-tank

Fact Sheet 1.5: (*Continued*)

in economics. Over the past 50 years, eight recessions have been recorded with an average length of 10 months. Some of the deepest have been (1) 1973–1975, due to the rapid rise in world oil prices and the end of the Vietnam War; (2) early 1980s, with the second oil crisis and tight monetary policy; (3) early 1990s, following the bursting of the Internet dot-com bubble, which led to a precipitous decrease in the prices of their stocks and the consequent decrease in the wealth of their shareholders; and (4) following the financial crisis of 2007–08. The following graph shows the official dates of the recessions by shaded columns.

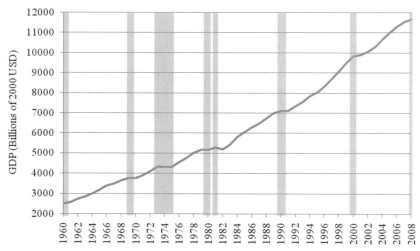

Box 1.5: The Fundamental Role of Economics as a Science

In studying macroeconomics, keep in mind that economics is a science. *A science is a discipline whose objective is to explain the real world.* This is done through its 'theories'. *Theories are attempts to understand specific segments of the economic reality.* The real world is too complex and has too many dimensions to encapsulate within the limited construct of theories. Therefore, theories are simplifications — such as caricatures — of reality. As such, they may be valid or not, or better for explaining some aspects of reality than others. Economics tries to judge their success or failure in explaining the relevant observation of the real world by intuition and statistical methods using data. Both are needed and useful in judging the validity and relative usefulness of theories. The science of using statistical data to test economic theories is known as *econometrics*, which is a component of economics.[14]

The role of economics in explaining the real world is also referred to as its '*positivist role*'. Another aspect of economics is its '*normative role*' — i.e., offering policy prescriptions to improve on the performance of the economy, hopefully as a means of increasing the welfare of its citizens, or of the functioning of one of its markets.

---

[14]The relationship between econometrics and economics is somewhat similar to that between engineering and physics.

Box 1.5: (*Continued*)

Theories/models in economics

A theory is a simplified system of relationships — in other words, a 'model' — for understanding or explaining some aspect of the real world. The AD-AS model discussed earlier is a theory. A theory may be valid (i.e., applicable) or invalid (i.e., at odds with the observations). Clearly, theories that are invalid should be discarded. All theories are invalid to some extent or under some circumstances, so that faith in them usually depends on experience about their degree of usefulness or failure.

Macroeconomics often continues to maintain several theories for explaining any given economic phenomenon — e.g., the current rate of inflation or unemployment. Using the inflation rate as an example of a variable whose determination is to be explained, economists have to choose that theory, among the competing ones, which does the best job in explaining the experienced rates of inflation. However, judgments on which theory performs best in this respect often differ among economists and lead to controversies.

As mentioned above, a science seeks to explain specific aspects of the real world. Economics is a science in this respect. However, not all of the theories in any of the sciences are valid under all conditions. Some sciences do a better job of explaining their field of reality than others, and are held in greater respect by the public than those that often do poorly. Historically, the public's faith in the accuracy and usefulness of economics, especially as a guide to policy, has tended to wax and wane.

Economics as the 'premier social science'

Sciences are broadly separated into two categories: the natural and the social sciences. The former deal with natural phenomena. Examples of natural sciences are biology, chemistry, and physics. Social sciences study aspects of society. Examples of social sciences are anthropology, economics, political science, and sociology. Economics is sometimes called 'the queen of the social sciences' because it is the most highly developed one of the social sciences. In general, the natural sciences have had historically a longer period of development than the social sciences. Further, the subjects of the social sciences are human beings, whose behavior seems harder to predict than natural phenomena. Part of the reason for this is that their behavior can change in response to policies based on the predictions of the theory. These provide some of the reasons the public is more sceptical about the success of economic policies in practice than of natural sciences.

Sciences differ from disciplines that do not try to explain the real world. Among the latter are languages, which are means of communication and analyses, and are built on systems of definitions and identities. Mathematics is a language in this sense. Economics needs to make extensive use of languages, including mathematics, in the formulation and development of its theories. Therefore, economic theories include identities among their relationships. However, theories must also include some relationships that are not identities but rather assertions about the real world — thereby imparting to the theory its critical element (as a component of a science) that it may not be valid for the phenomena that it seeks to explain.

1.13 Paradigms in Macroeconomics

There are several schools of thought or paradigms in macroeconomic. The currently dominant ones are the classical and Keynesian schools. The classical paradigm originated in the 18th century and periodically becomes the dominant doctrine in macroeconomics. It views the capitalist economy as one that tends to perform at full employment and produce full-employment output. It does allow for the possibility that the economy will sometimes produce less or more than this level, but views any such deviations from full-employment output as transitory and self-correcting, so that the central bank and the government do not need to pursue monetary and fiscal policies to speed the economy to its full employment level. As a corollary, even if the economy enters into an economic crisis, it can and should be left alone to recover. Further, the adherents of the classical paradigm maintain that intervention by the central bank and the government could worsen, or worsen as often or more often than improve, the performance of the economy.

The Keynesian paradigm originated in (John Maynard) Keynes' writings, especially with the publication in 1936 of his book, *The General Theory of Employment, Interest and Money*. This paradigm takes the view that the economy often does not perform at full employment; it may do so sometimes but not at other times. Further, the deviations from full employment are often not transitory and self-correcting. Hence, central banks and governments need to pursue monetary and fiscal policies to speed the economy to its full-employment level and to maintain it there.

1.14 Economic and Political Systems: Organization of the Macroeconomy

1.14.1 Capitalism

Capitalism is an economic system in which production, income distribution, and other aspects of the economy are controlled by individual economic units and allocations of products and inputs are based on prices determined by freely operating markets. In particular, capital (physical or financial) is owned by individuals and firms (which are owned by individuals). In a pure form of capitalism, the state's role in the economy is minimal and is confined to such public goods as providing law and order, defence, etc. In this form, the government does not engage directly in production and does not attempt to change the distribution of incomes in the economy. A corollary of the latter is that the government does not provide subsidies or make transfer payments either to firms or individuals.

The fundamental argument in favor of capitalism is based on the theory of prefect competition, which implies that individual economic units acting in their best interests (i.e., pursuing profit or utility maximization) maximize efficiency in production and allocation of inputs among different uses and firms under the existing technology. An additional argument in favor of capitalism is that it provides incentives in the form of higher profits and personal incomes for invention and innovation, which produce changes in production techniques and raise the growth rate of the economy over time.

1.14.2 Marxism and communism

There are also other approaches to the macroeconomy. One of these is that of the Marxist school, which is based on the writings of Karl Marx around the middle of the 19th century. In general, this school maintains that the capitalist system is inherently flawed. From a social perspective, it produces large (and unfair) income inequalities, which create a strong distinction between the working and capitalist classes, resulting in conflict and unrest. Further, the nature of the capitalist system is such that it periodically breaks down and collapses (as in crises, recessions, and Great Depressions). While the classical and Keynesian schools seek to understand the workings of the capitalist economy and to improve on its performance, Marxists see the replacement/overthrow of the capitalist system as the essential way out of its flaws. Marxist economic analysis provided the basis of communism, which has highly or fully centralized economies with the government controlling all production and distribution in the economy. While capitalism relies on markets to determine the prices of commodities, production, and income distribution, these roles are performed by bureaucrats in a communist system. While, in principle under the rather unrealistic assumption of perfect knowledge, such centralized/bureaucratic allocations can be made the same as under the market system, in practice they induce major inefficiencies in production and factor allocations. Further, compared with capitalism, the communist system does not provide incentives to individuals and production units to invent and innovate, so that the long-run growth rates of the economy tend to be lower under a communist organization of production than under a capitalist one.

1.14.3 Socialism

Compared with communism and capitalism, socialism (defined in such a way as to exclude communism) provides a system and philosophy that allows for a largely capitalist economy but wants to modify it in many respects. Some of these departures from capitalism include government ownership of production units,sometimes involving public ownership of industries as a whole (thereby excluding the private sector completely from the selected industries). The resulting macroeconomy with some production units owned by the government and some by private economic agents is often termed a 'mixed economy'. Other departures from the pure form of capitalism may not involve any ownership of production units or exclusive ownership of industries by the state but try to achieve a better income redistribution through progressive taxation, subsidies, and government expenditures. Social programs in this category include income support programs to individuals and households (often called welfare programs, intended to ensure that everyone has a minimum income level), child support, old age security, unemployment insurance, etc. The intent behind such programs is to obtain the allocative and production efficiency provided by a capitalist, market-determined, production system, while generally ameliorating the income inequalities that arise under capitalism, and reducing the uncertainty of incomes for the poorer segments of society.

Note that, sometimes, a country, e.g., China at present, tries to combine a communist political system (in China's case, inherited from the total communist system in earlier years) with a capitalist economic mode of production and factor allocation in specific economic sectors of the economy. The latter is intended to capture the allocative efficiency and long-run growth that private economic incentives in the form of higher profits and incomes tend to provide, thereby avoiding the inefficiency in production and lower long-run growth usually experienced under a communist economic system with allocation of inputs and production decisions by bureaucrats.

1.15 Conclusions

- The full, most productive use of the economy's factors — consistent with the desires of the owners of the factors of production and the structure of the economy — produces the full-employment level of output. This is called the long-run equilibrium level of output. Changes in aggregate demand do not change this output.
- The actual level of output in the economy at any given time can differ from the full-employment level. Some of these differences occur in short-run equilibrium, which allows increases (decreases) in output as aggregate demand increases (decreases). The actual output level may even differ from the short-run one if the economy is not in short-run equilibrium. Over the business cycle, trend-adjusted output increases in upturns and decreases in downturns.
- The rate of unemployment is negatively related to output. It increases in downturns and decreases during upturns in the economy.

- The statistical measures of national output and income are GDP (or NDP) and GNP (or NNP). These are calculated at market prices or at factor cost or by value added.
- For the real value of output, these measures are deflated by a price index. The most appropriate measure for deflating nominal GDP to arrive at real GDP is the GDP deflator. The CPI is the more appropriate index for studying changes in the standard of living of consumers. The CPI for Canada uses base-period weights for the quantities of commodities while the GDP deflator for Canada uses current-period weights.
- Growth, business cycles, crises, and booms are inherent features of free market economies.
- The role of economics is to explain the real world. It formulates theories and tests them for their ability to explain real-world and real-time economic variations. However, the core analytical apparatus of economics uses the analytical concepts of the long run and the short run, whose correspondence with the chronological passage of time — as in the real-time concepts of the short term and the long term — is at best very rough. Intuition plays a major role both in the formulation of theories and their application to real-time economies. Mathematics plays a major role in deriving rigorously the implications of theories.
- The two main paradigms in economics for the study of free market economies are the classical and Keynesian ones.

KEY CONCEPTS

Aggregate demand
Aggregate supply
Price level
Short-run aggregate supply
Long-run aggregate supply
Full-employment output
The natural rate of unemployment
GDP and GNP
GDP in market prices
GDP at factor cost

GDP deflator
Consumer price index
The rate of inflation
Identities versus equilibrium
  conditions
Short run versus short term
Long run versus long term
Business cycles
Short-run macroeconomic model
  versus growth theory

Paradigms in economics
Capitalism, communism,
  and socialism, and
The definition of a science,
  social sciences, economics
  as the queen of the
  social sciences.

CRITICAL CONCLUSIONS

- GDP per capita can be used as a proxy for living standards over time and across countries.
- The AD-AS diagram is an important tool for studying the determination of real output and the price level.
- The long-run level of output is called the full-employment level of output. The long-run level of unemployment is called the natural rate or full-employment rate of unemployment.
- Inflation may cause an increase in output in the short run but does not do so in the long run. It may reduce unemployment in the short run but does not do so in the long run.

- In the long run, increases in aggregate demand only cause inflation, not increases in output or decreases in unemployment.
- The long-run increase in living standards only comes from increases in output per capita, which depends on increases in capital per worker and technical change. These are studied in growth theory.
- Short run and long run are analytical concepts. These allow the study of economic changes in analytical time. Short term and long term are chronological concepts that are needed for the study of real-world, real-time economies. In general, the short-term effects — in the year ahead — of any shock include both short-run and long-run effects, but may not encompass even all the short-run effects.
- Business cycles are fluctuations of output and unemployment over time. They occur in real time. Business cycle fluctuations are explained by taking into account the structure of the economy and both the short-run and long-run effects of shocks originating in the supply and demand sides of the economy.
- Growth, business cycles and crises are inherent and interrelated features of free market economies.
- Identities always hold. They differ from equilibrium conditions, which hold when there is equilibrium but not when there is disequilibrium.
- Economics is a science. It uses theories/models to explain economic phenomena and to make predictions about the real world. It uses econometrics to test its theories.
- The common form of organization of modern industrial economies is the free market system arising out of capitalism, with socialism representing modified forms of capitalism to cure some of the perceived social and economic ill-effects of capitalism. Communism in its purest form replaces the free market economy by a centralized, bureaucratic-run one.

REVIEW AND DISCUSSION QUESTIONS

1. Show diagrammatically the long-run and short-run levels of real output and the price level with equilibrium at full employment. Now show the effects of (a) a permanent increase in demand, (b) a temporary (i.e., short run but without being long run) decrease in supply, and (c) a permanent (i.e., both short-run and long-run) decrease in supply.
2. What are the main components of aggregate demand (AD) in the open economy?
3. Why can output differ in the short-run from the full-employment one? Can it be even higher? How do you explain this?
4. Specify the equation relating the unemployment rate to the employment rate.
5. For the open economy, what are the two main methods of measuring gross income and output of the economy? What is the difference between their gross and net versions?
6. What are the three methods of calculating GDP and what are the differences between them? What is double counting?
7. Developing countries typically have much smaller participation of women in the labor force and produce a larger proportion of their consumption in home-produced goods. Their agricultural sector also produces a larger proportion of the food consumed by the farmers themselves. Would these patterns produce lower official values of GDP per capita than for the developed economies? Why? How might the measures of GDP per capita be adjusted to eliminate this mis-measurement of the standard of living in cross-country comparisons?

8. How does a closed economy differ from an open one? What are the main markets studied for the closed economy macroeconomics?

9. When would there be disequilibrium between aggregate demand and supply? Show diagrammatically? What do you expect to happen to prices in your shown situation? Define a stable equilibrium. Does your diagram indicate the stability of equilibrium? Give reasons for your answer.

10. Specify the distinctions between long-run, short-run, and actual output? Illustrate your answer with appropriate diagrams of the relationship between long-run and short-run output and the price level? Explain the reasons for the different relationships?

11. What are business cycles? What two types of explanations are possible for their causes? What explanation do the real business cycle theories favor?

ADVANCED AND TECHNICAL QUESTIONS

Basic model for Chapter 1

You are given the following information for the year 2000 on an economy. All amounts are in current dollars.

Goods and services produced by factories		10,000
Revenue from sales during the year (goods sold)		8,000
Labor costs	7,000	
Interest paid to domestic residents	1,600	
Interest paid to foreign residents	400	
Taxes paid by factories to the government	100	
Goods purchased by some factories from others for inputs	900	
Value of the factories as of January 1, 2000		150,000
Value of the factories as of December 31, 2000		150,000
Goods carried over in the economy on January 1, 2000		200,000
Value of home activities, such as meals, child-care, etc.		14,000
Interest and profits received by residents on foreign investments		100
Paid volunteer activities by NGOs		200
Unpaid volunteer activities, such as home visits to the elderly, by NGOs		300
Sales taxes paid by residents to the government		150

T1. For the basic model,

    a Calculate GDP for this economy by three different methods. Do these calculations yield the same amount?

    b Calculate GNP and the difference between GDP and GNP at market prices.

    c If the value of home production, such as care for the elderly, increases by $90, recalculate GDP.

    d If persons engaged in home production reorganize their production arrangements into factories and start selling all of their output to others, while buying back a corresponding amount for their own consumption, re-calculate GDP.

    e If the NGOs begin to raise the funds needed by donations from residents and pay all their (including formerly unpaid) volunteers, recalculate GDP.

T2. Assuming that real GDP remains constant, suppose that at the beginning of year 1, nominal GDP was $1000 and the price level was 2. If the inflation rate in year 1 was 10%, what would be their values at the beginning of year 2?

T3. Suppose that at the beginning of year 1, nominal GDP was $1000 and the price level was 2. If the inflation rate in year 1 was 10%, what would be their values at the beginning of year 2? If the inflation rate in year 2 was 25%, what would be their values at the beginning of year 3? What is the amount of inflation over the two years? Does it differ from the amount obtained by adding the inflation rates over the two years? If not, why not?

T4. Are productivity shifts endogenous or exogenous in the AD-AS model? Why? Suppose productivity increases. Show its effects on the two main endogenous variables of that model?

CHAPTER 2
Money, Prices, Interest Rates, and Fiscal Deficits

Some of the fundamental questions of macroeconomics concern the proper role of monetary, fiscal, and other policies in managing the economy.

Money is the medium of payments. The money supply and interest rates have important effects on the economy. Changes in the central bank's monetary policy on these variables are major determinants of aggregate demand in the economy and, therefore, of changes in the economy's output, unemployment, price level, and the inflation rate.

Governments usually run fiscal deficits or surpluses, which also impact on aggregate demand and interest rates, and then on output and unemployment.

Among the most important questions in macroeconomic analysis are whether, how and to what extent changes in the money supply, interest rates, the price level, and inflation affect the economy's real variables, especially national output and employment. The control of the money supply and interest rates rests with the central bank or '*the monetary authority*'. Its policies with respect to the money supply and interest rates are known as *monetary policy*.

The government or '*the fiscal authority*' determines the policies on government spending, taxes, and the fiscal deficit/surplus. Its policies with respect to these variables are known as *fiscal policy*.

Both monetary and fiscal policies impact on a considerable number of macroeconomic variables. In particular, they affect aggregate expenditures and interest rates in the economy.

2.1 What Is Money and What Does It Do?

2.1.1 The functions of money

Money is not itself the name of a particular asset and is best defined independently of the particular assets that may exist in the economy at any one time, since the assets which function as money tend to change over time in any given country and among countries. At a theoretical level, money is defined in terms of the functions that it performs. The traditional specification of these functions is:

  (i) medium of exchange/payments,
 (ii) store of value, sometimes specified as a temporary store of value or temporary abode of purchasing power,
(iii) standard of deferred payments, and
(iv) unit of account.

Of these functions, the medium of payments is the most essential function of money. Any asset that does not directly perform this function — or cannot indirectly perform it through a quick and costless transfer into a medium of exchange — cannot be designated as money. A developed economy usually has many financial instruments that can perform such a role, though some do so better than others. The particular instruments that perform this role vary over time, with currency being the only or main medium of exchange early in the evolution of monetary economies. It is supplemented by demand deposits with the arrival of the banking system and then by an increasing array of financial assets as other financial intermediaries become established.

2.1.2 The practical definitions of money

Historically, the definitions of money have measured the quantity of money in the economy as the sum of those items that serve as media of exchange in the economy. However, at any time in a developed monetary economy, there may be other items that do not directly serve as a medium of exchange but are readily convertible into the medium of exchange at little cost and trouble and can simultaneously be a store of value. Such items are close substitutes for the medium of exchange itself. Consequently, there is considerable controversy and disagreement about whether to confine the definition of money to the narrow role of the medium of exchange or to broaden it to include close substitutes for the medium of exchange.

The theoretically narrow definition of money is that it is the good that directly serves as a *medium of payments*. This *narrow definition of money* is given the symbol M1. It is defined in practical terms as the sum of the currency (i.e., notes and coins) in the hands of the public and the public's demand deposits in commercial banks. Payments for commodities are usually made by the transfers of currency and demand deposits (through checks and debit cards) from the buyer to the seller. Close substitutes to M1 are referred to as *near-monies*.

A broader definition of money that has won the widest acceptance among economists is known as the (Milton) *Friedman's (or broad) definition of money* and has the symbol *M2*. It defines money as the sum of currency in the hands of the public plus all of the public's deposits in commercial banks. The latter include demand deposits as well as savings deposits in commercial banks.

A still broader definition of money is *M2* plus deposits in *near-banks* — i.e., those financial institutions in which the deposits perform almost the same role for depositors as similar deposits in commercial banks. Examples of such institutions are savings and loan associations and mutual savings banks in the United States (USA); credit unions, trust companies, and mortgage loan companies in Canada; and building societies in the United Kingdom (UK). The incorporation of such deposits into the measurement of money is designated by the symbols M3, M4, etc., or by M2A (or M2+), M2B (or M2++), etc. However, the definitions of these symbols have not become standardised, so that their definitions remain country specific.

Financial institutions in the economy

Financial institutions are firms involved in the process that determines the money supply and interest rates. They also intermediate between the borrowing and lending processes in the economy. In practical terms, financial institutions include the central bank, commercial banks, near-banks such as credit unions, trust companies, brokerage companies, postal banks, pension funds, etc. They do not engage in the production or consumption of commodities but receive funds from some sources and channel them to others (i.e., invests them).

2.2 Money Supply and Money Stock

Money is a good, which, just like other goods, is demanded and supplied by the various participants in the economy. There are a number of determinants of the demand and supply of money. The most important of the determinants of money demand are national income, the price level, and interest rates, while that of the

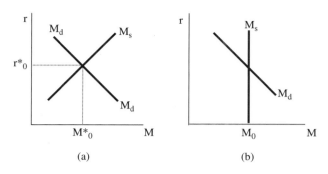

Figure 2.1

money supply is the behavior of the central bank of the country which is given the power to control the money supply and bring about changes in it.

The *equilibrium amount* in the market for money specifies the *money stock*, as opposed to the *money supply*, which is a behavioral function. These are depicted in Figure 2.1a with the nominal quantity of money M on the horizontal axis and the market interest rate r on the vertical axis. The money supply curve is designated as M^s and the money demand curve is designated as M^d. The equilibrium quantity of money is M_0^*. It equals the quantity of money supplied at the equilibrium interest rate r_0^*. Note that the quantity M_0^* is strictly speaking not the money supply, which has a curve or a function rather than a single value. However, M_0^* is the money stock that would be observed in equilibrium.[1]

The money supply and the money stock are identical in the case where the money supply is exogenously determined, usually by the policies of the central bank. In such a case, it is independent of the interest rate and other economic variables, though it may influence them. In this case, the money supply 'curve' will be a vertical line, as shown by the line M^s in Figure 2.1b, with the money supply as M_0. Much of the monetary and macroeconomic reasoning of a theoretical nature assumes this case, so that the terms 'money stock' and 'money supply' are used synonymously. One has to judge from the context whether the two concepts are being used as distinct or as identical ones.

Note that the symbol M in Figures 2.1a and 2.1b can represent any of the relevant money supply variables, i.e., $M1$, $M2$, etc. These symbols were defined earlier.

The control of the money supply rests with the monetary authorities. Their policy with respect to changes in the money supply and interest rates is known as *monetary policy*.

2.3 The Nominal Versus the Real Value of the Money Supply

It is important to distinguish between the nominal and the real value of the money stock. The *nominal value of money* is in dollars — i.e., in term of money itself as the measuring unit. The *real value of money* is in terms of its purchasing power over goods and services. Thus, the nominal value of a $1 note is 1 — and that of a $20 note is 20. The real value of money is the amount of goods and services one unit of money can buy and is the reciprocal of the price level of the commodities (goods and services) traded in the economy. It equals $1/P$ where P is the price level in the economy. The real value of money is what we usually mean when we use the

---

[1] M_0^* or M_0 (with 0 in the subscript) in these figures is different from the symbol M_0 used later to refer to the 'monetary base' — which is different from the money supply but related to it.

term 'the value of money'. The real value of $M1$ equals $M1/P$ and the real value of $M2$ equals $M2/P$, where P is the economy's price level.

The demand and supply functions of money are often stated in nominal terms in a general analysis involving *both* of them. However, the demand for money is mainly by the public, which is concerned not so much with its nominal as with its real value since the latter represents its ability to buy commodities. Therefore, the demand for money is usually investigated in real terms. However, the supply of money is mainly determined by the central bank in nominal terms.[2]

2.4 Bonds and Stocks in Macroeconomics

The common definition of a *bond* is that it is a financial instrument with a fixed payment, known as the '*coupon*', at pre-specified intervals plus the repayment of the principal amount at a designated time — known as the redemption or maturity date. Bonds are issued by the government (including those of the states/provinces and municipalities) and corporations and are normally traded/re-traded in the financial markets.

The common definition of a *share* — shares, *equities*, or stocks in the plural — of a corporation is that it is a financial instrument which entitles the shareholder to the declared dividends of the corporation and participation in the ownership rights of the corporation. Normally, shares do not have a (fixed) coupon payment and there is no designated redemption date. However, hybrid forms of shares and bonds also exist. An example of such a form is preferred shares and convertible bonds (i.e., bonds that may be converted to shares).

Bonds and shares are normally not acceptable to sellers in payment for their commodities. Since both bonds and stocks are financial instruments but neither qualifies as a medium of payments, macroeconomic analysis aggregates them into the single concept of 'bonds' in macroeconomics. Therefore, *the term 'bonds' in macroeconomics and in this book refers to non-monetary financial assets* and differs from its meaning in ordinary English language usage.

There exist in the economy many financial instruments that lie at the interface between money and bonds. Such instruments are not directly a medium of payments but can be easily and almost without delay or cost be converted into demand deposits or currency. Among these are savings deposits in commercial banks and other financial institutions. There is no hard and fast rule about their classification. For some types of analysis, they are included in money and excluded from bonds, while for other types of analysis they are included in bonds and excluded from money.

2.5 The Definition of the Money Market in Macroeconomics

The *money market* in macroeconomics is defined as the market in which the demand and supply of money ($M1$, $M2$, or a broader money measure) interact, with equilibrium representing its clearance. However, the common English language usage of the term 'money market' refers to the market for short-term bonds, especially that of Treasury bills. To illustrate this common usage, this definition is embodied in the term, *Money Market Mutual Funds*, which are mutual funds that invest in short-term bonds.

---

[2]Note that in the equilibrium equation setting money demand equal to money supply, the dimensions — which can be either real or nominal — of both the money supply and demand must be identical.

It is important to note that our usage of the term 'the money market' in this book will follow that of macroeconomics. To reiterate, *the 'money market' in macroeconomics means the market for money, not the market for short-term bonds.* The analysis of the money market is based on the demand and supply of money and of equilibrium between them.

2.6 A Brief History of the Definition of Money

The evolution from a *barter economy* to a monetary economy usually starts with a commodity money — i.e., a commodity used in consumption also begins to be used as a medium of payment. One form of commodity monies is currency in the form of coins made of a precious metal, with an exchange value that is at least roughly equal to the value of the metal in the coin. These coins were usually minted with the monarch's authority and were made *legal tender*, so that the seller or creditor could not refuse to accept them in payment.

Legal tender was in certain circumstances supplemented as a means of payment by the promissory notes of trustworthy persons or institutions and in the 18th and 19th centuries by 'bills of exchange'[3] in Britain. While these bills could be traded by the sellers to other buyers or banks, they did not became a generally accepted medium of payment. The emergence of private commercial banks in the 19th century in Britain led to note issues by them and eventually also led to orders of withdrawal (i.e., checks) drawn upon these banks by those holding demand deposits with them. However, while the keeping of demand deposits with banks had become common among firms and richer individuals by the beginning of the 20th century, the popularity of such deposits among the ordinary persons came about only in the 20th century. With this popularity, demand deposits became a component of the medium of exchange in the economy, with their amount eventually becoming larger than that of currency.

Until the mid-20th century, demand/checkable deposits did not pay interest but savings deposits in commercial banks did do so, though subject to legal or customary ceilings on their interest rates. During the 1950s, changes in banking practices caused these savings deposits to increasingly become closer substitutes for demand deposits so that the major dispute of the 1950s on the definition of money was whether savings deposits should or should not be included in the definition of money. However, by the early 1960s, most economists had come to measure the supply of money by $M2$ — that is, as $M1$ plus savings deposits in commercial banks — which does not include any types of deposits in other financial institutions. $M2$ is known as the Friedman definition (measure) of money, since Milton Friedman had been one of its main proponents in the 1950s and 1960s.

Financial innovation — i.e., innovation in financial instruments, institutions, and processes — has been extremely rapid in the last few decades. It has included innovations in the payments mechanism, which has included technical changes in the servicing of various kinds of deposits, such as the introduction of automatic teller machines and Internet banking (i.e., banking from home through the use of computers, etc.). It has also included the creation of new assets such as Money Market Mutual Funds. There has also been the spread first of *credit cards*, then of *debit/bank cards*, followed still more recently by the attempts to circulate *smart cards* (i.e., cards which embody a certain amount of money from which deductions can be made when making payments through them).[4] Further, competition among the different types of financial intermediaries in the

---

[3] Bills of exchange were promissory notes promising to pay a certain amount of money at a specified future date. They were issued by buyers of goods to the sellers in exchange for goods, and represented a method of extending trade credit by the suppliers of goods to the firms buying the goods.

[4] Examples of these include telephone cards, bus cards, etc.

provision of liabilities that are close to demand deposits or readily convertible into the latter, has increased considerably in recent decades. Many of these innovations have served to further blur the distinction between demand and savings deposits and also blurred the distinction between banks and some of the other types of financial intermediaries as providers of liquid assets. This process of innovation and the evolution of financial institutions into an overlapping pattern in the provision of financial services is still continuing.

2.7 The Current Definitions of Money and Related Concepts

We have already referred to several definitions of money. These definitions are not completely standardized across countries for $M1$ and $M2$. The *approximate generic definitions of* M1 *and* M2 *that we will use through this book* are:

$M1 =$ currency in the hands of the public plus checkable deposits in commercial banks and other financial institutions and

$M2 = M1$ plus (small or retail) savings deposits in deposit-taking financial institutions.

Note that $M1$, $M2$, and other measures of money exclude amounts held by the commercial banks, the government, foreign banks, and official institutions, since these amounts are not relevant to financing the public's expenditures. There are also many symbols — often differing among different countries — used for measures of money broader than $M2$. Some of these are illustrated in Box 2.1 from their usage in Canada, the USA and the UK.

Extended Analysis Box 2.1: Current Meanings of the Symbols for the Monetary Aggregates
in Selected Countries

The monetary aggregates for Canada

$M1 =$ currency in the hands of the public plus demand deposits in chartered banks[5]

$M1+ = M1$ plus personal checkable deposits and non-personal checkable notice deposits at chartered banks, trust and mortgage loan companies, and credit unions (including caisses populaires[6])[7]

$M2 = M1$ plus personal savings deposits and non-personal notice deposits at chartered banks

$M2+ = M2$ plus deposits at trust and mortgage loan companies and credit unions (including caisses populaires)

'Adjusted $M2+$' $= M2+$ plus Canada savings bonds and mutual funds at financial institutions

$M3 = M2$ plus non-personal fixed term deposits at chartered banks and foreign currency deposits of residents booked in Canada

The monetary aggregates for the USA

$M1 =$ currency in circulation among the public (i.e., excluding the Fed, the US Treasury, and commercial banks) + demand deposits in commercial banks[8] (excluding interbank and US government

---

[5]The chartered banks in Canada correspond to the commercial banks in our discussions.

[6]These are essentially credit unions in Quebec, Canada.

[7]TML is the abbreviation for trust and mortgage loan companies and CUCP is the abbreviation for credit unions and *caisses populaires*.

[8]Our usage of the term 'commercial banks' refers to 'depository institutions' in the USA.

Extended Analysis Box 2.1: (*Continued*)

deposits and those of foreign banks) + other checkable deposits including negotiable orders of withdrawal (NOW) + credit union (such as savings and loan associations) share draft accounts + demand deposits at thrift institutions (such as mutual savings banks) — cash items in the process of collection and federal reserve float

$M2 = M1$ + savings deposits, including money market deposit accounts + small time deposits under $100,000 + balances in retail money market mutual funds

$M3 = M2$ + time deposits over $100,000 + Eurodollars held by US residents at foreign branches of US banks and at all banks in the UK and Canada + money market mutual funds held by institutions

The monetary aggregates for the UK

$M1$ = currency plus current account (checking) sterling deposits in retail banks and building societies, held by 'UK residents'[9]

$M2$ = currency plus sterling deposits in retail banks[10] and building societies, held by UK residents

$M4$ = currency plus sterling deposits at the central bank, other banks and building societies, held by UK residents

As listed in Box 2.1, the detailed descriptions of $M1$ and $M2$ for Canada, the UK and the USA are more complex than their standardized generic definitions. However, these definitions are reasonable proxies. Note also that the definitions of the monetary aggregates beyond $M2$, e.g., $M3$ and $M4$, differ more radically among countries than of $M1$ and $M2$. For $M3$ and $M4$, the only common denominator is that they are broader than $M2$ and include, besides $M2$, other highly liquid assets held at financial institutions. The reliance on these specific wider aggregates usually reflects the peculiarities of the country's financial structure.

Note that currency holdings C (i.e., currency, which consists of notes and coins in the hands of the public) and $M1$ are becoming increasingly smaller proportions of $M2$ and wider aggregates. We illustrate the relevant magnitudes and ratios by the following. For Canada in 1995, the currency in the economy was $26.8b, $M1$ was $62.7b while $M2+$ was $618.4b, so that $C/M1$ was 42% and $C/M2$ was only 4%. The ratio of $M1$ to $M2+$ was only 10%. In the USA, at the end of 1995, the amount of currency in the economy was $379b,[11] $M1$ was $1,150b, $M2$ was $3,680b, and $M3$ was $4,954b. The ratio $C/M1$ was 33% and $C/M2$ was 10%. The ratio of $M1$ to $M2$ was only 31% and to $M3$ was 23%. For the UK in 1995, currency holdings were £20.8b, $M2$ was £439.4b, and $M4$ was £682.5b.[12]

Fact Sheet 2.1: Monetary Aggregates of the USA

This Fact Sheet illustrates changes in the relative importance of currency (held by the banks and the public), demand deposits in banks, $M1$, $M2$, and $M3$ by examining movements in these monetary aggregates for the USA. Since the 1970s, with banks providing ever closer substitutes for checking deposits and the increasing

---

[9]'UK residents' is meant to exclude the public sector and the financial institutions.

[10]Since 1993, these deposits include both non-interest-bearing and interest-bearing deposits.

[11]b stands for billion defined as 1,000 million.

[12]These figures are taken from *Statistics on Payment Systems in the Group of Ten Countries*, published by the Bank for International Settlements, various years.

Fact Sheet 2.1: (*Continued*)

use of debit and credit cards, broader monetary measures such as *M*2 and *M*3 have become ever larger proportions of the money supply.

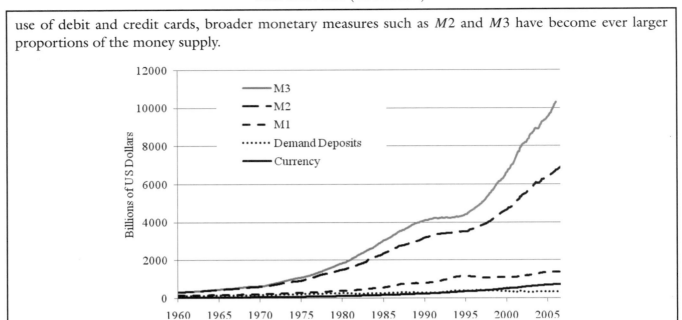

2.8 The Monetary Base and Bank Reserves

The money supply equals the *monetary base* — sometimes also called the *reserve base*[13] — multiplied by the *monetary base multiplier*, which is defined as the ratio of *M*/*M*0, where the symbol *M*0 (pronounced as 'M zero')[14] stands for the monetary base. It generic definition is:

$$M0 = \text{currency in the hands of the non-bank public} + \text{currency held by the commercial banks}$$
$$+ \text{deposits held by the commercial banks at the central bank.}$$

The reserves held by the commercial banks are called *bank reserves* and are designated by the symbol *R*. Bank reserves for the banking system as a whole are defined as:

$$R = \text{currency held by the commercial banks} + \text{deposits held by the commercial banks at the central bank.}$$

Therefore, we have:

$$M0 \equiv C + R.$$

Note the difference between the monetary base *M*0 and the money supply *M*1. $M1 = C + D$, where *D* is demand deposits of the public in commercial banks, while $M0 = C + R$.

---

[13]The monetary base is also known as *high-powered money*.

[14]The meaning of this symbol differs from that of M_0, which is meant to indicate a particular value of the money supply *M* and is pronounced as *M* sub zero.

2.8.1 The relationship between the monetary base and the money supply

The central bank controls the monetary base through its purchases and sales of bonds to the public. A purchase of bonds means that the central bank pays for them by transferring funds from itself to the public, which increases the monetary base. A sale of bonds means that the central bank receives funds from the public, which decreases the monetary base. These sales or purchases of bonds in the financial markets are called *open market operations*. They are a major element in the central bank's control of the monetary base and the money supply.

The money supply is related to the monetary base by the equation:

$$M1 = \alpha_1 M0, \tag{1}$$

where:

$$M1 = \text{narrow money supply,}$$
$$M0 = \text{monetary base, and}$$
$$\alpha_1 = \text{monetary base multiplier } (= \partial M1/\partial M0) \text{ for } M1.$$

The coefficient α_1 represents the increase in the money supply $M1$ for a unit change in the monetary base $M0$. Its value is usually greater than one. In fact, a value of three or four is not unusual for it for the modern economies. This implies that a change in the monetary base engineered by the central bank increases the money supply by the multiple α_1, so that it is called the monetary base (to the money supply) multiplier.[15] The broader the definition of the monetary aggregate, the larger will be the relevant multiplier. For $M2$, we have:

$$M2 = \alpha_2 M0,$$

where $\alpha_2 = \partial M2/\partial M0$ and is the monetary base multiplier for $M2$. Since $M2$ is always larger (because it also includes savings deposits) than $M1$, $\alpha_2 > \alpha_1$.

The use of monetary base and the money supply as instruments of monetary policy and their relationship to interest rates will be studied in Chapter 5.

2.9 The Quantity Equation

Any exchange of goods in the market between a buyer and a seller involves an expenditure that can be specified in two different ways.

1. Expenditures by a buyer must *always* equal the amount of money handed over to the sellers, and expenditures by the members of a group which includes both buyers and sellers must *always* equal the amount of money used by the group multiplied by the number of times it has been used over and over again.[16] Designating the average number of times money turns over in financing transactions during a given period as its velocity of circulation V, expenditures as $\$Y$, and the money stock in use as $\$M$, we have $\$Y \equiv \$MV$, where $\equiv$ indicates an *identity* rather than merely an equilibrium condition.

---

[15]The value of this multiplier depends upon the nature of the banking system, the public's demand for currency, the banks' demand for reserves and the monetary aggregate used.

[16]Thus, a person buying $100 of goods pays $100 to seller 1. Suppose the latter in turn buys $100 worth of goods from another seller (seller 2) of goods. The total expenditure was thus $200, the amount of money used was only $100 and it was paid over twice in financing the expenditures. Suppose now that the initial seller had bought only $50 worth of goods from Seller 2. Total expenditures would now be $150, the amount of money in use remains at $100 but it has been paid over only 1.5 times on average.

2. Expenditures on the goods bought can also be measured as the quantity y of the commodities (goods and services) traded times the average price of commodities.[17] Expenditures Y then always equal the quantity y of the commodities bought times their price level P, so that, $\$Y \equiv \$Py$.

Obviously, these two different ways of measuring expenditures must yield the identical amount. These two measures are

$$Y \equiv MV$$
$$Y \equiv Py.$$

Hence

$$MV \equiv Py. \tag{2}$$

Equation (2) is an identity since it is derived solely from identities. It is valid under any set of circumstances whatever since it can be reduced to the statement: in a given period by a given group of people, expenditures equal expenditures, with only a difference in the computational method between them. Equation (2) is *true* for any person or group of persons.[18] If it is applied, as it usually is, to the aggregate level for a country, the two sides of the identity and its four variables refer to all expenditures in the country. But if it is applied to the world economy as a whole, its total expenditures and the four variables will be for the world economy.

2.9.1 The quantity equation in growth rates

The quantity equation specified above was $MV \equiv Py$. This can be restated in growth rates (See Chapter 1, Box 1.3. Also consult Useful Mathematical Formulae for Economics page xliii of this book.) as:

$$M'' + V'' \equiv P'' + y'',$$

where $''$ indicates the rate of change (also called the growth rate) of the variable. This identity can be restated as:

$$\pi \equiv M'' + V'' - y'',$$

where π is the rate of inflation and is the same as P''. This identity asserts that the rate of inflation is always equal to the rate of money growth plus the growth rate of velocity less the growth rate of output. *Ceteris paribus*, the higher the money growth rate, the higher will be the inflation rate, while the higher is the output growth rate, the lower will be the inflation rate. Note that velocity also changes over time and can contribute to inflation if it increases, or reduce inflation when it falls. The spread of banks and automatic teller/banking machines (ATMs) has tended to increase velocity in recent decades.

2.9.2 The implications of the quantity equation for a persistently high inflation rate

In normal circumstances in the economy, velocity changes during a year but not by more than a few percentage points. Similarly, real output growth rate is usually only a few percentage points. For the quantity equation, we need only to consider the difference $(V'' - y'')$ between them. In the normal case, both velocity and output increase over time and the difference in their growth rates is likely to be in low single digits. *Adding this*

---

[17] Since the goods traded are generally of different kinds, there are obviously problems in thinking of an aggregate measure of goods in physical terms and of the price level to be associated with a unit of such a conglomerate or composite good. Both the 'quantity' or 'output' y of this good and its average price P must then be thought of as indices.

[18] Identities are said to be true or false. By comparison, propositions or relationships about the real world are said to be valid or invalid.

information to the quantity equation implies that high (high single digits or higher numbers) and persistent (i.e., for several years) rates of inflation can only stem from high and persistent money growth rates. This is particularly true of hyperinflations in which the annual inflation rate may be in double (10% or more) or triple (100% or more) digits or even higher.

To reiterate, the source of high and persistent inflation is high and persistent money growth rates. Therefore, if the monetary authorities wish to drastically reduce inflation rates to low levels, they must pursue a policy that achieves an appropriate reduction in the money supply growth.

Fact Sheet 2.2: Money Growth and Inflation in the USA, 1960–2008

The quantity theory asserts a close positive relationship from the quantity of money and the rate of inflation. The following graph is a plot of these for the USA during 1960–2008. If the quantity theory held perfectly during every period, we would expect to see a perfect positive trend along the 45-degree line between annual money supply growth and inflation. In reality, as we see that the relationship between the two is only slightly positive. However, because the effect of money supply on inflation is usually lagged by some quarters, we might expect that its effect on inflation will not be noticeable in the same period, but is likely to be more visible over longer periods of time (and in hyperinflation). In the interim, money growth impacts on output and velocity, which do not remain constant.

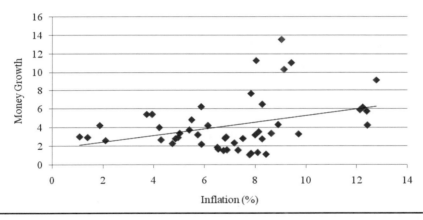

2.10 The Quantity Theory

The quantity theory was first formulated in the 18th century. It is the proposition that: *ceteris paribus, a change in the money supply in the economy causes a proportionate change in the price level.* This proposition only applies in the long run, with output at its long-run (full-employment) level. It does not apply if the economy is away from its full-employment level, as usually happens when the economy is in a recession with output below its full-employment level. It also does not apply while the economy is undergoing adjustments following a change in the money supply.

The quantity theory was dominant as a theory of the determination of the price level through the 19th and early 20th century, though more so as an approach than a rigorous theory. Its statement varied considerably among writers. One version of the form that it had achieved by the beginning of the 20th century is presented below from the works of Irving Fisher, an American economist in the early 20th century.

Extended Analysis Box 2.2: The Difference between the Quantity Theory and the Quantity Equation

The quantity theory is vitally different in spirit and purpose from the quantity equation. The quantity theory is not an *identity*, as is the quantity equation. The quantity equation is not a *theory*, as is the quantity theory.

A relationship or statement that *always* holds under *any* circumstances is said to be an *identity* or *tautology*. Identities generally arise by the way the terms in the relationship are defined or measured. Thus, the quantity equation defined (measured) expenditures in two different ways, once as *MV* and then as *Py*, so that it is an identity. Note that an identity is different from — and a much stronger statement than — an equilibrium condition which holds only if there is equilibrium but not otherwise — i.e., it does not hold if there is disequilibrium. Further, a *theory* may or may not apply to any particular economy in the real world or it may be valid for some states — e.g., equilibrium ones — but not for others, while an *identity* is true (or false) by virtue of the definitions of its variables and its logic so that its truth or falsity cannot be checked by reference to real-world, real-time observations. A theory usually includes some identities but must also include behavioral conditions — which are statements about the behavior of the economy or its agents — and often also equilibrium conditions on its markets. The quantity theory does so,[19] but not the quantity equation. Further, note that the quantity theory includes (long-run) equilibrium conditions. Since the quantity equation is an identity, it does not need to do so and does not incorporate any equilibrium conditions.

2.10.1 The transactions approach to the quantity theory

This approach is associated with the writings of Irving Fisher in the first quarter of the 19th century. He started with the quantity equation. He recognized it as an identity and added two assumptions:

(i) *Except during transition periods*, the economy's output is independent of the changes in the money supply.
(ii) *Except during transition periods*, the velocity of the circulation of money is independent of the money supply changes.

On assumption (i), the dominant theory of the 19th and early 20th century on output and employment in the economy implied that the labor market would be in equilibrium at full employment and that output would tend to stay at the full-employment level except in temporary disequilibria. This full-employment output is the long-run output, explained in Chapter 1. It is independent of the money supply and prices. Similarly, in the long-run equilibrium, the velocity V is also independent of changes in the money supply. We discuss this point further in a subsequent subsection.

Fisher's model can be stated as:

$$\text{Quantity equation:} \qquad MV \equiv Py$$
$$\text{Long-run equilibrium conditions:} \quad y = y^{f}$$
$$V = V^{*},$$

where $*$ and the superscript f indicate long-run values which do not change when M and P change. Hence, in the long run, $MV^{*} = Py^{f}$. Therefore, noting that the rate of growth of the price level (P'') is the same as the

---

[19]This is done through its statement that in the long run, both output and velocity are independent of the money supply and prices. This statement will hold in some economies but need not do so in all economies.

inflation rate π,

$$\pi^* = M'' + V^{*''} - y^{f''},$$

where π^* is the long-run inflation rate. Since the changes in M'' and π do not cause V^* and y^f to change, $\partial V^*/\partial M = 0$ (so that $V^{*''} = 0$) and $\partial y^f/\partial M = 0$ (so that $y^{f''} = 0$). Hence, for long-run equilibrium, changes in the money supply imply that:

$$\pi^* = M''.$$

That is, if we examine the effect of changes in the money supply in long-run equilibrium only, the inflation rate will equal the money growth rate. This is the quantity theory proposition.

The adjustment period relevant to the quantity theory

Note the qualification 'except during transition periods' to the quantity theory proposition. Following a change in the money supply by the central bank, the economy usually takes time to absorb it and to return to long-run equilibrium. During this adjustment, both output and velocity tend to change. The inflation rate is usually less than the money growth rate during the adjustment phase.

The adjustment period is often longer than a year, so that the real-world economies rarely have an inflation rate equal to the money-growth rate during the short term. This is even less likely if the real-world economy had started with a recession, so that it was already out of its long-run equilibrium, and increases in the money supply increase output. That is, for real-time economies, the assumption of continuous long-run equilibrium with full employment and long-run velocity is doubtful, so that the quantity theory does not apply over short periods.[20] However, most macroeconomic theories accept that the quantity theory holds under the assumptions of long-run equilibrium. This result is established in Chapter 7.

Is velocity constant over time?

Velocity (of the circulation of money in financing purchases) is the average number of times money changes hands in the economy over a given period. This can be formally derived from $MV \equiv Y$ which implies that $V \equiv Y/M$.

Velocity does not stay constant over time in real-world economies. It increases as real incomes rise because the income elasticity of real money balances is less than unity — usually about 0.7.[21] Since velocity is the ratio of real income to real money balances, velocity increases as income increases. Therefore, as income changes over the business cycle and over the long run of growth theory, velocity changes. There are also other reasons, such as innovations in the payments technology — an example of which is the spread of automatic teller machines — for changes in velocity both over the short and the long term. Hence, from a realistic perspective, velocity is continuously changing in the economy. Estimates of the annual fluctuation in velocity for the USA are about 3% to 4%.

Fisher's version of the quantity theory recognized, as does economic theory generally, the real-time variations of velocity. Hence, if you see a (fairly common) statement in some book that 'the quantity theory assumes velocity to be constant', you must take this statement to mean not the constancy of velocity in real time or in disequilibrium, because that would be patently invalid for any real-world economy in real time, but merely

---

[20] This deviation is studied in the short-run and disequilibrium macroeconomic models covered in Chapters 7 and 8.

[21] That is, if real income rises by 100%, the demand for real money balances rises by about 70%.

that velocity is independent of the money supply and the price level in long-run equilibrium — which is an analytical concept rather than a real-time one — with full employment.

Statistics on velocity are hard to collect directly. Therefore, the common procedure for deriving an index of velocity is to use the quantity equation. Under this procedure, $V \equiv Py/M$. We can use this identity and the easily available data on P, y, and M to calculate an index for velocity. It would normally show changes in velocity during the year as well as from one year to the next.

Fact Sheet 2.3: Velocity of Money in the USA, 1960–2008

This Fact Sheet illustrates movements in the velocity of $M1$, $M2$, and $M3$ from data for the USA. None of them is constant over the short term or the long term. Financial innovations like the interest-bearing checking accounts increased the demand for $M1$, which decreased $M1$ velocity (which equals $Y/M1$) in the 1980s. Interest rates on non-monetary assets (i.e., on savings deposits and bonds) fell after 1994, which raised the demand for $M1$ and further decreased velocity. Since savings deposits pay interest and are a component of $M2$, $M2$ velocity proved to be relatively more stable than that of $M1$. Nevertheless, $M2$ velocity did not prove to be constant.

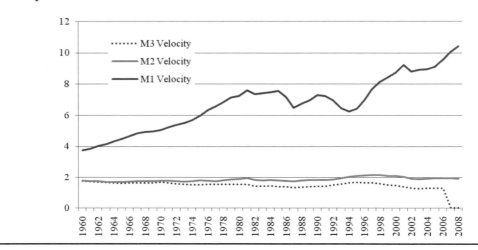

2.11 The Definitions of Monetary and Fiscal Policies

Monetary policies consist of changes in the money supply or in interest rates (induced by the central bank of the country) to bring about changes in the economy. The change in the money supply is usually brought about by the central bank through a change in the monetary base or in interest rates.

Fiscal policies are the use of government expenditures or taxes and the resulting fiscal deficits (or surpluses) to bring about changes in the economy. While government deficits can be financed through increases in the money supply (and surpluses be accompanied by decreases in it), *macroeconomics defines fiscal policy as one in which the money supply is held constant*, so that the deficits must be financed by government borrowing through increases in its bonds sold to the public. The reason for this definition of fiscal policy is to keep distinct the effects of monetary and fiscal actions on the economy.

In the real world, fiscal and monetary policies are intertwined, more so in some countries than others. However, macroeconomics treats them as conceptually independent policies and performs their analyses under the assumption that fiscal deficits are bond-financed.

2.12 The Central Bank and Monetary Policy

The control of monetary policy is usually allocated to the central bank of the country. This means that the central bank determines the changes it wishes to bring about in the money supply and in the interest rates in the economy. As we have shown earlier, the central bank usually induces changes in the money supply through changes in the monetary base, brought about through transactions (sales or purchases) in the bond market. It induces changes in the market interest rates through its changes in the monetary base and also by changing its own interest rate, known as the discount or bank rate.

If the control over monetary policy is shared between the central bank and the government — as is currently done in Britain — the term 'monetary authority' seems more appropriate.

The central bank of Canada is the Bank of Canada and that of the USA is the Federal Reserve System, often shortened to the term 'the Fed'. In both Canada and the USA, the central bank is effectively independent of the government and the legislative bodies (the Parliament in Canada and the Congress in the USA) and has sole jurisdiction over the formulation of monetary policy. However, there is normally extensive ongoing consultation between these central banks and their governments on the formulation of monetary policy.

2.13 The Economic Aspects of the Government and Fiscal Policy

Fiscal policy is pursued through changes in either government spending and/or its tax revenues, in such a way as to create a surplus or deficit in the government budget.

Government *spending*, defined as the sum of all payments made by the government,[22] can be classified into two broad categories:

(i) *Expenditures* on (currently produced) commodities (i.e., goods and services), with payments by the government in exchange for the goods and services purchased by it.

Examples of expenditures on goods and services are those on the civil service, the courts, and the military, as well as those on schools, hospitals, etc.

(ii) *Transfers* to the private sector, *without* a corresponding flow of commodities from the private sector to the government. This category includes:

a. payments to households under social programs,
b. subsidies to businesses, and
c. payment of interest on the public debt — which is the debt owed by the government to the public. This debt is accumulated through past borrowing by the government from the public in the form of bonds sold to the public (not the central bank).

Note the differences in terminology: '*expenditures*' for the purchases of currently produced goods and services, '*spending*' for total payments, and '*transfers*' for transactions in which the government does not receive currently produced goods and services in exchange. This usage will be maintained throughout this book. In 1999, total federal government spending in Canada was about $158 billion while the tax revenues were about $162 billion, with an estimated surplus of $4 billion. Expenditures on commodities were only about one-third of the total government spending while transfers were more than two-thirds of total government spending.

---

[22]Our focus is on the current account of the government. Therefore, the receipts (or payments) of funds in transactions involving the purchases (or sales) of bonds by the government are excluded from this definition of government spending/payments.

Tax revenues are collected from a variety of taxes. Among the most obvious taxes are income and corporate taxes, sales taxes and tariffs.

The government's spending and tax revenues represent the two sides of its budget balance sheet. If the two sides are equal, the budget is said to be 'balanced'. Otherwise, there is budget/fiscal[23] surplus or deficit. A fiscal surplus occurs if:

Fiscal surplus[= tax revenues (including transfers) − government spending (including transfers)] > 0.

If we define net tax revenues as net of transfers from the government to the private sector, we have:

Net tax revenues = total tax revenues − transfers to the private sector.

Therefore, we can redefine a fiscal surplus and deficit as:

fiscal surplus [= *net* tax revenues − government expenditures on goods and services] > 0 and

fiscal deficit [= government expenditures on goods and services − *net* tax revenues] > 0.

Therefore, a fiscal deficit occurs if the government buys goods and services worth more than its net (of transfers) tax revenues. These definitions of the fiscal surplus and deficit are the ones most directly related to the economic analysis of the commodity sector and we will adopt this usage.

2.13.1 The financing of fiscal deficits/surpluses and changes in the money supply

A fiscal deficit represents government spending in excess of its income. Just as with households, the government has to pay for its deficit. There are two ways in which the government can pay for it. They are:

(*i*) *Bond-financing of the deficit (without a change in the money supply)*
Under this method, the government raises funds through the sale of newly issued bonds to the public, receives money in exchange and then uses these funds to pay for the excess spending. The funds received by the government in this process are returned to the public through its extra spending (i.e., equal to the deficit) on commodities.

(*ii*) *Money-financing of the deficit (without a change in the public's bond holdings)*
Under this method, the government issues new bonds, which it sells to the central bank for newly created currency (notes and coins), which is then put into circulation in the economy by the government's expenditures on commodities. This creation of currency increases the monetary base and, as shown earlier, increases the money supply by a multiple.

A fiscal surplus represents government income in excess of its spending. Since the government usually has a lot of outstanding bonds, it can use its excess income to buy back some of the outstanding bonds and cancel them. There are two ways of doing this. They are:

(*i*) *Bond financing of the surplus, without a change in the money supply*
A fiscal surplus implies that the government collects more in taxes than it spends, so that it has surplus funds on its hands. In order not to change the public's money supply, it has to return these funds to the public. To do so, it buys bonds from the public. Hence, a 'bond-financed surplus' involves the purchase of an amount of bonds (equal to the fiscal surplus) by the government[24] *from the public*. The funds received

---

[23]To distinguish between this deficit and that in the balance of payments, the government's budget deficit is called the *fiscal deficit*.
[24]This operation is usually conducted through its banker, which is the central bank. The purchased bonds are almost always ones that the government had issued in the past and sold to the public. The government retires/destroys the bonds it buys.

by the government through its budget surplus are returned to the public in payment for the bonds. Therefore, the monetary base and the money supply do not change in this process — while the public's holdings of bonds decrease by the amount of the surplus.

(*ii*) *Money-financing of the surplus, without a change in the public's bond holdings*

A 'money-financed surplus' means a decrease in the monetary base equal to the amount of the fiscal surplus. To achieve this, the funds received by the government in taxes from the public are used by it to buy bonds *from the central bank* — which 'retires/cancels' the currency it gets back, so that it no longer circulates in the economy. In this process, the funds are not returned to the public, so that the monetary base decreases by the amount of the surplus, thereby decreasing the money supply.

Therefore, money-financed deficits increase the money supply while bond-financed ones do not do so. Money-financed surpluses decrease the money supply while bond-financed ones do not. *Fiscal policy* will be defined as running a bond-financed fiscal deficit or surplus with the *intention* of changing aggregate demand in the economy.[25] It does not change the money supply.

The implications of the independence of the central bank from the government for financing deficits

In Canada and the USA, since the central bank is independent of the government, the government cannot rely on the use of money creation, which is in the control of the central bank, for financing its deficits. Therefore, the usual method of financing deficits is bond financing, which increases the government debt but does not change the money supply. Similarly, fiscal surpluses also are 'bond-financed', which decreases the government debt but does not change the money supply.

Therefore, when the central bank is truly (i.e., factually and not merely legally) independent of the government, *monetary policy changes the money supply, while fiscal policy does not*. If fiscal deficits in a real-world economy are money-financed, macroeconomic theory considers them to be a mix of both fiscal and monetary policies.

2.13.2 The public debt

The public *debt* is the debt owed by the government to others (excluding the central bank). It consists of the bonds sold by the government in the past and not yet redeemed but held by the public (not the central bank). The part of this debt held by residents of foreign countries is called the *external debt*. The rest is held by domestic residents; this part of the public debt is called the *internal debt*.

A bond-financed deficit means that the value of the new bonds issued by the government equals the nominal value of the deficit. Therefore, the public debt increases by the nominal value of the fiscal deficit. Conversely, the public debt falls by the nominal value of the fiscal surplus.

Most countries have large public debts. In 1999, in Canada, the accumulated debt of the federal government was estimated to be about \$576 billion. The debt/GDP ratio was about 71% in 1995, dropped to about 60% in 1999, and continued dropping thereafter. The reasons of this drop were the rise in GDP and the decreases in the deficits, with surpluses emerging in the years after 1998.

---

[25]Fiscal deficits often occur because the government cannot collect enough revenue to finance its desired expenditures. Such deficits also change aggregate demand, but this is an inadvertent consequence of a failure to balance the budget. Our focus in the analysis of the government budget as a tool of fiscal policy is on those deficits and surpluses that are created so as to manage aggregate demand in the economy.

Interest has to be paid on the public debt. Payment of this interest is treated as a transfer in the government payments to the public.

2.13.3 The selective nature of government expenditures, taxes, and subsidies

Most aspects of government activity impact on some sectors of the economy more than on others. To illustrate, government expenditures for education support schools and universities, those for medicare support health services, subsidies for R&D expenditures encourage innovation, etc. Similarly, progressive tax rates are intended to reduce after-tax income inequality and taxes on cigarettes are intended to discourage smoking. Therefore, the government's policies on government expenditures, transfers, and taxes constitute more than merely a way of managing aggregate demand in the economy. However, the macroeconomic study of fiscal policy focuses only on its impact on aggregate demand.

2.14 Interest Rates in the Economy

The interest rate is the rate of return on a loan (bond). This rate of return has two elements: any fixed (also known as the 'coupon') payment on the bond — or the dividend in the case of a share in a corporation — each period and any capital gains and losses due to changes in the market value of the bond. Since some of these elements are not known at the time the bond is bought, we distinguish between the expected rate of return, and the actual rate of return — i.e., the rate that will eventually materialize.

The rates of interest on different bonds differ due to differences in the risk, the time to maturity of the bond, and other differences in their characteristics. In general, a riskier bond will yield a higher return, as will a bond with a longer maturity. However, for all bonds in the economy, macroeconomics envisages a common underlying element of the rate of return to which premiums are added for riskiness, the time to maturity and any other relevant characteristics.

Macroeconomics focuses on the common underlying component of the variety of interest rates in the economy. It, therefore, deals with a single rate of interest in the economy and studies its determination. In particular, macroeconomics studies the short-run and the long-run effects of monetary and fiscal policies, and of the rate of inflation, on this underlying interest rate.

One of the proxies used for the macroeconomic interest rate is the Treasury bill rate, also called the T-bill rate. *Treasury bills* are government bonds, usually with a 90-day term to maturity. They are riskless and have a very short maturity. Another proxy is a medium-term interest rate, which is usually interpreted as the rate of return on 3–5-year government bonds. A third proxy would be the long-term interest rate, which is usually interpreted as the rate of return on bonds with more than ten years to maturity.

2.14.1 The Fisher equation on interest rates

Assuming that the market for bonds — the 'capital market' — is perfectly competitive, Irving Fisher, in the early 20th century, derived what has come to be known as the *Fisher equation* (for the market/nominal rates of interest). The Fisher equation separates the market rate of interest into two components: the real rate of return and a premium or allowance for the expected inflation rate. It assumes that (a) lenders have the option of investing in riskless durable commodities, including capital goods, whose prices rise by the inflation rate and which do not have storage or transactions costs, so that the investor could risklessly receive the real return r^r

by investing in such commodities, (b) the capital markets are perfectly competitive and efficient, and (c) both borrowers and lenders hold identical expectations.

Most bonds in the economy are nominal bonds (i.e., paying a nominal interest rate), so that the interest rates observed in the economy are mainly *market (or nominal) rates.* However, there are sometimes also real bonds (i.e., paying a real interest rate).

The (proper form of the) Fisher equation relating real and nominal interest rates is:

$$(1 + R) = (1 + r)(1 + \pi^e),$$

where:

$$R = \text{market (nominal) rate of interest per period from the loan,}$$
$$r = \text{real rate of interest per period from a real loan, and}$$
$$\pi^e = \text{expected rate of inflation over the period of the loan.}$$

Note that π^e can differ from the actual inflation rate π, which is unknown at the beginning of the period, i.e., when the investment is undertaken. The explanation for the Fisher equation is as follows. An investor investing one dollar in a 'nominal bond' (i.e., paying a nominal rate of interest R) would receive $\$(1 + R)$ at the end of the period. If he/she was to buy a 'real bond' (i.e., paying a real interest rate r), he/she would receive $(1 + r)$ in real terms (commodities) at the end of the period. Given the expectations on inflation held at the beginning of the current period, the expected nominal value at the end of the period of this real amount equals $\$(1 + r)(1 + \pi^e)$. The investor will be indifferent between the nominal and the real bonds if the nominal return from both bonds was equal, i.e., $(1 + R) = (1 + r)(1 + \pi^e)$.

Expanding the preceding equation gives,

$$(1 + R) = 1 + r + \pi^e + r\pi^e$$

so that:

$$R = r + \pi^e + r\pi^e.$$

For small values of r and π^e, $r\pi^e$ would be approximately zero, so that the commonly used ('standard') form of the Fisher equation is:

$$R = r + \pi^\varepsilon. \tag{3}$$

Although this form of the Fisher equation is an approximation, we will use this form as the Fisher equation in further analysis. The intuitive justification for this equation is that the lenders want to be compensated for the expected loss of purchasing power due to the expected inflation, while the borrowers — mainly firms who benefit from the expected increases in the prices of their products — would be willing to so compensate.

The (simplified/standard) Fisher equation implies that:

$$r^e = R - \pi^e.$$

In this form, r^e is the real rate of interest that lenders *expect* to end up with at the end of the period: since they expect the inflation rate π^e for the period of the loan, the real return the lender *expects* to get from a nominal loan will be only $(R - \pi^e)$.

If inflation occurs during the period of a loan, the loan repaid at the end of the period is worth less by the rate of inflation than its purchasing power at the time the loan was made. We can then derive the *actual* — also called the *ex-post* — *real rate of return* from the nominal one by subtracting the actual rate of inflation from the latter. That is, the *actual real rate of return* is specified by:

$$r^a = R - \pi, \tag{4}$$

where r^a is the actual real rate of interest. The actual/realized real rate of return on loans (r^a) differs from the expected one (r^e) if actual inflation differs from the expected one, which does happen frequently.[26] Note that if the rate of inflation is greater than the market interest rate, the actual (*ex-post*) real return would be negative.

Fact Sheet 2.4: Nominal and Real Interest Rates in the USA, 1982–2008

The Fisher equation implies that the real interest rate is the difference between the nominal interest rate and the *expected* inflation rate. In simple applications, the expected inflation rate is approximated by the actual one. The following graph illustrates the relationship over time between the nominal interest rate on Treasury bills and the *actual* inflation rate using USA data. Their difference yields the *actual* real interest rate on Treasury bills. Since the real interest rate fluctuates much less than the inflation rate, very high nominal rates are usually due to very high inflation rates, as during the late 1980s. Since 2000, nominal interest rates have been quite low because the inflation rates have been low.

The real interest rate fluctuates due to changes in the real sectors of the economy and the monetary policy pursued by the central bank under interest rate targeting. In the USA, since 2000, the central bank has maintained the real interest rate at a fairly low level.

Note that while the nominal interest rate normally remains positive, the actual real interest rate can become negative if the expected inflation rate is below the actual one, as happened around 2003 and 2008.

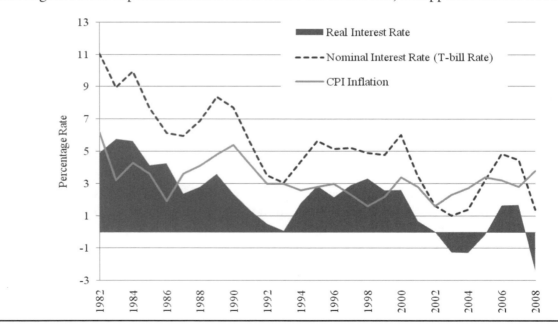

---

[26]In special circumstances, the actual real interest rate can turn out to be negative. However, the expected real rate on loans would always be positive if lenders have the alternative of investing — with the same transactions costs, including time and convenience — in physical capital (e.g., land and houses), whose nominal return will at least equal the expected inflation rate. If the expected real return on loans were negative while that on physical capital was positive, no one would want to make loans.

2.14.2 The concept of present discounted value (PDV) of a bond

A *bond* in ordinary English-language usage is a financial instrument that entitles the holder a fixed coupon payment at specified intervals and a payment at the specified maturity date. The general procedure for finding the *present discounted value* (PDV) of the amounts to be received (or to be paid) in the future requires discounting every future amount to its present value by dividing by the relevant *discount factor* and summing over the discounted values.[27] The nominal amount received at the end of the first period; is divided by $(1 + R_1)$, where R_1 is the interest rate in period 1. If the amount received is at the end of the second period, it is first divided by $(1 + R_2)$ to find its value at the beginning of period 2 (which is also the end of period 1) and then divided by $(1 + R_1)$ to find its value at the beginning of period 1. That is, the PDV of any amount received at the end of period 2 is divided by $(1 + R_1)(1 + R_2)$. Similarly, PDV of any amount received at the end of period 3 is divided by $(1 + R_1)(1 + R_2)(1 + R_3)$ and so on. Therefore, the PDV^b of a bond with a fixed coupon payment c and redemption value a^n after $(n - 1)$ periods[28] is:

$$PDV^b = \frac{c}{(1 + R_1)} + \frac{c}{(1 + R_1)(1 + R_2)} + \cdots + \frac{c}{(1 + R_1) \cdots (1 + R_n)} + \frac{a^n}{(1 + R_1) \cdots (1 + R_n)}, \quad (5)$$

where:

$p_1^b = $ price of the bond in period 1,

$c = $ coupon payment each period on the bond, assumed to be constant over time,

$R = $ market interest rate

$a^n = $ the expected price (i.e., amount received by the bond holder on sale or at maturity)
    after n periods $(= p_n^{be})$, and

$n = $ sale or redemption date.

The above formula assumes that c, a, and n are known, and that these are paid at the *end* of the relevant period. If there is no risk in holding the bond, investors would be willing to pay PDV^b to buy the bond, so that the bond market will establish this value as the price of the bond. Since government bonds are normally riskless, the above formula can be applied to government bonds. Since bonds issued by private firms are risky, the discount rate used has to be the one that takes account of this risk.

If we were to assume — as is usually done and as we did earlier — that the interest rates are going to remain constant at R, the discount factors become $1/(1 + R)$ for the first period, $1/(1 + R)^2$ for the second period, $1/(1 + R)^3$ for the third period, and so on. In this case, the PDV formula simplifies to:

$$PDV^b = \frac{c}{(1 + R)} + \frac{c}{(1 + R)^2} + \cdots + \frac{c}{(1 + R)^n} + \frac{a^n}{(1 + R)^n}. \quad (6)$$

The present discounted value of a stream of payments on the bond in the future is the sum of the present discounted value of each of these payments. In perfect capital markets, this is the amount that the investors in the bond will be willing to pay for it. Hence, in perfect capital markets, the price of a bond will be the present discounted value of the future receipts from it. That is:

$$PDV^b = p^b.$$

Given the price of the bond, the rate of return on the bond can therefore be calculated from the formula:

$$p_1^b = \frac{c}{(1 + R)} + \frac{c}{(1 + R)^2} + \cdots + \frac{c}{(1 + R)^n} + \frac{a^n}{(1 + R)^n}. \quad (7)$$

---

[27] For the constant interest rate R, the discount factor for funds received after one period is $1/(1 + R)$. For funds received after n periods, the discount factor is $1/(1 + R)^n$.

[28] This formula assumes that the future interest rates are known. Otherwise, the future interest rates would be replaced by their expected values, which would introduce risk into the equation.

The above formula can be used in two different ways:

1. It can be used to calculate the rate of return R on the bond for a given bond price p_1^b. The rate thus calculated is called the *internal rate of return*. The preceding formula shows that an increase in the bond's current price lowers its rate of return.
2. The second way is to derive the market price p_b of the bond for a given market interest rate R and given the expected resale value. An increase in the market rate lowers the bond price. Hence, there is an inverse relationship between bond prices and interest rates.

Therefore,

(a) If the aggregate demand for bonds increases in the economy, it would raise bond prices (of the existing bonds), and lower the economy's (macroeconomic) interest rate.
(b) If the central bank causes the market interest rate to rise, bond prices (of the existing bonds) will fall. Conversely, if the central bank causes the market interest rate to fall, bond prices will rise.

In the limiting case of a *perpetual bond* — also called a *'consol'* — defined as a bond with *a constant coupon payment per period and without a redemption date*, the above formula simplifies to:

$$p^b = c/R, \tag{8}$$

which clearly shows an inverse relationship between bond prices and the nominal interest rate.

2.14.3 Bubbles in asset prices

A *bubble* in the price of an asset is said to exist if this price differs from the 'fundamental value' of the asset, as determined by the present discounted value of the asset given its current and future returns and the market interest rate. The 'bubble' is the difference between the market price and the fundamental nominal value, as explained in Box 2.1. While the concept of a bubble is analytically clear, it is often difficult to determine this fundamental value for assets whose future returns are unknown and have to be based on very vague and incomplete, even possibly erroneous, information. This is usually the case in the valuations of corporations. Therefore, there are often disputes on whether or not there is a bubble in stock prices and the extent of the bubble.

A *positive (negative) bubble* is said to exist if the actual market price becomes greater (less) than the fundamental value of the asset. A bubble is said to burst when the stock price adjusts, as in a stock market crash, to its fundamental value. The bursting of a positive bubble is often followed by a negative bubble, i.e., the downward correction in the price gets overdone.

The importance of asset bubbles for output and business cycles

Bubbles in the prices of widely held assets, such as stocks, land, and houses, can cause severe fluctuation in output and employment. Positive bubbles in them cause household wealth to increase significantly and lead to an increase in consumption expenditures. Positive bubbles in the stock prices of corporations make it easier for them to obtain funds for investment, which leads to increases in investment expenditures. These increases in consumption and investment expenditures cause booms in economic activity. The reverse process is set in motion when the bubbles burst: the rapid fall in the prices of widely held assets sends the economy into a crisis and a recession, as happened when house prices in the USA in 2007 started collapsing after a positive bubble developed during 2000–2006. Chapter 16 on business cycle explains this process in greater detail.

Box 2.1: The Determination of Stock Prices

The present discounted value formula also applies to the prices of equities/shares. Assume perfect capital markets, a share with an expected dividend d_t^e at the end of period t, and a constant market interest rate R. The present discounted value formula implies that the price p_1^S of the share at the beginning of period 1 would be:

$$p_1^S = \frac{d_1^e}{(1+R)} + \frac{d_2^e}{(1+R)^2} + \cdots + \frac{d_n^e}{(1+R)^n} + \frac{p_n^{Se}}{(1+R)^n},$$

where the superscript S stands for the share and p_n^{Se} is the expected (designated by the superscript e) sale price of the share S at the end of period n. As interest rates rise, future receipts are discounted at a higher rate, resulting in a lower present value, so that there is an inverse relationship between the current share price and the market interest rate. There is a positive one between the share price and its expected dividends, as well as between the current share price and its expected future one (at the expected resale date n).

If there comes into being an expectation of higher (lower) future dividends or resale prices, this shift in expectations will raise (lower) the current price of the share. The average expectation in the financial markets is called 'market opinion' (i.e., the average degree of market optimism or pessimism on future share prices), so that a major determinant of current share prices is 'market opinion'. Since this opinion is often more volatile than the profits of firms or sectors, their share prices also tend to be volatile. Such volatility of stock prices can be seen in the fluctuations on a daily basis of the average values of stocks on stock exchanges, such as the New York Stock Exchange, the Toronto Stock Exchange, and the London Stock Exchange.

The volatility of the prices of the Internet and communications stocks at the end of the 1990s and the early years of this century is an example of the shifts in the market opinion about future prices causing volatility in current stock prices. The almost worldwide decline in stock markets in mid-2006 was at least partly due to the increases in interest rates induced by the central banks of many countries, especially the US Federal Reserve System, which raised their discount rates in an attempt to combat rising inflation.

To emphasize this conclusion, our analysis implies that, besides changes in stock prices due to changes in dividends or interest rates, *stock prices rise (fall) just because they are expected to rise (fall)*. The ways this volatility impacts on aggregate demand, output and prices in the economy is laid out in Chapter 9.

Bubbles in house and land prices

Just as stock prices can have bubbles, so can house and land prices. These are assets whose future resale value is not known, so that speculation about the future resale value can drive up (a positive bubble) or down (a negative bubble) the current prices.

An example of large bubbles in house and land prices occurred just prior to the East Asian crisis of the mid-1990s and the financial crisis in the USA before 2007. The bursting of the bubbles in these cases decimated the wealth of the public and sent the economies into severe recessions.

A bubble in tulip bulb prices!

Bubbles can occur in the price of any asset. To illustrate, a massive bubble in the price of tulip bulbs occurred in Holland in the 18th century soon after it was introduced to Europe from Turkey. The bubble was such that the prices of the bulbs of some desired varieties of tulips became greater than the prices of many middle class houses.

Conclusions

- Money performs the two main functions of the medium of exchange and the store of value, with the former being absolutely critical to the transactions role of money in the economy. These functions are performed by a variety of assets, with their liquidity characteristics and substitutability among them changing over time. Innovations in the types of assets and the changing characteristics of existing financial assets mean that the financial assets which meet the role of money keep changing over time.

- While currency was considered to be the only form of money at one time (prior to the 20th century), currency and demand deposits were taken to be the two components of money early in the 20th century, so that the appropriate measure of money was considered to be $M1$. By 1960, the measure of money had been expanded to include savings (including time) deposits in commercial banks, and therefore had become $M2$. In subsequent decades, as the liabilities of near-banks became more and more similar to the demand and savings deposits of banks, the measures of money were broadened to include the deposits in near-bank financial intermediaries.

- The recent incursion of electronics into banking in the form of automatic tellers, banking from home through one's computer or telephone, and the use of smart cards for payments, etc. represent a very fast pace of technical change in the banking industry. It is a safe bet that the empirically appropriate measure of money is changing and will keep changing in the future. Because of these changes, disputes about the proper measure of money have expanded beyond the monetary aggregates $M1$ and $M2$ to encompass broader and more complex forms.

- Given that the growth rates of output and velocity tend to be in low single digits, the quantity equation implies that high, sustained rates of inflation are due to high, sustained rates of increase in the money supply. This is particularly true of hyperinflations.

- The quantity equation differs from the quantity theory. The quantity theory states that, in long-run equilibrium analysis with full employment, an increase in the money supply will produce a proportionate increase in the price level.

- Monetary policy is controlled by the central bank. It consists of changes in the monetary base or in the interest rates set by the central bank.

- The central bank controls the money supply through changes in the monetary base. The money supply changes by a multiple of the change in the monetary base.

- The government has its own budget. If its total spending exceeds its revenues, it has a deficit, which has to be financed. An independent central bank forces the government to finance any deficits through the issue of new bonds rather than through the issue of newly created notes and coins. A bond-financed fiscal deficit increases the public debt and a surplus decreases it.

- Fiscal policy is controlled by the government. It consists of changes in government spending or revenues. In particular, it is exercised through changes in the amount of the fiscal surplus or deficit. Macroeconomics defines and studies fiscal policy under the assumption that any deficits are financed by the issue of new bonds while any surpluses are used to redeem a corresponding amount of the existing government bonds.

- The Fisher equation on interest rates shows that the macroeconomic market rate of interest rises with the expected rate of inflation. The expected and the actual real rates of return on bonds will differ if the expected inflation rate is different from the actual one.

- Bond prices are inversely related to the market interest rates.

KEY CONCEPTS

The functions of money
Money supply versus money stock
M1, M2, and broader definitions of money
An identity versus a theory

The quantity equation
The quantity theory
Fiscal deficits and surpluses
Public debt

The nominal rate of interest
The real rate of interest, and
The Fisher equation.

SUMMARY OF CRITICAL CONCLUSIONS

- The appropriate definition of money keeps changing. There are currently several definitions of money in common usage. These include *M*1, *M*2, and broader monetary aggregates.
- All definitions of money include currency in the hands of the public and demand/checking deposits in commercial banks.
- Banks are one type of financial intermediaries but are different from others in that their liabilities in the form of checking and savings deposits are the most liquid of all assets in the economy.
- The quantity equation is an identity while the quantity theory is a long-run equilibrium condition. The latter asserts that, in long-run equilibrium, increases in the money supply will produce a proportionate increase in the price level. This will not be so in the transition from an initial equilibrium to the subsequent one. The quantity theory does not hold in the short term since the commodities and the velocity of circulation of money usually respond (at least during the short-term disequilibrium phase) to changes the money supply or to changes in its growth rate.
- The velocity of circulation of money is not constant over time, but changes from one month to the next one, and from one year to the next one.
- There are numerous interest rates in the economy. The differences among them are mainly due to differences in the riskiness and the term to maturity of the loans on which they are paid.
- Monetary policy is the use of changes in the monetary base or in interest rates to influence the economy.
- Fiscal policy is the use of changes in government spending, taxes, and the resulting fiscal deficits or surpluses to influence the economy.
- The public debt is the total amount of government bonds outstanding in the economy. Bond-financed fiscal deficits increase the public debt and fiscal surpluses decrease it.
- The present discounted value formula explains how the price of a financial asset depends on its stream of expected returns (the coupon payment on the bond or the expected dividends on a share) and its expected resale price at the time the investor expects to sell it.

REVIEW AND DISCUSSION QUESTIONS

1. What does 'the medium of payments' mean? Are credit cards a medium of payment? Are debit cards a medium of payment? Are telephone cards a medium of payment? Discuss.
2. Define (a) currency, (b) demand deposits, and (c) savings deposits. What are their relative proportions that you tend to hold on average over a typical month? Explain their likely variation near Xmas?

3. What are the proportions of your holdings of currency, $M1$ and $M2$ relative to your own expenditures over a typical month and year? Does this proportion fluctuate? Using your own experience as indicative of the representative consumer's behavior, what can you conclude about the constancy of the velocity of circulation of money over time?

4. What is the definition of 'bonds' in macroeconomics and how does it differ from that of 'money'? Compare the definition of 'bonds' in macroeconomics with those of bonds and stocks in ordinary usage.

5. Define (a) treasury bills, (b) money market mutual funds, (c) coupon payment on a bond, and (d) a perpetual bond (consol).

6. Define the monetary base and specify its general relationship with the money supply ($M1$ and $M2$) in the economy.

7. Specify the quantity theory.

8. Specify the quantity equation. What does the quantity equation imply for the causes of persistently high rates of inflation in the real world? Explain your answer.

9. Can the actual real rate of return on loans become negative? Illustrate with an example.

10. What is the definition of monetary policy?

11. Specify the relationship between government spending and government expenditures (on goods and services).

12. Define fiscal deficits and surpluses in two ways (i.e., in terms of (a) government spending and (b) government expenditures on commodities).

13. Define the public debt. How do fiscal deficits and surpluses change its amount? What else changes the debt/GDP ratio?

14. Specify the present discounted value formula for the price of a bond. Explain the relationship it implies between the bond price and the market interest rate.

ADVANCED AND TECHNICAL QUESTIONS

T1. For a given value of $M0$, if $M2$ was five times the size of $M1$, what would be the relationship between their monetary base multipliers?

T2. [Optional] What were the magnitudes of $M1$ and a broader money measure for the last year (for which the data is available) for your economy? What were the relevant monetary base multipliers? How have these multipliers and the ratio of $M1$ to $M2$ changed in the past two decades? [Use the Internet for your sources and cite your sources.]

T3. [Optional] What were the magnitudes of government spending, government transfers revenues, and deficits/surpluses for the last year (for which the data is available) for your economy? What were the government expenditures on goods and services and government transfers? What were their proportions relative to each other and to government spending? How have these proportions changed in the past two decades? [Use the Internet for your sources and cite your sources.]

T4. What is meant by a theory versus an identity? Define these two terms and specify their differences. Is the Quantity Theory a theory or an identity? Explain your answer.

T5. Why is the interest rate paid by banks on savings deposits so much lower than those paid by them on money market mutual funds and those charged by banks on loans to the public?

T6. Stock prices rise if investors expect them to rise and fall if investors expect them to fall. Why? Why does this make stock markets volatile?

CHAPTER 3

Introduction to the Open Economy: Exchange Rates and the Balance of Payments

This chapter provides an introduction to the concepts and determinants of the foreign exchange rates and the balance of payments. It lays the basis for the open economy macroeconomics and the determination of the exchange rates in later chapters.

This chapter also presents the theories important for open economy macroeconomics. These are the purchasing power parity (PPP) and interest rate parity (IRP) theories.

This chapter introduces the economic concepts related to the openness of the economy. Its focus is on the understanding of the exchange rate and the components of the balance of payments.

Every economy nowadays has considerable commodity and financial flows with other economies. These flows — mainly of commodities, currencies, and financial capital, though sometimes also of people — between economies affect their domestic national income, employment, prices, and other endogenous variables, as well as the scope and effectiveness of national monetary and fiscal policies.

The flows of factors of production other than physical capital[1] are minor and are generally ignored in macroeconomic analysis. Further, the short-run analysis of an open economy assumes that the physical capital stock is fixed so that any flows of such capital that occur are out of currently produced output and do not affect the productive capacity of any economy. In fact, there is a special use of the word 'capital' in the context of international trade. This is in its financial usage. Therefore, the international flows of 'capital' are to be understood as being only financial flows, that is, a flow of the currency and other financial assets of one country to another country in exchange for financial assets. These flows have become quite considerable in the last few decades with the global integration of financial markets, and on a daily basis, are very much larger than the values of commodity flows for many countries.

The open economy has one more good than the closed economy. This good is *'foreign exchange'*, which is the designation for the medium of payments between the domestic and foreign economies. This good consists of foreign currencies, gold, and *Special Drawing Rights* (SDRs) at the International Monetary Fund (IMF). SDRs act as a kind of demand deposits of individual countries with the IMF. The price of the domestic currency against a foreign one is the exchange rate between the currencies. Since macroeconomic theory usually treats the rest of the world as a single unit, our analysis will be set out in terms of the composite category labeled 'foreign exchange' — meaning by it the foreign currencies of the rest of the world — and 'the exchange rate' between this composite and the domestic currency.

Flows of commodities and financial instruments occur between the domestic economy and the rest of the world. The flows of commodities among countries take the form of exports and imports of commodities, with the difference between them designated as *net exports* (of commodities), which is also called the *balance of*

---

[1]The remaining flows are of immigrants and transient migrants. While these are not very significant for most economies, there are a few countries, especially in the Middle East, for which such workers can be a significant proportion of the labor force.

trade. The flows of financial instruments — in the form of bonds and other ownership claims — are financial capital flows and are captured in the *balance of payments on capital account*. The flows of physical capital are counted in commodity imports or exports, rather than in international capital flows. They do not directly appear in the balance of payments on capital account.

3.1 Exchange Rates

3.1.1 Three concepts of exchange rates

Almost all countries have their own national currencies. The rate of exchange between a domestic currency and a foreign one is called the exchange rate between them. The exchange rates between currencies can be nominal, real or effective ones.

The (nominal) exchange rate

The *(nominal) exchange rate* is the rate at which a currency can be exchanged against another currency. This exchange rate between any two given currencies can be defined in two alternate ways. It can be defined as:

1. The price of the domestic currency ($) in terms of a foreign currency (£s). An example of this occurs if we cite the exchange rate for the British £ in Canadian dollars as £0.4 per C$. [News reports in Canada often use this definition of the exchange rate for the Canadian dollar in terms of the US dollar, as in 'today, in foreign exchange markets, the Canadian dollar traded at 85 US cents'.]
2. The price (per unit) of a foreign currency in terms of the domestic currency. An example of this occurs if we cite the exchange rate for the British £ in Canadian dollars as C$2.40 per £. This measure of the exchange rate is clearly the reciprocal of the former measure, so that the exchange rate as Canadian dollars per pound would be specified by £1 = C$1/0.4 = C$2.5. [News reports in Canada often use this definition of the exchange rate for the Canadian dollar in terms of the euro and the yen].

The definition of exchange rate that would be appropriate to use obviously depends upon convenience and preferences. There is no consensus on which definition is more useful. Both have certain advantages and disadvantages relative to the other. We prefer using the definition above. That is, *the (nominal) exchange rate will be defined as the amount (i.e., number of units) of a foreign currency required to purchase one unit of the domestic currency*. Taking the dollar as the unit of the domestic currency and the £ as the generic symbol for a unit of the foreign currency, the nominal exchange rate under our definition will be the amount of £s per $ in the foreign exchange markets — *compactly expressed as £/$*. We will use the Greek letter ρ (pronounced 'rho') for the nominal exchange rate. The dimension of ρ for our definition is £/$.

The real exchange rate

The *real exchange rate*, designated as ρ^r, is the amount of foreign commodities that can be exchanged for one unit of domestic commodities.[2] Its relationship with the nominal exchange rate is specified by:

$$\rho^r = \rho P / P^F, \tag{1}$$

---

[2]To illustrate this point, assume that we are comparing the price of an identical car that costs £10,000 in Britain and $24,000 in Canada, and the nominal exchange rate is £0.5 per $. Hence, for this car,

$$\rho^r = \rho P / P^F = 0.5 \times 24{,}000/10{,}000 = 1.2$$

The units of measurement of ρ^r, from $\rho P / P^F$ are:

(£ per $)($per Canadian car)/(£ per British car) = British cars per Canadian car.

where:

ρ = nominal exchange rate (£/$) (amount of foreign currencies per unit of the domestic one),
ρ^r = real exchange rate (amount of foreign commodities per unit of the domestic one),
P = domestic price level, and
P^F = foreign price level.

Therefore, the real exchange rate is the nominal exchange rate adjusted for the relative price ratio between the countries. As mentioned above, *the real exchange rate specifies the amount of foreign commodities required to purchase a unit of the domestic commodity.*

The best way of intuitively grasping the concept of the real exchange rate is to focus on a single commodity, say X. Suppose we had one unit of commodity X and were to sell this unit at home, convert the dollars thus obtained into the British currency (£) and then attempt to buy units of the same commodity in Britain. Let the amount of the commodity obtained in Britain be z units. Then, assuming that there are no transport or other transactions costs, one unit of the commodity in the domestic market allows us to purchase z units of the same commodity in Britain. Therefore, the real exchange rate is z (units of the foreign commodity per unit of the domestic one). If the commodity is (a) a standardized one, (b) without transport and other transactions costs, and (c) traded on competitive world markets, we would expect z to equal unity but it is unlikely to do so if any of these conditions are not met.

At the level of the economy as a whole with a very diverse set of commodities, different economies have different mixes of commodities, so that each economy's mix is treated as if it was a 'composite commodity'. The proxy for the price of this composite commodity is the price level. Hence, the relative price ratio (P/P^F) is used to adjust the nominal exchange rate ρ to derive ρ^r.[3]

Since the standardised composite commodity on a world-wide basis does not exist, many economists intuitively estimate the real exchange rate on their travels by using the price of a standard commodity such as a Macdonald's hamburger as they move from one country to another. To illustrate, a price of $1.20 in Canada and of £1 per hamburger in the UK, with a nominal exchange rate of £0.50 per $, gives a real exchange rate of 0.60. The calculation is as follows:

$$\rho^r = \rho P/P^F = 0.5(1.20/1) = 0.6.$$

Intuitively, in this example, it takes only 60% of a British hamburger to buy a Canadian one: the Canadian hamburgers are relatively cheaper (by 40%).

The effective exchange rate

There is obviously a different exchange rate for each foreign currency, even though economic analysis is formulated in terms of a single exchange rate for simplification purposes. Such a rate can be envisaged as an average exchange rate for all currencies, just as the 'price level' is an average of the prices of commodities in the economy. This average exchange rate between the domestic currency and all foreign currencies is called the *effective exchange rate*. As an average, the effective exchange rate is obtained by weighting the exchange rate against each foreign currency by the proportion of the domestic economy's total trade (exports and imports) conducted with the foreign country. Changes in this effective exchange rate provide a measure of the average change in the value of a currency in terms of all other currencies.

---

[3]Since the dimensions of ρ are £/$ and of P/P^F are $/£, the dimension of ρ^r is $[(£/\$) \cdot (\$/£)]$, where the £ and $ signs cancel out, so that the dimension of the real exchange rate is foreign commodities per domestic ones.

There can obviously be both a nominal and a real effective exchange rate. The effective rate is preferable for converting GDP, exports, imports etc. from one currency to another one for international comparisons.[4]

3.2 Fixed, Flexible, and Managed Exchanged Rates

The market for foreign exchange may be allowed to determine the exchange rate. Alternatively, the exchange rate may be set by the central bank (or the government). The former is known as the *flexible/floating* exchange rate case and the latter as the *fixed/pegged*[5] exchange rate case. In general, there are three *exchange rate regimes*: (i) fixed, (ii) flexible, and (iii) managed floating. The *managed floating exchange rate* regime covers the case where the central bank (and/or the government) buys or sells foreign currencies (from its reserves) in the foreign exchange market to limit the range of fluctuations in its foreign exchange rate. Most flexible exchange rate regimes tend to be managed ones to a greater or lesser extent.

Depreciation and appreciation of the domestic currency

If the exchange rate (£/$) decreases, say from £0.50 per dollar to £0.40 per dollar, the domestic currency decreases in value against foreign currencies and there is a *depreciation* (under floating exchange rates) or *devaluation* (under fixed exchange rates) of the domestic currency against other currencies. If the exchange rate depreciates, it costs more in the domestic currency to buy foreign goods and assets, while domestic goods and assets become cheaper in foreign currencies. Conversely, if the exchange rate increases, the domestic currency increases in value against foreign currencies and there is an *appreciation* (under floating exchange rates) or *revaluation* (under fixed exchange rates) of the domestic currency against other currencies. In this case, foreign goods and assets will become cheaper in terms of the domestic currency, while the domestic goods and assets will become more expensive in foreign currencies.

3.3 Purchasing Power Parity (PPP) as a Theory of the Exchange Rate

3.3.1 PPP at the level of a single commodity

PPP for a single, standardized and internationally traded commodity is that it must cost the same in different countries, once its prices in the different countries are converted into the same currency by the nominal exchange rate. The assumptions required for this condition are that:

- The commodity is identical in different countries.
- There is perfect competition.
- There are no 'transactions costs' (such as from transport, insurance, tariffs, quotas, etc.) to its movement or information asymmetries among the countries.

Under these conditions, the internationally traded commodity will cost the same (after conversion into any one currency) in different countries. If its price was higher in one country, there would be an inflow of imports

---

[4]The PPP index of nominal exchange rates — which is an index over time of the nominal exchange rate which makes the real exchange rate equal to unity — would be an even better measure for certain purposes such as comparing standards of living across countries.

[5]The term 'pegged' is more appropriately used where the exchange rate by the policymaker is changed periodically.

from other countries in sufficient amounts to reduce the domestic price to the foreign one. If the price was lower, domestic firms will export enough of it to other countries to raise the domestic price to the foreign one.[6]

Absolute PPP among countries

In the limiting (but unrealistic) case where *all* the goods and services between the domestic and foreign economies are of the above type, we have *absolute PPP between the domestic economy and the world one*. At this aggregate level, PPP is the condition that:

$$\rho^{\mathrm{r}} = \rho P / P^{\mathrm{F}} = 1. \tag{2}$$

PPP is often called the 'law of one price' (for commodities in the international context). All of the commodities in the economy do not meet the assumptions for PPP. Among the reasons for this are that many goods — for example, buildings and land, most kinds of services, etc. — are not internationally tradable. Further, some of the inputs of even internationally tradable goods, such as the labor services in retailing or local transportation or the usage of immovables such as buildings and land, etc., have to be local ones. Therefore, even for the internationally traded goods, these transportation and local retailing costs drive a wedge between the domestic prices of goods and the prices in other countries. Hence, the conditions for PPP are not met for all or possibly most final goods (i.e., at the retail level) in the economy, so that the above absolute version of PPP does not apply in practice.

Extended Analysis Box 3.1: Does PPP Apply in the Real World? An Illustration

On the question of whether PPP applies in the real world, we turn to the prices of hamburgers across countries as an intuitively appealing test. *The Economist* annually publishes the prices of McDonalds' Big Mac among countries.[7] Its reports invariably show very significant deviations from PPP. The data reported is on the price in the local currency, the exchange rate between the local currency and the US dollar and the implied dollar price. The article on 27 April 2000, showed the following:

	In local currency	In US$	Implied PPP* of the US$[8]	Actual US$ exchange rate[9]	% Overvaluation (+) against US$
USA	US$2.51	US$2.51	1.00	1.00	0
Australia	A$2.59	1.54	1.03	1.68	−39
Britain	£1.90	3.00	0.76	0.63	+20
Canada	C$2.85	1.94	1.14	1.47	−23
Mexico Peso	20.90	2.22	8.33	9.41	−12

The more detailed calculations for this table are given in the Appendix of this chapter. This evidence shows that, relative to the PPP implied values for the Big Mac as of 27 April 2000, the Canadian currency was undervalued by 23% and the Mexican one was undervalued by 11%, relative to the US dollar, even though these countries are neighbors of the USA. The British pound was overvalued by 20% relative to

---

[6]This activity is known as arbitrage, which consists of buying in cheaper countries and selling in more expensive ones so as to make a profit from the price differences.

[7]http://economist.com/markets/bigmac/displayStory.cfm.

[8]This is the domestic price of the Big Mac divided by its price in USA.

[9]Local currency per US dollar.

Extended Analysis Box 3.1: (*Continued*)

the USA. As a corollary, the British pound was overvalued relative to the Canadian dollar by about 50% ($=1.23/0.80 - 1$). There was also considerable under- or overvaluation even among the national currencies (in 2000) of the EU.

Over several years, *The Economist*'s time series of Big Mac prices do not usually show a strong tendency toward PPP; in fact, they sometimes even show movements contrary to it. This can be seen by comparing the Big Mac index over several years. The issue of *The Economist* on 18 July 2009, showed the following for the countries in the preceding table.

	In US$	Implied PPP* of the US$[10]	% Undervaluation (−) or Overvaluation (+) against US$
USA	US$3.57	1.00	0
Australia	US$3.37	1.22	−6
Britain	US$3.69	1.56	+3
Canada	US$3.35	1.09	−6
Mexico	US$2.39	9.34	−33

Comparing the extent of undervaluation and overvaluation in the preceding data for 2000 and 2009, the extent of undervaluation of the currency decreased for Australia and Canada, whose nominal exchange rates against the US dollar shot up in July and August 2009; and the extent of overvaluation of the currency decreased for Britain, whose nominal exchange rate against the US dollar fell in 2009. But, for Mexico, the extent of undervaluation increased from 12% to 33%. Therefore, PPP does not hold as a reasonably realistic assumption over fairly long periods, and its assumption in macroeconomic theory is unjustified.

Although the Big Mac is a fairly standardized product, its local cost of production only partly depends upon internationally traded inputs, such as meat and flour, which should adhere to PPP. Its cost of production also depends on inputs such as local labor, land, and buildings, which are not internationally traded and for which there is unlikely to be PPP. The degree of local competition for hamburgers could also differ, so that McDonalds may vary its profit margin among countries. These factors cause differences in relative prices among countries.

At the economy's level, most final products are similarly combinations of internationally traded and non-traded goods, and there are different degrees of competition for each country's goods. Therefore, PPP rarely applies to individual goods or to commodities as a whole.

3.4 Relative PPP and Shifts in the Relative Efficiency of Economies

If we assume that the real exchange rate has a particular value k, we have:

$$\rho^r = \rho P/P^F = k. \tag{3}$$

---

[10]This is the domestic price of the Big Mac divided by its price in the USA.

For absolute PPP, $k = 1$, so that commodities would cost the same at home and abroad. However, travellers from a country with k less than unity find that that the same commodities cost more abroad than at home — and vice versa. Appendix Box 3.1A derives the value of k for selected countries for 27 April 2000. k is less than 1 for Canada, Mexico, and Australia, so that the residents of these countries find a Big Mac more expensive in the USA than in their own countries. However, k exceeds 1 for Britain vis-à-vis the USA, so that Americans find a Big Mac more expensive in Britain than at home. One of the reasons for the divergence of k from unity for Big Macs is that some of the inputs — such as local labor and land — into their production and retailing are not internationally traded and the Big Mac is itself not internationally traded — i.e., cannot be exported or imported. Another reason arises from the impact of capital flows on exchange rates.

If a country's k exceeds unity, its exchange rate is said to be *overvalued* (relative to PPP). If k is less than unity, its exchange rate is said to be *undervalued*. The reasons why k can differ from unity, and, therefore, from absolute PPP, are:

- The price indices for P and P^F (such as the CPI) are based on the prices of a bundle of commodities, which include some internationally traded goods and others which are not internationally traded, e.g., services, buildings, etc.[11] The distinction between these types of commodities is relevant to the determination of the country's nominal exchange rate ρ, which is affected by its relative ability to produce and export internationally traded commodities more efficiently than other countries. The nominal exchange rate is not affected by the efficiency and costs of goods and services that are not internationally traded, even though they are included in the measurement of domestic and foreign price indices, which affect the derivation of the real exchange rate.
- The nominal exchange rate also reflects the ability to attract net inflows of capital. As explained later in this chapter and in Chapter 12, these flows are likely to be the dominant *short-term* determinant of exchange rates for countries with extensive capital flows. Countries that are attractive havens for capital attract large net capital inflows from abroad. These inflows push up the demand for their currencies, which increase their exchange rates, with the result that their value of k becomes greater than unity. The reasons for this attractiveness can be higher interest rates, better business opportunities, greater security of capital, etc. Countries that are relatively more attractive for capital inflows tend to have k greater than unity.
- Under fixed exchange rate regimes, another cause of the overvaluation (undervaluation) of the real exchange rate is if the government or the central bank sets the value of the country's exchange rate higher (lower) than P^F/P.

Empirical observation suggests that less developed countries often have values of k less than one relative to the developed ones. Even among the developed economies, countries that are attractive havens for capital have values of k higher than one relative to other developed economies.

3.4.1 Long-run changes in relative PPP

Rewrite the preceding equation of the relative PPP as:

$$\rho = k \cdot (P^F/P). \qquad (4)$$

In the long run, k will not be a constant since transactions costs, the relative competitiveness of the domestic economy in commodity production, the relative sizes of its internationally tradable and non-tradable sectors,

---

[11]Note that the price indices do not take account of capital flows.

and its relative attractiveness for capital flows can change over time. With k potentially varying in the long run, the rate of change in ρ would be given by:

$$\rho'' = P^{F''} - P'' + k'' = (\pi^F - \pi) + k''. \tag{5}$$

Note that $''$ stands for the rate of change in the accompanying variable and π is the rate of inflation.

This is the *long-run version of relative PPP*. It asserts that the rate of change in the nominal exchange rate reflects the difference in the inflation rates and the rate of change in the real exchange rate. An increase in the value of k for our currency — i.e., $k'' > 0$ — appreciates it. A decrease in the value of k for our currency — i.e., $k'' < 0$ — depreciates it.

3.4.2 Short-run changes in relative PPP

For the short-run analysis, the factors that determine k are assumed to remain unchanged so that k is treated as a constant (i.e., its rate of change k'' equals zero), so that in the short run:

$$\rho'' = P^{F''} - P'' = \pi^F - \pi. \tag{6}$$

This version of PPP is known as the *short-run version of relative PPP*.

Economists usually prefer using the relative version (either the long run or the short run one) of the PPP theory rather than its absolute version in explaining changes over time in exchange rates. However, PPP indices are often constructed and used for calculating the PPP-based GDP series for cross-country comparisons of output and output per capita. An example of these is given in Box 3.1.

3.4.3 Implications of short-run PPP for exchange rates and inflation rates

The short-run version of relative PPP is that $\rho'' = \pi^F - \pi^F$. This short-run version of relative PPP implies the following two theories, depending on whether the country is following a fixed or flexible exchange rate regime.

(i) Fixed exchange rate regime case: In this case, $\rho'' = 0$, so that $\pi = \pi^e$. That is, in the short run, the domestic inflation rate for a small open economy is determined by the foreign one. Therefore, the domestic central bank through its monetary policies cannot achieve an inflation rate different from the world one. Hence, *under a fixed exchange rate regime, PPP becomes a theory for the determination of the domestic inflation rate for a small open economy.*

(ii) Flexible exchange rate regime case: In this case, ρ'' can differ from zero. This assumes that the central bank through its monetary policies can bring about a domestic inflation rate different from the world one, so that the rate of appreciation/depreciation of the exchange rate will be given by: $\rho'' = \pi^F - \pi$. If the domestic inflation rate is maintained lower (higher) than the world one, the exchange rate will rise (fall) correspondingly. Therefore, *under a flexible exchange rate regime, PPP becomes a theory for determining the rate of change of the exchange rate for a small open economy.*

Box 3.1: International Comparisons of Standards of Living in Terms of PPP

The nominal GDP (or GNP) measure discussed in Chapter 1 was in domestic prices. The real GDP measure discussed in Chapter 1 was its nominal value divided by an index of the domestic price level (e.g., the CPI

Box 3.1: (*Continued*)

or the GDP deflator). The standard cross-country comparisons of GDP are made by converting its nominal value into a common currency, often the US dollar, at the nominal exchange rate between the domestic currencies and the US dollar. For example, Canadian GDP is converted to US dollars as:

$$\text{Canadian GDP in US\$} = (\text{Canadian GDP in C\$})(\text{US\$ per C\$})$$

or as,

$$\text{Canadian GDP in US\$} = \frac{\text{Canadian GDP in C\$}}{\text{C\$ per US\$}}.$$

This mode of conversion is quite useful for some purposes — e.g. comparing the relative sizes of economies in nominal terms for international trade purposes. However, the GDP per capita derived from it is not an appropriate measure of the relative standards of living among countries when the nominal exchange rate is not consistent with PPP.

Appropriate cross-country comparisons of real GDP and real GDP per capita require that each given commodity be given the same value among the different countries. For example, a cup of coffee, *ceteris paribus*, in one country should be properly counted as being equal to a cup of coffee in other countries, even though its domestic purchase price converted into the US dollars at the nominal exchange rate may be quite different from that in the USA. For this purpose, first, the exchange rates based on PPP have to be constructed.[12] These provide the values of the 'PPP exchange rate'. Second, the PPP exchange rates are used to convert GDP is the national currency into the PPP GDP. This is done for selected countries in the following table.

Using PPP real exchange rates for cross-country conversions of GDP raises the GDP figures for countries whose real exchange rates (derived from the nominal ones) are less than unity and lowers those for countries whose real exchange rates (derived from the nominal ones) are greater than unity. The following table[13] provides for a few selected countries the comparisons of GNP and GNP per capita based on the nominal exchange rate and those on PPP.

	GNP (1993)		PPP GNP (1993)	
	Total	Per capita	Total	Per capita
	(US $M)	(US $)	(US $M)	(US $)
USA	6,378,873	24,070	5,925,080	23,220
Canada	574,786	19,970	596,557	20,970
UK	1,045,994	18,060	941,413	16,302
Mexico	324,997	3,610	692,795	7,867
Australia	307,967	17,500	321,126	18,500
India	269,460	300	1,437,124	1,633
Kenya	6,844	270	29,024	1,176

---

[12]The mode of construction of this index first requires finding for a common, pre-selected bundle of commodities the domestic price and the foreign price. Suppose this bundle is labeled as A and its domestic price is P^{PPP} while its foreign price is P^{*PPP}. Under PPP, $\rho^{PPP} \cdot (P^{PPP}/P^{*PPP})$ will equal unity, where ρ^{PPP} is the PPP exchange rate. Hence, $\rho^{PPP} = (P^{*PPP}/P^{PPP})$.

[13]Source: John L. Allen, *Student Atlas of Economic Development*. Dushkin/McGraw-Hill, 1997, pp. 69–72.

Box 3.1: (*Continued*)

The general pattern in this sample of countries is for the PPP calculations to be different from the ('standard') calculations based on the nominal exchange rates. Some of the differences are very large. In particular, the less developed economies have much higher PPP values than the standard ones. For India and Kenya, the PPP-based per capita values are about five times those based on the market exchange rate. For Mexico, they are twice as much. This reflects a commonly observed pattern of the relative — i.e., relative to PPP — under-valuation of the currencies of the developing economies. But, for the UK, the PPP figures are lower, reflecting its relatively over-valued exchange rate. This over-valuation pattern also holds for France, Germany, and most of the other West European countries.

3.5 Interest Rate Parity (IRP) and the Determination of the Exchange Rate

3.5.1 The benchmark IRP theory

Corresponding to the PPP for commodity flows, the interest rate parity IRP condition is derived with reference to capital flows. It is based on the assumption that investors seek the highest return on their investments. Therefore, if the risk of investing in different countries were identical, for capital to be shared among countries, the rate of return must be the same among countries — otherwise, the country with a higher rate of return will get all the capital flowing into it. This argument leads to the IRP condition. Its assumptions are: (a) perfect capital markets (including the absence of controls on capital flows), (b) zero transactions costs, and (c) risk indifference or zero risk. Under these assumptions, an investor will invest his capital in the country that offers him the highest return.

The nominal rate of return from investing in domestic bonds is their yield, designated by the interest rate R. Designating the nominal yield on foreign bonds as R^F, the net nominal return (in the domestic currency) on foreign investments is R^F *less any expected appreciation* ρ''^e of the domestic currency — or alternatively, *plus any expected depreciation* of the exchange rate.

For this comparison, consider an investor who wants to invest \$100 for one year. If he/she invests it in domestic one-year bonds yielding 5% per year, he/she will get back \$105 at the end of the year. His/her alternative is to invest in British bonds at a current exchange rate of £0.50 per dollar, so that he/she will be investing £50. Let British bonds pay an interest rate of 6%, so that he/she will get back £53 after one year. Further, assume that he/she expects the exchange rate to become £0.51 at the end of the year, so that the £53 will give him/her \$103.92 (= £53/0.51) in dollars. He/She therefore benefits by investing in domestic bonds (which will pay \$105) — even though the domestic interest rate is only 5% against the 6% interest rate in Britain. The reason the British bonds provided a lower expected return in this calculation is that the exchange rate for the domestic currency was expected to appreciate (from £0.50 per dollar to £0.51 per dollar) and the effect of this appreciation had to be deducted from the British interest rate.

In general terms, investment of \$1 at home will yield \$$(1 + R)$. Investment of \$1 abroad will be worth £ρ in the foreign currency at the time of investment and therefore, would yield £$(\rho + \rho R^F)$ in the foreign currency. The latter's expected value in the domestic currency will be \$$(\rho + \rho R^F)(1/\rho^e)$. This equals \$$(1 + R^F)(\rho/\rho^e)$. Therefore, the return from investments at home and abroad is the same if:

$$(1 + R) = (1 + R^F)(\rho/\rho^e),$$
$$R = R^F(\rho/\rho^e) + (\rho/\rho^e) - 1,$$
$$= R^F(\rho/\rho^e) - [(\rho^e - \rho)/\rho^e].$$

Note that the denominator on the right hand side is ρ^e and not ρ. Also note that R in the IRP equation stands for the return including the coupon payment and any expected capital gains or losses. This is especially important for capital flows into equities whose values fluctuate a great deal and have a strong speculative component. Note that for relatively small changes expected in the exchange rate, the error induced by the approximation can be ignored for the sake of simplifying the presentation. It cannot be ignored for large expected changes, as illustrated in Chapter 2.

In the preceding equation, setting $[(\rho^e - \rho)/\rho^e]$ as ρ''^e and approximating (ρ/ρ^e) by unity for small differences between ρ and ρ^e, the above equation reduces to the approximation:[14]

$$R = R^F - \rho''^e, \tag{7}$$

where ρ''^e is the expected rate of appreciation of the domestic currency and equals $(\rho^e - \rho)/\rho^e$. This simplified version of the IRP equation is called the *benchmark IRP equation*. Interpreting intuitively this benchmark IRP equation, to be used for low interest rates and 'small' changes in exchange rates, investors compare the nominal yield R on domestic bonds with the expected return on foreign bonds. The latter equals $(R^F - \rho''^e)$. If $R < (R^F - \rho''^e)$, investors will get a higher expected return from investing abroad, so that they will only invest abroad. But if $R > (R^F - \rho''^e)$, investors (including foreigners) will get a higher return from investing in our country and will only invest in it. In equilibrium, under the assumption that the investments in each country have the same risk level, if the bonds of both countries are to be sold simultaneously, the return must be the same from the two forms of investment, so that market equilibrium requires that $R = R^F - \rho''^e$.

To reiterate, the benchmark IRP equation is an approximation and holds only for very small changes in exchange rates. While it is in common usage and we will continue to use it for further analysis, it is an approximation to the actual relationship between these variables. However, the approximation is quite good for very small changes in exchange rates and for relatively low interest rates.

3.5.2 The benchmark IRP as a determinant of the domestic interest rate

If the country follows a fixed exchange rate regime or the exchange rate is expected to remain unchanged, $\rho''^e = 0$, so that the benchmark IRP theory implies that $R = R^F$. That is, the domestic interest rate will equal the world interest rate. Countries with a fixed exchange rate, which is expected by the investors to remain unchanged, would clearly have this determination of the interest rate. Countries with a flexible exchange rate that is not expected to change will also experience the same restriction on their interest rate.

If the investors expect the exchange rate to change, then the IRP condition implies that the domestic interest rate will diverge from R^F by ρ''^e.

3.5.3 The benchmark IRP as a theory of the exchange rate under flexible exchange rates

If the exchange rate is expected to change during the investment period, IRP turns into a theory for the determination of the exchange rate. For this theory, note that $\rho''^e = (\rho^e - \rho)/\rho^e$, so that IRP can be written as:

$$\rho''^e = (\rho^e - \rho)/\rho^e = R^F - R.$$

---

[14]This is an approximate formula that does fairly well at low values of the expected rate of change in the exchange rate but not very well at high values. It is only approximate since it does not, for foreign investments, take into account the conversion of the earned interest rate into the domestic currency.

Hence,

$$1 - \rho/\rho^e = R^F - R,$$
$$\rho/\rho^e = R - R^F + 1,$$
$$\rho = (R - R^F + 1)\rho^e. \tag{8}$$

Given IRP, this equation determines the exchange rate for given values of the domestic and foreign interest rates and the given value of the expected future exchange rate. It implies that if the central bank raises the domestic interest rate relative to the foreign one, the country's current exchange rate will rise relative to the expected future exchange rate. Further, if the increases in the interest rate and exchange rate induce the financial markets to expect a further appreciation of the exchange rate (i.e., ρ^e rises), the exchange rate will appreciate even more.

A simple illustration of the above arguments is provided by the following example. Suppose that initially $\rho^e = \rho = 1$. The central bank now raises the interest rate by 5%. Keeping ρ^e unchanged at 1, IRP implies that the current value of the exchange rate ρ would rise by 5%. Therefore, the exchange rate is *expected to depreciate* to the lower future value, with this value equal to ρ^e, which remains at unity.

3.5.4 The role of speculative returns to stocks in capital flows and IRP

While the IRP theory is usually stated as if the capital flows were in and out of bonds, international capital flows arising from the purchase and sales of stocks have become increasingly important in recent decades, as evidenced by international mutual funds and stock index funds. These flows are dominated not by the present discounted value of a known stream of coupon payments on bonds, but by the unknown and highly speculative future stock prices (see Chapter 2). Consequently, the expected returns on stock prices tend to be speculative and very different from the returns on bonds. Further, the movements in bond and stock yields can follow very different patterns. In particular, bubbles in the stock prices (see Chapter 2) build up, often to different extents in different countries. These bubbles, rather than bond yields and movements in interest rates, can significantly influence capitals flows among countries and limit the straightforward application of the IRT theory as a determinant of capital flows and interest rates among countries.

3.5.5 Extending IRP to incorporate risk factors and risk aversion

The interest rate on an asset incorporates a premium to compensate investors for its riskiness. The extra risk ('exchange-rate risk') in investing in foreign countries includes the potential for future exchange rate appreciations and depreciations, which depend upon the possibility of different inflation rates in different countries and other factors. The latter in turn depend on the general health of the economy and the ability and willingness of governments and central banks to control inflation and promote growth. Further, the possibility of financial and exchange rate crises and that of the imposition of controls on the redemption of capital increase the risk for foreign investors and increase the required risk premium.

To compensate for the relevant risk premium α, the benchmark version of the IRP equation has to be modified to:

$$R = (R^F - \rho''^e) + \alpha.$$

Assuming a lower risk and/or a greater preference for investments at home than abroad, capital importing countries have to pay a premium to foreign investors as an inducement to send their capital, so that α would be positive. That is, capital importing countries have to maintain higher interest rates at home than capital exporting countries because of the risk premium required by foreign investors to send capital to them. Conversely, capital-exporting countries would have a negative value of α and relatively lower interest rates at home than capital-importing countries. Hence, under the preceding assumptions,

$$\text{For capital importing countries: } \alpha > 0, \text{ so that } R > R^F.$$
$$\text{For capital exporting countries: } \alpha < 0, \text{ so that } R < R^F.$$

In the general case, where countries are neither consistently capital importing nor exporting ones relative to each other, the sign and value of α will depend on many factors, which include the degree of risk aversion of investors, investor's perception of the degree of (country) risk involved in investing in at home versus abroad, etc. The latter depend on the likely future economic prospects of the economies. Therefore, as these factors shift, the sign and value of α can shift over time.

Fact Sheet 3.1: Interest Rate Differentials Between Countries

This Fact Sheet shows the interest rate differential (plotted as the USA Treasury bill rate minus the Canadian one) between USA and Canada, which have closely integrated financial markets, so that there should be perfect capital flows between these countries. The Interest Parity Theory implies that the interest rates should be identical between them. However, as the following graph shows, there is almost always a differential between them. The Canada T-bill rate was higher in Canada from the early 1970s to the mid-1990s; outside this period, the Canadian rate was sometimes higher and sometimes lower than in the USA. Therefore, the value of the interest rate premium/discount α is usually not zero, even for closely integrated economies, and also not constant over time.

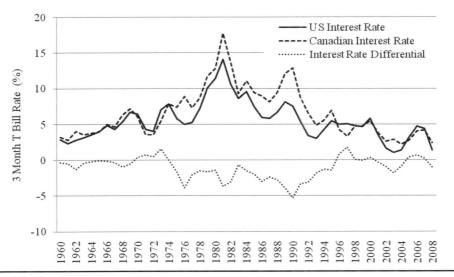

3.5.6 The relative importance of PPP and IRP in determining exchange rates

International capital flows are nowadays potentially much larger than the value of commodity flows for developed economies with open capital markets, so that anticipated changes in interest rates can set up massive capital flows. These flows — entering on either the demand or supply side of the foreign exchange market of a country — dominate over other flows and determine the exchange rate — unless the governments have fixed the exchange rate or try to manage it through offsetting sales or purchases of foreign exchange from their reserves.[15]

Further, since capital is extremely mobile and very large amounts can be transferred among countries with well-developed financial markets at a few minutes' notice, IRP determines exchange rate changes on a continuous basis in free exchange markets, while, as we have already argued, PPP holds at best in a long-run context. Hence, *in well-developed financial markets, IRP provides the short-term determination of the exchange rates while PPP or its relative version at best only provides a long-term tendency, so that exchange rates determined through IRP can deviate from PPP for considerable periods.*

3.6 The Balance of Payments

The balance of payments can be defined or presented in an economic or accounting form. Economic analysis focuses mainly on its economic form. *The (economic) balance of payments is a statement of the inflows and the outflows of funds from the domestic country and the difference between them.* If the economic balance of payments were arranged in the form of a table, it would specify each of the sources of the inflows and outflows of funds from a country, and the *difference* between them. This is illustrated in Table 3.1. The inflows of foreign exchange during a period are the sum of the payments we receive for commodities and financial assets sold to foreigners plus interest and dividends on our investments abroad and unilateral transfers (such as gifts) from foreigners. The outflows of foreign exchange are the sum of the payments we make for commodities and financial assets bought from foreigners plus interest and dividends on foreign investments in our country and unilateral transfers (such as gifts) to foreigners. Defining the (economic) balance of payments by B, we have:

$$B = \text{Inflows of foreign exchange} - \text{Outflows of foreign exchange} \tag{9}$$

$$= (X_c + Z_k + IR + IT) - (Z_c + X_k + OR + OT) \tag{10}$$

$$= (X_c - Z_c + IR + IT) - (X_k - Z_k + OR + OT),$$

where:

B = balance of payments,
X_c = value of exports of commodities (goods and services),
X_k = value of capital exports (against our purchases of stocks and bonds from foreigners),
Z_c = value of imports of commodities (goods and services),
Z_k = value of capital imports (against foreigners' purchases of stocks and bonds from us),
IR = inflows of interest and dividend payments,
IT = inflows of funds due to unilateral transfers (gifts and donations) from abroad,
OR = outflows of interest and dividend payments, and
OT = outflows of funds due to unilateral transfers (gifts and donations) to foreigners.

On the right side of the above equation, $(X_c + Z_k + IR + IT)$ are the inflows of foreign exchange, with X_c as the inflows against the exports of commodities and Z_k as the inflows against the outflows of bonds (including stocks and shares and other claims to ownership). $(Z_c + X_k + OR + OT)$ are the outflows of funds. Of these,

---

[15]The ability to do so depends upon the country's foreign exchange reserves (and other support it can arrange from other countries or the IMF) relative to the private capital flows. Since the latter can be potentially much larger than the former for most countries, countries now possess a very limited ability to manage exchange rates contrary to market forces.

Table 3.1 Stylized Balance of Payments Accounts

Credits (inflows of funds)		Debits (outflows of funds)	
The balance of payments on current account			
Merchandise exports	150	Merchandise imports	125
Rent	0	Rent	5
Interest	80	Interest	25
Dividends	100	Dividends	10
Wages and salaries	25	Wages and salaries	35
Transportation	5	Donations to foreign countries	
		Private	10
		Government aid (grants)	20
Total for current account	*360*		*230*
The balance of payments on capital account			
A. Private			
Sale of domestic shares to foreigners	15	Purchase of foreign shares	40
Sale of long-term bonds to foreigners	10	Purchase of foreign corporate bonds	20
Sale of short-term bonds to foreigners	20	Purchase of foreign government securities	10
Foreign demand deposits with local banks	5	Demand deposits with foreign banks	15
		Acquisition of foreign exchange by local banks	10
B. Government			
		Loans to foreign countries	100
Total for capital account	*50*		*195*
The balance of payments			
Total flows for balance of payments	410		425
Net balance of payments position	−15		
(= inflows − outflows = 410 − 425 (a deficit in the balance of payments of 15))			
Official settlements balance			
Official settlements balance	+15		
(= outflows from foreign exchange reserves, representing inflows into the foreign exchange markets)			
The accounting balance of payments			
Total inflows of funds	425	Total outflows of funds	425
(in/from the foreign exchange markets of the domestic economy)			

Z_c are the outflows of funds to pay for the imports of commodities and X_k are the outflows of funds to pay for our purchases of foreign bonds (including stocks and shares and other claims to ownership).

IR and IT represent inflows of funds without a corresponding reverse flow of currently produced commodities or bonds. IR captures the payments of interest and dividends on foreign bonds held by the domestic residents, with such bond holdings representing past investments rather than being a current cross-border flow of bonds. Similarly, OT captures the payments of interest and dividends on domestic bonds held by foreigners. IT and OT capture cross-border remittances or gifts, which do not involve explicit future debt obligations.

The preceding equations define the *balance of payments in an economic sense*. The balance of payments is thus a statement of the exports and imports of commodities and financial assets. Note that all of the magnitudes in this equation are in nominal form.

The balance of payments can be decomposed as:

Balance of payments = Balance of payments of current account
+ Balance of payments on capital account.

3.6.1 The components of the balance of payments

The (economic) balance of payments has two components:

(i) *The balance of payments on current account* (B^c):

$$B^c = (X_c - Z_c + NR + NT), \tag{11}$$

where $(X_c - Z_c)$ specifies the *net exports of commodities* and is also called *the balance of trade*. $NR (= IR - OR)$ is the net inflow of interest and dividend payments and $NT (= IT - OT)$ is the net inflow of transfer payments.

The balance of payments on current account has three components: net exports of goods and services, net interest and dividend income from foreign investments, and net unilateral transfers. If the sum of the *net* interest and dividend payments and net unilateral transfers were zero, the balance of payments on current account becomes identical with net exports, which is also known as the balance of trade. The common assumption on $(NR + NT)$ in the macroeconomic analysis for most developed economies is that this sum is zero or that it can be taken as exogenously given in short-run analysis.[16]

(ii) *The balance of payments on capital account* (B^k):

$$B^k = Z_k - X_k. \tag{12}$$

This balance specifies the *net* inflow/imports of funds resulting from (financial) capital flows. Z_k is the inflow of funds/capital resulting from the purchase by foreigners of financial assets from us while X_k is the outflow of funds/capital resulting from the purchases by domestic residents of financial assets from foreigners. Z_k is called capital imports and X_k is called capital exports.

Fact Sheet 3.2: United States Balance of Payments, 1976–2008

> This Fact Sheet illustrates movements in the balance of payments and its components by examining these for the USA. As this sheet shows, none of these is ever in equilibrium, i.e., equal to zero. The USA has had a large and increasing trade and current account deficit since abut 1984. Its capital account balance has tended to be positive since the USA attracts foreign capital flows because of its political stability and its economic performance.

---

[16]Such as assumption would be unrealistic for countries with large positive or negative values of either NR or NT. Among these are countries with a large externally held debt, as in the case of many developing economies, or large net remittances as in the case of some oil-rich countries on the Arabian Peninsula with a large number of foreign workers.

Fact Sheet 3.2: (*Continued*)

3.6.2 Equilibrium in the balance of payments

Clearly, the value of B need not equal zero. It could be positive, negative, or zero. If $B > 0$, there is said to be a surplus in the balance of payments, which is paid to us in foreign currencies so that our reserves of foreign currencies increase. If $B < 0$, there is said to be a deficit in the balance of payments, which we pay for through running down our country's reserves of foreign currencies. If $B = 0$, the balance of payments is said to be in *equilibrium*, so that there is no change in our foreign currency reserves. By comparison, if $B < 0$ or $B > 0$, the balance of payments is said to be in *disequilibrium*.

We have the following two implications of equilibrium in the balance of payments:

a. If the balance of payments is in equilibrium, $B = 0$ so that,

$$(X_k - Z_k) = (X_c - Z_c) + (NR + NT). \tag{13}$$

That is, in the balance of payments equilibrium, net capital inflows (outflows) equal the balance of payments surplus (deficit) on the current account. Hence, if our country is exporting more than it imports of commodities, it must also be a net exporter of capital, so that it increases its investments abroad on a net basis.[17]

b. Also, for $B = 0$, we have:

$$(Z_c - X_c) = (Z_k - X_k) + (NR + NT),$$

so that for the balance of payments equilibrium to exist, the net capital inflows (plus NR and NT) must be enough to cover the cost of net imports. Hence, countries with net imports of commodities must be importing capital or pay for them from their foreign exchange holdings.[18]

---

[17]A clear example is provided by the case of China in 2004 and 2006. It was both a net exporter of commodities and a net exporter of capital.

[18]A clear example is provided by the case of USA in 2004 and 2006. It was both a net importer of commodities and a net importer of capital.

3.6.3 The change in foreign exchange reserves

The difference between the inflows and outflows of funds equals the change in the nation's foreign exchange reserves. Evaluated in dollars, this amount is designated as ΔFR. Therefore,

$$\$\Delta FR = B$$
$$= (X_c + Z_k) - (Z_c + X_k) + NR + NT$$
$$= (X_c - Z_c) - (X_k - Z_k) + NR + NT, \qquad (14)$$

where \$FR stands for the foreign exchange reserves evaluated in the domestic currency (Canadian dollars).

Hence, the net change in our foreign exchange reserves is zero (i.e., ΔFR = 0) if the balance of payments is in equilibrium (i.e., $B = 0$). There is a net inflow of foreign exchange to the home country (ΔFR > 0) if the balance of payments is in surplus (i.e., $B > 0$) and a net outflow (ΔFR < 0) if the balance of payments is in deficit (i.e., $B < 0$). B is thus a measure of the change in the country's foreign exchange reserves.

Fact Sheet 3.3: US Foreign Exchange Reserves and Balance of Payments, 2005–2008

As explained in the text, balance of payments surpluses and deficits produce corresponding changes in foreign exchange reserves, so that movements in the balance of payment and foreign exchange reserves are closely related. This Fact Sheet illustrates this relationship for the USA. For the USA, both balance of payments and foreign exchange reserves experienced a drop in 2005, followed by a steady increase up to the last quarter of 2008.

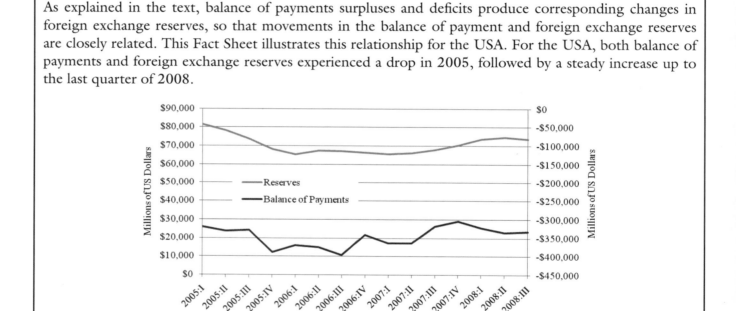

Equilibrium in the balance of payments

For pedagogical purposes, macroeconomic analysis assumes that the country in question desires equilibrium in its balance of payments.[19] This corresponds to the assumption that the desired level of the balance of payments and of the change in foreign exchange reserves is zero. This is clearly a simplification, though it is commonly used in open economy macroeconomics. We will also do so. In this case, ΔFR = B = 0, so that:

$$(Z_c - X_c) = (Z_k - X_k) + (NR + NT).$$

---

[19]However, note that in practice, central banks do often want to build up their foreign exchange reserves through $B > 0$. An example of this is provided by China in 2005 and 2010.

That is, the net capital inflows (plus NR and NT) must exactly cover the payments for the net imports of commodities, with the result that the change in foreign exchange reserves is zero.

Foreign exchange reserves and short-term bonds

Central banks often invest part of their inflows of foreign exchange in the short-term bonds, especially Treasury bills, of foreign governments, so that they can earn some income. These bonds are highly liquid and earn interest, while holdings of foreign currencies do not.

The country's official holdings of foreign exchange consist of its reserves of foreign currencies (including gold and SDRs) plus its holdings of short-term foreign bonds held by the government and the central bank.

3.7 The Balance of Payments in an Accounting Sense

Surpluses and deficits in the balance of payments have to be settled in foreign currencies. To capture the changes in the country's foreign exchange reserves, we define the *official settlements balance* B^s as the amount that has to be paid to 'settle' (or 'balance' for accounting purposes) the net indebtedness arising from the balance of payments deficits and surpluses. It is defined by the condition $B + B^s \equiv 0$, which makes B^s identical to $-B$.[20] To reiterate,

$$B^s \equiv -B. \tag{15}$$

That is, *the official settlements balance equals the negative of the balance of payments B*. Note that, with a balance of payments surplus, a positive value of B (but a negative value of B^s) represents an increase in our foreign exchange reserves.

The *accounting balance of payments* is given by $(B + B^s)$, which is identically equal to zero, since $(B + B^s) \equiv 0$. Hence,

$$[(X_c - Z_c + NR + NT) - (X_k - Z_k)] + B^s \equiv 0, \tag{16}$$

where $\equiv$ indicates an identity.[21] Hence, the *accounting* balance of payments is a statement of the receipts and payments to foreigners in a given period of time, in a form such that the total receipts *always* equal total payments.

The accounting balance of payments is related to the (economic) balance of payments by the identity $B + B^s \equiv 0$. The *accounting* balance of payments has three components:

1. The balance of payments on current account, B^c.
2. The balance of payments on capital account, B^k.
3. The official settlements balance, B^s, such that $B^s \equiv -B \equiv (-B^c - B^k)$.

Note that the balance of payments (in the macroeconomic sense of this concept) consists only of (1) and (2).

An illustrative form of the balance of payments accounts is shown in Table 3.1. For this tabular form, the inflows of funds are listed in one column and the outflows in another one, with the balancing item B^s being placed with an appropriate sign in one column or the other one. This table lists the flows by type of activity

---

[20]Note that $B^s > 0$ indicates an outflow of foreign exchange from the central bank's official reserves to pay for a balance of payments deficit ($B < 0$). Conversely, if there is a balance of payments surplus ($B > 0$), $B^s < 0$ and there is a corresponding inflow of foreign exchange reserves, which become an addition to the official reserves.

[21]This is an identity since the left side will always equal zero.

or function. While the items in this table are self-explanatory, a few comments would be useful. The interest and dividend payment flows are the return to past flows of capital and appear in the current account (of the balance of payments), while the capital flows — through the purchases and sales of bonds (including loans, equities, and deposits in foreign banks) — during the same period are part of the capital account.[22] Although there is a net surplus of 130 on the current account, the deficit on the capital account of 145 (because of net investments abroad) results in a net deficit of 15 on the overall balance of balance of payments. This deficit is settled by net sales of foreign exchange worth 15 by the country, so that the official foreign exchange reserves decrease by 15 — and the official settlements balance is +15.

To conclude, from the accounting perspective of Table 3.1, the inflows of funds from the exports of commodities, financial instruments, and foreign exchange equal 425. The outflows of funds from the imports of commodities, financial instruments, and foreign exchange reserves also equal 425. This is the essential aspect of an accounting balance of payments: both sides of the statement are always equal. The element in this balance sheet that ensures the identity of the two sides is the flows out/in of the country's foreign exchange reserves to settle the (economic) balance of payments deficit or surplus.

3.8 The Market for Foreign Exchange and the Changes in Foreign Exchange Reserves

3.8.1 The demand and supply of foreign exchange

As explained earlier, *foreign exchange* consists of all those assets that can act as media of exchange in international transactions. These include gold, currencies of foreign countries, and Special Drawing Rights (SDRs) at the International Monetary Fund (IMF). The SDRs are created by the IMF and held by individual countries as a form of demand deposits with the IMF itself, and are designated in a specified basket of the national currencies.

The *supply of our currency (\$) in foreign exchange markets* arises during the payments process when we buy from foreigners their commodities (which are our imports of commodities) or financial assets (which lead to our export of capital), pay interest and dividends or transfer funds as gifts to them. Conversely, *foreigners' demand for our currency* arises because they buy our commodities (which constitute our exports of commodities) or our assets (which constitute our imports of capital), pay interest and dividends or send gifts of currency to us.[23] Hence,

$$\$S^\$ = \$Z_c + \$X_k + \$OR + \$OT \tag{17}$$

$$\$D^\$ = \$X_c + \$Z_k + \$IR + \$IT, \tag{18}$$

where:

$S^\$$ = supply of our dollars in the foreign exchange markets,
$D^\$$ = demand for our dollars in the foreign exchange markets,
$OR\,(IR)$ = outflows (inflows) of funds for interest and dividend payments, and
$OT\,(IT)$ = outflows (inflows) of funds occurring due to unilateral transfers.

---

[22]High levels of net inflows (outflows) of capital over some years will imply increased outflows (inflows) for interest and dividends in subsequent years, creating a dynamic relationship between the present capital account and the future current account. The donations to foreign countries are unilateral flows and enter in the current account.

[23]Note that our exports (imports) of capital X_k would be equal to our imports (exports) of bonds (including equities) Z_b.

Note that $(IR - OR) = NR$ and $(IT - OT) = NT$, where NR is net inflows of interest and dividends and NT is net inflows of transfers.

3.8.2 Equilibrium in the foreign exchange market

Equilibrium requires the equality of demand and supply, so that, in equilibrium,

$$\$S^\$ = \$D^\$.$$

Since $\$S^\$$ corresponds to the inflow of foreign funds in the balance of payments and $\$D^\$$ corresponds to the outflow of funds, equilibrium in the balance of payments requires that $B = 0$.

Extended Analysis Box 3.2: The Demand and Supply of Foreign Exchange Stated in Foreign Currencies

In terms of foreign currencies, the *demand for foreign exchange* (£s) is the demand for an international mode of payment (other than one's own currency). This demand arises because the residents of the domestic economy wish to purchase, i.e., import either commodities or financial assets from other countries, pay interest and dividends and make transfer payments.[24] This demand corresponds to the outflow of funds in the balance of payments. The *supply of foreign exchange* (£s) to our economy arises because foreigners wish to purchase our commodities or financial assets, as well as pay interest and dividends to us, and send us gifts. This supply of foreign exchange to our economy corresponds to the inflow of funds in the balance of payments. The difference between the supply of and demand for foreign currencies becomes the inflow of foreign exchange funds into our economy. A net inflow (outflow) in the form of foreign currencies, gold and SDRs increases (decreases) the country's foreign exchange reserves.

The demand for *foreign currencies* (£D^F) by the domestic economy is the sum of our imports of commodities (£Z_c) and our imports of financial assets corresponding to our capital exports or outflows (£X_k). Similarly, the supply of foreign currencies (£S^F) to the domestic economy is the sum of our exports of commodities (£X_c) and our exports of financial assets (corresponding to our capital imports) (£Z_k), plus net transfers of interest and dividends (£NR) and net unilateral transfers (£NT). Therefore,

$$£D^F = £Z_c + £X_k + £OR + £OT \tag{19}$$
$$£S^F = £X_c + £Z_k + £IR + £IT, \tag{20}$$

where:

D^F = demand for foreign currencies,
S^F = supply of foreign currencies,
£$OR(IR)$ = outflows (inflows) of funds for interest and dividend payments, and
£$OT(IT)$ = outflows (inflows) of funds for unilateral transfer payments.

---

[24]Note that capital equipment and services such as shipping and tourism are already included in the definition of commodities (goods and services) and are part of imports and exports.

Extended Analysis Box 3.2: (*Continued*)

The *demand for foreign currencies* by a country ($£D^F$) has its converse in *the supply of dollars* ($\$S^\$$) by us to foreigners to act as an element of their foreign exchange balances. The *supply of foreign currencies* by foreigners ($£S^F$) is correspondingly the converse of the *demand for dollars* ($\$D^\$$) by foreigners from us. The market for foreign exchange, therefore, can be looked at from two different viewpoints: as the demand and supply of *dollars in the foreign exchange market* or as the demand and supply of foreign exchange/currencies. We will often find it convenient to switch from one to the other in the intuitive explanations of our analysis.

3.9 The Market Determination of the Nominal Exchange Rate

For the flexible exchange rate regime with efficient exchange markets, Figure 3.1 illustrates the market for foreign exchange and the market determination of the equilibrium exchange rate. The horizontal axis measures the quantity of dollars in the foreign exchange market, while the vertical axis specifies the exchange rate (in £s per $). This figure assumes that the curve for $\$D^\$$ follows the usual shape of demand curves and is downward sloping, while that for $\$S^\$$ follows the usual shape of supply curves and is upward sloping. Equilibrium between $\$D^\$$ and $\$S^\$$ is shown at the nominal exchange rate ρ^*. Exchange rates above this equilibrium rate would have $(\$D^\$ - \$S^\$) < 0$, so that there would be a deficit in the balance of payments. Exchange rates below this equilibrium rate would have $(\$D^\$ - \$S^\$) > 0$, so that there would be a surplus in the balance of payments.

Since the exchange markets for financially developed economies tend to be efficient (i.e., go to equilibrium rapidly), the market exchange rate for our economies would tend to be the equilibrium one. However, if the exchange rate has been fixed by the government or the central bank, it might be at the equilibrium level, or above or below the equilibrium level. If it was set above the equilibrium level, the economy would have a balance of payments deficit; if it was set below the equilibrium level, the economy would have a balance of payments surplus.

Since both commodity and capital flows are components of the demand and supply of foreign exchange, changes in the net exports of commodities and net capital flows both produce changes in the market exchange rate. In the short term, capital flows are usually more volatile, so that short-term fluctuations in the exchange rate are usually due more to fluctuations in capital flows than in commodity flows.

Chapter 12 will further expand on this analysis of the foreign exchange market.

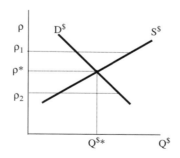

Figure 3.1

Fact Sheet 3.4: Exchange Rates against the US Dollar, 1980–2008

This Fact Sheet illustrates movements in the exchange rates in terms of the US dollar of the currencies of several countries. Some of these countries had pegged exchange rates for part of the selected period. For example, the decision to peg the national currency to the US dollar was taken by Argentina from 1980 to 1988 and from 1991 to 2001, by Mexico in the early 1990s, by Malaysia after 1997, and by China in 1993. When this peg became unsustainable, they switched to a floating exchange rate. The depreciation experienced after such a switch is evident for Argentina in 1988 and 2001 as well as for Mexico in 1991.

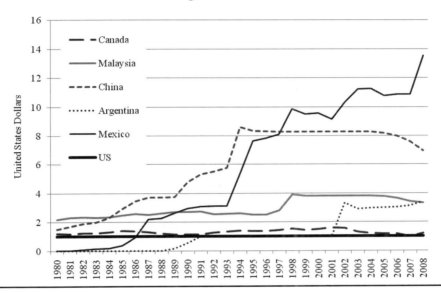

3.9.1 Hot money

Some of the capital flows among countries are extremely sensitive to expected interest and exchange rate changes, as well as to the political and economic insecurity in the country. Speculation about a possible devaluation/depreciation of the domestic currency can cause sudden, heavy outflows of short-term funds seeking protection from it, or trying to make a profit out of it. Funds whose flows among countries are very sensitive to expected exchange rate changes, interest rate fluctuations or security and convertibility (i.e., unhindered exchanges among currencies) considerations are known as *hot money*.

Investments in short-term bonds can move easily among countries, so that changes in them are part of hot money movements. Such investments can be a major part of financial capital flows among countries.

Box 3.2: National Policies on the Balance of Payments and Accumulation of Foreign Exchange Reserves

Countries hold reserves of foreign exchange with their central banks to meet the possibility of deficits in the balance of payments. Deficits draw down the country's foreign exchange reserves by the amount of the deficit and surpluses increase these reserves by the size of the surplus.

The size of the country's foreign exchange reserves, or changes in it, is a matter of national policy, so that ΔR^F may be positive or negative for long periods. For example, by the end of World War II in 1945, the USA had accumulated massive foreign exchange reserves that were really not needed for financing its international transactions and could have been reduced. It ran very significant deficits in its balance of payments virtually throughout the 1950s and the 1960s. Germany and Japan had hardly any foreign exchange reserves until the early 1950s and needed to build them up. As their economies recovered and exports increased, they maintained surpluses in their balances of payments for several decades as a way of building up their reserves. Neither the US nor Germany or Japan was especially concerned about their deficit or surplus for much of the 1950s and 1960s. This example illustrates that countries often deliberately accept continuing deficits or surpluses in their balance of payments for fairly long periods. In 2005 and 2006, China provided a clear example of continuing surpluses and the USA provided a clear example of continuing deficits.

3.10 The Persistence of Balance of Payments Deficits and Surpluses

A country may continue to have a balance of payments surplus even with flexible exchange rates if its central bank is willing to accumulate the resulting inflow of foreign exchange. Alternatively, if there is a deficit, it may be willing to sell the required foreign exchange from its reserves. As explained earlier, such a system is known as a managed exchange rate system. Under a managed exchange rate, the exchange rate is manipulated by the central bank through sales or purchases of foreign exchange from its reserves or changes in domestic interest rates. This provides one reason for the persistence over time of balance of payments surpluses and deficits. There are several additional reasons for the persistence over time of balance of payments disequilibrium. These have to do with the elasticities of the exports and imports of commodities and lags in the adjustment of foreign exchange markets from a disequilibrium position to equilibrium. These reasons will be discussed in Chapters 12 and 13 on the open economy.

Conclusions

- While some countries in the world have floating/flexible exchange rates, others have fixed/pegged ones. Many countries with flexible exchange rates try to control/manage the movements in their exchange rates.
- PPP and IRP provide the main theories for explaining the differentials between inflation rates, exchange rates, and interest rates across countries. These theories are especially likely to apply to countries with high ratios of exports and imports to GDP and with large inflows and outflows of capital.
- The weight of empirical evidence is that PPP does not strictly hold among countries even over several years. The empirical failure of PPP occurs mainly because of the existence of goods that cannot be traded across borders and because of capital flows.
- The weight of empirical evidence is that most currencies do not strictly possess interest rate parity with others. The empirical failure of IRP occurs because of imperfect capital markets and differences in the riskiness of domestic versus foreign assets, especially the 'exchange-rate risk' in investing abroad.
- Foreign exchange consists of foreign currencies, gold, and SDRs issued by the IMF. These serve as the media of exchange in international payments. A decrease in the demand for the domestic currency in the foreign exchange markets induces a depreciation of its exchange rate, while a decrease in the supply of the domestic currency in the foreign exchange markets induces an appreciation of its exchange rate.

	KEY CONCEPTS	

Exchange rates: nominal real, and effective
Purchasing power parity
Interest rate parity
Balance of trade

Balance of payments on current account
Balance of payments on capital account
The balance of payments
The accounting balance of payments
Official settlements balance

Foreign exchange reserves
The demand and supply of foreign exchange, and
Fixed, flexible, and managed exchange rates.

	SUMMARY OF CRITICAL CONCLUSIONS	

- The nominal exchange rate defines the value of a currency in terms of another currency.
- The real exchange rate defines the conversion rate between the commodities in one country and the commodities in other countries.
- The real exchange rate rather than the nominal one indicates the relative prices of commodities in different countries.
- Relative PPP rather than absolute PPP is more likely to apply among countries.
- IRP is an important determinant of interest rates across countries with perfect capital flows.
- While the accounting concept of the balance of payments is that the balance of payments will always be in balance, this is not so for the (economic) balance of payments, which can have a positive or negative value. The latter is said to be in equilibrium when its value is zero.
- Countries can have fixed, flexible, or managed exchange rates.
- Most countries with floating exchange rates usually try to manage the movements in the exchange rate.

Appendix

Extended Analysis Box 3.1A: Comparison of the Actual and PPP Costs of the Big Mac in Different Countries, 27 April 2000

	Big Mac price in local currency	Big Mac's implied PPP exchange rate	PPP check	Exchange rate = US$ per unit of local currency	Big Mac price in US$	% Overvaluation of local currency (+) against US$	k
USA	2.51	1.00	1	1.00	2.51	0.00	1.00
Australia	2.59	0.97	1	0.60	1.54	−38.58	0.61
Britain	1.90	1.32	1	1.59	3.00	20.15	1.20
Canada	2.85	0.88	1	0.68	1.94	−22.76	0.77
Mexico	20.90	0.12	1	0.11	2.22	−11.51	0.88

Notes:
Nominal exchange rate = US$ per unit of local currency.
Implied PPP exchange rate = foreign (US$) price of the Big Mac divided by the local price of the Big Mac.
PPP check is done by multiplying PPP-implied exchange rate by local price and dividing by foreign price.
This should equal 1.

US$ per unit of local currency is the actual nominal exchange rate.

Big Mac price in US$ = Big Mac price in local currency times the nominal exchange rate.

% Overvaluation (+) against US$ = (actual exchange rate – PPP exchange rate)/PPP exchange rate.

k equals the nominal exchange rate times the domestic price of the Big Mac divided by its US price.

Findings:

With *k* less than 1 for Australia, Canada, and Mexico, the Big Mac is relatively cheaper in these countries than in the USA.

With *k* more than 1 for Britain, the Big Mac is relatively more expensive in Britain than in the USA.

Source of original data: http://economist.com/markets/bigmac/displayStory.cfm.

REVIEW AND DISCUSSION QUESTIONS

1. What are the two ways of defining the nominal exchange rate? Which one is used in this book?
2. What is purchasing power parity? Explain its relationship to the real exchange rate.
3. What does relative purchasing power parity imply for changes in the nominal exchange rate?
4. Does PPP apply to different shops in the same city? Same country? Across countries? Illustrate with some examples. Give reasons for the deviations from PPP.
5. What is the relative importance over time of IRP and PPP in determining movements of the exchange rates?
6. Define equilibrium, surplus, and deficit in the balance of payments? What does each imply for changes in the country's foreign exchange reserves?
7. Is the accounting balance of payments always in balance? Give reasons for your answer.
8. Is the (economic) balance of payments always in balance? Give reasons for your answer.
9. Distinguish between fixed, flexible (floating), and managed exchange rates? Which does your country have at present?
10. Show diagrammatically the demand and supply of the domestic currency in the foreign exchange markets. For the figure as you have drawn it, is the equilibrium exchange rate stable or unstable? Explain your answer.
11. How is the payment of interest to foreigners treated in the country's balance of payments?
12. Why do countries with flexible exchange rates continue to have deficits or surpluses on their (a) current account, (b) capital account, and (c) balance of payments?

ADVANCED AND TECHNICAL QUESTIONS

T1. Suppose that a given bundle of commodities costs C$50 in Canada and £20 in Britain, and the exchange rate (£ per C$) is 0.5. What is the real exchange rate between these countries? Is this different from the real exchange rate that PPP requires?

T2. Why do underdeveloped economies tend to have real exchange rates less than unity? What difference does it make in comparing standards of living across countries?

T3. A simplified form of Canada's balance of payments on current account is presented below.

	1999 ($b)	2000 ($b)	2001 ($b)
Goods and services receipts	417	478	468
Investment income receipts	33	42	37
Transfer receipts	6	6	7
Goods and services payments	385	425	413
Investment income payments	65	69	65
Transfer payments	5	5	5

Calculate the values of (a) net exports of commodities, (b) net interest and dividend flows, (c) net transfers, and (d) balance of payments on current account.

T4. A simplified form of Canada's net inflows on capital account is presented below.

	1999 ($b)	2000 ($b)	2001 ($b)
Net flow of Canadian assets[25]			
Canadian direct investment abroad	−27	−65	−57
Canadian portfolio investment abroad[26]	−23	−62	−35
Other Canadian investment abroad[27]	5	−7	−16
Net flow of Canadian liabilities			
Foreign direct investment in Canada	37	94	43
Foreign portfolio investment in Canada	4	20	30
Other foreign investment in Canada[28]	−13	8	8
Statistical discrepancy	15	−7	−3

Calculate the balance of payments on capital account (including the statistical discrepancy)?

T5. Given the information in the preceding two questions, what was Canada's balance of payments in the three years? Was it in equilibrium, deficit or surplus?

---

[25] A minus sign indicates an outflow of capital due to an increase in our claims on nonresidents or a decrease in liabilities to them.

[26] This item includes bonds and stocks.

[27] This item consists of loans, deposits, official international reserves, etc.

[28] This item consists of loans, deposits, official international reserves, etc.

PART II
Short-run Macroeconomics

CHAPTER 4
Determinants of Aggregate Demand: The Commodity Market of the Closed Economy

This chapter presents the analysis of the commodity market of the macroeconomy. For this analysis, it encapsulates the relationships of the commodity market into the IS equation and curve.

Chapter 1 listed four types of goods in the closed economy. These are:

1. Commodities, usually referred to as goods and services, and including both consumer goods and physical capital
2. Money
3. Bonds (i.e., all non-monetary financial assets)
4. Labor

This chapter lays out the assumptions and their implications for the commodities market of the closed economy. It encapsulates this analysis into the compact IS relationship and curve.

4.1 Symbols Used

Many of these symbols used in this chapter have already appeared in the preceding chapters. However, for convenience, the meanings of the symbols used in this chapter are specified in Table 4.1.

In most cases, the small letter symbol will indicate the real value of the variable while the capital one will indicate its nominal (dollar) value. Thus, y is the real value of income/output while Y is its dollar value. One exception to this rule is the use of K to designate the real value of the physical capital stock.

The superscript d on a variable will indicate its demand and the superscript s will indicate its supply. The variable symbol without either of these superscripts will indicate its actual value. If there exists equilibrium, the actual value will be the equilibrium one, i.e., one at which the demand and supply for that variable are equal. Thus, n^d is the demand for labor and n^s is its supply, while n is actual employment.

The symbol $\equiv$ indicates an identity while the symbol $=$ indicates an equilibrium condition.

4.2 The Commodity Sector of the Closed Economy

As specified in Chapter 1, this book defines commodities as what are usually referred to in everyday English language usage as goods and services. This category includes both consumer goods and physical capital.

4.2.1 Uses of national income

Commodities are produced by firms with the use of inputs (factors of production). Firms incur expenses in the form of wages, profits, and rents, the sum of which is aggregate income. Therefore, real national

Table 4.1   Symbols used in this chapter.

Symbols	Meaning
y	aggregate quantity of commodities (also often referred to as output/national income)
y^d	aggregate demand for commodities
y^s	aggregate supply of commodities
y^f	full-employment output/income
e	aggregate expenditures (in real terms)
c	consumption expenditures
c_0	autonomous consumption
s	(private) saving
s^n	national saving
i	(planned) investment expenditures
i^u	unintended investment
i_0	autonomous investment
t	net taxes paid (government's tax revenues less government transfers to the public)
t_0	autonomous net taxes paid
g	government expenditures on commodities
r	real rate of interest
R	nominal/market rate of interest
P	price level
π	rate of inflation
π^e	expected inflation rate

Nominal national income is written as Y and equals Py.

income (y) represents both the aggregate cost of production of firms[1] as well as the aggregate income of all economic agents in the economy. In the closed economy, the recipients of national income y can spend it on consumption c, pay it in net taxes (i.e., total taxes paid to the government by the public less transfers from the government to the public) t or put it away for future periods as saving s.[2] That is,

$$y \equiv c + t + s. \tag{1}$$

Note that all the variables are in real terms, so that the data collected on their nominal values would have been deflated by the appropriate price index (see Chapter 1).

---

[1]Total output is assumed to be fully distributed to the factors of production within the same period. Some of this is done through contractual income in the form of wages, rents and interest payments. The remainder is considered the profits of the firms that produced the output. In equilibrium, the amount of profits would be 'normal profits', which is the amount that firms need to earn to produce the existing output and pay their owners for the capital investment in the firm.

[2]Note that the word 'saving' is in its singular form and represents the amount of currently produced commodities that are not paid in taxes and are not consumed (i.e., destroyed) in the current period. This saving is in real terms. It differs from the word 'savings' which is often used to refer to 'wealth' or to 'savings deposits' in banks. Wealth can be in a physical form, such as houses, or a financial form, such as bonds and stocks. Savings deposits are a form of money and are included in M2 (see Chapter 2) and are in nominal terms.

4.2.2 Sources of national expenditures

For the closed economy, the demand for commodities — which constitutes the sales revenue of firms — originates as consumption expenditures c, as government expenditures g on goods and services, or as (*desired*) investment expenditures i which are deliberately undertaken by firms. Such investment expenditures deliberately incurred by firms are for the purpose of intentionally increasing their capital stock used for production in future periods and are also known as 'desired', 'intended', 'planned', or '*ex ante*' investment. We will just refer to them as 'investment', leaving its adjectives as implicit. Designating the real aggregate expenditures on commodities as e, where e is, by definition for the closed economy, specified by:

$$e \equiv c + g + i, \tag{2}$$

where g is real government expenditures on commodities produced in the current period. Note that neither g nor t includes transfers from the government to the public (see Chapter 1).

4.2.3 Equilibrium in the commodity market

National income y is the sum of the payments to the inputs in the production process and is thus the aggregate cost of production in the economy. Aggregate expenditures e is the aggregate revenue from the sale of the output produced. Ongoing equilibrium in the production process (i.e., according to firms' production plans) requires that the firms' aggregate costs and revenues be equal. That is, the commodity market requires $y = e$ for equilibrium.

To check that $e = y$ represents the equilibrium position, examine what happens in the economy if $e > y$ or if $e < y$. If $e > y$, firms' revenues exceed their costs, so that they find it profitable to increase production — and also possibly raise their prices. To increase production, they will hire more workers and other inputs. This would increase income y, so that y would tend to increase toward e. If $e < y$, firms find that their input costs are higher than their sales revenue, so that they will cut back on production and employment of inputs. This would decrease employment and the incomes paid to the factors of production, so that y will fall toward e. Therefore, equilibrium will only exist in the commodities market if,

$$y = e. \tag{3}$$

When $e = y$, firms' expenses exactly equal their revenues, so that they do not have an incentive or compulsion to change their employment of factors of production. Therefore, $y = e$ represents equilibrium between income and expenditures in the commodity market *for the closed economy.*

Since $y = c + t + s$ and $e = c + i + g$, *equilibrium* ($y = e$) *in the closed economy commodity market* requires that:

$$c + t + s = c + g + i,$$

which is the same as:

$$t + s = g + i. \tag{4}$$

The equality of $(t+s)$ and $(g+i)$ is another way of stating the equilibrium condition for the commodity market for a *closed* economy. As Chapter 5 will show, it differs from the equilibrium condition for an open economy.

4.2.4 National saving

National saving s^n is defined as the sum of private saving s and government/public saving ($= t - g$), so that:

$$s^n \equiv s + (t - g). \tag{5}$$

This equation is a definitional identity — i.e., a way of defining a variable.

Therefore, another way of stating the equilibrium condition for the commodity market of the *closed* economy is:

$$s^n = i, \tag{6}$$

which asserts the equality of national saving and investment for equilibrium in the closed economy, and is another form of the equilibrium condition for a closed economy. Note that this equality of national saving and investment for the closed economy does not hold in disequilibrium in the commodity market and is not an identity.

4.2.5 The relationship between saving and investment

We specified i above as the firms' *desired* real investment expenditures undertaken for the purpose of increasing their capital stock. These are incurred because the firms *want* to change their capital stock. For achieving this, at the level of a single firm, the firm can buy the commodities from other firms or use some of its own output. The critical element in this definition, determination, and measurement of the macroeconomic concept of investment is not whether the firm buys commodities needed to add to its capital stock from other firms or uses some of its own output.[3] The critical element is whether the firm *wants* to change its capital stock and how much investment it wants to undertake for that purpose. For these reasons, this concept of investment is also known as *desired, intended, or ex ante investment.* Macroeconomics uses the single word 'investment' for this concept, thereby leaving the adjectives 'desired, intended, planned, or *ex ante*' as implicit. Note that this investment can be partly in terms of buildings, machines, etc., which will be used to produce more commodities in the future and partly in the form of desired changes in the firms' inventories of their goods to meet their future expected sales.

Real private saving is the 'residual' of current output left over after consumption and payment in taxes. This residual may be directly committed by the savers themselves for future production in the form of investment in physical capital (such as in a newly built house), but most of it tends to be lent to others in exchange for bonds (which includes the purchase of shares) or exchanged for money balances. Therefore, the overall investment expenditures on commodities may not equal the supply of saving in an economy in which other goods — such as bonds and money — exist. Further, saving is done by households on the basis of their utility maximization, subject to a budget constraint, while investment is undertaken by firms based on profit maximization. There is no reason to assume that the saving intentions of the myriad households in the economy will in the aggregate *just and always* produce the aggregate level of saving that will equal the aggregate investment expenditures undertaken by the myriad firms.

National saving is based on the plans of households and governments. There is again no basis for assuming that national saving planned by these will *always* be an amount equal to the investment intended by firms. What the above analysis shows is that the *equilibrium* of the commodity market, *when and if it comes about*, will show the equality of national saving and investment for a closed economy. But, this equality will not apply if there is disequilibrium.

4.2.6 The (physical) capital stock

For a firm, the *actual capital stock* of a given period is defined as consisting of all the commodities carried over from the preceding period. The actual capital stock can differ from the *desired capital stock*. Investment i is the

---

[3] One way of thinking about it would be to envisage each firm selling its output and then deliberately buying some of it back for its investment purposes.

desired change in the existing capital stock, and can differ from the actual change in the existing capital stock. Further, one of the simplifying assumptions of macroeconomics is that, in the short run, this investment does not become operational as capital in production use due to a gestation lag. Hence, the capital stock is held constant in short-run macroeconomic theory, even though this theory envisages investment as occurring.

Box 4.1: An Unjustified Oversimplification for a Modern Economy

---

If there is no government at all in the economy — which is quite an unrealistic assumption for the modern world — or if the government expenditures on commodities (goods and services) and the net taxes received by the government are equal, the budget is balanced, so that $g = t$. In this special case, the equilibrium condition simplifies to:

$$s = i. \tag{4'}$$

The equilibrium condition for the commodity market is sometimes expressed as (4'), which requires the equality of saving and investment for equilibrium in the closed economy. However, since this condition requires a balanced budget (which rarely occurs) or the absence of the government (which is now patently unrealistic), it is preferable to specify the equilibrium condition for the closed economy as $t + s = g + i$, rather than as $s = i$.

A cautionary note : $(s + t) = (i + g)$ and $s = i$ are not identities.

Since $s + t = i + g$ (or its simplified form $s = i$) is an equilibrium condition, it would not hold in disequilibrium. Since it does not hold under all circumstances — e.g., in disequilibrium — it is not an identity.

Further, saving and tax payments are done by households, while investment is undertaken by firms and government expenditures are expenses incurred by the government. There is no reason to assume that in the real world in real time, the actions of these very different economic agents will produce the value of $(s + t)$ that would be the same as that of $(i + g)$ over any given quarter or year. Whether they are equal for any given quarter or year would depend on whether the commodity market comes into equilibrium in that quarter or year. It may or may not. However, for analytical convenience, the analysis is pursued under the assumption of (short-run, though not short-term) equilibrium in the commodity market.

4.3 The Two Uses of Private Saving and the Drag of Deficits on Investment

We have so far derived the following alternative forms of the equilibrium condition for the closed economy.

$$s + t = i + g,$$
$$s^n = i.$$

We can restate the above conditions as:

$$s = i + (g - t).$$

This equation states that, in the closed economy, private saving can be used for two purposes: investment and a fiscal deficit $(= g - t)$. To the extent that the government absorbs private saving to finance its deficit (through borrowing by the issue of its bonds), it reduces the amount of commodities that can be used for investment. The less left for the latter, the slower the growth of the physical capital stock and the smaller will be the future production capacity of the economy. Current fiscal deficits, therefore, hurt future increases in output and the standard of living.

The above equilibrium condition can also be stated as:

$$s/y = i/y + (g - t)/y.$$

Hence, for a given level of fiscal deficits as a proportion of GDP, the higher is the domestic saving rate (i.e., s/y), the greater will be the investment/GDP ratio and the greater will be the growth rate of the future productive capacity of the economy. A high saving rate is, therefore, desirable for the economy.

4.4   Disequilibrium and the Role of Changes in Inventories in the Adjustment to Equilibrium

Note that there is no basis for assuming that a particular real-world economy will always or mostly have commodity market equilibrium. In fact, because the behavior of households, firms, and the government is constantly changing and causes variations in private saving, investment, and fiscal deficits, and because there are usually lags in commodity market adjustments, the more common state in the real world is likely to be one of disequilibrium, rather than of equilibrium. In this case, the relevant assumption is that when the economy is in disequilibrium, it does make adjustments to move toward equilibrium.

When the commodity market is not in equilibrium, we need to examine the mechanism that might take this market toward equilibrium. This mechanism operates through the responses of economic agents and markets. To illustrate this mechanism, start from an initial equilibrium and assume that a positive shock[4] increases expenditures such that national expenditures e become greater than national income y, i.e., $e > y$. Since $e > y$, firms face a higher demand for commodities than their production, since y represents not only national income but also the amount of commodities produced in the economy. To meet this demand, since an increase in production takes some time to implement, firms would have to deplete their inventories below the planned levels or raise their product prices. Firms' revenues are also higher than their costs. Hence, they have an incentive to increase production — as well as raise prices. To increase production, firms have to increase their employment of labor and other inputs, thereby increasing national income y in the economy.

Similarly, a negative shock to expenditures would produce for some time $e < y$. In this case, firms' revenues are less than their costs and they sell less than their output, leading to losses and the unintended accumulation of inventories of commodities. This will cause firms to decrease their production and employment of inputs, thereby decreasing factor incomes y. Such adjustments will continue until y equals e and the economy enters its equilibrium state. In this state, firms' demand and supply, as well as their revenues and costs, are equal and there is no tendency for them to further adjust their employment or output.

To recapitulate, national income y paid out by firms to inputs and national expenditures e received by firms from the sale of their products are not always equal. Over any given period, firms both individually and in the aggregate may end up with more or less sales revenue than their costs. If this happens, firms change their production plans and employment — as well as their product prices and payments to inputs. If and when these alterations bring about the equality of income and expenditures, we say that the commodity market has reached equilibrium. An efficient economy will continue with changes in the firms' production plans until the commodity market equilibrium is attained. But, since this process involves the production

---

[4]Examples of such positive shocks are those that increase consumption, investment, government expenditure, or reductions in tax rate.

and consumption plans of very large numbers of firms and households in the economy, any disequilibrium is unlikely to be eliminated instantaneously. Therefore, after a shock, the economy could be in disequilibrium for several quarters, if not years.

4.4.1 The role of unintended changes in inventories

Firms hold inventories of both unfinished and finished goods because production takes time and firms want to be able to meet orders for their products within a desired time. The total value of these inventories is part of the firm's capital stock. Changes in inventories can be desired or undesired ones. The major reason for the former is an increase in the firm's expected sales. Such desired changes in inventories are part of the firm's (desired) investment, as this term is defined in macroeconomics. Unintended changes in inventories are not part of the firm's (desired) investment. They reflect an unintended difference between the firm's output and its sales. Since inventories are costly to hold, the firm would want to reverse any unintended accumulation of inventories by cutting its production. It may also try to increase its sales through a reduction in the price of its product.

At the macroeconomic level, unintended changes in the economy's inventories are a reflection of the difference between the economy's output y and its sales e. Such changes are a symptom of disequilibrium in the commodity sector of the economy. Therefore, economic analysts pay considerable attention to the movements in inventories since they serve as an indicator of potential disequilibrium.

If $y > e$, firms will be producing more output than selling, so that there will be an unintended increase in inventories. Firms would cut back on production (a) to unwind any unintended accumulation of inventories and (b) to meet the lower demand level. They may also decrease their prices somewhat to increase sales. Conversely, if $e > y$, firms would have sold more than they had planned for and there would be an unintended decrease in inventories. Firms would increase production (a) to replenish inventories to reach their desired levels and (b) to meet the higher demand level. They may also try to reduce the quantity demanded by raising their prices.

Extended Analysis Box 4.1: A Simplified Diagrammatic Analysis: The 45° Diagram

For the simplest diagrammatic analysis at this stage, it is better to convert the variables into their *nominal* values. Figure 4.1a plots the equations:

$$\text{Equilibrium condition:} \qquad E = Y$$
$$\text{Composition of expenditures:} \quad E \equiv C + I + G,$$

where $E = Pe$, $Y = Py$, $C = Pc$, $I = Pi$, and $G = Pg$. Figure 4.1a shows E (nominal expenditures) on the vertical axis and Y (nominal income) on the horizontal axis. The 45° line represents $E = Y$ and is, therefore, the line for the first equation above, which is the specification of equilibrium in the commodity market. By the second equation above, national expenditures E are shown by the curve marked $C + I + G$. Figure 4.1a assumes that consumption C increases proportionately with income Y, while investment I and government expenditures G are independent of income. Equilibrium occurs at the point where the curve $(C+I+G)_0$ intersects the 45° line. This equilibrium is shown by the point a at which $E^* = Y^*$.[5] Points on the $(C+I+G)$ line, other than the point a, are ones of disequilibrium. On this line, points to the left of the 45°

---

[5]At this point, nominal national saving S^n equals nominal investment I.

Extended Analysis Box 4.1: (*Continued*)

line have $E > Y$,[6] so that firms will have an unintended decrease in inventories and/or not be able to meet the demand for their products. To restore inventories to their intended levels and to meet the higher demand, as well as increase profits, firms will increase production and/or prices. These will increase firms' revenues, which will raise national income. Therefore, Y will increase toward equilibrium. On the $(C+I+G)$ line, points to the right of the 45° line have $E < Y$,[7] so that firms will be paying more in factor incomes than they collect from sales revenues, which entails losses. They will also be left with unintended increases in inventories. They can restore inventories to the desired, lower levels, as well as increase profits by cutting back on production and employment, so that incomes will fall. Therefore, Y will decrease, moving the commodity market toward equilibrium, at which Y is lower than initially but now equals E. This type of the response pattern of firms to disequilibrium between Y and E ensures the stability of the commodity market equilibrium, which is the condition that $E^* = Y^*$.

Diagrams of the type used in Figures 4.1a and 4.1b are known as the 45° diagrams. The meaning of the symbols Y and E on the axes of these figures needs to be noted. In these figures, E is *nominal* national expenditures and Y is *nominal* national income. Suppose that firms become more optimistic about the future of the economy and increase investment. Let this increase in investment be such as to shift the

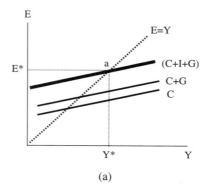

(a)

Figure 4.1a

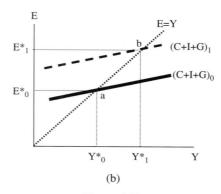

(b)

Figure 4.1b

---

[6]At these points, $S^n < I$.
[7]At these points, $S^n > I$.

Extended Analysis Box 4.1: (*Continued*)

$(C + I + G)$ curve from $(C + I + G)_0$ to $(C + I + G)_1$ in Figure 4.1b. The equilibrium of the economy moves from Y_0^* to Y_1^*.

Limitations of the 45° diagram for macroeconomic analysis

The use of this 45° diagram for the analysis of the commodity market suffers from two deficiencies:

- Since the price level is not determined in this diagram, the increase in *real* expenditures and income cannot be determined from this diagram. In reality, prices are likely to be pushed up by the higher expenditures and the consequent higher demand for commodities, so that we need a more elaborate analysis and diagram, which simultaneously determines real expenditures/income, prices, and real output. Such a diagram was the AD-AS one presented in Chapter 1. We will revert to the AD-AS diagrammatic analysis in subsequent chapters.
- The 45° diagram only captures the dependence of consumption on income but not that of investment on the interest rate. Because of the latter, there is likely to be interaction between aggregate expenditures and the interest rate, which is not captured in the preceding analysis and diagrams.

To avoid these deficiencies, we need to use the more elaborate IS-IRT and AD-AS analyses developed in Chapter 5.

4.5 For the Macroeconomic Analysis of the Closed Economy, Is There a National Income Identity and One Between National Saving and Investment?

It is sometimes asserted that there is an *identity* between real national saving and real investment[8] — that is, $i \equiv s^n$ — so that what is saved *automatically and instantaneously* becomes national investment. This is not true for the modern economy, whether or not there is a balanced budget. Intuitively, households and governments save while firms invest, and the motives of these agents are very different. It would be unrealistic to expect that, in the aggregate, the plans to save of the very large number of very diverse households and of the government will *identically* coincide with the plans to invest of the very large number of very diverse firms. Further, in the modern economy, most households do not even directly lend their savings to firms, but can hold them in currency or, more usually, lend it to financial intermediaries, who may choose to lend out only part of their own borrowing. Therefore, there cannot be a saving-investment identity in short-run macroeconomic analysis.

Correspondingly, there is no '*national income identity*' (i.e., $y \equiv e$) between national expenditures and income *in economic terms*. These variables can differ from each other, with a difference indicating disequilibrium in the commodity market and leading to adjustments in employment and output in the economy.

4.5.1 An accounting national income identity

What we have studied so far are *economic* relationships between the various variables, especially between national expenditures and income and between national saving and investment. We have to distinguish between these relationships — from the seemingly similar though quite different in economic theory — and *accounting*

---

[8]The alternative assertion in nominal terms is $I \equiv S^n$.

ones between the same variables. To do so, assume that there is disequilibrium in economic terms between expenditures and income. If expenditures are less than income/output, firms are forced to hold goods that they had intended to sell but could not sell. Hence, their inventories of goods increase to an undesired extent. Conversely, if expenditures exceed income, firms have to sell some commodities (out of inventories) that they had not intended to sell. Hence, their inventories of goods decrease to an undesired extent. Such *unintended changes in the inventories of goods constitute 'unintended investment'* and are identically equal to $(y - e)$. That is:

$$i^{u} \equiv y - e, \tag{7}$$

where i^{u} is unintended investment equal to the unintended increase in inventories. If $i^{u} > 0$, inventories increase — by an undesired amount — and if $i^{u} < 0$, inventories fall. Therefore:

$$y \equiv e + i^{u}. \tag{8}$$

To see why the preceding equation is an identity, substitute $(y - e)$ for i^{u}. This gives $y = e + y - e = y$, which is clearly an identity. Equation (8) is known as the *national income identity*. Expanding both sides of this identity,

$$c + s + t \equiv c + g + i + i^{u},$$

so that:

$$i + i^{u} \equiv s + (t - g).$$

Setting $i^{a} = i + i^{u}$ and calling i^{a} the *accounting measure of investment*, we have the identities:

$$i^{a} \equiv s + (t - g),$$

$$i^{a} \equiv s^{n}, \tag{9}$$

so that, for a closed economy, there is a national income identity between the accounting measures of investment and national saving. i^{a} is also sometimes called *actual or ex post investment*, so that the national income identity for a closed economy can also be stated as the equality of actual investment and national saving. Data is easier to collect on i^{a} than on i, so that the statistics on investment are usually based on i^{a}. This makes it difficult to judge from the national accounts data whether there is equilibrium or disequilibrium in the commodity market. Therefore, data on changes in inventories is usually used as an indicator of unintended investment and disequilibrium.

Extended Analysis Box 4.2: The Distinction Between the Meanings of Investment in Macroeconomics and the Accounting Definition of Investment

For the economic analysis, we included the investment expenditures of firms in national expenditures. At the level of the firm, investment is the amount of expenditures the firm (intentionally/deliberately) incurs in an attempt to maintain or add to its capital stock (i.e., the stock of commodities they want to possess for future production). As pointed out earlier, such investment is also known as *planned, intended,* or *ex ante* investment.

Accounting/actual investment equals these investment expenditures and the unintended accumulation of inventories, labeled above as unintended investment. At the level of the single firm, the latter results from the firm's unintended change in its inventories because of a failure to match production to the sum of actual sales and desired changes in inventories. It often results from a failure to correctly anticipate the demand for the firm's products. At the macroeconomic level, unintended investment results from the collective failure of firms to match production less the intended additions to inventories to aggregate demand. It often results from the failure of firms in the aggregate to correctly anticipate aggregate demand in the economy and is a symptom of disequilibrium in the commodity market — which will induce changes in national production and income.

The actual change in the capital stock and the definitions of investment

The capital stock is defined as the amount of commodities carried over one period — say the current one — to the next one. Most of these commodities consist of buildings, machines, roads, dams, etc., which contribute to the production of new commodities. But it also includes inventories of commodities, produced in the current or past periods and intended for sale in subsequent periods. In commodity market equilibrium, these inventories will equal their desired level. However, if expenditures are less than output in the current period, some of the commodities that the firm had produced with the intention of selling them will remain unsold. This amount will be added to inventories and will constitute an unintended change in inventories. The measurement of the capital stock at the end of the period will include them. Therefore, the change in the capital stock during a period is identical to the accounting definition of investment. That is:

$$\Delta K \equiv i^a \equiv i + i^u,$$

where ΔK is the actual change in the capital stock, which includes any unintended investment. As a corollary, the change in the capital stock differs from the investment i unless the commodity market is in equilibrium — which requires $i^u = 0$. But, since i^a is identically equal to s^n, ΔK is identically equal to s^n — but not to (the macroeconomic concept of) i!

4.6 Demand Behavior in the Commodity Market

In the closed economy, the only economic agents that create the demand for commodities are households, firms, and the government. We now study their demands for commodities.

4.6.1 Consumption expenditures

Consumption expenditures are expenditures by households on consumer (durable or non-durable) goods. Their most important determinant is current disposable income. The remainder (disposable income less consumption expenditures) is saving, which is meant to provide for known future consumption needs, such as for retirement, or because of the uncertainty of future incomes or consumption needs such as medical ones.[9]

Therefore, our model assumes that real consumption expenditures c depend linearly upon real *disposable income* y_d, which equals income y less *net* taxes t paid to the government.[10] Hence, disposable income y_d

---

[9]In some societies, objectives such as sumptuous children's marriages or building a house can also be significant determinants of saving.

[10]'Net taxes paid' equals total government expenditures less transfer payments by the government to the public. Since transfer payments are not being deducted from income in calculating disposable income, disposable income includes transfer payments.

equals $(y - t)$. Therefore, our consumption function is:

$$c = c(y_d) = c_0 + c_y y_d,$$

$$= c_0 + c_y(y - t) \quad 0 \leq c_y \leq 1^{11}, \tag{10}$$

where the symbol c in $c(y)$ stands as *a functional symbol* and is indicative of the dependent variable while c_0 and c_y are *parametric symbols*, indicating that they are exogenously determined (held constant unless a change in them is hypothesized) rather than variables. The names given to these two parameters are:

c_0 *autonomous consumption* — which is that part of consumption that does not depend upon variables in the model

c_y *the marginal propensity to consume* (MPC), since it specifies the change in consumption for a unit change in disposable income.[12]

On average, a one-dollar increase in income increases consumption expenditures by a positive amount but by less than one dollar since some of the income increase is put toward saving. Hence, c_y lies between zero and one, and is usually between 0.8 and 0.95 for developed economies.

Note that the above consumption function implies that real (private) saving s is given by:

$$s = y_d - c \tag{11}$$

$$= y_d - c_0 - c_y y_d \quad 0 \leq c_y \leq 1,$$

$$= -c_0 + (1 - c_y)y_d.$$

The linear form of the saving function can also be written as:

$$s = s_0 + s_y y_d. \tag{12}$$

Comparing the above two equations, we have:

$$s_0 = -c_0$$

$$s_y = 1 - c_y,$$

so that the marginal propensity to save (MPS) equals $(1 - \text{MPC})$. For c_y between 0.8 and 0.95, the MPS would be between 0.2 and 0.05.

Note that the average propensity to consume (APC) is measured by c/y and is different from the MPC, which is given by $\partial c/\partial y$ and equals c_y. Similarly, the average propensity to save (APS) is measured by s/y and is different from the marginal propensity to save (MPS), which is given by $\partial s/\partial y$ and equals $s_y(= 1 - c_y)$.

---

[11] The normal upper limit on both MPC $(= c_y)$ and APC $(= c/y)$ is specified as unity (i.e., one). It does apply over long periods. The reason for this is that one cannot indefinitely consume more than one's income. However, over short periods, APC does sometimes exceed unity, with the excess of consumption over income financed out of wealth.

[12] Some economists assume that consumption depends negatively on the rate of interest, so that the consumption equation should have included another term $(-c_r r)$ on the right side. The empirical dependence of consumption on the rate of interest, for the usual range of interest rates in the developed economies, is doubtful — and definitely much more doubtful than the dependence of investment on the rate of interest. Further, the impact of such a term within the macroeconomic model is identical with that of the dependence of investment on the rate of interest. Consequently, we have not included the rate of interest in the consumption function; by implication, the rate of interest will also not be in the saving function.

Fact Sheet 4.1: Consumption and Disposable Income in the USA, 1980–2008

This Fact Sheet uses US data to illustrate the relationship between consumption and disposable income. Plotting disposable income per capita against total consumption expenditures per capita for various years yields a virtually linear relationship, indicated by the line trend with an intercept (which corresponds to what the text has called as autonomous consumption). This suggests that the linear consumption function used in the text is a good approximation to actual consumption behavior.

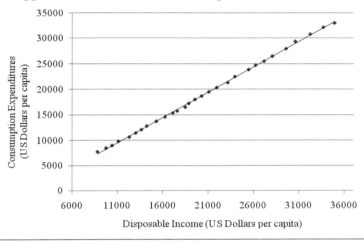

Figure 4.2a shows real consumption expenditures c and saving s as functions of real disposable income y_d. Autonomous consumption c_0 is shown by the intercept of the curve c. The slope of the consumption curve equals the MPC. The saving curve is marked s and represents the difference between the 45° line, which in this diagram represents $e = y_d$, and the c curve. Its slope is $(1 - c_y)$ and its intercept with the vertical axis is at $-c_0$. At y_{d0} $c = y_d$, thereby implying that at this point $s = 0$. The saving curve marked s shows the behavior of saving. Autonomous saving equals $-c_0$, which provides the intercept of the s curve with the vertical axis. The slope of the s curve is $(1 - c_y)$. For $c_y = 0.9$, the slope of the s curve is 0.1, while that of the c curve is 0.9. Therefore, the s curve will be very much flatter than the c curve.

Figure 4.2b shows the effect of an increase in autonomous consumption from c_0 to c_0'. This shifts the consumption curve up in a parallel fashion from c to c'. Note that a change in the MPC, c_y, will change the slope of the consumption curve.

4.6.2 The saving function

Since consumption is a function of disposable income, so is saving, which is defined as the part of disposable income that is not spent for consumption during the period in which income is received. Since both disposable income y and consumption c are in real terms, i.e., in commodity units, so is saving. Saving occurs every period and differs from the everyday usage of the term '*savings*', which is usually a synonym for wealth. Saving is also different from *savings deposits* in banks, which are in nominal terms and part of money holdings.

Some economists believe that saving depends not only on disposable income but also on the *real* interest rate, which are the return to saving if it were to be invested and not merely held in money (i.e., currency and

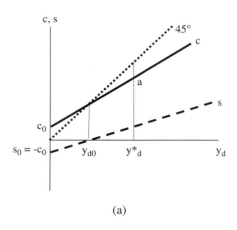

(a)

Figure 4.2a

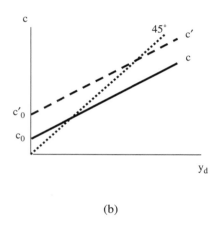

(b)

Figure 4.2b

bank deposits). Fact Sheet 4.2 shows for USA the relationship between saving and the *nominal* interest rate on Treasury bills (the T-bill rate). While this graph establishes a presumption that saving depends on the interest rate, it does not strictly establish that saving depends on the *real* interest rate.

Fact Sheet 4.2: Interest Rates and Saving in the USA, 1985–2008

This Fact Sheet illustrates the relationship between saving and the interest rate using US data. Note that the appropriate relationship is between the saving rate (i.e., saving divided by GDP) and the real interest rate, not the nominal one.

The graph below shows that saving and the real interest rate have followed similar fluctuations over the past 20 years. Each time interest rates rose, as in the late 1980s, between 1995 and 2000, and the mid-2000s, the saving rate also rose.

Fact Sheet 4.2: (*Continued*)

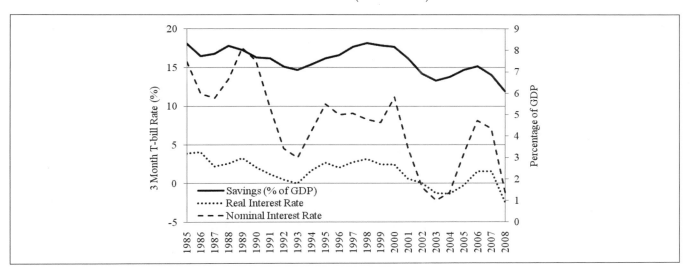

Extended Analysis Box 4.3: The Dependence of Consumption on Wealth, Interest Rates and Consumer Confidence

The concept of lifetime wealth as the present discounted value of future incomes

Assume that the individual consumer expects to receive labor income of y_t^L in period $t, t = 1, 2, \ldots, R$, until retirement at the end of period R. Further, he/she has a current amount of wealth a_1 in physical and financial assets. He/she expects the interest rate to remain constant at r. Then, according to the present discounted formula presented in Chapter 2, his/her expected lifetime wealth w_1^e at the beginning of the current period 1 equals his/her current assets plus the present discounted values of expected future labor incomes. That is:

Wealth ≡ Current assets plus the present discounted value (PDV) labor incomes over the lifetime.

$$w_1^e = a_1 + \frac{y_1^L}{(1+r)} + \frac{y_2^{Le}}{(1+r)^2} + \cdots + \frac{y_R^{Le}}{(1+r)^R}$$

where w_1^e is the present (i.e., in period 1) real value of wealth, a_1 is the real value of physical and financial assets, y_t^{Le} is the expected real labour income in period t, and R is the period at the end of which the person retires. Note that the real value of physical and financial wealth in terms of consumer goods is not definite, since their nominal values tend to fluctuate. Future labour incomes are also not known with certainty. Therefore, w_1^e is more or less uncertain.

The dependence of consumption on wealth and the interest rate

If we consider the individual's consumption over his/her lifetime, we would have to take account of the possibilities of substitution between present and future consumption and also replace current disposable income by his/her disposable lifetime wealth.[13]

---

[13] *Disposable lifetime wealth* is defined as the present discounted value of disposable income over the consumer's lifetime.

Extended Analysis Box 4.3: (*Continued*)

The cost of one unit of current consumption is unity. The present discounted cost of one unit of consumption next period is $1/(1 + r)$. The higher the interest rate, the cheaper a unit of future consumption becomes, so that it becomes tempting for the consumer to substitute more of future consumption for current consumption.[14] Doing so for a given level of budgeted expenditures on current and future consumption requires cutting down on current consumption and increasing current saving to invest it at the higher interest rate and increase future consumption.

Clearly, changes in the level of wealth also influence consumption: an increase in the consumer's lifetime wealth increases his/her consumption expenditures. Therefore, stock market booms tend to increase consumption, by increasing wealth, while stock market crises decrease consumption. Similarly, expected increases in future labor incomes increase the expected lifetime wealth and increase consumption.

Therefore, the analytical determinants of current consumption are often specified as current disposable income, the PDV of disposable wealth (i.e., net of taxes) and the interest rate r, so that the consumption function becomes:

$$c = c(\text{PDV of disposable wealth}, r),$$

where an increase in disposable wealth or a fall in the interest rate increases consumption. Note that current disposable income is a part, though usually a small part, of the PDV of disposable wealth. This consumption function can be restated as:

$$c = c(y_d, \text{PDV of future disposable wealth}, r),$$

where y_d is disposable income in the current period. This function adds to the standard consumption function we have used for building our model by explicitly adding future disposable wealth and r as two additional determinants of consumption.

Empirical evidence on the dependence of consumption expenditures and saving on interest rates

While expenditures on highly durable consumer goods that are financed by borrowing, such as the purchase of cars and houses financed by mortgages, are sensitive to changes in the interest rate, empirical evidence indicates that expenditures on non-durable consumer goods are not significantly sensitive to interest rate increases and decreases. Since the latter are the dominant part of total consumption expenditures, empirical estimates of the *direct* effect of interest rate changes on aggregate consumption expenditures (and, therefore, also on aggregate saving) do not show this effect to be very significant. We will therefore ignore it and drop the interest rate from the consumption function.

However, note that a rise (fall) in the interest rate usually lowers (raises) bond and equity prices, and is therefore associated with a decrease (increase) in wealth. A decrease (increase) in wealth lowers (raises) consumption expenditures. However, this *indirect* effect of changes in the interest rate, through wealth on consumption, is usually left to the analysis of the impact of wealth on consumption rather than directly of the interest rate on consumption. This effect is encompassed under the next heading.

The impact of changes in wealth on consumption

While changes in lifetime wealth clearly have an impact on current consumption expenditures, the standard macroeconomic models continue to specify the consumption function as:

$$c = c(y_d)$$

Extended Analysis Box 4.3: (*Continued*)

For this simplified/standard consumption function, changes in consumption induced by changes in wealth are treated as exogenous shifts in autonomous consumption and/or the marginal propensity to consume. To illustrate, a stock market boom that increases equity prices and raises shareholders' wealth (as happened in the late 1990s in the western economies) will increase their consumption. This increase will be captured through an exogenous shift of the consumption function and an upward shift in the consumption curve from c to c' in Figure 4.2b. Conversely, a crash in the prices of shares in the stock market (as happened in 2000 and 2001) will shift the consumption curve downwards.

To reiterate, the standard macroeconomic model operates with the consumption function $c = c(y_d)$, and treats the impact of changes in wealth as exogenous shifts in this function. The latter is a significant effect and will be studied again in Chapter 9.

The impact of changes in consumer confidence on consumption

Our broad statement of the consumption function is:

$$c = c(y_d, \text{PDV of future labour incomes, present value of financial and physical assets, } r)$$

Since the PDV of future labour incomes and even the present real value of financial and physical assets are usually quite uncertain, expectations of their value have a very significant impact on consumption expenditures. These expectations are represented by economists by the concept of '*consumer confidence*' in the current and future state of the economy – especially that on jobs and incomes. Over the short term, the influence of changes in consumer confidence on consumption tends to be even more significant than of changes in interest rates. Therefore, for the explanation of changes in consumption expenditures, economic analysts often have in mind a simple consumption function of the form:

$$c = c(y_d, \text{consumer confidence, stock market performance})$$

4.6.3 Investment expenditures

Investment was defined earlier as the amount of expenditures on currently produced commodities, which firms *intentionally* incur for the purpose of maintaining or adding to the capital stock. The real value of investment expenditures i depends on the real (rather than the nominal[15]) rate of interest, which is the real cost of borrowing funds to finance investment projects. Note that by the Fisher equation on interest rates (see Chapter 2), the real interest rate r equals the nominal/market interest rate R less the expected inflation rate

---

[14]The intuition behind this argument is as follows. Suppose a commodity costs \$1 this year and \$1 next year. If the commodity is not bought this year, the dollar saved will be invested at the interest rate r and yield $(1 + r)$ at the beginning of next year. As r rises, more of the commodity can be bought next year for each dollar's worth of its consumption during this year. That is, its future consumption has become cheaper relative to its current consumption, so that current consumption will be reduced. The amount thus saved will be invested at the higher interest rate, so as to buy a larger amount of next year's consumption. Hence, as the interest rate rises, future consumption is substituted for (is increased) at the expense of current consumption. This is an application of the substitution effect studied in microeconomics.

[15]Suppose a firm borrows funds in the loan market at the nominal interest rate R (10%) when the expected inflation rate is π^e (8%) and uses these funds to purchase commodities for investment. The value of the commodities purchased is expected to rise by the end of the year by π^e (8%), so that, to the firm undertaking the investment, the real cost of obtaining the funds is only $R - \pi^e$ (2%). It is this real cost, not the nominal one, which the firm compares with the (real) productivity of investment.

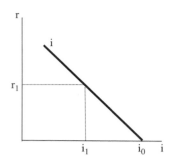

Figure 4.3

(π^e). Hence, we have for our model:

$$i = i(r),$$

which is simplified to the linear relationship:

$$i = i_0 - i_r r. \tag{13}$$

Since the real interest rate r is the real cost of borrowing funds for investment, an increase in the real interest rate will reduce investment, so that $i_r \geq 0$. The names given to the parameters of the investment equation are:

$$i_0 = \text{autonomous investment}$$

$$i_r = \text{the interest sensitivity of investment}^{16}.$$

The component $(-i_r r)$ of investment demand is the decrease in investment induced by rises in the interest rate and is often referred to as 'induced investment'.

Figure 4.3 plots the above investment equation and shows a downward sloping investment curve i. The intercept of this curve on the horizontal axis is at i_0 and represents the level of investment if $r = 0$. The slope of the curve equals $(-i_r)$: as the interest rate rises, the level of investment falls.

Fact Sheet 4.3 plots the relationship between investment and the interest rate on Treasury bills. Two curves are shown, one between investment and the nominal interest rate and other between investment and the real interest rate. Economic theory posits a relationship between investment and the real interest rate.

Fact Sheet 4.3: Interest Rates and Investment in the USA, 1960–2008

This Fact Sheet shows the relationship between investment and the real interest rate using US data.

The interest rate, being the cost of borrowing, plays an important role, along with real GDP as an indicator of expected sales, in investment decisions. The graph below shows that sharp drops in the real interest rate are often followed by periods of increased investment. Similarly, increases in the real interest rate, as in the late 1970s and late 1990s, sooner or later led to decreases in investment.

---

[16]If saving depends positively on the rate of interest, this can be easily incorporated into the model by redefining $(-i_r)$ to measure the decrease in investment and the decrease in consumption (or less the increase in saving) induced by the marginal increase in the rate of interest.

Fact Sheet 4.3: (*Continued*)

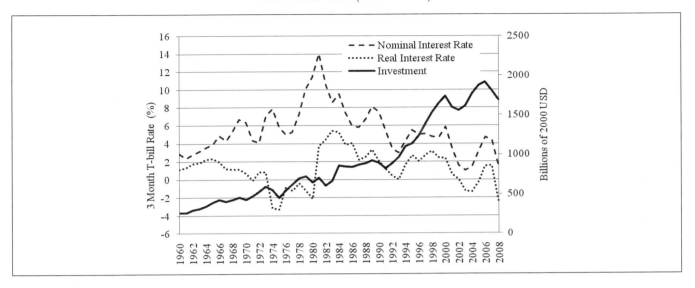

Extended Analysis Box 4.4: A more Realistic Investment Function

Investment expenditures by firms also depend on their desired capital stock, which depends on the projected demand for commodities, which equals y^e in equilibrium. Hence, the main determinants of investment are the interest rate r and expected future sales y^e. Therefore, the more realistic investment function is:

$$i = i(r, y^e).$$

For simplification, basic macroeconomic analysis simplifies this function by dropping expected future demand, so that investment becomes a function only of the rate of interest. That is, the standard macroeconomic analysis is based on the simplified investment function $i = i(r)$, so that shifts in the expectations of future demand are represented as exogenous shifts in the standard investment function.

The impact of business confidence on investment

In the short term, changes in the expectations of future sales do cause quite significant shifts in investment expenditures. Economic analysts try to capture these expectations in the concept of '*business confidence*', so that, for practical analysis, the investment function that is often used is:

$$i = i(r, \text{business confidence}).$$

Business confidence shows a great deal of variation over the business cycle and depends on political as well as economic events. These variations make investment the most volatile component of aggregate demand. Their role is examined under the concept of business confidence in Chapters 8 and 16.

4.6.4 Government expenditures and tax revenues

Government revenues are collected from a variety of taxes, of which two of the most significant ones are income taxes and corporate taxes. For given tax rates, tax revenues rise with the level of national income, so that the main determinant of government revenues is national income y (not disposable income y_d). Further, our concern is with the *net* tax payments, which exclude government transfers to the public in the form of business subsidies, income support (or welfare) payments, unemployment/employment insurance benefits, etc. The need for such payments decreases as incomes and employment rise. Further, as incomes rise, more of the taxpayers end up in higher tax brackets under a progressive tax system. Hence, net tax payments tend to rise with the level of national income, so that the *net tax revenue function* can be written as:

$$t = t(y), \tag{14}$$

where t is real net government revenues. Note that tax revenues have been made a function of national income y, rather than merely of consumers' disposable income y_d. Assuming for simplification that the tax function is a straight line, we have:

$$t = t_0 + t_y y \qquad 0 \le t_y \le 1, \tag{15}$$

where:

> t_0 = autonomous net tax revenues and
> t_y = marginal tax rate.

In the present context, autonomous net tax revenues are the amount collected when income equals zero. These represent that component of total tax revenues (or transfers) which does not change with changes in income. Major examples of these are poll taxes (taxes per head) or transfers to persons independent of their level of income, taxes on wealth rather than income, taxes on house values, etc. Note that t_0 can be negative, zero, or positive. It would be negative if the government has a net transfer (i.e., transfers exceed total tax revenues) to the public when national income falls to zero. This is a likely possibility in the short term, especially under a progressive tax system and income support programs in which the government ensures that each person has at least a minimum amount (private income plus income transfers from the government) each year.

The government expenditures on goods and services also depend upon a variety of elements. Here, the simplest assumption is that their amount is a matter of political choice by the government, rather than of the variables such as income, unemployment, and interest rates in the model. Their essentially political determination is reflected in the assumption that real government expenditures g are exogenously determined at g_0, so that,

$$g = g_0. \tag{16}$$

Note that g_0 are real government expenditures on goods and services (which would include civil service salaries) but do not include transfers from the government to the public. The latter are also not included in our corresponding variable t, which is tax revenues net of transfers. Hence, t represents government net 'withdrawals' of real income/output from the private economy, while g represents government 'additions' to the expenditures on commodities.

Figure 4.4 shows the net revenue function by the line marked t. Tax revenues increase proportionately with income, so that this line is upward sloping. This line assumes that the tax rate is held constant at the rate t_y. An increase (decrease) in autonomous taxes t_0 will shift the t curve up (down) in a parallel manner, while an increase (decrease) in the tax rate t_y will make this curve steeper (flatter). Government expenditures on goods and services do not increase with income, so that their line, marked g, is horizontal. The budget is balanced at the level of income y_{BB} (balanced budget income). If the actual level of income is below y_{BB}, there will be a fiscal deficit. If the actual level of income is above y_{BB}, there will be a fiscal surplus.

Some economists argue that the tax rates should be set at a level such as to yield a balanced budget at the full-employment level of income. If this is done, a fall in income below the full-employment level

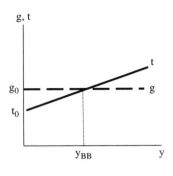

Figure 4.4

would automatically generate a fiscal deficit and an increase in income above the full-employment level would automatically generate a fiscal surplus. The former (latter) will increase (decrease) expenditures in the economy, so that the government budget provides, to some extent, an automatic stabilizing effect on national expenditures and aggregate demand in the economy. Such a stabilizing effect on aggregate demand occurs whenever the tax rates and government expenditures are held constant — while national income fluctuates. Therefore, the budget is one of the *automatic stabilizers* in the economy.

Fact Sheet 4.4: USA Fiscal Deficit, 1962–2008

This Fact Sheet illustrates movements in fiscal outlays, revenues and surpluses/deficits by using data for the USA. Before the 1970s, US governments generally followed the philosphy that, in peacetime, governments should aim at a balanced budget. However, since about 1975, the USA has usually run a fiscal deficit, observable as periods when total government outlays surpass total revenues. Notable exceptions include the late 1990s when the economic boom of the period raised incomes and the resulting rise in tax revenues created a fiscal surplus. The recession that followed caused a sharp drop in incomes and tax revenues, with the result that the government budget fell into a deficit.

After the financial crisis starting in 2007 turned into an economic recession, tax revenues fell while the US government pursued a fiscal stimulus policy, which created unprecedented peacetime budget deficits.

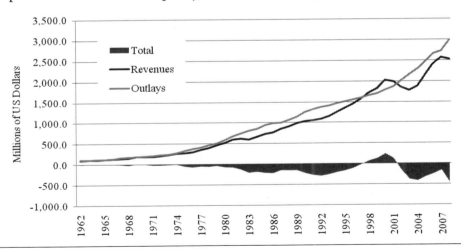

4.6.5 The commodity market and the price level

Note that all the variables specified for the commodity market have been assumed to be in real terms and independent of the aggregate price level. In one-period analysis, this assumption means that consumers and firms are free of price illusion in their consumption and investment decisions. It is a convenient one in macroeconomic models and is often made.[17]

4.7 The Commodity Market Model: The IS Equation/Curve

The above arguments collectively specify our model for the commodity sector *of the closed economy* as:

$$
\begin{aligned}
c &= c_0 + c_y(y - t) & 0 &\leq c_y \leq 1 \\
i &= i_0 - i_r r & i_r &\geq 0 \\
t &= t_0 + t_y y & 0 &\leq t_y \leq 1 \\
g &= g_0 \\
e &\equiv c + g + i \\
y &= e & &\text{equilibrium condition.}
\end{aligned}
$$

This model can be solved for y in terms of r, the policy variables and the various parameters in either of two ways:

1. One method is to use the equilibrium condition $s + t = i + g$, and substitute the functions for each of the variables in this equation.
2. The alternative method is to use the equilibrium condition $y = e$ and substitute for e its various components. We follow this procedure here. The steps are:

$$
\begin{aligned}
y &= e \\
&= c + i + g \\
&= c_0 + c_y(y - t) + i_0 - i_r r + g \\
&= c_0 + c_y(y - (t_0 + t_y y)) + i_0 - i_r r + g \\
&= c_0 + c_y y - c_y t_0 - c_y t_y y + i_0 - i_r r + g.
\end{aligned}
$$

To rearrange this equation to keep only y on the left side of the equation, take all the terms in y to the left side. This gives:

$$
y - c_y y + c_y t_y y = c_0 - c_y t_0 + i_0 - i_r r + g,
$$

which implies that:

$$
\begin{aligned}
y[1 - c_y + c_y t_y] &= c_0 - c_y t_0 + i_0 - i_r r + g \\
y[1 - c_y(1 - t_y)] &= c_0 - c_y t_0 + i_0 - i_r r + g,
\end{aligned}
$$

so that,

$$
y = \left[\frac{1}{1 - c_y(1 - t_y)} \right] (c_0 + i_0 + g_0 - c_y t_0 - i_r r). \tag{17}
$$

---

[17] It has to be modified if the analysis is over more than one period or if the economy is an open one.

This equation is derived from the equilibrium condition $y = e$, so that it is another form of the equilibrium relationship. It specifies the locus of values of y and r at which equilibrium exists in the commodity market and is known as the IS (investment-saving) equation.[18]

The only two variables in this IS equation are y and r. It expresses income y as a function of the interest rate r, exogenous parameters and the policy variables/parameters (g, t_0, and t_y) of the model. It implies that the equilibrium level of real income is a function of the rate of interest and not of the price level.[19] Note that y in this equation represents the demand for commodities as a function of the interest rate, not of the price level, so that *this equation is not the aggregate demand equation*. Further, in the above equation, y does not represent the output — that is, the quantity produced — of commodities in the economy; it only represents the demand for commodities as a function of the interest rate.

The writing of the IS equation can be simplified to:

$$y = a(c_0 + i_0 + g_0 - c_y t_0 - i_r r)$$

$$y = a c_0 + a i_0 + a g_0 - a c_y t_0 - a i_r r, \tag{18}$$

where:

$$\alpha = \left[\frac{1}{1 - c_y(1 - t_y)} \right]$$

As explained below, the name given to α is the '*autonomous investment multiplier*'. Note that all the terms in it are parameters, so that the value of α is treated as given (unless one of its parameters shifts), and does not change as the variables in the model vary.

The impact of investment fluctuations on income: a partial investment multiplier

We can use the IS equation to derive the impact of changes in the exogenous parameters and policy variables on income. Of all these, a common concern is with the impact of shifts in investment on income since investment is one of the most volatile components of expenditures and government expenditures are an important policy variable. The impact on income of a change in autonomous investment is captured by the following *multiplier*, which is derived from the IS equation above. For this derivation, note that all the parameters and variables on the right-hand side of the IS equation are to be held constant except for i_0. Let the change in i_0 be Δi_0. Then, $\Delta y = \alpha \Delta i_0$, which implies that $\Delta y / \Delta i_0 = \alpha$. We use the conventional symbolic term $\partial y / \partial i_0$ to replace $\Delta y / \Delta i_0$ when the change is very small, 'with all other things being held constant'. Therefore,

$$\frac{\partial y}{\partial i_0} = a = \left[\frac{1}{1 - c_y(1 - t_y)} \right] > 0. \tag{19}$$

This multiplier is the *autonomous investment multiplier*, which is defined as the increase in national income for a (very small) unit increase in autonomous investment. For $0 < c_y < 1$, $0 < t_y < 1$, this multiplier is positive and greater one.

For $c_y = 0.8$, $t_y = 0.2$, Box 4.3 derives the value of this multiplier as 2.78. But suppose that the MPC was higher at 0.9, so that the parameter values were $c_y = 0.9$ and $t_y = 0.2$. For these, the multiplier

---

[18] It was given this name since it was originally derived for a model without a government sector. Hence, it represented the equilibrium condition $i = s$.

[19] This general statement remains valid even if consumption depends upon income *and* the rate of interest, and even if investment depends upon the interest rate *and* income. For this variation of the IS model, use the general linear forms of the consumption and investment functions as: $c = c(y, r) = c_0 + c_y y - c_r r$ and $i = i(r, y) = i_0 - i_r r + i_y y$, with the assumption that $c_y(1 - t_y) + i_y < 1$.

equals 3.57. Hence, increases in the MPC increase the investment multiplier. Increases in the tax rate will lower it.

Box 4.2: The Mechanism of the Investment Multiplier: An Illustration

Assume that the MPC (c_y) equals 0.8 and the marginal tax rate (t_y) is 0.2. Now suppose that firms decide to increase their investment expenditures by $1. They spend it on commodities, so that expenditures rise by $1.

The firm that receives this dollar has higher sales revenue by $1, so that it pays out an extra dollar in incomes (wage and profits). With a tax rate of 0.20, disposable income only rises by 80 cents, so that the recipients of the additional dollar spend 64 cents (80 cents times MPC of 0.8) out of it and add 16 cents to their savings.

The 64 cents spent on commodities are received by firms who eventually pay them in wages and profits, thereby raising incomes by 64 cents. The recipients of this amount pay taxes of 12.8 cents (= 64 cents times 0.2), so that their disposable income rises by 51.2 cents. They spend 40.96 cents (= 51.2 cents times 0.8) as an increase in consumption and save the rest. These 40.96 cents further increase the sales revenue of firms, which will induce an increase in incomes of 40.96 cents and an increase in disposable incomes of 32.77 cents (= 40.96 time 0.8). This amount will cause a further increase in expenditures of 26.22 cents (= 32.77 times 0.8) — and so on.

This process continues until the last increase in expenditures becomes zero. Eventually, the increase in expenditures becomes:

$$\$1 + \$0.64 + \$0.41 + \$0.26 + \cdots$$

The total increase is given by the formula:

$$\frac{\partial y}{\partial i_0} = \left[\frac{1}{1 - c_y(1 - t_y)} \right] = \left[\frac{1}{1 - c_y(1 - t_y)} \right]$$

Two points about this multiplier are worth noting. One is that it depends on the MPC and the marginal tax rate. For most plausible values of these parameters, the multiplier will be greater than unity. The second point is that the process of expenditure increases and income payments is going to take quite some time. It would be several quarters at least, so that the increase in expenditures during the first quarter — called the *impact effect* — is substantially less than the full increase — called the full or *long-run effect*. The IS analysis, which does not incorporate real time and is based on analytical time, only uses the full/long-run increase.

The impact of fiscal policy on income: partial fiscal policy multipliers

The impact of an increase in government expenditures on income is:

$$\frac{\partial y}{\partial g} = a = \left[\frac{1}{1 - c_y(1 - t_y)} \right] > 0, \tag{20}$$

so that an increase in government expenditures increases income. Note that the government expenditures multiplier equals the autonomous investment one.

Correspondingly, the *autonomous net tax multiplier* — which is the effect of a very small change in t_0, with all other parameters and variables held constant — is specified by:

$$\frac{\partial y}{\partial t_0} = -c_y a = -c_y \left[\frac{1}{1 - c_y(1 - t_y)} \right]$$

$$= -c_y[\partial y/\partial g] < 0. \tag{21}$$

Hence, an increase in autonomous net taxes decreases income. Further, since $c_y < 1$, this reduction in income is less than that induced by a correspondence decrease in government expenditures.

Box 4.3: The Impact of a Balanced Budget: The Balanced Budget Multiplier

Suppose that the government always balances its budget — that is, $g = t$ — so that any increase in its expenditures is matched by an equal increase in its tax collection. The latter could be done through an increase in autonomous tax revenues or in the tax rate. If this is done, the increase in the government expenditures tends to increase income while the increase in tax revenues tends to decrease it.

We illustrate the balanced budget multiplier by examining the case when the tax rate (t_y) is zero, so that all net tax revenues are autonomous ones. In this limiting case (with $t_y = 0$), the balanced budget multiplier is unity, as shown by:

$$\frac{\partial y}{\partial g} + \frac{\partial y}{\partial t_0} = \left[\frac{1}{1 - c_y} \right] - \left[\frac{c_y}{1 - c_y} \right] \tag{22}$$

$$= 1.$$

To illustrate this value of the balanced budget multiplier, we use our earlier numerical example with $c_y = 0.8$, in combination with the additional assumption that $t_y = 0$. Then, the government expenditures multiplier will be 5 and the net tax multiplier will be 4. The increase in expenditures would be unity.

If the economy has a positive tax rate, which is always the case in modern economies, the balanced budget multiplier remains at unity whether the increase in tax revenues is due to a rise in autonomous taxes or in the tax rate, or some combination of the two. Note that to achieve this effect, the increase in tax revenues must equal the increase in expenditures, so that the budget remains balanced.[20]

A word of caution on IS multipliers

Note that while we have derived the investment and fiscal effects on income through the use of the partial multipliers based on the IS equation, they are deceptive and even erroneous for a monetary economy. The reason for presenting them is partly by way of an exercise in the illustration of multipliers and partly out of an attempt at uniformity of treatment with most textbooks in macroeconomics. The above multipliers are based on the commodity market, which is a very limited part of the economy, and ignore the monetary sector and the role of monetary policy, which are also needed for determining aggregate demand in the economy.

---

[20]For $c_y = 0.8$, $t_y = 0.2$, the government expenditures multiplier equals 2.78, while the autonomous tax multiplier has the value -2.22, so that if the increase in government expenditures of $1 was financed by an autonomous tax increase of the same amount, expenditures/incomes would rise by 0.56. In this example, if both government expenditures and autonomous taxes had increased by Δg, expenditures would rise by 0.56 times Δg. Therefore, the increase in income is only 0.56, which is less than unity. While this result seems to contradict the balanced budget multiplier proposition, it does not really do so. In this calculation, tax revenues rise for two reasons: the initial increase of $1 in autonomous taxes — equal to the increase in government expenditures — and the increase in tax revenues because of the constant tax rates on a higher income. The total increase in tax revenues becomes greater than the increase in government expenditures, so that the budget changes are not balanced, and the balanced budget multiplier does not apply.

Further, they ignore the supply side of the economy. The appropriate multipliers are those derived after a general analysis of all the sectors of the whole economy.[21] Therefore, the usefulness of the above multipliers for the commodity sector alone is only in studying the determinants of the position and shifts of the IS curve.

The IS curve

The IS equation specifies the income and interest rate combinations that ensure equilibrium in the commodity market. It is plotted in Figure 4.5 as the IS curve. The IS curve represents the set of points in the (y, r) diagram at which equilibrium exists in the commodity market. It has a negative slope since r has a negative coefficient in the investment function. The intuitive explanation for the negative slope of the IS curve is obtained by comparing points a and b on the curve marked IS_0. Starting from the point a, an increase in income y, along the horizontal axis, increases both consumption and saving, as well as increasing tax revenues. Equilibrium requires that investment must also increase by the combined increases in saving and tax revenues. This increase in investment has to be induced by a decline in the interest rate. Hence, if equilibrium is to be maintained in the expenditure sector, an increase in income must be accompanied by the appropriate decline in the interest rate.

Shifts in the IS curve versus movements along it

Movements along the IS_0 curve (e.g., from the point a to the point b in Figure 4.5) occur if there is an exogenous change in the interest rate r, while shifts in the curve occur if any of the parameters (e.g., c_0, c_y, i_0, i_r, etc.) or the policy variables (g, t_0, t_y) change. Some of these shifts will be parallel ones while others even change the slope of the IS curve.[22] As shown in Figure 4.5, an increase in autonomous investment or government expenditures will shift the IS curve in a parallel manner to the right from IS_0 to IS_1, while decreases in them will shift it, again in a parallel manner, to the left to IS_2.

Intuitively, at the given interest rate r_0 and the IS curve IS_0, induced investment will be constant. An increase in autonomous investment will raise the level of investment, which through the multiplier will increase

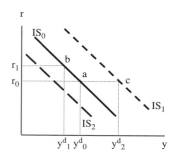

Figure 4.5

---

[21] For the open economy, the appropriate multipliers are those from the open economy model presented in Chapter 5.
[22] The slope of the IS curve depends on i_r, c_y, and t_y, so that the IS curve shifts in a parallel manner if these do not change but one of the other parameters or policy variables changes. Changes in one of these three parameters will change the slope of the IS curve.

expenditures from y_0^d to y_2^d. Hence, at the given interest rate r_0, the economy will go from the point a on IS_0 to the point c on IS_1.

The IS curve shifts to the right from IS_0 to IS_1 due to:

- An increase in private expenditures, either from an increase in autonomous consumption c_0 or in autonomous investment i_0 and/or
- An expansionary fiscal policy, which increases government expenditures g or reduces autonomous taxes t_0.

Conversely, the IS curve shifts to the left from IS_1 to IS_2 due to decreases in private expenditures or a contractionary fiscal policy.

Extended Analysis Box 4.5: The Slope of the IS Curve

The IS equation was derived above as:

$$y = \alpha(c_0 + 1_0 + g_0 - c_y t_0 - i_r r)$$

where α is the autonomous investment multiplier. It specifies the increase in y for a unit change in autonomous investment. Note that the increase in y caused by a unit increase in government expenditures also equals α.

First, note that a mathematician plotting this equation would put the variable on the left side, which is y, on the vertical axis and the variable on the right side, which is r, on the horizontal axis. However, economists have traditionally put y on the horizontal axis and r on the vertical one: y is the more important variable of interest and the IS equation reflects this by placing it on the left side. Second, note that the slope of the IS curve is $\partial r/\partial y$, which is the inverse of $\partial y/\partial r$. Third, we have to use the IS equation to first derive $\partial y/\partial r$ and then take its inverse to derive $\partial r/\partial y$.

From the IS equation:

$$\partial y/\partial r = -\alpha i_r.$$

Therefore, the slope of the IS curve is specified by:

$$\partial r/\partial y = \frac{1}{\partial y/\partial r} = -\frac{1}{\alpha i_r}$$
$$= \frac{1 - c_y(1 - t_y)}{i_r}$$

Since both α and i_r are positive, $\partial r/\partial y$ is negative, so that the IS curve slopes downwards.

Changes in c_y, t_y, and i_r change the multiplier value and the slope of the IS curve. An increase in the marginal propensity to consume c_y or a decrease in the tax rate t_y will decrease the numerator in the preceding equation, thereby reducing the slope of the IS curve and making it flatter. In terms of the multiplier α, which equals $1/(1 - c_y(1 - t_y))$, the increase in the marginal propensity to consume c_y and/or the decrease in the tax rate t_y will increase α. Since an increase in α reduces the slope $[1/(\alpha i_r)]$ of the IS curve, this would flatten the IS curve. Students can check on this effect by plotting the IS curve for the alternative sets of values: (i) $c_y = 0.8$, $t_y = 0.2$ and $i_r = 0.2$, (ii) $c_y = 0.9$, $t_y = 0.2$ and $i_r = 0.2$, (c) $c_y = 0.8$, $t_y = 0.1$ and $i_r = 0.2$.

4.8 Conclusions

- In the commodity market of the closed economy, the main components of expenditures are consumption, investment, and government expenditures. The main uses of income are for consumption, tax payments, and saving. Their main determinants are income or disposable income, wealth, and tax rates. The main determinant of investment is the interest rate.
- The equilibrium condition for the commodity market is the equality of national saving and investment. This condition is not an identity. This equilibrium condition yields the IS equation and curve.
- Increases in government expenditures or decreases in tax rates raise real aggregate demand (at the pre-existing price level).
- The division of an increase in aggregate demand between increases in the price level and the quantity produced of commodities also requires the specification of the aggregate supply curve.
- The balanced budget multiplier for equal increases in government expenditures and tax revenues is unity.

The nature and properties of the aggregate demand curve are analyzed in the next chapter.

KEY CONCEPTS

Consumption function
Investment function
Government expenditures, transfers, and spending
Investment multiplier

Fiscal multipliers
The IS relationship/curve, and
Aggregate demand.

SUMMARY OF CRITICAL CONCLUSIONS

- The IS curve shows the set of combinations of y and r at which the commodity market is in equilibrium.
- A change in investment or fiscal deficit changes the equilibrium value of y by a multiple. In practice, this process takes several quarters. The value of the multiplier depends on the consumption, investment, and tax revenue functions.
- An increase in investment or government expenditures increases expenditures on commodities at the existing interest rate and shifts the IS curve to the right.
- An increases in taxes, for government held constant, shifts the IS curve to the right.

REVIEW AND DISCUSSION QUESTIONS

1. Define (private) saving. What is the equilibrium condition for the closed economy involving private saving and investment?
2. What is unintended investment? Suppose this investment is positive. Discuss firms' responses to this and the impact on national income.
3. Is unintended nvestment positive, negative, or zero in equilibrium in the commodity market? Explain.

4. Define national saving. What is the equilibrium condition for the closed economy between national saving and investment?

5. Suppose the stock market booms and causes consumers to increase their marginal propensity to consume. Show its effect on the IS curve. Is there a change in the slope of the IS curve?

6. Suppose the stock market collapses and causes firms to substantially decrease their autonomous investment. Show its effect on the IS curve. Is there a change in the slope of the IS curve?

7. Suppose that a financial crisis reduces the credit that households can borrow to finance their purchases of consumer durables and that firms can borrow to finance their inventories and meet short-term obligations. Analyze their effects on consumption, investment, and the IS curve. Can fiscal policy reduce or eliminate this impact of the crisis and how?

8. Explain the impact of an increase in autonomous taxes on national income and consumption. Does it shift the IS curve? If so, how (parallel or not) does it shift the IS curve?

9. Suppose the government increases the income support (in the form of transfers per head) provided to seniors in the economy while holding its autonomous (poll) taxes and the tax rate constant. What effects would it have on: government expenditures, the net revenue function, consumption, and the IS curve?

10. What is meant by the government expenditures multiplier. Discuss the process by which income/expenditures would increase by a multiple following an increase of $1 in these expenditures.

11. If there is a balanced budget increase in government expenditures and autonomous taxes, does the IS curve shift and, if so, in which direction? Explain.

12. What is the 'national income identity'? Does it imply an identity between investment and saving? If so, in what sense of these terms? Explain.

13. Does the IS curve incorporate the national income identity and/or the identity between investment and *national* saving? Explain.

14. Suppose that the government wants to increase its expenditures *g* and has the options of financing it by higher taxes, bond issues or increases in the monetary base. Explain the impact of each of these on the IS curve and show diagrammatically the effect on the IS curve.

15. What is meant by the 'balanced budget multiplier'? Explain why it takes this value.

ADVANCED AND TECHNICAL QUESTIONS

National income accounts data

You are given the following information for the year 2000 on an economy. All amounts are in current dollars.

Goods and services produced by factories	10,000
Of which, goods and services sold during the year	8,000
Labor costs	7,000
Interest paid	1,600
Taxes paid by factories to the government	100
Goods purchased by some factories from others for inputs	900
Value of the factories as of January 1, 2000	150,000
Value of the factories as of December 31, 2000	150,000
Goods carried over in the economy on January 1, 2000	200,000

Value of home activities, such as meals, child care, etc.	14,000
Income taxes paid to the government	1,900
Government purchases of goods and services	2,400
Transfers by the government to persons and firms	250
National saving	3,000

T1. Using the above national income account data, calculate GDP, consumption, disposable income, government deficit/surplus, private saving, and the average propensities to consume and to save.

Basic (commodity sector) Model for the closed economy in Chapter 4:

$$c = 50 + 0.8y_d.$$

$$i = 100 - 50r.$$

$$g = 500.$$

$$t = -100 + 0.20y.$$

T2. Answer the following for the Basic (commodity sector) Model of this chapter.

(a) What is the equation that describes the IS curve? [Do not use the IS equation formula for this answer. Use step-by-step calculations. Start by calculating disposable income. Then, use the equilibrium condition $y = e$ for your further steps.] Draw this curve in the IS diagram.

(b) What is the IS curve if g becomes 600? Draw this curve in the IS diagram.

(c) Are the IS curves in (a) and (b) parallel?

(d) What is the IS curve if i_r becomes 60? Draw this curve in the IS diagram.

(e) Are the IS curves in (a) and (d) parallel?

Revised commodity sector model for the closed economy:

$$c = 0.8(1 - t_y)y$$

$$t_y = 0.25$$

$$i = 10,000 - 50r$$

$$g = 5,000.$$

T3. Answer the following for the revised commodity sector model:

i. What is the equation that describes the IS curve? [Do not use the IS equation formula for this answer. Use step-by-step calculations. Start by calculating disposable income. Then, use the equilibrium condition $y = e$ for your further steps.]

ii. If the interest rate were to be set at 0.02 by the central bank, what would be the equilibrium amounts of consumption, investment, and net tax revenues?

iii. If the interest rate were to be set at 0.02 by the central bank, what happens to the level of equilibrium investment if g increases to 6000? What is the reduction in private investment because of the increasing?

CHAPTER 5

Aggregate Demand in the Open Economy Under an Interest Rate Target: IS-IRT Analysis

This chapter extends the commodity market analysis of the closed economy in the last chapter to a small open economy with a flexible exchange rate.

This chapter further uses the assumption that the monetary policy being pursued sets an interest rate target, and the money supply is adjusted to support this target. Under these assumptions, it shows that the open economy aggregate demand curve has a negative/downward slope.

Under interest rate targeting, expansionary (contractionary) monetary and fiscal policies are both effective in increasing (decreasing) aggregate demand.

This chapter also discusses the demand for money and derives the money supply appropriate to the real interest rate target set by the central bank.

The preceding chapter covered the analysis of the commodity market through the development of the IS equation and curve for the closed economy. This chapter revises the closed economy treatment of the commodity market to accommodate trade in commodities and assets with other countries. It will be assumed that the home economy, also referred to as 'our economy', is small relative to '*the rest of the world*' so that changes in it do not induce changes in the values of the economic variables in other countries. Hence, the variables of the rest of the world can be taken as exogenous to the domestic economy in question. The resulting model is known as the *small open economy macroeconomic model*.

The IS curve analysis for both the closed and the open economy shows that the critical variable determining the aggregate demand for commodities is the interest rate. The determination of the interest rate depends on the policy pursued by the central bank. This policy can be classified broadly under the headings of *monetary targeting* or *interest rate targeting*. The former leads to the exogenous specification of the money supply, and leads to the IS-LM analysis presented in the next chapter. The latter leads to the exogenous specification of the interest rate, and leads to what we label as the IS-IRT analysis. The approach used in this chapter is based on the assumption of interest rate targeting by the central bank.

This chapter combines the IS curve analysis for the commodity market with a real interest rate target set by the central bank to derive aggregate demand in economy. It also examines the influence of the rest of the world on the domestic aggregate demand for commodities, as well as the impact of monetary and fiscal policies in the open economy.

The definitions of the symbols used in this chapter are as given in the preceding chapters.

5.1 The Number of Goods and Markets in the Open Economy

The open economy macroeconomic model has five goods: commodities, money, bonds, labor, and foreign exchange, and the corresponding five markets. Of these, in equilibrium, the results obtained from the analysis of four markets also provide the equilibrium solution for the fifth market, so that the explicit analysis of one market can be omitted. We will follow the conventional macroeconomic analysis to omit the bond market from explicit analysis, so that the analysis will proceed with the specification of the remaining four markets for commodities, money, labor, and foreign exchange. We will start with the last one in the next section and then proceed to analysis of the commodity market for the open economy. This will be followed by the analysis of monetary policy as pursued by most central banks and the determination of the aggregate demand for commodities.

5.2 The Foreign Exchange Sector of the Open Economy and the Balance of Payments, Review

Chapter 3 defined the balance of payments (B) as the net inflows of foreign exchange — that is, as the difference between the country's inflows of funds (from commodity exports, capital imports/inflows and the net inflows of interest, and dividend payments and unilateral transfers) and its outflows of funds for commodity imports and capital exports. These net inflows result in corresponding changes in the foreign exchange held in the domestic country. The usual assumption for macroeconomic analysis is that the foreign exchange authorities — usually the central bank — desire equilibrium in the balance of payments and achieve it, so that $B = \Delta FR = 0$. As Chapter 3 showed, the balance of payments B is specified as:

B = (inflows of foreign exchange from *net* exports of commodities)

+ (inflows of foreign exchange due to *net* imports of capital)

+ (inflows of foreign exchange from *net* interest payments to us)

+ (inflows of foreign exchange from *net* transfers to us).

Hence, in equilibrium,

$$B = \Delta FR = (X_c - Z_c) + (Z_k - X_k) + NR + NT = 0, \tag{1}$$

where:

 FR = foreign exchange reserves,
  B = balance of payments, in nominal terms,
 X_c = value of exports of commodities (goods and services, including physical capital goods),
 X_k = value of (*financial*, not physical) capital exports,
 Z_c = value of imports of commodities (goods and services, including physical capital goods),
 Z_k = value of (*financial*, not physical) capital imports,
NR = net interest and dividend inflows,
NT = net unilateral transfers (gifts and donations) to the domestic economy from abroad.

Chapter 3 had also defined the *real* exchange rate as:

$$\rho^r = \rho P / P^F,$$

where:

ρ = nominal exchange rate, defined as the amount of foreign currency (say, £s) required to purchase a unit, i.e., a dollar, of the domestic currency ($), so that the dimensions of ρ are £ per $ [not $ per £],
ρ^r = real exchange rate, defined as the amount of foreign commodities required to purchase a unit of the domestic commodity,

P = domestic price level, and
P^F = foreign price level.

We will henceforth simplify by assuming, unless otherwise explicitly specified, that both exports and imports have price elasticities greater than unity (see Chapters 12 and 13 for the reasons for this assumption). In this case, our volume of exports (x_c) and their value X_c decrease, as the real exchange rate $\rho^r(=\rho P/P^F)$ rises (which will occur if the domestic price level P rises, ρ rises[1] and/or the foreign price level P^F falls) since our commodities would become relatively more expensive compared with foreign goods. However, the nominal value of our exports also increases with an increase in foreign income y^F. Similarly, under the assumption that our imports have an elasticity greater than one, both the volume and the nominal value of our imports Z_c increase if ρ^r rises (since a unit of our commodities will buy more of foreign ones so that foreign commodities become relatively less expensive) or if domestic income y rises.

Capital flows depend upon a range of factors, of which the rates of return on domestic and foreign assets are likely to be the most important ones. It will be assumed that capital exports X_k decrease, and capital imports Z_k increase, as the yield on domestic bonds rises or as that on foreign bonds falls.[2] The domestic yield equals the domestic interest rate R, while the yield on foreign bonds to domestic investors is the sum of the foreign interest rate R^F and the expected appreciation of the domestic currency ρ''^e.

Putting these ideas formally into Equation (1), the equilibrium condition for the foreign exchange market becomes:

$$[X_c(\rho^r, y^F) - Z_c(\rho^r, y)] + [Z_k(R, R^F, \rho''^e) - X_k(R, R^F, \rho''^e)] + NR + NT = 0(5), \qquad (2)$$

where:

y = domestic national income,
y^F = foreign national income,
R = domestic nominal interest rate,
R^F = foreign nominal interest rate, and
ρ''^e = (if positive) expected appreciation of the exchange rate; (if negative) expected depreciation of the exchange rate.

NR (net interest inflows) and NT (net inflows of transfers) tend to be largely exogenous. To the extent that they are not exogenous, their dependence on incomes and interest rates can be captured in either commodity or capital flows.

We have assumed in the introduction to this chapter that the domestic economy is *small* relative to the rest of the world: that is, the variables P^F, y^F, and R^F would not be affected by changes in our exports and imports of commodities and capital. Therefore, they are exogenous variables, whose values are given for our economy. Omitting the variables y^F and R^F from Equation (2) since they are exogenous and omitting ρ''^e for simplification, we are left with the equation:

$$[X_c(\rho^r) - Z_c(\rho^r, y)] + [Z_k(R) - X_k(R)] + NR + NT = 0. \qquad (3)$$

---

[1]Remember that ρ falling (i.e., less £s per $) means that the domestic currency — the dollar — has depreciated. This would make our commodities cheaper to foreigners while making their commodities more expensive to us. To illustrate, if the exchange rate falls to half, the price to foreigners (in £s) of a $10 shirt will fall to half while the dollar price (to us) of a £20 trousers will double. This will make our goods cheaper for foreigners and increase our sales to foreigners (i.e., increase our exports), while making foreign goods more expensive for us and decreasing our imports.

[2]It is also assumed that the other endogenous variables such as incomes, prices and exchange rates are not likely to significantly affect capital flows from the viewpoint of a purely comparative static analysis.

By substituting $\rho P / P^F$ for ρ^r in Equation (3), we get:

$$[X_c(\rho P / P^F) - Z_c(\rho P / P^F, y)] + [Z_k(R) - X_k(R)] + NR + NT = 0. \qquad (4)$$

This equation — designated as the *BP* (equilibrium) *equation* — now becomes an element of the open economy macroeconomic model. Solving it for the equilibrium value ρ^* of the nominal exchange rate ρ yields $\rho^* = f(P / P^F, y, R;$ other exogenous variables and parameters in the BP equation).

For a country with a flexible exchange rate, the usual assumption for convenience in macroeconomic analysis is that the exchange rate will always be the equilibrium one, thereby ensuring *continuous* balance of payments equilibrium for the given values of R and y. Therefore, under flexible exchange rates, ρ^* from Equation (3) is substituted for ρ in the open economy IS equation to derive the final form of the IS equation and curve. We will return to this point later in the next section.

5.2.1 Net interest payments and net transfer payments

NR is the net inflow of interest and dividend payments from ownership of bonds, stocks, and physical capital in other countries. NT is the net inflow of transfer payments from gifts and remittances. It is commonly assumed in international economics that NR and NT are relatively insignificant compared with net exports and net capital flows for most countries, so that they are usually omitted from further analysis. However, this is not true of certain countries. For example, Saudi Arabia has a lot of foreign workers who send remittances back to their families, often in Pakistan and India. In these cases, the balance of payments analysis should explicitly take into account NR and NT and not omit them from balance of payments analysis.

5.2.2 Relationship between nominal and real interest rates

The nominal interest rate R is the appropriate interest rate for the analysis of the balance of payments since foreign investors are interested in the nominal, not the real, interest rate. However, the real interest rate r is appropriate for the analysis of investment and the commodity market. As Chapter 2 discussed, in prefect capital markets, the relationship between the nominal and the real interest rate is given by the Fisher equation on interest rates, which is:

$$(1 + R) = (1 + r)(1 + \pi^e),$$

where π^e is the expected inflation rate. The approximate form of the Fisher equation is:

$$R = r + \pi^e.$$

This chapter assumes that $\pi^e = 0$, so that $R = r$.

5.3 The Commodity Market of the Open Economy

Now consider the specification of the commodity market of the open economy. Let y stand for *domestic* output and national income, while e stands for real expenditures on *domestically produced* commodities. The symbol for consumption expenditures in Chapters 4 was c. The open economy has two types of consumer goods, domestically produced and imported ones. We now define c as the real value of all consumption expenditures. Therefore, the consumption expenditures on domestic commodities will equal total consumption expenditures c minus the expenditures in real terms on imported commodities. For simplification, we assume that investment is wholly out of domestic commodities. In addition, foreigners buy our commodities through our exports, so that foreigners' real expenditures on our exports, which equal x_c, have to be added to derive the expenditures e on domestic output.

Hence, the real expenditures e on the commodities produced in the *domestic* economy, which constitute the aggregate sales revenue of all the firms in the economy, are given by:

$$e = (c - z_c/\rho^r) + i + g + x_c = c + i + g + (x_c - z_c/\rho^r), \tag{5}$$

where all the variables are in real terms. Our exports are already in domestic commodities and are in real terms. $z_c/\rho^r (= (P^F/\rho P)z_c)$ are expenditures in real terms on imported commodities. Why divide z_c by ρ^r? Note that z_c is the *quantity* of imported goods bought at foreign prices P^F, so that £$P^F z_c$ is our expenditure in the foreign currency on imported goods. This amount has to be converted into the domestic currency by dividing by the nominal exchange rate ρ, so that \$$(P^F/\rho)z_c$ is the domestic/dollar price of the imported goods. This nominal amount in dollars has to be deflated into real terms at the domestic price level P to find the expenditures in (domestic) real terms on the imported commodities. Therefore, the real value of imported commodities in the above equation is not merely z_c but $(P^F/\rho P)z_c$, which equals z_c/ρ^r.[3]

In the aggregate over all domestic firms, firms' output equals their total payments to the factors of production, which together constitute national income. As in the closed economy analysis, national income can be spent by domestic residents on consumption c (which includes the consumption of both domestic and imported goods), saving s, and payments of net taxes t. Hence:

$$y = c + s + t, \tag{6}$$

where:

c = real consumption expenditures,
s = real private saving, and
t = real net taxes paid (net of transfers).

For equilibrium in the commodity market, we need (as in the closed economy models) the equality of national income (which constitutes the domestic firms' cost of production of commodities) and national expenditures (which equal their revenues from sales of commodities). That is, the generic equilibrium condition for the open, as for the closed, economy is:

$$e = y.$$

In this equilibrium, firms' revenues and costs are equal, so that they would maintain production at an unchanged level. As shown in Chapter 4 for the closed economy, if $e > y$, firms' revenues would exceed their costs and they would be tempted to expand production. If $e < y$, firms' revenues would be less than their costs and they would attempt to reduce losses by contracting production.

Hence, we equate e to y for equilibrium in the commodity market. Doing so yields:

$$c + i + g + x_c = c + s + t + z_c/\rho^r.$$

By cancelling out c, we get:

$$i + g + x_c = s + t + z_c/\rho^r. \tag{7}$$

This equation represents one of the forms of the commodity market equilibrium condition.

---

[3]Some textbooks do not divide z_c by ρ_r under the assumption that it always equals unity. This is done under the implicit assumption that Purchasing Power Parity (PPP) holds, which makes ρ_r equal to unity. However, as shown in Chapters 3 and 13, PPP does not normally hold, even over periods as long as 10 or 20 years. Therefore, we do not assume that $\rho_r = 1$.

Fact Sheet 5.1: Components of Aggregate Demand for USA, Canada, and Thailand, 2007

The following pie charts illustrate the breakdown of 2007 aggregate demand (gross national product) at market prices for three countries with quite different economies: USA is a large continental country with a large economy, both Canada and Thailand are small economies but Canada has a developed economy, and Thailand has a developing one. Consumption expenditures (including those on imported goods) are the largest item (59% or higher) for each country. Gross capital formation (which is another name for gross (i.e., including replacement for depreciation) investment) is the next largest item. While exports and imports are large for each country, the pie charts show only net exports (i.e., exports minus imports), which are a very smaller percentage of GNP. In 2007, both USA and Canada had negative net exports, meaning that they were net importers of goods and services. With a fast-growing, export-led economy, Thailand allocates a larger proportion of its annual production to net exports and investments than USA and Canada. Government expenditures are relatively bigger for Canada than for USA or Thailand because of Canada's greater provision of social services for its residents.

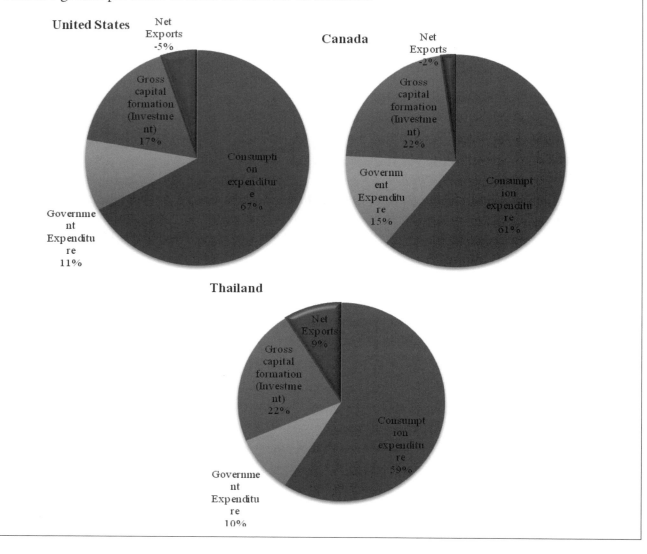

5.3.1 The uses of private saving in the open economy

The commodity market equilibrium condition above can also be rearranged to show the uses that can be made of private saving. For this purpose, rewrite this condition as:

$$s = i + (g - t) + (x_c - z_c/\rho^r) = i + \text{fiscal deficit} + \text{net exports of commodities}.$$

That is, private saving out of the currently produced output of commodities can be used to pay for domestic investment, the government deficit or be exported through positive net exports.

Uses of national saving

National saving s^n is the sum of private saving s and government saving $(t - g)$, so that:

$$s^n = i + (x_c - z_c/\rho^r).$$

Hence, national saving can be used for domestic investment or net exports. A fiscal surplus increases national saving, so that it increases domestic investment and/or net exports, or both. A fiscal deficit decreases national saving, so that it reduces the levels of domestic investment and/or net exports, or both. The fiscal deficit and the foreign trade deficit are thus closely connected.

5.3.2 Three gaps: saving, fiscal, and external

The preceding commodity market equilibrium condition can be rearranged as:

$$(i - s) + (g - t) + [x_c - z_c/\rho^r] = 0, \tag{8}$$

where $(i - s)$ is the (private) *investment-saving gap*, $(g - t)$ is the *fiscal gap*, and the last term $[x_c - z_c/\rho^r]$ is the *net export gap*, also called the *external trade gap*. Note that this equation expresses a relationship among the three gaps, but without specifying a *direction of causality* — that is, the initial change in which variable causes the other variables to change. However, additional information on the exogeneity of any one of the gaps will insert causality from an exogenous gap to the endogenous ones. For example, if it is assumed that the government sets its deficit exogenously of the economy, it would be better to rearrange the above equation as:

$$(s - i) + [z_c/\rho^r - x_c] = (g - t). \tag{7'}$$

With $(g - t)$ being given as exogenous, the exogenously created fiscal deficit will induce either an investment-saving gap and/or an external gap. To illustrate the implications of this relationship in the very unusual case when $i = s$, so that $(i - s) = 0$,[4] the fiscal deficit (i.e., $g > t$) would imply a balance of trade deficit of the same amount. Intuitively, a fiscal deficit means that the government is buying 'too much' of commodities. This is made possible through a net inflow of commodities from abroad. Conversely, a fiscal surplus would induce positive net exports. *In the general case*, in which saving does not necessarily equal investment, *fiscal deficits partly crowd out investment by making it less than saving and partly reduce net exports (e.g., by inducing imports)*.

---

[4]Note that there is no reason for this equality $(i = s)$ to hold in the open or the closed economy. In particular, it would not hold even in the closed economy — let alone the open economy — if there are budget surpluses or deficits, or if the commodity market is in disequilibrium. It almost never holds in the open economy.

Therefore, the above equation raises the presumption that countries with large fiscal deficits would also have balance of trade deficits while those with large fiscal surpluses would have trade surpluses. Hence, *the impact of fiscal deficits and surpluses is not confined only to domestic aggregate demand. They also have implications for the balance of payments and therefore, for the foreign exchange markets and the exchange rate.*

Fact Sheet 5.2: The uses of private saving in the USA, 1980–2008

This Fact Sheet uses US data to illustrate the allocation of private saving to investment, the fiscal deficit and net exports. In an open economy, equilibrium in the commodity market requires that private saving equal the sum of investment, the budget deficit, and current account balance. The following graph draws these variables as percentages of GDP. Both private savings and investments were positive, though with a declining trend, through the period, but investment was larger than saving. Further, the US government ran budget deficits for most of the period. The difference between investment and saving, plus the budget deficit had to be financed by a net inflow of foreign commodities, so that the current account had to be in deficit, as is clearly shown in the graph. To cover this external account deficit, the USA was a net importer of capital from other countries throughout the period.

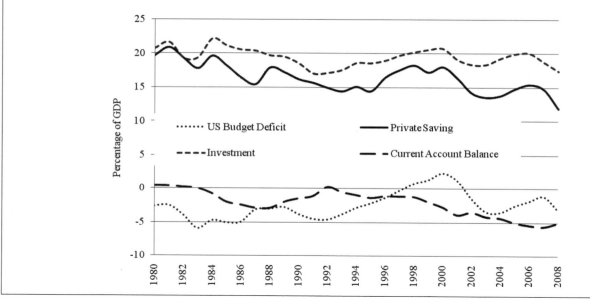

National saving and the two-gaps equilibrium condition

In Chapter 4, *national saving* was designated as s^n and was defined as:

$$s^n \equiv s + (t - g).$$

Therefore, the three-gaps version of the commodity market equilibrium condition for the open economy can be modified to a two-gaps one of the form:

$$(s^n - i) = (x_c - z_c/\rho^r) = \text{net exports of commodities.} \tag{7''}$$

That is, if we save more as a nation than we invest at home, then we must be exporting the excess national saving through positive net exports of commodities. But *if we save less as a nation than we invest at home, we must have positive net imports of commodities.*

5.3.3 Commodity market equilibrium and capital flows

We can combine the above condition for commodity market equilibrium with the condition for equilibrium in the balance of payments, derived earlier in this chapter. To do so, first convert the commodity market equilibrium condition into nominal terms by multiplying by the price level *P*. This gives the condition:

$$S = I + (G - T) + \text{Nominal value of net exports.}$$

The nominal value of net exports is specified by $[X_c(\rho^r) - Z_c(\rho^r, y)]$. Under the balance of payments equilibrium condition, the *nominal value of net exports of commodities* is related to *nominal capital flows* by the equation:

$$[X_c - Z_c] = [X_k - Z_k] - NR - NT,$$

so that combining the commodity market equilibrium condition and the balance of payments equilibrium condition gives the uses of nominal private saving. In nominal terms, $S = I + $ nominal fiscal deficit + net nominal exports of capital − nominal NR − nominal NT.

For countries for which we can justifiably assume that $NR = NT = 0$, this equation says that *nominal private saving can be used either for domestic investment, the government deficit, or net capital exports.*

Ownership of foreign assets and net external indebtedness

For *nominal* capital flows, the above condition for simultaneous equilibrium in both the balance of payments and the commodity market can be restated as:

$$S^n = I + \text{net nominal exports of capital} - \text{nominal NR} - \text{nominal NT.}$$

Note that net nominal exports of capital = change in foreign exchange assets (NFA) in the country.

For countries for which we can justifiably assume that $NR = NT = 0$, this equation says that *nominal national saving can be used either for domestic investment or for net capital exports.* The latter increase the country's claims on the rest of the world. High national saving is, therefore, a way of building the country's own physical capital and/or its ownership of foreign assets at a faster rate. Conversely, low national saving hinders the growth of the economy's own physical capital and/or increases foreigners' investments in our economy — thereby increasing the national indebtedness to foreigners.

The ownership of foreign assets, which occurs through the accumulation of net exports of capital, can take the following forms:

- ownership of foreign currencies,
- ownership of foreign bonds,
- ownership of foreign stocks, and
- ownership of foreign physical capital through foreign direct investment (FDI).

Extended Analysis Box 5.1: Financing high levels of domestic investment during the development stages and foreign exchange crises

Many countries, especially in their development stages, need to build up their physical capital at a faster rate than their own saving permits. For them, it is useful to turn the above equation to:

$$I - (S^n - \text{net nominal } \textit{outflow} \text{ of interest payments[5]}) = \text{net nominal imports of capital} + \text{nominal NT.}$$

[5]This equals −NR.

Extended Analysis Box 5.1: (*Continued*)

Note that past net inflows of capital have two effects:

1. If the past net inflows of capital increased investment in physical capital at home, domestic output, current saving, and capital would be higher. But if they were 'wasted' or used to finance consumption, they would not have increased current output and saving.
2. The past net inflows of capital increase the current net outflows of interest payments (on past capital imports). If net capital imports continue over time, this outflow for interest payments becomes a rising charge against both national saving and net exports.

If national saving increases because of higher output due to the investment of past capital inflows, the increased outflow for interest payments can be more easily accommodated and may not become a problem. If national saving did not rise sufficiently because of the past capital inflows, the increased outflow of interest payments reduces the domestic funds available for increasing the domestic capital stock. This scenario usually requires continuing net capital inflows and/or net unilateral transfers. If these do not occur to a significant extent, domestic investment will have to decrease.

Foreign exchange crises and debt forgiveness

Countries undergoing financial and exchange rate crises often have large net capital outflows. In such cases, there could come about negative investment — and a gradual reduction of the economy's physical stock — which reduces their future income and saving capacity. One way out of this trap is for the lenders to agree to some form of 'debt forgiveness' — which is essentially the canceling of all or part of some foreign debts. Lenders are reluctant to do so[6] but it has been done to a limited extent by some foreign lenders for the poorest countries with heavy foreign indebtedness. From 1989 to 1997, US$33 billion of debt owed by 41 countries designated as the Highly Indebted Poor Countries (HIPC) was forgiven.[7]

To see the potential of past capital inflows for causing financial crises, rewrite the above equation as:

$$\text{Net nominal outflow of interest payments} + \text{net nominal outflows of capital}$$
$$= S^n - I + \text{nominal NT}.$$

Countries sometimes build up a substantial external debt and, therefore, become committed to high outflows of interest payments. When these outflows as a percentage of domestic GDP become large, foreign investors tend to become reluctant to invest further in the country and domestic residents tend to choose foreign currencies or other assets, so that there would occur a massive net capital outflow. In such circumstances, the combination of the outflows (the left side of the above equation) is likely to exceed the right side of the above equation.[8] That is:

$$[\text{Net nominal outflows of interest payments} + \text{net nominal outflows of capital}]$$
$$> [S^n - I + \text{nominal NT}].$$

---

[6]One reason for refusing to do so is based on the argument that foreign aid was used by corrupt and/or inefficient governments with a pattern of misusing aid. Forgiving past debts would cause such governments to borrow more with the expectation that the debt will be forgiven, and/or they will use the debt forgiveness as providing a fresh opportunity to borrow again for similarly wasteful purposes.

[7]*Foreign Policy*, November/December 2001, pp. 20–26. New borrowing by these countries during the same periods was $41 billion.

[8]Note that the past accumulation of foreign debt implies that the country did not have enough national saving to finance its domestic investment.

Extended Analysis Box 5.1: (*Continued*)

We would also have:

[Net nominal outflows of interest payments + net nominal outflows of capital]

> [net nominal exports + net nominal outflows of transfers].

A country faced with such a scenario would have to default on its payments to foreigners, unless it follows policies to:

- Increase national saving. Since it is likely to be difficult to raise private saving rates, the government would have to cut its deficit drastically, by cutting its expenditures, possibly on transfers to the public (e.g., subsidies to the poor and corporations) and on programs such as health and education, and also by raising taxes.
- Reduce investment in domestic physical capital, which will hinder its productive capacity in the future.
- Increase exports and decrease imports. This can require massive depreciations/devaluations of its exchange rate, as well a decrease in domestic aggregate demand through monetary and fiscal policies.

Each of these possibilities comes at some cost, which can be economic, political, and social. Usually, all of the above policies have to be followed. Often, their cost on the economy and the standard of living of its citizens is quite heavy. Other policies — which are less painful in the short term and are therefore often followed — are:

- Increasing capital inflows, e.g., by borrowing from international organizations such as the International Monetary Fund, other countries' governments or from private foreign sources.
- Increasing net inflows in the form of transfers (e.g., grants, which do not require repayment or remittances by expatriates), or the waiver of past debts ('debt forgiveness').
- Arranging rescheduling of payments (interest and capital) on the existing debt, etc.

5.3.4 The open economy IS relationship

As specified above, the commodity market equilibrium condition for the open economy is:

$$y = c + i + g + x_c - z_c/\rho^r. \tag{9}$$

Our assumptions on the main variables of the commodity market (other than exports and imports) remain unchanged from those on the closed economy in Chapter 4. Therefore, the following equations from Chapter 4 are now taken to apply to the open economy.

$$c = c_0 + c_y(y - t) \qquad 0 \le c_y \le 1 \tag{10}$$

$$i = i(r) = i_0 - i_r r \qquad i_r \ge 0 \tag{11}$$

$$t = t_0 + t_y y \qquad 0 \le t_y \le 1 \tag{12}$$

$$g = g_0,$$

where the symbols have the standardized definitions in Chapter 4. Note that the above investment function assumes that the interest rate is a function of the *real* interest rate r rather than the nominal/market one R. The distinction between these and their relationship through the Fisher equation was specified in Chapter 3. The reason for the assumption that investment, which is in real terms in commodities, depends on the real rather than the nominal interest rate is that the firm is interested in the real cost, net of expected inflation, of the funds that it needs to borrow for its investments.

Further, for the small open economy, assume that the export and import functions are linear and are specified as in the following.

Export function

$$x_c = x_{c0} - x_{c\rho}\rho^r \qquad x_{c0}, x_{c\rho} > 0, \tag{13}$$

where x_c is the real amount of exported commodities and x_{c0} is autonomous exports — which are autonomous in the sense that their amount is independent of ρ^r and other endogenous variables, but can depend on exogenous variables, such as y^F. Exports decrease if the real exchange rate ρ^r rises, since this would make our exports more expensive in foreign markets. This is reflected in the last term $(-x_{c\rho}\rho^r)$, where $x_{c\rho}$ is the amount of the fall in exports for a unit increase in the real exchange rate.

Import function

$$z_c = z_{c0} + z_{cy}y_d + z_{c\rho}\rho^r \qquad z_{cy}, z_{cP} > 0, \tag{14}$$

where z_c is the real amount of imported commodities and z_{c0} is autonomous imports (i.e., the amount which is independent of disposable income y_d and the real exchange rate ρ^r, but can depend on exogenous variables). The marginal propensity to import out of y_d is z_{cy}, which is positive. Imports increase if the real exchange rate ρ^r rises/appreciates, since this would make imported commodities less expensive. This is reflected in the last term $(z_{c\rho}\rho^r)$, where $z_{c\rho}$ is the amount of the rise in imports for a unit increase in the real exchange rate.

The complete model of the commodity sector for the open economy

Gathering together the preceding equations, the open economy's commodity sector has the equations:

$$
\begin{array}{ll}
c = c_0 + c_y(y - t) & 0 \leq c_y \leq 1 \\
i = i(r) = i_0 - i_r r & i_r \geq 0 \\
t = t_0 + t_y y & 0 \leq t_y \leq 1 \\
g = g_0 & \\
x_c = x_{c0} - x_{c\rho}\rho^r & x_{c0}, x_{c\rho} > 0 \\
z_c = z_{c0} + z_{cy}y_d + z_{c\rho}\rho^r & z_{cy}, z_{c\rho} > 0.
\end{array}
$$

Equilibrium condition: $\qquad y = c + i + g + x_c - z_c/\rho^r.$

Substituting the equations for each of the variables on the right-hand side of the equilibrium condition gives us a long equation that has y in some terms on both side of the equation. If we rearrange this long equation to bring y to the left-hand side and all other terms to the right-hand side, we will get the following IS equation. Box 5.1 presents its derivation.

$$y = \left(\frac{1}{1 - c_y + c_y t_y + \frac{1}{\rho^r}z_{cy}(1 - t_y)} \right) \cdot$$
$$[\{c_0 - c_y t_0 + i_0 - i_r r + g + x_{c0} - x_{c\rho}\rho^r\} + (1/\rho^r) \cdot \{-z_{c0} + z_{cy}t_0 - z_{c\rho}\rho^r\}]. \tag{15}$$

This equation is the *IS equation for the open economy*. It makes y a function of r and ρ^r, where $\rho^r = \rho P/P^F$, so that replacing ρ^r by $\rho P/P^F$ makes y a function of r, ρ, P, and P^F, in addition to policy and exogenous variables and parameters. Under flexible exchange rates, the equilibrium value ρ^* of the nominal exchange rate is determined by the balance of payments equilibrium condition (Equation (3) earlier in this chapter). Replacing ρ by ρ^* gives the final form of the IS equation. In this form of the IS equation, y will be a function of P, r, the fiscal policy variables and the exogenous foreign variables P^F, R^F, and y^F, but ρ will no longer appear as a separate determinant of y. Since this form is considerably more cumbersome than Equation (15), our further analysis of the commodity sector will be based on Equation (15), with the understanding that ρ^r is replaced by $\rho P/P^F$ and ρ is replaced by its equilibrium value from the balance of payments equation equilibrium condition.

Equation (15) adds for the open economy the export and import functions to the closed economy IS equation. In particular, [.] has two terms involving the real exchange rate ρ^r, with both preceded by a negative sign, so that an appreciation of the exchange rate decreases national income/expenditures y. The first term is $x_{c\rho}\rho^r$. Its negative sign occurs because as ρ^r rises, exports fall, which decreases expenditures on domestic commodities.[9] The second term is $z_{c\rho}\rho^r$. Its negative sign occurs because as ρ^r rises, imports increase, so that the leakages from domestic income (similar to those due to taxes paid) rise, thereby decreasing the share of disposable income that can be spent on domestic commodities.[10]

Replacing (.) by α in the above IS equation, the IS equation can be written as:

$$y = \alpha[\{c_0 - c_y t_0 + i_0 - i_r r + g + x_{c0} - x_{c\rho}\rho^r\} + (1/\rho^r) \cdot \{-z_{c0} + z_{cy}t_0 - z_{c\rho}\rho^r\}], \tag{16}$$

where the symbol α has the meaning:

$$\alpha = \left(\frac{1}{1 - c_y + c_y t_y + \frac{1}{\rho^r}z_{cy}(1 - t_y)}\right) > 0. \tag{17}$$

Box 5.1: Derivation of the Open Economy is Equation

The equilibrium condition specified for the commodity market is that:

$$y = c + i + g + x_c - z_c/\rho^r.$$

Substituting the equations for each of the variables on the right-hand side, we get:

$$y = c_0 + c_y(y - t) + i_0 - i_r r + g_0 + x_{c0} - x_{c\rho}\rho^r - 1/\rho^r \cdot \{z_{c0} + z_{cy}y_d + z_{c\rho}\rho^r\}$$

where y_d and t are given by:

$$y_d = y - t$$

$$t = t_0 + t_y y.$$

Substituting for y_d and t in the equilibrium equation, we get:

$$y = c_0 + c_y y - t_0 c_y - c_y t_y y + i_0 - i_r r + g_0 + x_{c0} - x_{c\rho}\rho^r - (1/\rho^r) \cdot \{z_{c0} + z_{cy}(y - t_0 - t_y y) + z_{c\rho}\rho^r\}.$$

---

[9]Therefore, the IS curve will shift to the left and aggregate demand will fall.

[10]Therefore, the IS curve will shift to the left and aggregate demand will fall.

Box 5.1: (*Continued*)

Expanding and collecting the y terms on the left-hand side gives:

$$y - c_y y + c_y t_y y + z_{cy} y / \rho^r - z_{cy} t_y y / \rho^r = c_0 - t_0 c_y + i_0 - i_r r + g_{0+} x_{c0} - x_{c\rho} \rho^r + (1/\rho^r) \cdot \{-z_{c0} + z_{cy} t_0 - z_{c\rho} \rho^r\}.$$

Rewrite this equation as:

$$y(1 - c_y + c_y t_y + z_{cy}/\rho^r - z_{cy} t_y / \rho^r) = c_0 - t_0 c_y + i_0 - i_r r + g_{0+} x_{c0} - x_{c\rho} \rho^r + (1/\rho^r) \cdot \{-z_{c0} + z_{cy} t_0 - z_{c\rho} \rho^r\}.$$

This equation can be restated as:

$$y = \left(\frac{1}{1 - c_y + c_y t_y + \frac{1}{\rho^r} z_{cy}(1 - t_y)} \right) \cdot [\{c_0 - c_y t_0 + i_0 - i_r r + g_0 + x_{c0} - x_{c\rho} \rho^r\}$$
$$+ (1/\rho^r) \cdot \{-z_{c0} + z_{cy} t_0 - z_{c\rho} \rho^r\}].$$

This form of the IS equation for the open economy shows the commodity market's determination of y by the parameters and variables on the right-hand side of the equation. Since r and ρ^r are the variables on the right side of the equation, and $\rho^r = \rho P / P^F$, this equation implies that y depends on the variables r, ρ, and P/P^F, in addition to the policy variables and parameters.

The equilibrium value of ρ^* from the balance of payments is next substituted in the above equation to get the final form of the IS equation. The resulting equation would be quite complex and is omitted. The general form of the final IS equation would be:

$$y = f(r, P/P^F).$$

If P rises, our net exports fall, which will decrease expenditures on domestic commodities. Hence, domestic income y will fall. Therefore, for commodity market equilibrium, $\partial y/\partial P < 0$.

The open economy fiscal and investment multipliers

The government expenditures and autonomous investment multipliers for the preceding open economy IS equation are derived by the same procedure as used in Chapter 4. Briefly, this procedure was to expand Equation (5) to:

$$y = \{\alpha c_0 - \alpha c_y t_0 + \alpha i_0 - \alpha i_r r + \alpha g + \alpha x_{c0} - \alpha x_{c\rho} \rho^r\} - \alpha(1/\rho^r) \cdot z_{c0} + \alpha z_{cy}(1/\rho^r) \cdot t_0 - \alpha(1/\rho^r) \cdot z_{c\rho} \rho^r.$$

Now suppose that government expenditures g rise, with all other variables held constant, so that the change in them is zero. Therefore:

$$\Delta y = \alpha \Delta g,$$

which, for small changes in g, gives:

$$\partial y/\partial g = \alpha.$$

By similar reasoning when we only consider the effect of a small increase in autonomous investment i_0, we get:

$$\partial y/\partial i_0 = \alpha.$$

Hence, α specifies the autonomous investment and government expenditures multiplier for the open economy. As shown in Chapter 4 for plausible values of the parameters, this multiplier has a positive value, usually greater than one.

The multipliers for changes in exports and imports

Now suppose that autonomous exports x_0 rise, with all other variables held constant, so that the change in them is zero. Therefore:

$$\Delta y = \alpha \cdot \Delta x_0,$$

which, for small changes in x_0, gives:

$$\partial y / \partial x_0 = \alpha.$$

Therefore, the autonomous exports multiplier equals the fiscal expenditures and autonomous investment multipliers above. If α has a value greater than one, which is the usual case, an increase in exports increases aggregate demand in the economy by more than the increase in exports.[11] Similar reasoning implies that the multiplier specifying changes in aggregate demand due to changes in autonomous imports is:

$$\partial y / \partial z_{c0} = -\alpha(1/\rho^r).$$

Hence, an autonomous increase in exports increases y while an autonomous increase in imports decreases y.

5.3.5 The open economy IS curve

Plotting the open economy IS equation in the IS diagram, with r on the vertical axis and y on the horizontal one, gives the open economy IS curve, which has a negative slope. Figure 5.1a shows such a downward sloping IS curve. The reason for this negative slope is: an increase in income (from y_0 to y_1) increases saving and tax revenues, so that equilibrium requires an increase in investment, which requires a decrease in the real interest rate (from r_0 to r_1). Therefore, for equilibrium to be maintained in the commodity market, an increase in y

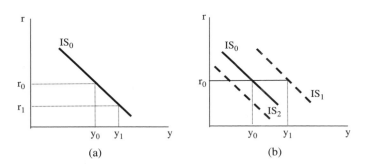

Figure 5.1.

---

[11] If α has a value between zero and one, the increase in exports increases aggregate demand in the economy by less than the increase in exports.

must be accompanied by a decrease in r. Hence, commodity market equilibrium implies a negative relationship between y and r.

5.3.6 Shifts in the open economy IS curve

The closed economy analysis of the IS curve implied that the IS curve would shift to the right if there were increases in autonomous consumption, autonomous investment, government expenditures, etc. The reasons for this shift should be reviewed at this stage. The same arguments also apply to the open economy IS curve. Such a shift to the right from IS_0 to IS_1 is shown in Figure 5.1b.

The open economy also has additional causes of shifts of the IS curve. Among these, at any given interest rate, an increase in autonomous exports increases expenditures on domestic commodities, so that the IS curve shifts to the right. Conversely, for any given interest rate, an increase in autonomous imports, for a given overall consumption, shifts expenditures from domestic commodities to foreign ones, so that expenditures y on domestic commodities fall. This shifts the IS curve to the left, as shown in Figure 5.1b by the shift of the IS curve from IS_0 to IS_2.

Extended Analysis Box 5.2: The Mathematical Derivation of the Slope of the IS Curve

Just as for the closed economy analysis of Chapter 4, the slope of the IS curve is given by $\partial r/\partial y$. To derive this, we note that $\partial r/\partial y$ is the inverse of $\partial y/\partial r$, whose value can be easily calculated from the above IS equation[12] as:

$$\frac{\partial y}{\partial r} = -\alpha i_r.$$

Hence, by using the inverse of this equation, the slope of the IS curve for the open economy is given by:

$$\frac{\partial r}{\partial y} = -\frac{1}{\alpha i_r} < 0.$$

Since α and i_r are both positive, this slope is negative.

Changes in the slope of the IS curve as the economy becomes more open

A more open economy is one with higher imports and exports as a percentage of its real GDP. The multiplier α becomes smaller as the imports/GDP ratio increases. This implies that the slope of the IS curve — which is given by $\partial r/\partial y = -1/(\alpha i_r)$ — becomes greater in absolute terms. Therefore, the IS curve will be *steeper* for a more open economy. Hence, as the Canadian and American economies, as well as most others, have become more open in the last several decades, their IS curves have become steeper.

Comparing the smaller, more open Canadian economy with the larger, less open American economy, the IS curve for Canada will be steeper than for the USA. That is, a 10% decrease in the interest rate will have a much smaller impact on aggregate demand in Canada than in the USA.

---

[12]For this derivation, first expand the IS equation by opening the brackets and rewriting it as:

$$y = \alpha c_0 - \alpha c_y t_0 + \alpha i_0 - \alpha i_r r + \cdots,$$

where $-\alpha i_r$ is the coefficient of r. To consider the effects on y of an exogenous change only in r, the parameters and any other variables on the right-hand side of this equation are held constant, so that the change in them is zero. Hence, this equation implies that $\Delta y = -\alpha i_r \Delta r$. For small changes in y and r, this transforms to $\partial y/\partial r = -\alpha i_r$.

Extended Analysis Box 5.2: (*Continued*)

Comparing the magnitudes of the fiscal multipliers for open economies

The fiscal multiplier depends on the propensity to import z_{cy}. Since z_{cy} is in the denominator of the multiplier, the autonomous investment multiplier α for a more open economy with a higher propensity to import z_{cy} is smaller in value than its counterpart for a less open economy. Hence, a larger, more diversified economy — such as that of 'continental' countries such as the USA, European Union, China, and India — is likely to have a larger multiplier than smaller, less diversified economies such as that of Canada or Britain. As a result, an increase of \$1 in government expenditures will have a smaller impact on aggregate demand in Canada than in the USA.

Further, as economies become relatively more open and increase the ratio of their imports to GDP, their fiscal and autonomous investment multipliers will decrease. This occurs since a larger part of the impetus to aggregate demand from the fiscal expansion leaks away in the form of higher imports and less is spent on domestic commodities.

Conversely, if foreign income y^F rises, exports and total expenditures on domestic commodities rise, which increases domestic income y. Therefore, while the economy has smaller fiscal and investment multipliers, its income rises because of higher exports.

The stability of aggregate demand in more open economies

With a smaller multiplier for a more open economy, national income will be more stable for a given change in domestic investment in the more open than in the less open economy. However, it will also be less responsive to a given change in government expenditures. Therefore, both the need for and the strength of stabilization policies will be less in the more open economy. The larger the marginal propensity to import z_{cy}, the stronger will be this effect. As against this greater stability in response to the domestic sources of disturbances, the fluctuations in imports and exports due to shifts in foreign economies will have greater impact on the domestic national income of a more open economy and may require offsetting stabilization policies.

5.3.7 The impact of exchange rate changes on the IS curve

The movement along the open economy IS curve when the interest rate or income changes

The relationship between the IS curve and the changes in the exchange rate is quite complicated and needs to be carefully specified. The nominal exchange rate ρ is determined by the equilibrium in the foreign exchange market. It rises if the domestic interest rate increases (because that induces capital inflows), but falls if income y increases (because that induces an increase in imports). Since the IS diagram has r and y on the axes, the impact of any change in ρ because of prior changes in r or y will produce a movement along (but not shift) the IS curve.[13] The reasoning behind this statement is illustrated by the following: starting from a given y_0,

---

[13]The formal reason for this has been specified earlier in this chapter. It is as follows. $\rho P/P^F$ is first substituted in the benchmark IS equation reported in this chapter. Then, the equilibrium value of ρ from the Balance of Payments equilibrium condition is substituted in the benchmark IS equation, thereby eliminating ρ from the IS equation. The resulting form of the IS equation will depend not only on the assumptions given earlier for the commodity sector variables but also on the balance of payments equilibrium condition and the assumptions on its components (especially commodity and capital flows). Therefore, the final IS equation will incorporate the adjustments in the equilibrium value of ρ.

an increase in r and R will induce capital inflows, thereby creating a balance of payments surplus, so that, in the flexible exchange rate case, ρ will appreciate to restore equilibrium in the balance of payments. But this appreciation will reduce net exports, which, through the multiplier, will reduce income y in the economy.[14] This reduction in y (due to the increase in ρ caused by the increase in r and R) is captured through a sliding movement upward to the new, higher, level of the interest rate on the existing IS curve. Conversely, a decrease in r and R will induce capital outflows, which will cause ρ to fall. This will increase exports, which will cause y to increase. Hence, the decrease in r will mean a movement downwards along the IS curve to a higher level of y. Similar analysis applies to an initial change in y. Therefore, for the flexible exchange rate case, if the change in ρ is caused by an initial shift in r or y, the IS curve does not shift, but there is a sliding movement along the IS curve to the new equilibrium levels of r and y.

The shift in the open economy IS curve when prices change

Since $\rho^{r} = \rho P / P^{F}$, an increase in the price level P increases ρ^{r}, which makes domestic goods more expensive to foreigners and causes net exports to fall. This will lead, because of the ensuing balance of payments deficit, to a decline in ρ. This depreciation will moderate the increase in ρ^{r}, which will moderate the reduction in net exports in the IS equation but net exports will remain below their initial level. The fall in net exports will reduce national expenditures and income below their original levels.[15] Since P is not on the vertical axis of the IS-IRT diagram, the reduction in y due to the increase in P is captured through a leftward shift in the IS curve, rather than through a sliding movement along it. That is, under flexible exchange rates, an increase in P causes a leftward shift of the IS curve. Conversely, a decrease in P causes a rightward shift of the IS curve.

Similar reasoning can be used to show that, under flexible exchange rates, increases in net exports induced by exogenous increases in P^{F} or in y^{F} will increase y for a given value of r and produce rightward shifts in the IS curve.

In the more complicated case where net exports change because of nominal exchange rate changes induced by changes in *both* the domestic prices and domestic interest rates, there will be a shift in the IS curve, as well as a movement along the curve.

The importance of the interest rate in determining national income/expenditures

The preceding IS equation and curve show that one of the critical *variables* determining the level of expenditures on domestic commodities is the interest rate. The determination of the interest rate depends on the financial sector of the economy and the policies followed by the central bank. On the latter, the central bank's policies can be classified broadly under the headings of money supply targeting or of interest rate targeting. The former leads to the exogenous specification of the money supply. The latter leads to the exogenous specification of the interest rate. The approach used in the remainder of this chapter and this book, except for Chapter 6, is based on the assumption of interest rate targeting by the central bank, and differs from that in most other macroeconomics textbooks, which assume money supply targeting. For completeness, the latter is presented in Chapter 6.

---

[14] Note that an increase in r will reduce investment, which also produces a movement up along the IS curve.

[15] Unless purchasing power parity holds, in which case ρ will depreciate in proportion to the increase P and net exports will not change.

5.4 The Formulation of Monetary Policy

In most modern and financially developed economies, the central bank has been allocated the role of determining monetary policy. The two main options of the central bank in the formulation of monetary policy are to:

1. determine the underlying nominal or real macroeconomic interest rate in the economy; and
2. determine the supply of money (or of another monetary aggregate).

Box 5.2: Money Supply, the Stock of Money and Their Relationship to the Interest Rate

Figure 5.2 shows the case of a money stock that is exogenously determined by the central bank at a given level M_0. In this case, the money supply curve is a vertical line. The exogenously determined money stock M_0 determines the equilibrium interest rate r_0^* along the money demand curve.

Suppose the following can be validly assumed.

- Stable money demand and supply functions (i.e., these functions do not shift).
- The existence only of the indirect transmission mechanism of money supply changes on national income (and the absence of the direct transmission mechanism).[16]
- An efficient money market — so that there are no lags in the impact of changes in the monetary base on the interest rate.[17]

Under these assumptions, it does not matter whether the central bank sets the interest rate or the monetary base supplied to the economy. If these conditions are not met, then it does matter which policy is adopted. In the real world, the economy's overall response occurs through three sequential lags:

1. from the change in the monetary base to the change in the money supply and thence to the change in the interest rate,
2. from the change in the interest rate to the change in investment, and
3. from the change in investment to the change in nominal national expenditures and income.

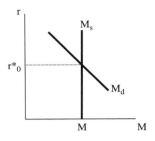

Figure 5.2.

---

[16]The indirect transmission operates through the impact of money supply changes on interest rates and, through them, on investment and aggregate demand. The direct transmission mechanism operates through the recipients of the increase in the money supply spending it directly on commodities, which increases aggregate demand.

[17]Note that the definition of an efficient market includes the absence of a lag in its reaching equilibrium, but does not exclude lags in the interaction from one market to another or from one variable to another.

Box 5.2: (*Continued*)

Each of these lags is of significant duration. Our concern here is with the central bank's choice between changing the monetary base versus changing the interest rate. In general, there is a significant lag between monetary base changes and its consequent interest rate changes. Therefore, the impact of a change in monetary policy on the economy would be faster if the central bank was to directly alter the interest rate than if it was to initiate the change by altering the monetary base. Consequently, most central banks tend to set interest rates and support them through monetary base changes, rather than set the monetary base and let the market determine the interest rate after some lag. An additional reason for using the interest rate as the monetary policy instrument becomes relevant if the money demand function is volatile and unpredictable, which it has proved to be in many developed economies for the past several decades. Therefore, the reasons for the central bank's preference for setting the interest rate rather than manipulating the money supply are:

- lags in the impact of changes in the money supply on the interest rate,
- instability of the money demand curve, and
- instability of the multiplier from the monetary base to the money supply, which makes the control of the money supply through the monetary base unpredictable.

The reasons for the central bank to manipulate the money supply rather than the interest rate are:

- Fragmented financial markets, several or all of which may not follow the lead of the central bank's change in the interest rate.
- Inability of changes in the interest rate to affect investment and consumer durable expenditures, because these are mainly financed out of the investor's own saving or their black money hoards.

In financially developed economies without fragmented financial markets and without significant amounts of black money, the central bank is better able to change aggregate demand, and to do so faster, by targeting the interest rate rather than the money supply. Therefore, the central banks of the USA, the UK, and Canada, as well as of many other countries, follow interest rate targeting. However, the standard macroeconomic analysis of aggregate demand in many textbooks is based on an exogenous money supply, so that it is based on the IS-LM analysis presented in Chapter 6.

5.4.1 Monetary policy through interest rate targeting

As Chapter 2 pointed out, the economy has a variety of nominal interest rates. The interest rate on a financial asset depends on many factors, including the risk of capital loss in holding it and, if it is a bond, its term to maturity. These interest rates tend to be related to each other, so that economists focus on an *underlying interest rate*, changes in which trigger corresponding changes in all other interest rates. As an approximation, this underlying interest rate is often taken to be the return on riskless bonds with short maturity, such as the 'T-bill rate' on three-month Treasury bills issued by the government. Financially developed economies normally also possess an interest rate on overnight loans (i.e., loans from late one day to the next day) among its major financial institutions, usually its commercial banks. In Canada and Britain, this rate is called the *overnight lending rate*, but is called the *federal funds rate* in the USA. Both the T-bill and the overnight lending rates are market/nominal rates.

The central bank can bring about changes in the interest rates by trading (i.e., open market operations) in the relevant financial market, which induces changes in the demand or supply in these markets. For example, its purchase of T-bills (i.e., Treasury bills, which are short-term government bonds) will push up the demand for them, increase their price and lower the interest yield on them. Conversely, its sale of T-bills will reduce the demand for them, reduce their price and raise the interest yield on them. Similarly, if the central bank wants to manipulate the overnight loan rate, it can change the demand for or supply of loanable funds in the market for overnight loans, and thereby alter the overnight loan rate.

In financially developed economies, financial markets are closely related and commercial banks are a major player in them, so that a change in any one interest rate — either in the cost of obtaining funds from the central bank (i.e., in the bank/discount rate) or in the overnight loans market (i.e., in the overnight loan rate) or in the yield on their assets (e.g., in the T-bill rate) — tends to trigger corresponding changes in the interest rates in all other markets. The central bank can therefore choose the interest rate that it wants to directly manipulate, while leaving it to the markets to adjust other interest rates in a more or less synchronous manner.

In some countries, the central bank is willing to lend to domestic commercial banks for short periods. The interest rate on such loans is called the *bank rate* (in Canada and the UK) or the *discount rate* (in the USA). Since the central bank is the lender in this market, it sets the interest rate that it charges.

In Canada, the Bank of Canada sets a range for the overnight loan rate, as well as specifying that the bank rate would be the maximum of the range it sets for the overnight loan rate. In the USA, the Federal Reserve System ensures its desired federal funds rate by trading in the market for overnight loans.

The value of the interest rate desired by the central bank is called its *target rate*. While central banks actually set nominal interest rates, their objective in doing so is to set the real interest rate. Our analysis will therefore assume that the target interest rate is the real one.

5.4.2 Rules versus discretion in setting the target interest rate

The central bank can determine its choice of the target rate by:

- Its evaluation of the current and emerging economic conditions or on some other basis without a pre-set rule. Such a policy is called a *discretionary policy*.
- A real *interest rate rule*. Examples of interest rate rules are:

i. Pursue a *simple rule* for determining the target real interest rate. The simplest form of such a rule occurs if the central bank maintains the target real interest rate at a constant level r_0 (while retaining the right to vary it when it so wishes).[18] According to this rule:

$$r_t^T = r_0. \tag{18}$$

Note that a *simple policy rule* does not have a feedback from the performance of the economy to automatically change the interest rate target r^T.

ii. Pursue a *feedback rule* for determining the target interest rate r^T. A feedback rule is one in which the feedback from the state of the economy (e.g., its inflation rate or unemployment, etc.) is allowed to change the target interest rate. An example of a feedback rule is provided by the popular *Taylor rule*. According to this rule, the central bank sets the real interest rate according to:

$$r_t^T = r_0 + \alpha(y_t - y^f) + \beta(\pi_t - \pi^T) \qquad \alpha, \beta > 0, \tag{19}$$

---

[18]In practice, central banks set the nominal interest rate R, not the real interest rate r. However, their objective in setting R is to aim at its corresponding value of r.

where r^T is the real interest rate target, y is real output, y^f is full-employment output, π is the actual inflation rate, π^T is the inflation rate desired by the central bank and the subscript t refers to period t. π^T is called the *target inflation rate*. Similarly, y^f is the *target output level*. $(y_t - y^f)$ is (minus of) the output gap. Under this rule, the central bank would increase its target interest rate if actual output (or the demand for it) was too high or if inflation was too high, relative to their long run or desired levels. The Taylor rule is a feedback rule according to which changes in the actual performance of the economy change the interest rate target: under this rule, the target interest rate is automatically decreased if output is below its full-employment level and raised if inflation becomes greater than the target rate.

This chapter restricts the analysis of interest rate targeting and its impact on the economy to the case of the simple policy rule specified in Equation (18), which is that the central bank exogenously determines the *real* interest rate that it sets for the economy. That is, our assumption will be that $r = r_0^T$, where the superscript T stands for the 'central bank target'.

5.4.3 Diagrammatic depiction of the interest rate target

The assumption made above on monetary policy is that the central bank successfully targets/sets the economy's real interest rate r at r_0. That is, under this simple interest rate targeting:

$$r = r_0^T. \tag{20}$$

Plotting this interest rate in the (r, y) space of the IS diagram, we have a horizontal line at the target real interest rate. This is shown in Figure 5.3a by the 'interest rate target' curve labeled IRT.[19]

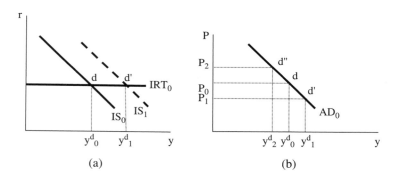

Figure 5.3.

5.5 The Determination of Aggregate Demand under Interest Rate Targeting

The equation for the aggregate demand for commodities — known as the aggregate demand (AD) equation — is obtained jointly from the IS equation for the commodity market and the monetary policy equation determining the interest rate. Our model now becomes:

---

[19]Note that the IRT curve replaces the usual LM curve (see Chapter 6), which is based on the assumption that the central bank targets/sets the money supply. The central bank can target/set either the interest rate or the money supply, but not both, so that the LM curve is not appropriate under interest rate targeting.

The IS equation:

$$y = \alpha[\{c_0 - c_y t_0 + i_0 - i_r r + g + x_{c0} - x_{c\rho}\rho^r\} + (1/\rho^r) \cdot \{-z_{c0} + z_{cy} t_0 - z_{c\rho}\rho^r\}], \tag{21}$$

where the symbol α stands for the (autonomous investment) multiplier and has the meaning:

$$\alpha = \left(\frac{1}{1 - c_y + c_y t_y + \frac{1}{\rho^r} z_{cy}(1 - t_y)}\right) > 0.$$

The monetary policy equation:

$$r = r_0^T. \tag{22}$$

Substitution of Equation (22) into (21) yields the *AD equation*, where y has been replaced by y^d to emphasize that this equation specifies the aggregate demand for commodities. This AD equation is:

$$y^d = \alpha[\{c_0 - c_y t_0 + i_0 - i_r r_0^T + g + x_{c0} - x_{c\rho}\rho^r\} + (1/\rho^r) \cdot \{-z_{c0} + z_{cy} t_0 - z_{c\rho}\rho^r\}]. \tag{23}$$

In this equation, the real exchange rate ρ^r equals $\rho P/P^F$, so that aggregate demand is a function of the price level, just as in a demand equation in microeconomic analysis. Further, aggregate demand y^d is likely to be negatively related to the price level P. This AD equation differs from the IS equation since the interest rate has been replaced by the exogenous target interest rate set by the central bank, so that in the AD equation, y^d is not a function of the interest rate.

5.5.1 Diagrammatic derivation of the AD curve

Aggregate demand in the economy is given by the intersection of the IS and IRT curves. This determination is shown in Figure 5.3a. The intersection of the IS curve and the given interest rate determines the level of the aggregate demand for domestic commodities. This level is shown as y^d. Further, at the given interest rate, a rightward shift of the IS curve because of increases in investment, government expenditures, exports, and the other reasons mentioned above will increase aggregate demand. A cut by the central bank in the real interest rate will also increase aggregate demand.

We concluded above that, under flexible exchange rates, a decrease in P causes a rightward shift of the IS curve. This shift in the IS curve, for a given target interest rate, increases aggregate demand, as shown in Figure 5.3a by the shift of the IS curve from IS_0 to IS_1, with a consequent increase in demand from y_0^d to y_1^d. Conversely, an increase in P causes a leftward shift of the IS curve, which decreases aggregate demand. Therefore, the aggregate demand curve AD in Figure 5.3b is downward sloping.

The reason for the downward slope of the AD curve under interest rate targeting in the open economy is that an increase in the domestic price level makes domestic commodities more expensive relative to foreign ones, so that foreign commodities are substituted for domestic ones in consumption. Consequently, the demand for domestic commodities falls. Therefore, as P rises, y^d decreases. Conversely, if P falls, y^d increases. This is shown by the downward sloping AD curve in Figure 5.3b.

Note that the open economy IS and AD curves incorporate within them the effects of changes in y and r on the nominal exchange rate ρ and through it on exports and imports. Note also that an increase in P (or decrease in P^F) shifts the IS curve to the left while a decrease in P (or increase in P^F) shifts it to the right. However, since P is on the vertical axis of the AD diagram, the changes in P do not shift the AD curve.

5.5.2 The downward slope of the AD curve in the open economy under an exogenous interest rate target: a reiteration

The open economy demand curve is downward sloping. To establish this for the open economy, suppose that the domestic price level rises, while the foreign price level and the nominal exchange rate held constant under the *ceteris paribus* clause. The price level increase raises the real exchange rate, which equals $\rho P/P^f$. This increase in the real exchange rate makes domestic goods more expensive relative to foreign ones. The substitution effect increases the demand for imported goods and decreases net exports,[20] which shifts the IS curve to the left, thereby decreasing aggregate demand at the given IRT. Hence, a rise in P reduces y^d. Conversely, a fall in P would increase y^d. Hence, the AD curve, which plots y^d against P, has a negative slope in the (P, y) Figure 5.3b.

5.6 The Policy Multipliers for the Open Economy Aggregate Demand

The policy multipliers measure the impact of changes in the exogenous policy variables on aggregate demand in the economy. The exogenous policy variables in our model are the fiscal ones of g, t_0, and t_y, while the monetary policy one is r_0^T. The more significant multipliers are the investment ones, the fiscal ones, and the monetary policy (target interest rate) ones. To derive these multipliers, we start with the simplified form of the AD equation, which was:

$$y^d = \alpha[\{c_0 - c_y t_0 + i_0 - i_r r + g + x_{c0} - x_{c\rho}\rho^r\} + (1/\rho^r) \cdot \{-z_{c0} + z_{cy} t_0 - z_{c\rho}\rho^r\}], \qquad (24)$$

where the symbol α stands for the (autonomous investment) multiplier and has the meaning:

$$\alpha = \left(\frac{1}{1 - c_y + c_y t_y + \frac{1}{\rho^r} z_{cy}(1 - t_y)}\right) > 0.$$

All of the elements of α are parameters, so that α can be treated as a constant whenever one of the variables of the model changes. This AD equation is almost the same as the open economy IS equation, so that its investment and fiscal multipliers are identical to the ones derived from the IS equation alone. The following subsections reiterate these briefly.

5.6.1 The impact of investment fluctuations on aggregate demand: the investment multiplier

The most volatile component of expenditures is investment, so that we want to capture the impact of shifts in it on aggregate demand. To do so, note that if only autonomous investment changes:

$$\Delta y^d = \alpha \Delta i_0 \Rightarrow \partial y^d / \partial i_0 = \alpha.$$

---

[20]This decrease in net exports would cause the nominal exchange rate to depreciate but not by enough to cancel out the initial appreciation of the real exchange rate. Further, under perfect capital mobility, capital flows would not change since the domestic and foreign interest rates would not have changed.

Therefore, α also gives the value of the autonomous investment multiplier for aggregate demand. This multiplier is identical with that derived for the commodity market alone. Note that the usual value of α is greater than unity.

5.6.2 The impact of fiscal policy on aggregate demand: the fiscal multipliers

The impact of changes in government expenditure on aggregate demand is specified by its multiplier. To derive this multiplier, assume that the government increases its autonomous expenditures by Δg, while keeping its other fiscal policy variables t_0 and t_1 constant. In this case:

$$\Delta y^d = \alpha \Delta g \Rightarrow \partial y^d / \partial g = \alpha.$$

Therefore, α is the value of the government expenditures multiplier for aggregate demand. This multiplier is identical with that derived for the open economy IS analysis alone. As the usual value of α is greater than unity, an increase in government expenditures increases aggregate demand by more than the increase in government expenditures.

Similarly, as shown in Chapter 4, the multiplier for the impact of an increase in autonomous taxes is given by:

$$\partial y^d / \partial t_0 = -c_y \alpha.$$

That is, an increase in taxes reduces aggregate demand and a decrease in taxes increases aggregate demand.

5.6.3 The impact of monetary policy on aggregate demand: the target rate multiplier

Under an interest rate target, the monetary policy multiplier for aggregate demand is given by $\partial y^d / \partial r$, which is the change in aggregate demand for a small increase in the interest rate. The value of this multiplier is given by:

$$\partial y^d / \partial r = -i_r \alpha.$$

Therefore, an increase in the target interest rate reduces aggregate demand in the economy. This effect depends on the impact $(-i_r)$ of the increase in the interest rate on investment and then on aggregate demand, so that the target rate multiplier depends on the value of i_r, which is the interest sensitivity of investment. Conversely, a reduction in the target interest rate increases aggregate demand in the economy.

5.6.4 The distribution of incomes, consumption patterns, and the size of the multiplier

The distribution of income in the population affects the consumption patterns, the average propensity to consume and the size of the multiplier. In particular, the marginal propensity to consume imported goods reduces the size of the multiplier. In developing countries, the rich usually have a much higher marginal propensity to import than the lower income groups. Therefore, if the initial increase in incomes accrues mainly to the rich, the multiplier will be smaller than if it enters the economy as an addition to the incomes of the poor. This point is relevant to the impact of government expenditures and transfers on the economy. Assuming all other things (including the saving propensity) being the same, income transfers to lower income groups, whose consumption is usually more of domestic goods and services than that of the rich, will have a higher multiplier and, therefore, a larger impact on aggregate demand than if the transfers were made to higher income groups. Further, the poor tend to have a higher marginal propensity to consume than the rich, which would further increase the size of the multiplier when the initial income goes mainly to the poor.

5.6.5 The impact of exports on domestic aggregate demand

The preceding model of aggregate demand shows that an increase in exports increases aggregate demand by a multiple. Conversely, a decrease in exports decreases aggregate demand. Such changes in aggregate demand tend to produce changes in the economy's output, at least for some time, so that fluctuations in exports become a major source of the transmission of business cycles across countries. This point is discussed further in Chapter 16 on business cycles.

5.6.6 The lag in the impact of changes in the interest rate target

Since investment depends negatively on the real interest rate, a reduction in the target real interest rate increases investment, which increases aggregate demand through the multiplier. In practice, this process takes quite some time. First, following the reduction by the central bank in the target rate, the financial markets act to reduce the various interest rates. Second, these reductions in the different interest rates induce increases in the related types of investment. Third, the multipliers related to the increases in the different types of investment have to work. As shown in Chapter 4, the multipliers take time to work through their various stages. Therefore, it is likely that the full expansionary impact of an interest rate reduction would take several quarters. Some estimates of this impact place it at six or more quarters, though some part of the impact may start to occur much earlier.

5.7 Diagrammatic Analysis of Fiscal and Monetary Policies

For both the closed and the open economy, an expansionary fiscal policy shifts the IS curve to the right. This is shown in Figure 5.4a by the shift of the IS curve from IS_0 to IS_1. At the given interest rate target r_0^T, aggregate demand increases from y_0^d to y_1^d. Conversely, a contractionary fiscal policy shifts the IS curve to the left and, at the given interest target rate r_0^T, reduces aggregate demand.

As shown in Figure 5.4b, an expansionary monetary policy in the form of a reduction in the interest rate target from r_0^T to r_1^T, shifts the IRT line downwards and increases aggregate demand from y_0^d to y_1^d. Conversely,

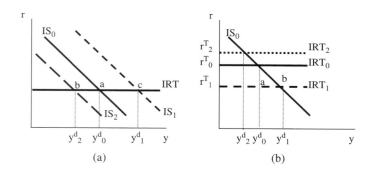

Figure 5.4.

a contractionary monetary policy in the form of an increase in the target interest rate target from r_0^T to r_2^T, shifts the IRT line upwards and decreases aggregate demand from y_0^d to y_2^d.

5.8 The IS, IRT Curves and the Determination of Output: A Caveat

Note that the intersection of the IS and IRT curves determines the aggregate demand for commodities and determines the AD function/curve used in Chapter 1. Their intersection does *not* determine the aggregate quantity of commodities that will be produced in the economy. This requires knowledge of both the demand and the supply functions/curves of commodities. Chapter 1 had shown this by incorporating both aggregate demand and supply in the AD-AS diagram.

Because the intersection of the IS and IRT curves only determines the demand for commodities but not output (i.e., the quantity produced), it is strictly inappropriate to interpret y on the horizontal axis of the IS-IRT diagram — as well as the AD-AS one — as the output (i.e., the quantity produced) of commodities. The symbol y on the horizontal section of both the IS-IRT and the AD-AS diagrams is to be interpreted as the '*aggregate quantity of commodities*', not as output (i.e., *the quantity produced*). This usage means that the intersection of the IS and IRT specifies the quantity demanded of commodities — not the output of the economy.

5.9 But What about the Monetary Sector and Its Money Demand and Supply Functions?

We have so far analyzed the determination of the interest rate, inflation, and output without any reference to the money market, which encompasses the demand and supply of money and the equilibrium between them. These are peripheral to the determination of aggregate demand under a successful interest rate targeting policy, since, as the preceding analysis has shown, knowledge of their values is not needed for determining aggregate demand.

However, for the successful achievement of the interest rate target, the central bank does need to know the money demand function and, thereby, to know the amount of money supply that it has to ensure for the economy. While the proper treatment of this topic is left to Chapter 6 on the money and other financial markets, we present below a limited part of the relevant analysis.

5.9.1 The demand for money

Theoretical and empirical studies show that the demand for *real* balances can be taken to be specified as:

m^d = transactions demand for real balances + portfolio demand for real balances. The transactions demand is the demand for money to finance individuals' purchases/expenditures. Since it is used to finance expenditures, which in equilibrium, equals national income, we assume that the transactions demand equals $m_y y$.

The portfolio demand for money is a component of the individual's portfolio. If we designate the nominal value of this portfolio by FW and assume that the portfolio includes only money and bonds (including stocks), the portfolio demand for money is given by:

portfolio demand for real balances

= real value of financial wealth − real value of the demand for bonds.

The real demand for bonds b^d will increase with their nominal return, which is the nominal interest rate R. Therefore, $b^d = f(R)$. We simplify by writing this demand function as $b^d = m_R R$, where $m_R \geq 0$. Hence, the portfolio demand for real (money) balances will equal $(FW/P - m_R R)$.

Therefore, the demand for real balances is given by:

$$m^d = m_y y + [FW/P - m_R R] \quad m_y > 0, \quad 0 \leq m_R \leq \infty, \tag{25}$$

where R is the nominal interest rate, which is related to the real one by the Fisher equation,[21] presented in Chapter 2. The preceding equation is usually simplified in short-run macroeconomic models to:

$$m^d = m_y y - m_R R \quad m_y > 0, \quad 0 \leq m_R \leq \infty, \tag{26}$$

where FW/P has been dropped from the equation. Although this simplification is traditional and almost universal in macroeconomic models, it does have some consequences for macroeconomic analysis when the rate of change of the nominal value of financial wealth is different from that of the commodity price level, as it usually is. This situation often occurs since bond and stock markets usually go up by more or less than commodity prices. Ignoring this issue so as to adhere to the traditional treatment of the money demand function, the demand function will be taken to be as specified by Eq. (26).

For the money demand function (26), the component of money demand represented by $m_y y$ is the *transactions demand for money* and the component of money demand represented by $(-m_R R)$ or, more accurately, by $(FW/P - m_R R)$,[22] is the *speculative or portfolio demand for money*. Note that these designations are just meant to be simplified ones for facilitating discussion of the reasons for money demand. The component $(-m_R R)$ or $(FW/P - m_R R)$ can also be referred to as the interest-sensitive component of money demand.

Figure 5.5 shows the demand curve for money by m^d. Note that the nominal interest rate R is on the vertical axis and the demand for real balances m^d is on the horizontal one. Since R is on one of the axes, changes in R imply movements along the curve. An increase in R reduces the amount of money demanded, so that there is a movement up along the existing m^d curve: a rise in R from R_0 to R_1 means going from the point a to the point b along this curve. However, income is not on one of the axes, so that for a given rate of interest R_0, an increase in income increases transactions demand and shifts the m^d curve toward the right from m_0^d to m_1^d. Correspondingly, a decrease in income reduces transactions demand and shifts the money demand curve left from m_0^d to m_2^d.

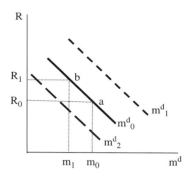

Figure 5.5.

---

[21]The Fisher equation is $R = r + \pi^e$ (see Chapter 2).
[22]If $m_R > 0$, an increase in the nominal interest rate will *decrease* the demand for money balances.

5.9.2 Ensuring equilibrium in the money market under an interest rate target and the determination of the money supply

Equilibrium in the money market requires that nominal money demand (Pm^d) equal the nominal money supply M^S. That is, under interest rate targeting, equilibrium requires that the money supply be given by:

$$M^s = Pm^d = P(m_y y^d + FW/P - m_R R). \tag{27}$$

We had assumed earlier in this chapter that monetary policy sets the real interest rate r. By the Fisher equation, $R = r + \pi^e$. With r set by monetary policy and π^e specified by the public's expectations, the value of R can be calculated. Plugging this value, as well as the value of y^d from our earlier IS analysis, into the above equation yields the nominal value of the money demand and the *required* amount of the money supply. For successful targeting of the interest rate, the central bank has to ensure the money supply given by the preceding equation.

5.10 Managing Aggregate Demand in the Open Economy: Monetary and Fiscal Policies under Flexible Exchange Rates

5.10.1 The effectiveness of fiscal policy for the open economy under interest rate targeting

Assume that the country in question has flexible exchange rates, with the initial general equilibrium shown in Figure 5.6a by the point a. Now suppose that an expansionary fiscal policy (i.e., an increase in government expenditures or decrease in tax revenues, resulting in a fiscal deficit) is pursued. Such a policy shifts the IS curve to the right from IS_0 to IS_1. This raises income from y_0 to y_1.

The intuitive sequence of effects is as follows. The expansionary fiscal policy increases income, which increases commodity imports, so that the supply of domestic dollars increases in the foreign exchange market. To restore equilibrium in the foreign exchange market, the exchange rate depreciates so that domestic products become relatively cheaper than foreign ones. This causes exports to rise and imports to fall, which further increases aggregate demand. Hence, there are two effects of the fiscal deficit:

1. A direct expansionary effect on aggregate demand and national income through the fiscal multiplier.

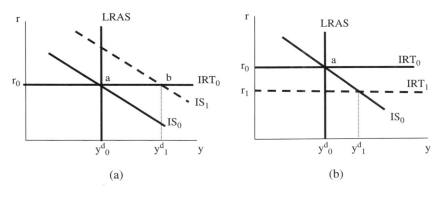

(a)   (b)

Figure 5.6.

2. An indirect expansionary effect on aggregate demand through the increase in net exports, which results from the fall in the exchange rate (which is itself due to the increase in imports resulting from the increase in income in the first point).

Both of these effects are incorporated in the slope and shift of the IS curve. Note that the fiscal expansion by shifting the IS curve to the right increases aggregate demand. This is shown by the intersection of the new IS curve IS_1 with the IRT curve in Figure 5.6a. Note that under interest rate targeting, the interest rate does not change since it has been exogenously set by the central bank. With domestic and foreign interest rates unchanged, there is no change in capital flows,[23] so that the impact of changes in capital flows on the exchange rate does not have to be taken into account. Therefore, even under a high degree of capital mobility, *the final effect of the fiscal expansion is to increase aggregate demand*. Hence, in the flexible exchange rate case with IRT, fiscal policy is a powerful tool for changing aggregate demand.

5.10.2 The effectiveness of monetary policy for the open economy under interest rate targeting

Now consider the impact under flexible exchange rates of an expansionary monetary policy, which in our context is a reduction in the target interest rate. This is shown in Figure 5.6b by the downwards shift of the IRT curve from IRT_0 to IRT_1. This policy pushes aggregate demand along the IS curve from y_0 to y_1.

The intuitive sequence of effects is as follow. As the interest rate falls, investment rises. The increase in domestic incomes (due to the rise in investment) increases imports and decreases net exports, which reduces the inflows of foreign exchange, so that the exchange rate falls. The lower interest rate also reduces capital inflows, thereby contributing to the depreciation of the exchange rate.[24] The overall depreciation makes domestic goods relatively cheaper compared with foreign ones, so that under the assumption of elastic net exports, imports fall and exports rise, which further increases domestic expenditures and income. All of these effects are incorporated in the final shape of the IS curve.

Therefore, under flexible exchange rates and elastic net exports, the effect of an expansionary monetary policy has two components. These are:

1. A direct expansionary effect on aggregate demand that occurs through an increase in investment at the lower interest rate and increases aggregate demand and income in the economy.
2. An indirect expansionary effect on aggregate demand brought about by an increase in net exports. This increase is brought about by the fall in the exchange rate, which itself occurs due to the rise in the imports of commodities (which themselves result from the higher income in the first point), as well as the fall in the net capital inflows due to the lower domestic interest rate.

Both of these effects are incorporated in the slopes and shifts of the IS and AD curves. Therefore, under flexible exchange rates, monetary policy is effective in increasing aggregate demand.

Hence, both monetary and fiscal policies are effective in changing aggregate demand, though their degree of effectiveness would differ. In both cases, expansionary policies increase aggregate demand, while contractionary policies decrease aggregate demand.

---

[23]To deal with the discrepancy between the market rates indicated by the intersection of the IS and *LRAS* curves and the interest rate set by the central bank, the central bank has to increase the money supply to maintain equilibrium in the domestic money and bond markets.

[24]This effect will be stronger in economies with greater capital mobility.

5.10.3 Limitations on the effectiveness of a policy of interest rate targeting

An expansionary monetary policy does not have an impact on aggregate demand if:

- If investment does not respond to changes in the interest rate, i.e., if $\partial i/\partial r = 0$. This case can occur if aggregate demand has fallen below full capacity production levels. For example, in a depreciation (such as that of the 1930s) or a deep recession (2007–2008), firms have excess capacity, so that they do not wish to increase their capital stock even if the cost of borrowing funds for investment falls. Note that these are precisely the conditions in which there is an urgent need to boost aggregate demand, but monetary policy is unable to do so to a significant extent.
- If changes in the monetary base will not increase the money supply, the central bank cannot bring about increases in the money supply. This can occur if banks become reluctant to lend to the public or buy more bonds, even when their reserves are increased, because the riskiness of bonds and loans has increased substantially or banks have become very risk averse. Such a situation occurred in the USA during the credit crises/crunch of 2007–2009 (see Chapter 16).
- Increases in the money supply do not lower interest rates, as in the liquidity trap (discussed in Chapter 6), or if the central bank cannot further reduce its interest rates, as for example if they have already been reduced to virtually zero.

All three cases are very likely in a depression or a deep recession, especially one due to a collapse of the financial system and markets. However, these are precisely the conditions under which policy needs to raise aggregate demand from its depressed level. During such conditions, many economists are doubtful of the success of expansionary monetary policies in increasing aggregate demand, and recommend the use of expansionary fiscal policies.

5.11 Internal Versus External Balance

Assuming that the net exports have an elasticity greater than unity (see Chapter 2 later for the analysis related to this elasticity), exchange rate flexibility provides the economy with the very useful equilibrating mechanism of changes in the nominal exchange rate brought about by market forces for handling the balance of payments deficits/surpluses. Together, exchange rate flexibility and domestic price flexibility eliminate the need for monetary and fiscal policies to return the economy to general equilibrium and full employment — *as long as* the authorities are willing to give the economy *enough* time to make its own adjustments to equilibrium *and* are willing to accommodate the possible reserve losses during the adjustment period. If they do pursue appropriate monetary and fiscal policies, the preceding analysis implies that expansionary monetary and fiscal policies increase aggregate demand, while contractionary monetary and fiscal policies decrease aggregate demand.

Internal balance is defined as the equality of domestic aggregate demand and domestic full-employment output, while *external balance* is defined as the equality of the demand and supply of foreign exchange. Flexible exchange rates maintain the latter equality, thereby freeing monetary policy to focus on maintaining the internal balance of the economy. By comparison, fixed exchange rates compel the use of monetary policy, especially in setting interest rates, to the maintenance of external balance, so that monetary policy is then much less able to maintain internal balance.

Extended Analysis Box 5.3: The Mundell–Fleming Model of the Open Economy

The Mundell–Fleming model of the open economy is based on the contributions of Robert Mundell and Marcus Fleming in the 1960s. It presented the analyses of monetary and fiscal policies for the open economy under the assumptions of (a) the *central bank targets the money supply*, so that it is exogenous, (b) elastic net exports, and (c) perfect capital mobility. Mundell and Fleming showed that, under *flexible* exchange rates, monetary policy is effective in changing aggregate *demand* while fiscal policy is not. Further, if it is assumed that the economy has (d) a fixed price level but variable output in responding to changes in aggregate demand, such changes will lead to corresponding changes in real output.

Parts of the Mundell–Fleming model are not relevant to our analysis under IRT because of their assumption that the central bank targets the money supply. For this assumption of money supply targeting, Mundell and Fleming had shown that for small open economies with *flexible* exchange rates, monetary policy would be effective in changing aggregate demand and output while fiscal policy would be ineffective.[25] This result does not hold in our model: as shown above, both monetary and fiscal policies are effective in changing aggregate demand.

Another distinctive part of the Mundell–Fleming model was its assumption that the price level is constant in the short run. This assumption implies a horizontal aggregate supply curve for commodities (see the sticky price model in Chapter 8). Our analysis in Chapters 7 to 9 will allow the possibility of three cases: a vertical LRAS curve for the long run, a positively sloped SRAS curve for the short-run equilibrium, and a horizontal supply curve under deficient demand.

While the Mundell–Fleming model is no longer as important to modern macroeconomic modeling as in earlier periods, it did make a considerable contribution to the development of the open economy analysis.

5.12 Conclusions

The adaptations of the closed economy model to the open economy introduced additional complexity into the analysis of the commodity market.

- A new good, foreign exchange, was brought into the macroeconomic model. Its 'price' which is the foreign exchange rate, could be flexible and determined by the supply and demand in the foreign exchange market, or managed by the central bank or the government or be fixed/pegged by them.

- For the open economy, the analysis of the IS curve was modified to include exports and imports of commodities.

- Under interest rate targeting by the central bank, expansionary monetary and fiscal policies are both effective in increasing aggregate demand. Conversely, contractionary monetary and fiscal policies are both effective in decreasing aggregate demand.

- An aspect of the changes in the intercountry flows in recent decades has been the increasing dominance of financial capital flows over the values of the net exports of countries. The former are more volatile and more susceptible to speculative forces than the latter. The dominance of the magnitudes of capital flows over net

---

[25]For the *fixed* exchange rate case and an *exogenous* money supply, the Mundell–Fleming model showed that monetary policy is ineffective in changing aggregate demand — and, therefore, ineffective in changing output under the horizontal supply curve assumption — while fiscal policy is effective.

commodity flows implies that, under flexible exchange rates, the exchange rate movements will be mainly determined, at least in the short term, by the interest rate differences among countries.

KEY CONCEPTS

Small open economy

Balance of payments curve

Three gaps: saving gap, fiscal gap, and external gap

The open economy commodity market equilibrium condition

The open economy IS curve

The interest rate as the operating monetary policy target of the central bank

Simple monetary policy rule

Feedback monetary policy

Taylor rule

IRT curve

Aggregate demand curve and its determination by the IS curve and the IRT curve

Effectiveness of monetary and fiscal policies in changing aggregate demand

Limitations on the success of expansionary monetary policies, and

Internal and external balance.

SUMMARY OF CRITICAL CONCLUSIONS

- A fiscal deficit crowds out some domestic investment and also induces a balance of trade deficit.
- The open economy aggregate demand curve has a negative slope (if the real exchange can differ from unity).
- Under interest rate targeting, the IS and the IRT curves determine aggregate demand.
- Under interest rate targeting by the central bank, both monetary and fiscal policies are effective in changing aggregate demand. Expansionary (contractionary) monetary and fiscal policies increase (decrease) aggregate demand.
- The aggregate demand (AD) curve neither shows the supply of commodities nor determines the quantity of commodities that will be produced or the price level at which they will be sold.

REVIEW AND DISCUSSION QUESTIONS

1. Define a 'small open economy'. Under this definition, is your country a small open economy? Is the USA a small open economy? Explain your answer.
2. What are the differences between the IS curves for the open and closed economy cases with respect to changes in the nominal exchange rate?
3. Under flexible exchange rates, assuming that net exports are elastic, what happens to the IS curve in each of the following cases:
   (a) foreign output rises,
   (b) domestic output rises, and
   (c) foreign interest rate rises.
4. Under flexible exchange rates, assuming that net exports are elastic, what happens to the IS curve in each of the following cases:
   (a) the central bank raises the domestic interest rate,
   (b) foreign demand for our commodities falls, and
   (c) our residents start taking much longer holidays abroad.

5. In a model with flexible exchange rates, what are the effects of an increased (domestic) demand for foreign commodities on the IS and AD curves?

6. "Given flexible exchange rates, elastic net exports and interest rate targeting, an expansionary fiscal policy is likely to be quite ineffective in increasing the level of aggregate demand." Do you agree or disagree? Present the relevant analysis.

7. "Given flexible exchange rates, elastic net exports and interest rate targeting, an expansionary monetary policy is likely to be ineffective in increasing the level of aggregate demand." Do you agree or disagree? Present the relevant analysis.

8. Assume a small open economy with elastic net exports, a flexible exchange rate and interest rate targeting. Discuss the effects of each of the following (one-at-a-time) on domestic aggregate demand:

   (a) an increase in the foreign demand for the country's exports,
   (b) an increase in government expenditures, and
   (c) a decrease in the central bank's target real interest rate.

9. Assume a small open economy with elastic net exports, a flexible exchange rate and interest rate targeting. Discuss the effects of each of the following (one-at-a-time) on domestic aggregate demand:

   (a) an increase in the world interest rates and
   (b) an increase in 'world income'.

10. Suppose that a banking and financial crisis reduces credit to households, which limits their purchases of consumer durables, and firms, which reduces their investment. Analyze the impact of this 'drying up' of credit (also called a 'credit crunch') on aggregate demand in the economy.

11. If a credit crisis in the USA (a 'very large economy') reduces its aggregate demand and output, discuss its effects on aggregate demand in the countries (i) which export extensively to it and (ii) whose financial institutions extensively borrow from and lend to financial institutions in the USA.

12. [Optional, based on Chapters 4 and 5 together]. For the general form of the macroeconomic model used in this and the preceding chapter, what are the differences between the multiplier for the open economy and that for the closed economy?

ADVANCED AND TECHNICAL QUESTIONS

Basic Model for this chapter

$$c = 0.8y_d$$
$$t = 0.2y$$
$$i = 1000 - 50r$$
$$g = 800$$
$$x_c = 200 - 0.5\rho^r$$
$$z_c/\rho^r = 500 + 0.1y_d$$
$$m^d = 0.25y - 60R$$

[R is the nominal interest rate, r is the real one, and, by the Fisher equation,

$$R = r + \pi^e]$$
$$y^f = 1{,}000$$

$$P^F = 1$$

$$\rho = 1$$

The central bank targets the domestic *real* interest rate, so that

$$r = r^T = 0.04$$

Benchmark Fisher equation: $R = r + \pi^e$

Assumption: $\pi^e = 0$

T1. For the Basic Model of this chapter, do the following questions:

(a) Derive the IS equation. [Do not use the IS equation formula for this answer. Use step-by-step calculations. Start by calculating disposable income. Noting that x_c and z_c depend on ρ^r, calculate ρ^r in terms of P. Then use the equilibrium condition $y = e$ for your further steps.]

(b) Given $r^T = 0.04$, derive the AD equation.

(c) If exports rise by 100, what is the new aggregate demand equation?

(d) If imports rise by 100, what is new aggregate demand equation?

T2. For the given target real interest rate and assuming $\pi^e = 0$, use the equality of money supply and money demand to derive the equilibrium money supply. [Hint: the money supply should be specified in nominal terms, so that, for equilibrium in the money market, it should equal $P \cdot m^d$.]

Revised Model for This Chapter

$$c = 1000 + 0.8 y_d$$

$$t = -100 + 0.2 y$$

$$i = 1000 - 50r$$

$$g = 0$$

$$x_c = 100 - 0.5\rho^r$$

$$z_c/\rho^r = 200 + 0.1 y_d$$

$$P = 4,\ P^F = 4$$

$$\rho_0 = 0.5.$$

The central bank sets the interest rate such that $r = 0.02$.

LR output: $y^f = 2000$

T3. (a) Derive the real exchange rate for this economy.

(b) Calculate disposable income as a function of income.

(c) Derive net real exports (i.e., exports — imports in domestic real terms) as a function of income. [Hint: imports in domestic real terms equal z_c/ρ^r.]

(d) Derive the IS equation.

(e) Derive the aggregate demand for commodities (y_0^d)?

(f) Suppose that the short-run output in the economy was determined only by aggregate demand, so that actual output equaled y^d. Calculate the budget deficit at this level of output.

(g) If the output was at the long run output level, specify government expenditures, revenues, and the full-employment budget deficit.

CHAPTER 6
Aggregate Demand Under a Money Supply Operating Target: IS-LM Analysis

This chapter presents the analysis of aggregate demand for the case where the central bank is able to control the money supply and set it at an exogenous level. With an exogenous money supply, money market equilibrium implies an LM equation/curve. In this monetary policy scenario, aggregate demand in the economy is determined jointly by the IS equation/curve and the LM equation/curve.

This chapter also presents the detailed analysis of money demand and money supply.

Chapter 4 presented the analysis of the commodity market and derived the IS curve for the open economy. Chapter 5 presented the determination of aggregate demand under the assumption that the central bank sets an exogenous interest rate target and derived aggregate demand for the open economy by the IS-IRT analysis. This chapter focuses on the money market under the assumption that the central bank sets an exogenous money supply target. This assumption implies an LM equation/curve when the money market is equilibrium. Further, with an exogenous money supply, the IS and LM equations/curves have to be used to derive aggregate demand in the economy. The name given to this analysis of aggregate demand is the IS-LM analysis.

The IS-LM and the AD-AS modes of analyses *together* represent the currently dominant *technique* for the exposition of the short-run macroeconomics. Neither is by itself a paradigm or a theory; each is only a mode of exposition of the underlying theory/model. Each of them encapsulates the information assumed on the macro markets of the economy into compact relationships — or curves in diagrammatic analysis — and studies the equilibrium properties of the assumed theory/model.

6.1 Monetary Policy

In most modern, financially developed economies, the central bank has been allocated the role of determining monetary policy. Here, as explained in Chapter 5, the two main options of the central bank are:

1. determining the underlying interest rate in the economy and
2. determining the value of a monetary aggregate.

The central bank either follows an interest rate target or a monetary target as its primary instrument. If it pursues an interest rate target, it lets the markets determine the monetary aggregates; if it pursues a monetary aggregate target, it lets the markets determine the interest rates. The pursuit of both targets in an independent manner, rather than in a coordinated, supportive one will mean that the central bank will most likely not achieve either of its targets. Macroeconomic analysis for each of these alternate targets pursued as the primary one (with the other variable changed in a supportive but not independent manner) is quite different. Chapter 5 presents the analysis for interest rate targeting while this chapter does so for monetary targeting.

6.1.1 Reasons for choosing interest rate targeting over money supply targeting, or vice versa

The main reasons for the central bank to select the use of the interest rate as the operating target of monetary policy for financially developed economies are:

- longer lags in the impact of money supply changes than in that of interest rates on aggregate demand and
- the instability of money demand.

The main reasons for selecting the use of the money supply as the operating target of monetary policy over interest rates are:

- imperfect and segmented financial markets, which occur in financially underdeveloped economies, especially if there is a large informal financial sector as well as black market holdings of money,
- the instability of the IS curve, which arises because of the instability of investments, exports, and other determinants of the IS curve, and
- lags in the impact of changes in the money supply on aggregate demand are shorter than of changes in the interest rate.

Lags in the impact of money supply changes versus those of interest rate changes

In financially developed economies to which the IS model developed in the preceding two chapters applies, an increase in the money supply increases aggregate demand by first lowering interest rates, which increases investment. The first part (that from money supply changes to interest rates) of this process not only takes some time to occur but may be uncertain and difficult to predict with sufficient accuracy. This part of the process can be cut out if the central bank directly targets interest rates, which implies that targeting interest rates would have a shorter lag in its impact on aggregate demand.

Instability of money demand

Financial innovations, such as the proliferation of credit and debit cards and Internet banking, in recent years have meant that the money demand function has become unstable, so that money demand cannot be predicted accurately. Since money demand and supply together determine the impact of money supply changes on interest rates, this impact has also become uncertain and unpredictable. This uncertainty and unpredictability can be avoided if the central bank was to directly change interest rates rather than to change the money supply and let the financial markets produce changes in the interest rates.

The informal financial sector and black money in developing economies

Many countries, especially underdeveloped ones, have a large informal financial sector (i.e., other than modern-style banks) and large holdings of black money. Further, much of their production is by very small firms. The informal sector generally takes the form of lending by small moneylenders and by friends and relatives to the small business owners. Interest may not be charged on such loans but, where the loans are by moneylenders, the interest rate tends to be very high with its variation dependent on local conditions, rather on the interest rate set by the central bank or that in formal financial markets.

In the less developed economies, the formal financial sector consists mainly of banks. They do not have significant number of other financial institutions such as investment banks, investment brokers, and pension funds. Their bond and stock markets are either non-existent or relatively insignificant.

Therefore, overall for the whole economy, the interest rate plays a very limited role in decisions on investment and consumer expenditures, while the money supply plays a more important role. This implies that money supply changes are likely to have greater impact on expenditures and aggregate demand in the economy than interest rate targeting, so that the former is the more essential tool for monetary policy. However, such economies also usually possess a somewhat developed sector which has large firms that use bonds and bank loans to raise capital, so that interest rate changes can play a supportive role to money supply changes, rather than vice versa.

6.1.2 Choosing the monetary aggregate as the target variable

Monetary aggregates are the monetary base ($M0$), narrow money ($M1$), broad money ($M2$), etc. The definitions of these aggregates were given in Chapter 2. These aggregates are related to each other by the structure of the economy, so that changes induced by the central bank in one of them trigger changes in the other ones. Instead of exercising direct control over interest rates, the central bank can choose to manipulate one or more of the monetary aggregates. The central bank has various options in doing so. These are:

- The central bank sets at its discretion the desired level (or growth rate) of the money supply — and achieves it through its control over the monetary base or/over interest rates. *In this case, the money supply is said to be exogenously determined by the central bank.*
- The central bank determines the money supply according to a feedback *policy rule*. An example of such a rule is a 'Taylor-type' rule, according to which it would increase the money supply when there is unacceptably high unemployment while decreasing it if there is unacceptably high inflation.

This chapter assumes that the central bank sets the money supply as the exogenous variable. Under this assumption, the central bank maintains the money supply at a particular level.[1] Hence, our assumption for the money supply function is that:

$$M^s = M, \tag{1}$$

where M is the *exogenously determined money stock*.[2] As explained in Chapter 2, the central bank controls the money supply through changes in the monetary base. These changes are often brought about through *open market operations* (i.e., purchases and sales of bonds from the private sector). The relationship between the money supply M and the monetary base $M0$ was given in Chapter 2 as:

$$M = \alpha M0 \quad \alpha \geq 1,$$

where α is the monetary base (to money supply) multiplier. The central bank can control the monetary base $M0$ but not its multiplier α, so that it needs to know the multiplier α reasonably well to be able to control the money supply.

Figure 6.1 shows the exogenous money supply curve by the M^s curve. Note that in this case, the horizontal axis represents the nominal money supply. The money supply curve M^s shown is vertical under the assumption that it is determined exogenously and, therefore, is independent of the interest rate. That is, an increase in the nominal interest rate from R_0 to R_1 leaves the money supply unchanged at M_0. The money supply is also

---

[1] If needed, it uses its control over the interest rates as an instrument to support the desired money supply.

[2] The actual determination of the money supply by the central bank is somewhat more complicated. The central bank directly controls only the monetary base, but can manipulate it to determine the money supply.

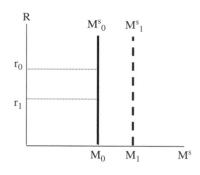

Figure 6.1

independent of output and the price level in the economy, so that the shifts in these variables will not move the M^s curve. When the money supply does not vary with the interest rate or any other variable, it is referred to as the *money stock*.

If the central bank increases the monetary base and thereby increases the money supply, it would move the money supply curve to the right from M_0^s to M_1^s in Figure 6.1.

6.2 The Demand for Money

As discussed in Chapter 2, money consists of items that serve as the medium of payments in the economy. In practice, it is represented by $M1$, $M2$, or one of the still broader monetary aggregates. The demand for money was also discussed in Chapter 5. The presentation below is an iteration and elaboration of the analysis of money demand presented in Chapter 5.

Holdings of money vary during each period. For example, the consumer may start a week with, say $100, and spend it during the week, ending the week with zero money holdings. To avoid dealing with such variations, macroeconomics focuses on the average money balances held during the week or period in question. Further, the consumer is taken to be free of money illusion and determines his demand for money in real terms, since the real value of money holdings is the proper indicator of their purchasing power in terms of commodities. Hence, the money demand variable is the real value of average money holdings over the period in question. The real value of these average money holdings is called '*real balances*'. To arrive at real balances m, divide the nominal balances M held by the public by the price level P, so that $m = M/P$.

Money balances are held by households and firms for several reasons, the most important of which are:

- Households hold money balances to facilitate their purchases of commodities; firms hold money balances to facilitate production of commodities and employment of inputs. Such balances depend on the cost of holding money. Since money holdings do not pay interest, the cost of holding them is the return foregone by not holding interest-paying bonds. The demand for money under this category is called the *transactions demand for money*. This transactions demand is a function of national income and the interest rate. It increases if income increases and decreases if the interest rate rises.
- Investors (including both households and firms) hold money balances for some time while switching among investments. This component of money demand is combined with the following speculative component of money demand.
- Both households and firms hold money balances to diversify their portfolios, so as to reduce their exposure to risk. For example, in riskier environments, when stock markets are volatile, investors increase the proportion

of their portfolio held in money, as well as of other highly liquid financial assets.[3] The money balances held for this reason depend on the return on investments and their perceived riskiness, as well as the size of the portfolio (i.e., amount of wealth). The return on investments is approximated by the interest rate on bonds, so that money demand depends on interest rates and wealth. This component of money demand is often called the *speculative demand for money*. It decreases if the interest rate rises and increases if wealth rises.

- Households hold money balances as a precaution against the possibility of sudden expenditures, e.g., due to an accident requiring sudden medical treatment, or reduction in incomes due to a job loss. This component of money demand is called the *precautionary demand for money*. It depends on income and the interest rate and is combined with the transactions demand for money in the first point above.

6.3 The Motives for Holding Money

Intuitive explanations of the demand for money often focus on the individual's *motives* for holding money. The two most important ones among these[4] are the following.

1. The transactions motive (related to income): this motive specifies the amount needed to finance expenditures on commodities through the use of money. The demand for money under this motive is called the transactions demand for money, which, when expressed in real terms, can be written as $m^{d,tr}$. When it is expressed in nominal terms, we give it the symbol $M^{d,tr}$. The real transactions demand for money is, for simplification, assumed to be a constant proportion of real expenditures/income y, so that it equals $m_y y$. Hence, $m^{d,tr} = m_y y$.
2. The portfolio/speculative motive (related to interest rates): this motive specifies the amount held in money rather than bonds and is an element of the overall desired portfolio of financial assets. It arises mainly because of the uncertainty of the actual yields on bonds, which includes any capital gains or losses arising from fluctuations in bond prices.

From the intuitive perspective, the portfolio/speculative motive for holding real balances (i.e., money in real terms) arises from the choice between money and bonds in investors' portfolios of financial assets. Let the total amount to be allocated between money and bonds be FW (financial wealth), whose real value will be FW/P, where P is the price level of commodities (not of financial assets). Since R is the return on bonds while money does not pay interest or pays much less than bonds do, bonds will become more attractive as the nominal interest rate R rises. Write the real demand for bonds as $b^d = m_R(R, \text{FW}/P)$. For simplification, let the amount invested in bonds equal $m_R R$, so that $m_R = \partial b^d/\partial R \geq 0$. The demand for money is the part of FW not held in bonds, so that it will equal $(\text{FW}_0 - m_R R)$. An increase in the interest rate R will induce investors to invest more in bonds, so that $m_R R$ will increase while the portfolio money holdings — equal to $(\text{FW}_0 - m_R R)$ — will decrease. Therefore, money balances held in the portfolio are given by:

$$m^{d,sp} = \text{FW}/P - m_R(R, \text{FW}/P) = (\text{FW}_0 - m_R R) \quad m_R \geq 0,$$

where $m^{d,sp}$ is the speculative demand for money. In this theory of the demand for money, the speculative demand is the interest sensitive component of money demand: an increase in the interest rate increases the demand for bonds and decreases the speculative demand for money.

---

[3]When the return on bonds and stocks becomes risky because of the volatility of bond and stock prices, investment brokers usually advice holding larger percentages of portfolios in money and treasury bonds, etc.

[4]Advanced macroeconomic analysis also considers two other motives for holding money balances. These are the precautionary motive and the buffer stock motive. For our analysis, these will be encompassed under the transactions motive.

Since total money demand is the sum of the transactions and speculative money demands, total money demand is given by:

$$m^d = m^{d,tr} + m^{d,sp} = m_y y + (FW/P - m_R R).$$

The transaction demand for money increases with income, while the speculative demand for money decreases when the nominal interest rate rises.

Note that the holdings of money balances cannot really be divided into separate holdings for each of the two motives or demand, so that any correspondence between the two terms on the right side of the money demand equation and motives/demand can only be rough and approximate. For ease of discussion, the traditional practice is to call the term $(m_y y)$ the transactions demand for money, and to call the term $(FW/P - m_R R)$ the speculative demand for money and associate it with the 'speculative motive' related to speculation in the financial markets. Also, note that changes in the real value of financial wealth, FW/P, will become important if the value of financial wealth (see Chapter 2 for some information on this value) does not change in proportion to changes in the price level of commodities, as it usually does not do in the real world.[5]

6.3.1 The volatility of the speculative demand for money

In the real world, the portfolio demands for money and bonds depend on the expectations of — rather than the actual — bond (and stock) yields. These yields include expected capital gains and losses, which depend on the expected future prices of bonds. These expectations are very volatile: an example of this volatility is the volatility of stock prices. An illustration of this occurs when an impending collapse in stock prices signals negative yields from holding stocks and drives up — 'a flight to liquidity' — money demand. This volatility induces volatility in the speculative demand for money, though more so in $M2$, $M3$, and broader money supply measures, than in $M1$, since $M1$ is now mainly kept for transactions purposes. The volatility in the expectations of the yields on bonds is not incorporated in the standard money demand function, so that the shifts in these expectations have to be captured through exogenous shifts in the standard money demand function. Such a shift is often referred to as a shift in '*liquidity preference*'.

6.3.2 Other reasons for the volatility of the demand for money

Recent years have witnessed considerable innovation in the types of instruments (checkable accounts, savings accounts, credit cards, debit cards, etc.) that can serve as a medium of payments and also in the technology of the payments system (e.g., the introduction and spread of automatic teller machines). These have shifted both the transactions and speculative demand for money. Overall, money demand in recent decades has proved to be unstable (i.e., shift frequently). Further, these shifts have proved to be difficult to predict.

6.4 The Standard Money Demand Function

Therefore, the total demand for real balances m^d is a function of real income y, the nominal interest rate R, and real wealth. Standard macroeconomic analysis simplifies by ignoring wealth and assumes that demand for real balances depends only on real income y and the nominal interest rate R, and that the money demand

---

[5]This will occur if the valuations of bonds and stocks in the bond and stock markets change more or less than the commodity price level.

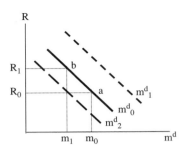

Figure 6.2

function is linear. Therefore, the *demand function for real balances* is simplified to:

$$m^d = m^d(y, R) = m_y y - m_R R. \tag{2}$$

As discussed earlier, the component of money demand represented by $m_y y$ is usually called the *transactions demand for money* and the component of money demand represented by $(-m_R R)$ [or, more accurately, by (financial wealth $- m_R R$)][6] is usually called the *speculative demand for money*. Note that these designations are just meant to be simplifications for facilitating discussion of the reasons for money demand. The component $(-m_R R)$ or, more accurately (financial wealth $- m_R R$), can also be referred to as the *interest-sensitive component of money demand*.

Figure 6.2 shows the demand curve for real money balances by m^d. Note that the nominal interest rate R is on the vertical axis and the demand for real balances m^d is on the horizontal one. Since R is on one of the axes, changes in R imply movements along the curve. An increase in R reduces money demanded, which means moving up along the existing m^d curve: a rise in R from R_0 to R_1 means going from the point a to the point b along this curve. However, income is not on one of the axes, so that, for a given rate of interest R_0, an increase in income increases transactions demand and shifts the m^d curve toward the right from m_0^d to m_1^d. Correspondingly, a decrease in income decreases transactions demand, which shifts the curve toward the left from m_0^d to m_2^d.

For financially developed economies, empirical studies indicate that, for $M1$, there are economies of scale in the transactions use of money: the *income elasticity* of real balances held in $M1$ (i.e., with respect to real income) is about 0.7, so that real balances to finance expenditures increase by 70% if real expenditures were to double. The *interest elasticity* of money demand with respect to the short-term (Treasury bill) interest rate is about 0.15, so that an increase of 1% in the interest rate decreases money demand by 0.15%.

Extended Analysis Box 6.1: Special Cases of Money Demand

There are two *theoretical extremes* of the money demand function. These are:

1. *The quantity theory case/range.* This occurs if $m_R = 0$, so that:

$$m^d = m_y y \quad 0 < m_y < \infty.$$

In this case, the demand for money does not depend on the rate of interest, which is the return on holding bonds, so that there is only a transactions demand for money. This case assumes that economic

---

[6]$(m_R R)$ is the part of the financial portfolio which is held in bonds, so that speculative money demand is obtained by subtracting this part from the size of the financial portfolio. As the interest rate rises, investors will increase their demand for bonds, so that $m_R \geq 0$. Doing so decreases their demand for money balances.

Extended Analysis Box 6.1: (*Continued*)

agents do not substitute between money and bond holdings. This is likely to be valid for economies with rudimentary financial systems in which bonds do not exist or are not accessible to most individuals, or if there is a very large informal financial sector in the economy.[7] It is not likely to be valid for the modern financially developed economies.

2. *The liquidity trap case/range.* This occurs if $m_R \rightarrow \infty$, where '$m_R \rightarrow \infty$' is pronounced as 'm_R goes to infinity'. In this case, the interest elasticity of money demand is infinite, meaning that the private sector is willing to increase its money holdings by any amount, however large, at the *existing* interest rate. This case will occur if the interest rate is too low to compensate for the costs and uncertainty of holding bonds, or if holding bonds is expected to lead to a net loss. The latter means that the expected rate of return on bonds is negative and occurs if the expected prices of bonds are expected to decline by more than the fixed coupon payments on them. This case may be more applicable in depressed economies but is not likely to be of macroeconomic significance in *normal* conditions in the financially developed economies. John Maynard Keynes, writing in the midst of the Great Depression of the 1930s, drew attention to this case as an analytical possibility while denying its empirical significance, and labeled it as the *liquidity trap*. To distinguish this trap from a liquidity supply trap defined below, we can more precisely call it a '*liquidity demand trap*'. However, note that this term is not in general usage, so that we will continue to use the term 'liquidity trap' for this case.

A liquidity supply trap

A '*liquidity supply trap*' or a '*monetary base trap*' occurs if an increase in the monetary base induced by the central bank does not result in an increase in the money supply. This situation occurs if commercial banks refuse to use the increases in their reserves (because of increases in the monetary base) to invest in private/corporate bonds or otherwise lend to private firms because of a perceived high risk in such lending, and/or an exceptionally high degree of risk aversion by lenders. This occurred in many countries, especially the USA and UK, during the financial crisis of 2007–2010, when the solvency of many firms (including major financial firms) was not easily transparent and was seriously being questioned.[8]

The impact of the extreme reluctance to lend to the private sector was that although the central bank increased the monetary base very substantially, the banks added these increases to their cash reserves or bought government bonds, mainly Treasury bills, but not commercial bonds. Consequently, bank deposits and the monetary base (whose main component is bank deposits) did not increase very much, while the excess reserves and liquidity of banks shot up. This failure of the money supply to expand in the face of increases in the monetary base meant that monetary policy became ineffective in changing the money supply, and, through it, aggregate demand in the economy. We can call this a '*money supply trap*', and define it as a situation in which increases in the monetary base do not cause significant increases in the money supply. Note that this is not a liquidity trap arising from the public's preference/demand for money

---

[7] In such a context, land and houses often become the alternative to holding money, especially over long periods.

[8] Even if old loans were rolled over, there was an increase in interest rates to such borrowers, often accompanied by a decrease in the quantity provided (i.e., quantity rationing). New loans to the private sector were hardly being given. However, such lack of confidence in lending to firms did not apply to government Treasury bills and bonds, so that they continued to be acceptable alternatives to holding money. Therefore, there was a switch from loans to the private sector to loans to the government.

Extended Analysis Box 6.1: (*Continued*)

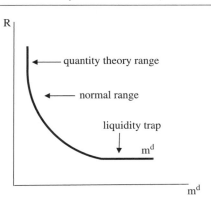

Figure 6.3.

holding rather than buying bonds, but arises from the behavior of the banking sector, which prevents the increases in the money supply in spite of increases in the monetary base.

Note that both the liquidity demand trap and the liquidity supply trap render an expansionary monetary policy ineffective.

The potential shapes of the money demand and LM curves

Figure 6.3 incorporates the two special cases of money demand, along with the normal case, into the money demand curve.

6.4.1 Equilibrium in the money market

Note that the definition of the *money market* for our macroeconomics purposes is that it is the market for money. Hence, the money market is the market for $M1$, $M2$, or a broader definition of money. It is not the market for short-term bonds, which is the common English language meaning of the term 'money market'. There is, therefore, quite a difference between the investors' and banks' usage of the term 'the money market' and the economists' usage.

Equilibrium in the monetary sector requires that money demand equals money supply. Hence, for equilibrium in nominal terms, with money supply exogenously given as M:

$$M = Pm^{\mathrm{d}}, \tag{3}$$

which gives,

$$M/P = m_y y - m_R R \quad m_y, m_R > 0. \tag{4}$$

Note that while the nominal stock of money is exogenously given and assumed to be in the control of the monetary authorities, the real value of that stock, (M^s/P), depends upon the equilibrium price level P in the economy and incorporates choices made by the public, including those on its demand for money.

Disequilibrium in the money market

The converse of equilibrium is disequilibrium. The money market is in disequilibrium if the demand for money differs from its supply. Suppose the former is greater than the latter: the public wants to hold more money than is available and there is excess demand for money. Applying this at the individual level, an individual with insufficient money balances will try to increase his money balances by selling some bonds, thereby receiving in exchange money from bond purchasers. In the aggregate, these sales of bonds by the public represent a decrease in the demand for bonds, which would push down bond prices. As Chapter 2 showed, a decrease in bond prices raises the return on them, so that the interest rate on bonds rises. In the money demand equation, this increase in the interest rate reduces the quantity of money that is demanded, and, therefore, reduces the excess demand of money. Households will continue to sell bonds until the interest rate rises sufficiently to eliminate the excess demand for money.

6.5 The LM Equation

The preceding Eq. (4) specifies those combinations of y and R that maintain equilibrium in the money market. It is called the LM equation or relationship — where L stands for liquidity preference — which is a term meaning the demand for money (i.e., liquidity) — and M stands for the money supply. We want to rearrange the LM equation to bring y to the left side. To do so, rearrange it as:

$$m_y y = M/P + m_R R,$$

so that the LM equation can be rewritten as:

$$y = \frac{1}{m_y}\left[\frac{M}{P}\right] + \frac{m_R}{m_y}R \quad m_y, m_R > 0. \tag{5}$$

This is the usual form of the LM equation, though any of its other forms are equally valid.

The impact of changes in the money supply M on income y, with interest rates held constant, is captured by the 'money (to income) multiplier', which is:

$$\frac{\partial y}{\partial M} = \frac{1}{m_y P} \geq 0, \tag{6}$$

so that increases in the money supply increase income by multiplying the increase in the money supply by $(1/m_y P)$.

6.5.1 The LM curve

The LM equation is plotted in Figure 6.4a as the LM curve. The LM curve is defined as the set of points at each of which there exists equilibrium in the money market. The LM curve has a positive slope.[9] The intuitive explanation for this positive slope is: for a given money supply and price level, an increase in y along the horizontal axis increases the transactions component of the demand for money, thereby requiring the public to reduce the amount of money held for speculative purposes — which the public will only do at a higher rate of interest. That is, an increase in real income must be accompanied by an increase in the rate of interest for equilibrium to be preserved in the monetary sector. Note that changes in y or R induce movements along the LM curve and not shifts in it.

6.5.2 Shifts in the LM curve

Shifts in the LM curve can be caused by changes in the money supply M or the price level P — or by a shift in the parameters m_y or m_R. We focus on the former in the following.

---

[9]Since $\partial y/\partial R = m_R/m_y > 0$.

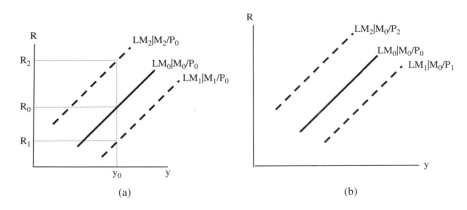

Figure 6.4

In Figure 6.4a, suppose that at the existing price level P_0 and the existing money supply M_0, the LM curve is $LM_0 \mid M_0/P_0$. Now suppose that the money supply increases from M_0 to M_1. Hence, the real money supply increases from M_0/P_0 to M_1/P_0. We examine its effects at a given level of income y_0. Since income is being held constant, the transactions demand for money does not change. Therefore, the public has extra money balances, which it will use to buy bonds. The increased demand for bonds will raise their prices — thereby lowering the rate of return on them, i.e., the interest rate R decreases. How far does it have to fall? It must fall by enough to persuade the public to willingly hold (i.e., increase money demand) all of the increase in the money supply. This will occur at the interest rate R_1 (at y_0) in Figure 6.4a. If we were to follow this reasoning for different levels of income, we would have a new set of points that will trace out the new LM curve as $LM_1 \mid M_1/P_0$ and pass through the point (R_1, y_0). This would lie to the right of $LM_0 \mid M_0/P_0$. Correspondingly, if the money supply decreases to M_2,[10] the LM curve will shift left to $LM_2 \mid M_2/P_0$.

Similar arguments can be applied to show the effects of changes in the price level P, holding the money supply constant. The position of the LM curve depends on the real money supply, so that an increase in the money supply or a decrease in the price level shifts the LM curve to the right. Conversely, a decrease in the money supply or an increase in the price level shifts the LM curve to the left. To reiterate the impact of changes in the price level on the LM curve, note that the price level P is a variable in the monetary sector and, therefore, in the LM equation, so that — since P is not on the axes of the IS-LM figures — a change in P must cause a shift in the LM curve. A rise in P decreases the supply of real balances which shifts the LM curve to the left while a fall in P shifts the LM curve to the right.[11] The effect of changes in the price level, with the money supply held constant at M_0, is shown in Figure 6.4b, with $P_2 > P_0 > P_1$.

The LM curve shifts to the right if:

- The money supply increases.
- The price level decreases.
- Money demand decreases because of shifts in the money demand function. From the money demand function, this occurs if the transactions demand per dollar of income (i.e., m_y) decreases or if m_R increases. In these cases, money demand decreases for given values of R and y.

---

[10] If the money supply decreases, the public tries to replenish its real balances by selling bonds, thereby driving down their prices and raising the interest rate.

[11] Note, however, that the price level is not an exogenous variable, so that a change in it must be determined and explained by reference to changes in some exogenous variables.

6.5.3 Shifts in the LM curve versus movements along it

The above discussion implies that the economy moves along the LM curve as the interest rate or income change and alter the demand for money. But it shifts if the money demand parameters (m_y, m_R), the policy variable M^s, or the endogenous variable P change.

In particular, an increase in the money supply shifts the curve to the right because this increases the real money supply (M/P). But an increase in the price level shifts the LM curve to the left because this decreases the real money supply. A proportionate change in the money supply and the price level leaves M/P unchanged, so that the LM curve would not shift.

6.5.4 Final comments on the LM curve

The modern economy has a money demand that is sensitive to the rate of interest but does not possess a liquidity trap. This was designated as the normal range of the LM curve. Except when we specifically try to explain the implications of the classical range or the liquidity trap, we will ignore these cases and draw the LM curve as an upward sloping straight line, as shown in Figures 6.4a and 6.4b. To emphasise the impact of the money supply and price level changes on the LM curve, we label this curve as $LM_1|_{M0/P0}$. An increase in the money supply from M_0 to M_1 shifts this curve to the right to $LM_0|_{M1/P0}$. An increase in the price level from P_0 to P_1 shifts this curve to the left to $LM_2|_{M0/P1}$. A proportionate increase in both M to M_1 and from P to P_1 leaves M/P unchanged and leaves the LM curve at LM_0, with $M_1/P_1 = M_0/P_0$.

Extended Analysis Box 6.2: The Potential General Shape of the LM Curve

The potential general shape of the LM curve, incorporating the liquidity trap range (when $m_R \to \infty$) and the quantity theory range (when $m_R = 0$), is as shown in Figure 6.5 by the curves labeled as LM_0 and LM_1, with the latter representing an increase in the money supply. The liquidity trap is the horizontal part of the LM curve and the quantity theory range is the vertical part of the LM curve. Between them lies the upward sloping part, which is the 'normal range' of the LM curve. Our earlier drawings of the normal part of the LM curve replaced the 'curve' by a straight line.

An increase in the money supply shifts the LM curve from LM_0 to LM_1, thereby elongating the liquidity trap part of it.

Financially developed economies in normal operation neither have the liquidity trap nor are in the quantity theory range for significant periods for relevance to the macroeconomy. They are in the normal range with a positively sloped LM curve.

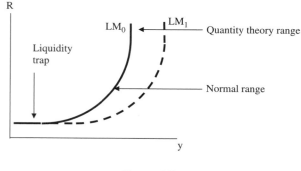

Figure 6.5.

6.6 Deriving the Aggregate Demand for Commodities by Combining the IS and LM Curves

6.6.1 The IS equation for the commodity market equilibrium

Chapter 5 had derived the IS curve for commodities for the open economy. Its derivation should be reviewed at this stage. The IS equation derived in Chapter 5 is:

$$y = \left(\frac{1}{1 - c_y + c_y t_y + \frac{1}{\rho^r} z_{cy}(1 - t_y)} \right)$$
$$\cdot [\{c_0 - c_y t_0 + i_0 - i_r r + g + x_{c0} - x_{c\rho}\rho^r\} + (1/\rho^r) \cdot \{-z_{c0} + z_{cy}t_0 - z_{c\rho}\rho^r\}]. \tag{7}^{12}$$

The definitions of the symbols are as given in Chapters 4 and 5. This equation is the *IS equation for the open economy*. Note that y is a function of r and ρ^r where $\rho^r = \rho P / P^F$, so that replacing ρ^r by $\rho P / P^F$ makes y a function of r, ρ, P, and P^F, in addition to policy and exogenous variables and parameters. Under flexible exchange rates, the equilibrium value ρ^* of the nominal exchange rate is determined by the balance of payments equilibrium condition (Eq. (3) of Chapter 5). Replacing ρ by ρ^* gives the final form of the IS equation. In this form of the IS equation, y will be a function of P, r, the fiscal policy variables and the exogenous foreign variables P^F, r^F (and R^F under the assumption that $\pi^e = 0$), and y^F, but ρ will no longer appear as a separate determinant of y.

Under an exogenous money supply, the IS and LM equations constitute the two components which together determine aggregate demand. However, note that the IS equation has the real interest rate r while the LM equation has the nominal interest rate R.

6.6.2 The relationship between the nominal and real interest rates

The nominal interest rate R is related to the real interest rate r in perfect bond markets by the Fisher equation:

$$R = (1 + r)(1 + \pi^e),$$

where π^e is the expected rate of inflation. The approximation to this relationship for low values of r and π^e is given by:

$$R = r + \pi^e.$$

The analyses behind the IS and LM curves is static and is used to examine changes in y, r, etc., when there is a *one-time* exogenous shift in the money supply, fiscal variables, and other variables and parameters. This analysis compares on equilibrium point prior to the shift with another equilibrium after the shift, and is called comparative static analysis. It does not study the dynamic path between the two equilibrium points. Since our analysis is comparative static, there is no inflation and no expected inflation at the equilibrium point prior to the shift and also none at the equilibrium point after the shift. Note that inflation and expected

---

[12]This is the IS equation without 'Ricardian equivalence', which assumes that private saving rises, and private consumption is cut back, exactly by the amount of any increase in the fiscal deficit. We do not make such an assumption in this chapter or book. A brief introduction to this concept can be found in Chapter 11. The form of the open economy IS equation that assumes Ricardian equivalence is different from the above equation but is not presented in this book.

inflation are aspects of the dynamic movements in prices, which are not relevant in comparative static analysis. Therefore, we will assume for our comparative static analysis that $\pi^e = 0$. In this case, $R = r$ and we could proceed with a diagram on whose vertical axis we can put either r or R. We choose to put r on the vertical axis.

Restating the LM equation

The LM equation derived above was:

$$y = \frac{1}{m_y}\left[\frac{M}{P}\right] + \frac{m_R}{m_y}R \quad m_y, m_R > 0. \tag{5}$$

Using the assumption that $\pi^e = 0$, so that $R = r$, we replace R in the money demand and LM equations by r. This turns the LM equation (5) into:

$$y = \frac{m_y}{m_R}y - \frac{1}{m_R}\left[\frac{M}{P}\right]. \tag{8}$$

Now substitute this value of the interest rate in the IS equation. The resulting AD equation for the open economy is:

$$y = \alpha[\{c_0 - c_y t_0 + i_0 + (i_r/m_R)(M/P) + g_0 + x_{c0} - x_{c\rho}\rho^r\} + (1/\rho^r) \cdot \{-z_{c0} + z_{cy}t_0 - z_{c\rho}\rho^r\}], \tag{26}$$

where:

$$\alpha = \left(\frac{1}{1 - c_y + c_y t_y + \frac{1}{\rho^r}z_{cy}(1 - t_y) + i_r m_y/m_R}\right).$$

6.6.3 Diagrammatic determination of aggregate demand

Figure 6.6a draws both the IS and the LM curves in the same diagram. The intersection point of the IS and LM curves provides those values of r (and R under our assumption that $\pi^e = 0$) and y at which there is simultaneous equilibrium in both the commodity and money markets. This point shows the aggregate demand for commodities, after incorporating the impact of the money market on the interest rate, which is needed to determine investment in the commodity market. The demand curve thus derived — just as for demand curves in microeconomic analysis — specifies the quantity demanded of commodities as a function of the price of commodities.

In Figure 6.6a, start with the IS curve and the LM curve, labeled as $LM_0 \mid M_0/P_0$. The latter is drawn for an initial money supply M_0 and an initial price level P_0. Their intersection at the point d_0 indicates the level of aggregate demand y_0^d, at the price level P_0. If, for the given money supply, the price level were somehow to fall to P_1 ($P_1 < P_0$), the LM curve would shift to the right to $LM_1 \mid M_0/P_1$. Then, the intersection of the IS and the LM_1 curves would occur at the point d_1, so that the level of aggregate demand would become y_1^d, at the price level P_1. That is, a fall in the price level produces a higher aggregate demand, in real terms, for commodities. Conversely, a rise in the price level will produce a lower real aggregate demand for commodities.

Hence, *the IS curve does not alone determine the level of aggregate demand*. The IS curve depends on investment which depends on the interest rate, which is jointly determined with the money market. This makes the LM curve an essential component for the determination of the aggregate demand for commodities — as well as of the interest rate.

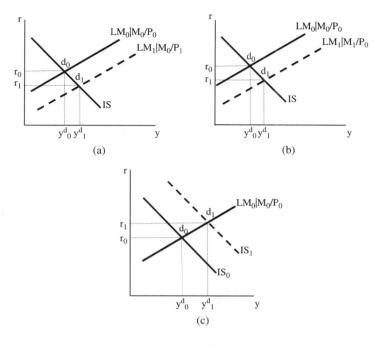

Figure 6.6

The IS, LM curves and the determination of output: a caveat

Note that the intersection of the IS and LM curves determines the aggregate demand for commodities and determines the AD function/curve used in Chapter 1. Their intersection does *not* determine the aggregate quantity of commodities that will be produced in the economy. This requires knowledge of both the demand and the supply functions/curves of commodities. Chapter 1 had shown this by incorporating both aggregate demand and supply in the AD-AS diagram.

Because the IS and LM intersection only determines the demand for commodities but not output (i.e., the quantity produced), it is strictly inappropriate to interpret y on the horizontal axis of the IS-LM, as well as the AD-AS, diagrams as the output (i.e., the quantity produced) of commodities. The symbol y on the horizontal section of both the IS-LM and the AD-AS diagrams is to be interpreted as the 'aggregate quantity of commodities', not as output (i.e., the quantity produced). This usage means that the intersection of the IS and LM specifies the quantity demanded of commodities — not the output of the economy — at the specific price level for which the LM curve has been drawn.

6.7 The Impact of Expansionary Monetary and Fiscal Policies on Aggregate Demand

In Figure 6.6b, suppose that the economy is initially in overall equilibrium at the point d_0 at the intersection of the IS and $LM_0|_{M0/P0}$ curves, where the $LM_0|_{M0/P0}$ is drawn for real balances M_0/P_0. At d_0, aggregate demand in real terms equals y_0^d at the price level P_0. Now suppose that an increase in the money supply to M_1 increases the real balances to M_1/P_0 and shifts the LM curve from LM_0 to $LM_1|_{M1/P0}$. The new equilibrium between the money and commodity markets is shown by the point d_1 and shows an increase in the real aggregate demand from y_0^d to y_1^d, with both evaluated at the price level P_0. Hence, an increase in the money supply increases aggregate demand at the pre-existing price level.

Conversely, a decrease in the money supply will shift the LM curve upwards and cause a decrease in the real aggregate demand for commodities at the pre-existing price level.

Now start with the given money supply as M_0 and the price level as P_0 and an initial IS curve as IS_0. Suppose that fiscal policy becomes expansionary with an increase in government expenditures. This would shift the IS curve from IS_0 to IS_1 in Figure 6.6c. At the pre-existing price level P_0, real aggregate demand would increase from y_0^d to y_1^d — i.e., from the point d_0 to the point d_1 at the intersection of the IS_1 and $LM_{0|M_0/P_0}$ curves.

The opposite pattern of effects occurs for a decrease in government expenditures or an increase in taxes.

6.8   Bringing Aggregate Supply into the Open Economy Analysis, a Preview of Chapters 7 to 9

6.8.1   The impact of an increase in aggregate demand on the quantity supplied and the price level

Since a change in the price level shifts the LM curve, further analysis requires the determination of the price level. This determination requires the specification of aggregate demand by the IS-LM analysis and that of aggregate supply set out in Chapters 7 to 9.

Would an increase in aggregate demand not raise the price level from its pre-existing level and shift the LM curve? To answer this question, we need to know not only the determinants of aggregate demand but also those of aggregate supply, which were briefly examined in Chapter 1 but are more rigorously examined in Chapters 7 to 9. Since the model specified so far in this chapter does not have the relevant aggregate supply curve, we are not yet able to determine either the change in the commodities produced or the price level at which they will be sold. The student who wishes to get an introduction to these effects at this point can do so by turning to the relevant analysis in Chapter 1. The more complete analysis of the supply side of the economy is in Chapters 7 to 9.

Hence, while the preceding sections have analyzed the effectiveness of monetary and fiscal policies in changing aggregate demand,[13] we also have to bring in aggregate supply, using the aggregate demand (AD) and aggregate supply (AS) curves in the (P, y) space. There is a long run LAS curve and a short run SAS curve for the open economy, as in the closed economy case. This would give us an analysis similar to that for the closed economy case, except that the AD curve is now susceptible to international influences through commodity and capital flows.

As Chapters 7 and 8 show, there are two different supply responses to an increase in AD. These depend on whether the economy is at full employment along the LAS curve or off it. In the latter case, it may be in short-run equilibrium and operate — as in the case of errors in price expectations or adjustment costs — along a SAS curve or the economy may be in disequilibrium.

6.8.2   The impact of monetary and fiscal policies on equilibrium output and price level in the open economy

For this analysis, we bring together two results:

1. For the flexible exchange rate economy with elastic net exports, an expansionary monetary policy is more efficacious in increasing aggregate demand than an expansionary fiscal policy.

---

[13]Note that an increase in aggregate demand due to an increase in the money supply or an increase in government expenditures has to be interpreted as a *real* increase in the aggregate demand for commodities at the *existing* price level.

2. Output is at its full-employment level y^f in the long run, but does increase in the short run as the price level rise. [This is explained in Chapters 1, 7, and 8.]

The short-run impact of aggregate demand changes on output and the price level

In the short run, an increase in aggregate demand increases both the price level and output. Therefore, the expansionary monetary policy, which does increase aggregate demand under flexible exchange rates, will increase both output and the price level.

Comparing expansionary monetary and fiscal policies under flexible exchange rates, the relative efficacy of monetary policy over that of fiscal policy in increasing aggregate demand means that the former will produce both greater output and higher inflation in the short run. Whether this makes monetary policy more desirable than fiscal policy depends on the economy's implied trade-off between inflation and the increase in output, and the policymaker's willingness to accept this trade-off.

The long-run impact of aggregate demand changes on output and the price level

In the long run, an increase in aggregate demand does not change the level of output from its full-employment level y^f, so that it only increases the price level. Therefore, in the long run, the expansionary monetary policy will only produce inflation, without a corresponding benefit in higher output. Hence, given flexible exchange rates, from the long-run perspective, monetary policy is worse than fiscal policy since the former is more efficacious in increasing aggregate demand. Of course, with employment and output maintained at their full-employment levels, neither policy serves a useful long-run purpose with respect to these variables. Therefore, neither policy should be pursued from the perspective of the long run.

6.8.3 Disequilibrium in the domestic economy and stabilization through monetary and fiscal policies

For the analysis of disequilibrium in the domestic economy, assume that the country has flexible exchange rates and these ensure continuous equilibrium in the balance of payments. Any disequilibrium, as in Figures 6.7a and 6.7b at the point d, will emerge as a difference between aggregate demand (shown by the point d) and aggregate supply (shown by y^f) and will be handled by the adjustment in the domestic price level. Assuming

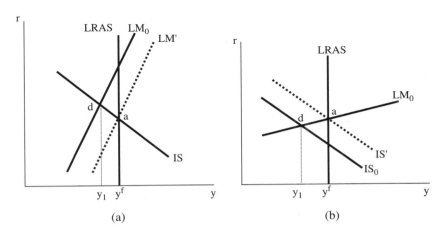

(a)   (b)

Figure 6.7

that the economy has price level flexibility, the price level will eventually fall to ensure equilibrium in the economy and monetary and fiscal policies will not be needed for this purpose. But this process can take real time.

If the authorities do not want to rely upon changes in the domestic price level to eventually restore full employment — e.g., because this process takes too long — they can pursue an expansionary monetary policy, as shown by shifting the LM curve to the right from LM_0 to LM' in Figure 6.7a. Alternatively, they can pursue an expansionary fiscal policy, as shown by shifting the IS curve to the right from IS_0 to IS' in Figure 6.7b. However, under flexible exchange rates and deficient demand disequilibrium, an expansionary monetary policy will be preferable since monetary policy is more efficacious than fiscal policy in increasing aggregate demand and output.

6.8.4 Summation on the roles of monetary and fiscal policies under flexible exchange rates

To sum up, exchange rate flexibility provides the economy with the very useful equilibrating mechanism of changes in the nominal exchange rate brought about by market forces for handling the balance of payments deficits. Together, exchange rate flexibility and domestic price flexibility eliminate the need for monetary and fiscal policies to return the economy to general equilibrium and full employment — *as long as* the authorities are willing to give the economy enough time to make its own adjustments to equilibrium *and* are willing to accommodate the possible reserve losses during the adjustment period. If they do pursue appropriate monetary and fiscal policies, the preceding analysis implies that:

- From the perspective of the long-run equilibrium analysis, monetary policy is less desirable than fiscal policy because the former's efficacy over the latter in increasing demand produces greater inflation, without any benefit in higher output. [The analysis behind this result is in Chapters 12 and 13.]
- In the short-run equilibrium analysis, an expansionary monetary policy produces both greater output and inflation than fiscal policy. Hence, the desirability of monetary policy over the fiscal one depends on the economy's trade-off between price and output increases and the central bank's preferences between them.
- In the case of deficient demand in the domestic economy, monetary policy is preferable to fiscal policy: the former is more efficacious in increasing aggregate demand and, therefore, in increasing output and employment.

Since the first and last points given above reverse the desirability of monetary over fiscal policy, the policymaker's preference for one over the other will vary with the existing state of the domestic economy and its propensity to maintain full employment or stay in deficient demand disequilibrium for significant periods.

Extended Analysis Box 6.3: The Mundell–Fleming Model of the Open Economy

The Mundell–Fleming model of the open economy is based on the contributions of Robert Mundell and Marcus Fleming in the 1960s. It presented the analyses of monetary and fiscal policies using the open economy IS-LM framework under the assumptions of elastic net exports, perfect capital mobility and *a fixed price level but variable output*. We can separate its analysis into two parts: that of the impact of the policies on aggregate demand and that of changes in the aggregate demand on real output. Chapter 12

Extended Analysis Box 6.3: (*Continued*)

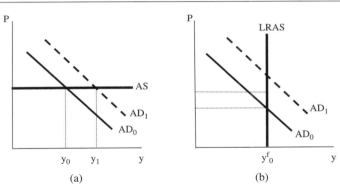

Figure 6.8.

and 13 shows that, under flexible exchange rates, monetary policy is more effective in changing aggregate *demand* than fiscal policy.

We consider here the effect of adding in the assumption of a constant price level and variable output. Under this assumption, the aggregate supply curve becomes horizontal. Therefore, as Figure 6.8a shows, changes in real output would equal the policy-induced changes in aggregate demand. Hence, monetary policy would be effective in changing aggregate output while fiscal policy is ineffective.[14]

Our analyses of aggregate supply in the subsequent Chapters 7 and 8 imply a vertical LAS curve for the long run and a positively sloped SAS curve for the short run. For further exposition with these differing slopes of the supply curves, we can truncate the Mundell–Fleming model by confining its analysis to the determination of aggregate demand. We can replace its assumption of a fixed price level and a horizontal aggregate supply curve by the SAS and LAS curves. This was done in our analysis of the impact of monetary and fiscal policies on output, and implied conclusions that differ from those usually associated with the Mundell–Fleming model. The biggest change occurs if the Mundell–Fleming assumption of a horizontal supply curve is replaced by the vertical LAS curve. As Figures 6.8a and 6.8b show, the Mundell–Fleming assumption in Figure 6.8a implies that an expansionary monetary policy increases real output and is desirable, while the vertical LAS curve in Figure 6.8b implies that it will only cause inflation and is undesirable. The SAS curve would have given an intermediate response: an expansionary monetary policy increases both output and the price level.

Under flexible exchange rates with perfect capital mobility, an expansionary fiscal policy does not change aggregate demand and, no matter what the shape of the supply curve, has no effect on output.

6.9 The Central Bank's Control Over the Money Supply

We now turn from the derivation of aggregate demand, output, and the price level to a detailed treatment of the determination of money supply.

---

[14]For the fixed exchange rate case, the Mundell–Fleming model showed that policy is effective in changing aggregate demand — and, therefore, output under the horizontal supply curve assumption — while fiscal policy is ineffective. Chapter 13 will present our analysis of the fixed exchange rate case.

The central bank controls the money supply through its instruments of monetary policy, which are:

- changes in the monetary base,
- changes in reserves requirements, which are imposed on commercial banks, and
- changes in the discount rate at which it lends to commercial banks.

6.10 The Central Bank's Instruments for Changing the Monetary Base

The central bank can change the monetary base through the following instruments at its disposal:

- open market operations,
- moving government deposits between itself and the commercial banks, and
- allowing the commercial banks to borrow from it.

6.10.1 Open market operations

Open market operations are the purchase (or sale) by the central bank of securities in financial markets, and results in corresponding increases (decreases) in the monetary base. Countries with well-developed financial markets and extensive amounts of public debt traded in the financial markets usually rely on such operations to change the money supply as their main tool of monetary policy. They — along with changes in the discount/bank rate[15] — are the most important tools of monetary policy in the USA, Canada, and the UK, and in most economies with well-developed financial sectors and capitalist economies. However, open market operations do not hold a corresponding degree of importance in very many other countries. In particular, financially underdeveloped economies generally do not possess sufficiently the size and depth of domestic bond markets required for adequate open market operations. This is also usually so in countries without a strong commitment to free enterprise and capitalism.

6.10.2 Shifting government deposits between the central bank and the commercial banks in Canada

The central bank usually acts as the government's bank, i.e., keeping and managing the government's deposits. Increases in these deposits with the central bank occur because of payments by the public to the government out of their deposits in commercial banks. This reduces the monetary base while decreases in such deposits because of increased payments by the government to the public increase the monetary base. One way of avoiding changes in the monetary base, because of payments to the government or receipts from it by the public, is for the government to hold accounts with the commercial banks and use them for its transactions with the public. The resulting increases and decreases in the government deposits with the commercial banks do not change the monetary base — while transfers of these deposits to the central bank reduces this base.

In Canada, the Bank of Canada manages the distribution of the government deposits between itself and the chartered banks in Canada as a way of manipulating the monetary base and, therefore, as a tool of monetary policy akin to open market operations. In current practice, such shifting of balances is more convenient

---

[15] In Canada, the shifting of government deposits between the central bank and the commercial banks is also used as a substitute for open market operations.

and has become more important than open market operations for changing the monetary base over short periods.

This practice is feasible for the Canadian banking system since it has a very small number (six) of very large banks, which are considered to be fully secure.[16] It would not be practical in a country with a large number of banks, as in the USA, nor in one where some of the commercial banks have a significant risk of becoming insolvent. The latter is likely to be the case in many developing countries.

6.10.3 A mechanism for commercial banks to change the monetary base

Central banks often allow commercial banks and other designated financial institutions to borrow from it at a designated interest rate called the *discount rate* (in the USA) or the *Bank Rate* (in Canada and the UK). Canada, the UK, and the USA have traditionally done so. Such borrowing from the central bank changes the monetary base. The level of the discount rate relative to the economy's ones at which banks can invest determines the willingness of commercial banks to borrow from the central bank, so that changes in the discount rate induces changes in the amount borrowed and thereby change the monetary base.

The central bank is not always able to accurately predict or achieve the monetary base at which the economy's interest rate will equal the target interest rate. A difference between them changes the incentives for the commercial banks to increase their borrowings from the central bank. For example, if the monetary base is not enough to ensure that the economy's rate is as low as the target one, the banks will increase their borrowings from the central bank, thereby increasing the monetary base. But if the monetary base is so large that it makes the economy's rate lower than the target one, the banks will reduce their borrowings, thereby decreasing the monetary base. Therefore, allowing the commercial banks to borrow from the central bank serves as a safety valve — and a fine-tuning mechanism — in adjusting the monetary base to the one required for equilibrium in the money market.

6.11 The Central Banks' Control Over the Monetary Base *Multiplier* through Reserve Requirements

The imposition of reserve requirements[17] has historically been a common tool of controling monetary aggregates for a given monetary base. In countries where the markets are too thin (small) for viable open market operations, or the monetary base cannot be controled for some reason, the monetary authorities often attempt to limit the creation of reserves by the banking system through the imposition of, or changes in, reserve ratios against demand deposits and sometimes also against other types of deposits. These ratios can range from 0% to 100%, though they are often in the range of 0% to 20%.

A decrease (increase) in the required reserve ratio increases (decreases) the amount available for loans to the public and increases the monetary base multiplier, so that it increases (decreases) the money supply. This tool for changing the money supply is often employed in developing economies. The change in the required reserve ratio is usually of the order of 0.25% or 0.5%.

---

[16]Besides security of deposits, there is also the question of equity in the distribution of government deposits among the commercial banks. This can be ensured by distributing the government deposits in proportion to the individual banks' holdings of private deposits. Note that commercial banks increase their revenues by investing increases in government deposits with them in interest-bearing bonds.

[17]In most countries, the required reserves have to be held by the bank in currency or in deposits with the central bank. These deposits normally do not pay interest.

6.12 The Impact of Discount Rate Changes on the Economy

A change in the discount rate serves as an instrument of monetary policy in three ways:

1. The change — or lack of a change when one was expected — acts as a signal to the private sector of the central bank's intentions about monetary policy.
2. The change affects the amount of borrowing from the central bank. Changes in the amount borrowed change the monetary base and the money supply.
3. The change cascades through various interest rates in the economy because of the institutional lending practices of the banks and other financial intermediaries.

6.12.1 The central bank's discount rate and interest rate differentials in the economy

The commercial banks and other financial intermediaries usually, though not always, follow the lead given by the discount rate changes to alter their own interest rates — such as the prime rate, the personal loan rates, and the mortgage rates — as well as in their purchases and sales of market instruments. This behavioral pattern results in a shift of the interest rates throughout the economy, while leaving the spread between any pair of rates to market forces.

The central bank's power to set its discount or bank rate does not extend over the differentials or spreads among the various interest rates in the economy. In particular, the spreads between the commercial banks' deposit rates and the short-term market rates, such as Treasury bills and money market mutual funds, are still outside the direct influence of the central bank and depend upon market forces. However, macroeconomics simplifies the analysis by making the assumption that the interest rate differentials remain unchanged for changes in the target interest rate and/or in the money supply.

6.13 The Determination of the Money Supply

As explained in Chapter 2, the quantity of money is usually measured by $M1$ (the sum of currency in the hands of the public and the demand deposits of the public in commercial banks), $M2$ ($M1$ plus savings deposits of the public in commercial banks), or a still broader measure. A related concept was the monetary base, for which we use the symbol $M0$. Chapter 2 should be reviewed at this point.

The generic definitions of the basic monetary symbols are:

$$M0 \equiv C + BR,$$

$$M1 \equiv C + D,$$

$$M2 \equiv M1 + S = C + D + S,$$

where:

$M0$ = monetary base,[18]
$M1$ = narrow definition of money,
$M2$ = broad definition of money,

---

[18]It is also called the reserve base or high-powered money.

C = currency in the hands of the (non-bank) public,
BR = commercial banks' reserves (in currency held by the banks or deposits with the central bank),
D = demand (checkable) deposits of the public with the commercial banks, and
S = savings deposits of the public with the commercial banks.

No matter whether the money supply in the economy is defined as $M1$ or $M2$ or some broader measure, there are three main participants in its determination. They are:

1. the central bank, which determines the monetary base and the reserve requirements for the commercial banks, and sets the discount rate at which it lends to the commercial banks,
2. the public, which determines its currency holdings relative to its demand deposits, and
3. the commercial banks, which, for a given required reserve ratio, determine their actual demand for reserves as against their demand deposit liabilities.[19]

There is considerable interaction among the behavior of the central bank, the public and the commercial banks in the money supply process. This interaction becomes of the greatest importance in studying the behavior of the central bank, which must take into account the responses of the public and the commercial banks to its own actions.

The relative importance of the major contributors to changes in the money supply varies between the business cycle and over long periods. Their contributions can be summarized as:

- The most important cause of the long-term (known as secular) growth of the money stock is the growth in the monetary base.
- Over the business cycle, the fluctuations in the currency ratio ($C/M1$) tend to have relatively large amplitudes, and can account for as much as half of the fluctuations in the growth rate of $M1$.
- Over the business cycle, fluctuations in the monetary base are another major source of the fluctuations in the growth rate of the money stock.

Over the business cycle, the reserve ratio (BR/D) can also fluctuate and be a source of the fluctuations in the growth rate of the money stock. The extent of this fluctuation varies among economies. In Canada, the reserve ratio is now at very low levels (less than 1%), so that the fluctuations in it are no longer a major source of fluctuations in the growth rate of $M1$. They play a more significant role in the USA and many other countries.

Extended Analysis Box 6.4: The Creation of Demand Deposits

Banks hold reserves to meet withdrawals by their depositors and any reserve requirements imposed by the central bank. One part of these reserves is held as currency in the banks' tills and vaults. Another part is held as a checking account with the central bank, to be drawn upon as needed. Individual banks' deposits with other banks are also part of their reserves. However, in the aggregate over all banks, interbank deposits cancel out and are not part of the reserves of the banking system. Therefore, for the banking system as a whole, bank reserves are currency held by the banks (not by the non-bank public) plus their deposits with the central bank.

---

[19]These are not the only actors in the money supply process. In particular, in open economies, the balance of payments surpluses (deficits) of a country can increase (decrease) its money supply. This relationship between the balance of payments and the money supply is discussed in Chapter 13.

Extended Analysis Box 6.4: (*Continued*)

Assume that the banks hold reserves against demand deposits in the proportion ρ, so that:

$$BR = \rho D,$$

where ρ (Greek letter 'rho') is the reserve ratio BR/D. As mentioned earlier, reserves are held for two reasons:

1. To meet a minimum reserve ratio set by the central bank. This ratio is called the *required reserve ratio*. Some countries have now eliminated such a requirement, while others maintain one. As an example, Canada requires banks to have a zero or positive reserve ratio at the end of each day, while the USA has a reserve requirement ratio of approximately 9%.
2. To meet the net withdrawals (i.e., withdrawals less deposits) by depositors on a continuous basis.

The reserve ratio ρ is usually greater than the required reserve ratio set by the central bank for the banking system because the banks need to hold extra reserves to meet withdrawals by the public from their deposit accounts. If the commercial banks have reserves equal to BR, our preceding equation implies that they can somehow create demand deposits equal to:

$$D = (1/\rho)BR.$$

This equation is the elementary deposit creation formula for the creation of deposits by the banks based on the reserves held by them.

What is the amount of reserves available to the banks as a whole? To answer this question, start with the identities:

$$M0 = C + BR$$
$$BR = M0 - C.$$

Therefore, the amount of reserves held by the commercial banks is determined by the monetary base $M0$ (provided by the central bank) less the public's desire to hold currency. Given this availability of reserves, banks create deposits equal to $(1/\rho)BR$. As an illustration, suppose that $\rho = 0.250$. In this case, banks create \$4 of demand deposits for every dollar of their reserves.

In most countries, ρ is less than unity, so that they are said to possess a *fractional reserve system*. In such a system, the commercial banks are the major player in the creation of the money supply, even when the initiative in changing the money supply rests with the central bank through its manipulation of the monetary base.

6.14 A Common Money Supply Formula for $M1$

To derive the quantity of $M1$, start with the accounting identities and definitions:

$$M1 \equiv C + D \tag{9}$$
$$M0 \equiv C + BR \tag{10}$$
$$c \equiv C/D$$
$$\rho \equiv BR/D,$$

where:

$M1$ = narrow money supply,

$M0$ = monetary base $\equiv BR + C$,

$\quad c$ = currency ratio of the public,

$\quad \rho$ = reserve ratio of the commercial banks,

$\quad C$ = currency in the hands of the public,

$\quad D$ = demand deposits of the public in commercial banks, and

BR = commercial banks' reserves.

The steps in the derivation are:

$$M0 = C + BR$$

$$= cD + \rho D \tag{11}$$

$$D = \frac{1}{c + \rho} M0 \tag{12}$$

$$M1 = C + D$$

$$= cD + D$$

$$= (1 + c)D$$

$$= (1 + c)\left\{ \frac{1}{c + \rho} M0 \right\}$$

$$= \frac{(1 + c)}{(c + \rho)} M0$$

$$= \left[\frac{\partial M1}{\partial M0} \right] M0, \tag{13}$$

where $[\partial M1/\partial M0]$ is the *monetary base multiplier*: it specifies the amount of $M1$ created by an increase in the monetary base by \$1. The above equation for $M1$ separates its basic determinants into changes in the monetary base and changes in the monetary base multiplier.

The dominant factor influencing the long-term (secular) growth in the money stock is the growth in the monetary base. For the long-term changes in $M1$, changes in the two ratios contribute much less than the changes in the monetary base. However, for *cyclical* movements in the money stock, the changes in the currency ratio are an important element of changes in the money supply. Changes in the reserve ratio have only a minor impact in stable, developed economies, but they can shift very significantly during a period of financial and economic crisis, as they did during 2007–2010 in the USA.

6.14.1 The monetary base multiplier

The monetary base multiplier is the multiple by which a change in the monetary base changes the money supply. Hence, for $M1$, it is specified by:

$$\frac{\partial M1}{\partial M_0} = \frac{(1 + c)}{(c + \rho)}.$$

This multiplier is itself determined by the reserve ratio and the currency ratio. Of these, the reserve ratio reflects the banks' demand for reserves. The currency ratio reflects the public's behavior on its demand for currency. Hence, the three main determinants of the money supply are: the monetary base determined by the central bank, the currency ratio determined by the public, and the reserve ratio determined by the banks.

6.14.2 Numerical examples

Suppose we have the following information: $c = 0.2$, $\rho = 0.1$, and $\$M0 = 100$ million. What would be the values of the monetary base multiplier, $M1$, C, and D?

$$\partial M1/\partial M0 = (1 + c)/(c + \rho) = 1.2/0.3 = 11.$$

$$M1 = 4(100) = 400 \text{ million.}$$

$$D = [1/(c + \rho)]M1 = (1/0.3)400 = \$333.33 \text{ million.}$$

$$C = cD = 0.2(333.33) = \$66.67 \text{ million.}$$

However, a reserve ratio of 10% is too high for many countries. Therefore, for another example, let $c = 0.2$ and $\rho = 0.02$, so that $\partial M1/\partial M0 = 1.2/0.22 = 11.411$. Then, for $M0 = \$100$ million, $M1 = \$545$ million. Comparing the multipliers and the money supply for the two values of ρ, we find that the lower the reserve ratio of banks, the greater is the monetary base multiplier and the expansion in $M1$.

Further, assume that the currency ratio rises to 0.3, while $\rho = 0.1$. In this case, $\partial M1/\partial M0 = 1.3/0.4 = 3.25$ and $M1 = \$325$ million. Hence, an increase in the currency ratio decreased the monetary base multiplier and the money supply.

It is left to the students to calculate the currency holdings and demand deposits in each of the above cases, and to provide the answer to the question: what do they show about the effects of increases in the currency ratio and the reserve ratio on currency holdings and demand deposits?

6.15 Conclusions

- In the money market, the two main elements of the demand for money are the transactions and the speculative ones. If the central bank pursues a policy of targeting the money supply, the nominal money supply is assumed to be exogenous.
- The two special cases of money demand are the quantity theory and the liquidity trap. These do not apply during normal conditions in the financially developed economies.
- One technique of analysis used in short-run macroeconomics with an exogenous money supply is that of grouping the relationships of the commodity and the money markets into the IS-LM format and the IS-LM diagram.
- Under an exogenous money supply, the intersection of the IS and LM curves shows the real aggregate demand for commodities at the pre-existing price level for which the LM curve was drawn.
- Increases in the policy variables of government expenditures and the money supply raise real aggregate demand (at the pre-existing price level). Increases in taxes reduce it.
- The division of an increase in aggregate demand between increases in the price level and the quantity produced of commodities also requires the specification of the aggregate supply curve.

KEY CONCEPTS

An exogenous money supply	*The LM relationship/curve*	*Monetary base multiplier*
Money stock	*The liquidity trap*	*Open market operations*
The demand for money	*The quantity theory range*	*Reserve ratio, and*
Transactions demand for money	*The determination of aggregate*	*Currency ratio.*
Speculative demand for money	*demand by IS-LM analysis*	

CRITICAL   CONCLUSIONS

- An increase in the demand for money shifts the LM curve to the left.
- An increase in the money supply shifts the LM curve to the right.
- An increase in the money supply is an expansionary monetary policy.
- In the normal context of the economy, both expansionary fiscal or monetary policies increase real aggregate demand at the existing price level.
- The intersection of the IS and LM curves determines the amount of commodities demanded at the price level for which the LM curve is drawn. It shows neither the supply of commodities nor its ability to determine the quantity of commodities that will be produced or the price level at which they will be sold.

Appendix

Determination of the LM curve

This appendix assumes an exogenous money supply. That is:

$$M^s = M, \tag{14}$$

where M is the *exogenously determined money stock*. The assumption on the money demand function is:

$$m^d = m_y y - m_R R \quad m_y, m_R > 0. \tag{15}$$

Money market equilibrium requires that:

$$M = Pm^d, \tag{16}$$

which gives,

$$M/P = m_y y - m_R R \quad m_y, m_R > 0. \tag{17}$$

Note that while the nominal stock of money is exogenously given and in the control of the monetary authorities, the real value of that stock, (M^d/P), depends upon the equilibrium price level P in the economy and incorporates choices made by the public, including those on its demand for money.

The preceding equation is called the LM equation and its corresponding curve is known as the LM curve. Its usual form is obtained by rearranging the above equation as:

$$y = \frac{1}{m_y} \left[\frac{M}{P} \right] + \frac{m_R}{m_y} R \quad m_y, m_R > 0. \tag{18}$$

This LM equation shows that y depends on positively on R and M, but negatively on P.

Derivation of aggregate demand for the closed economy from its IS and LM equations

Using the IS equation for the closed economy from Chapter 4, the above LM equation and the Fisher equation relating the real and the nominal interest rates, we have the complete model for determining aggregate demand.

This model is:

IS equation for the closed economy:

$$y = \left[\frac{1}{1 - c_y(1 - t_y)}\right](c_0 + i_0 + g_0 - c_y t_0 - i_r r). \tag{19}$$

LM equation:

$$M/P = m_y y - m_R R. \tag{20}$$

Fisher equation:

$$R = r + \pi^e.$$

The Fisher equation introduces an additional variable π^e, so that its determination needs to be specified. The simplest assumption for the mathematical derivation is one where $\pi^e = 0$.[20] We will make this assumption, so that for the following derivations, $R = r$.

To combine the IS and LM equations, first solve the LM equation for R in terms of y and P, which gives:

$$R = \frac{m_y}{m_R}y - \frac{1}{m_R}\left[\frac{M}{P}\right]. \tag{21}$$

Using the assumption that $R = r$, we replace R in the money demand equation by r. This turns Eq. (21) into:

$$R = \frac{m_y}{m_R}y - \frac{1}{m_R}\left[\frac{M}{P}\right]. \tag{22}$$

Now substitute this value of r ($= R$, under our assumption that $\pi^e = 0$) in the IS equation. The resulting AD equation for the closed economy is:

$$y^d = \alpha\left(c_0 + i_0 + g_0 - c_y t_0 + \frac{i_r}{m_R}\frac{M}{P}\right), \tag{23}$$

where:

$$\alpha = \left[\frac{1}{1 - c_y(1 - t_y) + i_r m_y/m_R}\right] = \left[\frac{m_R}{m_r - c_y(1 - t_y)_{m_R} + i_r m_y}\right].$$

This preceding AD equation specifies the aggregate real demand for commodities as a (negative) function of the price level P. Since P is in the denominator on the right side, an increase in P reduces y^d, so that $\partial y^d/\partial P < 0$. That is, the aggregate demand (AD) for commodities is inversely related to its price — which is the price level — so that we now have the equation with the usual form of a downward sloping demand curve.

For diagrammatic analysis, the above AD equation shows those combinations of (y^d, P) which simultaneously maintain equilibrium in the commodity and monetary markets.

Intuition

An increase in the price level reduces aggregate demand by reducing the real money balances (M/P) available in the economy. A reduction in real balances held by individual consumers implies that they cannot finance their previous level of purchases. In order to do so, they will try to sell some of their bonds. This will lower bond prices and raise their return — which is the interest rate. As the interest rate rises, investment falls, which reduces the expenditures on (demand for) commodities. For equilibrium to be maintained, this fall in expenditures reduces real income y.

---

[20]Another simple alternative is to assume that it is exogenously given.

Simplifying the AD equation for further analysis

We can rewrite the closed-economy AD equation as:

$$y^d = \alpha c_0 + \alpha i_0 + \alpha g_0 - \alpha c_y t_0 + \frac{\alpha i_r}{m_R} \frac{M}{P}. \tag{24}$$

There are only two endogenous variables, y and P, in this equation. There are also the policy variables of M, g, and the tax parameters (t_0 and t_1). Note that the interest rate is not a variable in this equation since it was dropped out in combining the IS and LM equations. We can now easily derive the effect of changes in the monetary and fiscal policy variables on aggregate demand.

We can plot this AD equation in a diagram with y on the horizontal axis and P on the vertical one, as in Figure 6.A.1. Since P is in the denominator in the above equation, an increase in P reduces y^d, which explains why the AD curve is downward sloping, as specified in Chapter 1.

Determination of the long-run *price level* under an exogenous money supply

Figure 6.A.1 shows the downward sloping AD curve. From the AD equation, we find that an increase in the money supply and/or in the fiscal deficit will shift the AD curve to the right from AD_0 to AD_1.

Figure 6.A.1 also shows the determination of the price level *in the long run*, that is, with a vertical LAS curve. The shift of the AD curve to the right from AD_0 to AD_1 increases demand at the existing price level P_0 to the point d. This demand exceeds the supply of commodities, which remains at y_0^f, so that the market pushes up the price level from P_0 to P_1. However, this price increase does not change the long-run output, which stays at y^f.

Derivation of aggregate demand for the *open economy* from its IS and LM equations

Using the IS equation for the open economy from Chapter 5, the above LM equation and the Fisher equation relating the real and the nominal interest rates, we have the complete model for determining aggregate demand in the open economy. This model is:

IS equation for the open economy:

$$y = \left(\frac{1}{1 - c_y + c_y t_y + \frac{1}{\rho^r} z_{cy}(1 - t_y)} \right)$$
$$\cdot [\{c_0 - c_y t_0 + i_0 - i_r r + g_0 + x_{c0} - x_{c\rho}\rho^r\} + (1/\rho^r) \cdot \{-z_{c0} + z_{cy}t_0 - z_{c\rho}\rho^r\}]. \tag{25}$$

Assuming that $\pi^e = 0$ in the Fisher equation, we arrive at the conclusion that $R = r$.

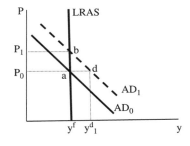

Figure 6.A.1

To combine the IS and LM equations, first solve the LM equation for R in terms of y and P, which gives:

$$R = \frac{m_y}{m_R} y - \frac{1}{m_R} \left[\frac{M}{P} \right]. \tag{26}$$

Using the assumption that $R = r$, we replace R in the money demand equation by r. This turns Eq. (26) into:

$$r = \frac{m_y}{m_R} y - \frac{1}{m_R} \left[\frac{M}{P} \right]. \tag{27}$$

Now substitute this value of the interest rate in the IS equation. The resulting AD equation for the open economy is:

$$y = \alpha[\{c_0 - c_y t_0 + i_0 + (i_r/m_R)(M/P) + g_0 + x_{c0} - x_{c\rho}\rho^r\} + (1/\rho^r) \cdot \{-z_{c0} + z_{cy} t_0 - z_{c\rho}\rho^r\}], \tag{28}$$

where:

$$\alpha = \left(\frac{1}{1 - c_y + c_y t_y + \frac{1}{\rho^r} z_{cy}(1 - t_y) + i_r m_y / m_R} \right).$$

REVIEW AND DISCUSSION QUESTIONS

1. What assumptions are made for the money supply in deriving the LM curve?
2. Suppose that firms and consumers increase their demand for real balances because of an increase in the income elasticity (use m_y as the approximation for this) of this demand. Show its effect on the LM curve. Is there a change in the slope of the LM curve?
3. What assumptions are made for the money demand function in deriving the normal shape of the LM curve? Show diagrammatically the normal ranges of the demand for money curve and the LM curve for a modern economy with well-developed financial markets?
4. Define the quantity theory (classical) range of the demand for money and show it diagrammatically by its versions of the demand for money curve and the LM curve.
5. Show the liquidity trap ranges of the demand for money curve and the LM curve? What justifies the liquidity trap? Discuss the likelihood of its occurrence for significant periods in modern economies.
6. Can we specify from the IS-LM analysis (i.e., without the commodity supply analysis) the impact on real output of changes in the money supply?
7. Using the IS-LM diagram, analyze the effects of a contractionary monetary policy (i.e., a decrease in the money supply) on the interest rate and aggregate demand in the economy.
8. Using the IS-LM diagram, analyze the effect of a contractionary fiscal policy (i.e., a decrease in government expenditures or increase in taxes) on the interest rate and aggregate demand in the economy.
9. If the central bank uses the money supply as its operating target, can it predict its impact on the interest rate? Or should it try to set the interest rate independently of the money supply? Discuss.
10. It is often contended that governments in LDCs have no choice but to fund at least some of their deficits by increasing the monetary base. Why and how does this happen? What are the effects of doing so on aggregate demand? Illustrate your answer by appropriate diagrams.
11. "While central banks in financially developed economies may be able to effectively control aggregate demand by only using the interest rate as their operating target, those in LDCs with under-developed financial markets need to use both the interest rate and money supply as their operating targets". What is the nature of the economies that justifies this argument?

ADVANCED AND TECHNICAL QUESTIONS

T1. The following equations describe the commodity market of an open economy:

$$c = 0.8y_d,$$
$$t = -100 + 0.2y,$$
$$i = 1000 - 50r,$$
$$g = 800,$$
$$x_c = 100 - 0.5\rho^r, \text{ and}$$
$$z_c = 500 + 0.1y_d + 0.2\rho^r.$$

Additional information: $P = 2$, $P^F = 4$, $\bar{\rho} = 4$ (i.e., the exchange rate has been fixed by the central bank at this level). [Hint: use this information to first derive the real exchange rate. Substitute this value in the export and import equations. Chapter 5 can provide the guidance on this.]

(a) Derive the IS equation? [Do not use the IS equation formula for this answer. Use step-by-step calculations. Start by calculating disposable income. Noting that x_c and z_c depend on ρ^r, calculate ρ^r in terms of P. Then use the equilibrium condition $y = e$ for your further steps.]

(b) Assuming $r = 2$, what is the value of y?

(c) Assuming $r = 2$, if the government increases its expenditures to 1000, what is the value of y?

(d) What is the fiscal multiplier?

T2. The following equations describe the money market of the economy:

$$m^d = 0.25y - 60R \quad \text{and} \quad M = 1000.$$

(a) Derive the LM equation?

(b) Given the commodity market model of question T1 and the money market model of this question, derive the aggregate demand equation.

(c) What is the autonomous investment multiplier for aggregate demand?

T3. Given the preceding information on the commodity and money markets and if the money supply were kept at 1000, derive the domestic interest rate determined by the economy? (Hint: this interest rate is determined jointly by the domestic commodity and money markets, i.e., by the intersection of the IS and LM curves. It will depend on y.)

CHAPTER 7
Full-Employment Output and the Natural Rate of Unemployment

The study of real output in the economy requires the analysis of the labor market and the aggregate supply of commodities for the economy. The main variables of interest in this analysis are the long-run levels of employment and output, and the natural rate of unemployment. Their derivation is distinct from that of the short-run behavior of the economy (covered in Chapter 8) and of the disequilibrium behavior of the economy (covered in Chapter 9).

The long-run behavior of the economy, captured under the notions of the full-employment level of output and the natural rate of unemployment, is presented in this chapter.

The counterpart of the aggregate demand for commodities is their aggregate supply. This chapter presents the derivation of the *long-run (LR) equilibrium levels* of employment and output. This expression is usually shortened to the 'long-run levels', thereby dropping the word 'equilibrium' but implying it nevertheless. The LR aggregate output in the economy is also known as the *full-employment output*.

As Chapter 1 explained, the full-employment output in macroeconomics is to be interpreted as the optimal output that can be produced on a *sustainable* basis over long periods from the efficient use of the economy's available factors of production and its available technology — given the economy's organizational and market structures,[1] the wishes of the owners of the factors of production,[2] as well as its economic, social, and political structures. This full-employment output is often more loosely referred to as the *'potential long-run output'* that can be maintained with the economy's current resources and structures. In more formal terms, the *full-employment level of output is defined as the long-run equilibrium level of output, where the term 'long run' refers to that analytical period when there are no rigidities, adjustment costs or expectational errors.*

The long run (equilibrium) requires the assumptions:

- If there exists uncertainty, the expected values of the variables are identical with the actual values.
- There are no labor contracts between firms and workers, and nominal and real wages adjust instantly and fully to reflect market forces.

---

[1] Whether the economy's industries have perfect competition, monopolies, or oligopolies clearly affects their production and employment levels.

[2] These wishes are relevant because the owners of the factors of production may choose to supply less than the full amount that exists in the economy. This means that, in the case of labor, labor supply may be, and usually is, less than the labor force. The owners of capital also usually do not choose to keep all their machines functioning all the time.

- There are no costs of adjusting prices or employment or output, so that the adjustments in these and other variables to their desired levels are instantaneous.[3]
- There exists equilibrium in all markets.

Given these assumptions, the economy's resulting employment level is said to be the full-employment one and its output is said to be full-employment output. Our symbol for this output level is y^f.

Alternatively, if there do exist rigidities or adjustment costs in the economy, the long run is that *analytical* period by which, following any shocks to the economy: (a) any discrepancies between the expected values of the variables (aggregate demand, prices, etc.) and the actual values have been eliminated, (b) all contracts based on such a discrepancy have expired, (c) all adjustments by markets and economic agents (households/workers, firms, and government) have been completed, and (d) all markets have reestablished equilibrium.

Note that the *actual* output in the economy can differ from its full-employment level because of the existence of rigidities, adjustment lags, expectational errors, and other factors. These can make the short-run output to be greater or lesser than its full-employment level.[4]

7.1 The Production Function

In industrialized economies, capital and labor are the dominant inputs in production, while land plays only a minor role and is normally not included in macroeconomic analysis. With this assumption, the remaining inputs in the production of commodities are labor and capital. The production function for the economy — as represented by that for 'the representative firm' — can then be written as:

$$y = y(n, K), \tag{1}$$

where:

y = output,
K = capital stock,
n = labor employed,
y_n = marginal product of labor (MPL),[5] and
y_K = marginal product of capital (MPK).[6]

In the short term, the flows of physical capital, labor and technology among countries are likely to be relatively limited, or limited in their impact on the economy, so that they are ignored in the short-run open economy analysis.[7] Further, since our analysis is short term, we assume that the domestic labor force, capital stock, and technology are constant.[8] With technology held constant for short-run analysis, the production function remains unchanged in going from the closed economy to the open one.

---

[3]Note that the capital stock, technology, and the labor force are still being held constant so that the overall context continues to be that of the short-run macroeconomic models.

[4]Hence, the long-run — or full-employment — output is not really the maximum output that the economy could produce at any time, e.g., if all its resources were used 24 hours a day, or even the equilibrium output that will be produced in the short run (see Chapters 1 and 8) or the actual output that might be produced when the economy is not in equilibrium (see Chapter 9).

[5]$y_{nn} < 0$ means that the MPL is diminishing.

[6]$y_{KK} < 0$ means that the MPK is diminishing.

[7]Over a longer term, domestic physical capital is increased by direct foreign investment and domestic technology improves by the adoption of better production methods from abroad.

[8]Both these could be affected by international flows in an open economy in the long run.

The stock of physical capital is also held (i.e., assumed to be) constant in the short-run macroeconomic analysis,[9] so that $K = \bar{K}$, where the line over the symbol indicates 'constancy' or 'exogeneity'. Hence, we have:

$$y = y(n, \bar{K}).$$

With this modification, labor is left as the only variable input, so that we can rewrite the production function as:

$$y = y(n). \tag{2}$$

We assume that the marginal product of labor (MPL) is positive and diminishing, i.e., successive increments of labor yield smaller and smaller increments of output.

Fact Sheet 7.1: Diminishing Marginal Product of Labor

This Fact Sheet illustrates the shape of the output curve usually assumed in economics and relates it to the marginal product of labor. Marginal product is given by the slope of the production function at any one point. The slope is assumed to be always positive, meaning that marginal product of labor is always positive and that an increase in labor supply will always produce an increase in output. Notice the slope at point C is lower than at point B and lower still than at point A. This is indicative of the diminishing marginal product of labor, since at higher levels of labor, additional units will produce less and less output.

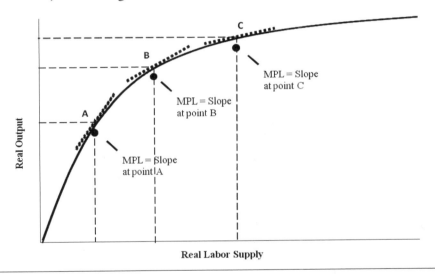

Figure 7.1a shows the usual shape of the production function. Its positive slope indicates that it has positive MPL as employment increases. Its concave shape reflects diminishing MPL. The shape of the MPL curve corresponding to the shape of the production function in Figure 7.1a is shown in Figure 7.1b. This shape is often simplified in textbook macroeconomics to the downward sloping straight line shown in Figure 7.2a.

---

[9]The assumption is that though investment occurs, such investment takes time to translate into physical capital in actual production. These are due to the 'gestation lag' for capital, caused by the time-to-build factories, machines, etc. and bring them into producing goods for sale. Further, as indicated earlier, the inflows of physical capital through direct foreign investment by foreigners are assumed not to alter the domestic capital stock in the short run. The impact of these inflows will then have to be treated as a shift in the production function.

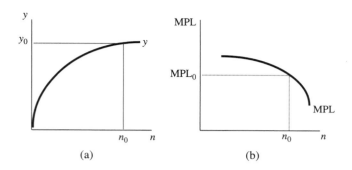

Figure 7.1

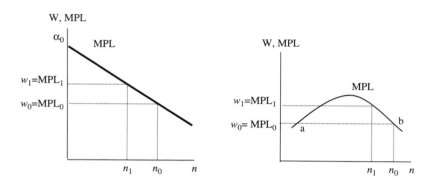

Figures 7.2

The general shape of the MPL curve is shown in Figure 7.2b. Along this curve, the MPL first increases and then decreases. The production function corresponding to this shape of the MPL curve has initially increasing MPL, followed by a segment with diminishing MPL. Such a production function is often used in microeconomics, and we will use it in the growth theory Chapters 14 and 15, but do not show it diagrammatically in this chapter.

Mathematical Box 7.1: Examples of Production Functions and the Derivation of the Marginal Product of Labor

The general procedure for deriving the MPL from the production function

Suppose we are given a production function of the form:

$$y = \alpha_0 n - \alpha_1 n^\beta,$$

where α_0, α_1, and β are parameters. The procedure for deriving the MPL (which in calculus corresponds to taking the first derivative of y with respect to n) is:

(a) Take the first term ($\alpha_0 n$) on the right-hand side of the equation. Note that the exponent on n is 1. Multiply the coefficient in this term by the exponent on n, and change the exponent on n by subtracting 1 from the initial exponent. This gives ($\alpha_0 \cdot 1 n^{1-1}$), which simplifies to α_0. This is the increase in output contributed by the first term.

Mathematical Box 7.1: (*Continued*)

(b) Take the second term $(-\alpha_1 n^\beta)$ on the right-hand side of the equation. Note that the exponent on n is β. Multiply the coefficient α_1 in this term by the exponent on n, and change the exponent on n by subtracting 1 from the initial exponent. This gives $[-\alpha_1 \cdot \beta n^{\beta-1}]$. This is the increase in output contributed by the second term. [If there are more than two terms on the right side, follow these steps for each term.]

(c) Add the increases in output contributed by the two terms to arrive at the MPL for the above production function. This gives:

$$\text{MPL} = \alpha_0 - \alpha_1 \cdot \beta n^{\beta-1}.$$

For the application of this procedure, we consider three production functions and derive their corresponding marginal product of labor.

i. *A linear production function*:

$$y = \alpha n \quad \alpha > 0,$$

where α is a constant. The marginal product of labor for this production function is:

$$y_n = \alpha \quad \alpha > 0,$$

so that the marginal product of labor is constant for all levels of employment. This violates the usual assumption of diminishing MPL, so that it is not appropriate to assume a linear production function.

ii. *A quadratic production function*:

$$y = \alpha_0 n - \alpha_1 n^2 \quad \alpha_0, \, \alpha_1 > 0,$$

where α_0 and α_1 are constants. The MPL for this production function is:

$$y_n = \alpha_0 - 2\alpha_1 n \quad \alpha_0, \, \alpha_1 > 0,$$

so that the MPL varies with employment. The MPL is positive but diminishing, as required.

For a numerical illustration of the quadratic production function, let $\alpha_0 = 1,000$ and $\alpha_1 = 0.75$. Then the production function is:

$$y = 1000n - 0.75n^2$$

and its MPL is:

$$y_n = 1000 - 1.5n.$$

This is plotted in Figure 7.2a and shows a downward-sloping straight line for the MPL. Note that the MPL declines as employment increases.

The quadratic production function has the severe disadvantage that the exponent on the second term $(-\alpha_1 n^2)$ is 2, which is much too high. This exponent should be about 0.6 or 0.7. However, using such values makes for greater mathematical difficulty in solving the model, so that the exponent of 2 is used for mathematical convenience — not realism.

iii. *The Cobb–Douglas production function* [*optional*]

A Cobb–Douglas production function, with labor and capital as inputs, is specified by:

$$y = An^\alpha K^{(1-\alpha)} \quad 0 < \alpha < 1,$$

Mathematical Box 7.1: (*Continued*)

where A and α are constants. This function has the special property that the income shares of labor (at α) and of capital (at $1 - \alpha$) are constant. With capital constant at $\bar{K}$, rearrange this function as:

$$y = (A\bar{K}^{(1-\alpha)})n^\alpha \quad 0 < \alpha < 1$$

and write it as:

$$y = Bn^\alpha \quad 0 < \alpha < 1, \ B > 0,$$

where B equals $(A\bar{K}^{(1-\alpha)})$ and is treated as a constant in short-run analysis. The MPL for this production function is:

$$\text{MPL} = \alpha Bn^{\alpha-1} \quad 0 < \alpha < 1, \ B > 0,$$

so that the MPL declines as employment increases. For many countries, the value of α lies in the range 0.6 to 0.7, so that their MPL is positive but diminishing, as required. If this MPL curve had been plotted (but was not), it would be a downward sloping concave curve rather than a straight line.

iv. *The general shape of the MPL curve*

A still more general shape of the MPL curve occurs if the MPL initially increases and then decreases. This is often the shape shown for the MPL curve. It is drawn in Figure 7.2b, and shows a concave curve with an initial upward sloping segment followed by a downward-sloping one. In this case, the profit-maximizing firm would employ workers up to the point where the MPL equals the wage rate on the downward — not the upward — sloping part of the MPL curve. This is explained in the next section.

7.2 The Labor Market

The specification of the labor market requires specification of the demand and supply functions of labor. The demand function for labor is derived from profit maximization by firms and the supply function for labor is derived from the utility analysis of households/workers. We here present the simplified functions used in standard macroeconomic models. These assert that both the demand and supply of labor depend only on the real wage rate.

7.2.1 Demand for labor

It is assumed that the representative firm maximizes profits in perfectly competitive markets and takes the price of its product and the nominal wage rate W as set by the market. The former is represented in aggregate analysis by the price level P. The microeconomic theory of perfect competition implies that the profit-maximizing firm would employ labor until the value of its marginal product (i.e., P times MPL) equals its nominal wage rate. The reason for this is that if the value of the MPL is more than the nominal wage, the firm will increase its profits by hiring an additional worker, since that worker's output contributes more to the firm's revenue than his wage. Conversely, if the value of the MPL were less than the nominal wage, the firm would increase its profits by reducing its employment. Therefore, profit maximization implies the equality of the value of the MPL to the nominal wage rate. The firm achieves this by choosing the appropriate level of employment. That is, employment will be carried to the point at which

$$P \cdot \text{MPL} = W, \tag{3}$$

where:

P = price level and
W = nominal wage rate.

Dividing both sides of this equation by P implies that, in perfect competition and in the aggregate, profit maximization requires that the representative firm employ labor up to the point where the real value of its marginal product equals its real wage rate. That is, $\text{MPL} = W/P = w$, so that:

$$\text{MPL} = w, \tag{4}$$

where w is the real wage rate and the MPL depends on the level of employment n. Solving the above equation for employment n, and designating this value as the demand for labor n^d by firms, we have:

$$n^d = n^d(w) \quad \partial n^d / \partial w < 0. \tag{5}$$

Since $w = W/P$, the demand for labor can also be written as:

$$n^d = n^d(W/P).$$

Diagrammatic analysis

The diagrammatic derivation of the labor demand curve is shown in Figure 7.2a for the linear MPL and in Figure 7.2b for the more general case where the MPL first increases and then decreases. To maximize profits, the firm increases employment until the MPL equals the market-determined real wage rate. Figure 7.2b shows two points of intersection at a and b between the market-determined wage w_0 and the MPL.[10] Of these points, b is the point of profit maximization at w_0, so that the firm would demand n_0 workers.[11]

In Figures 7.2a and 7.2b, the firm's initial labor demand is n_0 at wage w_0. If the wage rate rises to w_1, the firm's labor demand would fall to n_1 workers. The intuitive explanation for the fall in labor demand is that a rise in the wage rate makes labor more expensive, so that firms will hire less workers. Therefore, in Figures 7.2a and 7.2b, as the wage rate fluctuates up and down, it will trace out the demand for labor by the downward sloping part of the MPL curve, so that the labor demand curve is identical with the MPL curve if the upward-sloping part of the MPL is omitted. This labor demand curve is shown by the curve marked n^d in Figure 7.3. Hence, the demand for labor is negatively related to the wage rate: if the latter rises, the former falls.

7.2.2 Supply of labor

In microeconomics, an individual worker's supply of labor is derived by constrained utility maximization for a given real wage rate determined by the market and his time constraints (24 hours a day to be divided into work and leisure). For a worker, the real wage rate is the marginal return to an extra hour of work, as well as the opportunity cost of taking an extra hour of leisure. An increase in the wage rate causes the return to work

---

[10]Point a represents the minimum level of profits. At this point, increasing employment by one worker would increase output more than the wage rate, so that profits would rise. Therefore, the firm would increase employment beyond the point a, and continue hiring more workers until it reaches point b. Hence, the firm would never operate (i.e., employ workers) on the upward-sloping part of the MPL curve.

[11]If the firm were to increase employment beyond n_0, the increase in output due to the higher employment would be less than the wage rate, so that profits would fall.

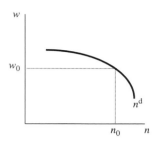

Figure 7.3

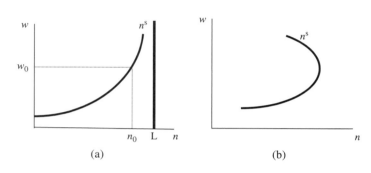

(a)   (b)

Figure 7.4

to rise. Conversely, it causes the opportunity cost of leisure to rise. Therefore, at higher wage rates, the worker will substitute more work for leisure and increase the supply of labor. As the wage rate continues to rise, the increase in the labor supply is likely to become lesser and lesser. Box 7.1 discusses the possibility that the labor supply of a given worker may eventually begin to fall, as in Figure 7.4b.[12] Short-run models assume that this fall does not happen. The justification for this assumption is given in Box 7.1.

The preceding paragraph implies that the worker's supply of labor depends upon the real wage rate, which is the marginal return to an extra unit of work, as well as being the marginal opportunity cost of leisure. For the economy, as the wage rate increases, some of the employed workers may increase their labor supply by working longer hours, some of those about to retire may postpone their retirement and continue to work, and others who were not in the labor force (students, housewives, etc.) may be induced by the higher wage to enter it. In addition to the real wage rate w, the economy's aggregate supply of labor over all workers would also depend on the labor force. Therefore, the labor supply function is:

$$n^s = n^s(w, L) \quad \partial n^s / \partial w > 0,$$

---

[12]This did occur over the 20th century. As the real wage rate rose from very low levels at the end of the 19th century to their present substantially high levels, workers chose to buy more leisure along with buying more consumer goods. The former translated into a decrease in the hours worked per week. However, such an effect occurs over long periods and for very substantial, rather than marginal, increases in wage rates.

where:

n^s = labor supply,
w = real wage rate, and
L = labor force.

The labor force L depends on the population and the labor force participation rate. The latter depends on the age, gender, geographic, and skill composition of the population. This participation rate can be altered by both social and economic changes, e.g., the labor force participation rates of women increased very considerably in the 1960s and 1970s in most countries. However, such shifts are treated as exogenous in the short-run macroeconomic analysis.

The cross-border flows of labor can be significant and endogenous for some countries — i.e., depend upon their unemployment rates and real wages — so that, for such countries, the labor force is not really exogenous.[13] However, with immigration strictly controlled by most countries, the annual inflows and outflows of labor to most economies are very small relative to their existing labor force, so that their labor force is not significantly affected by such movements in the short run. For such economies, the labor force is taken to be exogenous in the short run. Therefore, the labor supply function adopted for our open economy macroeconomic model is the same as it would be if the economy were closed. This function is specified as:

$$n^s = n^s(w) \quad \partial n^s/\partial w > 0, \tag{6}$$

so that the supply of labor n^s depends positively on the real wage rate w. Both n^s and w are for the current period. Since $w = W/P$, we can also write the supply of labor as:

$$n^s = n^s(W/P).$$

Note that the supply of labor depends upon the real rather than the nominal wage. That is, workers are free from *price and inflation illusion*. This illusion is the distortion caused when money wage rates and the prices of commodities rise by identical proportions but the workers, looking at the rising nominal wage rates, believe that they are better off, although the purchasing power of wages has remained unchanged. A proportionate increase in the nominal wage rate and the price level would leave the real wage unchanged, so that, without price illusion, the supply of labor also does not change.

Figure 7.4a shows the likely short-run shape of the labor supply curve. It shows that an increase in the real wage rate increases labor supply. We have drawn the labor supply curve with an increasing slope at higher wage rates since, as wages increase, the increases in the labor supply tend to become lesser and lesser. This is especially likely to occur as the labor supply becomes closer to the labor force level. Since the labor supply curve is upward sloping, it is often simplified for analytical convenience by a straight line with a positive slope.

Extended Analysis Box 7.1: The Intertemporal Analysis of Labor Supply

Economic theory implies that if the choices over time are considered (as in intertemporal analysis), the individual is likely to substitute between work in the current period and future periods — *if the employment patterns of firms allow such a choice*. In this analysis, the current period's supply of labor depends on the current wage rate and the present discounted value (PDV) of the future wage rate. In the two-period

---

[13] Examples of these are some of the countries of the Arabian Peninsula, the southern region of the USA with immigration from Mexico, etc.

Extended Analysis Box 7.1: (*Continued*)

analysis for periods t and $t + 1$, the current wage will be designated as w_t, and the PDV of the future wage rate is $w_{t+1}/(1 + r_t)$.

In the aggregate over all workers in the labor force, the supply of labor also depends on the labor force. Therefore, the supply function for labor can be expressed as:

$$n_t^s = n^s(w_t, \ w_{t+1}/(1 + r_t), \ L_t),$$

where:

n_t = labor supply in the current period t,
w_t = real wage rate in t,
w_{t+1} = real wage rate in $t + 1$ (i.e., future wage rate),
r_t = real interest rate in t, and
L = labor force.

In this labor supply function, an increase in the *expected future (but not the current) wage* or a decrease in the interest rate will induce the individual worker to reduce labor supply and increase leisure in the current period, while increasing labor supply and reducing leisure in the future. However, an increase in *both the expected future and the current wage* does not change the market rate of substitution between work in the current and future periods. Therefore, a temporary increase in the real wage will bring about a stronger increase in labor supply than a permanent increase.

Note that this tilt in the hours worked from the present to the future, or vice versa, requires the flexibility in working hours to be exercised at the employee's (not the employer's) option. For most workers in the economy, such a tilt is not an option allowed to them by their employers, at least not in the short run, so that the intertemporal substitution of labor may not be significant. However, there may be some workers such as self-employed ones, students working part time, those close to retirement, etc., who may possess some flexibility.

Empirical evidence usually reports that, over a quarter or a year, changes in the expected real wage lead to very limited changes in the hours worked, so that many economists do not consider the intertemporal substation of labor to be really significant. However, some other economists dispute this assessment of the empirical evidence and consider the dependence of current labor supply on future wage rates and the interest rate to be significant enough to use it in their explanation of the variations in unemployment over the business cycle.[14]

The Backward Bending Labor Supply Curve Over Long Periods

For many jobs in the 19th and early 20th centuries, work hours were as long as 60 hours or more per week. As wages and the standards of living rose in the 20th century, work hours per week fell. This phenomenon is the outcome of two effects of higher wages on labor supply. One of these is the *substitution effect*, which specifies the substitution of work for leisure as wages rise and makes leisure relatively more expensive. The other is the *income effect*, which specifies that as wages rise, incomes rise and workers can afford to purchase more commodities as well as more leisure. In fact, increased purchases of entertainment goods usually require more leisure to enjoy them. As the purchase of leisure per week increases, the labor supplied

---

[14]The theories doing so are called real business cycle theories. These are explained in Chapter 6.

per week falls. The overall effect of rising wages on labor supply represents the opposing pull of the substitution and income effects, which could produce an increase in labor supply for some increases in wages but a fall for larger increases in wages. This possibility is captured in the backward bending labor curve shown in Figure 7.4b.

Short-run macroeconomic theory usually simplifies by assuming that the net effect of rising wages is to increase the labor supply, i.e., the labor supply curve is upward sloping. This is a reasonable assumption for relatively small percentage increases in real wages that occur over short periods such as the business cycle. However, it cannot be taken for granted for large increases in wage rates over very long periods. In fact, the very long-term historical experience, starting with low wages and incomes, has been one of a gradual decrease of work hours per week. This pattern is also likely to occur in the very long term in those developing economies that currently have very high work hours per week.[15] Whether this pattern will continue to hold for further increases in wages in the *high income, developed, economies* remains to be seen.

If we look beyond the individual worker and focus on the family, the social norms on work by all its members — including children — become important. For *given norms* on the labor force participation rates of men, women, and children, the long-term impact of higher wages often means that the family as a unit decreases labor supply as wages and incomes rise. For instance, in recent decades, on average, children have continued their education longer and reduced their work hours per year. However, these norms can shift over time. One such shift has been the dramatic rise in the labor market participation of females since the 1960s, which has led to a dramatic increase in the average number of hours supplied *per family*.

7.3 The Long-Run Equilibrium Levels of Employment and Output

The equilibrium level n^* of employment is determined by the equality of the demand and supply of labor. Hence,

$$n^* = n^d(w) = n^s(w), \tag{7}$$

where n is employment and the asterisk (*) indicates its equilibrium value. Since this equation has only one variable, w, solving it would yield the equilibrium wage rate w^*. This wage rate, substituted in either the demand or supply function, yields the equilibrium level of employment n^*. This level of employment substituted in the production function would yield the equilibrium level of output y^* for the economy. Hence, we have:

$$y^* = y(n^*). \tag{8}$$

These equilibrium levels of output have been derived for the long-run case where there are no adjustment costs, expectational errors or rigidities. They are, therefore, the long-run equilibrium (LR) levels of employment and output. To reflect this, we will write y^* as y^f and n^* as n^f.

---

[15]For Canada, the average number of hours worked per week declined from 34 hours and 22 minutes per week in 1979 to 33 hours in 2003, mirroring a similar trend in other industrial countries. The annual average hours worked in 2003 were 1,718 for Canada, 1,792 for the USA, 1,354 for the Netherlands, and 2,400 for South Korea.

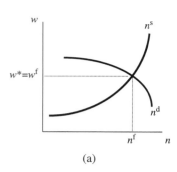 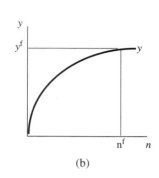 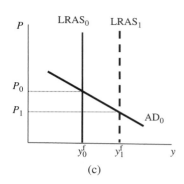

(a)   (b)   (c)

Figure 7.5

7.3.1 The impact on long-run output of an increase in the price level or inflation rate

Suppose that the price level or inflation increases for some reason. These variables have already been shown not to affect the long-run output level, so that the increase in them will not change output in the long run.

7.3.2 The diagrammatic analysis of employment and output

Figure 7.5a plots the demand and supply functions of labor, with the usual slopes for the demand and supply curves. LR equilibrium occurs at (n^f, w^f).

Figure 7.5b plots the production function: it plots output y against employment n and is labeled as y (output). This curve has a positive slope and is concave, representing the assumption of the diminishing marginal productivity of labor. The equilibrium level of employment n^f determined in Figure 7.5a is carried over into Figure 7.5b and implies the LR equilibrium — and profit-maximizing — output y^f.

Suppose the price level increases. It does not shift any of the curves in these diagrams, so that the LR levels of w^f, n^f, and y^f will not change. Therefore, if we plot y^f against P, as in Figures 7.5c and 7.6b, we would have a vertical curve. This curve was called the long-run supply (LRAS) curve in Chapter 1 and is shown by LRAS$_0$ in Figure 7.5c.

The effect on output of an improvement in labor productivity

Suppose that an improvement in the productivity of labor or an increase in labor supply increases the LR output of the economy, thereby shifting LRAS curve in Figure 7.5c to the right from LRAS$_0$ to LRAS$_1$. Hence, an increase is labor productivity increases the long-run level of output but decreases the price level.

7.3.3 The impact of aggregate demand on long-run output

Chapter 5 presented the analysis of aggregate demand under an interest rate target. The open economy AD equation derived in that chapter was:

$$y^d = \alpha[\{c_0 - c_y t_0 + i_0 - i_r r_0^T + g + x_{c0} - x_{c\rho}\rho^r\} + (1/\rho^r) \cdot \{- z_{c0} + z_{cy} t_0 - z_{c\rho}\rho^r\}], \qquad (9)$$

where the symbol α stands for the (autonomous investment) multiplier and has the meaning:

$$\alpha = \left(\frac{1}{1 - c_y + c_y t_y + \frac{1}{\rho^r} z_{cy}(1 - t_y)} \right) > 0.$$

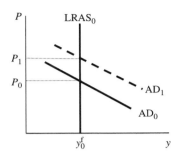

Figure 7.6

The meanings of the symbols are as given in Chapters 4 and 5. This aggregate demand equation implies that the aggregate demand curve AD has a negative slope, as shown in Figure 7.6.

The pursuit of fiscal policies

The IS-IRT analysis in Chapter 5 showed that an increase in government expenditures increases aggregate demand and shifts the AD curve to the right, as shown in Figure 7.6. With output at the full-employment level, the increase in aggregate demand will cause the price level to rise, but without any increase in output.

The pursuit of expansionary monetary policies

A cut by the central bank in its target rate constitutes an expansionary monetary policy. Suppose the bank pursues such a policy. This would increase investment and aggregate demand, as shown by the rightward shift of the AD curve in Figure 7.6. This would create excess demand. Its effects will be similar to the above ones for an expansionary fiscal policy: i.e., increase demand and lead to a price level increase, but without any increase in output.

7.3.4 The ineffectiveness of monetary and fiscal policies in LR equilibrium

Note that the LR levels of employment and output do not depend on any variables other than encapsulated in the production function (which determined labor demand) and the labor supply function (which depend on workers' work-leisure preferences). Changes in aggregate demand, prices and inflation do not change the production function and work-leisure preferences, so that they do not affect the LR employment and output. Since the impact of monetary and fiscal policies occurs through aggregate demand, these policies cannot change LR employment and output. This is an important conclusion. *It asserts the uselessness — and therefore, the inadvisability of pursuing — monetary and fiscal policies for changing LR output and employment.* Its message is reinforced by the following Mathematical Box 7.2.

Mathematical Box 7.2: The Derivation of the Demand for Labor, Employment, and Output

The *quadratic* production function for the representative firm in our earlier example was:

$$y = \alpha_0 n - \alpha_1 n^2 \quad \alpha_0, \alpha_1 > 0.$$

Its MPL was:

$$y_n = \alpha_0 - 2\alpha_1 n.$$

Mathematical Box 7.2: (*Continued*)

Since the profit-maximizing firm equates the MPL to the marker-determined real wage rate w, we have:

$$w = \alpha_0 - 2\alpha_1 n.$$

Solving for the demand for labor n^d, we get:

$$n^d = \frac{\alpha_0}{2\alpha_1} - \frac{1}{2\alpha_1} w.$$

If we let $a_0 = \alpha_0/(2\alpha_1)$ and $a_1 = 1/(2\alpha_1)$, we get the labor demand function:

$$n^d = a_0 - a_1 w \quad a_0,\ a1 > 0.$$

Assume that the supply function of labor is:

$$n^s = b_1 w \quad b_1 > 0.$$

In equilibrium, with $n^d = n^s$,

$$a_0 - a_1 w = b_1 w,$$

so that,

$$w^* = \left[\frac{a_0}{a_1 + b_1} \right].$$

Substitute this wage in the labor demand (or labor supply) function to derive the LR equilibrium level of employment as:

$$n^* = a_0 - \left[\frac{a_0 a_1}{a_1 + b_1} \right].$$

Substituting this level of employment in the production function provides the LR level of output as:

$$y^f = \alpha_0 \left[a_0 - \frac{a_0 a_1}{a_1 + b_1} \right] - \alpha_1 \left[a_0 - \frac{a_0 a_1}{a_1 + b_1} \right]^2.$$

The role of aggregate demand in determining output and the price level, an illustration

Since the long-run supply of output $y^{s,LR}$ depends only on parameters (whose values are exogenously given) and not on variables, its value can be specified by a number (a constant). Designate this value as y_0^f. That is.

$$y^{s,LR} = y_0^f.$$

Let the AD equation be simply of the form:

$$y^d = 1000 - 2r^T + 0.1g - 0.5P.$$

This AD equation implies that a reduction in the target interest rate and an increase in government expenditures increase aggregate demand. Further, an increase in the domestic price level P decreases aggregate demand (by causing consumers at home and abroad to switch from domestic commodity purchases to foreign ones). However, we can see from the LR aggregate supply equation that such increases in aggregate demand cannot change LR output, which will remain at y_0^f. Therefore, monetary and fiscal policies cannot increase LR output.

Mathematical Box 7.2: (*Continued*)

If the long-run AS and AD equations above are combined by substituting LR output into the AD equation, we get:

$$y_0^f = 1000 - 2r^T + 0.1g - 0.5P,$$

so that:

$$P = (2000 - 4r^T + 0.2g) - 2y_0^f.$$

Hence, P would increase if the monetary policy variable r^T was to decrease, the fiscal policy variable g were to increase, or if output y decreased.

The impact of expansionary monetary and fiscal policies

Suppose the interest rate target is reduced by 10% from its previous level. This reduction does not change any of the parameters in the LR employment and output functions. Therefore, it does not change LR output and employment. However, the price level would increase to adjust the larger aggregate demand to an unchanged output.

Suppose government expenditures are increased by 10% from their previous level. This increase also does not change any of the parameters in the LR employment and output functions. Therefore, it does not change LR output and employment, but would increase the price level.

This conclusion on the ineffectiveness of monetary and fiscal policies to change LR output and employment holds not only for the illustrative AD equation used above but also for any AD function. It is a very important analytical and policy conclusion on the long-run performance of the economy.

7.4 The Effects of an Increase in the MPL on LR Output and Employment

Increases in the MPL occur because of an improvement in technology and/or the increased use of capital and other inputs by firms. Assuming that the increase in the MPL is accompanied by an increase in the average productivity of labor, the output curve relating output to employment shifts up. An increase in the MPL increases labor demand, which means that the labor demand curve shifts up for any given level of employment. This increases both the real wage and employment. LR output rises for two reasons: higher employment (from the labor market) and higher labor productivity (from the positive shift in the production function).

Conversely, decreases in the MPL occur because of a regression in technology and/or decreased use/availability of capital and other inputs by firms. Assuming that the decrease in the MPL is accompanied by a decrease in the average productivity of labor, the output curve relating output to employment shifts down. A decrease in the MPL decreases labor demand, which means that the labor demand curve shifts to the left. This decreases both the real wage and employment. LR output falls for two reasons: lower employment (from the labor market) and lower labor productivity (from the negative shift in the production function).

While our general knowledge indicates that improvements in technology occur frequently over time, it is harder to envisage a regression in technological knowledge. It is much easier to envisage decreases in capital, which can occur through the destruction of factories and other capital facilities in a war, through the bankruptcies of firms because of a fall in demand, and through depreciation or obsolescence of older machines without adequate replacement by new ones.

A still more common possibility for a fall in the MPL is a reduction in the availability of inputs other than labor and capital, or a rise in their prices so that the firm reduces their usage. These inputs include raw materials and intermediate goods. Among these, energy and imported inputs are important elements. A rise in the price of oil, gas, or electricity would lead to a reduction in their usage per unit of labor and reduce labor productivity. Further, many developing countries often have to curtail imports of inputs, including intermediate goods and spare parts for machines, due to foreign exchange problems, which reduces labor productivity. These reductions in labor productivity decrease labor demand, the wage rate, employment, and output.

7.4.1 Diagrammatic analysis of the impact of an improvement in technology on output and employment

For this analysis, suppose that positive technical change in the economy shifts the production function up from y_0 to y_1 in Figure 7.7a and the labor demand curve right from n_0^d to n_1^d in Figure 7.7b. The latter shift increases LR employment to n_1^f which, in Figure 7.7a, increases LR output to y_1^f. In this case, equilibrium output has increased for two reasons: greater employment and higher labor productivity. Therefore, as in Figure 7.5c, the LRAS curve will shift to the right from y_0^f to y_1^f. As shown in Figure 7.7b, the increases in employment and output are accompanied by an increase in the real wage at full employment. This is related to the increase in labor productivity ($\equiv y/n$).

7.5 The effects of an Increase in Labor Supply on LR Output, Employment and Price Level

Labor supply depends not only on the wage rate but also on the labor force, which depends on the population size and its participation rate. The labor supply out of a given labor force depends on social norms, workers' preferences between work and leisure, expected future wages and consumption needs — which depend on family size and the number of dependants, longevity, etc. — and other sources of income such as the return on

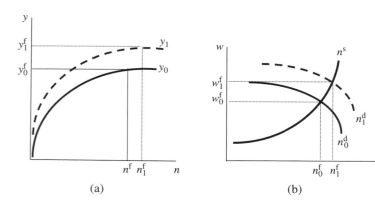

Figure 7.7

stocks and bonds. It also depends on factors such as unemployment insurance benefits, welfare, and minimum income support by the government, etc. Among examples of major increases in the labor supply out of a given labor force is the increasing participation in the last four decades of women in work outside the home, and significant immigration levels.

An example of a decrease in the labor supply is the decreasing participation rate of younger persons because of an increase in the number of years spent on education, with larger proportions of high school leavers continuing on to college and university education.

An increase in the labor supply shifts the labor supply curve to the right. It decreases the LR real wage rate but increases employment — which increases the LR output. As illustrated in the earlier Figure 7.5c, such an increase in output will be accompanied by a decrease in the price level. Conversely, a decrease in labor supply shifts the labor supply curve to the left. This increases the LR real wage rate but decreases employment — which decreases the LR output. This decrease in output will be accompanied by an increase in the price level.

Comparing the effects of a productivity increase with those of an increase in labor supply, increases in the labor supply or productivity raise the LR levels of employment and output. But the former decreases the LR real wage while the latter increases it.

Mathematical Box 7.3: The Effect of an Improvement in Technology

To see the effects of productivity improvements on employment and output, assume that initially the production function is as given in the Mathematical Box 7.2. Let there be a productivity increase such that the production function shifts to:

$$y' = 1.05(\alpha_0 n - \alpha_1 n^2) \quad \alpha_0, \alpha_1 > 0,$$

whose MPL is:

$$MPL' = 1.05(\alpha_0 - 2\alpha_1 n).$$

That is, the MPL (compared with that derived in the Mathematical Box 7.2) has increased for any given level of employment by 5%. The profit-maximizing firm would now equate this MPL to w, so that:

$$w = 1.05(\alpha_0 - 2\alpha_1 n),$$

which can be solved for the new demand curve for labor. This would be:

$$n^{d'} = -w/2.10\alpha_1 + \alpha_0/2\alpha_1.$$

If the original and the new labor demand curves are plotted, it will be seen that the labor demand curve would have shifted to the right. Since the increase in labor productivity shifts the labor demand curve to the right for any given wage, it increases the equilibrium levels of both the wage rate and employment. The latter increases the equilibrium level of output through the production function. The derivations of the solutions of this case for w, n, and y are left to the student.

The effect of an increase in labor supply

Suppose labor supply increases — due to a higher labor force participation rate or immigration — by 5% so that the labor supply function of the Mathematical Box 7.2 shifts to:

$$n^s = 1.05b_1 w \quad b_1 > 0.$$

Mathematical Box 7.3: (*Continued*)

Assuming the initial production function, MPL, and labor demand to be as in the Mathematical Box 7.2, the increase in labor supply would increase LR employment to:

$$n^* = a_0 - \left[\frac{a_0 a_1}{a_1 + 1.05 b_1}\right].$$

Since employment increases, the production function implies that output will also increase. But the LR real wage decreases to:

$$w^* = \left[\frac{a_0}{a_1 + 1.05\, b_1}\right].$$

Diagrammatically, the increase in labor supply has shifted the labor supply curve to the right, reduced w but increased n — which increased y.

7.6 Conclusions on Changes in the Equilibrium Levels of Employment and Output

The preceding analysis shows that the long-run equilibrium levels (w^{LR*}, n^{LR*}, and y^{LR*}) of the real wage rate, employment, and output depend on:

- the production function and
- the supply of labor.

Therefore, the factors that will change the LR values w^{LR*}, n^{LR*}, and y^{LR*} are shifts in the production function — with implied shifts in the demand for labor — and in the supply of labor. As established earlier, an increase in the MPL — which is illustrated in Mathematical Box 7.3 by increases in α_0 and/or α_1 — will increase the demand for labor and thereby increase the real wage rate, employment, and output. A decrease in the supply of labor — in Mathematical Box 7.2, because of a decrease in b_1 — will increase the wage rate but reduce employment and output. Conversely, an increase in the labor force participation rate would increase labor supply, decrease the wage rate while increasing employment and output.

These LR values w^{LR*}, n^{LR*}, and y^{LR*} do *not* depend upon:

- the price level or inflation,
- the aggregate demand for commodities, and
- monetary and fiscal policies.

Therefore, shocks to the economy which bring about shifts in aggregate demand and the price level will not alter the LR values w^{LR*}, n^{LR*}, and y^{LR*}. Among these shocks are changes in the policy variables, such as the target interest rate, money supply, and fiscal deficits, which are in the overall macroeconomic model but do not appear as arguments of the production function and the supply function of labor. This is a very strong implication for the equilibrium states of the above model. It implies that the aggregate demand policies such as monetary and fiscal policies cannot affect the LR levels of wages, employment and output in the economy. Similarly, the levels or shifts of consumption and investment do not alter the LR levels of output, employment, and real wages, but will change the price level.

7.7   Full Employment and the Full-Employment Level of Output: Definitions and Conditions

'Full employment' was defined in Chapter 1 and earlier in this chapter as the employment level that exists under certainty and in the absence of adjustment costs and lags, when all the (qualified and in the right locations)[16] workers who want jobs at the existing wage rate are employed while the firms can get all the workers that they want to employ at this wage rate. That is, *full employment* corresponds to the *long run* (i.e., once all adjustments have been completed) *equilibrium level of employment under certainty*. To reiterate, the conditions for the existence of full employment are:

- The absence of uncertainty about demand and prices. Full employment would also occur in the presence of uncertainty if the expected prices *and* expected demand corresponded to the actual ones — so that there were no errors in expectations.
- The absence of adjustment costs. Examples of adjustment costs are those of adjusting employment, output, and prices. Alternatively, if there are adjustment costs, as is normally quite likely, the economy's long-run responses captured in the analysis are only those after all the adjustments are over and the economy has again become stationary.
- The absence of labor contracts.
- Equilibrium in the labor market.

Since the analysis of this chapter has assumed certainty and the absence of adjustment costs, the condition for full employment is met at its equilibrium employment level n^{LR*}. To emphasise this property, we designate it as n^f. Its corresponding equilibrium output level y^{LR*} is the full-employment level of output y^f.

Our conclusions on the full-employment levels of output and employment are:

- These levels are uniquely determined by the production function and labor supply.
- They do not depend on aggregate demand, monetary, and fiscal policies, or the price level in the economy.
- They shift only if there are shifts in the production function and/or in the labor supply function.

7.8   The Role of Supply-Side Policies in Changing Full-Employment Output

As we have seen above, positive shifts in the production function and the supply of labor increase the full-employment level of output. Policies that do so are called *supply-side policies*. Among the examples of such policies are:

- Shifts in the production function induced by government subsidies to research and development (R&D).
- Policies that promote investment in the domestic economy — through government subsidies and tax breaks to firms to build factories or modernize their equipment — increase and/or make more efficient the capital stock and thereby increase labor productivity.
- Policies that increase labor supply include reductions in unemployment insurance benefits, thereby increasing the incentive to look for and accept job offers sooner. Other labor-oriented policies that increase employment include retraining schemes and those that increase the participation rate (which increases labor supply) or lower the minimum wage (which induces firms to hire more workers).[17]

---

[16]These qualifications are clarified in Chapter 8.

[17]This assumes that the minimum wage was initially above the equilibrium one for workers possessing the relevant skills.

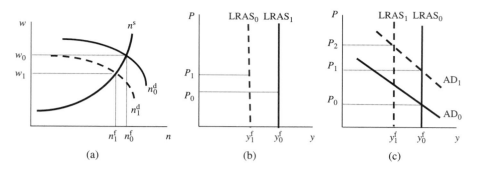

Figure 7.8

7.9 Stagflation

The condition in which output is static (stagnant) or falling while prices are rising is called *stagflation*. The increases in oil prices in 1973–1975 and 1980–1981 produced a negative shift in the production function and were among the sources of the fall in output, while the increases in aggregate demand induced by expansionary monetary and fiscal policies to offset the fall in output and employment were the main cause of stagflation during 1973–1975 and 1980–1981. The impact of rising oil prices on the economy is analyzed in Box 7.1 and Figures 7.8a and 7.8b. The following Fact Sheet provides information on the movements in the price of oil in recent decades.

Fact Sheet 7.2: The Price of Oil in the USA, 1960–2008

This Fact Sheet shows fluctuations in the price of oil, which is an important source of energy in the production of commodities. The price of crude oil is stated in terms of dollars per barrel. As we see in the graph below, both real and nominal prices of oil have fluctuated greatly since 1960. The 1973 and 1979 OPEC oil embargoes caused surging oil prices after 1973 and for most of the 1980s. However, the increases in oil prices since the early 2000s have also been considerable. High energy prices usually have a contractionary effect on output in oil importing countries since it is an essential input in production, but not for large oil exporting countries, which benefit from high oil prices.

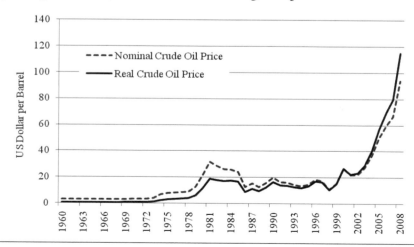

Increases in aggregate demand brought about by expansionary fiscal or monetary policies do not offset long-run decreases in output but will add to inflation. Such policies were attempted during 1973–1975 and again in 1980–1981 in an attempt to offset decreases in output due to the oil price increases. Their result was to increase the inflation rate in subsequent years, so that these policies contributed to the stagflation initiated by the oil price increases.

Box 7.1: The Impact of Oil Price Shocks on Full Employment and Full-Employment Output in Oil Importing Countries

Oil is a major source of energy in the production processes of the economy. Oil prices in real terms in the world economy increased substantially in 1973–1975, in 1980–1981 and again in 2000. At other times, they increased less dramatically. There were also many years during which they decreased. Our analysis is only concerned with the real or relative price of oil. By this, we mean the price of oil divided by the price level.

How do increases or decreases in oil prices impact on the economy? For the LR analysis, we will assume that the increase in oil prices is permanent and was fully anticipated, so that it was taken into account in the firms' production and employment decisions. We will also ignore any effects of this shift on investment and aggregate demand, and any adjustment costs and lags.

To properly incorporate the impact of oil prices on production, we need to modify our production function to:

$$y = f(n, O),$$

where O designates the usage of oil. The rationale for its inclusion is that oil is an essential energy source that affects the output produced by a given quantity of employment. Assume that both labor and oil are complementary in production, so that a reduction in oil usage will reduce the marginal product of labor. Since the MPL now depends on both employment and oil usage (as well as the capital stock and technology), we write it as $y_n(n, O)$. Therefore, the profit-maximizing condition for employment becomes:

$$y_n(n, O) = w.$$

An increase in the price of oil will reduce its usage and shift the MPL curve to the left. In Figure 7.8a, the oil price increase decreases its usage and shifts the labor demand curve to the left from n_0^d to n_1^d. The LR employment falls from n_0^f to n_1^f. Hence, from the production function, LR output will also fall. This fall in output occurs for two reasons: the fall in employment and the decrease in labor productivity. It is shown in Figure 7.8b by a leftward shift of the LRAS curve from $LRAS_0$ to $LRAS_1$. This causes the long-run output y^f to fall from y_0^f to y_1^f and the real wage to fall. The price level is also likely to rise (the analysis for this is given in Chapters 8 and 9). Since output falls, while the price level rises, an oil price increase produces stagflation.

Oil is only one of the elements of a factor of production that can be labeled as 'resources' (raw materials). The above analysis can also be used to find the impact of changes in the costs and availability of other resources on output, employment, prices, and real wages.

Stagflation (i.e., stagnant inflation) is the term used for a situation in which output is constant or falling, while the economy has inflation. It is a dynamic situation that can be caused, as explained above, by continual oil price increases, which, by shifting the LRAS curve left, keep reducing output and increasing the price level over several quarters or years. The resulting inflation is likely to be at low levels. It would increase further under expansionary monetary and fiscal policies, for which see below.

Note that rising oil prices will also worsen the balance of payments of oil importing countries, and are likely to cause decreases in their exchange rates against the currencies of oil exporting countries.

The impact of oil price increases on oil producing countries

Note that the preceding analysis strictly applies to oil importing countries. By comparison, countries that produce their own oil and even export some are likely to increase their oil production levels and thereby increase their GDP and their employment. If they are mainly oil producing countries, with most of their GDP originating in the oil sector, the raising oil prices are likely to shift their LRAS curve to the right, not to the left, thereby rising their GDP.

Can expansionary monetary and fiscal policies eliminate this stagflation?

As oil prices rose considerably in 1973–1975 and again in 1980–1981, they set up the potential for the fall in output. Many countries tried to offset this by expansionary monetary and fiscal policies. To see the LR effects of such a response, assume that aggregate demand is raised by such policies and shifts the AD curve to the right in Figure 7.8c from AD_0 to AD_1. This shift does not increase or change the (post-increase in oil prices) LR output from y_1^f but provides a stronger impetus to the price increases. Therefore, in the long run, there are two causes/components of the price level rise:

- The rise in the price level due to the oil price increase.
- The further raise in the price level due to the expansionary monetary and fiscal policies.

The LR analysis implies that since output falls from y_0^f to y_1^f, while the price level rises, these policies only made stagflation worse in the long run.

Extended Analysis Box 7.2: The Role of Demand-Side Policies in Changing Full-Employment Output

The preceding analysis has shown that n^f and y^f depend only on the parameters of the production and labor supply functions, and not on any of the parameters and exogenous policy variables that determine aggregate demand. In particular, they do not depend on the target interest rate, money supply, government expenditure, or deficits. That is, the long-run equilibrium effects are specified by:

$$\partial y^f / \partial r^T = 0$$

and

$$\partial y^f / \partial g = 0, \tag{11}$$

where r^T stands for the target interest rate. That is, the output level under full employment is independent of any demand influence, whether it is from investment, fiscal policy, or monetary policy, or the parameters of aggregate demand in the economy.

An implicit assumption in the above conclusions

Since the full-employment output is independent of the demand side of the economy, the preceding analysis has the implicit assumption: the economy has adequate and sufficiently fast reacting equilibrating mechanisms to force aggregate demand y^d into equality with the full-employment output y^f immediately or in a short enough time through price changes only, so that the deficit or excess demand do not affect production and employment by firms, nor do they affect the consumer demand and labor supply of household or investment by firms. A corollary of this assumption is that the firms do not react to changes in their current and expected future demand directly but only to the prices established by the markets for their products and assume that they will sell the amounts consistent with the full-employment levels of demand. Further, workers/consumers do not react — by changes in their consumption patterns or in the search for jobs — to changes in their current employment and incomes and future prospects for jobs and incomes directly but only to their market-established wages, and assume that the market will in fact ensure that the full-employment number of jobs will be available at this wage. These represent very strong assumptions and not all economies in all possible stages of development or of the business cycle meet them. When these assumptions are not met, we need to rely on the short-run equilibrium and/or disequilibrium analyses, which are presented in Chapters 8 and 9.

The LR analysis of full employment assumes that the above assumptions are met. In it, the equilibrating forces adjusting aggregate demand to the aggregate supply (at the full-employment level) determined in the production-employment sector bring about, in the long-run equilibrium, appropriate changes in the interest rate, real wages, and the price level. Therefore, we can assert that "*in the long-run equilibrium of this model, the equilibrium level of supply creates its own demand*" — through the equilibrating changes in prices, wages, and interest rates.

7.10 Crowding Out of Investment by Fiscal Deficits, Given the LR Supply of Output in the Closed Economy

'Crowding out' is a term which is applied to the decrease in investment and net exports by fiscal deficits. There are two reasons for crowding out. They are:

1. Interest-rate crowding out. This occurs if fiscal deficits financed by government borrowing in the form of new bond issues increase the interest rate in financial markets, which reduces investment. This form of crowding out occurs in the determination of aggregate demand if the money supply is being held constant by the central bank. This case of money supply targeting was discussed in Chapter 6. However, note that if the central bank targets the interest rate (as in the analysis of Chapter 5) and holds it constant in the presence of fiscal deficits, interest-rate crowding out does not occur.
2. Output-crowding out. This case occurs when output does not change in response to fiscal deficits, even if the deficits do increase aggregate demand. This occurs only if the economy was already producing the full-employment output and maintains this level of output in the presence of fiscal deficits. This is the context of the long-run analysis of this chapter. [However, it does not apply in the determination of output in the short run (explained in Chapter 8) or in the disequilibrium analysis of Chapter 9.]

The following analysis is that of output-crowding out based on the analysis of long-run output in this chapter. To start, first suppose that the fiscal deficit is caused by an increase in government *expenditures* directly on goods and services. In the long run, with $y = y^f$, the equilibrium between the LR output and the commodity sector specifies that:

$$y^f = c + i + g + (x_c - z_c/\rho^r). \tag{12}$$

Since the exogenous increase in g does not change the left side, the increase in g must reduce either c or i and/or net exports $(x_c - z_c/\rho^r)$. But the increase in g also does not alter disposable income, so that c does not change. Therefore, the *increase* in g must be matched by a corresponding *decrease* in either i or net exports, or both. This crowding out is being enforced by the LR supply constraint set by full-employment output on the economy, so that it belongs to long-run analysis.

Now suppose that the fiscal deficit is caused by an increase in government *transfers* to households. Hence, the public's disposable income increases, so that consumption c rises. Therefore, on the right side of the preceding equation, while government *expenditures* g do not increase (or change), c does. Therefore, the sum of investment and net exports must decrease by a corresponding amount.

Hence, government deficits, whether due to the increase in the government's provision of commodities for the public's consumption or in transfers to households, can be quite inimical to LR private investment and net exports by crowding out either one or both of them. On the crowding out of investment by government deficits, if the deficit is due to increases in government expenditures on capital projects, then it is preferable to focus on total investment (sum of public plus private investment). It is the crowding out of total investment by the consumption expenditures of either the government or the households that is of concern for the future growth of the economy's capital stock and wealth.

7.11 The Actual Level of Output in the Economy

Actual output in an economy in a given period can differ from the full-employment one. The components of the actual level of output can be differentiated in the form:

$$y = y^f + (y^* - y^f) + (y - y^*), \tag{13}$$

so that the actual level of output has three components:

1. y^f: the full-employment level of output. This is the LR equilibrium level — under certainty (or in the absence of price misperceptions under uncertainty) and once all adjustments have been completed. Alternatively, if there is uncertainty, economic agents do not make any errors in their expectations.
2. $(y^* - y^f)$: the deviation of the short-run equilibrium level of output from the full-employment one due to errors in expectations under uncertainty and adjustment costs.
3. $(y - y^*)$: the disequilibrium level of output, which would exist if actual output was not even in short-run equilibrium.

Therefore, the *actual* output in the economy can differ from the full-employment level for one or more of the following three reasons:

1. Under uncertainty, the difference between the short-run equilibrium and the long-run (full-employment) output due to errors in expectations.
2. The difference between the short-run equilibrium and the long-run full-employment output due to adjustment costs and lags.
3. The possibility that the economy may not even be in equilibrium.

Cases (1) and/or (2) lead to the short-run aggregate supply (SRAS) curve analyzed in Chapters 8. Case (3) represents disequilibrium and is analyzed in Chapter 9.

This chapter has only examined the determination of the LR (full-employment) level of output. Its analysis was under the assumption of certainty so that expectational errors were ruled out. Further, adjustment costs and lags were not allowed in the analysis. Therefore, by assumption, $(y^* - y^f) = 0$. Furthermore, this analysis was under the assumption of equilibrium in the labor market, firm's production, and workers' labor supply, so that disequilibrium was also ruled out by assumption, with the result that $(y - y^*) = 0$. However, we cannot take it for granted that the real-world economies will meet these assumptions for each period of our study, when these periods are as short as, say, a month, a quarter, or a year. We, therefore, resorted to the analytical notion of the long run, which is defined as the stage in which these assumptions are met, so that the economy can be said to be at the full-employment (LR) level of output.

Hence, the aggregate supply curve for the full-employment level of output is called the LR aggregate supply (LRAS) curve. It is applicable in the case of zero expectational errors, zero adjustment costs and lags, and equilibrium in the labor market and in production. It is strictly not applicable when these conditions are not met. However, *the LR levels of output and employment can be used as a benchmark or reference state toward which the economy will tend to move.* If it does not do so of its own volition or does not do so fast enough, macroeconomics (see Chapters 8 and 9) examines the policies that can induce such a movement.

7.11.1 Changes in the actual rate of output over time

The actual level of output alters over time because of changes in any or all of its three components since:

$$\frac{\partial y}{\partial t} = \frac{\partial y^f}{\partial t} + \frac{\partial (y^* - y^f)}{\partial t} + \frac{\partial (y - y^*)}{\partial t}. \tag{14}$$

As we have argued earlier, the full-employment level of output does change over time due to shifts in technology and in labor supply. The other two components of the actual level can also change and do change over the business cycle. In particular, they are positively related to the business cycle and tend to have positive values during a boom than during a recession. They can be changed by monetary and fiscal policies.

7.12 The Rate of Unemployment

This chapter has focused on the long-run analysis of output and employment. Changes in unemployment and its rate are the converse of those in employment, so that we now derive the implications of the long-run analysis for unemployment. Chapter 10 will present the treatment of unemployment in greater detail.

The level of unemployment was defined in Chapter 1 as:

$$U = L - n, \tag{15}$$

where:

U = level of unemployment and
L = labor force.

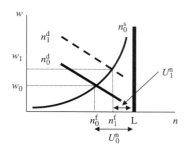

Figure 7.9

Since $n < L$, unemployment is always non-negative.[18] For our analysis at this point, we will make the simplifying assumption that the labor force is exogenously given and is independent of the wage rate. Figure 7.9 shows the initial demand for labor by n_0^d, the supply of labor by n_0^s and the labor force as L. LR employment is given by the intersection of labor supply and demand and equals n_0^f and LR unemployment equals $(L - n_0^f)$.

7.12.1 The LR equilibrium (natural) rate of unemployment

The *long-run equilibrium (full-employment) level of unemployment U^** is:

$$U^f = L - n^f. \tag{16}$$

The *rate of unemployment* is specified by:

$$u = U/L = 1 - n/L.$$

Therefore, the *long-run equilibrium rate of unemployment*, also called the full-employment rate of unemployment, u^f is:

$$u^f = U^f/L = 1 - n^f/L. \tag{17}$$

The long-run equilibrium (full-employment) rate of unemployment is called the 'natural rate of unemployment' and often designated as u^n. Alternatively stated, unemployment is at its natural rate when the economy is at full employment. Hence:

$$u^n \equiv u^f = U^f/L = 1 - n^f/L, \tag{18}$$

where u^f stands for the 'full-employment rate of unemployment'. To reiterate, the natural unemployment rate u^n is the *equilibrium rate of unemployment under certainty (or without errors in price expectations under uncertainty), and once all adjustments are over.*

For the initial n_0^d and n_0^s curves, Figure 7.9 shows the labor force L and full employment n_0^f. The difference between them is the level of natural unemployment U_0^n. This unemployment level divided by the labor force gives the natural *rate* of unemployment u_0^n.

Shifts in the natural rate of unemployment

The natural rate of unemployment changes if there is a shift in the production function or in the labor supply. To illustrate, an improvement in technology that increases the marginal product of labor and shifts the labor

---

[18] If L can be assumed to be exogenously given as L, so that it does not vary with the real wage, the labor force will be the sum total of workers who are able and willing to work at *any* wage. It will be the maximum amount of potential employment in the economy. If the number of workers willing to work increases as the real wage rises, the labor supply function will be $L = L(w)$, with $\partial L/\partial w > 0$. This is further explored in Chapter 10.

demand curve right from n_0^d to n_1^d in Figure 7.9 increases the full-employment level from n_0^f to n_1^f — which causes a reduction in the natural unemployment level to U_1^n. Hence, the natural rate of unemployment is not a constant. Nor is it likely to be a constant in real-time, real-world economies in which changes in productivity and labor supply occur frequently.

The natural rate of unemployment also varies among countries since the labor demand and supply functions tend to differ among countries. The lower the capital stock and the less efficient/advanced the technology, the greater is the likelihood of a higher natural rate. It would also be so if the labor force is less educated or skilled relative to the technology used by firms. It would also be so if the labor force has a higher preference for leisure. In general, LDCs (less developed economies) have higher natural rates of unemployment than the developed economies.

The lack of impact of monetary and fiscal policies on the natural rate of unemployment

Our earlier analysis showed that, for a given economy, n^f is independent of monetary and fiscal policies, as well as of any other determinants of aggregate demand, so that the natural rate of unemployment is also not altered by these policies. That is:

$$\partial u^n / \partial r^T = 0 \tag{19}$$

and

$$\partial u^n / \partial g = 0. \tag{20}$$

We want to reiterate this important conclusion: *for a given economy, both the level of full employment and the natural rate of unemployment are independent of changes in aggregate demand and therefore, of monetary and fiscal policies.*

7.13 The Long-Run Equilibrium (Natural) Rate of Interest

In the long-run equilibrium, the interest rate is determined by the intersection of the LRAS and IS curves. As such, it is the rate of interest at full employment and is called the LR or full-employment rate of interest. Its determination is shown in Figure 7.10. In this figure, the initial LR rate of interest is shown as being r_0^{LR}. An increase in investment or in government expenditures which shifts the IS curve from IS_0 to IS_1 will increase this rate of interest from r_0^{LR} to r_1^{LR}.

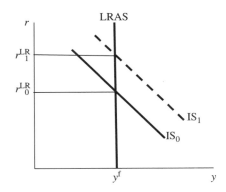

Figure 7.10

Since the LR rate of interest is not only determined by the supply structure of the economy but also changed by shifts in the commodity market components, applying the designation of 'natural' to it is less appealing than for the LR unemployment rate. However, some economists do apply the term '*the natural rate of interest*' to the LR rate of interest.

The ineffectiveness of monetary policy and inflation in changing the long-run real interest rate

In the long run, shifts in fiscal policies can alter the long-run equilibrium real interest rate. A monetary policy change in the interest rate can only cause the short-run interest rate to differ from the long-run one, but not change the long-run rate itself.[19]

The nominal interest rate will change because of changes in the real rate and the inflation rate. For the distinction between the real and the nominal interest rate, see the Fisher equation on interest rates presented in Chapter 2.

7.14 Conclusions

- The long-run prosperity of the economy depends on its ability to utilize its factors and technology at the most efficient sustainable level. The level of employment generated at this level of utilization for the given structure of the economy is referred to as its full-employment level and its corresponding output is the full-employment level of output.
- For a given social, political, and economic structure of country, the main determinants of the full-employment level of output are the production function and factor inputs. In the short-run analysis, the capital stock is assumed to be fixed, so that the only factor included in the determination of the full-employment level of output is labor. Shifts in the full-employment level of output occur due to shifts in the production function or in the supply of labor — or shifts in the availability or prices of resources such as oil.
- The economy does not always produce at the full-employment level of output so that the next two Chapters study the sources of deviations from this level.
- The rate of unemployment at the full-employment level of output is called the natural rate of unemployment. Its main determinants are the production function, the supply of labor and the labor force. Shifts in these alter the natural rate of unemployment, so that it cannot be taken to be constant over time. The actual rate of unemployment can — and usually does — differ from the natural rate.
- The long-run equilibrium level of the interest rate is determined by the intersection of the LRAS and the IS curves, and is independent of monetary policies, but not of fiscal policies.
- There are two types of crowding out of private investment and net exports by fiscal deficits. One is caused by the rise in interest rates due to bond-financed fiscal deficits and is called interest rate crowding out. This can occur if the central bank targets the money supply and holds it unchanged in the presence of fiscal deficits (see Chapter 6), but not if the central banks targets the interest rate (see Chapter 5). The other type is output-crowding out. This occurs in the long-run analysis when output is maintained at its full-employment level and is not changed by fiscal deficits. Full crowding-out is unlikely to occur in short-run analysis (Chapter 8) or disequilibrium analysis (Chapter 9).

---

[19]For guidance, see the analysis relevant to this point in Chapters 4 and 5.

KEY CONCEPTS

The demand for labor
The supply of labor
Equilibrium in the labor market
Full employment
Full-employment output
The employment–output relationship/curve

The long-run aggregate supply (LRAS) relationship/ curve
The natural rate of unemployment
The full-employment (natural) rate of interest

Ineffectiveness of monetary and fiscal policies in terms of long-run output and employment
Interest rate crowding out; output crowding out.

SUMMARY OF CRITICAL CONCLUSIONS

- The long-run equilibrium levels of full employment and full-employment output are under the assumptions of (a) certainty or the absence of expectational errors, (b) the absence of adjustment costs, or after the economy's adjustments are over, and (c) equilibrium in all markets. These levels are independent of aggregate demand — and of monetary and fiscal policies. Shifts in the private or public components of aggregate demand cannot change them.
- The natural level of unemployment and the natural rate of unemployment occur when there is full employment in the economy.
- The long-run (equilibrium) level of the interest rate occurs when there is full employment in the economy. It is determined by the LRAS and IS curves. Fiscal deficits increase it and fiscal surpluses reduce it.
- The long-run real interest rate is independent of money demand and money supply, as well as of the interest rate target rule adopted by the central bank.
- In the long-run with the full-employment output unchanged by fiscal deficits, fiscal deficits crowd out investment or net exports, or both.

REVIEW AND DISCUSSION QUESTIONS

1. What is the general form of the production function commonly used in short-run macroeconomics? What assumption does the short-run production function make with respect to physical capital? What is the justification for this assumption?
2. Show diagrammatically the relationship between output and labor, and specify its assumptions. Show in this diagram the effects of (a) an increase in the capital stock and (b) an increase in employment.
3. Show diagrammatically the downward-sloping curve for the marginal productivity of labor (MPL). Show the effects on this curve of (a) an increase in the capital stock and (b) an increase in employment. Discuss the derivation of the demand curve for labor (n^d curve) from the MPL curve and show the demand curve for labor.
4. Show diagrammatically the effects of an increase in the marginal propensity to consume on (a) aggregate demand and (b) LR output.

5. Show that the LR equilibrium rate of interest does not depend on (a) the demand or supply of money and (b) the interest rate target rule.
6. Does the natural rate of unemployment depend upon government expenditures on goods and services or on government transfers to the public? Give reasons for your answer.
7. Suppose an expansionary monetary policy is pursued. Would it change the natural rate of unemployment? Discuss in the context of the analysis of this chapter.
8. Would you expect full employment and full-employment output to (a) always exist in the economy and (b) hold in 2008 and 2009 in the USA, Canada, and other economies hit by the financial and economic crisis? Give reasons for your answer.
9. What is meant by an expansionary monetary policy in the context of interest rate targeting by the central bank? Does such a policy alter the following?

   (a) full-employment output and
   (b) the natural rate of interest.

   Explain your answer, using the appropriate diagrams.
10. Does an increase in government expenditures alter the following?

    (a) full-employment output and
    (b) the natural rate of interest.

    Explain your answer, using the appropriate diagrams.
11. Analyze, using diagrams, the impact of an increase in labor productivity on the natural rate of unemployment, full-employment output and the long-run equilibrium interest rate.
12. Show the long-run effects of a permanent increase in oil prices on the long-run equilibrium levels of output, employment, real wage, and interest rate.

ADVANCED AND TECHNICAL QUESTIONS

Basic AD Model for Chapter 7

Assume that the following equations describe the commodity markets of an economy and the interest rate targeted by its central bank.

$$c = 0.8 \, y_d$$

$$t = 0.25y$$

$$i = 1000 - 50r$$

$$g = 500$$

$$r = r_0^T = 0.04$$

$$x_c = 200 - 0.5\rho^r$$

$$z_c/\rho^r = 500 + 0.1y_d$$

$$P^F = 1$$

$$\rho = 1.$$

T1. Given the Basic AD model, now add the assumption that the long-run aggregate supply function is given by:

$$y^f = 1,000$$

(a) Derive the IS equation. [Do not use the IS equation formula for this answer. Use step-by-step calculations. Start by calculating disposable income. Noting that x_c and z_c depend on ρ^r, calculate ρ^r in terms of P. Then use the equilibrium condition $y = e$ for your further steps.]

(b) Derive the AD equation.

(c) Derive the equilibrium price level P_0^*.

Basic AS Model for Chapter 7

For the supply structure of the economy, assume the following.

The production function:

$$y = 10n - 0.1n^2.$$

The labor supply function:

$$n^s = 5w.$$

T2. For the Basic AS model, derive:

(a) The marginal product of labor.

(b) The labor demand function.

(c) Equilibrium real wage and employment.

(d) Equilibrium output.

T3. For the combined Basic AD and AS models, derive:

(a) The equilibrium levels of employment and output.

(b) The equilibrium price level P_2^*.

(c) The equilibrium values of the nominal and real wage.

T4. Starting with the combined Basic AD and AS models, assume that there is an increase in the labor force participation rate, which shifts the labor supply function to:

$$n^s = 10w.$$

Recalculate your answers to the preceding two questions.

Revised Model for Chapter 7

Assume the following:
The production function:

$$y = 4,000n - 0.1n^2.$$

The labor supply function:

$$n^s = 10,000 + 5w.$$

Labor force:

$$L = 20,000.$$

The aggregate demand (AD) function:

$$c = 7,000,000 + 0.8 y_d.$$

$$t = 0.25 y.$$

$$g = 7,000,000.$$

$$i = 5,000,000 - 50r.$$

$$x_c = 2,000,000 - 50\rho^r.$$

$$z_c / \rho^r = 1,000,000 + 0.1 y_d.$$

$$P^F = 1 \quad \text{and} \quad \rho = 1.$$

T5. For the revised model, calculate:

(a) The AD function.
(b) The long-run equilibrium wage.
(c) The natural rate of unemployment.
(d) The equilibrium price level.
(e) What will be the impact on the natural unemployment rate of (a) an increase in the target interest rate to 0.05 and (b) an increase in government expenditures by 10%?

T6. What do the answers to the preceding technical questions imply for the impact of on the long-run equilibrium levels of output, employment, unemployment rate, real wage rate, and the long-run equilibrium interest rate of:

(a) Increases in the target interest rate.
(b) Increases in government expenditures.

CHAPTER 8

Output in the Short Run: The Role of Expectations and Adjustment Costs

This chapter presents the short-run analyses of the labor market and the aggregate supply of output for the closed economy. There are several reasons for the deviation of the short-run equilibrium output from the full-employment one.

On the supply side, one of these reasons is the existence of uncertainty so that the economic agents have to form, and act, on their expectations of future prices. Expectational errors incorporated in wage contracts imply the Friedman supply rule, while those in the relative prices of commodities imply the Lucas supply rule. Both lead to the same conclusion: unanticipated inflation (deflation) increases (decreases) output above (below) its full-employment level. However, these deviations from the full-employment level are likely to be transient and self-correcting.

Actual output may also deviate from the full-employment one due to the existence of adjustment costs. These costs include those incurred by the firms in (i) adjusting prices in commodity markets, (ii) adjusting employment, and (iii) adjusting output. These costs can cause deviations in output and employment from their long-run levels.

This chapter studies the short-run equilibrium behavior of employment and output. The *short-run equilibrium* levels of output and employment can differ from their long-run (full-employment) levels for several reasons. Of these, macroeconomics focuses on:

- The existence of uncertainty, with errors in price expectations. The two main theories on this imply the Friedman and Lucas supply rules.
- Costs of adjusting prices in response to changes in demand and productivity. These lead to sticky prices for some products. The theory on this is called the menu cost theory.
- Costs of adjusting output in response to changes in demand and productivity.
- Costs of adjusting employment in response to changes in demand and productivity. These lead to variations in the work effort of employees. The theory on this is the implicit contract theory, which implies Okun's rule.

These factors imply that the short-run aggregate supply (SRAS) curve becomes different from the long-run aggregate supply (LRAS) curve: the SRAS curve has a positive slope while the LRAS one is vertical in the AD-AS diagram.

On (i), when there is uncertainty about the future value of an economic variable — for instance, the price level, the rate of inflation, the demand for products or employment, etc. — firms and individuals have to form expectations on its likely value. The two major hypotheses in economics for constructing the expected value of a variable are the *adaptive expectations hypothesis* (AEH) and the *rational expectations hypothesis* (REH). The former is a statistical procedure, while the latter represents an economic theory of expectations. On the role of expectations in macroeconomic theory, this chapter focuses on (a) expectations on the price level and the rate of inflation — rather than on demand and expected sales (which are considered in Chapter 9) — and (b) the use of the REH for modelling these expectations.

This chapter examines (i) the two main theories on the impact on output of errors in price expectations (Sections 8.1 to 8.11), (ii) the theory on the costs of adjustment of prices (Section 8.12), and (iii) the theories on the costs of adjusting employment and production (Sections 8.13 and 8.14). These theories *separately* and *collectively* imply that the short-run impact of changes in aggregate demand on output and employment will differ from the long-run impact and that, in the AD-AS diagram, the SRAS curve will have a positive slope, even though the LRAS curve is vertical. This chapter does not examine the role of a fall in aggregate demand below its full-employment level, which would cause a *demand deficiency* in the economy. Since such a situation in macroeconomics is considered a case of disequilibrium, rather than of short-run equilibrium; this analysis is left to Chapter 9, which focuses on disequilibrium in the economy. In addition, it does not present the analysis of the impact of a credit crisis on output, which is covered in business cycle theory (Chapter 16).

Note that actual output in the economy (i) can be at the long-run equilibrium (full-employment) level, (ii) not be at the long-run equilibrium (full-employment) level, but only at the short-run equilibrium level, or (iii) not be at the long-run or short-run equilibrium levels, but at the disequilibrium level, for numerous reasons. This chapter studies (ii), while Chapters 7 and 9 study (i) and (ii) respectively. To reiterate a point made earlier in this book, the long run and short run are analytical states (i.e., under specific assumptions about the economy), not real-world states existing in real, chronological time, while the data on the economy is on actual real output.

8.1   The Role of Uncertainty and Errors in Expectations

8.1.1   The theory of rational expectations

The theory of rational expectations was proposed during the 1960s, but was popularized in macroeconomics by Robert Lucas, among other economists, only in the 1970s. The REH is currently the dominant approach in macroeconomics to modeling expectations. This approach asserts that:

- Expectations are formed on the basis of all available information. This information includes not only past experience but also anything known or expected about the future. This knowledge will include knowledge of economic theories and the policy rules followed by the monetary and fiscal authorities.
- Systematic errors in expectations are costly; therefore, economic agents try to eliminate them by acquiring better information. They revise the theories and data on which they are based, until the remaining errors in expectations are purely random ones. Random errors have a zero mean (average value) and are not related to information known at the time the expectations are formed; therefore, they are not predictable. [However, the REH does not specify how long it will take to acquire and process adequate information for the errors to become merely random ones. This period can be exceedingly long, e.g., possibly even decades.]
- For simplification for analytical purposes, we can extend the assumptions of the long run in Chapter 7 by adding the assumption that it has no expectational errors (not even random ones). We will call this the *long-run (or expectational) equilibrium*, the important aspect of which is that it does not have errors in expectations.

Applying the theory of rational expectations to future inflation rates, the actual inflation rate — which will become known only in the future — can be decomposed into two components. These are:

1. The *rationally anticipated* (*or expected*) *inflation rate* (π^e), which has only random errors.
2. The *unanticipated* (*or unexpected*) *inflation rate* (π^u), which equals the actual inflation rate less the anticipated one. That is $\pi^u = \pi - \pi^e$. The *unanticipated inflation rate* can also be called 'errors in expectations' or 'expectational errors'.

Under rational expectations, the rational expectation of the future inflation rate will equal the 'mathematical expectation' (average) of the actual inflation rate. The rationally expected inflation rate will be sometimes above and sometimes below the actual one, but without any systematic — i.e., persistent — positive or negative bias in the difference between these rates. Therefore, the (currently) unanticipated component, i.e., expectational errors, will be random, which makes them unpredictable with a zero mean.

8.1.2 Random errors and their predictability

Some of the changes that occur are based on known information. If they are uncertain, the economic agent — i.e., households/workers, firms, and policy makers — forms expectations on them and attaches *subjective probabilities* (i.e., personal guesses on their likelihood) to the potential outcomes. These outcomes are said to be expected or anticipated.

Random errors are not based on any known information. Therefore, there is no basis on which to expect such an error to be negative or positive; there is also no basis for forming estimates of their magnitudes for a future period. Hence, random errors are inherently unpredictable — even to the extent that a subjective probability cannot be assigned to the actual value of the error in the next period. However, we can specify two properties for them. These are (a) the expected value of random errors is zero and (b) the sign and magnitude of the actual error that will occur are unpredictable.

8.1.3 Application of rational expectations to monetary and fiscal policies

Rational expectations implies that the systematic value of — and changes in — any variable relevant to economic agents will sooner or later be learnt by them so that they will anticipate any changes in it. Only the random variation of the variable will remain unanticipated. Applying the REH to monetary and fiscal policies implies that any systematically pursued monetary and fiscal policies will become anticipated by the public. Therefore, the future impact of such systematic policies on output and the actual inflation rate will also be incorporated into the public's expected values for them, so that such policies cannot cause unanticipated changes in production and employment. Only random alterations in monetary and fiscal policies — just as for shifts in consumption, investment, or net exports — could possibly cause unanticipated changes in production and employment.

8.2 Price Expectations and the Labor Market: Output and Employment in the Context of Wage Contracts

In industrialized economies, firms and workers negotiate the nominal wage rate through explicit contracts or implicit arrangements. This nominal wage rate is established in advance of the production and employment decisions by the firm and before the actual price level is known. The following considers the effects of this pattern of wage negotiations and production on employment and output. It defines the two stages of this process as:

1. The first stage during which wage negotiations take place and the nominal wage is set.
2. The second stage during which firms take the nominal wage as given and determine their employment and output.

8.2.1 Labor supply in wage negotiations during the first stage

To start, suppose that there is uncertainty about the price level P in the period ahead. Since workers want to know what the purchasing power of their nominal wage rate W is likely to be, they have to form expectations on P. Let the household's expected price level for the period ahead be P^{eh}. Workers supply labor on the basis of their expected real wage W/P^{eh}, so that their supply function can be written as $n^s(W/P^{eh})$, where W is the nominal wage. Similarly, let the firm's expected price level for the period ahead be P^{ef}, and their labor demand curve based on their expected real wage, equal to their marginal product of labor, be $n^d(W/P^{ef})$. Their negotiations yield a nominal wage given by equilibrium between labor demand and supply, i.e., by $n^s(W/P^{eh}) = n^d(W/P^{ef})$. The nominal wage thus established becomes the wage contract between workers and firms. This wage remains unchanged for the following period, during which production and employment take place.

An increase in the firm's expected price level increases its willingness to agree to higher nominal wages, and an increase in the household's expected price level makes workers demand higher nominal wages, so that either or both of them will result in a higher nominal wage set in the wage contract.[1]

The analysis further assumes that: (a) the contracted wage rate W^c is set for the duration of the labor contract and (b) workers will be willing to increase or decrease the amount supplied of labor without asking for a change in the contract wage during the contract period. This implies that workers will supply any amount of labor demanded by the firms at W^c. Hence, for the duration of the wage contract, the labor supply is as if it was horizontal at W^c in the (n, W) diagram,[2] so that the *ex-ante* labor supply curve is set aside in the analysis of employment for the contract period.

8.2.2 Employment during the contract period (the production stage)

At the time of production, the jth firm would know the actual price of its own product as an element of its joint production and pricing decisions, so that its actual demand for labor will be based on the nominal wage divided by the actual price of its product, rather than on the price which had previously been expected by it.

Hence, over the two stages,

1. As discussed earlier, an increase in the expected price level establishes a higher contractual nominal wage during the first stage's wage negotiations. This increase in the contracted nominal wage, *ceteris paribus*, increases the actual real wage, which makes labor more costly and reduces labor demand, during the second stage.
2. For the given contractual nominal wage, any increase in the actual price level during the second stage will lower the actual real wage, thereby making labor cheaper and increasing the employed.

---

[1] W^c will increase proportionately if both P^{ef} and P^{eh} increase by the same amount but not if only one of them increases.

[2] Clearly, this would only be so in the neighborhood (i.e., applying only to small changes) of the expected equilibrium employment level at W^c in the (W, n) diagram.

Hence, the introduction of uncertainty and wage contracts into the labor market analysis implies that employment will depend upon: (i) the duration of the wage contract, (ii) the price level expected by firms and households during wage negotiations, and (iii) the actual price level when employment occurs. Since output and employment are positively related through the production function, the above analysis implies that output will depend positively on the ratio P/P^e, which can be written as $y = f(P/P^e)$. For this function, a rise in P^e would raise the contracted nominal wage and make labor more expensive, thereby reducing employment and output, while a rise in P lowers the real wage for the pre-determined contracted nominal wage and makes labor cheaper.

8.2.3 Diagrammatic analysis

Figure 8.1a presents the labor demand $n^d(W/P_0^{ef})$ and the labor supply $n^s(W/P_0^{eh})$ curves for the coming period. These curves are drawn for the particular price levels expected by the firms and the households. Note that the vertical axis in this figure is the nominal wage rate W. The negotiated nominal wage will be set at the equilibrium level W_0^c, and has the expected employment level of n_0^e. An increase in P^{ef} will shift the labor demand curve to the right[3] and a rise in P^{eh} will shift the labor supply curve to the left,[4] so that each will raise

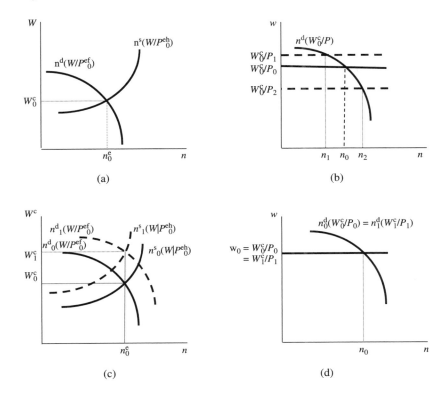

Figure 8.1

---

[3] As P^{ef} rises, labor is expected to become cheaper, so that firms will increase their labor demand for a given value of W, say W_0. This higher labor demand at the given W_0 implies that the n^d curve shifts right in the (W, n) diagrams.

[4] As P^{eh} rises and lowers the expected lower wage for a given nominal wage W_0, labor will require a higher nominal wage W to supply a given amount of labor, say n_0. The higher value of W for the given n_0 implies an upward shift of the labor supply curve in the (W, n) diagrams.

the nominal wage. However, the former will increase the expected employment level and the latter will decrease it. If both P^{ef} and P^{eh} increase proportionately, the two curves will shift proportionately and the nominal wage will increase in the same proportion, without a change in the expected employment level. Henceforward, to simplify further analysis, we will assume that the price level expected by both firms and households is identical and is designated as P_0^e.

Actual employment is determined not in Figure 8.1a but in Figure 8.1b, now with the actual real wage w — equal to W/P — on the vertical axis. For the contracted nominal wage W_0^c from Figure 8.1a, and a given price level P_0 equal to the expected one P_0^e (i.e., $P_0 = P_0^e$), employment in Figure 8.1b is n_0 — so that $n_0 = n_0^e$. However, with the contracted nominal wage still at W_0^c, a lower price P_1, with $P_1 < P_0^e$, will raise the actual real value of the contracted nominal wage to W_0^c/P_1 and decrease employment to n_1 with $n_1 < n_0$. Conversely, if the actual price level is above the expected one (e.g., $P_2 > P_0^e$), real wages would turn out to be lower (at W_0^c/P_2) and employment higher (at n_2) relative to their expected levels.

Note that no explicit labor supply curve was drawn in Figure 8.1b for the contract period. But workers remain willing to supply any amount of labor at the negotiated wage, irrespective of changes in the price level. Therefore, we can think of an implicit labor supply curve that is horizontal at W^c (in Figure 8.1a with the nominal wage W on the vertical axis and labor supply on the horizontal one), and at the actual real wage $(=W^c/P)$ (in Figure 8.1b with the real wage w on the vertical axis and labor supply on the horizontal one, as shown).

If there were no errors in expectations — that is, if $P^{ef} = P^{eh} = P$, actual employment n will equal n_0^e, as determined in Figure 8.1a; therefore, we can take this to be the full-employment level n^f or the 'expectational equilibrium' level n^*. If P is higher than both P^{ef} and P^{eh}, $n > n_0^e$, and vice versa. Therefore, the deviation — i.e., $(n - n_0^e)$ — in employment from its expected level n^e in Figure 8.1a is positively related to the errors $(P - P^e)$ in expectations.

The effect of a proportional increase in the expected and actual price levels

An identical increase in both the expected and actual price levels will not change the real wage, even though the nominal wage will rise proportionately, so that it will also not change employment. The diagrammatic analysis of this case is shown in Figures 8.1c and 8.1d. In Figure 8.1c, since the price level expected by both firms and workers rises by the same amount, both the labor demand and supply curves will shift up in such a way that at the equilibrium employment level n_0^e, the contracted nominal wage will rise (from W_0^c to W_1^c) proportionately with the increase in the expected price level. Although the contracted wage has risen, the actual price level has also risen in a proportionate manner, so that labor does not become either cheaper or more expensive and the labor demand curve does not shift from its initial position. In Figure 8.1d, the real wage also remains unchanged at w_0 (with $W_0^e/P_0 = W_1^e/P_1$). Therefore, if nominal wages and prices rise in the same proportion, employment does not change in spite of the increase in the nominal wage rate.

Conclusions from the contract wage analysis of production

Hence, our results for the SR equilibrium employment in the context of nominal wage contracts are that:

(i) If the actual and expected price levels are identical, the economy would have full employment and produce the full-employment level of output.

(ii) If the actual price level proves to be higher than the one expected at the time of the signing of wage contracts, the employment and output levels would rise above their LR (full-employment) ones.

(iii) If the actual price level proves to be lower than the one expected at the time of the signing of wage contracts, the employment and output levels would fall below their full-employment levels.

(iv) If the actual and expected inflation rates remain equal, with both changing proportionately, employment and output will not change.

The expectations augmented employment and output supply curves

The above implications of the contract-based analysis are captured by writing the equations for employment and output as:

$$n^* = n^f + \alpha(P^* - P^e) \quad \alpha > 0$$
$$y^* = y^f + \gamma(P^* - P^e) \quad \gamma > 0.$$

These equations assert that if the equilibrium price level P^* is greater than the expected price level P^e, both employment and output would be higher than their LR equilibrium (full-employment) levels. Remember that this result occurs because the unanticipated rise in the price level reduces the real wage below its anticipated level and makes workers cheaper to employ. Once the contracts are re-negotiated and embody the unanticipated higher price level, the increases in employment and output above their full-employment levels disappear — unless new positive errors occur in the price level expectations for the following period.

The above two equations are respectively the *expectations augmented employment and output/supply equations*. These are important equations describing the short-run equilibrium response of the economy to price changes and inflation. This output supply rule is also called the Friedman supply rule (FSR).

Implications of the expectations augmented employment and output supply equations for variations in employment and output over the business cycle

The curve for the FSR is shown in Figure 8.2. The LRAS curve results under the FSR if $P = P^e$ — and $\pi = \pi^e$. In this case, $y = y^f$. At a given expected price level P_0^e equal to P_0, the FSR generates the SRAS curve as $SRAS_0$. If $P > P^e$, the economy is on the SRAS curve to the right of y^f, but if $P < P^e$, the economy is on the SRAS curve to the left of y^f. If the expected price level rises to P_1^e equal to P_1, the SRAS curve moves up to $SRAS_1$. That is, for a given LRAS curve, there is a separate SRAS curve for each expected price level embodied in the labor contracts.

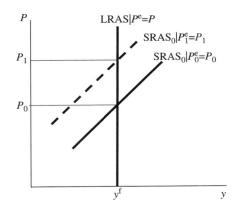

Figure 8.2

For applications to business cycles, we need to replace the price level P by the inflation rate π. In the upturns of most business cycles, while the rate of inflation is rising, its expected value tends to lag behind its actual value, so that the expected inflation rate becomes lower than the actual (*ex post*) one.[5] This causes employment to rise above its full-employment level. In the downturns of most business cycles, the inflation rate is falling, and its expected value tends to lag behind (i.e., become higher than) its actual value, which causes employment to fall below its full-employment level. Expectational errors especially tend to emerge when inflation is accelerating or decelerating, as compared with when the inflation rate is static/constant.

These cyclical variations in employment produce corresponding cyclical movements in output over the business cycle.

Box 8.1: Errors in Price Expectations, the Duration of the Wage Contract and Cost-of-Living Clauses

The deviation in employment from its expected level n^e — envisaged at the time of the signing of the wage contract — will only occur during the duration of the wage contract since the past errors in expectations will be eliminated when the wage contract is renegotiated. This is usually done through the 'catch-up' clause for cost-of-living increases in labor contracts. Therefore, continuously new errors will be needed to maintain employment above n^f. While this can occur for some time — the 'people can be fooled some of the time' syndrome — it cannot continue indefinitely — 'they cannot be fooled all the time'. The former usually has to take the form of accelerating inflation rates. The latter usually occurs in two ways:

1. The future expectations of inflation tend to 'jump' beyond the past — experienced — inflation rates in an attempt to capture the potential future acceleration in inflation.
2. In order to reduce or eliminate the loss in purchasing power through inflation, the duration of wage contracts is reduced or cost-of-living clauses[6] are built into them.

Therefore, while the errors in expectations can induce increases in employment — and do so during accelerating inflation — such increases can be only a short-term but not a long-term phenomenon in practice. Further, errors in expectations caused by inflation cannot be relied upon to occur over lengthy periods or at very high and persistent rates of inflation. Hence, over the longer term, the economy will revert to the long-run employment level n^f.

8.3 Friedman's Expectations Augmented Employment and Output Rules

The above expectations augmented employment and output equations were based on Milton Friedman's, and other economists', ideas for contract-based labor markets and we have named them after him. The Friedman employment rule for an inflationary context is:

$$n^* = n^f + \alpha(\pi^* - \pi^e) \quad \alpha > 0, \tag{1}$$

---

[5]The expansion of 2004–2006 in the USA and Canada was remarkable in that the inflation rate remained low (1% to 3%) and there seemed to be no perceptible errors in inflation expectations. This may have been due to the successful pursuit of interest rate targeting monetary policy during the period.

[6]Cost-of-living clauses in wage contracts ensure that nominal wages rise automatically with the price level.

where the inflation rate π has replaced the price level P. Note that the SR equilibrium employment level is predicated on labor market clearance in wage negotiations, so that this level is not a disequilibrium one.[7] Therefore, n^* is the SR equilibrium employment level, with * standing for SR equilibrium, while the superscript f stands for the long-run (full-employment level).

Correspondingly, since changes in employment produce changes in output, the Friedman supply rule (FSR) for output in an inflationary context is:

$$y^* = y^f + \gamma(\pi^* - \pi^e) \quad \gamma > 0, \tag{2}$$

where all the variables are in logs. The asterisk symbol ($*$) on a variable indicates that its value is the SR equilibrium one, while the superscript f indicates its LR equilibrium value. Note that:

- The expectations of inflation in these equations refer to those incorporated in wage contracts, and the economy deviates from its full-employment level due to errors in these expectations: if $\pi > \pi^e$, real wages are lower while employment and output are greater compared with the full-employment level, and vice versa. The mechanism of the FSR relies upon wage contracts established in advance of production, so that an increase in prices/inflation above the expected ones lowers real wages, thereby making it attractive to hire more labor than in the error-free LR equilibrium.

- Several assumptions were needed for deriving the FSR. Among these was the assumption of market clearance in the labor market at the wage contract stage. Further, at the production stage, given the contracted nominal wage, labor willingly supplies the amount of labor demanded by firms. Hence, the FSR does not allow for disequilibrium in the labor market, in which some workers may want jobs at the existing wage but cannot get them or firms want more workers at this wage but cannot get them. Further, the commodity market also clears. Therefore, the FSR represents the short-run equilibrium behavior of the economy.

- These deviations from full employment require a lack of adequate knowledge about the future and the existence of nominal wage contracts. The duration of their effects depends on the length of the wage contracts. In general, this length is reduced by firms and workers if inflation rates are quite high — e.g., during the late 1970s and 1980s, as inflation rates rose to double digits, the duration of many wage contracts was reduced from what used to be three years during the low-inflation periods of the 1950s and 1960s to one year. In some cases, cost of living clauses came to be inserted into the contracts.

Extended Mathematical Analysis Box 8.1: Labor Demand when There are Expectational Errors in the Context of Nominal Wage Contracts

To provide a mathematical illustration for the case of wage contracts with price uncertainty, let the labor market functions at the time of wage negotiations be:

$$n^s = b_1 W / P^{eh} \quad b_1 > 0$$

$$n^d = a_0 - a_1 W / P^{ef} \quad a_0, a_1 > 0 \quad a_1 > 0.$$

In equilibrium:

$$a_0 - a_1 W / P^{ef} = b_1 W / P^{eh}.$$

---

[7] Disequilibrium would occur if the market — or wage negotiations — do not bring about the equality of the demand and supply of labor. For this case, we would need the disequilibrium analysis presented in the next chapter.

Extended Mathematical Analysis Box 8.1: (*Continued*)

Hence, the contractual nominal wage will be:

$$W^c = a_0 \left[\frac{P^{ef} P^{eh}}{a_1 P^{eh} + b_1 P^{ef}} \right],$$

so that $\partial W^c / \partial P^{eh}$, $\partial W^c / \partial P^{ef} > 0$. Note that a proportionate increase in both expectation increases the nominal wage rate in the same proportion. The expected level of employment obtained by substituting this equation in the labor supply function is given by:

$$n^e = a_0 b_1 \left[\frac{P^{ef}}{a_1 P^{eh} + b_1 P^{ef}} \right],$$

which implies that a proportionate increase in both expectations does not change n^e.[8]

At the time of production, with the nominal wage set by the wage contract at W^c, the actual real wage and employment will be:

$$w = a_0 \left[\frac{P^{ef} P^{eh}}{a_1 P^{eh} + b_1 P^{ef}} \right] \left(\frac{1}{P} \right)$$

$$n = n^d = a_0 - a_1 a_0 \left[\frac{P^{eh} P^{ef}}{a_1 P^{eh} + b_1 P^{ef}} \right] \left(\frac{1}{P} \right).$$

Both w and n are independent of changes in P, P^{ef}, and P^{eh}. If P exceeds both of its expectations, the real wage will turn out to be less than its expectation in the wage contract and n will be greater than n^e and vice versa.

We now simplify the preceding equations by assuming that firms and households hold the same expectations, so that $P^{ef} = P^{eh} = P^e$, where P^e is the commonly held price expectation. This simplifies the above equation for employment to:

$$n = a_0 - \left[\frac{a_0 a_1}{a_1 + b_1} \right] \left(\frac{P^e}{P} \right). \tag{1}$$

The expectational equilibrium level of employment

If there are no errors in expectations, $P = P^{ef} = P^{eh}$, so that:

$$n^{e*} = n^f = a_0 - a_0 a_1 / (a_1 + b_1). \tag{2}$$

This expectational equilibrium level of employment n^{e*} is independent of the price level and is, therefore, the full-employment level. Positive expectational errors $(P - P^e)$ induce actual employment to be greater than this full-employment level and vice versa.

The impact of expectational errors on employment

To find this impact, subtract equation (2) from (1). This gives:

$$n^d - n^f = - \left[\frac{a_0 a_1}{a_1 + b_1} \right] \left(\frac{P^e}{P} - 1 \right) = -\alpha \left(\frac{P^e}{P} - 1 \right), \tag{3}$$

---

[8]Note that the employment level is not set in the wage contract and can deviate from n^e.

Extended Mathematical Analysis Box 8.1: (*Continued*)

where $\alpha = a_0 a_1/(a_1 + b_1) > 0$. Assuming that actual employment by firms will always equal their demand for labor, replace n^d by n. Therefore, the preceding equation implies that employment is given by:

$$n = n^f + \alpha \left(1 - \frac{P^e}{P}\right) \quad \alpha > 0. \tag{4}$$

This equation is usually simplified and written in a linear or log-linear form as:

$$n = n^f + \alpha(P - P^e) \quad \alpha > 0. \tag{5}$$

Since $\alpha > 0$, positive expectational errors (defined as $P > P^e$) raise employment above n^f, while negative expectational errors ($P < P^e$) reduce employment below n^f. This is the Friedman employment rule.

The Implications for Employment and Output of Wage Contracts with Expectational Errors in Prices

Our arguments have shown that, given nominal wage contracts conditional on expectations, firms would employ workers according to their labor demand. Substituting this level of employment from equation (4) in the production function implies that output will also depend on expectational errors in the price level. Hence, from (4), output is given by:

$$y = y^f + \gamma \left(1 - \frac{P^e}{P}\right) \quad \gamma > 0. \tag{6}$$

This equation is often written as:

$$y = y^f + \gamma(P - P^e) \quad \gamma > 0. \tag{7}$$

This equation is the Friedman supply rule (for output). These equations imply that:

$$\frac{\partial n}{\partial(P - P^e)} = \alpha > 0$$

$$\frac{\partial y}{\partial(P - P^e)} = \gamma > 0.$$

Hence, the Friedman supply rules imply that inducing unexpected positive errors (i.e., $P^* - P^e$) in the price level raises both employment and output above their full-employment levels. But unexpected negative errors in the price level will lower both employment and output below their full-employment levels.

8.4 Lucas Supply Rule with Errors in Price Expectations in Commodity Markets

In the 1970s, Robert Lucas proposed a short-run output function that came to be labelled as the Lucas supply rule. Like the Friedman supply rule, it implies that output will be above its full-employment level if the actual price level proves to be above the expected one. However, the Lucas supply rule is not based on nominal wage contracts but on firms' production behavior when they misinterpret the nature of changes in their product prices. The following exposition gives a simple and very brief glimpse into this analysis.

Lucas' analysis shows that at the beginning of the period, the representative firm will start with an *initial expected price level* P^e. During the period, it will observe the price of its *own* product, which on average over the whole economy is represented by the price level P. Part of the difference $(P - P^e)$ could be due to the rise in the firm's *relative price* (i.e., relative to the prices of all other commodities) but part of it could be due to a general inflation or deflation affecting all firms. The firm's opinion on the latter leads it to revise its initial expected price level. Lucas assumed that this revision cuts down the actual error in price expectations to $\alpha(P - P^e)$, where $1 \geq \alpha \geq 0$. α is the *revision factor* of the expected price level on the basis of a change in its observed product price. To reiterate, $(P - P^e)$ is the initial error in expectations based on prior information and α is the revision of this initial error on the basis of new information on changes in product prices. Under rational expectations, the magnitude of the revision factor α is heavily influenced by the firm's knowledge of the relationship between past variations in product prices and those in the price level — as well as such information about the future. Intuitively, if we were to focus only on the past information for simplification, if the past inflation rates were close to zero, firms are likely to expect that the price level is not going to rise even though they observe that their own product price is rising. That is, the increase in product prices will be interpreted as an increase only in relative prices (i.e., the product price divided by the price level), with α having the value one or close to it. But if the past experience was of hyper-inflation, an increase in product prices will be interpreted as an increase in the price level, so that the expected price level will be revised to equal the actual one. In this case, $\alpha = 0$. Experience indicates that the value of α will lie between zero and one.

The Lucas supply rule then specifies the economy's short-run supply function as:

$$y_t^s = y_t^f + \gamma\alpha(P - P^e) \quad \gamma > 0, 1 \geq \alpha \geq 0, \tag{3}$$

where γ is the response of output to a unit error in the expected price level, while α is the revision of the prior error based on new information on product prices. If α is positive, rather than zero, a 'positive expectational error' (with $P > P^e$) will raise output above its full-employment level. The Lucas supply rule specifies the short-run deviations in output from the full-employment level if firms make errors in the expectations of their relative product prices. By the definition of the long run, such errors will not occur in the long run, so that the long-run equilibrium output level is given by:

$$y^{LR^*} = y^f.$$

One of the short-run extreme cases occurs when $\alpha = 1$. In this case, $\alpha\gamma = \gamma$ and the Lucas supply rule becomes:

$$y_t^s = y_t^f + \gamma(P - P^e).$$

The second extreme case (usually if recent experience is one of very high inflation rates or hyperinflation) occurs when $\alpha = 0$, so that $\gamma\alpha = 0$. In this case, the Lucas supply rule, even for the short-run analysis, becomes $y_t^{SR} = y_t^f$. In this case, given a past history of very high inflation, expectational errors will not produce any deviations of output from full employment.

The Lucas supply rule implies that barring the case where $\alpha = 0$, the SRAS curve will have a positive slope, while the LRAS will be vertical, as shown in Figures 8.2, 8.3a, and 8.3b.

In terms of empirical applications, the Lucas analysis implies that:

- Countries going through hyperinflation are not likely to experience an increase in output due to inflation or further increases in inflation.[9]

---

[9]This is so because, in a hyperinflationary environment, firms are likely to view any inflation as merely due to changes in the price level, rather than due to changes in their relative prices.

- Countries with a history of stable prices will benefit from emergent inflation[10] because their output and employment will rise. Hence, starting from a period of stable prices, if a central bank pursues policies that increase the inflation rate, the economy's output will rise. However, as firms observe the higher inflation rates, two adjustments occur in the Lucas supply rule. One is that P^e will increasingly become closer to P, so that $(P - P^e)$ will become smaller. The other is that α will decrease in value. Both these adjustments will decrease the benefits from inflation; eventually the benefits will disappear at very high and persistent inflation rates.
- In the LSR just as in the FSR, the benefits from unanticipated inflation disappear as soon as accurate information becomes available to the public on the actual price level. In developed economies with speedy data collection and release, this period may be only one or two quarters; therefore, the increase in output from an inflationary policy would be quite transient. This is especially so for the LSR since it does not rely on labor contracts or rigidities in prices that could have induced lags in the impact of new information on output and employment.

Since any expectational errors become corrected by the accrual of new information, the deviations of output from the full-employment one under both the FSR and LSR will be automatically eliminated. Therefore, such deviations from full employment are *short-run, transient and self-correcting.*

8.4.1 Firms' responses to errors in expectations

Central banks in economies that start with stable low-inflation rates can increase output beyond full employment by expansionary monetary policies, provided that such policies generate unanticipated inflation. However, as inflation picks up, the experience of rising inflation rates causes two changes:

1. As soon as the actual inflation rate, and the error in the expected inflation rate, becomes known, firms learn that they had made an error in their price expectations. They cancel its effects by revising their expectations, which reduces or eliminates the error and the effect on output.
2. For future inflation or the acceleration in it, firms lower their value of their response factor α. Hence, the benefit of increasing inflation rates in raising output lessens. It disappears in hyperinflation.

Extended Analysis Box 8.2: Diagrammatic Analysis: Comparing the FSR and LSR Curves (FSR and LSR) and the LRAS Curve

> Both the Lucas supply rule (LSR) and the Friedman supply rule (FSR) are aspects of the short-run behavior of equilibrium output under expectational errors. Figure 8.3a illustrates both the SRAS and LRAS curves under the FSR and the LSR. For both hypotheses, the LRAS curve comes about if there are no errors in expectations. The aggregate demand curve AD has a negative slope, as derived in Chapter 5 for the open economy.
>
> For the SRAS, assume that the initial equilibrium price level P_0 is known — and, therefore, fully expected with $P_0^e = P_0$. If expected prices remain equal to this initial price level, an increase in P will create positive errors in expectations, implying, under both the FSR and the LSR curves, that the economy will increase

---

[10]This is so because, with a history of stable prices as the past experience, firms are likely to view (though mistakenly) any inflation as being due to an increase in their relative prices rather than an increase in the general price level.

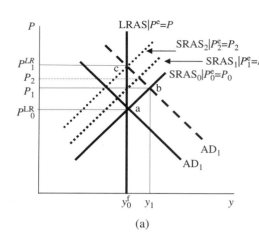
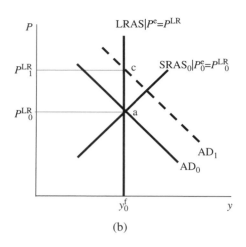

Figure 8.3

Extended Analysis Box 8.2: (*Continued*)

output in the short run. Therefore, the SRAS curve has a positive slope at the point a. In Figures 8.3a and 8.3b, start by assuming that an increase in aggregate demand from AD_0 to AD_1 shifts the actual price level to P_1, but without a shift in the expected price level, which still equals P_0. With $P_1 > P_0^e = P_0$, in the short run, the output supplied will be y_1 along the $SRAS_0$. Sooner or later, the public will learn about the positive error in its expectations, and revise upward the expected price level to P_1, i.e., P_1^e becomes equal to P_1. This will cause nominal wages to rise under the FSR. It would also cause the perception of relative price increases to decrease under the LSR. If the price level remains at P_1, so that the actual and expected prices become identical, output will revert to y_0^f, i.e., return to the LRAS curve. The resulting fall in output from y_1 to y_0^f is due to the elimination of expectational errors.

Now, if we were to start with a price level equal to P_1 and if the expected price level remains at P_1^e, equal to P_1, while the actual one varies, a new SRAS curve will be generated through the point (P_1, y_0^f).

Note that each upward shift in the expected price P^e produces a higher SRAS curve — e.g., $SRAS_2$ at $P_2^e = P_2$. In the limiting case, if P^e always equals P, only the LRAS curve will be observed. Therefore, the LRAS curve in Figure 8.3a was designated as $LRAS|P^e = P$. Further, under the LSR, the SRAS curve will become steeper (though this is not shown in Figure 8.3a) as higher prices are experienced.

Note also that the separate SRAS curves for the FSR and the LSR are likely to have different slopes. For the economy, the relevant SRAS curve will incorporate both influences of expectational errors on output, and, is therefore, an amalgam of the FSR and the LSR curves.

8.5 The Implications of the FSR and LSR for the Impact of Anticipated Demand Increases

Assume that the economy is initially in full employment and that aggregate demand increases in an anticipated manner. This increase could come from the private components of aggregate demand (e.g., through exogenous increases in consumption, investment, exports, etc.) or from the public components (government expenditures and taxes, or monetary policy). Since it has been assumed that the public anticipates such an increase, we will also assume that its impact on prices is anticipated. Therefore, the increase in demand will not produce any error in the expected price level or in relative prices, so that, according to both the FSR and the LSR, the economy will maintain full employment. Hence, the demand increase will not bring about any increases in output and employment, but merely cause proportionate price and nominal wage increases.

Figure 8.3b shows an increase in aggregate demand by the shift from AD_0 to AD_1. The economy is initially in equilibrium at the point a, with the price P_0^{LR} and output y_0^f. With the demand increase fully anticipated, the error in price expectations will be zero, so that the economy would operate according to the LRAS curve.[11] Along the LRAS curve, the shift from AD_0 to AD_1 takes the economy to the point c, with increases in the price level to P_1^{LR}, while leaving output unchanged at y_0^f. Conversely, an anticipated decrease in aggregate demand will merely lower all product prices, the price level and the nominal wage rate without changing the output of individual firms or aggregate output.

8.6 The Implications of the FSR and the LSR for the Impact of Unanticipated Demand Increases

In the case of unanticipated demand increase, the public would not be able to anticipate its impact on the price level, so that any price increase will also be unanticipated, thereby generating a positive error for the expected price level. Hence, in both the FSR and the LSR, output will increase. Under the FSR, this would be due to the negotiated nominal wage being too low, so that the real wage will fall and make labor cheaper. Under the LSR, the increase in output will occur because some of the observed product price increase will be attributed by individual firms to an increase in their relative price, which will induce them to increase their output.

Diagrammatically, the supply curve relevant to an analysis of unanticipated demand increases is the SRAS and not the LRAS curve. In Figure 8.3a, given the unanticipated increase in aggregate demand from AD_0 to AD_1 (with $P^e = P_0$) takes the economy to the point b along the $SRAS_0$ curve, thereby increasing the price level along $SRAS_0$ to P_1 while increasing output from y^f to y_1. Therefore, expansionary monetary and fiscal policies that cause unanticipated demand increases can push output and employment beyond the full-employment level. Conversely, unanticipated contractions in aggregate demand can push the economy into employment and output below their full-employment levels.

8.6.1 The impact of revisions in anticipations and real time

As explained earlier, after some delay, the public will come to learn of any demand increase. Further, the observed price increase to P_1 will sooner or later force the public to revise their price expectations. As this occurs and nominal wages rise to reflect the price P_1 and the expected rise in the relative prices decreases, the SRAS curve shifts up from $SRAS_0$ to $SRAS_1$, which raises the price level to P_2. This process will shift the SRAS curve up to $SRAS_2$ in Figure 8.3a, with $P_2^e = P_2$. Eventually, the price increase resulting from the demand increase will have become fully anticipated. This would make the expected price equal to its long-run level at P_1^{LR}, thereby shifting the short-run supply response of the economy to the long-run supply at y_0^f and ending in the new long-run outcome at (P_1^{LR}, y_0^f).

---

[11] It will not operate according to the SRAS curve for the anticipated demand increase since that has been assumed not to induce errors in price expectations.

8.6.2 Practical aspects of the FSR and LSR analysis

The above arguments raise the important practical question: how long does it take in real time to go from the point a to c? During the analytical interval in the shift from the short run to the long run, the economy has higher output — though with rising prices — from the demand increase. This analytical interval allows a positive short-run impact of aggregate demand increases on output and employment in the economy. The real-time counterpart of this analytical interval varies with the nature of the economy, the publication of accurate data and its dissemination, the alertness of the private sector, the stage of the business cycle and adjustment costs.

The FSR and LSR imply four aspects of the real time impact of increases in aggregate demand:

1. Under the FSR and LSR, any impact on output and employment occurs through changes brought about by the *markets* in prices and nominal wage rates, but not through any other channel, such as reacting directly to the changes in the quantities demanded or supplied. In particular, if the commodity and labor markets do not change prices and nominal wages in an unanticipated manner, there would be no impact on output and employment. Further, if these markets are slow in adjusting prices and nominal wages, economic agents may react (faster) by changing quantities demanded and supplied. The FSR and LSR do not provide the analyses of such possibilities, so that there is an implicit assumption that in terms of real time, the markets react instantly to bring about the changes, required to restore equilibrium, in prices and nominal wages for any anticipated shifts in aggregate demand and supply, and economic agents react subsequently to these changes.
2. In both the FSR and the LSR, the expected price level is replaced by its actual value as time passes and the information on the actual value becomes available, so that the impact on output and employment is transitory (except under the FSR where the duration of the wage contracts has to be considered). Therefore, any deviations of the expected price level from the actual price and, therefore, from full employment are *self-correcting*. Consequently, in the well-informed, modern, developed economies, this impact is unlikely to last for more than a few quarters.
3. Further, as the inflation rate accelerates from low single digits to higher ones, economic agents become more alert to the inflation rate and changes in it. They shorten the duration of their contracts and try to become better informed about the determinants of the future inflation rate. Hence, the relative magnitude and duration of the real-time impact of unanticipated inflation becomes shorter. Therefore, not only are the deviations from full employment transitory and self-correcting, their real-time duration becomes shorter in inflationary periods.
4. There is no benefit from increases in demand, prices, and inflation during hyperinflation.

Hence, in terms of real time for the modern economies, the FSR and the LSR imply that the fluctuations in investment, exports, and other components of demand should only cause *transitory* (only a few quarters) and *self-correcting* deviations in output from its full-employment level. Such deviations should, then, be hardly of much concern to the public or policymakers who are more concerned with real time rather than with analytical time.

Extended Analysis Box 8.3: The Implications of the FSR and LSR for the Impact of Monetary and Fiscal Policies

---

We have to differentiate between two different roles of monetary and fiscal policies, depending upon the stage of the economy prior to their pursuit. These roles are:

---

i. The stabilization role for monetary and fiscal policies

Stabilization policies are ones that are pursued to eliminate or reduce the economy's deviations from full employment. These deviations occur due to prior shifts in the private components of aggregate demand or shifts in aggregate supply. They are intended to stabilize output and employment at their full-employment levels.

The FSR and LSR imply that such deviations can occur. If these deviations take significant real time before the economy eliminates them, the policymakers can step in and pursue the appropriate policies to speed their elimination. Such policies are known as *stabilization policies*.

ii. The proactive role for monetary and fiscal policies

Policies intended to raise the levels of output and employment above their full-employment levels are said to play a proactive role. As we have shown above, based on the analysis of the FSR and the LSR, starting with a position of long-run equilibrium, expansionary monetary and fiscal policies can increase employment and output in the economy provided that they are not anticipated ones and create positive errors in the expected rate of inflation. Hence, the proactive role of policies under the FSR and LSR requires the creation of unanticipated inflation. However, in some ways, this represents an attempt to 'fool the public'.

Focusing only on the proactive role of central bank policies — irrespective of whether expectations are rational or not rational or whether systematic policy is fully anticipated or not — there are benefits and costs to any unanticipated expansion of the money supply. The benefits occur in the present in terms of higher employment and output. The costs come later. There are several types of costs.

One of these costs is the damage to the policymaker's credibility with the public since the central bank pursued policies that misled the public. This loss of credibility means that the public will become sceptical about the central bank's announced future targets for money supply growth and inflation.

Another cost occurs later when the central bank becomes concerned about high inflation and wants to switch to a policy of low inflation and uses a contractionary monetary policy, but the public refuses to adjust its inflationary expectations as fast. The result is unanticipated negative errors in the expected inflation rate, which pushes employment and output below their full-employment levels. Creating unanticipated inflation becomes a policy of 'benefit now, pay later', which raises doubts about the net benefits of such a policy.

Uncertainty about the future pursuit of policies and the rates of inflation and uncertainty increases, which makes business planning for investment more risky, and affects the long-term growth of capital accumulation and output growth.

If the economy already starts from a state of full employment and if the expansion in the money supply is anticipated, long-run equilibrium implies that it will have no effect on employment and output, but will only change the price level and the nominal wage — but not the real wage.

To conclude, under the FSR and LSR, monetary and fiscal policies can have a valuable stabilization role to play in the economy if the economy's deviations from full employment, caused by non-policy shifts, take significant real time before the economy can eliminate them. Their role in a proactive form has both benefits and costs.

The Implications of Rational Expectations for Systematic Monetary and Fiscal Policies

Rational expectations imply that the public will anticipate a systematic policy, whether monetary or fiscal; therefore, its implied price increase will also be anticipated. Further, the only type of policy that will not be anticipated will be a random one. Therefore, the FSR and the LSR imply that systematic monetary and fiscal policies will not shift the economy away from full employment, while random ones will do so.

However, a random policy does not make sense. To illustrate the nature of a random policy, a random monetary policy will increase the target interest rate or decrease the growth of the money supply in

Extended Analysis Box 8.3: (*Continued*)

magnitudes specified by a table of random numbers. Using money supply as an example, if the random number for the current quarter turns out to be 3%, the money supply would be increased by 3%; next quarter, the random number might turn out to be −10%, so that the money supply would be cut by 10%; and so on. In following this pattern of random numbers for growth rates, the central bank would not be pursuing a monetary policy related to the perceived needs of the economy. Hence, a purely random policy would not serve the interests of the economy.

Since the only types of policies that could change output and employment in the economy are random one and these do not make sense, adding rational expectations to the FSR and the LSR implies that the monetary and fiscal policies should not be pursued. The conclusion is that the monetary and fiscal authorities should leave the economy alone in the sense of not using their policies in a futile attempt at improving on its performance.

This is a very strong conclusion on the applicability and pursuit of monetary and fiscal policies, and, at the practical level, not all economists subscribe to it. Most central bankers do actively reduce or raise interest rates as they think fit, so that they do not follow the implications of the above conclusion.

The Scope for Monetary and Fiscal Policies for Stabilization when Private Demand is Volatile

Several of the private components of aggregate demand are volatile — i.e., change over time for reasons not encompassed in the model. The short-run analysis shows that this can induce movements in unemployment, output, interest rates, and prices that may not be desirable. Therefore, one of the roles for policies is the stabilization one aimed at offsetting any undesirable changes in aggregated demand coming from the volatility of its private components.

The preceding analysis implies a distinction between the effects of unanticipated, possibly random, changes in private demand and those of anticipated ones. In the latter case, the change would only be in prices and possibly interest rates, but not in unemployment and output, which will remain at their full-employment levels. If the policymakers are not bothered by the changes in prices and interest rates, they need not take any action. If they are bothered by even these changes, they can take counteraction designed to stabilize aggregate demand.

Unanticipated changes in the private components of aggregate demand will induce short-run changes in unemployment and output, as well as changing prices and interest rates. The policymakers may choose to tolerate them since they can be expected to be transient ones. Alternatively, the policymakers may consider them to be undesirable and try to offset them by appropriate counteracting policies. In practice, an unanticipated demand reduction is more likely to be considered undesirable since it increases unemployment and reduces output, than an unanticipated demand increase since this reduces unemployment and increases output in the short run. Therefore, our analysis implies that policymakers are more likely to try to offset unanticipated decreases in demand than other types of demand changes.

However, note that unless the policymaker has better information than the private sector, unanticipated demand changes in the private sector will also be unanticipated by the policymakers so that they can only try to offset them once they become known — by which time they will also be known to the private sector — and have become anticipated. Therefore, the stabilization role for policies has to be based on either:

a. Superior information available to the policymakers than to the private sector — which is an aspect of asymmetric (i.e., between the policymaker and the public) information, and/or

Extended Analysis Box 8.3: (*Continued*)

b. Long-time lags in the impact of private demand changes on the economy along with a faster impact of policy induced changes in demand.

The Scope for Monetary Policies and the Political Economy of the Government's Budget

Aggregate demand depends on the fiscal deficit. The size of the fiscal deficit is often determined by the expenditures needs of the government, including the size of the public debt and the payments on it, and the taxes it can raise, both of which are heavily influenced by the economic, political, and social context — including the desired levels of military spending, anti-poverty programs, wars, disasters, etc. This context may produce continuous deficits over many years and continuous surpluses over other years.

Therefore, the size of the deficit is rarely determined by the stabilization needs of the economy, so that monetary policy has to often assume the main — or the sole — burden of economic stabilization. In performing this role, it may not only have to offset undesirable fluctuations in the private components of demand but also redress the undesirable impact of the fiscal position on aggregate demand. Therefore, monetary policy is the pre-eminent stabilization policy in most developed countries. However, even in these countries, an expansionary fiscal policy is commonly used to supplement monetary policy in severe recessionary conditions induced by a fall in the private components of aggregate demand.

8.7 FSR and LSR: The Impact of Anticipated Permanent Supply Changes on the Economy[12]

As in the case of aggregate demand changes, the impact of anticipated supply changes differs from that of unanticipated ones. For anticipated supply shifts, assume that there is an anticipated permanent increase in productivity. This shifts the LRAS curve to the right, from $LRAS_0$ to $LRAS_1$ in Figure 8.4a.

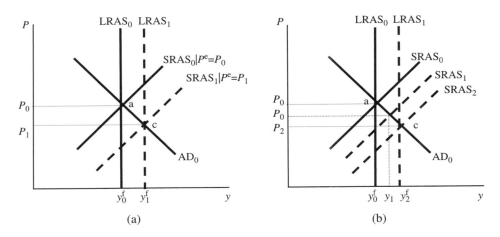

Figure 8.4

---

[12]This would include knowledge of past shifts in demand and supply and past variations in local and general prices, but can also include any available information about the future.

For the FSR, assume that the output supply increases and its effect on the price level was known when the wage contracts were signed, so that the wage contracts anticipated the new long-run price level. Therefore, under the FSR, the relevant SRAS curve would now go through the point c at the intersection of $LRAS_1$ and AD_0. For the LSR, assume that the firms know the impact of the LRAS shift on the price level, so that they know that there is no alteration of relative prices. Hence, there will not be any errors in relative price expectations. Therefore, under the LSR, the relevant SRAS curve would also shift so as to go through the point c at the intersection of $LRAS_1$ and AD_0. The SRAS curves were shown in this figure to elucidate the assumptions being made on expectations but are clearly not relevant to the long-run impact of the productivity increase on output.

Hence, for the anticipated positive supply increases, the long-run equilibrium of the economy will move from the point a at the intersection of $LRAS_0$ and AD_0 to the point c at the intersection of the $LRAS_1$ and AD_0 curves, with output increasing from y_0^f to y_1^f and the price level falling from P_0 to P_1.

8.8   The Impact of Unanticipated but Permanent Supply Changes on the Economy

Now consider the impact of an unanticipated but permanent increases in supply due to a positive productivity shift. For the FSR, we will assume that this shift was not known at the time the wage contracts were signed. In the new LR equilibrium, as seen in the preceding section, the MPL is higher but the equilibrium price level is lower, so that the value (P.MPL) of the MPL could become higher or lower at the new full-employment level (at the point c in Figure 8.4a) than at the old full-employment level (at the point a in Figure 8.4a). In the short run, under the FSR, the contracted nominal wages (Pw) proves to be (a) lower than justified by the new (unexpectedly higher) marginal product of labor, but (b) higher than justified by the new (unexpectedly lower) LR price level. The former increases employment while the latter decreases it. The net effect on employment could be positive or negative. But note that the increase in the MPL will raise output for any given level of employment, so that the SR employment could become lower while its accompanying output becomes higher.

For the LSR, the LR price level has fallen because of the positive supply shift. Assume that this positive supply shift introduces errors in relative price expectations: firms mistakenly expect a reduction in relative prices when it is a general price reduction due to the supply increase; therefore, they decrease output relative to the new LR full-employment level. Hence, while output tends to increase because of the productivity increase, the price fall acts under both the FSR and the LSR to hold back output and employment relative to their new long-run levels: employment would fall under both the FSR and the LSR.

In Figure 8.4b, the initial curves are $LRAS_0$, $SRAS_0$, and AD_0. The positive productivity increase shifts the LRAS curve to $LRAS_1$, with the new long-run output as y_2^f and the corresponding LR price level as P_2. The new SRAS curve (incorporating the old expected price level but the new productivity level) is $SRAS_1$. It lies below $SRAS_0$ but above the eventual $SRAS_2$ curve through the point c. The equilibrium between $SRAS_1$ and AD_0 has been shown as (y_1, P_1). As contracts are renegotiated and the expectational errors are rectified, the SRAS curve will move down to $SRAS_2$ to go through the long-run point c. Starting from (y_0, P_0), this movement produces continuing increases in output and reductions in the price level until the new LR equilibrium is reached at (y_2^f, P_2).

Hence, positive supply shocks tend to produce, over several periods, gradually increasing output and falling prices — or at least act to moderate the rate of inflation that would otherwise occur due to demand increases. However, over some of these periods, employment could fall even when output is rising.

We showed in Chapter 7 that oil price increases produce long-run declines in labor productivity and aggregate supply. The preceding analysis can be extended to derive the short-run effects of anticipated versus unanticipated changes in oil and other energy costs on the economy. This extension is left to the students to pursue.

Box 8.2: Cost of Living Clauses

Many wage contracts contain clauses to ensure that the nominal wage is automatically increased by the rate of inflation. Such clauses are called *cost-of-living clauses*. Their effect is to ensure that the negotiated wage rate embodied in the contracts becomes effectively the real wage rate. Other contracts in which a payment is agreed upon can have similar clauses.

Cost-of-living clauses are mostly inserted in contracts in periods of high, especially hyper, inflation rates. They serve to eliminate the effects of unanticipated inflation. Given such a clause in the wage contracts, the Friedman supply rule ensures that employment and output cannot be changed by inflation and will remain at the full employment levels.

8.9 The Short- and Long-Term Relationships between Output and Inflation

For the LSR, high and persistent (which approximates the long-run) rates of inflation over time will lead firms to expect that all price increases in their individual product prices are a reflection of the general price increase, so that they will not increase output. For the FSR, high and persistent rates of inflation will lead workers to adopt better mechanisms for predicting the price level or reduce the duration of wage contracts sufficiently. Alternatively, they may put cost-of-living clauses in wage contracts, so that nominal wages rise automatically with the price level. These reduce or eliminate the errors in price expectations and their impact on real wages will be reduced. As a consequence, under high and persistent inflation rates, the SRAS curve will be vertical or virtually so. The end result under both supply rules will be that high and persistent inflation will not produce significantly higher output than the full-employment one even in the short term.

As a corollary, high and persistent rates of increase in the money supply that produce high and persistent rates of inflation will also not increase output. Therefore, the economy's output will not show much variation in response to changes in the inflation rates and money supply growth rates in periods of high and persistent inflation.

Since the SRAS curve has a positive slope (because of both the FSR and the LSR) at low rates of inflation, unexpected increases in the inflation rates and money supply can produce some increases in output for some time. Therefore, at low rates of inflation, the economy will tend to show a positive relationship between output and inflation over the short term.

In an article published in 1973, Robert Lucas estimated a version of his output equation for a cross section of countries and found that countries with low rates of inflation (such as the USA in the 1950s and 1960s) showed evidence of a positive relationship between output and demand increases, while those with hyperinflation (such as Argentina in the 1950s and 1960s) did not, thereby concluding that this relationship shifts as inflation increases. This finding is consistent with the preceding analysis.

8.10 Empirical Validity of the FSR and the LSR

The major economic crisis of 2007–2009 in the USA and other countries was due to a fall in aggregate demand and a decline in credit availability brought about the mortgage-based financial crisis. It was not due to any significant initial decrease in the inflation rate, so that it was not due to errors in price or inflation expectations. Therefore, the FSR and the LSR cannot account for the decline in output and employment during this crisis.

For the overall validity of the FSR and LSR, we draw upon the 'Nobel Lecture' given by Robert Lucas (1996)[13] on his receipt of the Nobel Prize in economics. Robert Lucas wrote that:

> "… anticipated and unanticipated changes in money growth have very different effects" (1996, p. 679). However, on the models which attribute this non-neutrality to unanticipated or random changes in the price level, the evidence shows that "only *small fractions* of output variability can be accounted for by unexpected price movements. Though the evidence seems to show that monetary surprises have real effects, *they do not seem to be transmitted through price increases*, as in Lucas (1972)." (1996, p. 679; italics added).[14]

This quote on the empirical validity of the FSR and the LSR downplays their importance as a major contributor to valid explanations of the real-world deviations of output and employment from their full-employment levels. This assessment is consistent with the point emphasized several times in this chapter that deviations in output caused by errors in price expectations tend to be transient and self-correcting. Therefore, we need to look for additional sources of such deviations. This is done in the rest of this chapter and the next chapter.

8.11 Types of Adjustment Costs and Their Impact on Output

The preceding analysis in this chapter has focused on adjustments in prices and their expectations. However, there can also be other sources for deviations in output and employment from their long-run levels. Among these are costs of adjusting prices, employment, and production. Briefly, the three types of adjustment costs are:

1. costs to the firm of changing prices under imperfect competition,
2. costs to the firm of changing employment and the capital stock, and
3. costs to the firm of changing output at the pre-existing levels of employment and the capital stock.

Next, we consider these three types of adjustment costs in greater detail.

1. If firms operate under some form of imperfect competition and determine the price that they set for their products, there may be a cost to changing these prices. The costs of changing product prices are called '*menu costs*,' which refers to the cost of reprinting restaurant menus to indicate new prices. The theory of menu costs implies that prices will be sticky — i.e., left unchanged for some time — under certain circumstances, even though they are not rigidly set but would change under other circumstances.
2. Firms also face adjustment costs if they wish to change employment and the capital stock. To change employment, firms have to incur hiring and training costs. Further, firms usually need workers with some firm-specific skills, which can only be gradually acquired by workers while working in the firm in question.

---

[13]Lucas, Robert E. Jr. (1996). Nobel lecture: Monetary neutrality. *Journal of Political Economy*, 104, 661–682.
[14]Lucas, Robert E. Jr. (1972). Expectations and the neutrality of money. *Journal of Economic Theory*, 4, 103–124.

These factors lead to implicit or explicit contracts between the firm and its workers for long-term employment and labor hoarding in response to short-run fluctuations in aggregate demand and production. In a sense, the employment of workers and their hours worked become sticky, while that of the employee's work effort is made variable. To increase (decrease) the capital stock, the firm has to undertake investment (disinvestments), which the firm would be willing to do if the change in aggregate demand was expected to be permanent but not if it was expected to be temporary. Note that any change in the capital stock involves planning, investment, and integration of the new machines/capital into the existing ones, so that there are adjustment costs of changing the capital stock, which makes the capital stock also sticky. Firms get around this stickiness by changing the rate of utilization (e.g., by using them over more hours per day) of their capital stock.

Given the costs of changing employment and the capital stock, firms may try to increase their output with their existing employment and capital. They do so by varying the rates of utilization of their existing capital and the speed and work efficiency of their employees. However, in doing so, they again incur adjustment costs.

3. Costs to the firm of changing its output with the existing levels of capital and workforce. In the short term, firms can vary the level of effort of its employees, as well as capital utilization.

The following two sections consider the analysis of sticky prices for the commodity market and that of sticky employment for the labor market. These produce short-run commodity supply behavior that is different from the long-run one (when, by assumption, there are no adjustment costs). Note that for their analysis, the long run is being defined as that analytical period which has zero adjustment costs and lags.

8.11.1 Firms' responses to increases in the demand for their products

The preceding arguments imply that, when demand increases, firms have the following options:

- Raise prices, while leaving output unchanged (as under the long-run aggregate supply with full-employment output).
- Increase output to meet the demand increase, while leaving prices unchanged (the sticky price hypothesis).
- Not change output or prices, thereby leaving demand unsatisfied at the prices charged.
- Some mix of the above options.

In general, adjustment costs of various types individually and together imply that the short-run-term supply response of the economy to aggregate demand changes is slower than the long-run one[15] and slower than that posited by the Friedman supply function (FSR) and the Lucas supply function (LSR).

8.12 Menu Costs and Price Stickiness as the Explanation of the SRAS Curve

While some commodities in the economy are homogeneous and traded in perfectly competitive markets, many commodities — especially at the retail level — are differentiated by firms in some way or other. Such differentiation is often in the form of differences in color, packaging, location, associated services, or just established brand loyalty. Such differentiation in practice is usually not enough to create a monopoly for the firm but enables it to function in a monopolistically competitive manner. Profit maximization by a monopolistically

---

[15]The long run is that analytical period when there are zero adjustment costs and lags, and no uncertainty.

competitive firm implies that it is not a price taker, as firms are under perfect competition, but a price setter with a downward sloping demand curve for its product. Consequently, increases in the price it sets neither reduce its sales to zero nor do reductions in it allow it to capture the whole market for its industry. As a price setter, the firm sets the profit-maximizing price and supplies the output demanded at this price.

Changing the set price imposes a variety of costs, collectively known as *menu costs*. Examples of these are: reprinting price lists and catalogs, informing customers, re-marking the merchandise, etc. These costs, though often relatively small as a percentage of the price of the firm's product, can still be greater than the gain in revenue from a small price change. Further, even if there is a net gain from changing the price following an increase in demand, it may not be enough to persuade the firm to immediately raise its price since the inconvenience and costs to the firm's customers of frequent price changes are likely to be resented. Consequently, the firm may not find it optimal to respond to demand changes with price changes unless the demand changes imply large enough price changes. Over time, as demand increases accumulate, the optimal price change becomes large enough for the firm to be willing to incur the menu costs and change the actual price of its product. These arguments imply — though for a monopolistically competitive context rather than a perfectly competitive one — that:

- In the short run/term, the (monopolistically) competitive firm will change its prices infrequently, but will accommodate intervening changes in demand by changing its output at the existing price. In the limiting case of no change in the price but only a change in output to meet a change in demand, prices are said to be 'sticky' and the firm's supply curve becomes horizontal.
- In the long run/term, the competitive firm will adjust its prices to reflect demand changes.
- Even in the short run/term, if the demand change is large enough, the price adjustment will become profitable.

The aggregate economy is a mix of firms in perfect competition and monopolistic competition. Further, when aggregate demand increases, while some firms may be experiencing sticky prices, others may be coming out of such a phase. Hence, at any given time, the economy will only have some firms with sticky prices. An increase in aggregate demand will cause some sectors and firms, especially those with more competitive markets, to adjust their prices faster while others will not immediately do so but will respond to demand changes by changing output. Consequently, an increase in aggregate demand will be partly met by an increase in the price level and partly by an increase in aggregate output, so that the short-run supply curve will have a positive slope, as shown in Figure 8.5b, but not as steep as when none of the firms is suffering from sticky prices.

Conversely, a decrease in the demand for the products of the firm in monopolistic competition need not immediately cause it to lower its price unless the implied optimal price reduction was sufficiently large.

In the extreme case, if all firms in all sectors simultaneously have sticky prices, the average price level in the neighborhood of the initial equilibrium would become constant. In this extreme case, shown in Figure 8.5a, the price level is assumed to be constant at its initial level P_0. Prices are sticky at P_0, so that we can specify a short-run aggregate supply curve SRAS which is horizontal at P_0, while the LRAS curve still remains vertical at y^f. The increase in the aggregate demand from AD_0 to AD_1 raises the supply of output from y^f to y_1 at the sticky price P_0. Conversely, the decrease in the aggregate demand from AD_0 to AD_2 leads to the supply of output y_2 but again without an accompanying change from the sticky price P_0.

Therefore, the sticky prices theory implies that:

- Transient and small changes in aggregate demand are accommodated by a change in output.
- Cumulative or persistent changes in the same direction — or large aggregate demand changes — will, however, make it optimal for all firms to increase prices, so that the long-run response to such changes is taken to be along the LRAS curve.

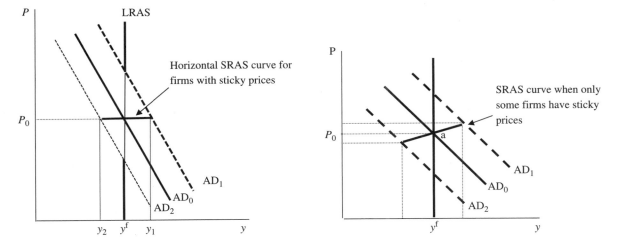

Figure 8.5

- Caution should be exercised in the use of a horizontal SRAS curve for the aggregate economy since this requires assuming that all firms will simultaneously have sticky prices. As pointed out earlier, the economy has a mix of perfectly competitive, monopolistically competitive, oligopolistic, etc., markets, so that the sticky prices argument does not apply to all commodities. Even for a given commodity, some producers may be in a sticky prices phase, while others are coming out of it, so that the adjustment of price lists is staggered. Therefore, even under the sticky-prices argument, the normal case for the aggregate economy is an upward-sloping SRAS curve rather than a horizontal one.

- Another caution, from the implications of the menu cost approach to price stickiness, is that prices will adjust faster the greater the increase in demand, so that the greater the demand increase, the more quickly will prices adjust and the less will be the effect of aggregate demand increases on real output. Hence, larger increases in aggregate demand and, therefore, potentially greater inflationary pressures, will produce smaller real effects. Hence, the sticky-price SRAS curve bends backward above a certain point.

8.12.1 Aggregate supply in the sticky-price hypothesis

The *supply equation under the sticky-prices hypothesis* can be illustrated by:

$$y_t^s = y_{t-1} + \beta(y_t^d - y_{t-1}),\qquad(4)$$

where $\beta > 0$ if $|(y_t^d - y_{t-1})|$ is 'small', while $\beta = 0$ if $|(y_t^d - y_{t-1})|$ is 'large'.[16] Note that the variation in output is from last period's level, not from the full-employment level. This sticky-prices short-term equation differs from the FSR and LSR by making the increase in demand, not in the price level, the engine for increases in output. Therefore, in the sticky-price model, expansionary monetary and fiscal policies have a direct impact on output without necessarily first producing an increase in the price level. This implication accords well with the stylized facts on the impact of changes in the money supply on output.

Corresponding to the output adjustment, there is a price adjustment equation, which can be illustrated by:

$$P_t = P_{t-1} + \alpha(y_t^d - y_{t-1}).\qquad(1')$$

Totally, sticky-price level would require $\alpha = 0$. However, more realistically, $0 \le \alpha \le 1$ in the short run.

---

[16]The magnitude of 'small' and 'large' depends on the firm's behavior.

8.12.2 Monetary policy and the sticky-price SRAS curve

The sticky-price analysis implies that, for the analysis of monetary policy, relatively small reductions in the target interest rate — and, hence, relatively small increases in aggregate demand — would increase output but larger reductions in the target interest rate — and, hence, relatively larger increases in aggregate demand — would produce smaller increases or no increase in output. Further, there is no direct causal relationship between from inflation to output; rather, the causal relationship runs from aggregate demand to output — as well as (later) to inflation. From the perspective of inflation, only relatively large increases in aggregate demand would necessarily cause significant inflation in the short term. These conclusions are very different from those of the theories (FSR and LSR) based on expectational errors in prices. However, the implications of the sticky-prices argument that concur with those of the theories based on expectational errors are:

- Any increase in output induced by an expansionary policy will be temporary. Prices will sooner or later adjust and output will return to its full-employment level.
- There is no clear-cut and strong case for the continuous or massive pursuit of *proactive* expansionary policies as a route to a *lasting* increase over several quarters and years in output and employment beyond their full-employment levels.

8.13 Costs of Adjusting Employment: Implicit Contracts as an Explanation of the SRAS Curve

The production function implies a unique relationship between employment and output. This is based on an implicit — and rather unrealistic — assumption that work effort and, therefore, the output per hour of work is constant at any given level of employment. Under this assumption, as employment and output increase, the marginal productivity of labor (MPL) declines, so that the real wage rate also declines.[17] Figure 8.6 shows the standard (long-run) labor demand curve as n^d. It has the downward slope derived earlier from the production function in the preceding chapter: the MPL (and average product of labor) decline as employment n increases from its long-run equilibrium at n^f. This decline implies that higher employment will be associated with lower real wage rates.

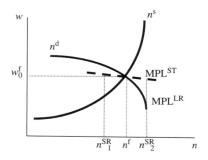

Figure 8.6

---

[17]Hence, they behave counter-cyclically over the business cycle.

8.13.1 Variations in work effort over the short term

In the short term, aggregate demand increases usually induce increases in the work effort of employees relative to their *long-run norm* at full employment. This moderates the decline in the MPL, which would have otherwise occurred as employment increases. Conversely, short-term decreases in demand induce a reduction in effort, so that the MPL does not rise as much as implied by the production function. Therefore, in Figure 8.6, instead of the standard (long-run) MPL curve labeled as MPL^{LR}, the short-term MPL curve becomes MPL^{ST}. This short-term MPL curve — and, therefore, the short-term n^d curve — is flatter than the long-run one for variations in employment induced by aggregate demand changes.

This theory, allowing variations in work effort, is known as the *implicit contract theory*. An implicit contract between two parties is an understanding or a verbal arrangement rather than a written, legal document. The implicit contract theory deviates from the standard production function in two ways.

1. It allows for variations in work effort, with variations in the MPL as aggregate demand changes.
2. It allows for long-term implicit contracts between firms and workers, with labor hoarding (i.e., retaining workers but using them at less intensity than at their normal long-run level) in demand-deficient periods and increased work effort during excess demand periods.

Box 8.3: Work Effort in Restaurants During the Day

Restaurants provide a good example of variations in work effort during the day. Restaurants experience spurts of demand during the lunch and dinner hours, with very little demand during other periods. They work at a faster pace during the high-demand hours while doing very little work during the low-demand hours. The average work intensity over the day can be thought of as the long-run work intensity for that type of restaurant, with short-run variations in work intensity induced by the fluctuations in demand. In particular, the restaurant does not resort to laying off some workers during the slack periods while hiring more during the busy ones, since these would increase hiring and training costs, poorer service by temporary employees, as well as a loss of staff morale. Holding onto excess staff during the slack periods and reducing their effort demanded of them is called *labor hoarding*.

If, during a particular week, the restaurant experiences an increase in its customers, it usually accommodates them by further increases in the work intensity of its existing employees, even if this exceeds the long-run norms on work intensity for that restaurant or class of restaurants. However, this level cannot be sustained on a long-run basis, otherwise employee morale will suffer, leading to increases in absenteeism, poor service, and resignations. If this demand remains exceptionally high over the longer term, the restaurant would increase its staff or raise its prices, or both. The former is often done whether the increase in demand is a relative one or a general one for the economy.

If the number of customers decreases, the restaurant is likely to respond by reducing the work effort of its staff without laying-off an appropriate number or changing its prices. Once it is realized that the decrease in demand is a longer-term one, the restaurant has the options of reducing its prices and laying-off some employees. The latter is often pursued, whether the decrease in demand is a relative one for the restaurant or a general one for the economy.

Work Effort by Students over the Term and the Calendar Year

Students follow similar patterns of variations in study effort during the academic term and the calendar year. At one extreme, there are vacation (and other!) days that are sometimes spent without any studies

Box 8.3: (*Continued*)

being done. At the other extreme, there are intense study days and nights near examinations. Students do not load up with extra courses on a short-term basis in slack periods and drop some when pressure builds up. Rather, they follow some notion of a long-run norm for the average work effort over the term and the year. Variations around this norm occur, leading to increased effort and productivity near examinations and reduced ones during slack periods.

8.13.2 The Flexibility of the Employment–Output Nexus in the Short Term

Chapter 7 had specified the relationship between output and employment by the production function, which is strictly a one-to-one relationship, so that a given level of output is associated with a unique level of employment. This relationship assumes a constant 'work-effort', which is to be interpreted as the intensity of work. However, the existence of costs of adjusting employment implies that firms may sometimes find it less costly to increase output by increasing the work effort of their employees rather than by increasing their employment, or do so by some combination of the two.

Long-term labor contracts and labor hoarding

Firms and workers often find it in their interests to enter into long-term implicit (non-written) and explicit (written) employment contracts when there are costs of hiring and training workers and/or workers possess some firm-specific skills, usually acquired through training and learning on the job. For such workers, the productivity of an existing skilled employee will be greater than that of new hires. The employed worker also benefits from this higher productivity through higher wages in his/her existing firm than if he/she was to quit and join other firms. This mutual benefit from continued employment implies that the firm would try to retain its skilled workers if it can do so through a period of reduced demand for its output, rather than laying them off immediately. The firm, therefore, finds it optimal to (temporarily) lay off less workers than justified by the fall in demand, leading to a form of labor hoarding during recessions. Such hoarded labor works less hard during recessions because there is less work to do or is often diverted to low-productivity tasks such as maintenance etc. In the case where a worker is laid off, the worker also has an incentive to wait to be recalled by his/her old employer rather than immediately accept a job with another firm in which his/her productivity and wage will be lower. The firm and its workers are then said to have an implicit contract for long-term employment under certain types and magnitudes of fluctuations in demand, with short-term fluctuations in work effort to permit output to respond to demand fluctuations. Therefore, reductions in aggregate demand in the short term partly lead to labor hoarding, with a consequent fall in average productivity, and partly to an increase in unemployment, with some of the laid-off workers being put on recall and voluntarily waiting to be recalled rather than actively searching for jobs.[18]

An implicit agreement between firms and its workers also means that workers accommodate increases in the demand for the firm's product with increased effort, even in the absence of wage increases, so that moving along the SRAS curve away from full-employment output will be partly accommodated by changes in work

---

[18]Note that the economy is quite diverse with some sectors resorting to labor hoarding while others not.

effort. Hence, increases in aggregate demand will increase the average product of labor (APL)[19] relative to its LR trend, and, therefore, increase aggregate output. The APL will be procyclical and output will fluctuate more than employment over the business cycle.

The short-term production function and the output supply function under the implicit contract hypothesis are:

$$y_t = f(n_t, e_t) \tag{5}$$
$$\Delta y_t = y_t - y_{t-1} = f(\Delta n_t, \Delta e(y_t^d - y_{t-1}))$$
$$\text{so that: } y_t = y_{t-1} + f(\Delta n_t, \Delta e(y_t^d - y_{t-1})),$$

where e stands for work effort, which varies with the excess or shortfall of demand relative to last period's output. Its implications are similar to those of the sticky-price output function. However, it differs from the latter in stressing that, proportionately, the variations in employment will be less than in output.

8.13.3 Okun's Rule: The Relationship between Unemployment and Output Changes

Okun's rule — named after Arthur Okun — is the statement that, in the short term, increases in the level of aggregate output are accompanied by less than proportionate decreases in the level of *unemployment*. To illustrate this with an example from one country, over the business cycle, one estimate of this relationship for Canada is that a 5% increase in the economy's output rate is accompanied by approximately a 3% decrease in the unemployment rate.

Okun's rule runs counter to the assumptions made for the production function, under which increases in output are accompanied by more than proportionate increases in employment (because of diminishing marginal productivity of labor) and more than proportionate decreases in the unemployment rate. The explanations for Okun's rule lie in (a) the short-run variations in labor effort and labor hoarding, and (b) the discouraged worker effect. (a) implies that as demand increases, the average level/intensity of effort increases so that the average productivity of labor also increases. Hence, employment rises — and unemployment falls — less than proportionately with output.[20]

Another reason for Okun's rule is the discouraged worker effect. During recessions, some workers are discouraged after looking some time for jobs and meeting rejections of their applications. In such circumstances, some workers close to retirement may choose to retire earlier. Both these drop out of the labor force and the measured unemployment rate. As demand increases and firms increase employment, the prospect of landing a job rises. This induces some of the discouraged workers to re-enter the labor force, so that the labor force increases, making the decrease in the unemployment rate less than proportionate to the increase in output.

Therefore, over the business cycle, the unemployment rate fluctuates less than the growth rate of output around its trend.

---

[19]This occurs since all employed workers, and not merely the marginal one, work harder. In this scenario, real wages are likely to be mainly determined by the long-run MPL, though short-term changes in wages are likely to be somewhat responsive to the short-run movements in the APL.

[20]Conversely, in the short run, as demand falls, firms decrease the average effort of their employees and resort to labor hoarding, in order not to lose valuable employees while waiting for the pick-up in demand. If this happens, average labor productivity falls.

8.14 The Implications of Adjustment Costs for Persistence of Output and Employment Fluctuations Over the Business Cycle

The long-run analysis (in Chapter 7) is based on the assumption of instant adjustment of the equilibrium price level to shifts in the demand and long-run supply functions. The analysis of this chapter shows that adjustments in output and prices by firms are not instantaneous but gradual because of the existence of costs in changing employment, prices, and output. Further, firms face costs in adjusting their capital stock, which, combined with the uncertainty of future sales, make their adjustment of physical capital much slower than the instantaneous one assumed in the long-run analysis. Consumers also have valid reasons for slower than instantaneous adjustments of their consumer demand and labor supply.

What these arguments translate into in terms of our macroeconomic diagrams is that the movements along the various demand and supply curves can be quite slow ones spread over several quarters, possibly years, rather than an almost instantaneous one. To illustrate, the slow adjustment of the capital stock implies that the change in investment specified by the investment function will occur over many quarters. Movements along the AD and AS curves will be slow ones. Movements along the labor demand and supply curves will also be slow. In fact, movements along any of the curves used for macroeconomic analysis are likely to be slow and gradual ones, rather than the instantaneous ones assumed in the AD-LRAS analysis.

In practical terms, starting with the economy at the peak of the business cycle, if aggregate demand or supply were to decrease because of exogenous shifts, the declines in output and/or prices will not come about instantaneously. If this were to happen, the economy would have gone instantly from the peak of the business cycle to its trough. Instead, output, prices, and employment tend to decline gradually in a stretched-out recessionary movement. Conversely, starting with the economy in the trough of the business cycle, if aggregate demand or supply were to increase because of exogenous shifts, the increases in employment, output, and/or prices will not come about instantaneously. If this were to happen, the economy would have go instantly from the trough of the business cycle to its peak. Instead, output, employment, and prices tend to increase gradually in a stretched-out upturn. Therefore, the existence of adjustment costs implies that the economy would not display sudden highs and lows of output and employment, but is likely to follow business cycle upturns and downturns of several years' duration.

A corollary of this argument is that there is a high degree of *persistence in output and employment fluctuations over the business cycle*. This persistence in the sign of output changes means that an increase in output (or employment) in one period is more likely to be followed by another increase rather than a decrease, and vice versa. By comparison, the instantaneous adjustment assumed in the long-run analysis would produce *random changes in output and employment* in response to random shocks to aggregate demand and supply. 'Random changes' in output means that an increase in output (or employment) in one period is as likely to be followed by another increase as a decrease, and vice versa. Business cycles clearly display persistence of the signs of changes in output and employment, rather than random changes, except at their peaks and troughs.

Therefore, the incorporation of the adjustment costs of employment and variations in work effort under implicit contracts implies that over the business cycle:

- Variations in output occur due to demand fluctuations, whether anticipated or not.
- Output fluctuates more than employment.
- The economy produces output higher (lower) than the full-employment one in response to demand increases (decreases).

- The APL increases as output rises in booms and decreases as output falls in a recession. Hence, the APL would be procyclical.
- Under Okun's rule, employment increases less than proportionately as output rises, especially in the early parts of an upturn. Conversely, employment declines less than proportionately as output falls, especially in the early parts of a downturn.

8.15 Implications of Adjustment Costs for the Impact of Monetary and Fiscal Policies

The essential implication of the analysis of this chapter is that the full impact of a significant shock, whether to demand or supply and whether from private or policy decisions, on output and employment is likely to be spread over some time. The behavior of the economy during this period is not necessarily identical with that which equilibrium analysis leads us to expect. In particular, the theories of sticky prices and implicit contracts imply that the responses to demand and supply shocks are likely to include changes in quantities, e.g., in output and employment, as well as in prices.

8.16 Stagflation and the Recessions of 1973–1975 and 1980

Stagflation occurs when the economy has inflation while its output is stagnant (i.e., not changing). In the more general case, the term stagflation means inflation with constant or falling (or at least not rising) output. Stagflation was also discussed in Chapter 7, Section 7.9. Fact Sheet 7.2 and Box 7.1 in Chapter 7 related the experience of stagflation in 1973–1975 and 1980 in many countries to increases in the price of oil.

As shown in Chapter 7, output would be stagnant in an economy (without growth) in the long run of a static economy (i.e., without technical change or capital or labor force growth), since output is constant at the full-employment level. In such a context, continuous increases in aggregate demand would produce an increasing price level, so that there would be inflation. Frequent causes of continuous demand increases are continuing expansionary monetary and fiscal policies.

A special case of stagflation occurs when output is falling (and not merely constant) while the economy has inflation. The fall in output can be due to a declining marginal product of labor, due to a negative shift in the production function, a decreasing physical capital stock or rising prices of inputs. On the last cause, Chapter 7 discussed the declines in output brought about by oil price increases in 1973–1975 and again in 1980–1982. These periods were marked by expansionary monetary and fiscal policies, meant to increase aggregate demand in the belief that the increase in the demand for commodities would increase output. In fact, output fell in many oil-importing countries because of the impact of the rising oil prices while their expansionary demand policies caused inflation. These two periods provide clear cases of stagflation.

Box 8.4: Empirical Evidence on Price Changes, Wage Contracts and Output Response

In a relatively low inflation context, one survey revealed that about 10% of firms change their prices less frequently than once a year, about 39% change their prices once a year, about 28% change them up to four times a year, while about 21% change them more often. Of the latter, about 10% change more frequently than once a week. Therefore, about 59% of firms change their prices four or more times a year. The most common reasons given for infrequent price changes were waiting for other firms to go first (about 60%), not changing prices until costs rise (about 55%), fairness to customers (about 50%), etc. The cost of

Box 8.4: (*Continued*)

changing prices was cited by only about 30% of the surveyed firms.[21] This seems to suggest limited support for the sticky-price hypothesis.

Empirical studies show that the average duration of wage contracts was about one year in the 1970s. All wage contracts are neither renegotiated on the same date nor do all price changes occur on one date. Both wage contracts and price changes are staggered and overlapping in the economy, so that the average nominal wage rate and the price level are never constant. Hence, even over the short term, the aggregate supply curve for output is never horizontal.

8.17 Stylized Facts and Intuition on the Theories Explaining Variations in Output

Note that this chapter has presented three major approaches (price expectations, sticky prices, and implicit contracts) and four theories (FSR, LSR, sticky prices, and implicit contracts) to explain variations in output from the full-employment level. How do these theories compare with the empirical evidence? For low-inflation economies, the *stylized facts* on the impact of aggregate demand on output are:

- Positive (negative) demand shocks, including both anticipated and unanticipated ones, have a positive (negative) impact on current aggregate demand and output. Demand shocks sometimes have a smaller impact on output than at other times. [This finding is consistent with the sticky prices and implicit contracts hypotheses. The variations in output in response to anticipated demand shocks are not consistent with the FSR and the LSR. The variations in output in response to unanticipated demand shocks are consistent with all four theories.]
- The impact of increases in aggregate demand or of the money supply on output does not always or necessarily require a prior impact on the price level or inflation. Not all of the impact of changes in aggregate demand on output filters through changes in prices or inflation. [This finding is consistent with the sticky prices and implicit contracts hypotheses, but not with the FSR and the LSR.]
- Current inflation is positively related to current output and an increase in the inflation rate causes it to exceed expected inflation for the current period. [This finding is consistent with the FSR and the LSR but not necessarily inconsistent with the sticky prices and implicit contracts hypotheses.]
- Past inflation is negatively related to current output. Past inflation leads to higher expected inflation rates for the current period. [This finding is consistent with the FSR and the LSR but not necessarily inconsistent with the sticky prices and implicit contracts hypotheses.]
- For economies with very high inflation rates, further increases in inflation or in aggregate demand do not tend to increase output and employment. [This finding is consistent with the FSR and the LSR but not necessarily inconsistent with the sticky prices and implicit contracts hypotheses.]
- Cutting back on aggregate demand or lowering the inflation rate significantly from past levels sends the economy into a recession and reduces output and employment. [This finding is consistent with all four theories.]

---

[21] Blinder, Alan S. (1994). On sticky prices: Academic theories meet the Real World. In N.G. Mankiw (ed.), *Monetary Policy*. Chicago: University of Chicago Press.

- Employment fluctuates less than output over the business cycle. [This finding is only explained by the implicit contracts hypotheses.]

8.18 Conclusions

- The FSR based on nominal wage contracts and the LSR based on errors in perceived relative prices imply that output and employment increase when there is an unanticipated increase in the price level.
- The FSR and LSR imply that expectation errors in prices generate the positive slope of the SRAS curve. Under rational expectations, only random policies can generate such errors. Systematic policies will not generate these errors and will not produce deviations from full-employment output.
- In the FSR, expansionary demand policies induce an increase in output through a reduction in real wages induced by an unanticipated increase in the price level. Any such reduction will be temporary, with a readjustment when wages are renegotiated or, even earlier, under pressure from disappointed workers and at the volition of firms. The LSR does not require a prior reduction in real wages.
- The FSR and the LSR assume optimization by both firms and households and clearance of the labor market in one way or another. Therefore, these theories rely on the assumption of equilibrium to derive the SRAS curve and its policy conclusions. In this equilibrium, firms can sell all that they want to sell and there are enough jobs for all the workers who want jobs at the existing wage. Note that involuntary unemployment does not occur along the LRAS curve, or along the SRAS one.
- The deviations from full-employment output due to errors in price expectations under the FSR and LSR are transient and self-correcting. They account for only some of the deviations that occur in the real world.
- The costs of adjusting prices lead to sticky prices, so that changes in demand are reflected in output changes. In the sticky-prices model, menu costs imply that firms' profits could fall if they were to adjust their prices by small amounts. Rather than change prices, firms find it profitable to accommodate changes in aggregate demand by changing output and employment in the short run. For these firms, the supply curve would be horizontal in the vicinity of their long-run position.
- At any given time, since not all firms in the economy find it profitable to maintain sticky prices, the sticky-price model does not really imply a horizontal SRAS curve for the aggregate economy. Further, more rapid increases in aggregate demand will produce smaller rather than larger increases in output.
- For firms experiencing sticky prices, an increase in aggregate demand increases their output without a prior or accompanying increase in prices. Therefore, the impact of monetary policy on output is not a function of the change in their prices but rather of the change in the aggregate demand — and through it, in the money supply — itself. In fact, any increase in prices reduces the impact of monetary expansion on output.
- In the sticky-price model, the impact of aggregate demand and the money supply on output is not uniform since relatively small increases in aggregate demand and the money supply increase output but very rapid increases in them induce larger increases in aggregate demand which produce more rapid price adjustments, with consequently smaller increases in output.
- Costs of adjusting employment explain the existence and nature of implicit contracts, which allow adjustment of work effort, with labor hoarding in recessions, so that labor productivity changes as aggregate demand changes.
- Changes in work effort imply that employment fluctuates less than output in response to demand fluctuations and that the marginal product of labor and real wages do not necessarily have to fall in upturns or rise in recessions, as they do under the long-run production function.

- In the FSR, expansionary demand policies induce an increase in output through a reduction in real wages (induced by the increase in the price level). Any such reduction will be temporary, with a readjustment when wages are renegotiated or, even earlier, under pressure from disappointed workers and at the volition of firms. The LSR and the sticky-prices models do not require a reduction in real wages.
- Each of these theories is based on optimization by both firms and households and clearance of the labor market in one way or another. Therefore, these theories rely on the assumption of equilibrium for their short-run/term analysis and its policy conclusions. In this equilibrium, firms can sell all that they want to sell and there are enough jobs for all the workers who want jobs at the existing wage under the existing explicit and implicit contract arrangements.

However, real-world economies do go through recessions and booms, and sometimes through depressions. Unemployment and output fluctuate very significantly over time. These casual observations suggest the possibility that there may be periods (of deflationary demand) during which the firms collectively cannot sell all the output that they produce if they offered full employment to workers in the economy. These may also be periods during which some of the unemployed workers — in spite of possession of the appropriate skills for jobs and the willingness to accept the existing wage rates for their skills — cannot get jobs. That is, there exists the possibility that the economy may experience levels of employment and output that are neither at the full-employment level nor on the short-run supply curve of the economy. The next chapter will explore this possibility.

KEY CONCEPTS

Price expectations
Adaptive expectations
Rational expectations
Expectational errors
Expectational equilibrium
Wage contracts
The short-run employment–output equation/relationship

The short-run aggregate supply (SRAS) curve
Friedman supply rule (FSR)
Lucas supply rule (LSR)
Imperfect competition
Implicit contracts
Firm-specific skills

Labor hoarding
Okun's rule
Sticky prices
Persistence in output and employment fluctuations, and Stagflation.

SUMMARY OF CRITICAL CONCLUSIONS

- Nominal wage contracts allow the impact of the errors in the expected rate of inflation on the real wage, employment, and output. This effect is captured in the Friedman supply rule/curve, which explains the deviation of output from its full-employment level due to the reduction in the real wage under unanticipated inflation. This rule is based on the errors in the expectations — of households and firms — embodied in nominal wage contracts.
- The Lucas supply rule/curve for output is based on the errors made by firms in their expectations of the relative prices of their commodities.
- The deviations in output from its full-employment level due to errors in price expectations are transient and self-correcting.

- The costs of adjusting prices, output and employment are also significant determinants of the short term deviation of output and employment from their long-run levels.
- Some firms, especially monopolistically competitive or monopolistic ones, find it best to maintain their prices in response to limited demand increases for their products, so that they are said to have sticky prices in the neighborhood of the full-employment level of output.
- In the short run, firms are able to vary the work effort of their employees, so that employment fluctuates less than output. Since the average productivity of labor rises in booms and falls in recessions, the APL moves procyclically over the business cycle.
- In the theories of sticky prices and implicit contracts, in the short term, changes in demand directly impact on output and employment rather than indirectly through prior price changes brought about by markets. In the FSR and LSR, demand changes must alter prices in order to have any impact on output even in the short run.
- The sticky-price hypothesis relies on some form of imperfect competition with firms able to manipulate their prices rather than under the strict assumptions of perfect competition.

REVIEW AND DISCUSSION QUESTIONS

1. Do rational expectations allow errors in the expected rate of inflation relative to its subsequent actual value? If so, explain the nature of this error.
2. Explain the two-stage process in the FSR for the determination of employment.
3. Specify the equation for output under the FSR. Why should an actual inflation rate higher than the expected one cause output to rise under the FSR? Explain.
4. Discuss the following in the context of the FSR: "The central bank has to keep on accelerating the inflation rate in order to continuously maintain employment and output above their full-employment levels".
5. "A boom due to accelerating inflation is bound to bust and end in a recession when the central bank is fed up with the ever-rising inflation and decides to lower it". Explain how this would happen in the context of the FSR.
6. Explain the contributions of Robert Lucas on the dependence of output and employment on errors in expectations. Why would the response of the economy to a rise in the inflation rate differ between economies that follow low-inflation strategies versus those that maintain very high-inflation rates?
7. [This question is based on interest rate targeting and, therefore, on the IS-IRT analysis]. Suppose the government cuts income taxes, show its impact in the long-run and the short-run output (i.e., along the LRAS and SRAS curves based on the FSR and the LSR) under two alternative assumptions:

   (i) The central bank uses interest rate targeting and keeps the target interest rate constant.
   (ii) The central bank uses interest rate targeting and changes the target interest rate to maintain aggregate demand equal to long-run supply.

8. What is stagflation? Describe a situation that could produce stagflation? Could the stagflation in the situation described by you have been avoided through an expansion of the money supply?
9. What is a cost-of-living clause in wage contracts? If all wages were indexed to the inflation rate, how would this affect the applicability of the FSR? Discuss the short- versus long-run effects of an initially

unanticipated but permanent increase in oil prices on output, employment, real wage, real interest rate, and the price level.

10. In the early 1990s, the Bank of Canada pushed up the economy's interest rates (and decreased the growth rate of the money supply) to reduce inflation in the Canadian economy. Analyze the effect of such a contractionary monetary policy on the interest rate, aggregate demand, and output in the economy:

    (i) If this monetary policy was unanticipated.
    (ii) If this monetary policy was anticipated.

    Use the IS-IRT and AD-AS diagrams for your answer.

11. Explain menu costs. What implications do they provide for the shape of the SRAS in industries with menu costs? What implications do they provide for the shape of the SRAS if the economy has some industries with menu costs and others without any such costs?

12. "The sticky-price hypothesis implies that the aggregate supply curve is horizontal in the short term". What is the sticky-price hypothesis? Is this statement likely to apply to modern economies in the short term? Discuss.

13. Discuss the following in the context of the sticky-price hypothesis: "The central bank has to keep aggregate demand in excess of long-run aggregate supply order to continuously maintain employment and output above their full-employment levels".

14. Suppose that firms can vary the work effort of their workers in the short run in response to variations in the demand for its products. How does this affect the marginal product of labor in the short run versus the long run? Explain.

15. Assume that firms face adjustment costs in changing their prices and employment. Suppose the government cuts income taxes. Show its impact in the long run and the short run under two alternative assumptions:

    (i) The target interest rate remains unchanged.
    (ii) The central bank adjusts its target interest rate to keep aggregate demand constant.

16. Explain the implicit contract theory.

17. In 2004 and 2005, the US government ran large fiscal deficits while the Federal Reserve System of the USA raised the Federal Funds rate several times to curb but not eliminate excess demand. Using only the general nature of this information (rather than the specific situation in the USA at the time), discuss the initial cause of excess demand as specified in this question? Using the analysis of adjustment costs, discuss the likely effects of the remaining excess demand on aggregate demand and output in the short run.

18. The demand expansion of 2004–2005 in the USA initially increased output without a corresponding significant impact on employment, but subsequently also led to a strong growth in employment. How can this pattern be explained by the relevant adjustment cost theories presented in this chapter?

19. What is Okun's rule? Provide the justification for this proposition.

20. What does Okun's rule imply for the relative variations in employment and output over the business cycle? What does Okun's rule imply for the relative variations in unemployment and output over the business cycle?

ADVANCED AND TECHNICAL QUESTIONS

Basic structural AD-AS model for this chapter [with interest rate targeting and an endogenous money supply]:

$$c = 0.8y_d$$

$$t = 0.2y$$

$$i = 1000 - 50r$$

$$g = 800$$

$$x_c = 200 - 0.5\rho^r$$

$$z_c/\rho^r = 500 + 0.1y_d$$

$$m^d = 0.25y - 60R$$

Output:

Long-run output: $y^f = 1,000$

Short-run aggregate supply function: $y = 1,000 + 0.1(P - P^e)$

[Note: depending on the context, the short-run aggregate supply can be stated as a positive function of the error in the expected price level or of the error in the expected inflation rate.]

Foreign trade sector:

$$P^F = 1$$

$$\rho = 1$$

The central bank targets (i.e., fixes) the domestic *real* interest rate, so that:

$$r = r^T = 0.04$$

T1. For the basic structural AD-AS model above,

   (a) Derive the IS equation? [Do not use the IS equation formula. Do the calculations step by step. To do so, first calculate the real exchange rate in terms of the domestic price level P. Then, calculate disposable income. Substitute these in the consumption, import, and export functions. Then, use the equilibrium condition $y = e$ to derive the IS equation for the information in this model.]

   (b) What is the level of aggregate demand y_0^d?

   (c) Equating demand and long-run supply, what are the long-run levels of real output and the price level? Designate this output as y_0^f and the price level as P_0^*.

T2. For the basic AD-AS model, assume that the economy was in long-run equilibrium in period 0. In period 1, the government raises its expenditures to 1,000.

   (a) Calculate the new level of aggregate demand (y_1^d).

   (b) Since $y_1^d > y^f$, calculate the new long-run equilibrium price level P_1^{LR} and output y_1^{LR}.

T3. [This question uses the rational price expectations hypothesis in which economic agents know the new *long-run* price level and their expected price level is equal to the appropriate long-run price level.] Using the basic AD-AS model and your answers to the preceding question, answer the following. Assume that, in period 1, the expected price level P_1^e equals the long-run price level P_1^{LR}, but, in fact, the actual price level in period 1 rises by only 50% of the increase required to move to P_1^{LR}. (a) Using the SRAS function, what is the price level P_1^{SR} and the level of output y_1^{SR}? Designate the latter as $y_1^{SR\#}$. (b) Explain the reasons provided by the FSR and the LSR for the change in output from y^f to $y_1^{SR\#}$.

T4. [This question uses the *static price expectations hypothesis, according to which the expected price level for the period ahead is the actual price level one period earlier.*] Using the basic AD-AS model and your answers to the preceding question, answer the following. Now, assume that in period 1, the public expects that prices will stay at P_0^* (i.e., $P_1^e = P_0^*$). Using the short-run supply function, calculate the output in period 1.

a. For period 1, calculate the increase in the short-run levels of real output.
b. What is the short-run fiscal (government expenditures) multiplier for real output in period 1? Is it zero? Explain your answer.
c. What is the long-run fiscal (government expenditures) multiplier for real output? Is it zero? Explain your answer.

T5. Comparing your results in questions T2 and T3. (a) Which provides a smaller deviation from full-employment output? (b) Which seems a more realistic expectations hypothesis as far as your own behavior is concerned? Discuss.

T6. [Optional] Note that in the preceding three questions, the target real interest rate had remained at r_0^{LR}, even though fiscal expenditures increased. Now assume for period 2 that the central bank realizes that aggregate demand has risen. It adjusts the target rate r^T to 20. Calculate the new equilibrium price level P_2^* and output y_2^*. Compare these to P_0^* and output y_0^*. Are they different? Why or why not? Explain your answer.

Basic reduced-form AD-AS model:

For the basic reduced-form AD-AS model, assume that the following equation describes the aggregate demand function for the economy.

IS equation:

$$y_t = 100{,}000 + 0.2g_t - 10{,}000r_t - 100P_t \quad t = 0, 1, \ldots, g_t = 1{,}000$$

The central bank's real interest rate targets are:

$$\text{In period } 0, r_0^T = 0.04$$

$$\text{In periods 1, 2, and 3, } r_1^T = r_2^T = r_3^T = 0.05$$

The money supply adjusts to be consistent with money market equilibrium at the interest rate target.

$$m^d = 0.25y - 60R$$

Fisher equation:

$$R = r + \pi^e$$

$$\pi_0^e = \pi_1^e = \pi_2^e = \pi_3^e = 0$$

Long-run output:

$$y^f = 90{,}000$$

Because of adjustment costs, the short-run aggregate supply function is given by:

$$y_t = 90{,}000 + 0.2(y_t^d - y_{t-1})$$

[*Note: in this specification of the SRAS, SR output is a function of full-employment output and the deviation of the demand for output from last period's output. This SR output function is in the Keynesian tradition, in which firms adjust output in the short run in response to changes in the demand for their products. Such an SR function is consistent with the menu cost theory, which is in the Keynesian tradition. For comparison, note that the classical tradition would make the derivation of SR output from the full-employment level an function of the error in prices, as in the FSR and the LSR.]*

Output in period $t-1$: The economy is in long-run equilibrium in period $t-1$ with $y_t - 1 = y^f = 90,000$. Price level: The economy maintains the price level in period 0 that is consistent with long-run equilibrium.

T7. Given the basic reduced-form AD-AS model, assume that the economy is in long-run equilibrium in period $t-1$ with y_{t-1} (=10,000) being the initial long-run output. The current period is $t = 0$.

(a) What is the level of aggregate demand in period 0? What are the levels of actual and long-run output in periods 0, 1, 2, 3, and 4? Discuss the impact of demand on the time pattern of actual output.

(b) [Optional] Suppose that g rises to 1200 in period 1. Calculate the output level for periods 1, 2, 3, and 4.

(c) [Optional] Using the above answers, calculate the fiscal (government expenditures) multipliers for actual output? What is the long-run fiscal (government expenditures) multiplier for output?

CHAPTER 9
Actual Output, Disequilibrium, and the Interaction among Markets

The economy is often not in short-run equilibrium, let alone in long-run equilibrium. If either the commodity or the labor market is not in full-employment equilibrium, the study of the interaction between these markets becomes important. The resulting disequilibrium analysis gives different results from the equilibrium ones on the determination of output and employment.

There can be numerous causes and symptoms of macroeconomic disequilibria. This chapter presents the analyses of two cases: when the economy develops a demand deficiency and when the real wage is too high, relative to their equilibrium levels. In each of these cases, the failure of a market to clear at the full-employment level (i.e., to have adequate demand to buy the full-employment output) impacts on the other markets. This chapter derives the impact of the resulting disequilibrium in the commodity and labor markets on output and employment, and the appropriate role of demand and supply side policies in such conditions.

The analysis of full-employment output under the long-run supply curve (see Chapter 7) and of deviations from it along the short-run supply curve (see Chapter 8), is based on the assumption of market clearance (i.e., the equality of demand and supply) in all markets, with economic decisions by households and firms taking it for granted that market clearance will, in fact, immediately occur following any shifts in demand and supply. Hence, both households and firms believe that they can buy and sell as much as they want at the existing market prices and act accordingly in making their decisions on consumption, investment, labor supply, labor demand, production, etc. This chapter examines the interaction between the commodity and labor markets when they are not in equilibrium (i.e., demand and supply are not equal, that is, they do not clear), so that consumers and firms, knowing this non-clearance and behaving rationally, modify their demand and supply for commodities and labor accordingly. It derives the implications of this interaction between the commodity and labor markets for output and employment.

However, the economy sometimes enters a situation in which there are not enough jobs for all the workers who are willing to accept jobs at the existing wage rate. In this case, the difference between the available number of jobs and the number of workers at the existing wage represents *involuntary unemployment*. The involuntarily unemployed workers are unable to sell the labor that they want to sell at the existing wage, even though they possess the requisite skills and are in the right locations, as evidenced by their employment just prior to the fall in aggregate demand. Unable to earn incomes, they reduce consumption expenditures, which reduces aggregate demand. Therefore, from household behavior, there is a special nexus, running from employment to the demand for commodities. This nexus is not fully apparent in the AD-AS analysis studied so far.

Similarly, the economy sometimes enters situations in which firms want to sell more commodities than they are able to sell. In particular, the demand for commodities becomes less than what the firms can produce if they were, collectively, to hire the number of workers specified by the full-employment level. Such a situation is known as that of deficient demand. In this case, since firms will not want to pile up unsold inventories, they will reduce employment below the full-employment level. Therefore, from firm behavior, there is a special nexus between the demand for commodities and employment, which translates into a special nexus between aggregate demand and unemployment. This nexus is also not fully apparent along the LRAS and SRAS curves.

Given the preceding arguments, we need to study the causes of the persistence of disequilibrium and the behavior of the economy during disequilibrium. This chapter does so. The worldwide economic crisis and recession of 2008–2010 attests to the empirical relevance and importance of the analysis of this chapter for the economy.

This chapter focuses on the potential deviations of actual output from the output shown by the LRAS and SRAS curves. The relevance of these curves depends on whether the economy is always in equilibrium or not. Some economists claim that the economy is always, or almost always, in or near this state, and, if it gets moved away from it, reverts quite fast and on its own to this full-employment state. Most economists and economic policy makers, however, believe that the economy can be out of equilibrium for several quarters, if not years. This occurs because, following a shock, the economy's required adjustments to reach the new equilibrium are varied and take time. The fluctuations in unemployment and the existence of recessions and booms provide casual empirical validity to the economy being sometimes out of its equilibrium state.[1]

When the deviations from equilibrium occur, the roles of monetary and fiscal policies become quite different from those derived so far from the LRAS (see Chapter 7) and the SRAS (see Chapter 8). In particular, since such deviations can be brought about by shifts in the private components — such as consumption, investment, and money demand — of aggregate demand and the economy has lags in restoring equilibrium, monetary and fiscal policies acquire the very useful and important role of stabilizing the economy at or close to its full-employment level. This stabilization role of demand-management policies does not occur if the economy is *always* in full-employment, as in Chapter 6.

The Three Components of Actual Output

As a reminder, note that Chapter 7 had divided actual output into three components. These are repeated in the following identity.

$$y = y^f + (y^* - y^f) + (y - y^*),$$

where:

y^f: long-run (full-employment) level of output (see Chapter 7).
$(y^* - y^f)$: the deviation of the short-run equilibrium level of output from the full-employment one due to errors in expectations under uncertainty and adjustment costs (see Chapter 8)
$(y - y^*)$: the deviation, in disequilibrium, of output from its short-run equilibrium level (this chapter)

This chapter focuses on the last component: that is, on the deviations of output from even the short-run equilibrium level. Real-world economies do not continuously maintain equilibrium in the commodity and labor markets. In many instances, demand and supply shocks cause the economy to initially move away from its equilibrium. While it may soon start adjusting towards equilibrium, this process takes real time during which the economy is in disequilibrium and away from its equilibrium employment and output levels. During this

---

[1] However, not all economists agree that recessions are evidence of labor market disequilibrium.

adjustment period, which can take several quarters or even years, the powerful conclusions on the ineffectiveness of monetary and fiscal policies in long-run equilibrium derived in Chapter 7 do not apply. Further, the channels of adjustment may not be as specified in the short-run supply hypotheses in Chapter 8. This chapter focuses on the likely adjustment scenarios and the roles of monetary and fiscal policies during this adjustment period.

Fact Sheet 9.1 shows the relationship between money supply growth and real output growth in the USA. This relationship occurs because an increase in money supply growth causes aggregate demand to increase, which stimulates output, thereby creating a positive relationship between money growth and real output growth, so that increases in money supply growth are followed by increases in output growth, and decreases in money supply growth are followed by decreases in output growth. This relationship is better explained by the disequilibrium analysis of this chapter than by the short-run analysis of Chapter 8.

Fact Sheet 9.1: Money Growth and Output Growth in USA, 1960–2008

This Fact Sheet illustrates the relationship between money supply growth and real GDP growth. The graph below illustrates this positive relationship using US data: both variables follow a similar zigzag pattern during the 1970s, increase in economically prosperous times such as the early 1980s and late 1990s, and fall during the late 1980s and early 2000s. Further, peaks and troughs in money supply precede peaks and troughs in real GDP growth, so that the former cause the latter.

As a corollary, this graph shows that in real time and for real-world economies, money supply shifts do not leave either real output or velocity unchanged/constant, as asserted by the quantity theory of money.

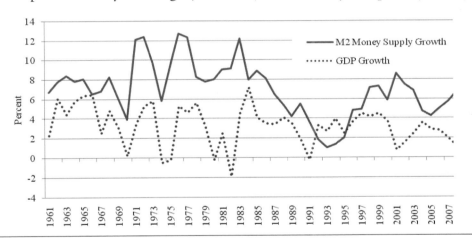

9.1 The Relevance of Expectations on Variables Other Than Prices

The short-run analysis of Chapter 8 had considered the impact of firms' and households' expectations on prices and that the optimal supply responses of firms to changes in demand take adjustment costs into account. This chapter argues that there are also other reasons for firms to form expectation on the future demand for their products, as well as for workers to form expectations on the future demand for their labor. Therefore, the expectations formed by firms are on:

(i) the quantity that they would be able to sell,
(ii) the price at which their product will be sold, and
(iii) on wages to be paid.

Similarly, workers form expectations on jobs, wages, and nominal and real incomes. These expectations, just as those on prices, play important roles in the decisions of firms and households/workers. For example, firms' expectations of future sales strongly influence their investment and the number of jobs they want to offer. Households' expectations of being employed or becoming unemployed, as well as their expected incomes, strongly influence their consumption.

The role of the expectations formed on the 'quantities' of the (real) variables and their nominal values was excluded from the short-run analysis provided by the Friedman and Lucas supply rules (Chapter 8) in constructing the SRAS curve. However, their role is important enough for economic analysts to construct indices of '*business confidence*' and '*consumer confidence*' to explain what is happening to output and employment in real time in the real world. Some aspects of this role of the expectations formed on the nominal and real values of the real variables are captured through the disequilibrium analysis specified in this chapter.

Another component of this chapter's analysis is the interaction between the commodity and labor markets when one of these fails to achieve equilibrium. This analysis will be irrelevant to economies if prices and wages change instantaneously to ensure their equilibrium values. It becomes relevant when they do not do so. In the latter case, there is spillover of disequilibrium between markets.

This chapter explores the role of expectations on variables other than prices and of deviations from the equilibrium levels of employment and output when there is interaction between the labor and commodity markets.

9.2   Shocks to Aggregate Demand and Supply

The shocks to — that is, shifts in — aggregate demand can come from the domestic private sector, the foreign sector, the central bank, and the government. Shocks from the central bank and the government are discussed as aspects of the pursuit of policy. Shocks to aggregate demand from the domestic private sector occur because of shifts in consumption, investment, net exports, or the demand for money. Each of these variables tends to vary over time, often on a daily basis. We illustrate some of the major sources of shocks to these variables.

Examples of shocks to consumption

First, consider the shocks to consumption. Clearly, the seasonal variations in climate and in holidays cause variations in consumption over the calendar year. More important for macroeconomics is the impact of changes in wealth on consumption. The major components of household wealth are houses, bonds, and stocks. The prices of bonds and stocks are determined in the bond and stock markets and do not consistently mirror either the rate of inflation or the changes in the physical stock or the sum of the two. To illustrate the shifts in wealth that can occur, Table 9.1 presents the change in the Dow Jones Industrial Index — which serves as a rough indicator of the stock market prices in the United States — during the 20th century and up to 2008.[2]

Table 9.1 provides a very rough indication of the changes in the nominal and real values of the financial wealth held in stocks over the last century by examining changes in the (USA) Dow Jones Industrial Index for the New York Stock Exchange. These variations affected consumption, pushing up consumption if the stock markets were doing particularly well, and pushing it down if they were doing badly, relative to income. They also affected firms' ability to raise funds for investment. The resulting variations in consumption and investment expenditures led to variations in aggregate demand.

---

[2]For the decades up to 1940, the percentages have been rounded to the nearest 5%. Data for each year is for 31 December.

Table 9.1   Changes in the Dow Jones industrial index (DJII)

Period	% Change in DJII	% Change in CPI	ΔDJII − ΔCPI (%)
1900–1909	50	8	42
1920–1929	150	−15	165
1930–1939	−40	−17	−23
1940–1949	52.9	70	−17.1
1950–1959	188.57	21	167.6
1960–1969	29.9	24	5.9
1970–1979	−0.02	87	−87.0
1980–1989	185.6	50	135.6
1990–1999	336.5	27	309.5
2000–2004	−0.05	10	−10.1
2005–2008	−18.1	12	−30.1
2000	−6.17	3.36	−9.5
2001	−7.10	2.85	−10
2002	−16.76	1.58	−18.3
2003	25.32	2.28	23.0
2004	3.15	2.66	0.5
2005	−0.61	3.39	−4.0
2006	16.29	3.23	13.1
2007	6.43	2.85	3.6
2008	−33.84	3.84	−37.7

The largest single item of wealth in household portfolios is the value of owner-occupied houses. House prices fluctuate considerably, often rising for several years and sometimes falling for several years. Increases in house prices increase household wealth, which for a given level of income, persuades households to increase their consumption expenditures and reduce their saving.

Another source of shocks to consumption comes from changes in *consumer confidence*. Consumers go through episodes of optimism (especially in economic booms) or pessimism (especially in recessions) about their future job prospects and wages. Optimism encourages a reduction in precautionary saving which is partly a hedge against future job loss or fall in the value of accumulated wealth, so that consumption expenditures increase. This is represented by either an increase in autonomous consumption or in the marginal propensity to consume, or in both. Conversely, if consumers become pessimistic about the future, precautionary saving rises and consumption expenditures fall.

At current levels of income and wealth in the developed economies, the impact of changes in wealth on the expenditures on durable consumer goods, such as kitchen appliances, TVs and other entertainment units, automobiles, etc., tends to be much greater than those on non-durables, such as food and rental units.

Examples of shocks to investment and net exports

Investment is often the most volatile component of aggregate demand. Changes in it are caused by shifts in:

- Technology, of which changes in information technology (IT) have been very noticeable in the last few decades.
- Firms' existing physical capital relative to current aggregate demand.

- Availability of qualified workers.
- Costs and availability of external funds. The cost of such funds is approximated in the investment function by the interest rate.
- Expected future demand for commodities and workers.
- Business confidence.
- Firms' ability to raise funds from external sources. Firms use short-term credit and long-term bonds and stocks for their external sources of funds. The availability of such funds is also an important consideration in determining the actual levels of investment (see Chapter 16). Rapid increases in the stock market prices of a firm's shares improve its ability to raise additional funds for investment, while rapid decreases in the stock market prices of a firm's shares are detrimental to its ability to raise additional funds for investment. The availability of short-term credit is also important for investment in the short term.

The uneven pace of investment over time, due to shifts in one or more of its determinants above, is the most frequent and significant cause of fluctuations in aggregate demand.

After investment, exports are the next most volatile component of aggregate demand. Shifts in exports occur due to changes in the real exchange rate, foreign incomes, and domestic supply constraints. Their determinants are discussed in Chapters 3, 5, 12, 13, and 16.

Shocks to money demand and supply

Money demand is influenced by many factors, among which are the returns on stocks and bonds, which are affected by speculation in the stock and bond markets. Many economists believe that the speculative component of money demand is very volatile since it depends on the subjective expectations of returns in the highly speculative bond and stock markets. These expectations are often based on inadequate information and are influenced by 'herd behavior' and 'contagion'.[3]

Shocks to the cost and availability of credit

Credit provided by banks and other financial institutions to households is a major determinant of their purchases of durable goods and houses, etc. Credit provided to firms is a major determinant of their investment, especially in inventories, and of exports (since there is a time lag between production of exported goods and payment for them by buyers abroad). Therefore, reductions in credit, whether due to a reduction in the money supply or a perception by financial institutions of an increase in the risk of lending to consumers and firms, reduce consumption, investment and exports, so that aggregate demand falls.

9.2.1 Shocks to the aggregate supply of commodities

Shocks to aggregate supply occur through:

- shifts in the production function,
- the supply behavior of labor and the supply of other inputs, and
- the supply of credit and other funds to firms.

---

[3]'*Herd behavior*' occurs when economic agents tend to follow each other, as can be observed in stock market manias and collapses. '*Contagion*' is the spread of a shock in one market, or one country, to others, as happens when a foreign exchange crisis occurring in one country spreads to other countries in the region. Another example is when the collapse of the price of the shares of one major corporation also brings about a collapse in the share prices of other corporations in the same industry. Herd behavior and contagion were very evident in the stock market boom in the late 1990s, the collapse from 2000 to 2002 of the prices of Internet and telecommunications stocks, and the worldwide financial crisis of 2007–2010.

Of these, the shifts in the production function depend upon changes in technology, which is rarely a smooth and even process over time. However, in general over the whole economy, shifts in technology tend to be less volatile in terms of the frequency of occurrence and relative magnitudes than shifts in the private components of aggregate demand.

In addition, shocks can also occur to the prices of most of the inputs, including the wage rate, energy prices, and the interest rate, which can affect the cost of production and, therefore, the supply of output.

The financial crisis of 2007–2010 in major economies also showed that reductions in credit limit the ability of firms to finance production. Production firms employ labor and buy other inputs in advance of sales of their products, so that they have to bridge the time gap between their cost disbursements and receipt of revenue. This is partly done through credit borrowed for short periods from financial institutions directly in the form of loans or through sale of short-term bonds in bond markets. Therefore, reductions in credit supply reduce the production that can be undertaken, thereby reducing aggregate supply in the economy.

9.3   An Analysis of the Disequilibrium Following a Demand Shock

9.3.1   The assumptions for disequilibrium analysis

The analysis of disequilibrium for any given comparative static (equilibrium) model is tricky since there can be many possible disequilibrium patterns. Hence, we should not expect a consensus on the particular pattern that will hold. In particular, the disequilibrium patterns depend on the specific assumptions made for behavior in disequilibrium. To limit these patterns, we will maintain the assumptions of the rationality of economic behavior by households and firms in the light of the information available to them. [4] However, we will dispense with the assumption of instant market clearance in each individual market and instant restoration of general equilibrium in the economy, i.e., our analysis will allow the possibility of some disequilibrium for some time, since these assumptions are quite unrealistic ones.[5]

To start this analysis, take the economy to be initially in full-employment equilibrium. Now suppose that aggregate demand falls for some reason such as an exogenous decrease in consumption, investment, fiscal expenditures, or an increase in taxes — or an increase in the central bank's target interest rate. Such a fall in aggregate demand is shown in Figure 9.1 by a shift from AD_0 to AD_1. We need to analyze the plausible dynamic responses to it by rational economic agents in the modern economy.

Effective aggregate demand and supply

Effective demand is the actual demand that exists in the economy. It is based on the actual consumption of workers, actual investment by firms, actual government expenditures, and actual net exports. It differs from the level of demand that would exist if the economy was in full employment, and expected to continue functioning in full employment. This level of demand is called *notional demand*. Effective demand will be less than notional demand if there is not sufficient demand for full-employment output. This is called '*deficient demand*'. If effective demand is greater than notional demand, the economy is said to have '*excess demand*'. An economy with excess demand will usually be in a boom (see business cycle theory in Chapter 16).

---

[4]Hence, for uncertainty scenarios, the rational expectation hypothesis (see Chapter 8) will be maintained Further, we maintain the usual assumptions on the absence of money illusion and adequate flexibility of prices and wages to *eventually* (but not instantly) restore equilibrium following any shifts or shocks in their demand and supply functions in their respective markets.

[5]In addition, we dispense with the assumption that firms can sell all that they want at the existing price. This means that firms are in monopolistic competition, which is the dominant mode of industrial economies.

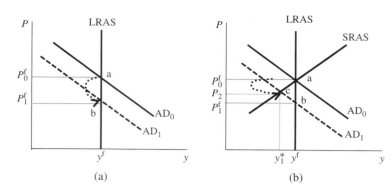

Figure 9.1

The *effective supply* of commodities is the actual supply that exists in the economy. It differs from *notional supply*, which exists when the economy is functioning at full employment. Effective supply will be less than notional supply in recessions caused by a fall in aggregate demand, since firms then produce enough to meet actual demand. Effective supply is usually greater than notional supply in booms caused by an increase in aggregate demand, since firms then try to produce enough to meet the higher demand.

In general, during disequilibrium in the economy, effective demand will be less (recessions) or more (booms) than notional demand and supply will be less or more than notional supply. This chapter studies the behavior of the economy and the need and impact of monetary and fiscal policies in such situations (recessions and booms), since disequilibrium is usually the most common state in which real-world economies normally function.

Extended Analysis Box 9.1: The Dynamics Required for the Maintenance of a Full-Employment Scenario

First, consider the response pattern *if* the economy (without any action on monetary or fiscal policy pursued by the central bank and the government) were to adjust to the fall in aggregate demand while constantly maintaining *full-employment* output. Note that since the central bank has been assumed to not take any action, the money supply remains constant at its pre-existing level and exerts an influence on aggregated demand, so that the LM curve and the price level for calculating the real money supply become relevant. Therefore, the relevant AD curve is the downward-sloping one.

In Figure 9.1a and b, the market is initially at (P_0^f, y^f), but is suddenly faced with the fall in demand to AD_1. To outline the required responses, start with the assumption that firms *continue* to keep employment at n^f and maintain their output at y^f even though demand for their products has fallen.[6] Since demand will have become less than the output supplied, which is at y^f, prices and nominal wages will fall in response to the lower demand, while the marginal product of labor (MPL) and the real wage will remain at their full-employment levels.

In Figure 9.1a, the price fall required to clear the commodity market will be from P_0^f to P_1^f. At P_1^f, there is adequate aggregate demand in real terms to buy the full-employment output. This occurs because the decline in the price level sufficiently increases the real value of the given money supply, so that the LM curve in the IS-LM diagram would have shifted to the right. With real aggregate demand restored to its initial level, the firms' policy of maintaining full-employment output will have been validated. However, the

---

[6]This assumption is made so that the SRAS curve is excluded from the analysis at this stage. It implicitly assumes that there are no price misperceptions or adjustment costs. If either of these exists, the relevant curve would be the SRAS curve.

Extended Analysis Box 9.1: (*Continued*)

dynamics of this full-employment analysis require that the economy go *instantly* from P_0^f to P_1^f, *without changing output in the process. Therefore, firms never become doubtful about their ability to sell all of their full-employment output and do not resort to a reduction in employment and output.* The realism of these dynamics is highly questionable for real-time, real-world economies.

9.3.2 A plausible dynamic scenario

Initial effects of the emergence of a demand deficiency

Firms do at times develop doubts about their ability to sell all the output that they can produce with their existing equipment and employment, and worry about mounting inventories of unsold products. When they do so, they do usually reduce output and employment. Therefore, consider the following components of an intuitively quite plausible dynamic scenario. As aggregate demand falls, the rational firm in the economy shares in this experience and believes, or even finds, that it cannot sell its former level of output, so that with production in advance of sales, it ends up unintentionally accumulating inventories. To run these down and to adjust to its reduced sales, its optimal response is to cut back on production, rather than wait for the economy's aggregative markets to clear. It is also likely to reduce the price for its product.[7] This reduction in output by the representative firm takes the economy below the equilibrium output y^f, with jobs offered falling below full employment.

Secondary effects of the demand deficiency

As output falls below its full-employment level, so does employment. This fall in employment results in a reduction in the incomes received by workers who have become unemployed, so that they cut their consumption expenditures. Further, some of the employed workers find or believe their jobs to be at greater risk than normal at the full-employment level, so that the employed workers on average will increase their precautionary saving and reduce their consumption expenditures. This process accentuates the initial decrease in aggregate demand, leading to further reductions in output and prices by the representative firm.

Facing a fall in sales, the firms are also likely to cut back on their investment plans, thereby contributing further to the fall in aggregate demand. This is especially so since the reduction in sales and sales revenue would reduce their ability to service their existing debt and maintain their share prices, as well as reduce their ability to raise funds for investment through new bond and share issues.

Let us now assume that the economy eventually returns to equilibrium. However, the economy would have spent some real time at less than full employment. In Figure 9.1a, the economy will not have gone from the initial equilibrium at (y^f, P_0^f) to the new equilibrium at (y^f, P_1^f) *instantly*. Output will loop from the point a to the point b, with the output in the loop falling for some period below the full-employment level. This loop occurred not because of price misperceptions or adjustment costs, for none were assumed, so that it represents disequilibrium positions.

The transition from the old equilibrium to the new one

If the economy does not move directly to its long-run equilibrium but instead moves to its short-run one, it will move from the initial position a in Figure 9.1b to its short-run equilibrium at c (at the intersection of

---

[7]This implicitly assumes some degree of monopolistic competition rather than perfect competition.

the AD_1 and SRAS curves), but through disequilibrium positions. These positions are depicted by the loop from *a* through *c* in this figure. In this case, output would have fallen for some time even below its short-run equilibrium level y_1^*.

Hence, the rational production responses of firms and the rational consumption responses of households work in ways that do not always make for an instant restoration of general equilibrium but could accentuate the departure from equilibrium for some time. Note that this scenario allowed prices and wages to be flexible, so that there was no assumed rigidity of prices and either nominal or real wages.[8] What was relevant was the firms' and households' information set. Firms did not observe or know either the new long-run price level (P_1^f) or the new short-run equilibrium price level (P_2) in Figure 9.1b, corresponding to the fall in aggregate demand, since the markets did not establish these instantly. Their observation was that their sales were lower due to a decline in aggregate demand.

Note that if the long-run equilibrium output is stable, both the short-run equilibrium position and the disequilibrium ones are 'transient ones'. *The chronological time taken by this transition is usually significant and depends on many factors — among which are the severity of the fall in aggregate demand, firms' and households' expectations on the magnitude and duration of the fall and their reactions to these expectations.*

Output-price adjustment function [Optional]

The above arguments suggest that firms adjust both prices and output whenever demand differs from full-employment capacity. To capture this effect, we posit the output adjustment in a simple linear form as

$$\Delta y_t = b(y_t^d - y_{t-1})/y_{t-1} \quad 0 \le b \le 1.$$

The price adjustment can also be posited as a function of the fall in demand relative to that in the previous period. A simple linear form of the price adjustment function is

$$\Delta P_t = a(y_t^d - y_{t-1})/y_{t-1} \quad 0 \le a \le 1,$$

where *P* is the price level. For both adjustment functions, the adjustment has been posited to depend on the deviation of current demand from the preceding period's output level.[9] The relative adjustment ratio b/a will depend on many factors, including the extent of the decrease in aggregate demand and the expectations of its duration. These differ among recessions, so that the adjustment in output relative to that in prices will differ among recessions.

Box 9.1: The Nature and Critical Role of Expectations in Dynamic Adjustments

As we have seen in the above arguments, expectations play a critical role in the dynamic process that is actually followed by the economy. We have already discussed two different types of expectations that are relevant to the macroeconomic analysis. These are:

(a) Expectations of future prices
(b) Expectations on the future values of the real and nominal values of the relevant variables, such as sales, incomes and employment prospects, interest rates, etc.

The macroeconomic analysis of Chapter 8 had captured the role of price expectations through the Lucas and Friedman supply rules. The macroeconomic analysis of this chapter captures the role of expectations held on the real values of the variables in the disequilibrium analysis.

---

[8]There has also been no assumption of money illusion by either firms or workers.
[9]In a dynamic context, *P* is usually replaced by the inflation rate π.

Box 9.1: (*Continued*)

In planning production and investment expenditures, firms form expectations on their expected sales. In planning consumption expenditures versus saving, households form expectations on their expected employment and incomes. These expectations are reflected in:

- *Business confidence on expected demand and sales*
- *Consumer confidence on jobs and incomes*

We illustrate their very important role for the economy's dynamic adjustments by starting with full employment and examining two polar expectation scenarios:

(a) A fall in aggregate demand that is expected by firms to be mild and temporary and occurs in an overall intertemporal pattern of enough demand to absorb the full-employment output in the aggregate economy. In this case, the representative firm's profit-maximizing response is likely to be to maintain full employment rather than lay off some trained employees whose replacement, when the expected demand pickup occurs, would impose hiring and training costs. With employment by firms maintained at its full-employment level, labor incomes would not fall, so that consumers will not reduce their consumption. In this scenario, output may remain at full employment, with some accumulation of inventories, or be decreased somewhat through changes in the work effort of existing employees. There is also likely to be some softening of prices (e.g., in the form of more than the usual sales and discounts, etc.) but no significant price reduction. In retrospect, the initial fall in demand is not worsened by decreases in consumer expenditures and firms' investment expenditures, since these do not occur in this scenario. The economy remains at or close to full employment and its initial price level. Aggregate demand is soon restored to its full-employment level, thus validating firms' expectations.

(b) A significant fall in demand expected by firms and households to last for a significant period. In this case, often backed by the experience of earlier recessions in the firms' information set, business and consumer confidence declines. Firms reduce their employment and output — which takes the economy onto a dynamic path below full employment. As workers lose jobs, they reduce their consumption demand. Other workers may also do so in order to increase their precautionary saving. The consequent further fall in demand validates and strengthens firms' earlier pessimistic expectations and provides *ex post* justification for their cuts in employment and production. It may make firms even more pessimistic about future sales.

What are the critical differences between these two scenarios? The first scenario requires firms to continue producing y^f output and employing n^f workers at a w^f wage rate, even when they observe the initial fall in demand. They are only likely to do so if they are, individually and collectively, convinced that the fall in demand is very temporary and will be reversed very soon, so that they can temporarily accommodate any output that is not sold. However, there are many instances of reductions in aggregate demand which are not so transient or at least firms generally do not take them to be such, so that the actual response of firms would be to reduce output, thereby reducing employment and leading the economy into a recession. Hence, aggregate demand shocks can have none or minor effects on output and employment, or large ones, depending on business and consumer/worker expectations and confidence.

From the policy perspective, the irony of the above scenarios is that the deliberate pursuit of aggressive policies to maintain aggregate demand at the full-employment level leads to expectations by consumers and firms which maintain full employment, while a policy of leaving the economy alone may, for larger demand shocks, bring into play dynamic responses which take the economy below full employment.

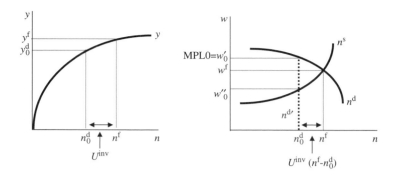

Figure 9.2

9.4 Diagrammatic Analysis Following a Fall in Aggregate Demand

Assume that the demand and supply functions for labor are as shown in Figure 9.2b and that initially the economy is at full employment n^f and full-employment output y^f in Figure 9.2a and b. Now assume that a shock reduces aggregate demand to y_0^d in Figure 9.2a so that a demand deficiency — such that the firms are not able to sell the full-employment output y^f at the existing price level — emerges in the economy. *Also assume that firms do not consider this decrease in demand to be very transitory.* The actual aggregate demand y_0^d can be supplied by the employment of n_0^d workers.

In Figure 9.2b, the marginal product of labor for employment equal to n_0^d is MPL_0, which is above the full-employment wage w^f. However, if firms were to employ more than n_0^d workers, they would not be able to sell the extra output so that their *marginal revenue product* would be zero. Hence, if aggregate demand falls to y_0^d, firms would cut employment to only n_0^d workers in order not to exceed their desired levels of inventories. This causes the emergence of involuntary unemployment u^i, one measure of which is $(n^f - n_0^d)$, which equals the deficiency of jobs relative to the full-employment level. These workers want jobs for which they were fully qualified in the old equilibrium and would prove to be fully qualified once the aggregate demand needed for full employment is restored — but in the mean time they cannot get jobs at the existing wage.[10]

In Figure 9.2b, these n_0^d workers can be paid a nominal wage rate which can change, as can the price level, with the resultant real wage being anywhere in the range w_0' and w_0'', without a change in the firms' employment of n_0^d workers, so that the real wage rate could drift up or down from the initial equilibrium level of w^*.[11] Hence, the decrease in employment (from n^* to n_0^d) can be accompanied by either an increase or a decrease in the real wage rate of the employed workers.[12]

The above effects are only *partial* or initial ones. Since the unemployed workers do not receive any incomes, they cut back on their consumption demand, which worsens the recession in output. The higher risk of losing the job leads the still employed workers to increase their precautionary saving by cutting back on their consumption.

---

[10]Involuntary unemployment and its different measures are discussed in the next chapter.

[11]Real wages will rise if the price level falls faster than nominal wages; they will fall if the price level falls more slowly than nominal wages, and will stay constant if both prices and wages fall in the same proportion.

[12]Wages may, therefore, follow a pro-cyclical or counter-cyclical pattern: some recessions and some parts of a given recession could show wages falling while others show them to be rising. If wages rise, it could be claimed that the rise in wages is the cause of falling employment, when this rise is itself only an effect while the true cause was the initial fall in aggregate demand.

Would a cut in the real wage rate restore full employment? If wages were cut below w^f, the lower incomes of the employed workers would also lead to a reduction in their consumption.[13] The resulting fall in aggregate demand further shifts the effective demand curve to the left[14] and worsens the recessionary effects derived in the preceding paragraph. Hence, a reduction in the real wage rate due to a fall in aggregate demand could drive the economy further from full employment, rather than towards it.

Effective demand for labor

Firms want to hire the amount of labor whose output can be actually sold. Therefore, the *effective demand for labor* is that level of employment for whose output there is adequate demand. In Figure 9.2a, if the demand for commodities is only y_0^d, the effective demand curve for labor in Figure 9.2b will be n_0^d. This curve differs from the usual (notional) demand curve marked n^d, which is the labor demand curve if firms had no problem selling all their output.

9.5 Disequilibrium with Flexible Prices and Wages

The above scenario is not the only one that can be sketched but it does seem to capture the most common response patterns of actual firms, consumers, and workers to a significant fall in aggregate demand. Critical to this scenario is not any rigidity in prices and wages (either nominal or real), for none has been assumed, nor the absence of an eventual return of the economy to equilibrium, but the critical role of expectations (or optimism versus pessimism) on the real and nominal values of sales, incomes and jobs, the absence of a mechanism for *instantly* restoring equilibrium,[15] and at least some adjustment in production by firms and in consumption by households.

Extended Analysis Box 9.2: The Relative Rapidity of Commodity Markets in Adjusting Prices versus those by Firms and Consumers in Adjusting Production, Employment, and Prices

The above disequilibrium analysis placed particular focus on the failure of immediate/rapid clearance in the commodities and labor markets. In particular, the main initial impulse was a fall in aggregate demand due to a fall in investment, in consumption or government expenditures, or an increase in economy's interest rate. Firms responded to this demand deficiency not solely by reducing prices *but also by reducing output and employment*, with the latter, in turn, reducing labor incomes and inducing a reduction in consumption demand. This fallback in consumption demand further increases the demand deficiency in the commodity markets, which is likely to persuade firms to further reduce output and employment. While the economy

---

[13] For many employed workers, the fall in employment usually increases the subjective risk of staying employed, so that such workers also tend to cut back on consumption in order to increase precautionary saving to provide for the eventuality of becoming unemployed.

[14] The new demand curve is not the classical notional one n^d but an effective one, and one cannot proceed with analysis using n^d. A notional demand function for labor assumes that firms can sell all the output they find profitable to produce, which was implicit in the derivation of the n^d function and curve. An effective demand function for labor is one for which output there is enough demand.

[15] Note that the assumption of perfect competition does not *a priori* specify the chronological time needed by the 'invisible hand of competition' to return an economy, follow a shock, to its full-employment equilibrium. Because of this, some models resort to a process known as tâtonnement with recontracting, which solves the problem analytically. However, since this process does not exist in the real-world economies, its usage represents in some ways an escape from answering the relevant question of how long does it take the real-world economies to return to equilibrium.

Extended Analysis Box 9.2: (*Continued*)

may eventually return to equilibrium, this process may take a sufficiently long time, during which the economy would have less than full employment.

As the demand for commodities falls, why does the price level not fall instantly to restore equilibrium in the commodity market? The reason is that the commodity market is not a unified market with a homogeneous product. It is really a collection of very diverse markets with an enormous variety of products. Further, not all of the markets for products operate with perfect competition or perfect efficiency (i.e., the immediate adjustment of prices to equate demand and supply). *In a large number of industries, in fact for most industrial goods, firms sell differentiated products and set their own prices in price lists, rather than taking the prices of their products as given by the market. The result is that there is no mechanism for an orchestrated simultaneous reduction in all prices in response to the aggregate demand reduction.* Therefore, firms operating along upward sloping marginal cost curves respond by both reducing their prices as well as reducing their output supply.

If the firms' reduction in output also leads to a reduction in employment, the latter lowers labor incomes and also increases the uncertainty of future expected incomes of those still employed. This induces a reduction in consumption and therefore in aggregate demand. Hence, the representative firm's response to a reduction in aggregate demand is a *multi-pronged* one — including reductions in price, employment, and output — and could be a destabilizing one that worsens or prolongs the effects of the initial fall in aggregate demand. *The sluggishness or failure of the market mechanisms in adjusting the price level and the real wage relative to the faster responses of the firms in adjusting their employment, output, and prices lie at the heart of the real-world dynamic adjustments in the modern economy.* Many additional factors, including the reactions of the stock markets and the financing of investment and consumer durable goods purchases, contribute to this scenario.

The failure or sluggishness of the labor market in adjusting nominal wages versus the faster responses of firms and workers in adjusting employment and consumption

In the labor market, as unemployment emerges, why does the real wage not instantly fall to restore full employment or at least short-run equilibrium? The reasons are that:

(a) The labor market is also not a unified market with a homogeneous good. It is really a collection of very diverse markets in skills, occupations, and locations.
(b) The labor market does not possess a mechanism for a *simultaneous general* reduction in real or nominal wages.
(c) In most jobs, wages are usually negotiated in nominal, not real, terms and are often fixed in contracts.

Therefore, if a reduction in real wages is required for the return to full employment, the labor market usually takes too long for the required reduction in real wages. Moreover, even when real wages do fall, this could reduce labor incomes, which further reduce consumption demand and worsen the demand deficiency in the economy. This, in turn, induces firms to further cut back on output and employment. Hence, *while the reduction in real wages is required by theory as a critical market equilibrating mechanism, it could in reality become a potentially destabilizing mechanism that could worsen and prolong unemployment.*

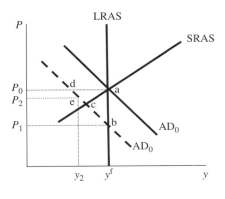

Figure 9.3

9.6 If the Real-World, Real-Time Economy is not on its LRAS or SRAS Curve, Where will it be?

If actual output that can be sold differs from its long-run equilibrium level, the economy would not be on the LRAS curve but could be on the SRAS curve. But if actual output that can be sold differs from its short-run equilibrium level, the economy also cannot be on the SRAS curve. Therefore, in disequilibrium, the economy must be off both the SRAS and LRAS curves.

Suppose that a decrease in aggregate demand has driven the economy into disequilibrium. The AD-AS Figure 9.3 illustrates the possibilities. Out of both the long- and short-run equilibrium, the actual economy is neither at *a*, *b* or *c*. *If* we assume that there continues to be equilibrium in the income–expenditure process, the economy will be on the aggregate demand curve. This assumption limits the number of possible positions in Figure 9.3 to those between *d* and *c*. *If prices were rigid*, the economy would be at the point *d*. *If the price level adjusted fully* to its short-run equilibrium level, the economy would be at the point *c*. But it is more likely that prices do fall somewhat — or rather soften through sales discounts, refund coupons, etc. — and do so gradually, but the *required* short-run reduction in prices does not occur fast enough. Under this scenario, the economy would move to a lower price level than P_0, as well as a lower output than given by the point *c*. Such a point is shown as *e*.

Note that, as mentioned earlier, that both points *e* and *c* in Figure 9.3 are transient ones for a stable economy. However, the movement of the economy from the point e towards its short-run equilibrium at *c* can take real time. Further, the movement from the point *c* to the long-run equilibrium at *b* can also take real time. The duration of these periods will depend on the causes and magnitudes of the initial fall in aggregate demand and the actual dynamics of business and consumer confidence. Therefore, this duration will differ between recessions for a given economy and among economies for a given initial fall in aggregate demand.

9.7 Can the Economy Get Stuck Below Full Employment?

If the real-world, real-time economy stays below full employment for some time and does not seem to be moving rapidly towards full employment, we might designate its state as that of a temporary equilibrium or of under-full-employment equilibrium, where 'equilibrium' is being defined as the state from which there is no significant and inherent tendency to change. Alternately, observing some (though relatively slow) movement in the economy, we can say that the situation is one of disequilibrium; though the economy's inherent forces or mechanisms are weak, they will eventually get the economy to full employment. These are two different ways of describing a slowly adjusting economy, analogous to describing a glass as being 'half full' or 'half empty'. How long is 'eventually' in real time? In practical terms, leaving aside semantics and dogma, an economy in such a disequilibrium situation might spend several quarters or even years below full-employment output.[16] In such situations, policy could play a very useful role in speeding up the return to full-employment equilibrium.

Impact of the disequilibrium on the long run: hysteresis

Can the dynamic path during disequilibrium affect the short-run and long-run equilibrium positions for the future? This would occur if it alters the accumulation of skills and physical capital while the economy is away from equilibrium. Less of these are accumulated in recessions than in booms, so that drawn-out recessions and booms can leave their impact on the economy beyond their own duration. Such an effect of the short-run adjustment on the long-run path is called *hysteresis*. Mild recessions and booms would not have a significant hysteresis effect, while long and deep recessions and strong booms are likely to leave behind their impact on the long-run of the economy.

9.8 Optimal Monetary and Fiscal Policies for the Demand-Deficient Economy

The policy cure for an economy suffering from the hangover of a demand deficiency requires a policy-induced expansion in aggregate demand. This could come from expansionary fiscal and monetary policies.[17] However, note that fiscal policies can be notoriously slow to implement as a stabilization tool in some countries, while monetary policy — through reductions in interest rates supported by appropriate increases in the money supply — can be implemented much faster.

The use of expansionary monetary policies

To derive the optimal role and impact of monetary policy in a demand-deficient economy, assume that the economy is already at n_0^d of employment and y_0 of output in Figure 9.2a and b. Further, suppose that the central bank believes — on the basis of its information, including its past experience of recessions — that the economy if left to itself would take several quarters to return to equilibrium. Therefore, to speed up this process, the central bank decides to pursue an expansionary monetary policy (through a cut in the target interest rate, supported by the appropriate increase in the money supply), so that there is a reduction in the economy's interest rate and an increase in its aggregate demand. To see its effects, we need to supplement Figure 9.2a and b with Figure 9.4a and b, and start with the assumption that the central bank had originally set the interest rate target at r_0^T. Figure 9.4a shows the pre-existing position of the economy at (y_0^d, r_0^T), so that there exists deficient demand (i.e., $y_0^d < y^f$). For this level of demand deficiency, Figure 9.4b shows the *effective* amount of labor demanded (i.e., the level of employment whose output can, in fact, be sold, so that it determines the pre-existing employment) as n_0^d. Now suppose that the central bank lowers the target

---

[16]It did so in the Great Depression of the 1930s and in many deep recessions.

[17]In open economies, it could also come from a policy-induced devaluation of the exchange rate to increase net exports. This is discussed in the open economy Chapters 12 to 13.

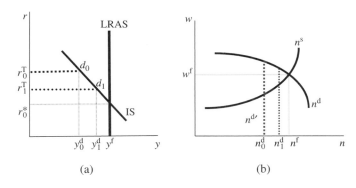

Figure 9.4

interest rate from r_0^T to r_1^T. This reduction in the interest rate stimulates investment, and through the multiplier, increases aggregate demand at the pre-existing price level from y_0^d to y_1^d. Firms confronted with the increase in demand would increase output, thereby shifting the *effective* amount of labor demanded (though not the labor demand curve labeled n^d) in Figure 9.4b from n_0^d towards n^f (say to n_1^d) and increasing output closer to its full-employment level.

In this process, since the pre-existing situation was one of deficit demand and involuntary unemployment, output increases in response to the increase in aggregate demand. Since firms also make some adjustment in prices in response to excess demand, there may also be some increase in prices. This price increase will depend on how deficient the earlier demand was and how large was the earlier excess capacity in the economy, but, in any case, the expansionary monetary policy would have succeeded in increasing real output in the economy. The real wage may rise or fall, depending upon where it was earlier in relation to the full-employment wage w^*.

Limits to the effectiveness of monetary policies in a demand-deficient recession

The above policy recommendations of an expansionary monetary policy in a demand-deficient economy would not be appropriate if the fall in aggregate demand had led to excess productive capacity — that is, firms were left with more physical capital than required to meet actual demand for their products. In this case, the decreases in interest rates are less likely to stimulate investment — thereby reducing the ability of monetary policy to revive aggregate demand in the demand-deficient disequilibrium. During the financial and economic crisis of 2007–2010, the central banks of many countries found themselves in such a position. While they reduced the interest rates, in some cases close to zero, and increased the monetary base, investment, consumer demand and aggregate demand did not pick up fast enough (see Chapter 16).

The use of fiscal policy: increases in government expenditures and/or cuts in taxes

In a demand-deficient situation, an expansionary fiscal policy (i.e., a cut in taxes and/or an increase in government expenditures) would also raise output and employment. Its analysis is similar to the above one for an expansionary monetary policy. However, there is one major difference: a fiscal deficit increases aggregate demand without requiring a prior increase in investment and makes fiscal policy especially valuable if the economy has excess productive capacity. In the economic crisis of 2007–2010, the governments of many countries, led by that of the USA, pursued massive fiscal deficits in their attempts to revive aggregate demand.

The policy dilemma

The above arguments raise the question: if aggregate demand falls and the market adjustments in prices and nominal wages are sluggish, which of the following approaches is preferable.

(i) Leave the market alone to make the needed adjustments. These require:

  (a) Decline in the price level, so that the real value of the money supply increases sufficiently to raise aggregate demand to the appropriate level
  (b) Decline in the market interest rate (without a pre-emptive reduction by the central bank in the interest rate that it had set, i.e., the central bank follows rather than leading the market in changing interest rates) sufficient to increase effective demand
  (c) Fall in nominal wages corresponding to or more than the fall in the price level

(ii) The central bank takes the initiative to increase aggregate demand. It cuts the interest rate (or increases the money supply) and/or the government increases its deficit to increase aggregate demand

From the perspective of the time taken for each of the steps, (ii) is clearly more rapid, especially for the central bank's pursuit of monetary policy. Further, (a) requires all or the majority of firms to cut their prices. Firms in modern industrial economies hardly ever do so. Further, (ib) requires reductions in nominal wages, which workers resent, so that workers' reactions induce delays, industrial unrest, and productivity losses. Consequently, firms are reluctant to attempt reductions in the nominal wages paid, especially to existing employees. (ii) avoids these major barriers to market-determined downward adjustments of prices and nominal wages, and can be much faster as a means of restoring aggregate demand. However, (ii) requires the central bank to have adequate knowledge to act in time and have the willingness and the will to pursue the appropriate monetary policy by the right amount. These requirements are only met sometimes, so that some economists believe that the central bank should pursue an expansionary monetary policy only in clear cases of a very significant and clearly observable fall in demand, but not attempt to offset small variations in aggregate demand. The latter is sometimes referred to as fine-tuning the economy, and the recommendation is to avoid such fine-tuning, since the possibility of errors in observations and the wrong policy being pursued is greater for small variations in aggregate demand.

Fact Sheet 9.2: Economies in Disequilibrium: USA During the Great Depression

The graphs of this Fact Sheet provide an illustration of changes in consumption, investment and aggregate demand, and the roles of monetary and fiscal policies, during the Great Depression of the 1930s. After the stock market crash in 1929, the USA, just as many other industrialized countries at the time, entered into a period of deep economic recession marked by significant drops in output, personal consumption, and investment. As seen below, the lowest point of the depression occurred in 1933, though a second smaller decline can be seen in 1937. As unemeployment rose sharply, aggregate demand fell dramatically, which caused reductions in output, saving, and investment.

The 1930s started with a strongly held belief in the USA in 'fiscal responsibility', which requires that governments should keep their budget balanced. This implied that as tax revenues fell with rising unem-ployment, government spending was also cut. However, government spending did rise with Roosevelt's New Deal, initiated in 1933 in an attempt to provide jobs and care for the unemployed. Between 1929 and 1933, many banks failed in the USA, so that money supply fell. The deep contraction of the money

Fact Sheet 9.2: (*Continued*)

supply allowed by the Federal Reserve System until 1933 is considered by many to have exacerbated the economic downturn. The eventual end of the Great Depression in the USA, as in European countries, was due less to economic policies but to the start of the Second World War, which led to rapid increases in employment in war-related production and conscription into the armed forces, and to large fiscal deficits and rapid money supply growth to finance the war efforts.

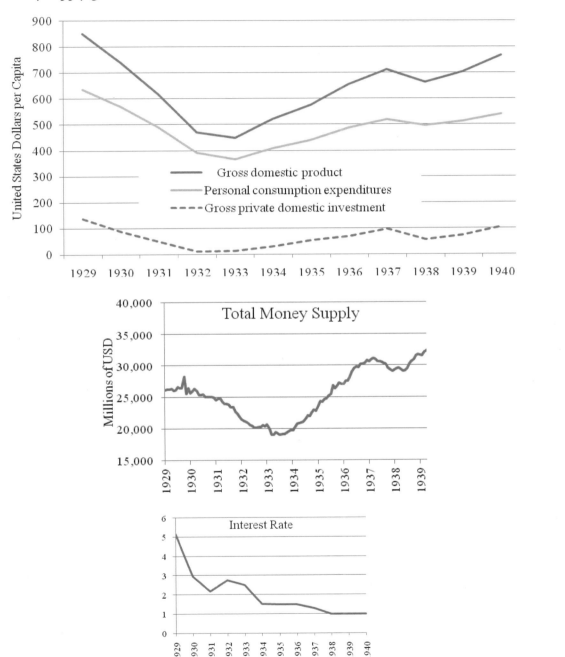

Fact Sheet 9.2: (*Continued*)

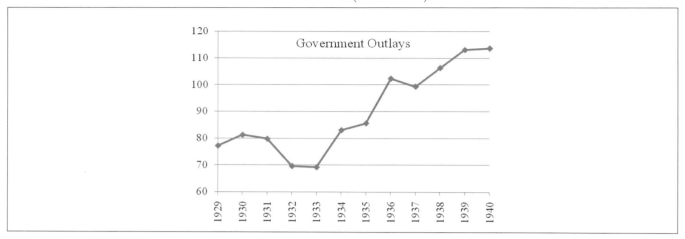

Recapitulation of the roles of monetary and fiscal policies in a demand-deficient economy

The preceding arguments imply that in demand-deficient economies with $y = y^d < y^f$, the results for monetary and fiscal policies are likely to be:

$$\partial y/\partial M \geq 0 \quad \text{and} \quad \partial y/\partial r \leq 0, \tag{1}$$

$$\partial y/\partial g > 0. \tag{2}$$

These effects of expansionary monetary and fiscal policies on aggregate demand and output in the demand-deficient economy differ from the zero values of these multipliers for the full-employment equilibrium along the LRAS curve derived in Chapter 7. Given these differences in the multiplier values between the LR equilibrium and the disequilibrium phases of the model, the policy maker has to be concerned with the real time the economy will stay at recessionary levels, and what it can do to speed up the return to full employment.

These arguments imply that:

- For real-time, real-world economies, there is no straightforward relationship between expansionary monetary and fiscal policies and real output. This relationship depends upon the initial state (full-employment, inflationary or recessionary) of the economy and the extent of the monetary and fiscal expansions.
- The transmission of the impact of the monetary and fiscal policies on output does not always require — and need not mostly go through — price level increases.
- The over-riding concern for policy makers becomes one of the determination of the actual existence of equilibrium or disequilibrium in a specific period — *even if the economy is inherently one which can eventually adjust on its own to full-employment output* — and with the duration which will have to be spent below full employment if the policies to revive aggregate demand are not undertaken.
- Expectations, reflected by consumer confidence on jobs and incomes and business confidence on sales and ability to obtain funds for investment, have a significant impact on the time path of employment and output.
- Deep recessions and depressions, as in the 1930s and 2007–2010, can reduce the effectiveness of an expansionary monetary policy. In such circumstances, an expansionary fiscal policy is more likely to revive aggregate demand and output.

Extended Analysis Box 9.3: Disagreements Among Economists on the Appropriate Policies in Real Time for a Real-World Economy

The analysis of this chapter provides considerable scope for disagreements among economists on the particular stage of the economy at any given time and the policies that are appropriate to it. These disagreements can be broadly classified as of two types:

(a) There are often disagreements on whether the economy, at a given time, is in disequilibrium, in SR equilibrium or in LR equilibrium. Unfortunately, there is no convincing statistical procedure for determining this.

(b) Even when it is agreed that the economy is in disequilibrium, there is considerable scope for disagreement on the extent of the departure from full employment, how long it would take the economy to reach it, and on the strength and timing of the policy doses that are appropriate. Again, the statistical techniques do not provide generally accepted answers to these questions.

(c) There are often disagreements on where the new long-run equilibrium is.

Hence, economists' opinions tend to differ considerably on practical issues. The policies that are recommended by economists as well as those that are followed by policy makers usually depend on judgement calls in a context of inadequate and imperfect information. These issues are further discussed in Chapters 11 and 16.

9.9 Excess Demand[18] in the Economy and Appropriate Policies

We have so far considered the dynamics of demand *declines* from a full-employment level. But suppose aggregate demand *increases* when there is already full-employment output. This demand increase could again come from a change in consumption, investment, money demand, or net exports. Most firms seeing an increase in the demand for their products would, besides raising their prices, tend to increase the supplies of their commodities. This could occur through increases in employment, overtime worked, as well as increases in the work effort of employees and their efficiency. Each of these is feasible in the short term. The increase in employment beyond the initial full-employment level could come about through increased working hours of part-time workers, through students delaying resumption of studies and through increases in the overtime put in by employed workers, through potential retirees postponing their retirement and through increases in effort, etc. While such increases in employment and output above their full-employment levels can and do occur in the short term and yield increases in output for several years, their scope becomes eventually limited and constrained by workers' long-run preference for work (workers eventually get tired of putting in undesired overtime, etc.). Hence, the (analytical) long run assumes that such increases in employment and output beyond the full-employment levels cannot occur in the long run but the disequilibrium and short-run analyses allow such increases.

When the private components of demand have been expansionary enough to pose serious risk of inflation, contractionary and fiscal monetary policies can be used to reduce aggregate demand and thereby reduce the inflationary pressures, though such a policy would also forego the associated disequilibrium and short-run increases in output beyond the full-employment level. Examples of such contractionary monetary policies are

---

[18]Excess demand occurs when the demand for commodities exceeds their supply, especially when the latter is at full employment.

the commonly observed increases in interest rates and decreases in the money supply by the central bank when the economy is working above its capacity level. Contractionary fiscal policies require a budget surplus.

9.10 *Asymmetry* in the Economy's Responses to Deficient and Excess Demand

Note that there is a significant difference in the economy's constraints — or in their short-term flexibility — and responses between increases and decreases in aggregate demand. While the increases in aggregate demand can increase output and employment for some time beyond their full-employment levels, the increase in prices is more likely and faster than the fall in prices in response to a decline in demand from the full-employment level.[19] Usually, firms are readier to increase prices than to reduce them. Consequently, the dynamic response patterns are different between the demand-deficient and excess-demand cases. This asymmetry is vital to differentiating between the stabilization roles of monetary policy when the private economy generates demand below full employment versus when it generates demand above full employment. But there is a role in both cases.

9.11 An Analysis of Disequilibrium Following a *Supply Shock*

The sources of supply shocks are usually specified as changes in productivity, the capital stock, and the labor supply. However, the worldwide recession of 2008–2009 showed that a shock to supply can also come a decline in credit to firms.

9.11.1 Supply shocks from labor productivity

Assume that there is a positive shock to the marginal productivity of labor. For an anticipated shock, long-run analysis implies that this will cause the full-employment output of the economy to increase, and actual output will rise correspondingly. Further, employment and the real wage will also rise, as shown in Chapter 6. However, these changes rarely happen smoothly and we need to look into the plausible behavior patterns to derive the likely dynamic patterns.

There are clearly many possibilities for the possible dynamic path followed by the economy after a positive supply shock. Two different scenarios of this path are:

(i) The markets adjust all prices *instantly* by the required amounts for taking the economy to the new full-employment equilibrium, the firms know these prices and respond by adjusting their output and employment accordingly.
(ii) Firms set prices, while markets are slower in establishing the market-clearing price level that equates aggregate demand to the new level of the full-employment output. The following expands on a plausible pattern for this scenario.

Suppose that the positive productivity shock shifts the LRAS curve from $LRAS_0$ to $LRAS_1$ in Figure 9.5a. This implies that the long-run price level will have to fall from P_0 to P_1. But firms will not observe/know the new LR price level since the market has not yet established it.[20] Assume that the firms experiencing the increase in productivity do not fully and instantly lower prices to the new equilibrium price level for the economy, but

---

[19]Further, workers are always happy to get nominal wage increases while resisting cuts in them.
[20]What the firms observe/know is that the labor productivity has increased.

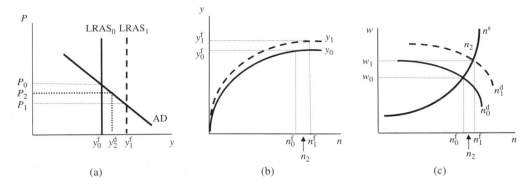

Figure 9.5

lower their prices *gradually and marginally* in order to increase their market share. Hence, let the actual price level only fall to P_2. At P_2, the aggregate demand is only y_2^d, which is inadequate to buy the new long-run output of y_1^f. In Figure 9.5b, aggregate demand at y_2^d implies employment of n_2, which, in Figure 9.5c, is below the new full-employment level n_1^f. Note that the new employment level n_2 has been drawn to show an increase in employment relative to n_0^f. However, there exists the possibility that the new employment level could have been to the left of this point, so that employment could have fallen from its initial level y_0^f. Hence, in this scenario, following a *positive productivity shock, firms' gradual groping towards a new set of prices could increase output, while decreasing employment or increasing it less than the increase in the full-employment level.* If this happens, involuntary unemployment emerges during the dynamic adjustments even though the nation's output is rising.

This scenario was based on the assumption that the firms experiencing an increase in productivity gradually lower their prices. This 'groping' process is a common pattern in periods with productivity increases and falling costs of production. The economy may eventually reach its new full-employment level, but there could be an interval of involuntary unemployment and possibly even of employment below the old full-employment level. This is a seemingly paradoxical result: *a positive productivity shock can increase output while creating involuntary unemployment for some duration, even among the otherwise qualified workers.*

Another reason for an increase in unemployment is that some of the previously employed workers will not possess the right skills for the new technology and will become redundant. Further, workers employed in declining industries will need to shift to expanding ones, which would take time and re-training, which may be too late for older workers and not practical for others.

The scope for monetary and fiscal policies

Now consider the policy implications of this scenario. The critical element of the emergence of involuntary unemployment was the failure of the price level to decrease sufficiently — and to do so sufficiently fast — to increase the quantity demanded[21] of commodities to meet the increase in their long-run supply. In this scenario, if the monetary and fiscal authorities were to increase aggregate demand sufficiently through expansionary monetary and fiscal policies to match the increase in supply, the new long-run supply would occur at the

---

[21]This occurs through an increase in the real value of the money supply for a constant money supply and lower price level. The resulting shift of the LM curve to the right in the IS-LM diagram increases aggregate demand.

pre-existing price level. Its result would be that the economy would have made a smoother transition to its new long-run position.

Box 9.2: Demand Shocks Emanating from Shifts in Long-Run Supply

In some periods (but not always), a demand response emerges from a positive shift in the long-run equilibrium output of the economy. An instance of this occurred in the late 1990s when the rapid technical change occurring in the computer, internet, and telecommunications sectors both increased the productivity of the economy and also caused a mania for the stocks of companies in these sectors. This enthusiasm for their stocks spread to the stocks of companies in other sectors, and caused a stock mania. With the increase in stock prices, there was an increase in the ability of companies to raise funds for new investment and an increase in stockowners' wealth, which increased their consumption. These caused increases in aggregate demand. These increases were greater than in the productive capacity of the economy, so that employment rose and unemployment rates fell through much of the 1990s.

Hence, technical change can have two effects: increasing the long-run level of full employment and increasing aggregate demand. Their net effect can then be of a decrease in the unemployment rate.

However, such a response of aggregate demand to technical change cannot be taken for granted. The collapse in stock prices from 2000 to 2002 produced a fall in investment and in aggregate demand. This fall, in a period of continuing positive shifts in technology, sent the economies into recessions and raised unemployment rates in many of them. The subsequent recovery during 2002–2006 produced increases in output but did not, for the first couple of years, produce increases in overall employment because the productivity of labor had increased in the meantime while the increase in aggregate demand was not strong enough to require firms to increase employment. In the USA, the very large fiscal deficits following the Iraq war and the bubble in house prices during 2003–2006 eventually led to a sufficiently strong increase in aggregate demand for employment to rise and unemployment to fall. However, such an increase in aggregate demand did not occur in western Europe whose economies struggled with high unemployment levels well into 2006. Unemployment rate rose further during the worldwide recession of 2007–2010.

9.11.2   The impact of a decline in credit supply on the effective supply of commodities

Firms borrow extensively to finance their operations. In developed financial economies, the amounts borrowed are usually from other firms in the form of trade credit, banks in the form of loans and bond markets. We can classify these amounts into two categories: (short-term) credit and long-term bonds, of which credit encompasses amounts borrowed through inter-firm trade credit, bank loans, and short-term bonds, such as through the issue of 'commercial paper' (usually three month to one-year bonds). Firms use credit to finance their inventories, payroll expenditures, and other rotating needs for funds. A sudden unexpected cutback in funds forces them to cut back their orders for inputs and lay off some workers, so that aggregate supply of commodities falls. The credit crisis of 2007–2010 illustrates the impact of a credit restraint on the production of commodities: it shifted the *effective supply* of commodities to the left of the long-run and short-run supply curves, thereby causing a recession in output.

The appropriate policies in this scenario require a credit increase to meet the production needs of full-employment output. However, monetary and fiscal authorities do not normally directly lend to firms, so that their policies have only an indirect and delayed effect on the supply of credit. In the interval before the reduction in credit is eliminated, the reduction in credit would cause a reduction in output. The 2007–2010 period shows the impact on output and employment of the reduction in credit from banks and other lenders. Further, it shows that even though the expansionary monetary policy drastically increased the monetary base and governments ran deficits to prop up the credit supply, the restoration of credit to normal levels was too slow to restore output to a full-employment level for many quarters.

Chapter 16 provides more detailed analysis of these issues.

9.12 'Crowding-Out' or 'Crowding-In' of Investment by Fiscal Expenditures in a Demand-Deficient Economy?

Crowding-out is defined as the crowding out (i.e., reduction) of investment by a fiscal deficit. Such crowding-out can occur due to (1) interest rate increases, caused by increased borrowing to finance the deficit by issues of government bonds, and (2) the output constraint of full-employment output in the long-run analysis. These were also discussed in Chapters 7 and 8.

On (2), the long-run analysis of output in Chapter 7, with y given by y^f, implies that firms' purchases of commodities for investment will be fully crowded out in a closed economy by increases in the government's purchases of commodities — because output does not increase while the government, with a deficit, takes a bigger cut out of it, so that less is left for investment (and/or net exports in the open economy analysis). The short-run analysis along the SRAS curve moderates this degree of crowding out since it allows some increase in output beyond y^f.

In deficient-demand conditions, the increases in government expenditures would reduce the degree of demand deficiency and raise output, thus lessening the degree of crowding out. Further, the increases in aggregate demand and sales due to the increase in government expenditures will tend to boost business confidence and raise the expected demand for their products. This would induce increases in firms' investment to raise their production capacity. Therefore, instead of any crowding out, an expansionary fiscal policy could increase private investment. This will mean 'crowding-in' (i.e., increase in) investment because of the fiscal deficit.

Hence, *for the real-world economies in recessions, there could be positive effects of increases in government expenditures on private investment, rather than the strong negative one that full crowding out implies for the analytical long run or the partial crowding out that the short-run analysis implies.*

Similar effects would follow a cut in the central bank's interest rate target. In this case, the increase in investment would occur for two reasons:

(i) For the given investment function, the cut in the interest rate increases investment.
(ii) In a demand-deficient recession, the expected increase in aggregate demand due to (i) boosts business confidence for future sales and causes them to further increase investment. There would also be an increase in consumption due to the boost to consumer confidence. These increases in investment and consumption would further increase aggregate demand and output in the demand-deficient context.

9.13 Disequilibrium (Involuntary Unemployment) in the Labor Market due to a High Real Wage

Assume that a shock (such as a fall in the price level or in aggregate demand, or union action, etc.) has pushed (or left) the real wage rate above its full-employment level. Since firms employ along their demand curve for labor, their employment would be less than the full-employment one and the economy would have involuntary unemployment . In this case, the involuntary unemployment would not be due to a demand deficiency but due to the real wage being too high.

Further, assume that this high real wage is maintained even if the price level were to rise, i.e., the factors that brought it about cause nominal wages to rise in proportion to any inflation. In this case, an expansionary monetary policy cannot reduce the real wage or decrease the involuntary unemployment.

Hence, there are two reasons for employment and output to be below their full-employment levels:

(i) A demand deficiency
(ii) A high real wage

The policies appropriate to each of these possibilities differ, so that there has to be a prior diagnosis of the causes of the involuntary unemployment and the responsiveness of the real wages to inflation, before the adoption of policies to address involuntary unemployment.

Expansionary monetary policy as a means of lowering the real wage and restoring equilibrium in the labor market

Suppose that the current real wage exceeds its full-employment level and that nominal wages do not increase proportionately with the price level so that inflation will reduce the real wage and involuntary unemployment. In this case, an expansionary monetary policy can be pursued to achieve these goals. The central bank will have the following three options:

(a) Leave the economy alone to move on its own to lower the real wage to the full-employment one.
(b) Pursue expansionary monetary and fiscal policies that cause a rate of inflation sufficient to reduce the real wage to the full-employment one.
(c) Pursue a policy of changing labor market structures to lower labor's resistance to wage cuts.

Each of these policies involves some time lags and has side effects. Judgements on these differ among economists. Some claim that the labor market adjusts fairly fast to lower the real wage whenever there is involuntary unemployment, so that (a) is the best policy. Others claim that there are significant impediments and lags in the economy's adjustment to a fall in real wages. Further, for this adjustment to occur, many economists claim that it is not the market, which lowers nominal wages but that individual firms have to do so, not only for new employees but also for all employees. When individual firms try to cut the nominal wages of their employees below the existing ones, workers' resentment over the cutbacks leads to strikes, work slowdowns, vandalism, and other types of disruptive 'industrial action', which makes firms reluctant to cut nominal wages. Therefore, a less painful and speedier adjustment of real wages would be through expansionary monetary policy, which creates sufficient inflation to bring about the appropriate reduction in the real wage for the existing nominal wage,[22] so that some economists favor (b). However, in practice, this policy prescription may only work for relatively small differences between the actual real wage and the full-employment one, and correspondingly appropriately small inflation rates. In particular, it is unlikely to work if the policy creates hyperinflation — in which case workers are likely to both be very alert to the actual rate of inflation and promptly negotiate nominal wage increases to match the inflation rate. In this case the long-run remedy for high real wages is (c), not (b).

---

[22]This policy will not work if nominal wages rise by the rate of inflation, which will mean that real wages do not fall. This could happen if the high real wage is due to labor market imperfections (including excessive union power), higher minimum wages set by the government, etc.

The third approach, as in (c) above, was followed by President Ronald Reagan of the USA.

Extended Analysis Box 9.4: Is the Preceding Demand-Deficient Analysis a Reflection of Market Failure or of Markets' Sluggishness in Adjustment of Prices and Nominal Wages?

The underlying theme of the dynamic analysis presented in this chapter can be interpreted as one of the 'failure of the market' — or of the competitive forces in the economy — to adjust the price level *instantly* to levels consistent with full employment. However, such instant adjustment seems to be asking too much for a very heterogeneous and dispersed economy, even if the economy had high levels of competition. Our analysis really did not assume that the markets did not adjust prices when demand or supply shift or that they do not initiate changes to move towards equilibrium. Our arguments were based on the relatively slower adjustment of prices by the markets relative to the faster adjustments by firms, consumers, and workers. These economic agents adjust production, employment, consumption, and money demand — in addition to the adjustment of prices by firms. Further, governments and central banks may adjust their expenditures, taxation, and the target interest rate (or the money supply) faster than the market adjusts prices and interest rates. These adjustments by economic agents — especially the quantity adjustments in production, employment, and consumption — lie at the core of the dynamic analysis of this chapter. They become especially significant when aggregate demand changes and firms and consumers adjust output and employment in response.

Some economist would call these results as those of '*market failure*', while others see them as merely — though dragged out in real-time — dynamic adjustments on the way to eventual equilibrium at full employment. No matter what they are called, they provide an important, stabilizing role for monetary and fiscal policies in the real-time, real-world economies.

9.14 The Dual Implications of a High Saving Rate

The saving rate plays a dual role for the closed economy:

(i) An increase in the saving rate promotes the growth of productive capacity and, therefore, improvements in future output and standards of living. This would shift the future long-run aggregate supply curve (LRAS in Chapter 1) to the right and raise the long-run levels of future full-employment income.

(ii) An increase in the saving rate reduces consumption expenditures and aggregate demand for commodities. This demand can cause the economy to reduce output below its full-employment level by moving it along its short-run aggregate supply curve (see the SRAS curve in Chapters 1 and 8). In other cases, as shown in this chapter, the fall in aggregate demand below the current productive capacity of the economy can push it for some time into a demand-deficient disequilibrium, so that the economy goes into a demand-deficient recession with high unemployment. This disequilibrium effect can be of serious concern in the context of real-time, real-world economies.

The paradox of a high saving rate — also known as the paradox of thrift

Note that the amount saved depends on the saving rate multiplied by national income/output. Suppose that the economy does not adjust fast enough to prevent a demand-deficient disequilibrium and production falls because of inadequate demand. If output falls more than in proportion to the rise in the saving rate, the amount actually saved will fall. Therefore, we could have the seeming paradox: an increase in the saving rate can cause a decrease in output and the amount saved. Note that this paradox does not occur if output does not fall or falls less than in proportion to the rise in the average saving rate.

9.15 Conclusions

For the study of disequilibrium and dynamics to be a potentially useful exercise requires the belief that the shocks from the private sector or by the monetary and fiscal authorities can drive the economy away from its full-employment equilibrium state for significant periods of time. Intuitively, continuous general equilibrium requires the belief that the economy responds to a shock by remaining in — or fairly soon returning to — equilibrium, whether along its LRAS or SRAS curve. To illustrate this from the use of monetary policy, this belief requires that an expansionary policy would *immediately* cause a proportionate increase in the price level and that a decrease in it would not cause a recession in output and employment. There is considerable evidence to show that these requirements are not always, or are not most of the time, met in most real-world economies.

The usefulness of monetary and fiscal policies clearly depends on the lags in the response of the economy to the shocks coming from investment, consumption, and money demand, and on the lags in the formulation and impact of monetary and fiscal policies.

The disequilibrium/dynamic analysis of this chapter has shown that:

- There are numerous types of shocks that constantly impinge on the economy. They can be from the demand or the supply side of the economy.
- For the private sector, the shocks from the demand side can come from shifts in consumption, investment, money demand, and exports, etc.
- The shocks to supply come from shifts in the production function due to technological change, shifts in industrial structure, in the supply of labor, minimum wage laws, etc.
- Adjustments in response to shocks are made by markets (to prices), by firms and households (to output, employment, and prices) and by policy makers (to fiscal and monetary policies). Their relative speeds of response are essential to understanding the dynamic adjustments of the economy and how long the economy stays away from full employment, and whether the pursuit of monetary and fiscal policies is useful or not.
- Once a shock hits the economy, competition, flexible wages, and prices, and the economic rationality of firms and workers are not enough to always ensure that the economy will immediately revert to full employment after an aggregate demand shock. It may do so for some types and some magnitudes of shocks but not for others.
- The expectations of firms and households — represented by business and consumer confidence — on the likely duration of deficient or excess demand play very significant roles in whether the economy will move away from equilibrium or not, and even on whether it may do so in a stabilizing or a destabilizing fashion. The emphasis in these expectations is not on the expectations of prices but of sales, incomes, and jobs.
- The economy sometimes behaves in a manner that takes its output to a level below full employment, with movement back to full employment sometimes being very hesitant and imperceptible. Such a situation can be interpreted as one of disequilibrium or equilibrium — where equilibrium is defined as the state from which there is no inherent tendency to change. From a policy perspective, it does not matter what name is assigned to this situation.

- It is not enough for the economy to *eventually* bring nominal wage rates and prices to their equilibrium levels consistent with full employment. These processes must occur fast enough, since, otherwise, the firms will act on the fall in their demand by cutting their output and employment and workers will react to the loss of employment by cutting consumption. Further, the interest rates must also change appropriately and the increase in investment must occur adequately and fast enough.
- The likely reactions of competitive markets, firms, and households to demand decreases can include cutbacks in nominal wages and prices, as well as in production, jobs, investment, and consumption. The former can be of the type that could take the economy to equilibrium, but they could, alternatively, be of the type that worsens the demand deficiency — and increase involuntary unemployment. The latter would move the economy away from full-employment equilibrium — rather than towards it.
- In demand-deficient economies, government deficits can cause crowding in.

A caveat is necessary here. Some economists are likely to disagree with the position that the economy can be in disequilibrium for significant periods of time following some types of shocks. Other economists may disagree with the above dynamic analysis because they may consider other scenarios to be more plausible. Econometric studies have not unambiguously answered these questions. Intuition should be used in establishing one's own responses to them. The arguments of this chapter were intended to provide some guidance on this intuition.

If the actual economy under consideration has a strong tendency towards equilibrium and can be expected to reach it in a short while, focusing the analysis and policy prescriptions on the equilibrium properties only would be justified. However, economic theory and econometric tests provide some but not full guidance for determining this. Consequently, the policy makers are also forced to rely on their 'feel' and 'perception' of the state of the economy. Further, they can never be sure of the intensity and timing of the impact of their policies. Therefore, even though economics is a science, *the formulation and pursuit of economic policies becomes 'an art rather than a science'*.

KEY CONCEPTS

Disequilibrium	*Involuntary unemployment*	*Crowding-in versus crowding out*
Dynamic analysis	*Market failure*	*The pursuit of economic policies*
Effective demand, excess demand	*Real time versus analytical time*	*is an art rather than a science*
Demand deficiency	*Real-world economies versus*	
Business confidence	*analytical/model economies*	
Consumer confidence	*Economics is a science*	

SUMMARY OF CRITICAL CONCLUSIONS

- The usefulness of dynamic disequilibrium analysis occurs when real-world economies take a significant amount of real time in reaching general equilibrium. Casual observation of booms, recessions, and depressions and the pronouncements and behavior of central banks — as well as many empirical studies — indicate that this is so.
- The dynamic behavior of real-world economies takes account of the relevant speeds of reaction of markets, firms, households/workers, and policy makers to exogenous shifts.
- In particular, markets may be relatively sluggish in changing prices to re-establish equilibrium after a shock, compared with the adjustment speeds of firms and consumers in changing output, employment, consumption, etc.

- If firms cut employment in response to a fall in aggregate demand, involuntary unemployment emerges. The latter can reduce consumption and further reduce aggregate demand.
- If involuntary unemployment has emerged due to a demand deficiency, expansionary monetary and fiscal policies may be able to — depending on their speed of formulation and implementation and the speed of response of the economy to them — shorten the period during which the economy stays below full employment. This is a stabilization role for these policies.
- Involuntary unemployment can also occur if the real wage is too high relative to its full-employment level. Expansionary monetary policies, which cause inflation, may serve to lower the real wage and, therefore, reduce involuntary unemployment — faster than the (sluggish) market-induced reduction in the real wage.
- Competition incorporates the 'invisible hand of competition' to guide the economy towards equilibrium through market-induced price changes. But this hand may be slow enough to leave the economy out of equilibrium for significant periods of real time — in which case, assuming a faster impact on aggregate demand, production and employment, the pursuit of policies may become preferable.
- In a deficient demand context, expansionary fiscal and monetary policies can boost private investment and result in 'crowding-in'.
- Monetary and fiscal policy makers rarely possess accurate and timely information on the actual state of their real-world economy. They also do not accurately know the timing and impact of their policies, or the strength/intensity of the policies that would be best. They have to formulate their policies on the basis of their limited knowledge, guesswork, and impressions of the economy, so that their pursuit of economic policies is an art rather than a science.

REVIEW AND DISCUSSION QUESTIONS

(1) Present the diagrammatic analysis of the impact on output caused by a fall in aggregate demand, when nominal wages and prices remain unchanged.

(2) Present the diagrammatic analysis of output caused by a fall in aggregate demand, with prices falling but the nominal wage remaining unchanged.

(3) Assume that the economy was initially at full employment. The central bank raises the target interest rate (and appropriately reduces the money supply), which causes a reduction in aggregate demand. Discuss, using diagrams, its effects on employment and output.

(4) What is meant by 'business confidence' and what can cause changes in it? Why should changes in it alter investment? List three other types of shocks or shifts in the economy that can cause shifts in investment.

(5) Discuss the likelihood that real-world firms respond to a fall in the demand for their products by reducing their production but only softening (through temporary discounts etc.) their prices. If they do so,

   (a) Discuss, using diagrams, the effect on unemployment.
   (b) In the context of interest rate targeting, what monetary policies are appropriate in this situation?

(6) Discuss how a demand-deficient disequilibrium can come about even when prices and nominal wages are flexible.

(7) What are the main reasons for disagreements among economists on the appropriate policies to follow in a recession?

(8) Start with the full-employment equilibrium position at $(y^f, n^f, r^{LR}, P^{LR})$, where LR indicates long-run equilibrium values. Suppose that a reduction in investment reduces aggregate demand, and that the markets are sluggish in adequately adjusting prices downwards. Answer the following:

(a) Analyze the behavior of firms hit with a fall in the demand for their products. If this analysis shows that employment is reduced below n^f, discuss the likely consumption responses of households and show diagrammatically their impact on aggregate demand.

(b) If these responses of firms and households imply a movement away from $(y^f, n^f, r^{LR}, P^{LR})$, what equilibrating mechanisms will come into play to bring the economy back to $(y^f, n^f, r^{LR}, P^{LR})$.

(9) Which do you think is more powerful and has a faster response to changes in the demand for firms' products: the market-based equilibrating mechanism of price adjustments for the commodity market as a whole or the adjustment responses of firms and households? What difference do the relative speeds of adjustment make to the continued maintenance of full employment when there are fluctuations in aggregate demand?

(10) Discuss the reasons why an economy may develop 'unduly high' real wages and the barriers to its reduction.

(11) If a recession is caused by a fall in investment and generates unemployment, would this be due to demand deficiency or a high real wage? Would monetary policies be appropriate in this case? Use diagrams for your analysis.

(12) If a recession is caused by an increase in oil prices and generates unemployment, would this be due to demand-deficiency or a high real wage? What monetary policies would be appropriate in this case? Use diagrams for your analysis.

ADVANCED AND TECHNICAL QUESTIONS

Basic AD-AS model I, with interest rate targeting

Assume that the following equation describes the aggregate demand function for an economy.

IS equation:

$$y_t = 50,000 + 0.2i_{0,t} + 0.2g_t - 10,000r_t - 200P_t \quad t = 0, 1, \ldots$$

$$i_{0,0} = 250,000$$

$$i_{0,1} = i_{0,2} = i_{0,3} = \cdots = 200,000$$

$$g_t = g_0 = 2,000.$$

The central bank's real interest rate targets are:

$$\text{In period 0, } r_0^T = 0.04.$$

$$\text{In period 1, } r_1^T = 0.04.$$

$$\text{In period 2, } r_2^T = 0.02.$$

The money supply adjusts to be consistent with money market equilibrium at the interest rate target

$$m^d = 0.25y - 60R.$$

Fisher equation:

$$R = r + \pi^e,$$

$$\pi_0^e = \pi_1^e = \pi_2^e = \pi_3^e = 0.$$

Long-run aggregate supply function:

$$y^f = 80,000.$$

T1. For the Basic AD-AS model,

   (a) Assume that the economy was in the long run in period 0. Derive the aggregate demand equation for period 0.
   (b) For period 0, derive the long-run price level P_0 and the aggregate amount demanded y_0^d at P_0.

T2 In the Basic AD-AS model, let autonomous investment so that for periods 1, 2 and 3, it becomes:

$$i_{i,1} = i_{i,2} = i_{i,3} = 200,000.$$

For period 1, derive the aggregate demand equation. Then, solve for the long-run levels of P and y. Designate these respectively as P_1^{LR} and y_1^f.

T3. Assume that, in period 1, instead of the price level adjusting to its long-run equilibrium level, the price level in period 1 remains unchanged from its level in period 0. That is, $P_1 = P_0$. Calculate the actual level of aggregate demand. Designate it as y_0^d.

   At the actual level of demand in period 1 at P_0,

   (a) What is the extent of demand deficiency?
   (b) Now assume that firms adjust their production so as not to have to add unsold commodities to their inventories. Derive the level of output under this behavior. Designate it as y_1.

T4. Given your answers to the preceding questions, following an unexpected fall in investment,

   (c) What adjustments in employment and output are profit-maximizing firms likely to make when they are faced with a fall in aggregate demand, which the markets have not cleared because of their sluggishness?
   (d) What adjustments are the markets likely to make to the fall in demand?
   (e) Compare these and discuss their likelihood in the short term.
   (f) Will the market response take the economy to full employment? Discuss.
   (g) If not, what will take the economy to full employment? Discuss.

T5. In period 2, in a delayed response to the fall in aggregate demand in period 1, the central bank lowers the interest rate target to 0.02. Given that the price level remains unchanged at P_0, what are the actual levels of aggregate demand y_0^d and real output y_2.

T6. For period 3, again assume that the price level has not changed from that in period 0. Calculate the real interest rate that the central bank needs to set as its target if actual output were to equal the full-employment one. If this interest rate turns out to be negative, discuss whether a negative nominal interest rate is possible in the economy.

T7. [Optional.] This question assumes that the deviation of demand from the preceding period's output is split by firms into an output change and a price change. Further, periods 0 and $t - 1$ are assumed to have the long-run solutions for output and the price level (i.e., full-employment output and the price level which equates aggregate demand to this output). Calculate the long-run output and price level for the Basic model before answering this question.

   For the output function of the Basic Model in a *dynamic* context, assume that the firms' *output adjustment pattern* depends on excess demand according to

$$y_t = y_{t-1} + 0.4(y_t^d - y_{t-1})/y_{t-1},$$

where, for $t = 0$, $y_{t-1} = y^f = 80,000$. The economy is in full employment in periods 0 and -1.

Further, assume that the economy adjusts the price level each period according to the following *price adjustment equation*:

$$P_t = P_{t-1} + 0.6(y_t^d - y_{t-1})/y_{t-1},$$

where for $t = 0$, P_0 is the market clearing price at which $y_t^d = y^f$.

Calculate the time path of output, the price level, and inflation for the first five periods $(0, 1, \ldots, 4)$ and the inflation rate for periods 1, 2, 3, 4. [Hint: first calculate y_0^d for period 0; then use it to derive the level of output y_0 under the output adjustment equation above; then use y_0^d and y_0 to determine the price P_0 according to the *price adjustment pattern*. Use a similar procedure to calculate the required values for periods 1, 2, 3, 4.] Arrange your answer in the form of a table with the columns as year, y, P, and π.

Basic AD-AS model II

[*Note: The aggregate demand parts of the following model were also used in Chapter 8*]
Aggregate demand function for the economy is specified by the following information.

IS equation:

$$y_t = 100,000 + 0.2g_t - 10,000r_t - 100P_t \quad t = 0, 1, \ldots g_t = 1,000.$$

The central bank's real interest rate targets are:

$$\text{In period} \quad 0, r_0^T = 0.04$$

$$\text{In periods} \quad 1, 2, \text{and } 3, r_1^T = r_2^T = r_3^T = 0.05.$$

The money supply adjusts to be consistent with money market equilibrium at the interest rate target.

$$m^d = 0.25y - 60R.$$

Fisher equation:

$$R = r + \pi^e,$$

$$\pi_0^e = \pi_1^e = \pi_2^e = \pi_3^e = 0.$$

Long-run output:

$$y^f = 90,000.$$

In periods 0, 1, 2, 3, and 4, the economy has deficient demand. The economy's markets are sluggish in adjusting the price level, so that firms respond to deficient demand by changing the economy's output. The short-run aggregate supply function when there is deficient demand in periods 0, 1, 2, 3, 4, is given by

$$y_t = 5,000 + 0.2(y_t^d - y_{t-1}).$$

Price level: before period 0, the economy has the price level that is consistent with long-run equilibrium. The economy maintains this price level for all subsequent periods. That is, $P_0 = P_1 = P_2 = P_3 = P_4 = P^{LR}$.

T8. [Optional.] Given the Basic AD-AS model II, assume for this question that the economy has deficient demand equilibrium in periods 0, 1, 2, 3, 4. The *short-run* output function *for periods 0, 1, 2, 3, 4*, is

$$y_t = 5,000 + 0.2(y_t^d - y_{t-1}).$$

The economy has full employment before period 0. [Note: this assumption allows the long-run price level to be calculated. Start answering this question by first calculating this price level, and using it for all periods.]

(a) For the preceding information, what is the level of aggregate demand in period 0? What are the levels of actual output in periods 0, 1, 2, 3, 4?

(b) What is the shortfall of actual output from the full-employment one in periods 0, 1, 2, 3, 4?

(c) For period 1, suppose that the central bank, observing the demand deficiency in period 1, reduces its target interest rate r^T to 0.02. What becomes the level of aggregate demand in period 1? What are the levels of actual output in periods 1, 2, 3, 4? What is the shortfall of actual output from the full-employment one in periods 0, 1, 2, 3, 4?

T9. Discuss the impact on actual output of the expansionary monetary and fiscal policies under the assumption that following a change in demand, markets are slow in adjusting prices while firms react faster by changing their output: (a) when output starts by being at the full-employment level, (b) when output is initially at a deficient demand level.

CHAPTER 10
Employment, Unemployment, and Inflation

This chapter provides a detailed treatment of the types of unemployment. Of these, structural and frictional unemployment, but not involuntary unemployment, can exist in the long-run or short-run equilibrium. Involuntary unemployment, in addition to the other two types, can also occur in disequilibrium.

This chapter also presents the analysis of unemployment and inflation. Their relationship is usually expressed by the Phillips curve and the expectations augmented Phillips curve. However, neither may be a stable curve since each is somewhat deficient.

This chapter also discusses the costs of unemployment and inflation.

This chapter studies the determinants of unemployment and inflation in the economy and the relationship between them. The analytical basis for this study has already been laid out in the preceding chapters, so that much of the analysis in this chapter represents a re-arrangement and elaboration of earlier arguments.

A particular focus of this chapter is on the relationship between unemployment and the rate of inflation. This relationship is usually encompassed in the Phillips curve. Related to the Phillips curve, though somewhat distinct, are Friedman's and Lucas' versions of the expectations augmented Phillips curve.

Among other topics presented in this chapter are the costs of unemployment and inflation.

10.1 Definitions of the Labor Force and Labor Supply

Workers in the labor force have an enormous variety of education and skills, live in a variety of locations, or otherwise differ in the characteristics relevant for the labor market. Similarly, jobs also differ in their characteristics. Further, a given worker — with a given set of characteristics — is often able to get several offers with different wages and working conditions. Our earlier definitions of the labor force and labor supply did not clearly recognize this variety. The following definitions do so.

(i) The maximum labor force (L^{max})
   This is the number of workers who have a job or are looking for a job — no matter how high the wage rate that they want and what skills they possess.
(ii) The labor force (L)
   This is the number of workers who already have jobs or are looking for work at the current wage, irrespective of their own productivity. It does not include workers who want a higher wage than the current one, though they are included in (L^{max}). The unemployment ($L^{max} - L$) of such workers is called *voluntary unemployment*.

(iii) The labor supply (n^s)

This is the number of workers who already have jobs or would be willing to accept a job, if offered one, at the current wage appropriate to their skills. It excludes those workers who do not have a high enough productivity for employment at the current wage.

If all workers and all jobs were identical, the supply of labor would equal the labor force. However, workers are heterogeneous, and differ in physical characteristics, education, aptitudes, and technical, management, and interactive skills, etc. Some workers are more productive than others, and only some have productivity equal to or higher than the current wage. The number of workers in the labor force who do not have the requisite skills and other characteristics, etc., for the jobs available at the current wage, constitute *structural unemployment*, which arises from the structure of the economy in terms of the requirements of the available jobs and the workers' own characteristics.[1] Structural unemployment includes the *seasonal unemployment* of workers who work in seasonal industries, such as fishing, logging, and farming, which offer substantially more employment in some seasons than others.

Therefore, labor supply excludes structural (including seasonal) unemployment, which equals ($L - n^s$).

The above concepts are compactly expressed in the following relationships:

$$L = L^{\max} - \text{voluntary unemployment, and}$$

$$n^s = L - \text{structural (including seasonal) unemployment.}$$

The above three concepts are illustrated in Figure 10.1a to c. The maximum labor force (i.e., at any wage) is shown as $L^{\max}$. The labor force is shown by the L curve. The labor supply is shown by the n^s curve. The labor market is in long-run equilibrium (i.e., with $n^s = n^d$) at the market-clearing wage w_0^* and long-run employment n^f.

10.1.1 Frictional unemployment and actual employment in labor market equilibrium

The labor market is not a single market with identical jobs, identical workers, trade taking place in one spot and with perfect information. Workers differ in the characteristics that firms require for the available jobs and jobs differ in the characteristics that workers want. Some of these characteristics are objective and can be precisely specified, while others are much more subjective and have to be determined through interviews. Further, there is imperfect information on both the characteristics of the jobs (including the nature of the managers, co-workers, the work place environment, etc.) and those of the workers. These factors make the labor market a *complex* one, in which the matching of workers and jobs takes time.

The labor market is also a *dynamic* market because of continuous changes to the available jobs and workers. Jobs change because of the emergence of new industries and skill requirements while some of the existing jobs get eliminated. The turnover of workers in the labor force occurs because some of the existing workers retire or otherwise leave the labor force, while new ones enter the labor force. The new entrants primarily consist of young workers who have recently completed their studies. The entrants to the labor force differ in educations, skills, and experience compared with those leaving it.

The labor market is, therefore, both complex and dynamic, which together imply that the matching of workers to the available jobs takes time. Assuming that vacancies equal the number of workers looking for jobs, unemployment occurring because of the time required for finding the appropriate job is called *frictional*

---

[1] For given levels of these, structural unemployment would be higher at higher wages.

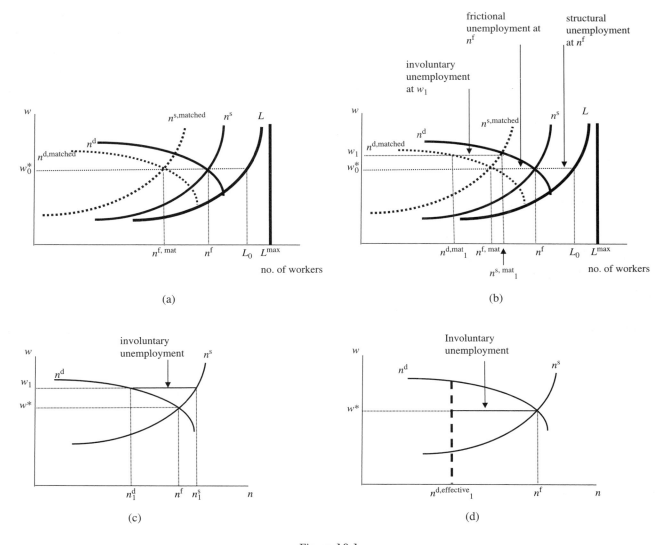

Figure 10.1

unemployment. That is, frictional unemployment consists of the number of workers who remain unemployed for some time even when enough suitable job vacancies are available. Frictional unemployment will be higher if the economy is more dynamic (i.e., with greater turnover of jobs and workers), has greater differences in the location of workers and jobs and has less accurate information on vacancies and available workers. One component of frictional unemployment is *search unemployment*, which consists of workers who have already received a job offer but have decided to remain unemployed while searching for a better job offer. The remainder would be workers who have not yet received job offers.

Labor market equilibrium, which is the equality of labor demand and supply, is defined to allow for frictional unemployment. On the labor supply side, such unemployed workers have the appropriate characteristics and are willing to accept jobs at the current wage. However, they are temporarily unemployed because finding the right job takes time. On the labor demand side, a corresponding number of jobs remain vacant because finding the right worker takes time. If such unemployed workers could be allocated immediately to the vacant jobs, frictional unemployment would be zero. Therefore, labor demand (supply) refers to the number of jobs (workers) *if* the cost and time taken to find the appropriate job/worker were zero and the match between vacancies and the relevant workers were instantaneous. However, this cost is not zero, so that matching workers and jobs involves frictional unemployment.

Note that frictional unemployment does exist even within the analytical concept of full employment but is counted as part of unemployment. In general, for any individual worker searching for a job when there is an appropriate job vacancy for his skills and location, it is expected to be of short duration.

The notions of matched labor supply and matched labor demand in the presence of frictional unemployment

Since the match between vacancies and the matched workers is not instantaneous, *actual employment* is strictly less than the number specified by the equilibrium between labor demand and labor supply by the amount of frictional unemployment. As a corollary, 'full employment' incorporates frictional unemployment, with job vacancies corresponding to the amount of frictional unemployment. Suppose that, for the given amount and commitment devoted by workers and firms on finding appropriate workers/jobs, we deduct the amount of frictional unemployment, from labor supply and call it the '*matched labor supply*' ($n^{s,\text{matched}}$). The matched labor supply curve in Figure 10.1a will be to the left of the n^s curve. Further, we deduct the amount of frictional unemployment from labor demand, and call it the '*matched labor demand*' ($n^{d,\text{matched}}$). The matched labor demand curve in Figure 10.1a will be to the left of the n^d curve. The two 'matched curves' will intersect at the same wage as the n^d and n^s curves. However, employment will be less than that given by the intersection of the n^d and n^s curves by the amount of frictional unemployment. Note that the intersection of the n^d and n^s curves is what is designated in macroeconomics as the full employment level n^f, even though it is the intersection of the $n^{s,\text{matched}}$ and $n^{d,\text{matched}}$ curves that specifies the numbers of workers who will in fact be employed in equilibrium.

Hence,

$$\text{matched labor supply} = n^{s,\text{matched}} = n^s - \text{frictional unemployment and}$$

$$\text{matched labor demand} = n^{d,\text{matched}} = n^d - \text{frictional unemployment.}$$

The number of workers actually employed in equilibrium is that when matched labor supply equals matched labor demand.

10.1.2 Discouraged workers

A *discouraged worker* is one who does not currently have a job, had searched for one in the past but stopped looking after some time. He does not meet the requirement of currently 'looking for a job' and, therefore, is neither included in the labor force nor in the labor supply.

Over the business cycle, discouraged workers play a volatile role by dropping out of the labor force in downturns when jobs take too long — and become too difficult — to find, while re-entering the labor force in upturns as jobs become easier to find. The existence of such workers is most evident when the economy is below full employment.[2] Therefore, the labor force and supply curves shift over the business cycle because of changes in the number of discouraged workers.

---

[2]The full employment state includes frictional unemployment, which consists of workers who are qualified for the available jobs but are unemployed for short periods while they get matched to jobs. This period is likely to be fairly short so that such workers do not become discouraged workers — and leave the labor force.

10.1.3 Other determinants of the equilibrium level of unemployment

The equilibrium level of unemployment not only depends on technical and economic factors but also on institutional and political factors. One of the institutional causes is encompassed in the theory of *insider–outsider unemployment*, which claims that existing job holders (insiders) exert pressure on firms to push the wages for the employed workers above the market-clearing level. Such pressure is exerted not only by unions[3] but also by non-unionized employees. Firms accede to such pressure to maintain a more harmonious work place. Pressures on the government, as well as social and political considerations, can also result in setting or raising the minimum wage above the full-employment one.

Workers differ in efficiency and can vary their work effort by either shirking or speeding up. Firms can provide an incentive for better performance by offering wages higher than the market wage. Doing so enables firms to select workers from larger numbers of applicants and also to retain better workers, since they know they are being 'well paid'. The theory which focuses on this reason for the wage being higher than the market-clearing one is called the *efficiency wage theory*. It implies that unemployment will be correspondingly higher than at full employment.

Among the political factors affecting the equilibrium unemployment are the legal and political environment which governs the bargaining power between firms and workers, and the non-wage costs of employment. Among the latter are the laws governing the security of employment, such as the legally acceptable conditions for hiring or layoff and severance pay. Equilibrium unemployment is also affected by the terms (amounts, duration, eligibility, penalties, etc.) of employment/unemployment insurance benefits and income support (social assistance) programs provided by the government to the unemployed since these affect the attractiveness of accepting a job readily versus not accepting one.[4] Reducing such payments to the unemployed reduces their *reservation wage* — which is the minimum wage a worker wants in order to accept a job offer — and increases their willingness to accept lower-paying jobs.

Further, *social attitudes and norms* such as the acceptability of not having a job, of mothers of young children working or not working, of the 'normal' retirement age, etc., also affect labor force participation and are among the determinants of the labor force. They also affect the pressures to accept a job sooner rather than later and the unemployment rate. These social attitudes and norms tend to differ among countries and among different social, sex, and age groups.[5] Another factor that affects labor force participation is the time needed to achieve desired educational levels. The desired educational level has been rising in most countries in recent decades and has been a factor in reducing participation rates. However, increasing longevity has persuaded many workers to retire later than in earlier decades, which has tended to increase participation rates.

Box 10.1: The Labor Force Participation Rate

> The labor force participation rate specifies the labor force — which consists of the employed and unemployed workers — as a percentage of the working age population. The latter is the sum of the labor force

---

[3] Union pressure is often proxied by the percentage of workers who are unionized. This number has been declining in recent decades in Western countries.

[4] Some economists claim that one of the reasons for the higher unemployment rates in Canada and Western Europe compared to those in the United States are the more generous unemployment insurance benefits and income support levels in the former.

[5] It is sometimes claimed that one of the reasons for the higher unemployment rates in Europe than in the United States is the social acceptance (or absence of social and family disapproval) of being without a job.

Box 10.1: (*Continued*)

and those working age people who are not in the labor force. The working age is usually specified to be between the ages of 15 to 24 years for youth, 24 to 65 years for adults, and 15 to 65 years for the overall classification. Cultural factors, family needs and health, number of children and their ages, the availability of time-saving home appliances and nurseries, job opportunities, and wages are the most important determinants of the participation rate. These determinants vary among countries and even cultural groups within a country, so that the labor force participation rate of women tends to differ among countries and even cultural groups within a country.

The participation rate of working-age females has been of special significance for changes in the labor force in recent decades, since this rate was quite low until the 1960s and then began to increase rapidly. In Canada, the participation rate for the 15 to 65 years age group was 78.6% for men and 49.7% for women in 1979, changing to 72.5% for men and 58.9% for women in 1999. The overall participation rate for both sexes taken together was 64.0% in 1979 and 65.6% in 1999.

The non-employment rate

The use of the unemployment rate for cross-country comparisons has some disadvantages since different countries are likely to use different ways of measuring unemployment. Further, the discouraged worker effect can give an erroneous picture of the true number of workers who would like to have jobs but are not employed. Therefore, for cross-country comparisons, some economists prefer to compare the *non-employment rate*, which is the percentage of the population in the working age bracket that does not have jobs. This rate is measured by the number of unemployed workers plus those not in the labor force as a percentage of the working age population. The non-employment rate in western countries is usually between 35% and 55% . Among countries and even among groups within a country, besides economic factors, culture and traditions play an important role in determining this rate.

The use of the non-employment rate has its own disadvantages. One of these is that it includes persons who choose not to seek paid work outside the home and, therefore, are voluntarily without a job. Historically, many women chose to be housewives and would have been counted as non-employed. Since this pattern has changed in recent decades, the use of the non-employment rate for time series comparisons poses problems as does its use for cross-country comparisons.

Shifts in labor force participation rates in recent decades

Labor force participation rates vary over time and depend on real wages, which is the potential return, i.e., when employed, for being in the labor force, and on many cultural, technological, and economic factors. While both male and female participations can change, the labor force participation rate of women, especially in the developed economies, has increased considerably since the early 1960s when the birth control pill was invented and became easily available to the public. Over the same period, the male participation rate decreased significantly. Part of the latter is due to the increase in the family incomes resulting from the rising participation rate of women.

Fact Sheet 10.1 provides a glimpse at the shifts in the participation rates in USA and Canada since 1960. In both Canada and the USA, over these 48 years, while this rate decreased by about 10% for males, that for females increased by about 20% for the USA and about 32% for Canada. The total participation rate for both males and females increased significantly in both countries.

Fact Sheet 10.1: Participation Rates in Canada and the United States, Male and Female, 1980–2008.

The following table classifies participation rates in Canada and the United States as the fraction of the total working age population (over 15 years old) currently in the work force.

	1960	1970	1980	1990	2000	2008
United States						
Males (%)	83.3	79.7	77.4	76.1	74.7	73
Females (%)	37.7	43.3	51.6	57.5	60.2	59.5
Total (%)	59.4	60.4	63.8	66.4	67.2	66
Canada						
Males (%)	82.8	77.8	78.3	76.1	72.4	72.9
Females (%)	30.1	38.3	50.6	58.5	58.9	62.8
Total (%)	56.2	57.8	64.3	67.1	65.8	67.8

Source: For data 1960–1970 Constance Sorrentino, International comparisons of labor force participation, 1960–1980. CANSIM V2062816 for Canada 1980-2008. Bureau of labour statistics for US 1980–2008

10.2 The Components of Unemployment

The above definitions of the labor force and labor supply imply several concepts of unemployment. An unemployed worker can belong to any one of four categories:

Voluntary unemployment ($U^{\text{voluntary}} = L^{\max} - L$): those workers who do not have jobs because they want a wage higher than the current one for their skills. Macroeconomics does not consider such workers as really a part of unemployment, so that such persons are not included in the measures of unemployment.

Structural unemployment (including seasonal one[6]) ($U^{\text{structural}} = L - n^s$): those workers who are in the labor force but do not have jobs because they do not possess the requisite characteristics (skills, location etc.) to get jobs with a productivity which would cover the going wage.

Frictional unemployment ($U^{\text{frictional}} = n^s - n^{s,\text{matched}}$): those workers who have the requisite characteristics and for whom there are enough jobs in the economy but who are temporarily unemployed while they search for an appropriate job.[7]

Involuntary unemployment ($U^{\text{inv}} = n^{s,\text{matched}} - n^{d,\text{matched}}$): those workers who are in the labor force and the labor supply but for whom the economy does not have enough jobs. Such workers have the appropriate characteristics for jobs for the current nature of the economy and do seek jobs at the current (or even lower)

---

[6]Seasonal unemployment affects workers who work in industries with seasonal production, such as fisheries and construction.

[7]One part of frictional unemployment is *search unemployment*, which is usually defined as the number of unemployed workers who have received job offers but are choosing to stay unemployed while searching for a job with a better offer. For such workers, economists use the theory of search unemployment to explain why they chose to stay unemployed. The remaining part of frictional unemployment consists of workers who have not yet received job offers though there are enough jobs for their skills and other characteristics.

wage, but cannot get jobs because firms do not have enough jobs to offer. The usual reason for the inadequacy of jobs is deficiency of aggregate demand in the economy. Involuntary unemployment is in addition to frictional and structural unemployment. Note that it is zero if labor demand equals labor supply at the current wage — i.e., the labor market clears.

Macroeconomics focuses on only the last three components of unemployment and defines the *level of unemployment U* as:

$$U = U^{\text{structural}} + U^{\text{frictional}} + U^{\text{inv}}.$$

Note that voluntary unemployment is excluded from this definition of unemployment.

The rate of unemployment (u) is defined as the level of unemployment (U) divided by the labor force (L). That is, $u = U/L$. u is often expressed as a percentage of the labor force.

In practice, structural unemployment is long term, since it is often related to skills no longer consistent with the evolving technology or shifts in the location of jobs. For an individual unemployed worker, it could last many years, even the rest of his life. Frictional unemployment is short term, since it is related to the time taken to find a job, when there are sufficient job vacancies to absorb the workers currently unemployed. It usually lasts a few months. The duration of involuntary unemployment depends on whether it is due to a high real wage or a demand deficiency. The latter is related to the duration of recessions, which normally last about two years.

The diagrammatic depiction of the components of unemployment

The difference between the labor force and the labor supply is structural unemployment. At the equilibrium wage rate w_0^* in Figure 10.1b, structural unemployment is shown by $(L_0 - n^{\text{f}})$.

At the equilibrium wage rate w_0^*, the difference between the actual employment and that given by the equality of labor demand and the labor supply n^s is frictional unemployment. It occurs because of delays in matching workers and jobs. In Figure 10.1b, at the wage w_0^*, frictional unemployment equals $(n^{\text{f}} - n^{\text{f,matched}})$.

Natural unemployment is the sum of structural (including seasonal) and frictional unemployment at the LR equilibrium (i.e., at full-employment). At the wage w_0^* and employment n_0^{f}, it equals $(L - n^{\text{f,matched}})$.[8]

For our further arguments and diagrams, we ignore the distinction between labor demand and supply and their matched versions, and take the intersection of the labor demand and supply curves as indicating the number of workers actually employed at full employment. This is the standard practice in expositions of the labor market in macroeconomic theory.

10.3 Involuntary Unemployment

Involuntary unemployment (U^{inv}) is the difference between actual unemployment U and natural unemployment U^{n}. That is, $U^{\text{inv}} = U - U^{\text{n}}$. As discussed in Chapter 9, involuntary unemployment can occur due to two reasons:

(1) Involuntary unemployment due to a 'high real wage' but without an aggregate demand deficiency.

---

[8]As can be seen from Figure 10.1b, an increase in the wage rate (from w_0^* to w_1) can increase or lower structural and/or frictional unemployment and, therefore, change their sum. However, at any time, the change in the structural and frictional unemployment — and their sum — from their natural levels will only be a small part of their total amounts. This variation is being ignored as a simplification.

(2) Involuntary unemployment due to the emergence of a demand deficiency even without a real wage above the LR equilibrium level.

In some cases, the economy can experience involuntary unemployment due to the simultaneous existence of both a demand deficiency and a high real wage.

Involuntary unemployment due to a high real wage

Note that the labor market will not be in equilibrium if the real wage is above the full-employment one. This is shown in Figure 10.1c at the wage w_1, which is above the full-employment wage w^*, so that involuntary unemployment at w_1 will equal $(n_1^s - n_1^d)$. Therefore, one cause of involuntary unemployment is a 'high real wage' (i.e., one above the full-employment one).

Involuntary unemployment due to the emergence of a demand deficiency

The second and more common cause of involuntary unemployment is *aggregate demand deficiency* which makes firms employ less than the full-employment number of workers. For this, start with the assumption that the economy's effective aggregate demand for commodities has fallen and is met by the *effective* labor demand (and employment) at $n_1^{d,\text{effective}}$. This possibility was covered in Chapter 9 and should be reviewed at this stage. For this scenario, suppose that the economy continued to maintain the full-employment wage w^*, even though employment had fallen because of a demand deficiency to only $n_1^{d,\text{effective}}$.[9] This is shown in Figure 10.1d. In this case, involuntary unemployment will depend only on the demand deficiency and will equal $(n^f - n^{d,\text{effective}}1)$.

However, since, at $n_1^{d,\text{effective}}$, the marginal productivity of labor exceeds the real wage w_0^*, firms can afford to raise the real wage of their employed workers. But, with more workers unemployed and greater scarcity of jobs, the increase in unemployment would put downward pressure on real wages. The real wage could, therefore, rise or fall relative to the initial full-employment one at w_0^*. The greater and the longer-lasting the rise in unemployment, the stronger will be the tendency of the real wage to fall. However, the (up or down) change in the real wage would not change involuntary unemployment since it arises from inadequate demand for commodities, rather from the real wage being too high.

Involuntary unemployment due to a credit crisis

As analyzed in Chapter 9 (and later in Chapter 16), a credit crisis, defined as a fall in credit supply sufficient to finance full-employment production levels, can reduce output and employment so that employment falls. The resulting increase in unemployment is involuntary unemployment due to a credit deficiency. It would be eliminated ('in the long run') once credit is restored to adequate levels but this process can take several quarters.

Note that, in some periods, the economy could have a high real wage, a demand deficiency, and a credit deficiency, so that each could contribute to the causes of its involuntary unemployment.

The variation in the number of discouraged workers with the state of the economy

Discouraged workers are not included in the above categories of unemployed workers, but need to be considered in judging the performance of the economy since such workers were in the labor force and will re-enter

---

[9]Note that, under these conditions, the employment–wage relationship is not given by the labor demand curve.

it as economic conditions improve.[10] From the statistical perspective, such workers dropped out of the labor force, so that they are not in any of the unemployment categories. Yet, from their own personal viewpoint, they consider themselves as unemployed, even though not actively looking for a job. Further, from the social viewpoint, discouraged workers without a job represent loss of some output, just as for the unemployed but not discouraged workers. Further, in assessing the performance of the economy, its need for job creation and the loss from unemployment, we have to focus on the sum of unemployed workers (as defined above and in official data) and discouraged workers. Hence, a more realistic statement of the economy's performance is provided not by u (the unemployment rate) but by $(u + d)$ (i.e., the sum of the unemployment rate and the discouraged worker rate).[11]

10.4 The Actual Rate of Unemployment

The relationship between the unemployment rate and employment was derived in Chapter 1. It was specified as:

$$u = U/L = 1 - n/L. \tag{1}$$

As discussed in Chapters 7 to 9, the actual rate of unemployment in the economy in any given period can be separated into three components in the following manner:

$$u = u^{n} + (u^{*} - u^{n}) + (u - u^{*}), \tag{2}$$

so that the actual rate of unemployment has three components.

 (i) The natural rate of unemployment. This is the rate that exists in LR equilibrium (full employment). It is the sum of the structural and frictional unemployment rates at the full-employment levels.
 (ii) The short-run deviation of the equilibrium unemployment rate from the natural rate due to errors in expectations under uncertainty and/or the existence of adjustment costs.
(iii) The disequilibrium rate of unemployment. One way of measuring it was earlier specified as the difference between the labor supply at the full-employment wage and the labor demand at the current wage. Such unemployment was also labelled as the involuntary unemployment rate.

The actual unemployment rate varies across countries, as is illustrated in Fact Sheet 10.2. However, the data plotted in this Fact Sheet is not strictly comparable across countries since they tend to measure unemployment in different ways and with different degrees of accuracy. Unemployment rates should be high in developing economies with a large migration of rural labor to the urban areas. However, this is often not reflected in the reported measures, which are often based on different definitions of unemployment, so that accurate comparisons across countries become difficult. The unemployment rate in any given country also varies over time, as is shown in Face Sheet 10.2 and more clearly in Fact Sheet 10.3 for the USA. The latter reports movements in the unemployment rate over the past century. This rate was especially high in the USA, as in most industrialized economies of the time, during the Great Depression years from late 1929 to 1939, when it reached more than 20% and stayed exceptionally high for a decade.

---

[10]One way of measuring the rate of discouraged workers is given by D/L, where D is the number of discouraged workers. It would equal $[L(w) - L(w^{f})/L^{f}]$, where L is the actual labor force and L^{f} is the labor force that would occur at the full-employment wage w^{f}. For $w < w^{f}$, $L(w) < L(w^{f})$.

[11]It could also be represented by $(u^{i} + d)$ (i.e., the sum of the involuntary unemployment rate and the discouraged worker rate). However, the data on the rate of involuntary unemployment is usually not available or in dispute.

Fact Sheet 10.2: Unemployment Rates in Selected Countries, 1985–2008

This Fact Sheet reports unemployment rates in five countries, two (USA and Canada) of which are developed ones and three (China, Malaysia, and Thailand) are developing ones. The unemployment rate in each country varies over time, rising in recessions and falling in booms (and wars). With truly free movement of labor between countries, unemployed workers would migrate from their own countries to countries with lower unemployment, so that the unemployment rates among countries would be approximately the same. However, the labor market of each country is especially partitioned from that of others by very limited and controlled legal immigration. USA and Canada, two otherwise considerably integrated neighbors, follow a similar pattern of unemployment but still do not show equal unemployment rates.

For Malaysia and Thailand, the early 1990s brought economic prosperity and with it decreases in their unemployment rates. However, the Asian Crisis of the mid-1990s meant the loss of many jobs, especially in Thailand, causing a substantial rise in their unemployment rates during the following decade. China has been going through an economic boom, especially for the last decade, so that it should show a fall in its unemployment rate. However, its graph shows otherwise, probably because the reported unemployment rate is for urban areas and there has been a rapid influx of workers from the rural areas to the cities. Unemployment rates across countries are defined and measured in different ways, making accurate international comparisons difficult, so that it would be erroneous to conclude from this graph that the developed countries have higher unemployment rates than developing ones. Intuitively, the opposite is quite likely.

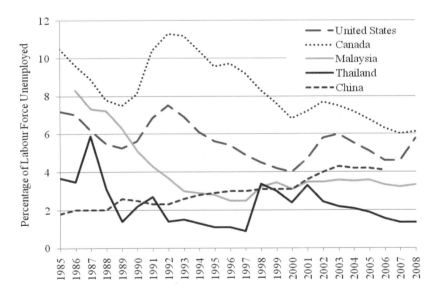

This Fact Sheet illustrates the variations in the actual unemployment rate over time by examining those for the USA. Since 1980, unemployment in the United States has exhibited both a downward trend and a cyclical pattern with peaks in the early 1980s, 1990s, and 2000s. There is likely to be another peak in 2009 or 2010 resulting from the financial and economic crisis, which started in 2007. Since the unemployment rate has a countercyclical pattern, it is relatively low during booms in the economy and higher during recessions.

Fact Sheet 10.3: (*Continued*)

Looking at unemployment rates over the past century demonstrates how much the unemployment rate has varied and its sensitivity to real-world events and policy shifts. The United States experienced its highest unemployment between 1929 and 1940 during the Great Depression when the unemployment rate reached 23%. Other episodes of high unemployment were due to the dislocation following two World Wars, the oil supply shocks of the 1970s, and the stagflation of the late 1970s and early 1980s. Exceptionally low unemployment rates occurred during the First and Second World Wars due to military needs and expenditures.

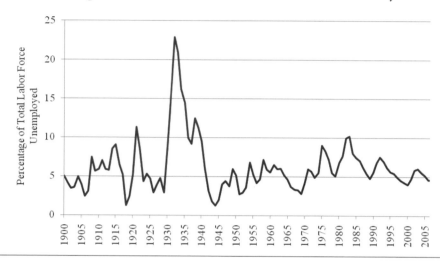

10.4.1 The division of unemployment into natural and cyclical unemployment

Some treatments of unemployment divide actual unemployment into two components:

(1) Natural unemployment
(2) Cyclical unemployment

Cyclical unemployment is defined in terms of the difference between actual unemployment and the natural one, where the latter is the sum of structural and frictional unemployment in full-employment equilibrium.[12] Cyclical unemployment is the sum of involuntary unemployment and the short-run variations in structural and frictional unemployment from their full-employment levels.[13] That is,

Cyclical unemployment = involuntary unemployment + the deviation of short-term equilibrium unemployment from the natural unemployment $= U^{inv} + (U^* - U^n)$.

In practice, cyclical unemployment is usually identified with involuntary unemployment due to fluctuations in aggregate demand. Cyclical unemployment decreases during an upturn and increases during a downturn of the economy. Hence, it is countercyclical (i.e., higher in recessions and lower in boom) and makes total unemployment also countercyclical.

---

[12]Note that involuntary unemployment — even when it exists — is not included in the natural rate of unemployment.
[13]Some textbooks simplify by assuming that they always remain at these levels, so that cyclical unemployment becomes synonymous with involuntary unemployment.

10.4.2 Changes in the actual rate of unemployment over time

The actual rate of unemployment over time can change because of changes in any or all of its three components,[14] since,

$$\frac{\partial u}{\partial t} = \frac{\partial u^n}{\partial t} + \frac{\partial (u^* - u^n)}{\partial t} + \frac{\partial (u - u^*)}{\partial t},$$ (3)

where $\partial u / \partial t$ is the change in the unemployment rate over time t. Hence, changes in the actual rate of unemployment can occur due to:

(i) Changes in the natural rate of unemployment
(ii) Changes in the deviation of the SR equilibrium rate from the natural rate due to variations in the errors in expectations under uncertainty and/or adjustment costs
(iii) Fluctuations in the disequilibrium rate of unemployment, i.e., changes in involuntary unemployment

The natural rate of unemployment does change over time. The other two components of the actual rate can also change and do change over the business cycle. In particular, they are negatively related to the business cycle and tend to have smaller — sometimes even negative — values during a boom than during a recession.

Short-run and long-run variations in the natural rate of unemployment

The natural rate of unemployment depends, among other variables, on the available technology and the supply of the factors of production. Short-term shocks to non-labor inputs make the natural rate deviate from its long-run level. For instance, a decline in the price of imports, especially of energy, reduces the natural rate; an increase raises it. Thus, the oil price shocks of 1973–1975 and 1980–1981 raised the natural rate, while the decline in the relative price of oil over the following two decades lowered it. A war which destroys part of the country's capital stock will also raise the natural rate. Such variations can be designated as *short-term variations in the natural rate*, as against the *long-term variations* resulting from permanent changes in technology and the secular growth of the capital stock.

Fact Sheet 10.4:

	Unemployment Rate, % of Labor Force		Unemployed for more than 1 Year, % of Unemployment	
	1985	2005	1985	2005
North America				
Canada	10.6	6.8	12.2	9.6
United States	7.2	5.1	9.4	11.7
Asia				
Japan	2.6	4.4	13.1	33.3
China	1.8	4.2	—	—

---

[14] It can also change because of changes in the number of discouraged workers. The discouraged worker rate changes over the business cycle but is being omitted from the following discussion.

	Unemployment Rate, % of Labor Force		Unemployed for more than 1 Year, % of Unemployment	
	1985	2005	1985	2005
Malaysia	8.3	3.6	—	—
Thailand	3.7	1.9	—	—
Europe				
United Kingdom	11.2	4.8	50.2	22.3
France	9.6	9.3	43.7	41.3
Germany	—	10.6	47.8	54
Spain	17.8	9.2	56.6	32.5
Italy	8.2	7.7	66.2	52.1

Source: OECD Source for OECD members, IMF IFS for rest.

Thailand	3.7	1.9	—	—
Europe				
United Kingdom	11.2	4.8	50.5	20.4
France	9.6	9.3	42.1	38.0
Germany	—	10.6	—	56.5
Spain	17.8	9.2	67.7	28.8
Italy	8.2	7.7	75.4	49.5

Source: OECD Source for OECD members, IMF International Financial Statistics for the rest.

Estimating the natural rate of unemployment

The actual rate of unemployment can differ from the natural one, so that it is very difficult to find a proper measure of the latter. A simple procedure used for calculating the natural rate uses the assumption that the economy maintains its full-employment level on average over the business cycle, with symmetrical cyclical fluctuations around this level.[15] Under this procedure, the average unemployment rate over one cycle is said to be its *short-term natural rate*,[16] with the difference between the actual rate and this rate specifying the cyclical variation. The average rate over several cycles is a proxy for the *long-term natural rate*.

---

[15]Another procedure for estimating the natural rate regresses unemployment on various macroeconomic variables, and proxies the natural rate by the estimated one.

[16]This procedure gives erroneous estimates of the natural rate if the cycle is not symmetrical or if full employment is not reached over the business cycle, as occurred in the case of cycles within the Great Depression from 1930 to 1939.

***Fact Sheet 10.5*:** Unemployment and Trend Unemployment in the United States, 1980–2008

This Fact Sheet uses USA data to illustrate movements in unemployment and in trend unemployment. Unemployment had a cyclical pattern (with a period of approximately 10 years), and was greater than the trend rate in the first half of the 1980s, the early 1990s, early 2000s and 2008–10.

The trend can be estimated over each business cycle or over several business cycles. The former procedure yields three distinct trends over the three business cycles since 1980. The three period trends differ in their slopes and intercepts, but with a clear downward movement in each of the trends during the three periods and in the overall trend over the whole period. If the business cycle had been perfectly symmetrical, the period trends would have been perfectly horizontal. The decline in the trend rate of unemployment indicates the influence of technological change, shifts in labor supply and factors other than purely cyclical ones.

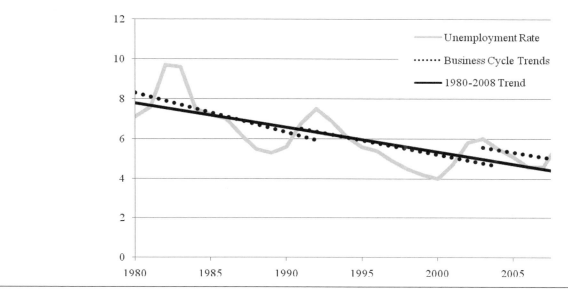

10.5 Policies to Reduce Structural Unemployment

Structural unemployment consists of workers unemployed by reasons of having inappropriate skills and education or being in inappropriate locations, etc. (relative to those required to produce the equilibrium marginal product of labor) in the current state of the economy. Structural unemployment results from differences between the characteristics of workers and the available jobs. A reduction in such unemployment requires the reduction of such differences, through either changes in job requirements or in workers' characteristics. For example, if the jobs are in one part of the country, while the unemployed workers are in another part, either firms with the jobs are moved to the location of the workers or the workers are moved to the location of the jobs. Changes in educational patterns and re-training schemes can improve the match between job requirements and workers' skills.

Seasonal unemployment consists of unemployed workers whose jobs are in seasonal industries but who do not currently (in the off-season) have jobs. Creating offsetting seasonal industries to provide jobs in off-seasons can reduce seasonal unemployment. Alternatively, migration of workers in the off-seasons to other locations and industries could help. We have incorporated seasonal unemployment in structural unemployment.

Extended Analysis Box 10.1: Changes in Structural Unemployment

Structural unemployment depends upon the supply structure — that is, the labor market relationships and the production function — of the economy and will change as the supply structure shifts. Technical change and changes in educational and skill requirements, the level of education of the labor force, the availability of information on jobs and workers, the location of industries, etc., are thus likely to change the rate of structural unemployment. This rate is, therefore, itself a variable and not a constant. As already pointed out, shifts in the supply side of the economy can change the structural rate.

Structural unemployment can also be changed by shifts in aggregate demand (in addition to shifts in the distribution of this demand among the sectors of the economy), including those brought about by the pursuit of monetary and fiscal policies. A decline in demand will hit some industries and job categories harder than others. Conversely, an increase in aggregate demand will benefit some industries and some job categories more than others.[17]

The impact of fiscal and monetary policies on structural unemployment

The impact of fiscal policy on structural unemployment has to be examined in the following manner. The public sector has different educational and skill requirements than the private sector. Therefore, changes in the relative size of the government sector shift the demand for different types of education and skills and can impact on the level of structural unemployment. Monetary policy would not have such an effect.

Increases in fiscal spending or tax concessions usually occur selectively among industries, locations, and firms. They can occur as increases in the subsidies for: education, re-training unemployed workers, the relocation of industries or workers, the employment of targeted groups with high unemployment rates, such as those of youth, handicapped, or workers discriminated against in employment. They can subsidize R&D expenditures or the expansion of certain industries. They can also increase (or decrease) unemployment insurance benefits, welfare benefits such as to mothers of young children so that they do not have to seek outside employment, etc. All such policies affect either the demand or the supply of labor and, therefore, affect structural unemployment.

Fiscal deficits change aggregate demand, which can alter structural unemployment because of changes in the structure of demand among occupations and industries.

Therefore, for economies which stay at full employment on their own, fiscal policies mostly affect structural unemployment through changes in the relative size and efficiency of the government vis-à-vis the private sector and through their selective nature.

Monetary policies tend to be general in nature rather than selective. General monetary policy acts on the economy through aggregate demand and only affects structural unemployment outside the full-employment state.

---

[17]Disequilibrium in the economy due to a 'high' real wage or deficient demand can also change structural unemployment since the change in aggregate demand and employment is not proportionately shared among all types of commodities and industries.

10.6 Policies to Reduce Frictional Unemployment

Frictional unemployment consists of workers who are unemployed because of the time involved in matching workers to appropriate jobs. Such unemployment is short-term, usually lasting a few months on average. Speeding and improving the information flows on available jobs and workers looking for jobs can reduce frictional unemployment. These can be affected by selective fiscal policies, such as those which improve the flow of information through the financing of job centers, internet posting of vacancies and available workers, financing the travel of workers to interviews, etc.

10.7 Measuring Involuntary Unemployment

Two ways of measuring involuntary unemployment

There are two ways of measuring the level of involuntary unemployment, which we denote by U^{inv}, with the rate of involuntary unemployment designated by u^{inv}. As we have defined earlier, involuntary unemployment consists of qualified workers — i.e., those with the requisite skills, location, etc. — who are willing to accept jobs at the current wage but do not have jobs or job offers. This implies that involuntary unemployment could be defined as the difference between labor supply (that is, the number of workers with jobs or job offers which they are willing to accept at the given wage) and labor demand (that is, the number of jobs at that wage). For this definition, Figure 10.2 shows this measure of involuntary unemployment by $(n^s - n_1^d)$, where n^s depends on the real wage that has come into being. If the real wage had become w_1, labor supply would equal n_1^s, so that involuntary unemployment would be $(n_1^s - n_1^d)$.

Involuntary unemployment could also be defined as the difference between full employment and actual employment, with the latter being equal to labor demand. Figure 10.2 shows this measure of involuntary unemployment by $(n^f - n_1^d)$ for this definition and given employment at n_1^d (either because of a demand deficiency or because of a high real wage equal to w_1).

The rationale for the second definition is that as the wage falls, labor supply will fall with it, so that (ii) measures the amount of unemployment that needs to be eliminated to get the economy to full employment. We

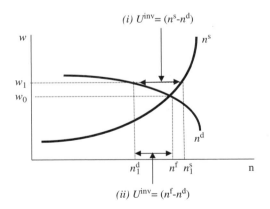

Figure 10.2

will use the second definition as the more relevant one for measuring the need for policy to take the economy to full employment. Note that involuntary unemployment is zero when there exists full employment.[18]

Many economists consider involuntary unemployment to be synonymous with the disequilibrium unemployment, so that it is used as an index of the extent of disequilibrium in the latter.

Monetary and fiscal policies to reduce involuntary unemployment

The ability of monetary and fiscal policies to ameliorate (or cause) involuntary unemployment depends on which of the two types of involuntary unemployment exists in the economy. Therefore, we have the following results.

- Expansionary monetary and fiscal policies can reduce an existing demand deficiency and, thereby, reduce involuntary unemployment.
- Conversely, contractionary monetary and fiscal policies can create involuntary unemployment and have been known to do so for several quarters and even years. Many recessions are known to have been caused by sharp contractions in the money supply. Part of the rise of unemployment — and the amount of involuntary unemployment — in such recessions is of a short-run equilibrium type until expectations adjust to the lower actual inflation rate, but part of it would also be a disequilibrium one while the economy adjusts to a lower level of demand.
- If involuntary unemployment is due to a high real wage without a demand deficiency, and if nominal wages rise proportionately with price increases, expansionary monetary and fiscal policies cannot address the root cause of such unemployment. Expansionary policies will merely create excess demand for commodities and inflation.

Box 10.2: Causes of High Unemployment in Canada and Europe Relative to the USA

This box discusses the variations in the unemployment rate in the USA, Canada, and a few European countries. Canada and most countries of the European Union (EU) have had persistently much higher unemployment rates during the last two decades than the United States. The average unemployment rate for the EU started to increase rapidly in the mid-1970s and had reached over 10% by the mid-1980s. It started to fall after about 1992, but was still above 8% in 2000. The unemployment rate in Canada also started to increase from about 6% in the mid-1970s to a high of 11.2% in 1992 and then started to decrease. It was about 7.5% in 2000. By comparison, the US unemployment also started rising in the mid-1970s, peaked at about 9.7% in 1982, and then decreased steadily, reaching about 4.5% in 2000.

The reasons for the rise in the unemployment rates in the mid-1970s were due to three shared factors: the two sharp hikes in oil prices (1973–1975 and 1980–1982), slowdown of productivity growth in the early 1970s and 1980s, and high real interest rates in the 1980s. But why did the unemployment rates in Canada and the European Union in the 1980s not decline as much as they did in the United States?

---

[18]Defining u^{inv} as $(n^{\text{f}} - n^{\text{d}})/L$, i.e., as the difference between full employment and labor demand divided by the labor force, u^{inv} has two components, as in:

$$u^{\text{inv}} = (u^* - u^{\text{n}}) + (u - u^*)$$

where $(u^* - u^{\text{n}})$ occurs because of the deviation of short-run equilibrium unemployment along the SRAS curve from unemployment in LR equilibrium along the LRAS curve. Though the economy is in SR equilibrium at u^*, $(u^* - u^{\text{n}})$ can nevertheless be considered to be a part of involuntary unemployment since the individual worker who becomes unemployed when $u^* > u^{\text{n}}$, does want a job at the existing wage rate but does not have a job. $(u - u^*)$ is the disequilibrium element in the involuntary unemployment rate.

Box 10.2: (*Continued*)

Generous unemployment insurance benefits in the former were one reason, since these reduce the incentive to return to work. Extensive regulations on layoffs and dismissals were another. Note that the longer the workers stay out of work, the greater the deterioration in their skills, and the greater the reluctance of employers to hire them, so that sustained high unemployment tends to perpetuate itself.

Canada cut back drastically on its unemployment insurance benefits in 1996, both in terms of its duration and coverage. These seem to have had the effect of decreasing overall unemployment by decreasing frictional unemployment and even structural one, by forcing unemployed workers to accept jobs earlier, seeking retraining for new skills or shifting to less suitable jobs.

In recent decades, several European countries similarly reduced income support for the unemployed workers. Among these was Ireland, which cut back the ratio of unemployment insurance benefits to after-tax wages from 77% to 64% in 1994, as well as reducing other income support for the unemployed. Netherlands also cut back on such benefits in 1986–1987, and gradually reduced the real minimum wage. Other initiatives included wage moderation, reduction in income taxes and taxes paid by firms for each worker, barriers to part-time work, etc. These programs reduced the unemployment rates in both Ireland and Netherlands over the 1990s to less than 5%, well below the European Union's average rate of about 8% in 2000.

10.8 The Costs of Unemployment

The main economic costs of higher unemployment are:

(1) Lost output and lower incomes, since those who become unemployed do not produce output nor do they receive any income. The cost to the economy of higher unemployment in lowering output is specified by Okun's rule, which was explained in Chapter 8.
(2) There may also be a long-term *hysteresis effect*, for which see below (and Chapter 9).
(3) Changes in unemployment are also usually accompanied by changes in the distribution of income. The impact of higher unemployment on the distribution of income occurs in three ways:

  (i) Unemployment among the less educated and less skilled members of the labor force increases more than proportionately, as compared with that among the more educated and more skilled workers, whom firms are more reluctant to lose.
  (ii) The wages of the workers who are still employed are more likely to suffer downward pressure, translating into wage decreases, less promotions, etc.
  (iii) Frictional unemployment increases, especially for certain groups in the economy. In particular, it increases for new entrants into the labor force (such as recent graduates) and those subject to discrimination, who find it harder and take longer to find jobs suitable to their qualifications — and when they do get jobs, they may have to settle for inappropriate occupations and lower wages than otherwise.

Most economists believe that the distribution of income — and not merely that of labor income — becomes more unequal in recessions as the unemployment rate increases: the poor suffer relatively more in lost incomes than the better paid workers and labor as a whole suffers relatively more than the owners of capital. However, some economists dispute this, claiming that the wealthy also suffer since the stock markets do badly, so that the return on capital falls and may fall more than labor incomes in some recessions, while falling less in other recessions. Further, the government's social programs — such as the income-support, unemployment insurance ones, etc. — provide a safety net for the fall in labor incomes. Therefore, which groups lose more in recessions cannot be established on a purely theoretical basis. It is likely to depend on the causes and the effects of the recession, such as a collapse of stock market prices, a decrease in aggregate demand due to contractionary monetary and fiscal policies, transitory increases in unemployment due to shifts in the industrial structure of the economy, etc.

The hysteresis effect

The impact of higher or lower current unemployment on the future long-run unemployment is called *hysteresis*. There can be a long-term cost/effect for the economy of high unemployment in recessions. This occurs through the deterioration of the skills of the unemployed workers. Further, workers slotted into lower skilled jobs do not get the chance to learn the skills appropriate to better and more productive jobs, so that when the economy recovers, the economy's productive capacity is lowered.

Non-economic aspects of hysteresis include the social and psychological costs of not having a job or accepting an undesirable job during a recession for the sake of a pay check but getting locked into otherwise undesired careers for long years.

10.9 Relationship Between Unemployment and the Inflation Rate from the AD-AS Analysis

The AD-AS analysis, in combination with the production function, determines the level of employment. This, in combination with the labor force specification, determines the rate of unemployment.

The determinants of the aggregate supply of commodities were specified in Chapters 7 to 9. They include the technology of production and labor supply. The labor supply depends on the population and its age and skill distribution, as well as the participation rate. The determinants of the aggregate demand for commodities were specified in Chapter 5. They include the central bank's target interest rate, money supply and fiscal deficits, as well as net exports in the open economy. Therefore, the AD-AS model implies that there are many determinants of the actual rate of unemployment.

Further, as shown in Chapter 8, under uncertainty, the SRAS curve based on the Friedman and Lucas supply rules implies that output rises when there is an *unexpected* increase in the price level. Therefore, in the short run, as the price level unexpectedly rises, unemployment falls. Furthermore, as shown in Chapter 9, the dynamic disequilibrium analysis implies that as aggregate demand increases, output and the price level rise while unemployment falls. Hence, the AD-AS analysis implies that

$$u = f(P), \quad \partial u / \partial P < 0,$$

where P is the price level. In the usual dynamic context of real-world economies, we replace the price level by the inflation rate and write the relationship as

$$u = f(\pi), \quad \partial u / \partial \pi < 0,$$

where u is the actual unemployment rate and π is the inflation rate. This relationship asserts that the unemployment rate falls as the inflation rate increases. This negative relationship between the actual unemployment rate and the rate of inflation for a given country is shown by plotting its unemployment rate on the horizontal axis and its inflation rate on the vertical one. The resultant curve is called the Phillips curve shown in Figure 10.3b.

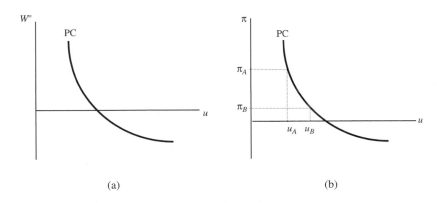

Figure 10.3

10.10 Phillips Curve (PC)

In 1958, A.W. Phillips plotted the rate of change of nominal wages against the rate of unemployment for the U.K. over several periods from 1861 to 1957, and found that the data showed a downward sloping curve. His original plotted relationship was of the form

$$W'' = f(u), \quad \partial W''/\partial u < 0, \tag{4}$$

where W'' is the rate of increase of the nominal wage rate, u is the actual rate of unemployment, and $\partial W''/\partial u < 0$ indicates that the rate of increase of nominal wages falls as unemployment rises. This occurs because a higher unemployment rate weakens workers' bargaining power relative to that of firms. Therefore, the unemployment–wage relationship is of the form shown in Figure 10.3a, which has the rate of change in nominal wages W'' on the vertical axis and the actual rate of unemployment u on the horizontal one. The estimated forms of this curve proved to be convex to the origin, i.e., decreases in unemployment cause successively greater increases in nominal wages.[19] This relationship soon evolved into its inverse — that is, $u = f(W'')$ — and then into a relationship of the form

$$u = g(\pi) \tag{5}$$

where π is the rate of inflation and $\partial u/\partial \pi < 0$. This equation is called the Phillips curve (PC) equation and is drawn as the curve PC in Figure 10.3b, with the rate of inflation π on the vertical axis. The PC states that increases in the inflation rate reduce the unemployment rate. Its convex shape indicates that at higher inflation rates, further increases in inflation produce smaller decreases in unemployment.

The transition between the above two equations comes from the link between the nominal wage rate and inflation: nominal wages represent the main element of the cost of production so that an increase in nominal wages will induce firms to increase their prices; alternatively, an increase in prices causes labor to ask for compensation in the form of wage increases. Hence, there is a positive relationship between W'' and π, and a negative one between these variables and unemployment.

In the 1950s and 1960s, numerous studies for many countries, including Canada, Britain, and the USA seemed to confirm the validity of the PC. Even though the relationship seemed to shift between periods and countries, the general form of the relationship seemed to be valid for the 1950s and 1960s. During the late 1950s and the 1960s, many economists came to embrace this curve, incorporating it in their macroeconomic

---

[19]Both the average level and the distribution of unemployment among industries together determine the Phillips curve relationship.

modeling in preference to a structural specification (labor demand and supply functions and equilibrium) of the labor market.

10.10.1 Use of the Phillips curve as a policy trade-off

Assume that the PC has been constructed for a country A and that it is known to be stable, especially with respect to changes in the inflation rate and the unemployment rate. The PC shows that lower unemployment — a desirable objective — can only be obtained at the cost of higher inflation — an undesirable side-effect. The central bank of the country can then use its PC to choose the levels of inflation and unemployment that it considers more desirable. Suppose that country A has the PC curve shown in Figure 10.3b and that it chooses the combination (u_A, π_A). It then adjusts the target interest rate and the money supply to ensure the inflation rate π_A, and the economy delivers the unemployment rate u_A. Using the PC for making this policy choice means that it is being used as a *policy trade-off* curve between inflation and unemployment.

Different countries or policy makers may make different choices along a given PC. For example, if country B has the same PC as in Figure 10.3b, its central bank could choose the combination (u_B, π_B). Comparing B's choice with that of country A, country B's choice indicates a relatively greater dislike (disutility) for inflation than for unemployment. In reality, different countries would most likely have different Phillips curves. Therefore, the actual levels of inflation and unemployment in each country would differ for two reasons: different u–π trade-offs as embodied in the PC and different choices made by the policy makers.

In the 1960s and early 1970s, the monetary and fiscal authorities of many countries assumed that the Phillips curve was stable and used it as a policy trade-off between inflation and unemployment. Using this curve as a policy trade-off, the policy makers tried to manipulate aggregate demand to achieve the desired inflation rate and its concomitant desired unemployment rate. In pursuing this agenda, the authorities wanted to achieve better levels of output and employment than the economy would have generated if left on its own. They seemed to be successful for some years in lowering the unemployment rate. However, continued success in this endeavour required that the PC be stable with respect to changes in the inflation rate. Around the mid-1970s, it became clear that this was not the case and that the PC shifts up as inflation accelerates.

10.10.2 Instability of the Phillips' curve

Subsequent analysis showed that the PC is not stable if inflation increases, so that the use of the PC for policy choices had severe pitfalls. The fundamental flaw of the PC is that both its shape and position depend on the expected inflation rate π^e, which in turn depends on the actual inflation rate π. It is this impact of π on π^e which shifts the PC and renders it unstable. Therefore, a decision of the policy makers to raise the inflation rate so as to get lower unemployment would sooner or later increase the expected inflation rate and shift the PC to the right. The instability of the PC for this reason is brought out in the Friedman and Lucas supply rules and their implied versions of the expectations augmented Phillips curve.

10.11 Deviations of the SR Equilibrium Unemployment Rate from the Natural One

These deviations can occur because of errors in expectations or adjustment costs. The impact of the errors in expectations on output and unemployment can occur through the labor market or the commodity market. Milton Friedman focused on the former and Robert Lucas on the latter, as explained in Chapter 8.

Fact Sheet 10.6: Historical Phillips Curves in the United States, 1960–1995

This Fact Sheet uses US data to illustrate the Phillips curve and its shifts. Note that the Phillips curve shifts with the expected inflation rate, which shifts with the actual one.

In the following graph, at least three periods can be easily identified as portraying a negative relationship between inflation and unemployment, characteristic of a downward sloping Phillips curve. The first period, spanning the 1960s, occurred in relatively low and stable inflationary environment. As expectations began to adjust to the higher inflation rate in the 1970s, the Phillips curve shifted. The expansionary monetary policies of the 1970s resulted not in lower unemployment but the stagflation of the mid- to late-1970s. Although a Philips curve can also be seen from 1976 to 1981 and from 1985 to 1991, it is obvious these are only short-term patterns. Looking over the whole period of the graph with numerous changes in the actual and expected inflation rates, there is no clear evidence of a downward sloping Phillips curve.

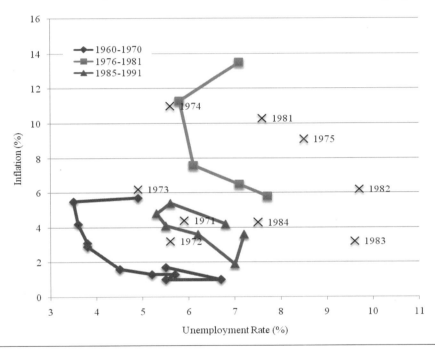

10.11.1 Friedman and the expectations augmented Phillips curve[20] (EAPC)

The Friedman supply rule, presented in Chapter 8, argued that if the inflation rate were perfectly *anticipated*, the labor contracts would reflect it so that the nominal wage would increase by the expected rate of inflation. Consequently, the expected rate of inflation would not affect the real wage rate, so that it will not affect employment or output. Hence, at the expected rate of inflation, the rate of unemployment would be the natural rate. However, the *unanticipated* rate of inflation[21] was not incorporated into the nominal wage set in wage contracts, since the contracts were negotiated in advance of the knowledge of the unanticipated inflation rate. Positive unexpected inflation, that is (i.e., $(\pi - \pi^e > 0)$), lowers the real wage. Since this reduces labor

---

[20]The formal derivation of this curve was presented in Chapter 8 which discusses expectations and wage contracts.

[21]This equals $(\pi - \pi^e)$.

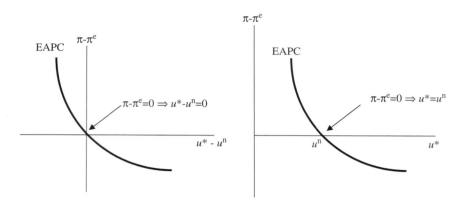

Figure 10.4

costs, employment and output rise while unemployment falls. Conversely, negative unexpected inflation (i.e., $(\pi - \pi^e < 0)$), raises the real wage, and causes a short-run increase in unemployment. This analysis deals with short-run deviations of unemployment from the long-run one. Therefore, only unexpected inflation can cause deviations in the short-run unemployment rate u^* from the natural rate u^n, so that, according to the FSR and LSR, the correct equation for the unemployment rate is

$$u^* - u^n = f(\pi - \pi^e), \quad \partial u^* / \partial (\pi - \pi^e) < 0, \quad f(0) = 0. \tag{6}$$

This equation asserts that the proper relationship between u^* and π is not the PC but between the deviation of unemployment from its natural rate and the unanticipated inflation rate.[22] This relationship is known as the expectations augmented Phillips curve (EAPC). The EAPC can be drawn in two different ways, as shown alternatively by the curves marked EAPC in Figure 10.4a and b. Note that the horizontal axis of Figure 10.4a has $(u^* - u^n)$, while that of Figure 10.4b has only u^*. The vertical axis of both figures measures unanticipated inflation $(\pi - \pi^e)$.

The EAPC in Figure 10.4b differs from the PC in two ways:

(i) The horizontal axis for the PC diagrams has the actual unemployment rate u while the EAPC in Figure 10.4b has the short-run equilibrium rate u^* on this axis.
(ii) The vertical axis for the EAPC figures is $(\pi - \pi^e)$, while that for the PC is π.

Empirical research and the widespread experience of stagflation in the mid- and late-1970s in the industrialized economies seemed to show that the PC was unstable in a period of accelerating inflation. Further, the EAPC seemed to perform much better in such periods, especially at high and accelerating rates of inflation. Many economists after the 1970s preferred dropping the PC/EAPC curve from their models, and replacing it by full labor market specification (i.e., with labor demand and supply equations and an equilibrium condition).

Similar to the arguments for going from the FSR for output to the EAPC, the Lucas supply rule (LSR) for output also implies that:

$$u^* - u^n = f(\pi - \pi^e), \quad \partial f / \partial (\pi - \pi^e) < 0, \quad f(0) = 0, \tag{7}$$

which has the same generic form as Friedman's version of the EAPC.

---

[22]To convert Friedman's relationship between n^* and P to that between u^* and π^*, $(u^* - u^n)$ is negatively related to $(n^* - n^f)$. Therefore, with $(n^* - n^f)$ positively related to $(P - P^e)$, $(u^* - u^n)$ is negatively related to $(P - P^e)$. In a dynamic context, $(P - P^e)$ is replaced by $(\pi - \pi^e)$, so that $(u^* - u^n)$ becomes negatively related to $(\pi - \pi^e)$, thereby giving the EAPC relationship.

We, therefore, have two types of EAPC relationships. One of these is Friedman's version which is based on errors in expectations in labor market and contractual nominal wage rigidities during the duration of the labor contract. The other is based on the Lucas supply rule which is based on errors in the expectations of relative prices in commodity markets. We will call the latter as the Lucas version of the EAPC. In both versions of the EAPC, the decrease in unemployment is a consequence of the unanticipated increase in inflation. Hence, the increase in aggregate demand does not reduce unemployment unless it first causes an unanticipated increase in the inflation rate.

10.11.2 Expectational equilibrium and the natural rate

Define expectational equilibrium as one when there are no errors in expectations — which is an assumption of the long-run equilibrium. In this LR (error-free) equilibrium,

$$\pi^e = \pi. \tag{8}$$

Therefore, the EAPC implies that in the expectational equilibrium (i.e., with $P^e = P$):

$$n^{LR} = n^f, \tag{9}$$

$$u^{LR} = u^n, \tag{10}$$

which assert that, in expectational equilibrium, employment and the natural unemployment rate are the full-employment ones and are independent of the inflation rate or the price level. Deviations from these occur because of expectational errors, with positive errors [i.e., $(\pi - \pi^e) > 0$] causing an increase in employment and a decline in the unemployment rate. Conversely, negative errors [i.e., $(\pi - \pi^e) < 0$] cause a decrease in employment and an increase in the unemployment rate.

Extended Analysis Box 10.2: The Friedman and Lucas Supply Rules

Chapter 8 presented the Friedman supply rule (FSR) based the price expectations incorporated in wage contracts. It had also presented the associated concept of Friedman's expectations augmented employment function. The FSR is:

$$y^* = y^f + \beta(P - P^e), \quad \beta > 0, \tag{11}$$

where all the variables are in logs, y^* is the SR equilibrium output and y^f is the LR equilibrium output.
Correspondingly, the *expectations augmented employment function* was

$$n^* = n^f + \alpha(P - P^e), \quad \alpha > 0, \tag{12}$$

where n^* is the SR employment and n^f is the LSR full-employment level. The diagrammatic analysis of these equations was given in Chapter 8.
Note that the relationship between the short-run equilibrium level of employment n^* and the short-run equilibrium unemployment rate u^* is:

$$u^* = (L - n^*)/L = 1 - n^*/L,$$

where L is the labor force. Hence, equation (12) can be converted from employment to unemployment and implies that

$$u^* = u^n + f(P - P^e) \quad \partial u^*/(P - P^e) < 0, \tag{13}$$

Extended Analysis Box 10.2 (*Continued*)

where f is a functional symbol. In a dynamic context, $(P - P^e)$ is replaced by $(\pi - \pi^e)$, so that we have

$$u^* - u^n = f(\pi - \pi^e), \quad \partial f/\partial(\pi - \pi^e) < 0, \quad f(0) = 0. \tag{14}$$

Note that several assumptions were needed for deriving Friedman's EAPC. Among these were:

a. EAPC assumes market clearance in the labor market at the wage contract stage. At the production stage, labor willingly supplies the amount of labor demanded by firms. Further, commodity markets clear. Hence, *the EAPC does not allow for disequilibrium in the labor market* — in which some workers may want jobs at the existing wage but cannot get them or firms want workers at this wage but cannot get enough — or in the commodity market — in which firms cannot sell all that they want to produce.

b. Friedman's EAPC captures the impact of one type of errors in expectations: that is, those embedded in wage contracts. The Lucas supply rule captured the impact of expectational errors in commodity markets and leads, as shown below, to a similar EAPC.

Expectational errors and the commodity markets: The Lucas supply rule

The Lucas supply rule presented in Chapter 8 considered the impact of errors in forecasting changes in relative prices versus those in the price level. We can modify this analysis to forecasting errors in the rates of increase in relative prices versus those in the general rate of inflation. The LSR then implies that the deviations of output from the full-employment rate are positively related to the unanticipated inflation rate. Since changes in output and employment are positively related, changes in the unemployment rate and output are negatively related (i.e., $\partial u/\partial y < 0$), so that an increase in unanticipated inflation $(\pi - \pi^e)$ reduces unemployment. Hence, similar to the arguments for going from the FSR to the EAPC, the Lucas supply rule implies that

$$u^* - u^n = f(\pi - \pi^e), \quad \partial f/\partial(\pi - \pi^e) < 0, \quad f(0) = 0. \tag{15}$$

This equation has the same generic form as Friedman's version of the EAPC.

10.12 The Implications of the EAPC for Shifts in the Phillips Curve and for Policy

The EAPC implies that there is a distinct Phillips curve for each expected rate of inflation: the higher the expected inflation rate, the higher the Phillips curve. Figure 10.5a shows three Phillips curves and the long-run PC (i.e., for which $P^e = P$) as PC^{LR}.[23] PC_0 is the PC for $\pi^e = 0$. It cuts the PC^{LR} at $\pi = 0$ and the (natural rate) of unemployment u_0. If the expected inflation rate rises to 5% $(= 0.05)$, the Phillips curve shifts to PC1 which cuts the PC^{LR} at $\pi^e = \pi = 0.05$. But if the expected inflation rate accelerates to 10% $(= 0.10)$, the Phillips curve shifts to PC2 which cuts the PC^{LR} at $\pi^e = \pi = 0.10$.

Therefore, the PC is not stable if the monetary authority changes the rate of inflation which induces the public to change its expected rate of inflation. However, it will be stable if the expected inflation rate does not change. Therefore, the PC does not shift during the period of unanticipated inflation but does shift once its occurrence has been realized.

---

[23] In the long run, both the PC and the EAPC are identical — and vertical at u^n — since there are no price misperceptions, adjustment costs, or disequilibrium.

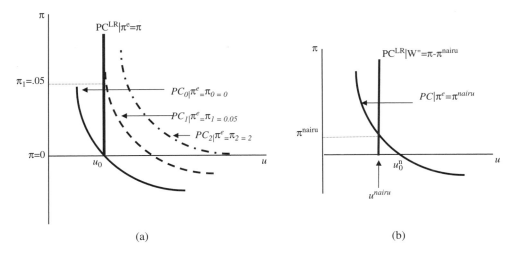

Figure 10.5

The relationship between the Phillips' curve and the EAPC

The dependent variable of the Phillips curve is u. We can express u as

$$u \equiv u^n + (u^* - u^n) + (u - u^*),$$

where u^* is the short-run equilibrium unemployment rate specified by the FSR and the LSR. These rules assert the EAPC, which is the statement that

$$u^* - u^n = f(\pi - \pi^e).$$

Further, $(u - u^*)$ is involuntary unemployment u^{inv}. Therefore,

$$u \equiv u^n + f(\pi^* - \pi^e) + u^{inv}.$$

If we were to draw the relationship between u and π in a PC type diagram, the curve would shift with shifts in u^n and π^e. The above equation is the proper statement of the PC, with the EAPC being only one part of the PC. *As a corollary, the EAPC is not an accurate explanation of fluctuations in u*, unless it could be validly shown that the economy in question never has u^{inv}.

Since u^{inv} varies over the business cycle, the impact of u^{inv} occurs over the business cycle between recessions and booms. Involuntary unemployment u^{inv} is positive in deficient-demand recessions. An expansion of aggregate demand is likely to impact on both output and prices,[24] with the impact depending on the extent of the demand deficiency: with a large demand deficiency and high u^{inv} and excess capital capacity, the impact is likely to be much greater on output than on prices, as in a deep trough, while, as the economy nears full employment, the impact is likely to be much greater on prices than on output. This coincidental effect of changes in aggregate demand on both u, through u^{inv}, and π creates a negative statistical relationship between u and π. This relationship is likely to be non-linear and convex.

Note that another part of the relationship between u and π occurs through the EAPC component of the above equation. This part varies with positively with $(\pi - \pi^e)$, as demonstrated by the FSR and the LSR.

---

[24]This impact occurs because profit-maximizing competitive firms operate along their marginal cost curves, which are upward sloping.

10.13 The EAPC and the Non-Accelerating Inflation Rate of Unemployment

The EAPC implies that if $\pi^e = \pi$, the economy will be at the natural rate of unemployment. Further, it implies that only PC is stable if $\pi^e = \pi$. If $\pi > \pi^e$, the PC curve would shift up as expectations adjust to the actual inflation rate. It would shift down if $\pi < \pi^e$.

However, in real-world economies, there is almost continuous improvement of products and the creation of new ones, so that the public might regard a small amount of inflation (say π^{nairu}) as a reflection of such improvements. In this case, workers would ask for compensation only for $(\pi - \pi^{nairu})$ but not for the full inflation rate. Therefore, the presence of inflation less than or equal to π^{nairu} will not produce nominal wage increases or further inflation,[25] so that the unemployment rate corresponding to π^{nairu} will not generate inflation and is called *NAIRU* — translated as the *non-accelerating inflation rate of unemployment*. Given that $\pi^{nairu} > 0$, the NAIRU-modified PC^{LR} will cut the PC at π^{nairu} and not at $\pi = 0$, as is shown in Figure 10.5b. The EAPC with this modification is

$$u^* - u^n = f[(\pi - \pi^{nairu}) - \pi^e].$$

From the policy perspective, NAIRU implies that the central bank can create or allow inflation equal to π^{nairu} without causing a shift of the Phillips curve. It can thereby lower unemployment on a long-term basis to u^{nairu}, which is less than the natural rate, as shown in Figure 10.5b.

10.14 The Implications of the EAPC for the Impact of Anticipated and Unanticipated Demand Increases

Assume that the economy is initially in full employment and that aggregate demand increases in an *anticipated* manner. This increase could be due to an increase in investment or expansionary monetary and fiscal policies. Since it has been assumed that this increase is to be anticipated by the public, we will also assume that its impact on the rate of inflation is also anticipated. Therefore, the increase in demand will not produce any errors in the expected inflation rate, so that, according to the EAPC, the economy will maintain the natural rate of unemployment. Hence, anticipated changes in inflation make the economy move along PC^{LR}: the demand increase will not bring about a decrease in unemployment, but merely cause a proportionate price increase.

In the case of *unanticipated* demand increases, the public would not be able to anticipate their impact on the inflation rate, so that the unemployment rate will fall. Under the Friedman version of the EAPC, this would be due to the negotiated nominal wage being too low, so that the real wage will fall and make labor cheaper. Under the Lucas version of the EAPC, the increase in output will occur because some of the inflation will be attributed by individual firms to an increase in their relative price, which will induce the firms to increase their employment, thereby decreasing unemployment. Hence, *unanticipated changes in inflation make the economy move along PC^{SR}*.

10.15 The Determinants of Inflation

As illustrated by the following Fact Sheet 10.7, inflation rates vary considerably over time for a given country and across countries. Inflation rates in very high double or triple digits are called hyperinflation.

---

[25] In general, this non-accelerating inflation rate is taken to be 2% or less.

Fact Sheet 10.7:

European and North American countries generally keep their inflation rates within single digits. With this objective, when inflation rates reached low double digits in the late 1980s, the central banks of countries such as UK, Canada, New Zealand and many others pursued contractionary monetary policies to bring inflation back to low single digits. In the 1990s, many adopt inflation targeting, with inflation targets as low as 2% or 3% on average.

Developing countries often have higher inflation rates than developed ones. Several South American countries experience hyperinflation during the 1970s and 1980s, as did Israel in 1980. Currently, Zimbabwe has hyperinflation, with the inflation rate becoming over 24,000% in 2007. It increased further in 2008 and 2009.

	1985	1990	1995	2000	2005	2006	2007	2008
North America								
Canada	4.0	4.8	2.2	2.7	2.2	2.0	2.1	2.4
Mexico	57.7	26.7	35	9.5	4	3.6	4	5.1
United States	3.6	5.4	2.8	3.4	3.4	3.2	2.9	3.8
South America								
Argentina	672.2	2314	3.4	−0.9	9.6	10.9	8.8	8.6
Bolivia	11,749.6	17.1	10.2	4.6	5.4	4.3	8.7	14
Brazil	226	2947.7	66	7	6.9	4.2	3.6	9.8
Nicaragua	—	—	—	7.1	9.6	9.1	11.1	19.8
Peru	163.4	7481.7	11.1	3.8	1.6	2	1.8	6.6
Asia								
China	—	3.1	16.9	0.3	1.8	1.5	4.8	5.9
India	5.6	9	10.2	4	4.2	5.8	6.4	8.4
Malaysia	0.3	2.6	3.5	1.5	3	3.6	2	5.4
Thailand	2.4	5.9	5.8	1.6	4.5	4.6	2.2	5.5
Other								
Czech Republic	—	—	9.5	3.9	1.8	2.5	2.9	6.4
Israel	304.6	17.2	10	1.1	1.3	2.1	0.5	4.6
Russia	—	197.5	20.8	12.7	9.7	9	14.1	
Ukraine	—	—	376.7	28.2	13.5	9.1	12.8	25.2
Zimbabwe	8.5	17.4	22.6	55.9	302.1	1096.7	24411	—

The AD-AS analyses of Chapters 5 to 9 provide the determinants of inflation. Basically, these are:

(i) Demand factors
(ii) Supply factors
(iii) Equilibrium versus disequilibrium in the commodity market

The AD-AS analysis showed that increases in aggregate demand cause inflation, while decreases in aggregate demand moderate inflation. Decreases in aggregate supply cause inflation, while increases in aggregate supply moderate inflation. Further, past inflation affects expectations of the current inflation rate. The AD-AS model implies that:

$$\pi = f(\text{change in AD, change in AS, a measure of disequilibrium, past inflation rates}).$$

The determinants of AD can be spelled out by several different proxies. Among these are the target interest rate, the money supply, and fiscal deficits, and, in the open economy, the level of net exports.

The determinants of AS can also be spelled out by several different proxies. Among these are the average unit cost of the production of commodities — which captures the improvements in productivity, changes in wage rates, and changes in the cost of resources, especially oil and other energy sources. Another determinant of AS in the open economy is the domestic price of imported goods, which depends on changes in exchange rates. Note that the shifts in aggregate supply will capture the shifts in the natural rate of unemployment.

Deviations of the unemployment rate from the natural one can be used as a proxy for the extent of disequilibrium (AD-AS) in the economy.

The economy usually shows *inertia* and *persistence* in the rate of inflation, which is partly due to the dependence of expected inflation on past inflation and partly due to the costs of adjusting prices rapidly. Therefore, past rates of inflation are an additional element in explaining the current inflation rate. This inertia means that inflation tends to lag behind the growth of aggregate demand, including that of the money supply. Over the business cycle, although inflation is procyclical, it picks up relatively slowly at the start of upturns and falls relatively slowly as the economy turns into a downturn.

Another way of stating the determinants of inflation

The types of inflation are sometimes classified as:

(1) '*Demand pull*' inflation, caused by increases in aggregate demand;
(2) '*Cost push*' inflation, caused by decreases in aggregate supply. Among the factors often listed in the cost push category is the demand by workers, especially by unions, for higher wages, with firms unable or unwilling to resist these demands. This pressure increases nominal wage rates, which increase firms' costs of production, so that firms react by raising their prices, thus resulting in inflation. Cost push inflation can also occur due to increases in the prices of inputs other than labor. For example, increases in oil and gas prices increase the cost of production and cause firms to raise their prices.

10.16 The Costs of Inflation

The costs of inflation depend upon whether it is anticipated or not, and upon the relative economic and political power of the different economic agents.

10.16.1 Inflation under perfect competition with fully anticipated inflation for all future periods: the costs of inflation in the analytical long-run case

Define *fully anticipated inflation* as one which is anticipated by *all* economic agents on both sides of all 'bargains' (formal and informal contracts) in the economy over *all relevant future* periods — a rather tall assumption. Further, assume that:

(i) All markets are in perfect competition and are fully efficient, i.e., adjust the prices immediately to equilibrium after any shock to demand and supply functions.
(ii) No (private or public) agent has special power to take advantage of the inflationary situation.
(iii) There are no costs of adjustment or 'inflexibilities' of any type which prevent instantaneous adjustments in prices or quantities.

Under these assumptions, rational agents taking part in any negotiations or decisions would agree to increase the relevant nominal variables proportionately with the inflation rate. Therefore, all prices, nominal wages, and interest rates — as well as the nominal values of other variables such as mortgages, pensions, minimum wages set by the government, etc. — would increase proportionately (and immediately) with the inflation rate. Consequently, the economy will operate at its long-run level, and employment and output would remain at their full-employment levels. There would be no losers or gainers from such inflation, so that its costs and benefits would not be significant. One could, therefore, ignore such inflation as inconsequential from a purely economic viewpoint.

From the perspective of realism, there are several objections to the realism of the assumptions made in arriving at the above result. Among these are:

(i) In the modern economy with explicit or implicit long-term contracts — for example, on employment, loans/bonds, pensions, etc. — fully anticipated inflation would require accurate anticipations over several decades. This does not occur in real time.
(ii) The economy always has some deviations from perfect competition and efficient markets.
(iii) Economic and political power is always unevenly distributed among economic agents, of which the government is the most powerful one. For example, the government exercises a preponderant power, e.g., in the payments made out for various types of social benefits, and in setting tax rates and tax brackets, etc. It often does not adjust these fully to the anticipated inflation rate, or even *ex post* to the actual inflation rate. Firms — especially if they are large and/or multinationals — also often tend to have greater clout than workers — especially if the latter are not unionized — so that nominal wages often do not increase instantly and proportionately with the inflation rate, with the result that real wages fall, usually when inflation accelerates.
(iv) There are always some adjustment costs or inflexibilities in the economy, so that even fully anticipated inflation imposes some economic costs. For example, interest is not paid on currency and some other components of money, so that the purchasing power of such holdings decreases by the inflation rate and their holders lose. As another example, firms have to post prices in price lists, which can only be changed at some cost, labeled in Chapter 8 as 'menu costs'.
(v) Further, even under the very restrictive and rather unrealistic assumptions made for the long run, fully anticipated inflation always imposes some non-economic costs, including psychological, social, and political ones. For example, the continuous confrontation with the ever-rising prices of products imposes a psychological cost/shock on consumers and a 're-calculation cost' when confronted with higher prices at the point of purchase (e.g., in a supermarket). Furthermore, practical experience indicates that very high inflation rates, even if they are anticipated, tend to result in strikes, demonstrations, and public dissatisfaction and increasing conflict among social classes, etc., thereby tearing at the economic, social, and political fabric of the country.

In any case, fully anticipated inflation over all future periods never occurs in real-time economies. The following makes a more limited assumption on the extent to which inflation is anticipated.

An intermediate scenario: anticipated inflation in the commodity and labor markets for some quarters ahead

A more realistic set of assumptions than made for the long run is that the inflation rate is anticipated for the next few periods (a few quarters) only. Also assume that this degree of anticipated inflation is all that is needed for economic decisions in the commodity and labor markets. These include those on labor supply and demand, on the duration of labor contracts and the production decisions of firms. Further, assume that there is perfect competition in these markets and they are fully efficient. Under these assumptions, the FSR and the LSR showed that such anticipated inflation will not produce short-run deviations from full employment or change the real wage.

Further, according to the Fisher equation on interest rates, since the inflation rate is anticipated for the next few periods, the *short-term* market interest rates will rise by the rate of inflation, so that the *short-term* real rates of interest will not be affected.

However, there are several costs of such limited anticipations of future inflation. These include:

(i) Longer-term expectations may still prove to be erroneous, so that long-term contracts would be based on incorrect expectations. Consequently, long-term bond holders may gain or lose, as may pensioners, and others locked into numerous long-term arrangements. In general, such limited anticipations would cause changes in the wealth distribution.

(ii) In addition, markets are not perfect and economic power is not evenly balanced in the economy. Administratively set payments, e.g., in social programs run by the government, may not be — and usually are not — fully adjusted even to the current (known) inflation rate, let alone to next period's anticipated rate. Further, the salaries of government and para-government employees may not adjust fully to inflation plus average productivity growth in the economy. Any adjustments that occur depend on political factors.

(iii) Under a progressive income tax system, the '*bracket creep*' of nominal incomes caused by inflation puts some tax payers into higher tax brackets — unless these are themselves indexed to the inflation rate — and increases tax payments in real terms. It correspondingly reduces the real disposable income of the public.

(iv) Since interest is not paid on currency and some other components of M1, holders of these lose by the decrease in their purchasing power.

10.16.2 The costs of unanticipated inflation

Unanticipated inflation imposes costs and benefits additional to those of anticipated inflation. These are:

• If we start with full employment in the economy with the expected inflation rate equal to the actual one, an unanticipated inflation produces a decrease in the real wage rate but a short-run increase in employment and output along the SRAS curve. However, once the inflation rate becomes anticipated, this gain disappears. Further, if the authorities subsequently decide to lower the inflation rate and the public does not immediately lower its expectations correspondingly, employment and output would fall below the full-employment one. Hence, the initial gain in employment and output from rising inflation has to be compared with a subsequent loss in them when inflation is reduced.

• Asset prices, such as of equities, bonds, and houses, do not adjust proportionately to the change in commodity prices, so that their owners either lose or gain in real terms.

• As inflation accelerates, real wages fall for the duration of nominal wage contracts, so that workers lose.

• Nominal interest rates do not incorporate the unanticipated inflation rate, so that lenders lose and borrowers gain.

- Recipients of all kinds of fixed incomes, including pensions, social benefits, etc., lose in the process.
- The tax brackets and collections of the government cannot be adjusted to neutralize the effects of unanticipated inflation on nominal incomes.
- Since interest is not paid on currency and some other components of M1, holders of these lose by the decrease in their purchasing power during unanticipated inflation.
- Once the past inflation rate is realized, various types of adjustment costs, including the menu costs of changing price lists, have to be incurred.

A caveat

The assumption that the average inflation rate is anticipated hides the following economic aspects usually experienced in the real world:

Inflation, irrespective of whether its average level is anticipated or not, never occurs in the form of a simultaneous proportionate increase in all prices. Some commodity prices increase earlier than others, and the wages of some workers increase faster than those of others. This imposes all kinds of adjustments on the economy, and some economic agents gain while others lose.

Actual experience also indicates that inflation is never fully anticipated over the next few years, even by what are supposed to be the most knowledgeable economic agents in this respect. Even central banks and financial institutions often make mistakes, sometimes with severe losses.

Inflation does not occur evenly over time. This increases uncertainty about the pattern of future inflation rates. This has many consequences. We illustrate two of these. For firms, uncertainty about the pattern of future inflation rates increases the uncertainty of the future profitability of investments and affects their investment plans. Lenders with an aversion to the risk inherent in uncertain rates of inflation increase the required risk premium in making loans, which increases the real interest rates.

Box 10.3: The Impact of Hyperinflation on Long-Term Output Growth and the Standard of Living: Practical Experience in Contrast to Theory

Economic theory implies that anticipated inflation does not affect the real variables. Further, under rational expectations, any unanticipated future inflation is random and the effects of any unanticipated inflation are eliminated as time passes and it becomes anticipated. Therefore, the theoretical prediction is that increases in inflation rates would not do much damage to the economy in terms of reducing the growth rates of output, output per capita, or have a long-term impact on unemployment rates. Many empirical studies confirm this finding.

However, studies of the economic history of hyperinflationary economies and their development seem to indicate that such economies usually do much more poorly than low inflation economies over long numbers of years. Comparison of this experience with the theoretical implications seems to imply that economic theory does not encompass all the effects of hyperinflation. Among the possible effects which are ignored can be following.

(i) Hyperinflation increases uncertainty about the future returns to physical and human investment, and destroys consumer and business confidence in the future economic performance of the economy. Investment in both physical and human capital decreases.

(ii) Invention and innovation suffer.

(iii) The increased conflict among the social classes, and between firms and workers, is detrimental to economic performance.

10.17 The Sacrifice Ratio

Both unemployment and inflation impose costs on the economy. We can use their sum (or weighted sum, with the weights chosen by society or the policy makers) to provide an index of the sacrifice by the population over time. This index is called the *sacrifice rate* or ratio, and has been used in some studies to provide a rough measure of the failure of the economy to perform relative to a full-employment, zero-inflation state.

Fact Sheet 10.8: Sacrifice Ratio in the United States, 1950–2008

This Fact Sheet illustrates movements in the sacrifice ratio (defined as the sum of the inflation rate and the unemployment rate) by looking at that for the USA. While one could argue that its constancy over time would be desirable as a social objective, in reality, the sacrifice ratio has varied dramatically over the past 60 years. The relatively high sacrifice ratio in the 1970s and the early 1980s was a result of stagflation, when the central banks pursued expansionary monetary policies in an attempt to offset the decline in GDP growth and the consequent rise in unemployment due to increases in oil price increases during that period. They failed to do so but instead resulted in higher inflation rates.

   Note that the Phillips curve, even if it was stable, does not imply the constancy of the sacrifice ratio.

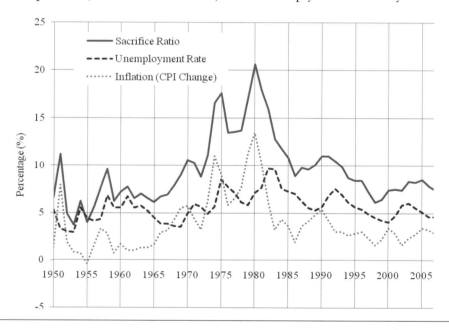

10.17.1 Gradualist versus Cold Turkey Policies of Disinflation

After a period of high and rising inflation rates, central banks often try to reduce the inflation rate. However, the expected inflation rates do not fall as fast. The Friedman and Lucas supply rules imply that disinflation in a period in which expected inflation rates become above the actual ones causes output to fall and unemployment to rise. Given this cost, central banks could follow either a 'cold turkey' or a 'gradualist' policy of disinflation. Under a cold turkey policy, the central bank pursues a contractionary monetary policy — increase in the target interest rate, supported by a decrease in the money supply — strong enough to *immediately* lower the inflation rate to its desired level, even though this causes a considerable gap between actual and expected inflation rates and large losses of output. Under a gradualist policy, the central bank pursues more moderate contractionary policies but over a longer period of time so as to decrease the actual inflation rate gradually to the desired one. This pattern allows the expected inflation to drift along with the actual inflation to lower levels. The gap between the two remains more limited and so do the losses in output from disinflation.

However, expectations tend to adjust faster after the jolt of the cold turkey policy, so that the recessionary period with output below its full-employment level is shorter than under a gradualist policy. Therefore, the cold turkey policy involves a bigger loss of output but over a shorter period while a gradualist policy involves a smaller loss of output but over a longer period. These two extreme patterns provide the central bank a choice of the disinflation pattern that it would want to follow. The preferred policy is likely to depend on the extent of the output losses involved, the rapidity of adjustment of expectations, the central bank's preferences, and the reaction of the public to rising unemployment.

10.17.2 Indexation to the rate of inflation: should nominal wages and interest rates be indexed?

Indexing nominal wages to the price level, which is a proxy for the cost of living, prevents inflation from reducing real wages in an unanticipated manner (see Chapter 8). Therefore, some economists favor such indexation and support the idea of a cost-of-living clause (i.e., one which adjusts nominal wages by the change in the price level) in nominal-wage contracts. Similarly, indexation of the nominal interest rate to the rate of inflation ensures that the real interest rate does not change because of inflation. A similar argument applies to pensions, unemployment insurance benefits, minimum wages, and other forms of payment. However, such indexation raises several questions, some of which are:

- Should indexation be privately determined in contracts (e.g., in wage contracts negotiated by firms and unions), or should it be legally imposed?
- Should governments also be bound to index wages, welfare payments, pensions, tax brackets, etc.?
- Should government bonds set a real interest rate, so that their nominal coupon rate rises by the inflation rate?
- Should indexing be by the inflation rate or the inflation rate consistent with NAIRU?

Eliminating the costs and the pain imposed by inflation reduces the pressures to reduce it, so that inflation tends to continue much longer. Should indexing not be done so as to retain this motivation for its reduction?

If indexation is such a good thing, why does the central bank not avoid the needed continual adjustments of nominal wages, etc., by just maintaining stable prices?

These questions are deliberately not answered here but are raised in order to encourage their discussion.

10.18 Conclusions

- The actual unemployment rate has three components. Of these, the structural component of the natural unemployment rate u^n does not depend on aggregate demand, the price level, or the rate of inflation. However, errors in price expectations and adjustment costs can cause positive or negative values of the deviation of the SR equilibrium rate from the natural rate, i.e. $(u^* - u^n)$. This component of unemployment depends on the adjustment costs and errors in the expectations of the price level and the rate of inflation. Disequilibrium in the labor market can cause positive or negative values of the disequilibrium component $(u - u^*)$. This component of unemployment depends on the extent of the demand deficiency for commodities or a real wage higher than the full-employment one.
- The PC is a real-world, real-time relationship between the actual unemployment rate and the inflation rate in the economy. Changes in the actual unemployment rate include variations in the natural rate, changes in

the short-run deviations of the unemployment rate from the natural one, and changes in the disequilibrium level of unemployment.

- The EAPC only considers the short-run deviations of the unemployment rate from the natural one due to errors in price expectations. The disequilibrium level of unemployment is not encompassed in the EAPC. The EAPC is an analytical relationship focusing exclusively on the impact of errors in price expectations, while the PC curve also includes other economic forces not captured in the EAPC. However, the EAPC does validly show that the PC will shift with changes in the expected inflation rate and that the latter will depend upon changes in the actual inflation rate. Therefore, the PC cannot be taken to be stable. It cannot be used by policy makers as a durable trade-off between inflation and unemployment. The long-run PC is vertical under the definition of the long run since this definition excludes adjustment costs or disequilibrium.

- The EAPC cannot be used as a durable trade-off or guide for the central bank's choice of the inflation rate and its accompanying unemployment rate. Meaningful policy increases in demand and policy-induced inflation cannot be random but must be systematic, which, under the EAPC, cannot change the unemployment rate. Further, any systematic demand increases or inflation, disguised or misinterpreted as being random ones, will sooner or later lose their efficacy as their systematic nature becomes understood. Hence, according to the EAPC, the policy makers cannot rely upon systematic aggregate demand and inflation increases to reduce the unemployment rate. Correctly anticipated inflation policies — such as would be the case if they generated a constant or steadily increasing inflation rate — generate a vertical EAPC, thereby not providing a durable negative trade-off between unemployment and inflation. While such a trade-off might be observed for short runs of data due to temporary misinterpretations of the nature of inflation, a durable trade-off will not exist.

- On the impact of monetary and fiscal policies in changing the actual level of unemployment in the economy, such policies change aggregate demand which can change structural unemployment and frictional unemployment, if they lead the economy out of long-run equilibrium. However, their effect on involuntary unemployment is greater.[26]

- Empirical evidence has often rejected the stability of the Phillips curve during inflationary periods. This curve shifts up with an increase in the experienced rates of inflation, raising the presumption that this curve is vertical in the limit, thereby providing justification for the concept of the natural rate of unemployment. However, empirical evidence does not support the constancy of the natural rate of unemployment. Nor does it show the inability of expansionary monetary policies to reduce unemployment under demand deficient conditions.

- These arguments lead to two competing paradigms — i.e., broad approaches — to the study of unemployment and provide an introduction to a topic not addressed so far in this book. These paradigms are:

  1. *The classical paradigm* which focuses on fluctuations in the natural rate itself both over the business cycle and the long run, and uses the EAPC to explain the deviations of the actual rate of unemployment from the natural rate. It rules out demand deficiency as a significant source of the actual unemployment or changes in it. Involuntary unemployment due to a demand deficiency is not a component of the actual rate of unemployment in the classical paradigm.[27]

---

[26]Unanticipated policies may be able to change both $(u^* - u^n)$ and $(u - u^*)$ by causing unanticipated inflation. Anticipated policies can change $(u - u^*)$ if there was an existing demand deficiency or by causing a demand deficiency when the expected inflation rate does not adjust instantly.

[27]However, the classical paradigm does allow involuntary unemployment due to a wage higher than the equilibrium one brought about by administrative actions or market imperfections.

2. *The Keynesian paradigm*, which allows — but does not emphasize — changes in the natural rate, but focuses on the deviations of the actual rate of unemployment from the natural one due to the EAPC and also due to fluctuations in the demand for commodities and labor. According to the Keynesian paradigm, involuntary unemployment due to a demand deficiency is considered to be a common and significant component of the actual unemployment rate.

Therefore, the Keynesians argue that the authorities should keep a close watch on the economy. When there is significant involuntary unemployment due to a deficiency in aggregate demand, they should use monetary and/or fiscal policies to increase demand by an appropriate amount. If they succeed, the economy will eliminate such involuntary unemployment and perform at its equilibrium level, which is the state assumed by the classical paradigm. Chapter 11 discusses these paradigms in detail.

KEY CONCEPTS

Structural unemployment

Frictional unemployment

Natural rate of unemployment

Involuntary unemployment

Voluntary unemployment

Wage contracts

Hysteresis

The Phillips curve

Friedman's expectations augmented Phillips curve

Lucas' expectations augmented Phillips curve

Costs of unemployment

Costs of inflation

Benefits of inflation

SUMMARY OF CRITICAL CONCLUSIONS

- The Phillips curve plots the relationship between the actual rate of unemployment and the actual rate of inflation.
- The EAPC shows that unemployment deviates from the natural rate if there are errors in price expectations.
- Friedman's version of the EAPC is based on the errors in the price expectations — of households and firms — embodied in nominal wage contracts.
- Another version of the EAPC is implied by the Lucas supply rule for output. This is based on the errors made by firms in their expectations/perceptions of the prices of their commodities relative to the price level.
- Unanticipated inflation induced by unanticipated policies can bring about changes in the deviation of the equilibrium unemployment rate from its natural level.
- Both anticipated and unanticipated policies can bring about changes in the deviation of the actual rate of unemployment from its equilibrium level.
- Involuntary unemployment can be a significant component of the actual unemployment rate over the business cycle.
- Both anticipated and unanticipated inflation have costs and benefits. Unanticipated inflation causes greater changes in output, employment, the real interest rate, and the distribution of wealth.
- The major economic cost of unemployment is the loss of output that would have been produced if these workers had been employed. There may also be a long-term cost through the hysteresis effect.

REVIEW AND DISCUSSION QUESTIONS

1. Define the Phillips curve (PC). What is its justification?
2. What are the determinants of the natural rate of unemployment? Show how changes in their values would change the natural rate.
3. Define the Expectations Augmented Phillips curve (EAPC). What justification for it arises from Lucas' contributions?
4. What is the difference between rationally expected inflation and fully (i.e., accurately) anticipated inflation?
5. Is the EAPC under rational expectations vertical in the long run? Is the EAPC under rational expectations vertical in the short run?
6. Define involuntary unemployment. What is the justification for it? Is its existence likely in a recession?
7. What can the government (excluding the central bank) do to reduce structural unemployment?
8. What can the government (excluding the central bank) do to reduce frictional unemployment?
9. What can the government (excluding the central bank) do to reduce involuntary unemployment?
10. What does NAIRU mean? What is its justification? What does it imply for the position and use of the PC as a policy trade-off between unemployment and inflation?
11. What costs occur, and to whom, if nominal wages do not increase by the rate of inflation? Should nominal wages be indexed? Discuss.
12. What is a (a) cold-turkey policy, (b) gradualist policy, of reducing inflation rates through a restrictive monetary policy? What are the differences in their effects?
13. Why do governments rarely, if ever, index income tax brackets? What are the consequences of not doing so (a) for the government budget, (b) for the economy? What are the consequences of doing so?

ADVANCED AND TECHNICAL QUESTIONS

T1. Suppose that the data on the economy shows that:

Population	22
Civilian population between ages 18 and 65	20
Armed forces	0.5
Unemployed but stopped looking for work	0.2
Employed, civilians, full-time	12
Unemployed	0.8
Employed part-time	0.9

Define and derive:
 (i) The labor force.
 (ii) The labor force participation rate.
 (iii) The employment rate.
 (iv) The (measured) unemployment rate; the discouraged worker rate.
 (v) If the labor force and those employed both increase by 3%, recalculate your answers to the preceding questions.

(vi) Starting with the initial data, if the unemployed increase by 5%, what would become the new unemployment rate?

(vii) Because of the increase in unemployment in (f), some workers become discouraged. If the discouraged workers increase by 10%, what would become the labor force and the unemployment rate?

T2. [On involuntary unemployment due to deficient demand.] Suppose that the economy was initially at full employment with a wage rate w^*. Now assume that aggregate demand falls, so that output produced and its accompanying employment fall below the full-employment level, but the wage rate (w_2) rises to equal the MPL $(= MPL_2)$. Show diagrammatically the two ways of measuring 'involuntary unemployment' at the wage rate w_2 under the two definitions of this term? Explain why both of these can be considered to be appropriate alternative measures of involuntary unemployment.

T3. [On unemployment due to a high real wage.] Suppose that the economy was initially at full employment with a real wage rate w^*. Now assume that a shock to the real wage increases the wage rate to w^3, which is above w^*. Show diagrammatically the amount of involuntary unemployment at w^3? Can monetary policy reduce such involuntary unemployment?

T4. Suppose that the economy was initially at full employment with a real wage rate w^*. Now assume that a shock to the real wage increases the wage rate to w_3, which is above w^*. Show diagrammatically the levels of structural and frictional unemployment at w_3? How do they differ from those at full employment? Does the natural rate of unemployment change?

T5. Assume that the Phillips curve has the relationship:

$$u = 0.06 - 0.005\pi + 0.001(\pi_{Oil} - \pi),$$

where π_{Oil} is the rate of increase of oil prices. Draw the two PC curves (i) for $\pi_{Oil} = 0.02$ and (ii) for $\pi_{Oil} = 0.10$.

(a) What is the economy's trade-off $(\Delta u / \Delta \pi)$ between unemployment and inflation?

(b) Calculate (and show diagrammatically) the shift in the Phillips curve if oil's inflation rate increases to 1.2, so that $\pi_{Oil,1} = 1.20$.

(c) Explain why the change in oil's inflation rate shifts the Phillips curve?

T6. Suppose that the correct relationship is not the Phillips' curve but the expectations augmented Phillips' curve of the form:

$$u_t = 0.06 - 0.005(\pi_t - \pi_t^e),$$

where π_t^e is the expected inflation rate for period t. What is the natural rate of unemployment? Draw the curves for $(u_t - u^n)$ against $(\pi_t - \pi_t^e)$ and for u_t against $(\pi_t - \pi_t^e)$.

T7. In the context of an EAPC such that

$$u_t = 0.06 - 0.005(\pi_t - \pi_t^e)$$

suppose the inflation rate had become 10% and was expected by the public to remain at this level.

(a) What monetary policy is needed to decrease the inflation rate to zero?

(b) What would be the impact of this policy on the unemployment rate if a cold-turkey policy (i.e., immediate reduction to a zero inflation rate, without a change in the expected one) is followed?

(c) What would be the impact of this policy on the unemployment rate in the long run once expectations adjust to a zero inflation rate?

(d) Explain, using the PC diagram, the impact of the reduction in the inflation rate on the unemployment rate in the impact period and in the long run.

T8. Suppose that in the context of an EAPC such that

$$u_t = 0.06 - 0.005(\pi_t - \pi_t^e),$$

with $\pi_t = \pi_t^e = 10\%$, the central bank in period $t+1$ brings the inflation rate down from 10% to its target inflation rate of 3% by a cold-turkey policy. What would happen to the unemployment rate (a) in the impact period (specify your relevant assumptions for this period), (b) in the long run (specify your relevant assumptions for this period)?

CHAPTER 11
Paradigms in Macroeconomics

There are two major paradigms in macroeconomics, the classical and Keynesian ones. The classical paradigm evolved over the past two and a half centuries. Its theories focus on the long-run (full-employment) equilibrium of the economy. Its theories are hierarchical in nature. The currently dominant formulation of this paradigm implies that any deviations from full employment occur due to expectational errors and are transitory or self-correcting. In full-employment equilibrium, changes in aggregate demand, brought about by systematic monetary and fiscal policies, can only cause changes in the price level, but not in output or employment.

The Keynesian paradigm has developed since the 1930s. It differs from the classical one in not focusing on the long-run equilibrium, (full-employment) state of the economy, but rather on its actual state, whether an equilibrium or disequilibrium one. Its theories imply that any deviations from full employment in the real-world, real-time economy are not always transient and self-correcting, so that the economy could function at less than full employment for significant periods. These deviations can arise from a variety of quite different causes. Therefore, the Keynesian paradigm has different theories corresponding to the different causes of the deviations from full employment. These theories usually imply that an increase in aggregate demand can increase output and employment, and that appropriate monetary and fiscal policies can improve on a macroeconomy working at less than full employment.

There are several paradigms for studying the macroeconomy, as it exists in most industrialized countries. The fundamental aspect of these economies is a largely market-based system of production and allocation of factors of production. Production in most of the sectors of these economies is by private enterprises, often operating in some type of competition, though governments have come to play significant roles in the production of goods and services and as employers of labor and capital in the economy as a whole. Among the existing paradigms for analysis of the macroeconomy, the dominant ones are the classical and Keynesian ones. This chapter focuses on these two paradigms and their various component schools. It neither presents any material on less common schools of thought, such as Marxism, post-Keynesian, Kaleckian, and Austrian for studying industrialized economies nor presents any treatment of political systems such as capitalism, socialism, and communism. A brief specification of these was given at the end of Chapter 1.

The two major paradigms in economics are the classical and the Keynesian ones. Their distinguishing elements are:

- The classical paradigm assumes that the market for each of the goods (so far specified in this book as commodities, money, bonds, labor, and foreign exchange) in the economy always clears, so that their demand and the supply will be in equilibrium, which could be a long-run or short-run one. Since one of the markets is the labor market, its clearance implies that every worker who wishes to supply labor at the existing wage will have a job and each firm will be able to employ all the workers that it wants to at the existing wage. In the absence of rigidities (leading to expectational errors and adjustment costs), this equilibrium state is that of long-run equilibrium with full employment. Under uncertainty, errors in expectations can occur, thereby producing a short-run equilibrium in which output and employment can differ from the full-employment ones. Such deviations from full employment are transitory and self-correcting (see Chapter 8). Therefore, a hallmark of the classical paradigm is that it tends to focus on the long-run (full-employment) equilibrium of the economy, with any deviations from it being transitory and self-correcting.

In view of the classical paradigm's emphasis on labor market clearance, this implication of long-run equilibrium is often turned around and stated as if it was an assumption. The literature, therefore, abounds with the statement that 'the classical models assume full employment', which is strictly not correct.[1] If full employment were used as an assumption, it would rule out the deviations from full employment, which occur under the Friedman and Lucas supply rules (see Chapter 8), which are part of the classical paradigm.

In the presence of uncertainty, short-run deviations from this full-employment equilibrium are allowed due to expectational errors in prices but the assumption of equilibrium — in this case, a short-run one — is maintained. These short-run deviations are as specified by the Friedman and Lucas supply rules, and are taken to be transitory and self-correcting — since expectations will adjust to eliminate expectational errors as soon as enough information becomes available and contracts are renegotiated.

- The Keynesian paradigm maintains that full employment may exist sometimes but not always. When it does not, the economy could be in (a) short-run equilibrium different from the long-run (full-employment) one or (b) disequilibrium, for significant periods. Further, if it is away from the full-employment equilibrium, the deviation is not necessarily self-correcting and/or transient enough to be ignored. Among the major reasons adduced for the deviation from full employment are the costs of adjusting prices, employment, and production, errors in the expectations of future demand and demand deficiency arising from the failure of markets to reestablish market-clearing prices instantly after a demand shock.

There are several schools or models within each of the two paradigms, without a consensus on the proper delineation of either the paradigms or their component models. This chapter sets out our classifications and definitions. However, no claim is being made to our taxonomy being acceptable to all economists.

Stylized Facts on Money, Prices, and Output

The usefulness of different theories can be judged by the stylized empirical facts about the economy. Among these are:

- Over long periods, there is a roughly one-to-one relationship between the money supply and inflation.
- Over long periods, there is no significant relationship between inflation and output growth. This is also so for money growth and output growth, though some studies show a positive correlation between these variables, especially for low inflation countries (while others show a negative one).
- Over long periods, changes in interest rates tend to reflect changes in inflation.
- In the short run, changes in money supply have a strong impact on both aggregate demand and real output. Unanticipated money supply changes affect output, as do anticipated ones. Negative shocks to money supply have a stronger impact on output than positive ones.

---

[1] The difference between an assumption of full employment and one which is an implication of the equilibrium state is that the former rules out the derivation of the properties of the system when it is in disequilibrium; the latter does not necessarily do so.

- Increases in short-term interest rates lead to a decline in output.
- On monetary policy dynamics in the short run, monetary policy shocks (i.e., changes in money supply or interest rates) build to a peak impact on output and then gradually die out, so that there is a 'hump-shaped pattern' of the effect of monetary policy on output, with the peak effect occurring with a lag longer than one year, sometimes two to three years.
- As a corollary of the preceding point, the impact of monetary shocks on prices and inflation occurs with a longer lag than on output.
- For the short run, since inflation responds more gradually than output to monetary policy changes, expected inflation also responds more gradually. Therefore, errors in price or inflation expectations do not provide a satisfactory explanation of the response of output to monetary policy shifts.
- Unanticipated price movements explain only a small part of output variability. The impact of unanticipated monetary shifts on real output does not occur through prior price increases.
- The responses of output and prices to monetary shocks differ over different stages of the business cycle. They are also stronger for contractionary than for expansionary monetary episodes.
- Contractionary monetary policies to reduce inflation do initially reduce output significantly, often for more than a year.

11.1 An Analogy for the Two Main Paradigms in Macroeconomics

We will use an analogy between the full-employment state of the economy and the healthy state of the human body, and that between the deviations from this full-employment state and the pathology (illnesses and breakdowns) of the human body. This analogy provides insights into the study of the economy by reference to personal experiences and knowledge on the performance of the human body.

We know that the human body sometimes functions in perfect health and sometimes suffers minor illnesses of a brief expected duration and without any need for the help of a professional (physician) to get back speedily to normal health. But it does sometimes suffer from serious illnesses and breakdowns from which the recovery may occur but be slow and be speeded up by the help of a physician, or even suffer ones from which there is no recovery without the intervention of a specialist to return speedily to normal health. There may also be illnesses from which there is no cure and no recovery, but we do not include this limiting state within our analogy. Among the serious illnesses, note there can be many possibilities: infection by bacterium A rather than B, infection by a bacterium versus a virus, infection versus collapse of lungs, collapse of lungs rather than heart attack, etc. The list of the possible sources of the deviations from the healthy state can be endless.

This analogy of the macroeconomy with the human body leads to the following two fundamental — and highly plausible — axioms on the performance of the macroeconomy:

α Axiom:

The economy, just as the human body, may sometimes function well and sometimes not. Hence, it is essential to study both the healthy and the 'sick' states, with the former serving as the benchmark for the treatment of the latter. This axiom implies that economists need to study the determinants of both the full employment state of the economy and of deviations (both small and large) from full employment.

β Axiom:

When the economy, just as the human body, is not functioning properly, the causes, symptoms, and effective treatments of the malfunction can be quite varied. The justification for the β axiom is that one cannot plausibly attribute all possible departures from the healthy body to a single underlying cause or attribute all potential causes to an overarching single source. This axiom implies that economists cannot assume that each of the deviations from full employment are due to a single cause and can be captured by just one model. Different models need to be formulated to deal with different potential causes of deviations from full employment, and the model used needs to be tailored to the actual cause of the breakdown of the economy.

11.1.1 The approach of the classical paradigm to the pathology of the economy

The focus of the classical paradigm is on the study of the 'healthy' state of the economy, meaning by this the state in which all available factors of production are used efficiently and are fully employed, so that output in this state is at its full-employment level. When the classical paradigm does envisage deviations — e.g., along the SRAS curve with the (Friedman and Lucas) EAPC due to expectational errors in prices[2] — away from this healthy state, the deviations are supposed to be minor, transitory, and self-correcting. Under it, while the economic body may become ill, the illnesses are never serious or long lasting, so that outside intervention (by the government or the central bank) never becomes necessary or will not really be worth the hassle and the cost — and/or its success will be uncertain.

Since the classical paradigm focuses on the single state — the healthy one — for the economy or self-correcting and transient deviations from it, its various component models tend to have a close relationship among them. Further, its models have almost a hierarchical nature, with subsequent models continuing on from the earlier ones, with modifications representing, in general, further refinements of the assumptions and analyses.

11.1.2 The approach of the Keynesian paradigm to the pathology of the economy

The Keynesian paradigm focuses on the pathology of the economy. An implication of the β axiom is that this pathology cannot be properly encapsulated within one model with one root pathogen. Hence, the Keynesian paradigm, if it is to do its job properly, has to be a disparate and, at best, a rather loose collection of models: the deviations from the full-employment (healthy) state of the economy state can be due to different pathogens or breakdowns of the different components of the economy. Further, the Keynesian paradigm envisages the possibility of serious departures from the full-employment state. Furthermore, it allows for the possibility that the recovery may sometimes be slow and could be speeded up with professional help (from the government and the central bank). It also has to allow for the possibility that, in extreme and rare instances, the recovery may never occur without such help.

To reiterate, by the nature of their attempts to deal with the pathology of the economy, the Keynesian models have to be, and are, quite varied. If they are to do their job properly of dealing with the different types of deviations, such models need not — in fact, must not — all focus on the same types of deviations from the overall equilibrium state or make the same recommendations for policies to address the impact of very different sources of deviations. Unfortunately, this aspect of the Keynesian paradigm is often not recognized. Frequently, the presentations and discussions of the Keynesian models miss this requirement for variety within the Keynesian paradigm and seek to force the various Keynesian models into a single format or view it as one

---

[2]See Chapter 8 for this analysis.

unified model. The danger in doing so is that a single policy prescription could be given as a cure-all for very disparate causes and be inappropriate for many.[3]

Extended Analysis Box 11.1: The Fundamental Assumptions of the Classical Paradigm

---

The classical paradigm is based on six fundamental assumptions. It analyzes equilibrium levels of output and employment along the LRAS curve for the long run (see Chapter 7) and along the SRAS curve, arising from expectational errors (see Chapter 8), for the short run.

- No money illusion in demand and supply functions

    Changes in the price level or the rate of inflation do not change the demands and supplies of goods in real terms. In particular, the demand and supply of labor depend on the real and not the nominal wage.

- Flexible prices and wages

    The prices of all the goods in the economy are assumed to be flexible and adjust to equate demand and supply in the relevant market. They increase if there is excess demand and decrease if there is excess supply. These prices include wages, which is the price of labor.

- Continuous market clearance (market coordination)

    Each market clears continuously, so that we can focus on the study of the general equilibrium in the economy and its properties, while largely ignoring the disequilibrium values of the variables. Continuous market clearance requires some mechanism for bringing about the continuous equality of demand and supply. One such mechanism is that of centralized coordination in a bureaucratic system;[4] another is that of markets in a free enterprise system. The mechanism for the latter is often referred to as the 'invisible hand' of competition. [However, it is highly questionable whether either of these mechanisms can, or ever delivered, the continuous equality of demand and supply in all the markets of any real-world economy.]

- Transparency of equilibrium prices

    All agents in making their demand and supply decisions assume that such market clearance will occur instantly after any disturbance and know/anticipate (or are informed by a 'market coordinator') the prices at which it will occur.[5]

---

[3]An example of this was economists' inappropriate policy prescriptions, based mainly on the traditional classical ideas, during the early stages of the Great Depression in the 1930s. These worsened the depth of the fall in GDP and lengthened the depression — and contributed to the demise of faith in the traditional classical ideas. Another example of inappropriate policies, based on the aggregate demand management approach in the Keynesian paradigm, occurred in response to the supply shocks of 1973 and 1974. This led to stagflation and contributed to the demise of faith in the Keynesian paradigm.

[4]For example, under the centralized economic system that used to exist in the former Soviet Union and several other communist countries, the bureaucrats made the decisions on production, employment, prices etc.

[5]In particular, if there are delays in establishing these prices or communicating their knowledge, it is assumed that all production and trade is put on hold during the delay and that any such delay does not impose costs on economic agents. This is known as recontracting.

Extended Analysis Box 11.1: (*Continued*)

- Notional demand and supply functions

   All economic agents assume that they will be able to buy or sell as much as they want to at the equilibrium prices. They plan to produce, consume, demand money, and supply labor at only these equilibrium prices. The demand and supply functions derived under this assumption are known as notional demand and supply functions. In particular:

   - Workers act on the assumption that they will be able to sell all the labor that they want — that is, there will be full employment — so that they can incur consumption expenditures based on full-employment income. [However, this is assumed to be so even if actual employment falls below full employment and the unemployed workers do not receive any income.]
   - Firms must act as if there will be enough demand to sell all the output that they want to sell, so that they produce at the full-employment level. [However, this is assumed to be so even if there is not enough demand for the full-employment output, though production by firms at this level would mean an unplanned accumulation of inventories.]

- Under uncertainty and errors in price expectations, short-run equilibrium analysis for the SRAS curve:

   The short-run analysis of the classical paradigm is based on price misperceptions under uncertainty, as presented in Chapter 8 for the Friedman and Lucas supply curves. Otherwise, the preceding assumptions are maintained. In particular, households maximize utility and firms maximize profits, and markets clear on a continuous basis.

Note that each of the above fundamental assumptions is related to the others but is still distinct. Any one or more of these assumptions may not be relevant to and valid for a particular stage of the business cycle or at a particular time in a real-world economy.

11.2 Defining and Demarcating the Models of the Classical Paradigm

All the models or schools within the classical paradigm share the common beliefs that the real-world economy under consideration — and not just the models — functions at full employment in the long run and that it does not stay very long out of the full-employment state, so that it never gets stuck in an under-full employment disequilibrium or equilibrium. Therefore, states with less than full employment are either transitory states of disequilibrium or short-run equilibrium during which the economy continues to adjust fairly rapidly toward its full-employment equilibrium — and not away from it. Further, one of the characteristics of the long-run equilibrium for all the classical schools is the independence of the real variables from the financial ones, so that money is neutral in the long-run equilibrium.[6] A major difference among the classical schools is whether the real-world economy adjusts so fast as to maintain virtually continuous equilibrium (so that it will not show any evidence of disequilibrium) or whether there can exist transitory disequilibrium states for some

---

[6]The empirical evidence on this issue is provided by the stylized facts presented at the beginning of this chapter. The evidence that money is not neutral in the short run or during disequilibrium (in the economy in general or following a change the money supply itself) is very strong.

duration.[7] It refinements over time have, in general, tended to exclude disequilibrium states, but allow short-run equilibrium states which deviate from the long-run full-employment equilibrium state. However, these deviations, as shown by the Friedman and Lucas supply rules in Chapter 8, arise not from the failures of markets to clear but from the errors in the expectations held by economic agents on market prices (not on sales and job prospects). These errors in expectations are transitory and self-correcting, so that the deviations of the short-run equilibrium from the long-run one are also transitory and self-correcting.

The following classification of the models of the classical paradigm has been chosen for reasons of clarity in separating each model from the others, rather than leaving their differences ambiguous. Our classification attempts to maintain consistency with the writings and folklore in the history of economic thought.

11.2.1 The traditional classical approach

'The traditional classical approach' consists of the somewhat disparate ideas on the macro structure of the economy from the origin of macroeconomics in the middle of the 18th century to the publication of Keynes' *The General Theory* in 1936. To quite a considerable extent, these ideas were diffuse, varied among authors and changed over time. In any case, there was no single compact version of the overall exposition, though we do now treat them as if there had been a compact model.

The common themes of the traditional classical approach were:

- A microeconomic approach to economics, especially after the 1870s, with market clearance and long-run equilibrium (see Chapter 7 for the underlying assumptions of this approach).
- Loanable funds (or bond market) theory of the rate of interest, under which the long-run rate of interest in a closed economy was determined solely by full-employment national saving and investment (see Chapter 7).
- The quantity theory for the determination of prices (see Chapter 2). It applied in the full-employment equilibrium of the economy. But outside this equilibrium, during the adjustment phase, changes in the money supply could change output and employment.
- Most of the traditional classical economists did not believe that the economy functioned so well that it always maintained full employment or that it did so most of the time. In fact, recessions and crises — any of them originating in the banking sector or financial speculation or occurring due to the response pattern of the financial sector to real shocks — were common during the 19th century. The widely held belief among economists at that time was that such crises did affect output and employment. Hence, the traditional classical school allowed for the existence of disequilibrium to exist for significant periods. That is, they did not assume continuous full employment. They also recognized that changes in the money supply do cause changes in employment and output over the short term and over the business cycle.
- Accompanying the economic analysis was a general conservative approach to politics and public finances, which espoused (a) a small size of government and (b) 'fiscal responsibility' by the government. Fiscal responsibility meant that the government should not spend more than its revenues, especially in peacetime, so that it should aim for a balanced budget.[8]

The Great Depression of the 1930s with its massive unemployment over a decade destroyed the public's and economists' faith in the traditional classical approach and especially in its prediction that the economy will

---

[7]Note that disequilibrium remains a hypothetical, analytical (but not necessarily a real-time) state within all the models of the classical paradigm. The difference among them is about its significant occurrence in the real-world economies.

[8]It also advocated that the central bank should be 'prudent' in the way that private banks have to be. This implied that it should not lend to commercial banks which are illiquid and in danger of insolvency, so that the central bank should allow the markets to determine whether private banks fail or not.

normally be at or close to full employment. Its doctrines and predictions were clearly remote from the public's own economic experience. Further, economic policies based on it tended to worsen the economy. Their failure prepared the public and the economics profession for the acceptance of an alternative paradigm that would explain the failures of the economy to maintain full employment, especially in response to serious declines in aggregate demand, and to provide more appropriate policy prescriptions during these failures. The theory of why the economy can be away from full employment, and the relevant policy prescriptions, were provided by the Keynesian paradigm, which originated in 1936 in the midst of the Great Depression.

Extended Analysis Box 11.2: The Founders of the Classical Tradition in Macroeconomics

---

DAVID HUME (1711–1776)

Hume was a philosopher who made several contributions to economics. These included the quantity theory of money, the loanable funds theory of interest, and the benefits to the nation from international trade. On the quantity theory, presented in Chapter 2, Hume argued that the long-run effect of changes in the money supply was to proportionately increase the price level. Gold coins were the main form of money in Hume's time, so that the changes in the amount of gold in the nation were synonymous with changes in the money supply.

On the loanable funds theory, Hume argued that the long-run rate of interest was determined by the equality of national saving and investment. Hume's observation on the saving behavior of the three main classes of society, the aristocrats, the merchants, and the peasants (including the workers) was that the aristocrats and peasants spent all their incomes on current consumption (including wasteful expenditures) and did not save while the merchants tended to save any increases in income and to invest them, often in their own small businesses. Since increases in the money supply in the hands of the merchant classes supplement saving and are lent, their short-run effect was to lower the interest rate and increase national economic activity — a code phrase meaning national output and employment in the modern terminology. This short run could last several years since prices tended to change rarely — be sticky. However, once the additional money supply was fully integrated into the economy, both the interest rate and economic activity would return to their long-run levels, but the prices would have increased proportionately.

Therefore, national prosperity flowed from the amount of capital, the workforce and its diligence, rather than the amount of gold and money in the nation. This prosperity increased with trade with other nations. Such trade helped poorer nations to export commodities, as well as learn the technology of other nations, which promoted growth and development. It also benefited richer nations by increasing their exports.

ADAM SMITH (1723–1790)

Although many economists, including David Hume, had earlier written on economic matters, Adam Smith is widely called the 'father' of economics because his analysis of the benefits from capitalism, greater competition and free trade had very considerable impact on the formulation of economic policy in Britain and other countries. His most influential work was *The Wealth of Nations* (1776), which assumed that people act according to their own self-interest — which is the fundamental postulate of modern economic analysis. Competition organized the individuals' self-interest into exchanges that were of benefit to both parties to the exchange and ensured the maximization of national welfare. The pursuit of self-interest promoted national interest, as long as competitive forces were allowed. As a corollary, state interference in economic matters through regulation decreased national welfare and impoverished the nation. The role of the government was to be limited to providing public goods, such as defence, legal, and police systems,

Extended Analysis Box 11.2: (*Continued*)

and the provision of goods with large externalities — i.e., effects on other than the producer and/or the consumer.

To Smith, specialization in production and the division of labor promoted greater production and growth. The larger the market, the greater the scope for them. Therefore, the lesser the barriers to trade within the country and among countries, the more prosperous the nation. His famous example of this division of labor was that of production in a pin-making factory. It showed how the division of the tasks among workers permitted greater production than if each worker were to produce the whole pin.

DAVID RICARDO (1772–1823)

Ricardo provided the first rigorous analysis of several topics in economics. Among these were: the theory of distribution of income into rents, wages, and profits; the theory of comparative advantage according to which nations benefit by specializing in the production of items in which they have a comparative advantage; the theory of value or relative prices, according to which the relative prices of commodities would depend on their relative cost of production in the long run and their scarcity in the short run.

Ricardo was a supporter of the quantity theory of money, proposed by Hume, under which changes in the money supply cause proportionate changes in the price level.

At the level of the economy as a whole, Ricardo maintained that there could not be general excess supply (i.e., output > aggregate demand) in the economy.[9] That is, the economy will always have enough aggregate demand for the purchase of the economy's output at full employment. This proposition was later designated as Say's Law, whose compact statement is that '(full-employment) output creates its own demand'. This proposition amounts to the denial of the empirical possibility of deficient demand and involuntary unemployment, whose analysis was presented in Chapter 9. While this proposition is consistent with the long-run equilibrium of the economy, it does not hold when there is disequilibrium, especially in the commodity and labor markets.

11.2.2 The neoclassical model

This name was given to the restatement of the traditional classical ideas rebottled and reflavored in the *post-General Theory* period in a new compact framework. The new bottle was the IS-LM technique or mode of analysis, first proposed in 1937 by John Hicks to explain the arguments of Keynes' *The General Theory*. In some ways, this rebottling represented a radical departure from the traditional presentation of the classical ideas, in that the latter did not have an analysis of the commodity market equilibrium while the IS-LM technique starts with a presentation of the analysis of the commodity market. Note that the IS-LM and the IS-IRT analyses of the commodity market embody the concept of the multiplier, which was unknown to the traditional classical economists and was not developed until the early 1930s. Chapters 4 to 6 incorporate the multiplier analysis.

Further, certain elements of the traditional ideas such as the Quantity Theory were discarded in the rebottling process and the analysis of the money market was incorporated through the LM curve — again a concept not familiar to the traditional classical school.

---

[9]Ricardo's contemporary, Thomas Malthus, disputed this proposition though Malthus did not offer an acceptable theoretical basis for his viewpoint. Another contribution of Malthus was to growth theory. This contribution is presented in Chapter 14.

The neoclassical model continued to have both equilibrium and disequilibrium aspects, and did not assume instant market clearance. In this, it represents the ideas of the traditional (pre-Keynesian) classical economists more faithfully than does the modern classical model.[10]

The classical paradigm — and its traditional classical and neoclassical versions — was rejected by the majority in the economics profession from the 1940s to the 1970s, though it continued to exist as an outcast. However, refinements and additions to it continued to be made during these decades. The dominant paradigm in these decades was the Keynesian one. Following the Keynesian policy debacle of the mid-1970s that erroneously addressed supply-side shocks (oil price increases) by expansionary monetary and fiscal policies and led to stagflation, the classical paradigm roared back in the 1970s and has since then taken various forms. These are the 1970s Monetarism, the modern classical model and the new classical model.

Box 11.1: Some Major Misconceptions about Traditional Classical and Neoclassical
Approaches in the Classical Paradigm

A common misconception nowadays is that the traditional classical and neoclassical economists believed that the economy functioned well enough to maintain full employment most of the time or that it had a fast tendency to return to full employment following a disturbance and a decline in employment. In fact, many traditional classical economists believed that "the economic system is essentially unstable" (Patinkin, 1969, p. 50).[11] Another misconception nowadays is that the traditional classical and neoclassical economists believed that money was neutral in practice and in theory for the real world over the short term.

It was generally recognized that "cycles and depressions [are] an inherent feature of 'capitalism'. Such a system must use money, so that the changes in the money supply and in its velocity were major sources of business fluctuations." Further, many traditional classical economists believed that these fluctuations were heightened by the 'perverse' behavior of the banking system, which expands credit in booms and contracts it in depressions. Among the reasons given for the real effects of changes in the money supply and velocity changes was that firms' costs have a tendency to move more slowly than do the more flexible selling prices. In view of this, monetary policy was often envisaged and recommended as a stabilization tool.

However, fiscal policy for the stabilization of aggregate demand was usually not even considered a possibility nor was its analytical basis known to the traditional classical (pre-Keynesian) economists. Its consideration and recommendation as a major stabilization tool was due to Keynes and the Keynesians, and needed as its basis the concept of the investment multiplier, first derived in the 1930s. As a counter-reformation, Barro's Ricardian equivalence theorem (which implies that aggregate demand cannot be changed by fiscal deficits and surpluses) was proposed to again remove fiscal policy from the set of potential demand management tools. This theorem is not presented in this book but can be found in more advanced macroeconomics textbooks.

---

[10]This modern classical model is also different from the traditional classical model in other ways. One of these relates to the existence of speculative money demand in the modern classical model while the quantity theory component of the traditional classical model did not have such money demand.

[11]The various quotes are taken from Patinkin, a prominent neoclassical economist, even though many of them are from passages quoted by him from other writers. The relevant references are to: Patinkin, D. The Chicago tradition, the quantity theory, and Friedman. *Journal of Money, Credit and Banking*, **1**, 1969, 46–70 and Friedman on the quantity theory and Keynesian economics. *Journal of Political Economy*, **80**, 1972, 883–905.

11.2.3 The 1970s monetarism

Monetarism and monetarists have been defined in a variety of ways. In a very broad sense, monetarism is the proposition that money matters in the economy.[12] In a narrow sense, monetarism was associated with the St. Louis School (named after the Federal Reserve Bank of St. Louis, whose researchers popularized monetarism) in monetary and macroeconomics. We will define monetarism in this narrow sense. This version of monetarism is called the 1970s or the St. Louis School Monetarism. Its ideas became quite popular in the late 1970s and early 1980s. It was essentially a simplification of the neoclassical model for empirical tests of the impact of money supply changes and fiscal deficits on aggregate demand and on real output.[13] Much of the work was statistical and econometric in nature and provided a simple empirical procedure for estimating the relationship between nominal income, money supply, and fiscal variables.

The empirical and theoretical bases of the 1970s Monetarism was provided by the economists at the Federal Reserve Bank of St. Louis. The main tenets of this school were that:

- The short-run versions of their model neither assumed full employment nor implied continuous full employment in the economy. Therefore, it allowed for the possibility of involuntary unemployment in the short run and supported the positive short-run impact of monetary policy on nominal income, real output, and employment. In this, it was relatively close to the then-Keynesian models. However, it denied on empirical grounds the Keynesian claim of the efficacy of fiscal policy.
- In its long-run version, it belonged to the classical paradigm. In the long run, changes in the money supply could not change full-employment output but would cause proportionate changes in the price level.
- Among its empirical findings for the USA were:
  - The lags in the impact of money supply changes on nominal income were fairly short — about five quarters.
  - Fiscal policy had a small positive impact on nominal expenditures followed by a negative one, roughly canceling out over about five quarters.
- This school also recommended that the central bank should aim at controling and targeting one of the monetary aggregates rather than interest rates.
- In general, the monetarists tended to be more conservative than the Keynesians in their general political and economic philosophy. Along with a recommendation that fiscal policy not be used as a stabilization tool, they tended to favor lower taxes and smaller government.
- Another aspect of the general ideas of the Monetarist school was that the central bank and the government neither possess an inherent superiority of information on the economy nor do they always manage to improve on the performance of the economy: their actions have worsened it at times. In these beliefs, the monetarists agreed with Milton Friedman. Their difference from Friedman was on an empirical issue: the duration of the lag in the impact of money supply changes on nominal income. Friedman's estimates showed that this lag was long (6 quarters to 21 quarters) and variable, so that it was dangerous to pursue monetary policy. The monetarists' estimates showed that this lag was relatively short (five quarters), so that monetary policy could be followed with predictable effects.

---

[12]In this sense, John Maynard Keynes and the Keynesians — along with Milton Friedman — were all monetarists, while the modern classical school is somewhat less monetarist since it downplays the impact of money supply changes on the real variables of the economy.

[13]Friedman's ideas are presented later in this chapter.

In many ways, the 1970s monetarism was a hybrid between the neoclassical model and the Keynesian paradigm, and made the switch away from Keynesianism palatable for many economists. However, it had a short life and was replaced in the early 1980s by ideas truer to the classical paradigm, which eventually took the form of the modern classical paradigm.

11.2.4 The modern classical model

This model is a statement of the classical paradigm under the assumptions of continuous labor market clearance and rational expectations. Because of the former assumption, it incorporates continuous full employment, except in the short run when the economy operates along the SRAS curve — which occurs due to errors in price expectations (including asymmetric information among economic agents) in the Friedman and Lucas supply rules. Given full employment as the long-run equilibrium state, rational expectations imply that systematic monetary policy will not be able to change real output and unemployment in the economy, though random changes in the money supply can affect them. Further, for unanticipated changes in the money supply and interest rates brought about by monetary policy, the economy deviates from full employment but reverts to it soon.

The modern classical model differs from the neoclassical one since the former assumes continuous labor market clearance, while the latter allows the possibility of disequilibrium in labor markets. Further, the former allows for uncertainty — addressed through the rational expectations hypothesis — while the neoclassical one does not.

Hence, the constituents of the modern classical macroeconomic model are:

- An emphasis on the microeconomic basis of macroeconomics, maximization of profits by firms, maximization of utility by households, and general equilibrium.
- The neoclassical model, modified by the additions of:

  - Perfect competition and continuous market clearance (especially of the labor market, so that there will not be any involuntary unemployment). This requires that markets are efficient in establishing the price level that equates aggregate demand and supply.
  - Rational expectations hypothesis when dealing with uncertainty.
  - Friedman and Lucas supply rules when there is uncertainty about prices and inflation.

Intuitively, the modern classical model focuses on the economy in good health (i.e., functioning at peak performance). Deviations from this state can occur along the SRAS curve and are analyzed using the Friedman and Lucas supply rules. These deviations are self-correcting and transient (i.e., short-lived). The full-employment state serves as the benchmark of what the economy can do at its best. It implies that there is no need for systematic governmental policies, either monetary or fiscal ones, to try to improve on this level of performance. In fact, the economists of this school point to the potential dangers of trying to do so.

Between about 1980 and 2006, the modern classical school seemed to be the dominant one in macroeconomic theory but not necessarily among policymakers.[14]

---

[14]Example of policy makers' refusal to follow the recommendations of the modern classical approach occurred during the recessions of 2000–2002 and 2008–10 when central banks hastened to intervene in the economy by lowering interest rates and increasing the money supply. These policies constituted intervention in the economy and represented Keynesian prescriptions for macroeconomic policy.

11.2.5 The new classical model

The new classical model imposes the assumption of Ricardian equivalence on the modern classical model. Intuitively, Ricardian equivalence is an aspect of intertemporal rationality and the extreme democratic notion that the government is nothing more than a representative of its electorate and is regarded as such by the public in making the decisions on its own consumption. This government provides just the goods that the population wants and its bonds, held by the public, are regarded by it (the public) as a debt owed by the public to itself. For bond-financed deficits, the implications of Ricardian equivalence are that, in order to provide for the future tax liability[15] imposed by a bond issue, the public increases private savings by the amount of the deficit. In doing so, private consumption is reduced by the amount of the deficit. Since the deficit increases aggregate demand while the decrease in consumption cuts it, the two effects cancel each other, so that the bond-financed deficit does not change aggregate demand. Therefore, deficits do not even change nominal national income and interest rates, let alone the real value of the economy's output.

The constituents of the new classical model are:

- The modern classical model, modified by the addition of,
- Ricardian equivalence.

The only difference between the implications of the modern classical and new classical models is that the former implies that fiscal deficits will change aggregate demand (shift the IS curve), national saving, and interest rate while the latter implies that they will not do so. Their other implications are identical. Among these are:

- Both models do possess money supply changes as a policy tool for changing aggregate demand in the economy.
- Both models imply the neutrality of systematic (which gets to be anticipated) money supply changes in the full-employment state, so that the impact of the systematic money supply and velocity changes can only be on the price level and not on real output and employment.
- Both models allow for the short-run deviations from full employment due to expectational errors in prices when the money supply changes are unanticipated.
- Both models imply that the deviations from full employment are at most minor, transitory, and self-correcting, so that there is a strong tendency for the economy to revert to full employment within a relatively short period after any shock. Hence, there is neither need nor scope for systematic monetary policy for changing the levels of output and employment in the economy, so that such policies should not be pursued.

Extended Analysis Box 11.3: The Founders of the Classical Approach in the Modern Period

---

MILTON FRIEDMAN (1912–2006)

We present the ideas of Milton Friedman in sufficient detail elsewhere, so that we add little to them here. We have already studied the Friedman supply rule (Chapter 8) and its associated expectations augmented Phillips curve (Chapter 10).

---

[15]This liability is to make the periodic interest payments and repay the principal on maturity.

Extended Analysis Box 11.3: (*Continued*)

Friedman was the foremost defender of classical ideas — at that time called the 'neoclassical approach' — during the Keynesian ascendancy from the mid-1930s to the mid-1970s and contributed extensively to updating the theories inherited from the traditional classical approach. He espoused an emphasis on the long-run equilibrium analysis, which implies the natural rate of unemployment and full-employment output. However, he also accepted the possibility that unemployment could be higher than its natural rate and that money supply increases could lower it. Friedman tried to modernize the quantity theory.

Friedman was, however, sceptical about the discretionary use of monetary policy since he believed that there were long and variables lags in its impact, so that monetary policy could in effect, end up worsening the economy as often, or more often, rather than improving it. He recommended following a set policy rule that would increase the money supply at a low, constant rate. He did not believe that fiscal policy was an effective policy tool.

Friedman also argued for competition in the provision of services in the various sectors of the economy, including education, health, etc, and was opposed to government regulation.

ROBERT LUCAS (1937–)

Robert Lucas is the most prominent contributor to the modern classical modeling of macroeconomics and is currently its best-known exponent. His approach is to base macroeconomics on a microeconomic foundation. Economic agents — households and firms — are rational (utility and profit-maximizing subject to the relevant constraints) and hold rational expectations. Markets clear. Since this tends to maintain full employment and full-employment output, economic management of the economy by the government and the central bank is not needed. We have already studied some of Lucas' ideas on the Lucas supply curve (see Chapter 8). Lucas has also contributed extensively to other areas of economics, including endogenous growth theory (presented in Chapter 15).

Note that the basing of macroeconomics purely on microeconomics means that the former is just an extension of the latter. This approach has led some economists to argue that macroeconomics is not a distinct field within economics; some have even argued that there is no such subject as macroeconomics. Milton Friedman occupies a special place in the counter-reformation from Keynesian economics to the neoclassical and modern classical ones. His major contributions from the 1940s to the 1970s laid the basis for challenging the then current versions and assumptions of the dominant Keynesian school. This school in the 1940s and 1950s had downplayed the impact of money supply changes on the economy and had a relative preference for fiscal over monetary policy.

In the 1950s, Friedman showed through his theoretical and empirical contributions that 'money matters' — that is, changes in the money supply change nominal national expenditures and income — as against the then general view of the Keynesian school that changes in the money supply brought about through monetary policy did not significantly affect the economy or did so unpredictably.[16] On the latter, Friedman argued and tried to establish through empirical studies that the money–income multiplier was more stable than the investment–income multiplier, so that monetary policy was not less important or less predictable than fiscal policy in its impact on nominal national income.

Other aspects of Friedman's agenda to reestablish the doctrine that money matters were to set out in the 1950s and 1960s the theory — and to establish it empirically — that the demand function for money was stable, with the result that the velocity of money also had a stable function. Therefore, changes in the money supply had a strong impact on aggregate demand. These arguments were accepted by the profession

Extended Analysis Box 11.4: The Economic Contributions of Milton Friedman

by the early 1960s, and contributed to the conversion of the Keynesian macroeconomics to the Keynesian-neoclassical synthesis[17] on aggregate demand expressed by the IS-LM model for the determination of aggregate demand.

On the relationship between the nominal variables and the real side of the economy, Keynesians in the late 1950s and 1960s had relied on the Phillips' curve, which showed a negative trade-off between the rate of inflation and the rate of unemployment. Friedman argued that the natural rate of unemployment — and, therefore, full-employment output — was independent of the anticipated rate of inflation, so that the fluctuations in output and the rate of unemployment were related to the deviations in the inflation rate from its anticipated level. This relationship came to be known as the expectations augmented Phillips' curve and incorporated his contributions on the natural rate of unemployment.

While Friedman brought the role of anticipations on the rate of inflation into discussions on the role and effectiveness of monetary policy in the economy, he did not have the theory of rational expectations. The rational expectations hypothesis had not yet entered the literature and Friedman had relied on adaptive expectations (see Chapter 8) in his empirical studies. Consequently, for Friedman, the unanticipated rate of inflation — equal to the errors in inflationary expectations — was not random with a zero expected value. Further, since Barro's contribution on the Ricardian equivalence theorem had not yet been made, Friedman's writings also did not incorporate this hypothesis. Hence, Friedman was a precursor of the modern classical school but not fully a member of it. Nor does this school follow all of his ideas.[18]

11.2.6 Milton Friedman and the Keynesians

Milton Friedman was closer to the Keynesians in one important respect than to the later modern classical school. He believed, as did the Keynesians, that the economy does not always maintain full employment and full-employment output — and does not always function at the natural rate of unemployment, even though this concept was central to his analysis. Hence, policy induced changes in aggregate demand could induce short-term changes in output and employment. Therefore, money mattered even to the extent that changes in it could induce changes in employment and output, depending upon the particular stage of the business cycle. While this view was shared with the Keynesians, Friedman tilted against the Keynesians on the pursuit of discretionary monetary policy as a stabilisation tool — especially for 'fine tuning' the economy — because of his belief that the impact of money supply changes on nominal income had a long and variable lag. He reported on the outside lag of monetary policy that:

> The rate of change of the money supply shows well-marked cycles that match closely those in economic activity in general and precede the latter by a long interval. On the average, the rate of change of the money supply has reached its peak nearly 16 months before the peak in general business and has reached its trough over . . . 12 months before the trough in general business. . . . Moreover, the timing varies considerably from cycle to cycle — since 1907 the shortest time span by which the

---

[16]Many Keynesians held this view in the 1950s and 1960s. It argued that the money stock was only a small part of the liquidity of the economy, which included short-term bonds, trade credit, overdrafts at financial institutions, etc. Further, the degree of substitution between these components to any contraction of the money supply was so high as to render the impact of the contraction on aggregate demand negligible.

[17]See Chapter 5.

[18]For example, Friedman believed that the economy does not always operate at full employment in which case changes in the money supply would change real output, as well as prices.

money peak preceded the business peak was 13 months, the longest 24 months; the corresponding range at troughs is 5 months to 21 months. (Friedman, 1958)

With such a long and variable lag from changes in the money supply to nominal national income, the monetary authorities cannot be sure when a policy induced increase in the money supply would have its impact on the economy. Such an increase in a recession may, in fact, increase aggregate demand in a following boom, thereby only increasing the rate of inflation at that time. Consequently, Friedman argued that discretionary monetary policy, intended to stabilize the economy, could turn out to be destabilizing. Friedman's recommendation on monetary policy was, therefore, that it should maintain a low constant rate of growth.

11.2.7 The relationship between the Monetarists and Friedman

As we have explained earlier, the St. Louis Monetarism was based in large part on Friedman's ideas. The St. Louis Monetarists believed, as did Friedman and the Keynesians, that changes in the money supply have a significant and positive impact on real output, and prices, in conditions of less than full employment. But, for the Monetarists, as with Friedman but not the Keynesians, the economy tended to full employment in the long run, so that the long-run impact of money supply changes would only be on the price level.

However, the estimations of the St. Louis equation indicated a much shorter and more reliable lag than Friedman had found. Therefore, contrary to Friedman's recommendations and consistent with Keynesian ones, Monetarism was consistent with the stance that monetary policy could be reliably useful for short-term stabilization of the economy.

On the transmission mechanism, the St. Louis Monetarists supported the direct transmission mechanism — from the money supply to expenditures, rather than indirectly from the money supply to interest rates, then to affect investment, which changes aggregate expenditures — espoused by Friedman. However, their estimation techniques were not fine enough to separate the direct from the indirect channel of monetary policy effects.[19]

The St. Louis Monetarism represented a transitional stage in the transition from Keynesian ascendancy in economics in the decades before 1970 to the ascendancy of the neoclassical and modern classical schools in the 1980s and 1990s. In many ways, it was an amalgam of Keynesian and Friedman's ideas in macroeconomics, and led the way to the reemergence of the classical doctrines.

11.2.8 Friedman and the modern classical school

While both Friedman and the modern classical economists are opposed to the pursuit of discretionary monetary policy, they arrive at this position for quite different reasons. For Friedman, money supply changes can change output and employment but the long and variable lags in this impact make a discretionary policy inadvisable. It could make the economy worse rather than better. For the modern classical economists, the economy maintains full employment, so that systematic policy changes in the money supply cannot change output and employment, but only change the price level. This joint stance against the pursuit of monetary policy hides a subtle difference. For Friedman, money matters for the real sectors of the economy, and changes in the money supply can alter output but are not advisable because of long and variable lags. For the modern classical economist, there are no lags in the impact of systematic money supply changes, and there is no impact on output, so that from the perspective of output and employment, it really does not matter what the money supply is.

---

[19]The modern classical school has abandoned the direct transmission mechanism in favor of the indirect one.

On the transmission mechanism from money supply changes to income changes, Friedman supported Fisher's direct transmission mechanism — from money supply changes directly to expenditures changes — over the indirect one, which is from the money supply to interest rates to investment, as in Keynesian and IS-LM models. Friedman had, therefore, recommended that the central bank should target monetary aggregates rather than interest rates in its pursuit of monetary policy. However, neoclassical and modern classical models espouse the indirect transmission mechanism, just as the Keynesians do — rather Friedman's direct one so, than that they recommend, as do the Keynesians, that the central bank should target interest rates rather than monetary aggregates.

11.3 The Keynesian Paradigm

The Keynesian paradigm studies the pathology of the macroeconomy. It focuses on the causes, implications and policy prescriptions for the potential deviations of the economy from a full-employment equilibrium. Since there can be many causes of such deviations, their appropriate study requires not one unified model but many, not all of which need be variations on a theme or even compatible with one other. This chapter provides a sample of their diversity. The original version of the Keynesian paradigm was Keynes' own ideas as set out in his book *The General Theory*, followed by a number of evolving versions of the Keynesian framework.[20] Keynesianism has been evolving over time, so that there is no single version of it.

The common strand in the Keynesian approaches is the anxiety over the performance of the economy, and especially of the labor market. In particular, the Keynesian models assume that:

- Even fairly or fully competitive markets in the real-world modern economy are not fully efficient: they do not continuously bring about the price level that would produce continuous market clearance. Alternatively stated, even if there exists a high level of competition, the 'invisible hand of competition' is not efficient and fast enough to ensure continuous and simultaneous equilibrium in all markets. There is also no other coordinating mechanism for achieving this. This is often stated as 'market failure'[21] or 'coordination failure'.[22]
- Given the sluggish response of markets relative to that of firms in establishing the price that would equate supply and demand, firms make and act on their profit-maximizing decisions on production and employment in response to changes in the demand for their products. These decisions include changes in their output, as well as changes in their prices.
- The labor markets do not perform well enough to ensure full employment as a continuous or almost continuous state for a variety of reasons. One of the basic reasons for this is that the labor markets cannot be taken to always clear at the current wage rate. They may do so, but not necessarily always, nor is there always

---

[20]There is considerable dispute as to whether any of the Keynesian models represents Keynes' own work or not. A close reading of Chapters 2 and 3 of *The General Theory* shows that they do not. It is therefore appropriate to make a distinction between the Keynesian models and Keynes' own analysis, though the former arose out of interpretations of the latter.

[21]However, this phraseology seems to indicate a rather harsh judgment on a mechanism that works amazingly well for a complex and dynamic economy — and definitely better than any system of administrative coordination of demands, supplies, and prices, which are attempted in centralized, communist countries. If the actual performance of competitive, free economies is assessed against realistic alternatives, the former comes out very well.

[22]The term 'coordination failure' is relative to the perfect coordination of markets under the hypothetical and mythical construct of an all-knowing 'auctioneer' or 'state planner' who can instantly work out the changes in prices following any shifts of demand and supply for individual commodities and announce them to buyers and sellers. The assumption of such an entity is unrealistic and can lead to erroneous conclusions relative to how households, firms and markets actually function.

a strong and rapid tendency for them to move from a disequilibrium state to the equilibrium one. The latter is related to the observation that the firms and the workers in the labor market do not even negotiate a real wage but rather negotiate and set a nominal wage. Further, there are very significant imperfections in the labor market for various reasons, including the fixity and firm-specificity of acquired skills, the differing geographical distributions of jobs and workers, explicit and implicit contracts, etc.

- Information on the future is often incomplete and vague. This is a source of considerable fluctuations in business and consumer confidence, whose impact on investment, consumption, money demand, and bond purchases and sales cause fluctuations in economic activity.
- There are various types of market imperfections and departures from perfect competition in the economy.

Extended Analysis Box 11.5: The Founders of the Keynesian Paradigm

---

KNUT WICKSELL (1851–1926)

Wicksell made contributions in both microeconomics and monetary economics. In monetary economics, Wicksell shifted the focus of monetary theory from an emphasis on the quantity of money to that on interest rates. His most famous analysis on this topic was based on a pure credit economy, which does not use currency but only uses checking accounts with the banks for all payments.

Wicksell argued that banks set the market rate of interest while saving at full employment and the marginal productivity of capital determine the natural rate of interest. If the market interest rate is lower than the natural rate, firms can increase their profits by borrowing more from the banks and investing these funds. This increase in investment increases employment and income in the short run. The money supply also increases in the process, but this increase is a consequence of the divergence between the market and natural interest rates, not the cause of it. This process continues until the banks raise their interest rate to equal the natural rate.

Conversely, if the market interest rate set by banks is above the natural rate, firms will reduce their borrowing, with the result that investment and economic activity will fall. The money supply will also fall. Economic activity thus depends on the market interest rate and investment, so that unemployment will also depend on them. This analysis was quite different from that of the quantity theory in several ways: its primary emphasis was on interest rates and investment, and output and employment could be altered by changes in the interest rate charged by banks. It is more in tune with the modern banking system and macroeconomic analysis, and served as a prelude to the foundation of modern macroeconomics outlined by Keynes.

JOHN MAYNARD KEYNES (1883–1946)

If Adam Smith is designated as the father of economics, Keynes deserves to be regarded as the father of modern macroeconomic analysis. There was no distinct field known as macroeconomics prior to the publication of Keynes' *The General Theory of Employment, Interest and Money* (known as *The General Theory*) in 1936. Keynes was a well-established economist and had published several books by that time. These represented expositions of the traditional classical ideas. *The General Theory* was a radical departure in many ways from these ideas and represented a broad attack on the fundamental ideas of the traditional classical school. It was written six years after the onset of the Great Depression, with massive unemployment year after year, and is based on the notion that while general equilibrium of the classical framework shows full employment, the economy rarely shows evidence of this state. *The General Theory* for the first time sets out a theory of employment and output, under which these variables can deviate from their full-employment

Extended Analysis Box 11.5: (*Continued*)

levels under the impact of aggregate demand changes. Keynes viewed investment fluctuations, acting through the multiplier, as a major source of these deviations. Another source of fluctuations was the speculative demand for money since it was based on expected returns in the highly speculative bond markets. Keynes dismissed the quantity theory of money, as well as the notion that the labor market clears on a continuous basis to ensure full employment or at least does so sufficiently fast not to leave excessive unemployment over lengthy periods.

In the analogy with the human body used in this chapter, Keynes' focus corresponded to that on the pathology of the economy and its pathogens. By contrast, the focus of the classical ideas corresponded to that on the healthy state of the body and only transient deviations from it.

The ideas of *The General Theory* were sufficiently novel for various expositions or 'guides' to explain it to the economics profession. One of these, by John Hicks in 1937, became the source of the IS-LM analysis. Out of *The General Theory* and its numerous expositions came the modern definitions of many terms which are now basic to macroeconomics: saving, investment, the multiplier, the speculative demand for money, effective demand, failure of markets to clear and the dynamic analysis relevant to this stage, the indirect transmission mechanism, etc.

11.3.1 Development of the Keynesian schools after Keynes

In the decades since 1936, variants of Keynes' ideas have been incorporated into a variety of quite different models. These models are known as Keynesian models. In one version or another, they dominated macroeconomics until the mid-1970s. Their major strength was in their analysis of demand shocks and the policies for dealing with them. Their major lacuna was their failure to consider supply shocks and the policies relevant for economies reacting to such shocks. The resurgence of classical economics in the mid-1970s, at a time of intense supply shocks from the dramatic increase in oil prices, pushed the Keynesian paradigm into the background. The classical paradigm still continues to be the dominant one. The limitations of the classical paradigm were to be revealed by the recessions of 2001–2002 and even more forcefully by that of 2008–10 in the world economy.

Both of these recessions experienced collapse of aggregate demand, both in investment by firms and consumer demand by households. The economy responded by decreasing output and employment, as predicted by the Keynesian analysis of demand-deficiency (see Chapter 9), so that the governments and the central banks were forced to pursue the Keynesian recommendations of expansionary monetary and fiscal policies — by cutting interest rates, increasing the money supply, and creating fiscal deficits.

11.3.2 Frequent themes in the Keynesianparadigm

A common concern of the Keynesian models is with the potential for involuntary unemployment, which is the deviation of actual employment in the economy from its full-employment level. Consequently, these models tend to pay special attention to the structure of the labor market: its demand and supply functions and whether or not equilibrium holds between them. Within this focus, some Keynesian models assume nominal wage rigidity, often justified by theories of nominal wage contracts between the workers and the firms. However, other Keynesian models do not do so but consider the deviations from general equilibrium that could occur even when the nominal wage is fully flexible.

The assumption of the rigidity or stickiness of prices in the economy is often regarded as another common theme of Keynesian models. While this assumption can impose deviations from a general equilibrium, it need not be the only cause or reason for potential deviations. Therefore, models within the Keynesian paradigm need not, and should not, all be based on price rigidity. There is, consequently, also a place for Keynesian models that consider the deviations from general equilibrium that could occur even when the prices are fully flexible.

While some of the Keynesian models assume equilibrium in the macroeconomic models, others do not do so. While some assume a special form of the labor supply function, others assume the same general form of the labor supply function — that is, labor supply depends on the real wage, not the nominal one — as the classical paradigm. While some assume nominal wage rigidity of some form, others do not do so. Similarly, while some models assume price level stickiness or rigidity, others do not do so. This variety in modeling within the Keynesian paradigm becomes even more evident when the Keynesian and the neo-Keynesian models are compared.

To reiterate, the variety of modeling — though perplexing and sometimes seemingly contradictory, among different models — in the Keynesian paradigm is essential to the proper study of the pathology of the economy. As our comparison with the pathology of the human body illustrated, it would be a mistake to force the Keynesian models into a single straightjacket, even though this would impart an attractive uniformity and a single model for the Keynesian paradigm as a whole.

New Keynesian economics

New Keynesian economics emerged as a distinct integrated model of the economy in the 1990s and has become increasingly popular. It has IS equations, a new Keynesian Phillips curve based on a price–adjustment equation and a Taylor rule for monetary policy.

11.3.3 The variety of Keynesian models

Given the complexity of the functioning of the labor market, the Keynesian models have resorted to a variety of simplifying assumptions about it. At the risk of oversimplification, the differing critical assumptions leading to different models of the Keynesian paradigm have been:

- The nominal wage is fixed (1940s and early 1950s). [Not presented in this book.]
- The nominal wage is variable but the supply of labor depends on the nominal and not the real wage (1950s and 1960s). [Not presented in this book.]
- The structure of the labor market can be replaced by the Phillips curve (late 1950s and early 1960s). [The Phillips curve was presented in Chapter 10.]
- A fall in demand leads to a demand deficiency relative to full-employment output because of the failure of commodity markets to instantly reduce the price level to the appropriate extent. Firms react faster and adjust output and prices. This leads to deficient demand models, which assume that when the demand for commodities falls, firms react faster than the economy and adjust the quantity produced (from Keynes' *The General Theory* in 1936 onwards). [Deficient demand analysis was presented in Chapter 9.]
- In the labor market, given hiring and training costs, it is optimal for firms and workers to enter into wage contracts, which tend to be staggered among firms and industries. In the presence of such contracts, the demand and supply of labor depend on the expected real (not nominal) wage but that the expectations on prices, needed to derive the expected real wage from the negotiated nominal one, are subject to errors and asymmetric information between firms and workers (1970s and 1980s). [The implicit contracts theory was presented in Chapter 8.]

- In the commodity markets, given the 'menu costs' of changing price lists etc., it is optimal for firms to resort to sticky prices (neo-Keynesian economics, 1980s and later). [The menu cost theory was presented in Chapter 8.]
- Workers' effort on the job is variable, leading to the efficiency wage theory of wages and employment. (neo-Keynesian economics, 1980s and later).
- An integrated macroeconomic model with sticky prices fixed by monopolistically competitive firms resulting in slow staggered adjustment of prices, Taylor rule for monetary policy and an IS equation (new Keynesian model, since mid-1990s).

As discussed earlier, the focus of the Keynesian analyses is on states other than full employment.

Monetary and fiscal policy effects in Keynesian models

The fundamental implication of the various forms of Keynesian models is that in conditions of aggregate demand deficiency and less than full employment, aggregate output depends upon aggregate demand and, therefore, on the demand management policy variables of fiscal expenditures, taxation, and the money supply. On the impact of monetary policy on real output, the major implications of the Keynesian analyses are:

- This impact will depend upon the existing demand deficiency in the economy, so that a linear relationship between real output and the money supply, with constant coefficients, is not a proper representation of the Keynesian implications. Notably, an increase in the money supply at full employment will mainly or wholly produce inflation, without much impact on output. But the same increase in the money supply when the economy is below full employment with considerable excess capacity will have a significant impact on output, though it may also produce some inflation.
- At any given stage of the business cycle, both the unanticipated and the anticipated values of the money supply — as also of the fiscal variables — will affect output equally, as against the classical assertion that only the unanticipated values do so. Therefore, the distinction between the effects of anticipated and unanticipated changes in demand are not very relevant to Keynesian models.
- The impact of money supply changes on employment and output does not necessarily proceed through changes in the price level. In fact, the impact of a money supply change on employment and output is greater, the smaller is the concomitant price level change. By comparison, along the expectations augmented Phillips curve associated with the classical paradigm, the change in output is greater the greater the price level change.

11.3.4 The critical role of dynamic analysis when aggregate demand falls

The introduction of demand deficiency in a dynamic context does away with the Keynesians' need to assume the rigidity of prices and nominal wages, or on the irrationality of the labor supply function based on nominal rather than real wages. For such analysis, given a fall in aggregate demand, the central issue is the nature of the individual firm's response to a fall in the demand for its product and the nature of the worker's response who is laid off or whose job no longer seems to be secure, in a context where the numerous markets of the economy cannot realistically be assumed to come into macroeconomic equilibrium instantly. This represents a shift in the debate from comparative static to dynamic analysis. There can be numerous plausible dynamic paths corresponding to any one comparative static macroeconomic model, and not all necessarily lead to full employment or do so within a short time. This implies a role for Keynesian demand management policies depending upon the state of the economy and the speed at which it is expected to redress deficient demand or involuntary unemployment.

Box 11.2: The Keynesian-Neoclassical Synthesis on Aggregate Demand

On the product, money, and bond markets, most Keynesians seem willing to accept the IS-and LM relationships and the aggregate demand analysis, as are those in the neoclassical model. This acceptance within the main Keynesian approach is often labeled as the Keynesian-neoclassical synthesis (of aggregate demand analysis). This synthesis evolved in the 1960s through the acceptance by both the neoclassical economists and the Keynesians of the IS and LM specifications for the demand structure of the economy. This synthesis excluded both the quantity theory range and the liquidity trap from the normal shape of the LM curve. Consequently, both fiscal deficits and money supply increases would be effective in increasing aggregate demand.

However, not all Keynesians go along with the acceptance of this synthesis, with some Keynesians — especially post-Keynesians — disputing the nature and/or the stability of the IS and LM curves and their accuracy in representing Keynes' own ideas in *The General Theory*. At the other end of the spectrum, some classical economists would wish to discard the IS-LM analysis while retaining the AD-AS analysis.

11.4 The Reformulation of Keynesian Approaches

11.4.1 NeoKeynesian building blocks for the reformulation of Keynesian macroeconomics

With the resurgence of classical macroeconomics in the 1970s and 1980, Keynesians sought to rebuild the foundations of their approach. This rebuilding in its early stages (1970s to 1990s) consisted of contributions on various aspects of macroeconomic modeling. These contributions were:

- The model based on menu costs, with a staggered price adjustment. This was discussed in Chapter 8.
- Staggered nominal wage adjustments model, based on staggered wage contracts. This was also discussed in Chapter 8.
- Implicit employment contracts based on hiring and training costs and/or firm-specific skills. Their implications for labor hoarding were discussed in Chapter 8. Such contracts can lead to staggered adjustment of employment among firms.
- The efficiency wage model based on variable effort and the incentives to increase it.

Each of the above implies that monetary policy can be used to change output and employment in the economy for the short run but not for the long run. This implication for the short-run effects of monetary policy is shared — though not always the assumptions on which it is based — with the earlier Keynesian models.

The models with one or more of these features were often labeled as neo-Keynesian ones. Note that in these neoKeynesian approaches, as in some of the earlier Keynesian ones, since the (sticky) price level does not rise in response to an increase in aggregate demand, the short-run increase in output occurs without a prior or accompanying increase in prices, so that the impact of monetary policy on output is not a function of the change in prices but rather of the change in the money supply itself. In fact, any increase in prices reduces the impact of monetary expansion on output. Therefore, in the neo-Keynesian approaches, the implication for monetary policy is that it is neutral in the long run but not in the short run. Further, higher rates of monetary expansion could evoke lower rather than higher increases in output. This impact of monetary policy does not require a reduction in real wages since the real efficiency wage — higher than the market-clearing one — creates a long-run pool of involuntary unemployment.

Many economists see the newer Keynesian approaches as replacing the earlier Keynesian ones. However, there are several distinctive elements in the earlier ones. Noteworthy among the elements of the earlier Keynesian school were the lack of a macroeconomic mechanism for instantly reaching equilibrium and the possibility of deficient demand. (see the deficient demand analysis of Chapter 9), compare with their absence in the neo-Keynesian approaches. Therefore, the newer Keynesian approaches should be taken to be another addition — rather than complete replacement of — to the stable of the models of the Keynesian paradigm.

11.4.2 Taylor rule and its incorporation into Keynesian macroeconomics

The Taylor rule is that the central bank pursues monetary policy by targeting the interest rate according to the equation:

$$r_t^T = r_0 + \lambda_y(y_t - y^f) + \lambda_\pi(\pi_t - \pi^T).$$

In the Taylor rule, r is the real interest rate, $(y - y^f)$ is the real output gap — i.e., the difference between actual and full-employment output — and $(\pi - \pi^T)$ is the difference between the actual and target inflation rates. Such a rule can be used in the context of any model that allows actual output to differ from the full-employment one for significant periods and implies that the economy can benefit from changes in aggregate demand brought about by monetary policy. Both these propositions are not consistent with the major proposition of the modern classical model that the deviations from full employment are, at most, transient and self-correcting. Both are consistent with the models of the Keynesian paradigm, so that the Taylor rule, first proposed in the 1990s, came to be incorporated into some of the subsequent formulations of Keynesian macroeconomics.

11.4.3 The new Keynesian model

Since the Taylor rule arose in the 1990s, at a time when the other components of the neo-Keynesian ideas were being refined and organized into a cohesive structure, some modern Keynesians have made it an essential component of their models. The cohesive form of the latest type of Keynesian models, developed since the mid-1990s, incorporates most of the building blocks of neo-Keynesian economics as well as Taylor's rule. This model has been labeled as New Keynesian economics. Its main components are:

- The IS curve analysis of the commodity market.[23]
- Staggered price changes (from the 'sticky-price' theory), based on the assumption of monopolistic competition rather than perfect competition, and staggered wage adjustments (from the wage-contract theory).
- Taylor rule for the specification of monetary policy on interest rate targeting.

The above components specify the short-run model and determine the deviation of output in the short run from the long-run one. For the long run, the economy is taken to function at full employment, with all prices and wage adjustments having been completed.

---

[23]The new Keynesian IS equation is somewhat different from the standard one presented in Chapters 4 to 6 of this book, and incorporates expectations about the future.

11.5 The Credit and Economic Crisis of 2007–2010: Which Theory Can Explain It?

The credit and economic crisis of 2007–2010 originating in the USA and spreading to many other countries, as well as Asian crises of the mid-1990s (see Chapter 16), provide an acid test of the validity of the various macroeconomic theories and schools. The stylized facts of these crises include:

- The crisis in financial (money, credit, and stocks) markets caused a fall in aggregate demand.
- The fall in aggregate demand caused a fall in output and rise in unemployment. Output clearly fell below the full-employment level and stayed below that level for several quarters and years.
- Money and credit were not neutral and a credit collapse was a major determinant of the depth and duration of the recessions. The prices of assets, such as houses, land, and stocks were also not neutral, and their rapid declines were contributors to the crises.
- There occurred a reduction in the number of available jobs, so that many workers who were otherwise qualified became involuntarily unemployed. Hence, the economies clearly had involuntary unemployment.
- The recovery in aggregate demand required substantial monetary and fiscal expansions; otherwise the economy would have had a worse and longer recession, so that such policies speeded up the return toward full employment.
- The collapse of credit played a key role in reducing aggregate demand and aggregate supply, and delaying their recovery.
- The financial collapse and economic crisis spread rapidly from the USA, the world's largest economy, to many other countries.

Economics is a science and if its theories are to be valid and useful, they must explain the preceding facts. The models of the classical paradigm, especially the modern and new classical ones with their emphasis on the full-employment general equilibrium state with minor, transitory, and self-correcting deviations, does a fairly poor job of explaining the above facts. Keynesian models as a whole do much better since they imply the non-neutrality of money and credit, the impact of credit, the occurrence of involuntary unemployment, etc. However, the new Keynesian model, with its emphasis on general equilibrium, seems to do poorly. The disequilibrium analysis of Chapter 9 is clearly very relevant to explaining the above facts, so that an exclusive focus on long-run or short-run equilibrium, as in many presentations of macroeconomic models, would be inappropriate and invalid.

Does macroeconomics as a whole provide an adequate explanation of the above stylized facts, and adequate guidance for policymakers? The answer to this has to be mainly in the affirmative. Macroeconomics does provide a fairly good understanding of the causes of the various crises and recessions and what monetary and fiscal policies needed to be pursued.[24] What it did not provide is precise enough knowledge of the extent and timing of the required policies. This extent and timing belong to the realm of dynamic analysis, which is as yet imperfectly developed. In any case, the dynamic patterns of the economy tend to differ from one recession to another. Their recognition and prediction in any one recession at best remains an art rather than a precise science, causing numerous differences and disputes among economists in diagnoses and policy recommendations.

---

[24] However, it still seems to lack an adequate understanding of the role of credit, which proved to be central to the cause and duration of the economic crisis of 2007–2010, as of many other crises.

11.6 Which Macroeconomic Paradigm Should One Believe In and Use?

While most textbooks and economists consider this to be a legitimate question, our remarks above suggest that it is an improper — and quite likely dangerous — one for the formulation of economic policies. The proper study of the economy requires the study of both its healthy state and its breakdowns. Since we cannot be sanguine that the economy will always operate in general equilibrium, the models of the Keynesian paradigm must not be neglected. Since we cannot be sure that the economy will never be in general equilibrium, the models of the classical paradigm must also not be neglected. Both paradigms have their relevance and usefulness. Neglecting either of them can lead to erroneous policies that impose high costs on the economy and its citizens.

For the practical formulation of monetary policy, the relevant and 'interesting' question is not the *a priori* choice between the classical and the Keynesian models, but rather the perpetually topical one: what is the current state of the economy like and which model is most applicable to it? There is rarely a sure answer to this question. Consequently, the judgment on this question and the formulation of the proper monetary policy are an art, not a science — and very often rest on faith in one's prior beliefs about the nature of the economy.

While one cannot dispense with one's beliefs and economists rarely give up their conception of the nature of the economy, the fundamental role of economics must be kept in mind. This is that economics is a positivist science, with the objective of explaining the real world. This is done through its theories, which, by their very nature, must be simplifications — more like caricatures — of reality. As such, they may be valid or not, or better for explaining some aspects of reality rather than others, or seem to be valid for some periods rather than others. Intuition and econometrics are both needed and useful in judging their validity and relative value.

A side implication of the positivist objective of economics is its normative role — i.e., the ability to offer policy prescriptions to improve on the performance of the economy, (hopefully) as a means of increasing the welfare of its citizens. Both the Keynesian and the classical paradigms are essential to these roles.

Box 11.3: The Anatomy of Two Quite Different Recessions: 1973–1975 and 2001–2002

The recession of 1973–1975 was mainly in response to increases in oil prices, engineered by the OPEC oil cartel. During this period, oil prices roughly quadrupled. This was a supply shock to the economy, which seemed to be permanent. In any case, this rise in oil prices was not only maintained through the 1970s but also further supplemented by another doubling of oil prices in 1980–1981. The economy responded by severe reductions in output and employment. The Keynesian economics of the day recommended expansionary demand management policies to reduce or eliminate these reductions. Such policies were attempted but — in hindsight — were clearly an inappropriate demand-based response to supply shocks. The results were recessions in 1973–1975 and 1980–1981, along with a lengthy period of stagflation.

The recession of 2001–2002 was triggered by a collapse of stock prices, starting with those of the Internet and computer stocks, which led firms to cut back on their investment and employment. This was soon followed by a collapse of consumer confidence and fall in consumer demand, further supplemented by the economic pessimism following the terrorist attacks on the World Trade Center in New York and the Pentagon. Severe and successive cuts in interest rates seemed to be ineffective in reviving investment since the firms had excess capacity relative to the perceived demand for their products. The classical paradigm would have predicted a severe fall in prices and wages to soon restore full employment. These did not occur.

Box 11.3: (*Continued*)

> The economy went into a severe recession, and the policymakers were forced to resort to expansionary fiscal and monetary policies.
>
> The recession of 2008–2010 and the East Asian crises of the mid-1990s have been discussed earlier in this chapter and are again discussed in Chapter 16 on business cycles and crises.

11.7 Paradigms and Policies

11.7.1 Stabilization versus pro-active policies

Stabilization policies are ones that attempt to stabilize aggregate demand at the level sufficient to buy the full-employment output of the economy at the current price level. Proactive policies are those that seek to increase the economy's output above its full-employment level by increasing aggregate demand.

11.7.2 Rules versus discretion in the pursuit of policies

Both stabilization and proactive policies can be pursued according to a rule (i.e., a set pattern) or in discretionary manner (i.e., not according to a set pattern but as the central bank thinks fit under the emerging conditions in the economy).

The Taylor rule, according to which the central bank's target interest rate depends on the output gap, has the objective of manipulating interest rates, and through them aggregate demand, to produce full-employment output. The Taylor's rule is an example of a stabilization rule.

11.8 The Role of the Government in the Macroeconomy

There has always been a role for the government in the economy. At the minimal level, this meant the provisions of some of the public goods, such as defence of the country, coinage, law and order, etc., provided by kings in earlier times. At its most extreme, it can encompass total control over the economy, including ownership of all production units and allocation of factors of production to different uses and payments to them, as under a communist system.

Modern industrialized economies tend to be largely, though not wholly, capitalist ones, with production and income distribution determined by markets and private economic agents (firms and individuals). The role of the government in such an economy tends to vary among countries and depends on their political system, philosophy, and history. Within the context of a democratic country with a largely capitalist economy, the 'conservative' approach argues for a 'small government' which focuses mainly on providing only public goods, with minimal regulation of the non-government sectors of the economy. Those in favor of this philosophy argue that governments, which are run by bureaucrats, are inefficient and often impose regulations that make the economy worse rather than better. Their arguments usually rely on the efficiency of production and factor allocation in the economy with perfectly competitive markets and flexible prices and wages. Such a system ensures that individuals and firms acting in their own interests (i.e., maximizing utility or profits), and without government interference and regulation, will maximize the economy's output and produce the socially optimal combination of commodities. This argument had produced during the 19th century the economic philosophy and approach to economic policies of *laissez faire*, discussed earlier in this chapter. The economic policies of Reaganomics and Thatcherism followed in the USA and UK during the 1980s and mentioned earlier in this chapter followed this 'small government' philosophy. By comparison, the more 'liberal' approach focuses on the income inequalities produced by the capitalist, free enterprise system, the failures of the market in the case of externalities, and the departures of many sectors of the actual economies from competition. The proponents of the liberal approach argue that governments should interfere in the economy to provide the goods that can be more efficiently provided by the government than by the existing market structures, and the government should regulate in the national interest firms and industries which tend to have monopolistic or oligopolistic structures. Further, government should pursue social objectives such as ensuring a minimum level of standard of living, children's welfare, access to medical care, and unemployment insurance. Because of its usual inclusion of social objectives, this liberal approach is now often associated with socialism.

There is no country in the world which has perfect competition and perfectly efficient markets in all their sectors, so that the actual economic structure does not provide the theoretical basis for the *laissez faire* approach to economic policies. There is also now hardly any country in the world which follows a pure capitalist philosophy. Further, the social and political philosophy of most countries does ask for the pursuit of certain social objectives. Therefore, nowadays, virtually all governments do actively pursue economic and social policies, though some do so more than others. Among the countries with somewhat lesser pursuit of economic and social objectives through government policies than others is the USA. European countries tend to be called socialist since their governments are more active in pursuit of social objectives than the USA. Most developing countries possess similar social objectives, but often lack the fiscal means to pursue them effectively to any significant extent.

11.8.1 Evolution of ideas about the role of the government

On the whole, the success of the capitalist economies versus those of the communist ones and of less regulated ones versus those of the more highly regulated ones since World War II produced by the end of the 20th century a general belief that controled and highly regulated economies led to lower growth of output and standards of living. This practical demonstration led to a movement in most countries during the last three decades of the 20th century toward a smaller government size than had earlier existed, with less ownership of production units and industries by the government and less regulation of the economy in general. Conversely, there was a move toward promoting competition both within the country and across countries. The latter helped the process of globalization, the spread of multinational corporations, and the expansion of international trade that occurred in the past three decades. In these decades, the free markets ideology seemed to have won the battle between market economies and centralized ones, many of which had been communist ones. The starkest example of this victory was the fall of state-dictated communist economies in several countries, many of which were earlier in the Soviet Bloc, and their transition to democratic socialism. In the case of China, while the political system of communism was retained, economic reforms after 1980 opened up significant parts of the economy to private market forces, thereby allowing the economic incentives of capitalism, which permit income differences and private wealth accumulation, to enhance production and improve economic efficiency. As a result, the output growth rates of both Russia and China shot up. In the domestic context of the USA, the supporters of capitalism and small government seemed to have won against the liberal ideology, with the words 'liberal' and 'socialist' often becoming somewhat pejorative in the US politics during the 1980s and 1990s.

The worldwide economic crisis of 2008–2010, initiated by problems in the financial sectors of the US economy, were seen by many observers as an outcome of a largely unregulated, free market, and capitalist financial system. This belief led to demands for more regulation of financial firms in terms of their capital requirements, the riskiness of their investments, auditing of their accounts and in many other aspects.

11.8.2 Classical and Keynesian approaches and the debates on the size of the government

How do the Keynesian and classical schools relate to the debates between small versus large government, between liberalism or liberal socialism and communism, or market versus centralized running of the economy? The Keynesian and classical paradigms are modeling approaches on the functioning of the macroeconomy. Since they study the workings of largely market-based economies, neither studies the communist, bureaucratic economies. Beyond that, the analyses of the Keynesian and classical schools can be applied to economies with small or large government, and purely capitalist or liberal socialist economies. However, since Keynesian economics focuses on the pathologies of the economy and the need for governments to interfere through monetary and fiscal policies in improving the performance of the macroeconomy, while classical economists focus on the full-employment level of the economy and argue against the need for monetary and fiscal policies, Keynesianism is often loosely associated with a larger government size than recommended by the classical economists. Further, Keynesianism is associated with greater regulatory role of the government over the economy and for the active pursuit of monetary and fiscal policies to stabilize the economy at full employment.

11.9 Conclusions

- There are currently two dominant paradigms in macroeconomics. These are the classical and Keynesian ones.
- The implications drawn from the classical paradigm are usually for its full-employment equilibrium states. For such states, output is also at the full-employment level. Since the objective of policy is normally specified to be the maintenance of full employment, which occurs anyway in the equilibrium of this model, there is no need or role for systematic demand management policies in such a state. Further, since the classical economists usually assume that full employment is restored within a reasonable or acceptable period, the classical prescription even for the disequilibrium states is that the economy should be left alone to return to full employment.
- Not all economists believe that the economy always achieves full employment or remains reasonably close to it. In particular, the Keynesian paradigm believes that the economy does not always perform at full employment for a variety of reasons.
- John Maynard Keynes was the founder of the Keynesian paradigm. It is now accepted that Keynes did not assume that workers based their supply behavior on nominal rather than real wages and did not assume that the nominal wages were rigid. While the classical paradigm focuses on price adjustments in response to demand or supply shocks, Keynes' analysis focused on quantity adjustments by firms in such situations to derive the disequilibrium paths of output and employment. If the adjustment toward equilibrium were a slow one, a shortfall in demand would result in a reduction in output and employment for periods of significant duration. If the economy was beset by fresh disturbances arising frequently, such as through bouts of pessimism or optimism about the future among firms' managers, the disequilibrium state would be a persistent phenomenon, with varying levels of employment or output.
- Neo-Keynesian economics came into being in an attempt to rebuild the Keynesian framework after the decline of faith in the 1970s in the Keynesian models and their policy prescriptions, and the resurgence of classical economics in the 1980s and 1990s. The efficiency wage hypothesis of neoKeynesian economics asserts the short-run rigidity of real wages, in contrast to that of nominal wages, which had been a component

of some of the earlier Keynesian ideas. The neo-Keynesian theory does provide a new basis for the short-run rigidity of prices through its hypothesis of menu costs in monopolistic competition. Both the Keynesian and the neo-Keynesian theories agree that monetary policy need not be neutral in the short run.

- In the presence of uncertainty, expectations play an important role in both paradigms. However, the classical paradigm assumes that economic agents formulate their expectations on the market-clearing prices and base their supplies of labor and commodities on these expected equilibrium prices. The Keynesian paradigm assumes that firms formulate their expectations in terms of the future demand for their products and produce accordingly, while households formulate their expectations on employment and determine their demand for commodities based on their expected income. These differing approaches to the formulation of expectations and subsequent responses by the two paradigms produce very different dynamic paths of output and employment in response to demand and supply shocks to the economy.

- Both the classical and Keynesian paradigms are consistent with the rational expectations hypothesis and can incorporate it. This implies that, in both cases, expectations are based on all available information. However, the application of this idea — and, therefore, of rational expectations — differs between the two paradigms. For the classical paradigm, since full employment is the normal state of the economy and any deviations from it are transient and self-correcting, the rational expectation is always that of the full-employment values of the economy's variables. For example, if the available information indicates that aggregate demand is falling, the rational expectation is that the economy will adjust fast to restore it to its full-employment level, so that at this rationally expected value of sales, the firms will continue to produce at the full-employment level. For the Keynesian paradigm, since the economy can stay away from full employment for considerable periods, rational expectations are those based on the expected actual state of the economy for the period ahead. For example, if the available information indicates that the economy is moving into a recession and will have lower demand than the current one, the rationally expected value of sales will be that they will fall — thereby leading firms to cut production and employment, which would take the economy away from full employment.

- In principle, interest rate targeting can be consistent with both the Keynesian and classical paradigms. However, the output gap in the Taylor rule implicitly incorporates the notion that the economy can stay away from full employment for significant periods. This possibility is more in line with the spirit of the Keynesian paradigm than of the modern classical model.

Keynesian versus classical economics in relation to the real world and real time

The classical and Keynesian paradigms represent different views of the self-adjusting dynamic nature of the capitalist economy. The former views it as being in full-employment equilibrium or close to it, with the dynamic forces providing a strong tendency to return to full employment after any deviation. The Keynesian paradigm allows the possible existence of full employment but is concerned that the economy does not always, or most of the time, perform at full employment. Further, a demand deficiency for output can generate dynamic forces creating involuntary unemployment that could subsist for extensive periods because there is no adequate and rapid equilibrating mechanism, or the likely mechanisms are destabilizing.

From the perspective of monetary policy, it does not matter whether the economy is away from full employment is described as being in disequilibrium, in temporary equilibrium or in equilibrium, or even whether there do exist mechanisms, such as the wage and price adjustments which will eventually bring the economy to full employment. If the economy left on its own can stay away from full employment for some time, the appropriate question for monetary policy is whether it is optimal for such policy to hasten the economy's return to full employment. On this issue, the neoclassical, and especially classical and new classical, economists claim that it is better to leave the economy alone, no matter what its state happens to be, while the Keynesians claim that monetary policy can have a positive optimal role in certain states of the economy.

Historically, faith in these positions has tended to vary considerably. The Great Depression of the 1930s in the industrial economies destroyed faith in the traditional classical belief in a self-regulating economy. The fairly stable macroeconomic performance of such economies in the 1950s and 1960s, though with active Keynesian demand management policies, produced shallow, and short-lived recessions and led to a slow revival of neoclassical economics — under the rubric of the Keynesian-neoclassical synthesis. This was followed in the 1970s — a time of stagflation, partly due to the Keynesian policy errors — which tended to restore faith in the general classical beliefs. The dominant paradigm was the classical one from the 1970s to the middle of the first decade of the 20th one.

The dragged out recession of the early 1990s and the increase in the rate of unemployment to double digits in many industrialized countries in the early 1990s was widely blamed on the restrictive monetary policies pursued in these years to reduce the rates of inflation, followed or accompanied by deficit-cutting strategies. The length of the recession and the tempered recovery until the mid-1990s seemed to indicate that the monetary and fiscal policies do affect real output and employment for significant periods, as the Keynesians claim. Further, the recession of 2001–2002 was induced by the collapse of stock market prices following the mania in Internet and computer stocks, leading to a collapse of business and consumer confidence. These were heightened by the terrorist attacks on the USA on September 11, 2001. The result was a severe fall in aggregate demand, to which the economies did not respond by a quick and sufficient fall in prices. Instead, firms cut back on output and employment, with some moderation of prices. The financial and economic crises of the world economy in 2007–2010 indicate the role of both financial factors (bank solvency and reductions in the availability of credit) and aggregate demand in causing severe declines in output. This causation strongly supports the Keynesian paradigm.

To conclude, the financial and economic crises of 2007–2010 and the collapse of credit markets (see Chapter 16), attributed by many to the largely unregulated financial sector in the USA in the preceding decades, brought serious doubts about the policies recommended by the classical economists. In the ensuing backlash against such policies, aggressive monetary and fiscal policies, as suggested by the Keynesian paradigm, were pursued by many countries to prevent the crisis from turning into a depression. There were also widespread calls for greater regulation of the financial sector by government agencies, all of which are in line with Keynesian ideas. Consequently, Keynesian doctrines, rejuvenated in newer forms during the preceding three decades, were brought into popularity by the recession of 2008–2010 and may become the dominant ones for the next few decades.

KEY CONCEPTS

Classical paradigm
Keynesian paradigm
Traditional classical approach
Neoclassical model
Modern classical model
New classical model

New Keynesian model
Reaganomics and Thatcherism

Comparison of the recessions
   of 1973–1975, 2001–2002
   and 2008–2010

Comparison of the booms of
   the 1960s and 1990s, and
The differing interpretations
   of rational expectations in the
   classical and Keynesian paradigms.

SUMMARY OF CRITICAL CONCLUSIONS

- The main paradigms in economics are the classical and Keynesian ones. Each consists of several different schools and theories.
- The classical paradigm focuses on the full-employment state of the economy and transitory deviations from it due to price misperceptions.
- The main branches of the classical paradigm are the traditional classical school, the neoclassical one, the modern classical one, and the new classical one.
- The St. Louis Monetarist School represented a transition from the Keynesian period to the modern classical one.
- An abiding theme in Keynesian models, originating with Keynes' *The General Theory*, is the failure of the economy to attain or maintain full employment. This is attributed to the imperfect and slow functioning of the competitive price mechanisms, and the likely responses of firms and households in terms of quantity adjustments (production and consumption) in disequilibrium. The Keynesian approach asserts that this failure is especially symptomatic of the labor market, so that involuntary unemployment is a common occurrence in the real-world economies.
- The Keynesian model based on this deficiency in the macroeconomic environment is the demand-deficient model. This approach posits that the rational dynamic responses by firms and households to conditions of inadequate demand and involuntary unemployment do not always take the economy to full employment or do so within an acceptable period.
- The new Keynesian theories rely on rational long-run behavior resulting in implicit contracts, staggered wage contracts, sticky prices due to menu costs, etc.

REVIEW AND DISCUSSION QUESTIONS

1. What are the underlying themes (or theme, if only one) of the classical paradigm?
2. What are the underlying themes of the Keynesian paradigm? Do they justify the study of just one model, one variety of models, or several different varieties of models? Why?
3. In order to explain the performance of the economy in economic recessions and booms, would you rely on either the classical paradigm or the Keynesian one, or sometimes on one and sometimes on the other? Explain your answer with reference to the different phases of the business cycle.
4. What are the distinguishing features of the modern classical model relative to the traditional classical approach to the macroeconomy?
5. What explanations for a high actual rate of unemployment are consistent with the modern classical model?
6. What explanation is offered by the Keynesians for unemployment when it is above its natural rate?
7. Specify the main tenets of the St. Louis Monetarism.
8. Specify the major components of the new Keynesian approach.
9. Milton Friedman showed that changes in the money supply could have a strong impact on national income and output. He also believed in the possibility of long and variable lags in the impact of monetary policy. What do these propositions taken together imply for the effective pursuit of monetary policy? Discuss.

10. What are the major reasons for the 1973–1975, 1980–1982, 1990–1992, and 2001–2003 recessions in the USA?

11. [Optional] What were the major reasons behind the strong expansion in output and employment of the late 1990s?

12. In the USA, President George W. Bush in 2000 and President Barack Obama in 2008–2009 proposed to Congress massive fiscal deficits, which they justified as being needed to fight the shortfall in aggregate demand at the time. In doing so, were they following the Keynesian or classical policy prescriptions? What had caused the shortfall in aggregate demand?

13. What is the Taylor rule? Explain why it is more in the spirit of the Keynesian paradigm than in that of the modern classical school.

ADVANCED AND TECHNICAL QUESTIONS

T1. (a) Are there levels of real output, interest rates, and the price level other than the full-employment ones in the neoclassical model? (b) How would the economy move from a disequilibrium position resulting from an unanticipated decline in investment to full employment? (c) Discuss the likely responses of firms and households following such a shock.

T2. High real wages is sometimes the explanation offered by the classical economists for unemployment above its natural rate in some countries (e.g., in Europe). What is meant by high real wages in this explanation? Show this diagrammatically. What can cause such high wages? Discuss whether or not these provide a likely cause of the last recession in your country?

T3. What were the main elements of Milton Friedman's macroeconomics?

T4. During the 1980s and 1990s, many economists argued that Keynesian economics give little guidance or even wrong prescriptions for dealing with the current economic problems in Canada (or the USA or Britain or any other country of your choice). What justified such comments? What are your views on this issue and how would you justify them for the country of your choice over booms and recessions?

T5. Sometimes, governments run fiscal surpluses and use these to reduce the public debt. Discuss the effects of such surpluses and debt reduction on aggregate demand, interest rates, and output. Very often, in running fiscal surpluses, it is not the intention of the government to follow Keynesian or classical policy prescriptions? What are some other reasons for running a balanced budget or one with a surplus?

T6. Write an essay on the causes of the credit and economic crisis in USA during 2007–2010. How did it spread to other countries? What policies were used by the monetary and fiscal authorities to fight these crises? What are the arguments for and against the decision of many governments to bail out their banks and other financial institution?

T7. Write an essay on the likely impact of the worldwide financial and economic crises of 2007–2010 on general views on the validity of the Keynesian versus classical economics.

PART III
Topics in Open Economy Macroeconomics

CHAPTER 12
The Foreign Exchange Market, IMF, and Globalization

This chapter presents the analysis of the foreign exchange market and the determination of the equilibrium value of the exchangerate. It also discusses the role of the international monetary fund (IMF) in assisting countries with balance of payments problems. It also includes a presentation of the economics aspects of globalization of commodity and capital flows.

Chapter 3 had presented the basics of the open economy concepts. This chapter starts with a brief review of the nominal and real exchange rates, as well as of purchasing power parity (PPP) and interest rate parity (IRP). Then, it proceeds to the analysis of the foreign exchange market and movements in exchange rates. The domestic country is again designated as 'our' country, and the rest of the world is designated as 'the world', 'foreign country', or 'foreign countries'.

Chapter 3 had defined the (nominal) exchange rate as *the number of units of a foreign currency required to purchase one unit of the domestic currency*. Using the dollar ($) as the unit of the domestic currency and the £ (British pound) as the generic symbol for a unit of the foreign currency, the nominal exchange rate is £s per $ (£/$). The Greek letter ρ (pronounced 'rho') is our symbol for the nominal exchange rate. The dimension of ρ for our definition of the nominal exchange rate is £/$. Note that some other textbooks define the exchange rate as dollars per pound ($/£).

The real exchange rate, designated as ρ^r, is the amount of foreign commodities required to purchase one unit of domestic commodities. Its relationship with the nominal exchange rate was specified in Chapter 3 by:

$$\rho^r = \rho P / P^F, \tag{1}$$

where:

ρ = nominal exchange rate in units of the foreign currency per unit of the domestic one (£/$),
ρ^r = real exchange rate,
P = domestic price level, and
P^F = foreign price level.

Therefore, the real exchange rate is the nominal exchange rate adjusted for the relative price ratio between the countries.

The nominal exchange rate may be left unregulated by the national authorities to adjust, demand, or supply pressures in the foreign exchange market or its movements may be controled rigidly by the central bank or allowed to vary within certain specified limits. An uncontrolled exchange rate is said to be a *flexible* (*or floating*) exchange rate. A rigidly specified exchange rate is said to be a *fixed* (*or pegged*) exchange rate. There are many combinations of these two basic practices. Thus, the authorities may operate a system whereby the exchange rate is allowed to vary within wide limits or is altered at pre-specified intervals.[1] The exchange rate regime is said to be a *managed* one if the exchange rate is flexible but the central bank intervenes (i.e., buys or sells foreign exchange) at its discretion in the foreign exchange market to 'manage' the magnitude of the movements in it.

12.1 Review of PPP

Chapter 3 presented three versions of PPP. These are the absolute version, the short-run relative version, and the long-run relative version. The absolute and relative versions of PPP are:

Absolute PPP:

$$\rho^{\mathrm{r}} = \rho P / P^{\mathrm{F}} = 1. \tag{2}$$

Relative PPP:

$$\rho'' = P^{\mathrm{F}''} - P'' + k'' = (\pi^{\mathrm{F}} - \pi) + k'', \tag{3}$$

where $k(k \neq 1)$ stands for the degree of deviation from absolute PPP, and depends upon: (i) barriers (tariffs, quotas, shipping, and other costs) to trade in commodities, (ii) the proportion of non-tradable goods in the calculation of the two price levels (P and P''), (iii) significance of capital flows, and (iv) imperfections in foreign exchange markets. k'' is the rate of change in k. In the short run, k may be taken as constant, which would make $k'' = 0$. In the long run, the determinants of k are definitely likely to change, so that k'' need not equal zero. Hence, the two versions of relative PPP are:

Short-run relative PPP:

$$\rho'' = P^{\mathrm{F}''} - P'' = (\pi^{\mathrm{F}} - \pi). \tag{4}$$

Long-run relative PPP:

$$\rho'' = P^{\mathrm{F}''} - P'' + k'' = (\pi^{\mathrm{F}} - \pi) + k''. \tag{5}$$

Of the various forms, economists prefer the short-run relative PPP equation over short periods. As argued in Chapter 3, under floating exchange rates relative PPP explains changes in the exchange rate, while under fixed exchange rates, it explains movements in the domestic inflation rate. However, in neither of these roles does this theory do well empirically. In modern economies, a major reason in addition to the existence of non-traded goods, for the failure of PPP is the dominance of capital flows in determining the demand and supply of foreign exchange for the country. This is so for most modern economies with free and large flows of foreign exchange on a daily basis. However, PPP and its relative version can be quite validly taken to represent *one* of the forces operating on the domestic inflation and exchange rates, but not the only one, and quite possibly not the dominant one in the short term for economies with large and sensitive capital flows.

---

[1]For example, under the *Smithsonian Agreement* reached in August 1972 between the USA and 19 other major trading nations, which are members of the IMF, the exchange rates between the US$ and the currencies of certain specified countries were allowed to vary within ±2.25% of the designated exchange rates. It had fluctuated within a band of ±1% of the designated rates earlier. In March 1973, the US$ was set free to float against other currencies.

12.2 Review of Interest Rate Parity (IRP) Theory

12.2.1 IRP as a theory of the interest rate

While PPP deals with commodity flows, the theory of IRP deals with *capital flows*. It was pointed out in Chapter 3 that the capital flows in international trade signify *financial capital* flows — not physical capital flows,[2] which are included under commodity flows. These financial capital flows are flows of money in exchange for financial assets (stocks and bonds) and ownership of physical ones (as, for example, when a domestic firm buys land and factories in other countries or a foreign firm buys land and factories in our country). When we buy foreign assets, the amount paid for them to foreigners represents an export (outflow) of the domestic currency from our economy. Conversely, when foreigners buy our assets, the amount paid to us represents an import (inflow) of foreign currencies to our economy.

Chapter 3 presented the IRP theory. It asserts that, in perfectly competitive markets,

$$(1 + R) = (1 + R^{F})(1 - \rho''^{e}), \tag{6}$$

where R is the domestic interest rate, R^{F} is the foreign one, and $\rho''^{e} = (\rho^{e} - \rho)/\rho^{e}$. $(1 + R)$ is the amount received from an investment of one dollar in domestic bonds after one period and $(1 + R^{F})(1 - \rho''^{e})$ is the amount expected to be received from an investment of one dollar in foreign bonds after one period. This equation is known as the *uncovered interest rate parity equation*. By expanding this equation, we have:

$$(1 + R) = 1 + R^{F} - \rho''^{e} - R^{F}\rho''^{e},$$

$$R = R^{F} - \rho''^{e} - R^{F}\rho''^{e}.$$

For very small values of R^{F} and ρ''^{e}, $(R^{F} \cdot \rho''^{e})$ is even smaller, so that the IRP condition is often simplified to the *benchmark uncovered IRP condition*, stated in Chapter 3, as:

$$R = R^{F} - \rho''^{e}, \tag{7}$$

where:

   $R =$ domestic nominal interest rate,
   $R^{F} =$ foreign nominal interest rate, and
   $\rho''^{e} =$ expected appreciation of the domestic currency[3] $[= (\rho^{e} - \rho)/\rho^{e}]$.

If there are differences in transactions costs, in the risks of investing at home or abroad[4] or in the degrees of risk aversion applied by investors to domestic and foreign investments, the benchmark form of the IRP condition was modified to allow for a premium or discount (see Chapter 3 for this analysis). The modified form is:

$$(1 + R) = (1 + R^{F})(1 - \rho''^{e}) + \alpha, \tag{8}$$

whose simplified approximate version is:

$$R = R^{F} - \rho''^{e} + \alpha. \tag{9}$$

---

[2] Such physical capital flows occur if a firm exports the components (which are in our category of commodities) of a factory and sets up the factory abroad. This action does not generate purchases or sale of foreign currency.

[3] Note that in the following expression, ρ^{e}, not ρ, is in the denominator. If period analysis is used, ρ^{e} will be represented by the expected future exchange rate ρ^{e}_{t+1} while ρ will be the actual current exchange rate ρ_{t}.

[4] These risks depend on the likely fluctuations in the exchange rate, the extent of political and economic uncertainty, home country advantage in information, etc.

Chapter 3 had shown in Fact Sheet 3.1 (reproduced below as Fact Sheet 12.1) for the USA–Canada differential in Treasury bill rates that α was positive or negative but was rarely equal to zero, so that IRP does not hold strictly even among developed economies with closely integrated commodity and capital markets. The sign and value of α depend on many factors, including the perceived riskiness of investing at home or abroad, the future prospects of the economies in question, the relative degree of knowledge of the relevant investment vehicles and economies, the degree of risk aversion, whether the country is a capital importing or exporting one,[5] etc. Therefore, the sign and value of α cannot be assumed to be constant over time. They tend to vary over time, as the determinants of α shift.

Taking accounting only of the fact that the country in question is a capital importing or exporting one. It is likely that α is negative for a capital exporting country if the general preference of its investors is for investing at home, in which case $R < (R^F - \rho''^e)$, so that the domestic return will be less than the foreign one. But α would be positive if the general preference of its investors is for investing abroad,[6] in which case $R > (R^F - \rho''^e)$.

The importance of stock market returns for capital flows: a problem for the IRP theory

As Chapter 3 pointed out, the major (and possibly the dominant) component of capital flows for certain countries are international investments in stocks, rather than in bonds. The expected returns in stocks are more speculative than those in bonds: the profits, dividends, and future resale prices of stocks are all uncertain while the coupons and redemption value on maturity are certain for bonds. Further, bubbles in stock prices tend to be more common and more pronounced than bubbles in bond prices, as discussed in Chapter 2. Therefore, the expected return on stocks can differ quite significantly from bond yields. They also fluctuate in different patterns.

Since international movements of capital due to investments in stocks can nowadays be much larger than those in bonds, the former limit the simple and straightforward application of IRP theory among countries, so that, in practice, the interest rates on bonds are rarely identical among countries.

Fact Sheet 12.1: Interest Rate Differentials between Countries

This fact sheet duplicates Fact Sheet 3.1 in Chapter 3. It shows the interest rate differential (plotted as the USA rate minus the Canadian Treasury bill rate) between the USA and Canada, which have closely integrated financial markets, so that there should be perfect capital flows between these countries. Interest Parity Theory implies that the interest rates should be identical between them. However, as the following graph shows, there is almost always a differential between them. The Canada T-bill rate was higher in Canada from the early 1970s to the mid-1990s; outside this period, the Canadian rate was sometimes higher and sometimes lower than in the USA. Therefore, the value of the interest rate premium/discount α is usually not zero and also not constant over time.

---

[5]Given a general preference for investing at home, capital exporting countries usually have lower domestic interest rates and capital importing countries have higher ones.

[6]LDCs and countries with political uncertainty usually fall in this category.

Fact Sheet 12.1: (*Continued*)

Simplified form of the benchmark IRP for short-run analysis

For simplification in comparing the rates of return among the developed, politically stable economies and considering only riskless government bonds, α is usually taken to be constant for purely short-run analysis. Further, it is usually set at zero for analytical convenience. That is, the *short-run benchmark IRP* condition is usually specified as:

$$R = R^{F} - \rho''^{e}.$$

Since our focus is on the short-run analysis[7] for such countries, this chapter will henceforth continue further with the use of the benchmark form of IRP with $\alpha = 0$, thereby implicitly making several assumptions. These are that investors do not have a preference between investing at home or abroad or that the risks are the same, the economies have similar future prospects, there are no differences in the brokerage costs of buying and selling domestic and foreign bonds, etc. Under the assumption of this simplified short-run IRP, funds will flow to the country that has the highest *expected return*.

Covered versus uncovered IRP

A *forward contract* in the foreign exchange market is a contract for the purchase (or sale) of a designated amount of a foreign currency at a specified future date at a specific exchange rate, with the contract being agreed to at the present time. The market in which forward contracts are traded is called the *forward market* (for foreign exchange). The financially developed economies tend to have several such markets for buying and selling foreign exchange at some of the future dates.

In the context of IRP, a dollar invested in foreign bonds will yield $(1 + R^{F})$ after one period in the foreign currency. To eliminate the risk of exchange rate changes during the investment period, the investor can contract *now* to sell the end-of-period receipt of $(1 + R^{F})$ in the foreign currency at the forward exchange rate. Designate the *forward exchange rate* as ρ^{For} and note that the current value ρ of the exchange rate is the *spot exchange rate*.

---

[7]Note that the determinants of α can vary for long-run analysis, since, as normally assumed in the definition of the long run, the factors determining its sign and value would not be *a priori* held constant .

For an investor to be indifferent between investing at home or abroad, and under the assumption that α equals zero, we need:

$$(1 + R) = (1 + R^{\text{F}})(1 - \rho''^{\text{For}}),$$

whose approximation is:

$$R = R^{\text{F}} - \rho''^{\text{For}}, \tag{10}$$

where $\rho''^{\text{For}} = (\rho^{\text{For}} - \rho)/\rho^{\text{For}}$. That if, for covered IRP, we replace in the IRP condition the expected exchange rate ρ^{e} by ρ^{For} and ρ''^{e} by $(\rho^{\text{For}} - \rho)/\rho^{\text{For}}$. This gives the *covered IRP condition* as:

$$R = R^{\text{F}} - (\rho^{\text{For}} - \rho)/\rho^{\text{For}}.$$

The difference between the original, *uncovered IRP condition* and the covered one is that in the former, the expected exchange rate change (ρ''^{e}) is not known, so that there is an exchange rate risk in making foreign investments, while, in the *covered IRP*, the forward rate is known, so that there is no exchange rate risk involved in covered foreign investments. Effectively, there exists *covered IRP* if the investors protect themselves against exchange rate fluctuations through forward contracts and *uncovered IRP* if they do not do so. For covered IRP to exist in the foreign exchange markets, there must be forward markets with zero or relatively low transactions costs. While these normally exist to some extent in economies with well-developed financial markets, they do not usually exist for most of the LDCs, which do not have organized and competitive forward markets for foreign currencies.

12.2.2 IRP as a theory of the exchange rate

To turn the benchmark IRP into a theory of the exchange rate, we used the following procedure in Chapter 3. The simplified version of IRP (under the continuing assumption that $\alpha = 0$) can be written as:

$$\rho''^{\text{e}} = R^{\text{F}} - R. \tag{11}$$

Hence, $R < R^{\text{F}}$ implies that $\rho''^{\text{e}} > 0$. That is, if the central bank lowers the domestic interest rate below the foreign one, the public must expect an appreciation of the domestic currency against the foreign one. This does seem counterfactual, since everyday experience indicates that a decrease in the domestic interest rate is usually followed by a depreciation of the domestic currency. The reconciliation between the theoretical and empirical observation is often explained in the following manner. Given perfect capital flows and the cut in the domestic interest rate, foreign bonds will pay a higher return than domestic ones. This will immediately translate into net capital outflows sufficient to cause a big depreciation of the country's exchange rate. From this low-exchange rate, the currency is expected to appreciate. For the expected appreciation to be validated, the IRP condition requires that the initial exchange rate depreciation must *overshoot* the eventual one.

Figure 12.1 illustrates the preceding scenario. It assumes that the domestic and foreign interest rates are initially equal and the exchange rate is stable at ρ_0, without a change in the demand and supply of foreign exchange rate. At time t_0, the central bank lowers the domestic interest rate below the foreign one. Investors react by sending abroad a sufficient amount of capital to immediately to drop the exchange rate to ρ_1. From this low level, the exchange rate gradually appreciates,[8] as required by IRP, so that it will eventually return to its

---

[8]The overshooting hypothesis does not explain why this adjustment is gradual and why the exchange rate does not immediately adjust to its eventual value.

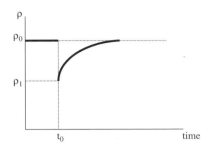

Figure 12.1

initial value of ρ_0. This appreciation would be expected by investors, so that the expected appreciation implied by the IRP condition occurs, as if instantly. Note that the drop in the exchange rate at t_0 is excessive relative to its eventual level. This excessive depreciation is called '*overshooting*' relative to the eventual exchange rate.

The inconsistency between the IRP's implications and common observations

The scenario shown in Figure 12.1 asserts that the cut in the domestic interest rate relative to foreign ones will immediately produce a sudden depreciation from ρ_0 to ρ_1, followed by a gradual appreciation (i.e., $\rho'' > 0$) *for quite some time*. This implication runs counter to the frequent real-world observation that a cut in the domestic interest rate by the central bank is not accompanied or followed by an appreciation but is followed by depreciations (i.e., $\rho'' < 0$) for quite some time (several quarters). While this observation might be explained by assuming that the exchange markets are imperfect and slow to adjust the exchange rate in response to shifts in the demand and supply of foreign exchange, exchange rate markets in the financially developed economies are known to be very efficient and adjust the exchange rate on a continuous basis. Therefore, our explanation, offered below, for the persistence in exchange rate movements does not rely on the claim that the *capital markets* are not efficient and are slow in adjusting the exchange rate to demand and supply shifts.

Our preferred main explanation for the observed relationship (i.e., depreciations following an interest rate cut) relies on:

- Capital flows are not only for investment in short-term bonds but also for investment in medium- and long-term bonds, as well as shares of firms. The return on shares is never very certain. While the current interest rate on bonds is known, future changes in interest rates are uncertain and can cause capital losses or gains from investment in bonds. Further, since future movements of exchange rates are uncertain, there is usually an exchange rate risk in investments in foreign bonds and stocks.
- Foreign exchange markets are efficient in the sense that they equate demand (orders to buy) and supply (orders to sell) instantly.
- Slow adjustments of portfolios by investors due to inertia, brokerage costs, and the uncertainty of yields and future bond/stock values.

    Following a reduction in the domestic interest rate, investors do not immediately make their long-run desired switch from domestic bonds and stocks to foreign ones but do so gradually.[9] Some investors adjust their portfolios immediately, then others and then still more, and so on. Further, even for a given investor, the uncertainty about the future course of interest rates and exchange rates often causes the investor to

---

[9]The reasons for this cautious switch of portfolios lie in the uncertainty of future domestic and foreign bond returns and prices, and in the uncertainty of the future course of domestic and foreign interest rate policies, so that there is uncertainty about the optimal composition of the portfolio over the future.

shift his/her funds gradually rather than in an abrupt manner to the new optimal long-run composition of his/her portfolio, which is never definite anyway. Overall, as the domestic interest rate is cut relative to the foreign ones, the capital markets see a slow and cautious switch from domestic bonds to foreign ones.[10] The resulting gradual net outflow of funds will, under the assumption of efficient capital markets, only gradually reduce the exchange rate. Therefore, a cut in the domestic interest rate will usually be followed by exchange rate depreciations for some time (i.e., $\rho'' < 0$). Rational investors will anticipate this pattern of depreciations, so that they will expect exchange rate depreciations (i.e., $\rho''^e < 0$), rather than the appreciation (i.e., $\rho''^e > 0$) implied by the IRP theory. These expectations of exchange rate changes will in fact be substantiated by the resulting movement in the exchange rate.

- The dependence of the exchange rate on the expected one and on the actual pattern of adjustments in the expected exchange rate value.

  In the real world, expectations on exchange rates are not dictated by the IRP theory but at least to some extent may be determined independently of it. Among these determinants is the past experience on the non-random part of exchange rate movements. This experience indicates persistence of exchange rate movements (i.e., depreciations usually followed by depreciations and by appreciations usually followed by appreciations) and expectations on future capital flows.

The depreciations may accumulate to an amount such that the exchange rate overshoots the long-run relationship asserted by IRP between the domestic and foreign interest rates. However, given the slow adjustments of portfolios by investors, any overshooting may occur not all at once but over several quarters. Note that the IRP theory implies that an overshooting depreciation phase will be followed by appreciations.

The different phases (depreciations, overshooting of the depreciations, and eventual appreciations) do seem to occur in the real world, since it is commonly observed that certain currencies do continue depreciating for quite some time, that these depreciations continue to a level which seems to be excessive/unjustified in terms of the performance of the domestic economy relative to foreign ones, and that they eventually begin to appreciate. An example of this pattern is provided by the Canadian dollar, which fell against the US dollar from about US$0.80 in 2002 to as low as US$0.62 in mid-2004, then climbed to about US$0.85 by the end of 2005 and to US$0.92 by mid-2006. It then fell to about US$0.85 in early 2007, but then shot up in late 2007 and touched US$ 1.08, before falling to about parity (i.e., one for one) in December 2007. The Canadian dollar fluctuated between 0.80 US cents and 0.90 US cents during much of 2009. The Euro–US$ exchange rate followed a somewhat similar pattern.

12.2.3 The impact of expectations on exchange rates

Rearrange the benchmark-covered IRP equation in the following manner:

$$\rho''^e = R^F - R, \tag{12}$$

where ρ''^e was our compact symbol for $(\rho^e - \rho)/\rho^e$, so that $\rho''^e = (\rho^e - \rho)/\rho^e = 1 - \rho/\rho^e$. Hence,

$$1 - \rho/\rho^e = R^F - R,$$
$$\rho/\rho^e = 1 + R - R^F,$$
$$\rho = (1 + R - R^F)\rho^e. \tag{13}$$

---

[10]Remember that there is always uncertainty about whether foreign countries will soon follow by corresponding cuts in their interest rates. Further, a considerable part of capital flows are for investment in foreign equities, whose returns are never known with any degree of precision, so that small cuts in the domestic interest rate on bonds rarely lead to immediate massive outflows of capital.

Hence, the current exchange rate not only depends on the interest rate differential between the interest rates at home and abroad but also depends positively on the expectations of the future exchange rate. One of the determinants of ρ^e is the interest rate differential $(R - R^F)$. If the rise in R increases $(R - R^F)$, the expected exchange rate would increase, which implies that ρ will rise, rather than fall, as implied by the IRP condition.

The expected exchange rate can clearly differ from the existing one. The expectations of future exchange rates can be volatile and sometimes shift rapidly. Suppose that investors suddenly form the expectation that the exchange rate is going to depreciate. This raises the expected return on foreign investments and sets up an outflow of funds, leading to the potential for a balance of payments crisis and a decline in the actual exchange rate to match the expected decline in it. If the central bank wants to avert this, it will have to raise the domestic interest rate drastically to compensate for the expected depreciation. However, sometimes, even such a rise in interest rates does not avert the foreign exchange outflows, with the consequence that the exchange rate would depreciate and continue to depreciate for some time.

12.3 PPP and IRP Combined

PPP and IRP represent two equations for deriving the exchange rate. They are:

$$\text{Relative PPP: } \rho'' = k'' + \pi^F - \pi. \tag{14}$$

$$\text{IRP: } \rho''^e = R^F - R + \alpha. \tag{15}$$

Long run analysis

For the long run, including the assumption that the errors in expectations are zero, we have $\rho''^e = \rho''$. This allows us to combine the IRP and PPP conditions, which yield:

$$R = \alpha + R^F + (\pi - \pi^F) - k''. \tag{16}$$

Note that this is a long-run condition. It shows that, *ceteris paribus*,

- An increase in the foreign interest rate will force the domestic one to rise.
- An increase in the inflation differential $(\pi - \pi^F)$ will raise the domestic interest rate. The intuitive explanation for the effect of the inflation differential on the domestic interest rate is that higher domestic inflation will lead to a depreciation of the exchange rate,[11] so that the domestic interest rate has to be higher than the foreign one to compensate for this depreciation.

Short run analysis

Short-run analysis takes k to be a constant, so that k'' equals zero. Therefore, assuming $\rho''^e = \rho''$, the short-run determination of the domestic interest rate under flexible exchange rates is given by:

$$R = \alpha + R^F + (\pi - \pi^F). \tag{17}$$

This equation can be rearranged as:

$$R - \alpha - R^F = (\pi - \pi^F).$$

---

[11] Remember that domestic inflation higher than the foreign one will make our commodities more expensive relative to foreign ones and decrease net exports. This will cause a balance of payments deficit, so that the exchange rate will be expected to depreciate. To offset this expected depreciation, investors will seek a higher interest rate from domestic bonds than from foreign bonds.

Hence, in the short run,

$$R = \alpha + R^{\mathrm{F}}, \quad \text{if } \pi = \pi^{\mathrm{F}},$$
$$R > \alpha + R^{\mathrm{F}}, \quad \text{if } \pi > \pi^{\mathrm{F}},$$
$$R < \alpha + R^{\mathrm{F}}, \quad \text{if } \pi < \pi^{\mathrm{F}}.$$

Further, in the short run:

- The domestic nominal return will rise relative to the foreign one only if the domestic inflation rate rises above the foreign one.
- For a small open economy, since the foreign interest and inflation rates are taken as given, the interest rate differential can be changed by altering the domestic inflation rate — for instance, by an expansionary or deflationary monetary policy.

For most countries, the cross-country differentials in interest rates do not always differ by a constant from the differentials in inflation rates for daily, quarterly, or even annual data.[12] There are several reasons for the departures from the implications of the joint PPP and IRP theories: ρ''^{e} does not always equal ρ'', the indices for inflation include the prices of non-traded goods and investors adjust their portfolios gradually because of uncertainty. Further, for some countries, capital markets are not perfect for international capital flows. While the above relationship does not apply in a precise form in real-world economies, its following two major implications are important and valid on average.

(i) *An increase in the domestic inflation rate tends to raise the domestic interest rate.* Note that this conclusion also comes from the Fisher equation on the nominal versus the real interest rate, so that there is a very strong basis for it.
(ii) *An increase in the foreign interest rate tends to raise the domestic interest rate.*[13] In practice, this conclusion is especially likely to apply to small developed economies whose net inflows of capital are quite sensitive to interest rate differentials.

12.4 The Market for Foreign Exchange, a Review

Chapters 3 and 5 had presented the analysis of the foreign exchange market. Both the demand and supply of foreign exchange are functions of the exchange rate as well as of other variables. If the exchange rate is permitted to be completely flexible and the foreign exchange market is efficient and stable, the exchange rate adjusts to equate the demand and supply of foreign exchange.

We supply our dollars *in the foreign exchange market* when we buy foreign goods (our imports) or foreign financial assets (for which we 'export capital') and need to pay for them.[14] The total payments for these sum to the supply of our currency ($S^{\$}$) in the foreign exchange markets. That is, the supply of our dollars ($S^{\$}$) arises when we import commodities (Z_{c}) or export capital (X_{k}).

---

[12]Note that this observation is about the short-term — not the short-run or the long-run — behavior of interest rates.

[13]An exception to this occurs if the central bank targets the domestic interest rate and chooses not to raise it. However, in this case, the central bank will have to balance the net capital outflows by selling foreign exchange out of its foreign exchange reserves.

[14]This supply of our dollars ($S^{\$}$) in the foreign exchange markets can also be looked at as the demand for foreign currencies ($D^{\pounds}$) since we need the foreign currencies to pay foreigners for their goods and financial assets.

Correspondingly, foreigners demand our currency, so that they can buy our commodities and financial assets and make unilateral payments to us on a net basis. In other words, the demand for our dollars ($D^\$$) *in the foreign exchange market* arises from foreigners' purchases of our commodities (our exports X_c) or of our stocks and bonds (which constitute our 'capital imports' Z_k) or because of net unilateral inflows of funds from abroad.[15] The net unilateral flows consist of two items: net interest and dividend payments NR to us (in excess of those we have to pay foreigners) and net gifts and donations NT (in excess of those we give foreigners).

Therefore, the supply and demand of our dollars in the foreign exchange markets are specified by:

$$
\begin{aligned}
S^\$ &= \text{Supply of our dollars in foreign exchange markets} \\
&= \text{Nominal value in dollars of our purchases of foreign commodities} \\
&\quad + \text{Nominal value in dollars of our purchases of foreign assets} + \text{OR} + \text{OT} \\
&= Z_c(\rho^r, y) + X_k(R, R^F, \rho''^e) + \text{OR} + \text{OT}. \\
&\qquad {+}\ {+} \qquad\ {-}\ {+}\ {-}
\end{aligned}
\tag{18}
$$

$$
\begin{aligned}
D^\$ &= \text{Demand for our dollars in foreign exchange markets} \\
&= \text{Nominal value in dollars of foreigners' purchases of our commodities} \\
&\quad + \text{Nominal value in dollars of foreigners' purchases of our assets} \\
&\quad + \text{IR} + \text{IT} \\
&= X_c(\rho^r, y^F) + Z_k(R, R^F, \rho''^e) + \text{IR} + \text{IT}, \\
&\qquad {-}\ {+} \qquad\ {+}\ {-}\ {+}
\end{aligned}
\tag{19}
$$

where:
X_c = value in dollars of exports of commodities (goods and services),
X_k = value in dollars of capital exports,
Z_c = value in dollars of imports of commodities (goods and services),
Z_k = value in dollars of capital imports,
IR = interest and dividend inflows in dollars,
OR = interest and dividend outflows in dollars,
IT = unilateral transfers (gifts and donations) to the domestic economy from abroad, and
OT = unilateral transfers (gifts and donations) out of the domestic economy.

A positive (negative) sign under a variable means that an increase in the value of that variable increases (decreases) the value of the variable on the left side of the equation. The determinants of imports and exports have been inserted in the above equations.

An appreciation in the nominal exchange rate ρ means an increase in the real exchange rate ρ^r, which makes our goods more expensive relative to foreign ones. Assuming that both exports and imports of commodities are elastic[16] with respect to price changes, increases in our prices cause X_c and $D^\$$ to decrease, while Z_c and $S^\$$ increase. Capital flows depend on the return R on domestic investments relative to the expected return ($R^F - \rho''^e$) on foreign investments, so that X_K and Z_K depend on R, R^F and ρ''^e. An increase in either the

---

[15] From another perspective, the supply of foreign currencies ($S^\pounds$) to us arises when foreigners buy our commodities (our exports) or buy our financial assets (which becomes our imports of capital) or make unilateral payments to us, and pay for them in foreign currencies.

[16] That is, the quantities imported (or exported) have elasticity greater than unity with respect to changes in their prices, so that the nominal expenditure on them rises as their price decreases.

domestic interest rate R or an increase in the expected rate of appreciation of the domestic currency increases the net inflows of capital.

Fact Sheet 12.2: Interest Rates and Net Capital Flows in the USA, 1985–2008

This Fact Sheet uses US data to provide some evidence on the dependence of net capital flows on the interest rate. It shows that net capital inflows (measured by the right-hand scale) are positively related to domestic interest rate (measured by the left-hand scale) over some periods but not over others.

There is a positive relationship between these variables since about 1997, but no clear-cut relationship before 1997.

Economic theory implies that capital flows would depend on the interest rate differentials among countries and not merely on the domestic interest rate. Since the USA is the world's largest economy, changes in its interest rate are often soon followed by those in other countries, so that the assumption of 'all other things being the same' (meaning constant foreign rates) would not be valid in this case. Further, capital flows depend on expectations of exchange rate depreciations and appreciations, and a host of other factors, including the stage of the business cycle among countries, riskiness of investment across countries, political events, etc.

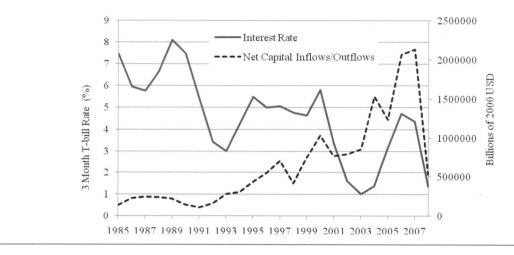

12.4.1 The relationship between the balance of payments and $(D^\$ - S^\$)$

Chapters 3 and 5 had presented the definition of the balance of payments. The balance of payments B is the amount of the net inflows (receipts less outflow) of foreign exchange into the economy. These net inflows, evaluated in dollars, equal the demand for our dollars by foreigners less the supply of our dollars in foreign exchange markets. This amount also equals the change in our foreign exchange reserves, which is measured in dollars by $\Delta R^\$$. That is,

$$B = \Delta R^\$ = (D^\$ - S^\$). \tag{20}$$

12.4.2 Diagrammatic analysis

If the nominal exchange rate rises (so that our currency appreciates), foreign goods become relatively cheaper (and our goods become relatively more expensive), so that our quantity of imported commodities increases.

With the elasticity of imports assumed to be greater than unity, the (nominal) expenditures on our imports also increase, so that our supply of dollars in the foreign exchange market increases. Hence, the supply curve of our dollars in foreign exchange markets has a positive slope. Conversely, as the nominal exchange rate declines (i.e., depreciates), our commodities become relatively cheaper for foreigners, so that the quantity of our exports increases. With the elasticity of exports assumed to be greater than unity, foreigners' expenditures on our exports also increase, so that the demand for dollars in the foreign exchange market rises. Hence, the (foreigners') demand curve for dollars has a negative slope. Therefore, the demand curve for our currency in the foreign exchange markets has a negative slope while the supply curve has a positive one, as shown in Figure 12.2a.

Figure 12.2a shows the demand curve $D^\$$ and the supply curve $S^\$$, with the nominal exchange rate ρ on the vertical axis and the quantity $Q^\$$ of dollars exchanged against foreign currencies on the horizontal axis. Net capital inflows $(Z_k - X_k)$ plus $(NR + NT)$ are held constant in drawing the curves in this diagram. The curves shown assume that the elasticities of both imports and exports are greater than unity. The equilibrium value of the nominal exchange rate is ρ^*. In Figure 12.2a, if $\rho > \rho^*$, as at ρ_2, there exists an excess supply of dollars (the domestic currency) in the foreign exchange market, which leads to the depreciation of its exchange rate. This lowers the exchange rate to ρ^*. But if $\rho < \rho^*$, as at ρ_1, there exists an excess demand for our dollars in the foreign exchange market, which leads to their appreciation, thereby pushing the exchange rate to ρ^*. Hence, the equilibrium exchange rate ρ^* is stable. This stability is indicated by the direction of arrows toward the equilibrium exchange rate.

Figure 12.2a has several limitations. These are:

- It only focuses on the impact of exchange rate variations on commodity flows, while holding the interest rates and the expected future exchange rate constant under the *ceteris paribus* clause since these variables are not on one of the axes of the figure. As a consequence, this figure keeps capital flows constant (or insignificant) and gives the erroneous impression that the changes in the commodity flows alone determine the movements in the exchange rate.
- The foreign exchange markets are financial markets that adjust the exchange rate on a daily basis to shifts in demand and supply, so that the shifts in capital flows — under interest rate parity — become the main short-run determinant of exchange rate changes. This is particularly so in the modern period in which capital markets have become increasingly globalized.
- The responses of commodity imports and exports to exchange rate changes are subject to significant lags.

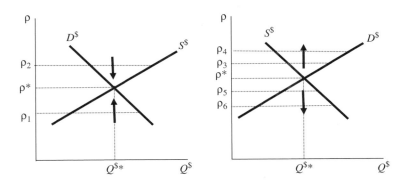

Figure 12.2

- As pointed out earlier, the assumption underlying the curves in Figure 12.2a is that the quantities of both the exports and imports of the country are elastic with respect to exchange rates and prices. Note that this assumption does not always hold, as discussed in the next section.

12.5 Demand and Supply Elasticities

The slopes of the demand and supply curves shown in Figure 12.2a assume that our imports and exports are elastic (i.e., with their elasticity being greater than one) with respect to changes in the real and nominal exchange rates. This means that, as our exchange rate depreciates and foreign goods become more expensive relative to ours, the *expenditures* (and not just the quantity) on our imports decrease and those on our exports increase.[17] However, this need not be so for all countries at all times. Even if it applies in the long run for a given country, it need not be the case in the short term while the buyers and suppliers take some time to make adjustments to their purchasing and production patterns as a consequence of a change in the exchange rate. Since our main concern here is with the value of net exports rather than with the values of imports and exports separately, we posit the following two scenarios.

1. An *inelastic short-term* pattern where the elasticities of imports and exports are such that the *value* of net exports *decreases* in response to a depreciation.
2. An *elastic long-run* pattern in which the elasticities of imports and exports are such that the *value* of net exports *increases* in response to a depreciation.

Figure 12.2a shows the long-run pattern. An extreme version of the short-term pattern, in which *both* imports and exports are inelastic, would have $D^\$$ sloping upwards and $S^\$$ sloping downwards. This case is shown in Figure 12.2b.

To compare the stability of the exchange rate in the Figures 12.2a and 12.2b, suppose that a disturbance causes the exchange rate to fall to ρ_1 below ρ^* in Figure 12.2a. Excess demand exists at ρ_1. The excess demand for dollars below ρ^* forces an increase in their value until equilibrium is restored at ρ^* through an exchange rate appreciation. However, in Figure 12.2b, an accidental fall in the exchange rate to ρ_5 will cause an excess supply of dollars, which will further lower their value — that is, cause a depreciation to ρ_6 — so that the market adjustments will lead to a movement away from equilibrium. Conversely, in Figure 12.2b, an accidental exchange rate appreciation to ρ_3 will cause a further appreciation to ρ_4, rather than a return to the equilibrium rate ρ^*. Hence, while the equilibrium exchange rate is stable in Figure 12.2a, it is unstable in Figure 12.2b. Therefore, depending upon the price elasticities of imports and exports during the relevant period, a depreciation of the exchange rate can cause either a decrease or increase in the net supply of foreign exchange.

12.6 The J Curve for the Value of Net Exports in Real Time

There are considerable disputes in the literature about the elasticity versus inelasticity of net exports for the industrialized economies in the *short term*. Some empirical studies do support such a possibility while others deny it. Intuitively, the *impact* or *short-term elasticities* for many commodities are often lower for some time,

---

[17] If the *supplies* of both imported and exported goods are infinitely elastic, the demand elasticities required for stability are known as the Marshall–Lerner condition. This is the requirement that the absolute values of the import and export *demand* elasticities sum to more than unity. The Marshall–Lerner condition ensures that the trade balance improves in response to a devaluation or depreciation of the domestic currency (assuming that the supply elasticities of commodities are infinite).

say for a year or more, than their long-run ones. There usually exists, some household inertia and lags in switching consumption between domestic and foreign goods, especially when there is product differentiation. There are usually also lags in switching production. In some, perhaps most cases, the short-term elasticities of net exports can be less than unity for a given economy for some quarters, so that a depreciation will worsen the balance of trade — i.e., reduce the value of net exports — in the short term, even though this balance eventually tends to improve in the long run.

Following a depreciation of the domestic currency, if the value of net exports initially falls and then rises, the net nominal exports follow a pattern resembling a J.[18] This pattern is called a *J curve* and is applicable to many countries. Such a curve is shown in Figure 12.3a. In this figure, assume that the net exports were negative and there was a balance of payments deficit at the pre-existing exchange rate ρ_0 at time t_0. This balance of payments deficit causes the exchange rate to depreciate (say to ρ_1 at time t_0), which leads to the time-path of the (value of) net exports shown by the curve marked net nominal exports: these fall for some time and then increase. That is, the elasticity of net exports is initially less than unity but increases over time to become greater than unity. Note that this figure shows the time path of net exports following a *single* specific depreciation. However, while net exports are falling, the balance of payments worsens[19] and causes further deprecations of the exchange rate,[20] so that the unstable market behavior induces a *cumulative* string of depreciations, before net exports do pick up and reverse some of the depreciations.

The corresponding figure for the exchange rate appreciations is Figure 12.3b, with an 'inverted J curve'. For this case, start at time t_0 with a balance of payments surplus at the pre-existing exchange rate ρ_0. This surplus causes an appreciation of the exchange rate (say to ρ_2) at time t_0. In the short term, this appreciation increases the value of net exports, which leads to further appreciations. There occurs, then, a cumulative string

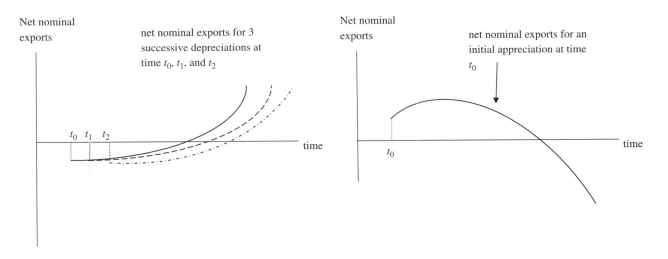

Figure 12.3

---

[18] Along the J curve, the elasticity of net exports is less than one for some time after a depreciation or devaluation but increases over time until it becomes greater than one.

[19] Capital flows are being held constant under the *ceteris paribus* assumption.

[20] Each succeeding depreciation would create a new J curve emanating off the preceding one. Figure 12.3a illustrates this by showing three J curves for depreciations at times t_0, t_1, and t_2.

of appreciations, with successive shifts in the J curve. Note that Figure 12.3b is drawn to show only the impact of the initial appreciation on net exports. Eventually, net exports do fall and the overall appreciation is partly reversed through depreciations.

Hence, the J curve analysis indicates the possibility that the exchange rate depreciations and appreciations will exceed — *overshoot* — their long-run amounts because of the short-term inelasticity of the net exports of commodities.

Under flexible exchange rates, the existence of a J curve for a country poses two types of problems in the short run:

1. A shock that appreciates the domestic currency will be followed for some time by further appreciations, with the trade balance developing a larger surplus, i.e., improving rather than worsening under the impact of the appreciation for some time. Conversely, a shock that depreciates the domestic currency will be followed for some time by further depreciations, with the trade balance worsening rather than improving under the impact of the depreciation.
2. The cumulative movements in exchange rates and the trade balance are likely to trigger supporting speculative flows of capital, thereby increasing the former's impact on the balance of payments and intensifying the extent and duration of the exchange rate movements, as well as surpluses or deficits in the balance of payments.

This analysis provides one of the reasons for:

- The observed persistence of trade deficits and surpluses even under flexible exchange rates.
- The observed overshooting of the exchange rate, with depreciations followed by further depreciations and appreciations followed by further appreciations over the short-term, relative to its long-run value.

12.6.1 Limitations of the commodity-based exchange market analysis

Note that the preceding commodity flow analysis of the foreign exchange market assumes that capital flows are either insignificant, which applies to few economies nowadays, or that we can hold the interest rates, expected exchange rate changes and hence capital flows constant under the *ceteris paribus* assumption while the value of net commodity exports takes its time to adjust in response to disturbances in the exchange rate. But the faster pattern of dynamic capital market responses often dominate the slower commodity flow responses and can turn a case of stability into an actual case of instability in the overall foreign exchange market, at least for some time — and vice versa. These capital flows are even more likely to accentuate a case of the basic instability, due to the J curve arising out of the commodity induced foreign exchange flows. In such a context, the central banks are often tempted to intervene in the foreign exchange market by buying or selling, as required, foreign currencies to try to stabilize the exchange rate of their currency against what they perceive to be short-term destabilizing influences.

12.6.2 Policy implications of the J curve

If a country needs to depreciate its currency to correct a balance of payments deficit and has a J curve, it needs sufficient foreign exchange reserves to ride out the worsening of the balance of payments during the early parts of the J curve. Alternatively, it could borrow foreign exchange from other countries or international financial institutions. In addition, it could raise its interest rate to boost capital inflows.

Extended Analysis Box 12.1: The General Experience of Industrialized Countries
and LDCs on the J Curve

The J curve analysis helps to explain the observed persistence and swings of exchange rate changes among countries. These depend on the duration of the declining part of the J curve, which is determined by the composition and nature of the country's exports and imports, their substitutes in consumption and/or production, and upon the supply conditions.

Even industrialized countries can possess a J curve for some time following a depreciation of their currency. The reasons among these include inertia in changing demand patterns between home and foreign products, production and marketing delays, imperfect competition and deviations from PPP, etc. Some empirical studies have supported the existence of such a curve, even for such advanced economies as those of the USA, Canada, Germany, and Japan.

Many developing countries export traditional types of products with low elasticities of demand in foreign markets and low supply elasticities at home. Their imports normally consist of industrial goods, which in general have imperfect domestic substitutes with limited production, so that the imports on the whole also have a low elasticity of demand. This scenario corresponds to the unstable case shown in Figure 12.2b for the foreign exchange market. Hence, these countries often face the possibility of the trade balance worsening in response to a depreciation of their currency and doing so for a longer period than for the industrialized countries. For many of the developing economies, attempts to eliminate the trade deficit and that in the balance of payments through a devaluation/depreciation of the currency often increase, rather than decrease, these deficits, at least for a significant period. As pointed out above, this requires that devaluations/depreciations have to be accompanied at least for some time by selling foreign exchange from the country's reserves or from loans from other countries to support the balance of payments and the exchange rate. They also often require other policy measures — such as contractionary monetary and fiscal policies to decrease domestic aggregate demand, import controls, etc. The long-run solution has to rely more on increasing net exports and higher net capital inflows.

The declining part of the J curve also implies that any devaluation/depreciation of the currency needs supportive monetary, fiscal, and other policies to prevent cumulative devaluations/depreciations. This need would depend upon the shape of the J curve and differ among countries. The existence of the J curve also points to the need of a country faced with a depreciation or devaluation to have either adequate foreign exchange reserves or access to a line of credit from the IMF and other countries, as a way of riding out the declining part of the J curve.

Implications of the above analysis for movements of exchange rates under flexible exchange rates

The preceding analyses of trade flows implied that, in the absence of significant capital flows or constant ones,

- If the elasticity of net exports is greater than unity (as in the stable case depicted in Figure 12.2a for the foreign exchange market), the exchange rate moves toward its equilibrium value. If shifts in exports and imports were to produce a balance of payments deficit (surplus), the exchange rate would depreciate (appreciate) to restore equilibrium in the balance of payments. If this return to equilibrium is sufficiently rapid, the central bank need not interfere in the foreign exchange market by buying or selling foreign exchange.
- If the elasticity of net exports is less than unity (as in the unstable case depicted in Figure 12.2b for the foreign exchange market) the exchange rate moves away from its equilibrium value. If shifts in exports and imports were to produce a balance of payments deficit (surplus), the exchange rate would still

Extended Analysis Box 12.1: (*Continued*)

depreciate (appreciate) but this would further worsen the deficit (increase the surplus) in the balance of payments. If this tendency is sufficiently powerful, the central bank may have to undertake offsetting sales (purchases) of foreign exchange to stop the series of depreciations (appreciations) from continuing.

The standard assumption of macroeconomic analysis is that the foreign exchange market is stable (first bulletted point) in the *long run*. Further, many economists assume that this stability also applies in the *short term*. If the market is unstable for the *impact period* of the devaluation/depreciation, the market returns to the stable case within an acceptable period and at an acceptable loss (if any) of foreign exchange reserves. That is, the assumption of the elasticity of net exports being greater than unity is reasonable for analytical and policy purposes. This is more likely to be valid for economies that mainly export homogenized industrial and agricultural products than for ones exporting specialized products in segmented markets.

The general view among economists is that it is acceptable for the central bank to offset random and transitory variations in its exchange rate. However, it is difficult to offset fundamental increases in the demand for foreign exchange or decreases in its supply — since these will cause continuing balance of trade deficits — by the (continuing) sales of foreign exchange from the country's foreign exchange reserves or from funds borrowed abroad. In this case, it is better to allow market-determined fluctuations in the exchange rate and, if needed, limit the potentially cumulative depreciations imposed by the J curve through the pursuit of various policies — including restrictive monetary policies — at the command of the central bank. This policy pattern is that of managed exchange rates within a flexible exchange rate regime.

12.7 Historical Experience with Flexible Versus Fixed Exchange Rates

Whether a country has a stable or unstable foreign exchange market in real time is an empirical question and generally one whose answer varies with the circumstances. Up to the late 1960s, the common belief in economics was that the foreign exchange markets tended to be unstable, so that it was in general preferable to have fixed exchange rates. This belief was embodied in the rules and recommendations of the IMF, with strong support from the USA from the founding of the IMF in 1945 to about the early 1970s. However, many of the major industrialized economies, especially that of the USA, suffered systematic imbalances in their balance of payments toward the end of the 1960s. Given these imbalances, combined with the speculative runs on several currencies, it proved impossible to maintain fixed exchange rates among currencies, and between the US dollar and gold.[21] In the early 1970s, the economics profession generally began to recommend flexible exchange rates and the IMF and the USA became strong advocates of flexible exchange rates.

In the years since the early 1970s, most of the world's largest trading nations have had flexible exchange rates[22] and unhampered flows of financial capital, without seemingly excessive exchange rate volatility, though

---

[21] The USA is the world's largest single trading nation and has enormous amounts of capital inflows and outflows. The currencies of most of the other major trading nations of the world had their exchange rates fixed directly or indirectly in terms of the dollar before March 1973. However, at that time, some of the currencies, such as the Canadian dollar, had a floating exchange rate against the dollar. Therefore, the US dollar, faced a mixed case of fixed and flexible exchange rates. The US dollar was set free in March 1973, to float against gold. Most other industrialized countries also moved to flexible exchange rate regimes during the 1970s.

[22] Over the last three decades, the European Union as a regional bloc including several major trading countries moved increasingly closer to a system of fixed exchange rates among its members, with flexible rates vis-à-vis other countries not in the union. In the earlier part of this period, the national currencies were permitted a limited float in a pre-designated narrow band, known as a 'snake'.

bouts of severe volatility have occurred for several emerging and transitional — mainly East European countries in the transition from communism to capitalism — economies. In general, this period has been one of the very fast growths in the international flows of both commodities and capital, accompanied by very rapid technical change (such as shifts in labor productivity and innovation) and other shifts in the comparative advantage of countries. These changes constitute potential pressures for changes in the exchange rates. Such pressures have been accommodated well by the flexible exchange rate system, while a fixed exchange rate system would most likely have created severe imbalances in the balance of payments of countries, which, reinforced by speculative and chaotic runs on the exchange markets, would have forced periodic changes in the fixed exchange rates.[23] Consistent with this experience, many economists believe that the flexible exchange rates provide greater stability in practice, especially in periods of significant shifts in the underlying determinants of the demand for and supply of foreign exchange.

However, the Latin American and Asian exchange crises during the 1990s seem to indicate a high degree of volatility in the exchange rates of individual countries. Part of the reason for this is that the extent of currency speculation that can potentially occur into or out of a currency can be a very significant proportion of the country's trading flows of foreign exchange and of its reserves. This is especially so for the smaller developing economies. In such cases, a speculative run into or out of the country's currency has the potential of creating large fluctuations in its exchange rate.

Economic theory and historical evidence do not make it unambiguously clear whether a flexible or a fixed exchange rate regime acts as a greater disincentive to such runs and/or contains them better. In general:

- Flexible exchange rates are better than fixed exchange rates at accommodating long-run shifts in the foreign exchange markets related to fundamental changes in commodity flows — e.g., from differential developments of technologies, different inflation rates, etc. — and to fundamental changes in the pattern of capital inflows resulting from shifts in the relative profitability of investment among countries.
- But flexible exchange rates and high capital mobility open the door to more frequent and potentially severe speculative runs into and out of individual currencies — especially for countries with unstable political systems and weak financial markets.

12.8 Measures to Reduce Balance of Payments Deficits

Remember that:

$$B = \Delta R^\$ = [X_c(\rho^r, y^F) - Z_c(\rho^r, y)] + [Z_k(r, r^F, \rho''^e) - X_k(r, r^F, \rho''^e)] + [NR + NT]. \tag{21}$$

There exists a balance of payments deficit — i.e., an outflow of foreign exchange — if $\Delta R^\$ < 0$. The measures that can be undertaken to reduce a deficit are:

- Assuming the elasticity of net exports to be greater than unity, devalue the exchange rate (if it is a fixed one), or allow it to depreciate (if it is a flexible one).
- One of the components of the balance of payments is net exports, $(X_c - Z_c)$, which — assuming the elasticity of net exports to be greater than unity — increase if domestic prices fall relative to foreign prices.

---

[23]The substantial fall in the exchange rates of Thailand, Indonesia, Korea, and some other Asian countries in the late 1990s is at first sight indicative of the volatility and instability of floating exchange rates. However, many of these exchange rates were not fully flexible but tied to the US dollar or the Japanese yen, and had became overvalued in effective terms against other currencies. The final assessment of whether this experience is indicative of the instability or not of flexible exchange rates is still pending.

Net exports also increase if domestic income falls and reduces imports. These require a fall in aggregate demand. Therefore, domestic deflationary policies, such as an increase in the interest rate (accompanied by the appropriate money supply decrease) or a reduction in the fiscal deficit (or increase in the fiscal surplus), can be employed to reduce domestic aggregate demand and domestic prices, which will increase net exports and reduce the balance of payments deficit.

- Another component of the balance of payments is net capital exports, $(X_k - Z_k)$, which depend on domestic interest rates relative to foreign ones and on the expected rate of change of the nominal exchange rate. Therefore, raising the domestic interest rate, through monetary policy, can increase domestic interest rates, which induce increases in capital inflows and reduce balance of payments deficits.

- Other measures that can be used to reduce a balance of payments deficit include increases in tariffs and/or reductions in import quotas,[24] which reduce imports and increase net exports. However, the country's maneuvrability to do so is usually subscribed by its international trade agreements, such as the North American Free Trade Agreement (NAFTA) and World Trade Organization (WTO) rules.

- Countries can also try to reduce their net interest payments to foreigners (i.e., increase NR). These can occur through readjustments of the interest rate or in the payment schedules related to foreign debts through renegotiations with foreign creditors of the outstanding external foreign debt. In a few cases, especially those relevant to the poorest countries, it may occur through 'debt forgiveness' by the foreign creditors, especially the IMF and foreign governments.

- Further, countries can try to increase their unilateral inflows of transfers (NT), e.g., by pursuing policies that promote higher remittances by expatriates living abroad.

From a long-term perspective, what is needed to curb balance of payments deficits is increases in the productive efficiency of the economy and an improved ability to compete in foreign markets. These need to be supplemented by measures to increase the attractiveness of the country for capital inflows. This requires both higher domestic returns and greater security of capital inflows, as well assurances to foreign investors that they would be able to repatriate their profits and capital.

12.9 The International Monetary Fund (IMF)

National policies on exchange rates have to be formulated in the context of the existing international financial system and arrangements. A core element of this system is the IMF.

The IMF was set up under an international agreement reached at Bretton Woods, New Hampshire, in 1945, and started functioning in 1947. Its main mandate was to be an international financial institution to oversee the member countries' payments arrangements and exchange rate policies, and to provide short-term financial assistance to members with balance of payments problems. Member countries were required to maintain fixed exchange rates and to devalue their currencies only in the case of a fundamental disequilibrium in their balance of payments and only after prior consultation in a specified manner with the IMF. The underlying support to this system of fixed exchange rates was provided by the decision of the USA to be on the gold exchange standard by maintaining a fixed exchange rate for its dollar against gold (at US\$35 to an ounce of gold) and convertibility of the dollar against gold. This system came to be known as '*The Bretton Woods system*'.

---

[24]The implications of such policies for the open economy require a respecification of the IS-LM model and are dealt with in the next chapter.

The imbalance in trade balances, especially large US deficits leading to turbulence in the foreign exchange markets, in particular the speculative runs on the US dollar at the end of the 1960s and early 1970s, led the USA to abandon the gold exchange standard in 1971 and let the US dollar float against gold. Further, in 1973, the European countries allowed their currencies to float against the US dollar. In 1974, the IMF adopted guidelines promoting managed floating exchange rates among its member countries. The encouragement and management of flexible exchange has since then been a central tenet of IMF policies. These changes meant an end to the Bretton Woods System.

Central to the IMF's role with respect to exchange rates is its mandate to exercise '*surveillance*' over its members' exchange rate policies and their macroeconomic and related structural policies. It promotes policies aimed at the elimination of balance of payments deficits, the creation of efficient and sound financial institutions, and limits on fiscal deficits, etc.

In recent decades, the IMF has been a strong supporter of the unrestricted international flows of both goods and capital, considering these to be essential for continued economic growth and prosperity. It uses its influence and powers to promote liberal trade practices and the free movement of capital among countries. Its power to influence a country's policies becomes especially effective when the country runs into severe balance of payments problems and needs large loans from the IMF.[25]

12.9.1 The IMF and disequilibrium in the balance of payments of the member countries

A core function of the IMF is to provide short-term loans to its member countries with balance of payments problems, whether due to negative net exports or capital outflows. Such loans are often in the form of a '*stand-by arrangement*' — that is, a line of credit — and are usually accompanied or followed by additional loans by other creditors. The stand-by loans are made subject to certain conditions, which often include an explicit commitment by the borrowing country to take specific and quantitative remedial economic measures, including the reduction of fiscal deficits and money growth rates. The objective of these is to reduce balance of payments deficits and to make it more feasible to repay international loans by specified dates. The policies and conditions accompanying the IMF loans are known as '*conditionality*'.

Extended Analysis Box 12.2: IMF Conditionality

In providing short-term loans to countries to cover their foreign exchange shortages, the IMF performs a function similar to that of national central banks when they act as a lender — at times, as that of last resort — to their respective commercial banks. While such a role is needed and of considerable benefit to member countries facing severe shortages of foreign exchange, it also carries *moral hazard*. Moral hazard arises because the availability of a loan or a line of credit reduces the compulsions and incentives for the borrowing country to contain its balance of payments deficits by appropriate policies.[26] Conditionality is a

---

[25]An example of the need for such loans occurred for Argentina in late 2001 and early 2002 to offset speculation against the devaluation of its currency, the peso. Argentina was not willing to meet the conditions required by the IMF, so that it was refused the required loans. Argentina defaulted on its interest payments on its bonds held by foreigners and, among other steps taken in January 2002, devalued the peso by 40%.

[26]Therefore, the existence of moral hazard implies that the borrower is more likely to resort to more risky choices if the loan is made than if it is refused. The loan transfers some of the consequences of the risky choices from the borrower to the lender.

Extended Analysis Box 12.2: (*Continued*)

device for containing moral hazard, since the loan will be made contingent on the pursuit of the economic adjustments required to enable the borrowing country to repay the loan within a specified period — usually within three to five years. The conditions often take the form of:

- An (often drastic) exchange rate devaluation or the requirement of floating the exchange rate of the domestic currency.
- Strict limits on fiscal deficits as a proportion of tax revenues or of GDP.[27]
- Low monetary growth rates.
- Increased liberalization, internally and externally, of the economy in the form of reductions in the tariffs and controls on foreign trade and on domestic industries.

In recent years, conditionality has had an underlying philosophy advocating free markets, competition, and democratic political structures, which some countries have resisted. At the international level, conditionality has consistently taken the form of supporting the liberalization of import and export flows. The required pursuit of policies under conditionality can have relatively minor consequences or, as in the case where the exchange crisis needs for its resolution major structural changes, have considerable economic, social, and political repercussions — which the borrowing country may not wish to incur. Many LDCs and economists have often contended that these repercussions seem to be ignored by the IMF. Further, it is often argued that the IMF policies on loans are really for the benefit of the richer nations, which gain by more prompt payment of their loans, as well as by the enforced import liberalization in the borrowing countries that increase the lending countries' exports.

For whose benefit are the IMF policies?

The IMF, the World Bank and the World Trade Organization (WTO) are currently the three dominant international organizations of the world economic system. Their policies are determined by their member countries and are in practice dominated by their wealthier members, especially the USA. They have often been accused of catering to the economic interests of the richer, rather than the economic and social interests of the poorer, nations. For the IMF, this accusation takes the form that the conditions imposed on the borrowing countries are not necessarily beneficial to their economies and often ignore their impact on the poor in those countries.

12.9.2 The IMF and capital flows

The original Articles of Agreement of the IMF signed in 1945 had allowed the use of controls by member countries on capital movements. Among the reasons for this was the aim of preserving for the member countries a degree of control over their monetary and fiscal policies. These controls also enabled the European countries to decrease or limit their balance of payments deficits and/or rebuild their reserves from extremely low levels at the end of World War II. Many countries, including most European ones, did maintain such controls for several decades after 1945. But, in recent decades, with the very considerable integration of the national markets for goods and services into the global economy, and in the current context of flexible exchange rates, the IMF

---

[27]These usually imply reductions in social welfare and anti-poverty programs. Such policies are unpopular with the public since they tend to lower incomes and increase poverty.

has strongly supported the liberalization of capital flows. Among the reasons for it is the belief that obstacles to capital flows reduce growth.

However, unrestricted capital flows also pose a risk since a major part of them is highly liquid and susceptible to sudden reversals — giving their most liquid component the name of '*hot money*'. These reversals can be due to shifts in the fundamental economic determinants of capital flows or be merely due to non-fundamental factors, such as (unjustified) shifts in the investors' perceptions of the riskiness of investment in the country in question. Reversal in capital flows can also occur because of international developments, such as the decisions of other countries to raise their interest rates or because other countries or regions come into 'fashion' as more attractive investment havens. With the considerable increase in international capital flows, the role of the IMF as a lender has become of even greater importance than in earlier decades. A country faced with a capital account crisis usually requires relatively large financial support at a few days' or few weeks' notice. If this strategy or 'cure' works, the loan can be repaid promptly; if it does not, there will be still greater demand for loans.

12.9.3 Special drawing rights (SDRs)

Under the initial arrangements made in 1945, the IMF was not envisaged as a central bank with the power to issue its own currency. This changed in 1969 with the creation of the *Special Drawing Rights* (*SDRs*) and their allocation to member countries. The SDRs are an international financial asset, which can be traded among member countries and used to settle payments imbalances among them. The IMF has increased the outstanding amount of SDRs at various times, allocating the increases among the members in proportion to their quotas in the IMF, which differs from the open market operations by which national central banks bring about increases in the monetary base. The total outstanding amount of SDRs is still a relatively small fraction (about 1.7% in 1997) of the non-gold reserves of the member countries, so that increases in it do not significantly affect the world money supply and the world price level.

With the replacement in 2001 of several European currencies by the Euro, a unit of SDRs is now[28] a weighted average of four currencies, the US dollar, the European euro, the Japanese yen, and the British pound, with its value calculated daily. As a weighted average, its stability is more than that of any of the individual currencies. Besides serving as a reserve asset for the member countries, it is also used as a unit of account in many international transactions and even for denominating private financial instruments. Countries can peg their currencies to the SDR, if they so wish, though, so far, few have done so. The SDRs are essentially a unit of account and their holdings are in the form of deposits. They do not have a physical existence and are not traded in national markets.

The interest rate charged by the IMF on its SDR loans is also a weighted average of the yields on specified short-term (mainly three month Treasury Bills) instruments of the countries (USA, UK, the European Union, and Japan) whose currencies are used for computing the value of the SDR.

Extended Analysis Box 12.3: The World's Demand for Liquidity

The need for assets that can serve as an international medium of payments arises from the world's transactions need for liquidity to finance international commodity and capital flows and as precautionary reserves held by individual countries against unanticipated net outflows of capital. This need for liquidity can be

---

[28]Initially, an SDR was a weighted average of four currencies, which are the US dollar, the euro, the Japanese yen, and the British pound.

Extended Analysis Box 12.3: (*Continued*)

met by holding foreign currencies and short-term foreign bonds. It is currently being met mainly in this manner by the large outstanding supply of US currency and short-term bonds to the world (non-US) economy. This gives the US Federal Reserve System the role of providing liquidity to the world economy. A somewhat similar, but more limited, role is also imparted to the central banks of other countries, such as Britain, European Union, and Japan, whose currencies and short-term bonds are widely held by other countries. However, national central banks are likely to put the interests of their own economies before the interests of the world economy. If they are in conflict, the world economy's interest is likely to suffer.[29] Therefore, it is preferable to have a central bank that is sufficiently remote from individual national interests and can focus more directly on the interests of the world economy and more impartially balance the conflicting interest of the individual countries.

Exchange and financial crises

At the international level, capital flows are now large, volatile, and subject to contagious movements, thereby providing the potential for exchange and financial (i.e., banking) panics. For a country with a flexible exchange rate, a panic attack will force a sharp and severe depreciation of the exchange rate. A country with a fixed exchange rate will usually be forced to devalue. In both cases, the country's financial institutions faced with panic withdrawals of funds are likely to become subject to exceptionally high failures, which can spread to firms in the production and trading sectors. The resulting fall in domestic liquidity will contract aggregate demand and output in the economy. All these effects tend to be excessive and often cumulative if the panic is unchecked. They can be moderated if the panic is managed through the provision of emergency financial assistance and management of the panic by the national central bank with adequate foreign exchange support provided by a world lender of last resort. The IMF is at present the only existing international financial institution that might evolve to fill this role.

Is the IMF a central banker for the world?

The IMF was neither set up to function as a central bank for the world nor yet fully evolved into this role. It is still much less than a world central bank since it is not able to control or change the world's liquidity, which national central banks can do for their economies. It does neither issue a widely traded currency nor have much influence on the world money supply or the total reserves of foreign exchange held by its member countries. The IMF's main similarity with national central banks is in its role as a short-term lender to member countries, especially during exchange crisis and also to provide them with liquidity while they tackle their balance of payments problems. This role is sometimes viewed as that of a lender of last resort for member countries, but is, in reality, somewhat different from and significantly less than the extent to which the national central banks can perform this function for their own commercial banks.

While the IMF has acquired considerable respect — mainly among the lending countries, but not necessarily among the borrowing countries on whom it has imposed severe and unpopular conditions — for its recommendations and considerable leverage over the macroeconomic policies and financial practices of

---

[29]The Great Depression was intensified by the absence of a world lender of last resort and the failure of any of the major national banks to address the international dimensions of their policies.

Extended Analysis Box 12.3: (*Continued*)

the countries that seek assistance from it, these still fall short of the powers exercised by national central banks over their financial sectors. Further, some of the member countries, especially the USA, exert greater influence on the world financial system and on short-term lending to countries with exchange crises than the IMF does.

Does the world economy need a central bank?

Two of the critical roles of a national central bank are the power to issue a financial instrument that can serve as reserves for private financial institutions and to be a lender of last resort. In the international context, the former requires that the world central bank — if the IMF was to become one — have the power to issue an international financial instrument that can be part of the foreign exchange reserves of the individual countries. While the SDRs do serve this role, the ability of the IMF to create them is severely limited and their current total amount is grossly inadequate as the main element of the foreign exchange reserves of the member countries.

Some economists have argued that the limitations on the power of the IMF to create an international currency or to do so to the required extent need not prevent its acting, at least partially, as if it were central bank. It can act to ensure liquidity for a country in crisis by being a 'crisis manager' and standard bearer in approving loans and imposing conditions, by the coordination of loans from national and private lenders, and generally by the signals its loans and assessments provide to the world markets.

The rising demand for the IMF to create a world currency

While the IMF has already created SDRs as an international reserve currency, their amount as of 2009 is relatively insignificant as a proportion of the foreign exchange reserves of countries or the world's need for an international medium of payments. However, the very severe US financial crisis starting in 2007 (see Chapter 16) and the continuing large outflow of dollars from the USA through the large and continuing deficits in its trade balance, as well as its large fiscal deficits, have created doubts in the world financial community whether the US dollar will maintain its value in the coming years. Its depreciation will mean that its holdings outside the USA will suffer corresponding losses, so that foreign countries would prefer to hold a more stable unit of international payments and foreign exchange reserves.[30] This has led to speculation among economic analysts about whether or not the IMF should create enough SDRs to meet the world demand, or a sufficiently large proportion of it, for increases in international reserves. Any such step is likely to represent a depreciation of the US dollar, as well as probably cause a global foreign exchange crisis. It would also mean very significant losses on the large amounts of US dollar assets held outside the USA, so that such a move is likely to be resisted by the USA and some of the countries with existing large holdings of US dollar assets. In view of these, any decision to allow the IMF to create assets that can displace the US dollar assets is likely to be a difficult political one, and is unlikely to come about easily or soon.

---

[30]During 2009, there were rumors that China and some other foreign holders of substantial US dollars wanted to decrease their foreign exchange holdings of US dollars and shift to other currencies. There was even discussion of the need for the IMF to create large amounts of SDRs, and the replacement of the US dollar by SDRs as the key currency for holding foreign exchange reserves.

12.10 The International Transmission of Crises and Business Cycles

Modern economies are closely linked through exports and imports of commodities and capital (see Chapter 16 on business cycles). Hence, a recession or a macroeconomic crisis in one large economy, especially that of the USA, which is the largest one, can affect other economies by reducing commodity imports from them, as well as reducing capital exports to them. This linkage is increased by the high degree of international integration known as 'globalization'. As an illustration, the financial crisis that originated in the mortgage market of the USA in 2007 immediately affected financial firms in many countries and its development into an economic recession in 2008 spread to other countries.

12.11 Economic Globalization

The effective globalization of the market for a single commodity would be the integration of the national markets for that commodity into a single one. However, the word '*globalization*' means *the integration of the national and regional economies as a whole into the world economy. Full globalization* would require the effective unification of all markets on a world scale, where the relevant markets are those of commodities, financial capital, and factors of production, including labor. The world markets and economies have not yet become integrated to this extent, so that the current stage of globalization is '*truncated globalization*'. The past three decades saw a major push for globalization in commodity and financial capital flows, though not very much in labor flows. In its current phase, globalization has to be thought of as the *process* of increasing integration of national commodity and capital markets into world ones.

The market system provides strong incentives in the form of larger profits for firms to increase the size of the markets for their output and inputs, first within the nation and then across nations. The latter requires the reduction of national barriers (such as tariffs and quotas) to trade, thereby implying liberalization of commodity flows. In the limit, the profit incentive to expand the market size would result in a single world market for the firm's products — i.e., globalization of the market. This expansion of the market requires: (a) a market-oriented system among countries, (b) the dismantling of tariffs and quotas, and (c) the reduction of communication and transport costs.

Historically, in the individual west European countries, the expansion of the market had been more or less completed through effective political unification and dismantling of regional barriers to trade by the beginning of the Industrial Revolution in the late 19th century.[31] The spread of railways, steamships, and the telegraph during the late 19th century deepened this process within nations by reducing communication and transport costs. Further, during the 19th century, the incorporation of the world into the empires of the European nations, promoted this process across nations, so that some internationalization of trade was already in place by the beginning of the 20th century. This process was interrupted by World War I, the rise of protectionism during the Great Depression of the 1930s during which nations tried to protect their national markets from foreign competition, and World War II. It picked up momentum after World War II under the aegis of the General Agreement on Tariffs and Trade (GATT), which was the precursor of the World Trade Organization (WTO). Both GATT and WTO set limits to the barriers that member countries can place on imports and subsidies to exports. However, the Communist countries that constituted a significant part of the globe were not members of GATT. Several factors in the last quarter of the 20th century produced a massive push

---

[31] This is never completely so. For instance, several provinces in Canada still maintain barriers to the flows of commodities and labor from other provinces.

toward internationalization of trade. One of these was the collapse of the communist system in several countries, accompanied by their adoption of market systems of production and exchange. Countries with mixed economies — i.e., with a mix of socialist and capitalist systems — decreased their regulations on production and exchange, as well as privatized many formerly nationalized industries. The information technology (IT) revolution reduced communication costs and the reduction in airfreight charges very considerably reduced transport costs and times. The net effect of these developments intensified the push toward effective globalization. This was accompanied by the unprecedented expansion of multinational corporations across the world.

For individual countries, the push for the globalization of commodity markets means that their international trade (usually measured as the sum of exports and imports)[32] as a proportion of GDP increases substantially. One estimate of the amount of this trade in 2000 was $6.6 billion per day. For individual countries, the globalization of financial capital flows means that the inflows plus outflows of financial capital also increase very substantially as a proportion of their GDP. The spectacular increase in foreign exchange transactions in the last few decades resulted in about $1.5 trillion a day of such transactions at the end of the 20th century. In addition, the transnationalization of production through direct foreign investment and ownership of plants in different countries by multinational corporations has increased very substantially. This trend toward globalization is most evident among the countries of Europe, North America, Japan, and some of the rapidly developing countries, such as South Korea and Taiwan. But there are few countries in the world that have not been affected by it.

The globalization of production and exchange is by no means complete or even dominant relative to national markets. The high-income countries, especially the USA, Europe, and Japan, have gone farthest along this route and been the main beneficiaries of globalization. More recently, developing countries, especially several Asian ones, have increasingly joined this movement. Overall, the process of the integration of the national economies into a global one is still in its early stages and has much further to go.

12.11.1 Causes of the push for global markets

The forces that have brought about the increasing internationalization of trade are:

- The reductions in transport and communication costs and delays. Among the former are the very substantial reductions in airfreight charges. Among the latter is the IT revolution.
- The self-interest of the world's major economic and political powers, which require ever-larger markets for their output and capital. Pre-eminent among these countries is the USA.
- The strengthening of the IMF, the WTO and the World Bank and their support for liberalization.
- The implementation of regional blocs and trade treaties, such as NAFTA.
- Political and economic unions, whose most successful instance is the European Union.

Most countries seem to have benefited considerably by opening up relatively closed economies to the international forces and the integration of their economy into the world one. Globalization imparts its economic benefits for several reasons.

- It increases competition from foreign firms, thereby forcing domestic firms to adopt the newer technologies (equipment, production techniques, managerial methods, etc.). This usually results in rationalization of domestic firms into larger and more efficient ones to compete with foreign ones.

---

[32]The 'openness' of an economy is usually measured by the sum of exports and imports, not by net exports.

- It increases the size of markets and permits specialization based on comparative advantage. These allow industries to benefit from economies of scale. It also allows diffusion of the stages of production among several countries (vertical diffusion) based on comparative advantage in production.
- It forces a considerable shift from state regulation and/or domination of national production and exchange to their determination by market forces. The former tends to be relatively inefficient and promotes corruption.
- It allows the inflow of knowledge on more advanced production and management techniques. The impact of this factor on output growth will be considered in Chapter 15.
- For firms, the integration of capital markets increases the availability of the amount and sources of external capital and reduces its cost.

These factors force the modernization of production, increased competitiveness, and specialization based on comparative advantage, which lead to higher output growth rates. Many economists consider globalization and market domination of economies, along with the IT revolution and other technological innovations, to be the major forces behind the rising growth rates of the 1990s in most countries and support the dismantling of barriers to openness of economies. These benefits become more visible once the institutions and technology of the domestic economy have adapted to the new economic forces brought about by globalization. However, it is likely that certain firms and groups that were among the beneficiaries under the old regime could lose from the shift to the new economic forces. It is also likely that certain firms and types of labor would suffer losses during the adjustment phase to the new long run, or from their failure to adapt to the new economic and political realities. Overall, at the level of the country, the general assumption borne out by the experience of most countries is that the losses will be less than the benefits, as well being of shorter duration and mainly during the adjustment phase, relative to the benefits, which are long run in nature, so that the countries participating in the globalization process will experience rising growth rates in their standards of living.

12.11.2 Measures of the extent of globalization

The extent of globalization is never absolute but one of degree, so that it has to be measured by indices of internationalization. It can be measured by various indices, among which the most important ones are:

- The level of trade flows relative to GDP.

  Smaller and more industrialized open economies tend to have larger ratios of trade flows relative to their GDP. Measuring trade flows by exports, the ratios of exports to GDP at the end of the 20th century were about: 61% for Holland, 39% for Germany, 28% for France, 25% for the UK, 10% for the USA, 5% for China, and 2.5% for India. For the world as a whole, exports as a percentage of GDP grew from about 5.5% in 1950 to about 10% in 1973 and then to 17% in 1998.
- The composition of trade.

  As international trade intensifies and industrial production rises, the composition of trade tends to shift from agricultural to manufactured products, and then to service industries. This ratio is higher for the industrialized economies than for others. For the world economy, more than three-fourths of exports now consist of manufactured goods.
- Capital flows relative to GDP.
- Foreign direct investment flows and the transnationalization of production.

  The transnational expansion of production within a firm occurs through foreign direct investment (FDI) in the countries in which the firms' plants are allocated. The amount of FDI in 2000 was over US$1.25 trillion.

Profit-maximizing firms attempt to cut costs by dividing their production into various components, which are produced in the firm's plants in different countries on a cost minimizing basis. This expansion leads to the transformation of national firms to multinational or transnational ones.[33] A considerable part of international trade now consists of the 'within-firm' trade of multinational corporations. One estimate of the extent of this trade relative to total exports is about 40%. Multinational firms have an especially strong incentive to push for free trade and have become the driving force behind the acceleration of globalization and its contemporary characteristics.

- The extent of foreign exchange trading relative to GDP.

The globalization of trade and capital flows has dramatically increased the trade in foreign currencies. By 1998, the amount of daily foreign exchange trades was over US$1.5 trillion, which was over 100 times the daily world exports.

12.11.3 Other aspects of globalization

Economic globalization often implies major changes not only in the economic policy and structure of the economy but also in the political and social spheres. Among the latter are:

- It has reduced the political and economic independence of governments and increased the power of international trade organizations, such as the WTO and NAFTA.
- It has reduced the power of governments relative to multinational corporations. It has favored a more laissez faire stance by governments toward the activities of multinational corporations.
- It has increased the impact of external shocks on the domestic economy.
- It has led to 'cultural internationalization', with their threat to national cultural patterns and industries. It has also diluted national control over the environment and social programs.
- The market orientation of economies seems to have increased income inequalities, at least in the short term, while lessening the ability of governments to redress this through progressive taxation and social welfare programs. As against this increase in economic inequality, the growth rate of GDP and wealth per capita have increased very significantly in most countries that liberalized foreign trade. This has reduced poverty and produced higher standards of living, even if income inequality did increase.

Most less developed nations that opened their economies seem to have benefited in economic terms. However, some have suffered, at least in the short term, on a net basis from some of its effects. In some countries, globalization has meant de-industrialization from the displacement of domestic production by cheaper or better quality imports and the take-over of domestic firms by foreign ones. Many have also experienced rising inequality between the capitalist class and the working one, and between the working classes. It has also heightened exposure to external shocks, which the relatively small and backward economies are ill equipped to handle.

12.11.4 Globalization and modernization

Although modernization and globalization are in principle different from each other, it is difficult to separate their effects in practice. *Economic modernization* is the process of the adoption of up-to-date production techniques and the appropriate education and training of the labor force. Inventions and innovations change

---

[33] One estimate of the number of the parent multinational firms is over 64,000 in 2000, with over 850,000 foreign affiliates.

these over time, sometimes drastically as in the Industrial Revolution or, more recently, by the technological revolution in data processing and communications. The adoption of newer techniques raises productivity, wages, and profits. Since technology keeps improving, modernization is a continuing process. Competition forces firms to adopt the newer technologies earlier than they would otherwise do. The experience with modernization over several centuries has established that over the long-term modernization brings considerable and continuing increases in productivity and standards of living for the population as a whole, so that it is highly desirable for the country.

Globalization increases both competition and the exchange of information on new processes and products, so that it is a major contributor to the modernization process. Since much of the improvement in technology may first originate in other countries, interaction with other countries is essential for continuation of the modernization process. Another part of this interaction occurs through foreign trade, which tends to boost modernization by forcing domestic firms to become more efficient in their attempt to remain competitive with foreign firms. Hence, globalization of the economy boosts its modernization. In turn, continuing modernization boosts the ability to compete internationally and therefore tends to increase exports. Conversely, withdrawing from the process of globalization often means falling behind in the continual modernization process. This reduces productivity growth and the growth in the standards of living.

Note that the modernization process often involves restructuring of the economy in which some sectors expand and some firms and workers benefit (in terms of job opportunities and wages), while other sectors, firms and workers lose. These losses can be quite significant, sometimes dramatic, over the short term for the affected sectors, firms and groups of workers. Firms and workers which cannot make a successful shift to the new technology and the sectoral shifts lose on a long-term basis while those which do so may only suffer short-term losses. Long-run analysis assumes that such adjustments have already been made, so that the losses during the adjustment process are ignored in discussions of the long-run consequences of globalization.

12.11.5   The persistence of nationalistic mercantilism — globalization limited to truncated globalization

Mercantilism is the economic form of nationalism and consists of the pursuit by countries of their own national advantage in the international sphere. The economic tools of mercantilist are tariffs, subsidies, quotas, and other devices to prevent competition from foreign countries. The latter include administrative delays at the borders, ban on imports based on (sometimes unjustified) charges of lack of safe production techniques abroad and unfair trading practices (dumping), etc. Since countries try to pursue their own national advantage, the international free trade agreements and globalization tend to be truncated (i.e., limited), so that the actual form of globalization in practice can be labeled as *truncated* (or *tilted*) *globalization*. The particular form of the truncated globalization put into practice by the international or regional trade agreements/agencies tends to favor countries with greater political and economic power. Therefore, many economists and countries claim that the rich industrialized nations only pursue international liberalization, through their policies or those imposed through international institutions such as the WTO, for those industrial goods in which they have comparative advantage. In general, the industrialized countries collectively seek to do so for high-tech industrial goods in which they possess a comparative advantage over the poorer, less technologically developed countries, while blocking the imports of low-tech goods from the latter. The textile and apparel industries are relatively low-tech and are among the first industries to develop en route to industrialization. They are also among the ones to which the economically richer and more powerful countries have been least willing to allow unhindered imports. Another such industry is agriculture. The industrialized countries have protected such industries through tariffs, subsidies, administrative rules, etc., and continue to do so extensively. While the barriers to textile and apparel imports from the developing countries have been gradually reduced, those to agricultural imports, especially though subsidies to domestic farmers, remain high. Such charges are often leveled at the USA, the European Union, and Japan.

12.11.6 The possibility of net losses from globalization

While, as pointed out above, the general experience has been one of significant increases in standards of living and average wealth levels in countries that joined the globalization bandwagon, some economists and organizations believe that under the existing form of truncated globalization, some countries, especially the poorer ones at lower technological levels, experience net negative effects from globalization. One reason for this net effect is that while the rich industrialized nations pursue the liberalization for industrial goods, their agriculture remains protected through tariffs, subsidies, administrative rules, etc., in which the agriculture-based poor countries might have a comparative advantage.[34] Another reason for this net effect arises from the restrictions on the diffusion of new technologies through the long-duration patents by the rich industrialized nations. The result of the tilted pattern of liberalization and globalization in practice becomes lop-sided in terms of net benefits across the two types (i.e., predominantly agricultural versus industrial) of economies.

However, as economic internationalization has progressed, the economic cost of maintaining closure to market forces and international competition has increased, so that few countries can now afford to keep their economies closed or isolated. There is considerable empirical evidence that the refusal to adopt the market system and to participate effectively in the international exchange of commodities and capital results in economies which become increasingly inefficient and technologically backward, with low per capita output and low growth rates. As a consequence, there are few countries that choose to remain closed to the international trade in commodities and/or continue to have state domination of production.[35]

The preceding focus on the net costs and benefits to the country as a whole hides the distribution of these net benefits across the different income and social groups within each country. Increasing the openness of the economy benefits those sectors (owners and workers) that are able to compete in the international sphere and expand; it has net costs for sectors that are not able to compete and decline. The more skilled workers who can adapt[36] to the skill requirements of the expanding industries benefit through greater demand for their skills see increases in their wages, while less skilled and less adaptable workers tend to lose.

12.11.7 Effects of globalization on commodity and capital flows

The globalization of commodity and capital flows has had both positive and negative effects. Among these are:

- They have substantially increased world trade, capital flows, and world economic growth, which have raised living standards significantly in all countries.
- They have increased the chances and scale of exchange crises and heightened the adverse impact of such crises on individual economies, especially smaller ones.

---

[34]Of course, the rich industrialized nations also try to protect those of their industries for which they do not have a comparative advantage.

[35]An excellent example of this is provided by China with a communist system, which is in principle opposed to the capitalist basis of globalization. Over the last two decades, it has chosen to accommodate the capitalist forces in many spheres, and benefited from very much higher growth rates than if had remained a closed economy.

[36]These are often the recent graduates and the young while the older workers tend to be less adaptable.

- They have also increased the possibility of the *contagion of crises*, with an exchange rate crisis for one country spreading to other countries, often in the same region. This is a worrisome externality of the closer integration of economies and world trade.
- The spread and size of multinational corporations have magnified dramatically. This has increased the economic power of multinational corporations relative to that of national governments, especially in the case of some of the smaller and poorer countries. Some experts view this as a disturbing erosion of national sovereignty.
- The increase in the size, competitiveness, and power of *markets* over that of national governments has increased substantially, raising the levels of competitiveness and efficiency in production and exchange. The power of governments to control and regulate trade and production has correspondingly decreased. Given the past record of many governments in this respect and the corruption that it fostered, the relative increase in the power of markets over governments is generally viewed as a very positive consequence of the liberalization process.

The responsibility of the IMF to act as a *lender at short notice and of last resort* — that is, when no other lenders/countries may be willing to lend to the country in question — to the national central banks and governments is, consequently, now of vital importance to the stability of exchange rates and the performance of the national and world economies. The IMF performed this role to a significant extent during the 2007–2009 worldwide banking and economic crises when commercial banks in the USA and Europe drastically reduced their lending not only to other domestic banks but also to foreign governments and banks.

12.12 Conclusions

- The world economy has experimented extensively with fixed, flexible, and managed exchanged rates. The post-World War II period started with a strong belief in the greater benefits of fixed exchange rates over those of flexible ones, and over the belief that devaluations other than those for really fundamental imbalances in the balance of payments were to be discouraged. The modalities of this determination were embodied in the rules established in 1946 for the IMF whose permission was needed before member countries could devalue their currencies relative to others.
- Another strong belief in 1946 was in the desire to maintain some form of control over the world's money supply through some form of the Gold Standard or the Gold Exchange Standard.[37] After 1946, this was done through setting a fixed exchange rate for the world's strongest currency, the US dollar, against gold at the rate of US$35 to an ounce of gold. The exchange rates for other currencies were set against the US dollar or against one of the world's other major currencies, such as the British pound or the French franc.
- As the economies of the world recovered from their war-torn states and expanded extensively during the 1940s and 1950s, the relative strength of the economies and the relative competitiveness of their export sectors had changed markedly by the later 1960s from their status in 1945. In particular, by the end of the 1960s, there were persistent deficits in the US balance of payments, which caused persistent speculative runs on the US dollar, as well as on many other major currencies, including the British pound (£). The fixed exchange rate system came to be viewed as an undesirable and unmanageable constraint on needed

---

[37]These are explained in Chapter 13. The Gold Standard was a system of fixed exchange rates in which the national currencies were fixed in value against gold. The Gold Exchange Standard was a system under which the national currencies had a fixed exchange rate against a key currency (mainly the US dollar), which had a fixed exchange rate against gold.

adjustments and on world trade. Eventually, in a series of steps taken during the late 1960s and early 1970s, the twin pillars of the fixed price of gold in terms of US dollars and the fixed exchange rates among currencies were abandoned. The general pattern of exchange rates among countries since that period has been one of flexible, though managed, exchange rates, though with relatively fixed ones by a few countries, of which (as of 2009) China was the one with the largest economy.

- Even though the trade in commodities grew enormously in the second half of the 20th century, that in capital flows came to dominate the foreign exchange markets on a short-term basis. Consequently, the short-term behavior of exchange rates, especially for countries with developed financial systems, is now explained by the interest rate parity condition. The application of purchasing power parity, especially in its relative form, for the equality of inflation rates is reserved for the long-run movements in exchange rates. The actual foreign exchange markets also exhibit a great deal of randomness, so that the deviations from the exchange rates implied by the interest rate parity occur on a daily basis.

- International flows of capital for certain countries are dominated by investments in stocks rather than in bonds, and the expected yield in stocks can have a different pattern than the yield on bonds. The capital flows for investments in stocks limit a straightforward application of the interest rate parity doctrine. Hence, for this and other reasons such as a home or foreign country preference for investment and the differences in risk, the interest rates among countries are rarely, if ever, equal.

- National economies have become more complex and more closely integrated into the world economy. Economists' opinions and national policies have gone from favoring fixed exchange rates among currencies — as in the years from the end of World War II to the early 1970s — to a strong recommendation for flexible exchange rates. The latter are now regarded as more suited to ensure balance of payments equilibrium in the face of day-to-day and longer-term shifts in the commodity and capital flows among countries. In particular, the IMF now advocates flexible exchange rates. However, there continues to be concern that a flexible exchange rate regime can expose the national currency to destabilizing speculative runs and thereby contribute to the volatility of its exchange rate. This is especially likely to happen in smaller or poorer countries if their exchange reserves are small relative to their potential inflows and outflows of financial capital.

- The general adoption of flexible exchange rates since the 1970s seems to have mitigated the potential disruption from fundamental shifts in the competitive positions of countries and protected the domestic economies from the differences in the inflation rates among countries. However, flexible exchange rates do hold the potential of large speculative runs on the currencies of selected countries and of the depreciation of their currencies in excess of what is implied by the fundamental economic forces. Combined with the short-term inelasticity of net exports as encompassed in the J curve, these speculative episodes can become self-reinforcing and damaging for the affected domestic economy, as well as for its trading partners.

- Expectations play a very significant role in speculation in the foreign exchange markets. To illustrate, the interest rate parity condition incorporates the difference between the expected rate and the spot foreign exchange rate. Speculation arising from differences in expectations and shifts in them can buffet currencies through speculative runs.[38] This is especially so since the amounts of liquid assets at the disposal of the world's major financial institutions, private firms, and even some individuals are extremely large, and shifts

---

[38] A speculative 'run' (i.e., a movement by many in the same direction) occurs if a lot of speculators simultaneously buy (or sell) the domestic currency. The cause of the run is the occurrence of a general belief among investors that the domestic currency is going to appreciate (depreciate). The result of the run under flexible exchange rates is to cause the currency to appreciate (depreciate). Under a fixed exchange rate, such a run requires the belief that the exchange rate can be made to change, and its purchases (sales) are called a speculative 'attack'.

in them of even small percentages from a given currency to others can cause major changes in the demand and supply of foreign exchange for the given currency, and thereby in its exchange rates against other currencies.

- The integration of national economies into a world economy is known as globalization. Its actual form is still a truncated one.

In terms of the short-run macroeconomic models, taking account of the existence of foreign trade and capital flows modifies the assumptions of our earlier closed economy models, so that the specifications of the expenditure and monetary sectors for the open economy change. These are dealt with in the next chapter.

KEY CONCEPTS

Purchasing power parity

Interest rate parity

The demand for the domestic currency (dollars) in the foreign exchange markets

The supply of the domestic currency (dollars) in the foreign exchange markets

Elasticity of net exports

The J curve

Fixed versus flexible exchange rates

Hot money

International Monetary Fund (IMF)

The Bretton Woods System

Special Drawing Rights (SDRs)

IMF conditionality

Globalization

Mercantilism

Truncated globalization, and

The IMF as a central bank.

SUMMARY OF CRITICAL CONCLUSIONS

- Purchasing power parity occurs under perfect commodity flows without transactions costs and is the doctrine that the real exchange rate between countries will be unity. Relative purchasing power parity is the doctrine that the depreciation of the domestic currency in terms of another will equal the difference between the inflation rates of the relevant countries.

- Interest rate parity occurs under perfect capital flows and is the statement that, under fixed exchange rates, the domestic and foreign rate of return on riskless assets will be identical. Under flexible exchange rate, the domestic interest rate will (approximately) equal the foreign one less the expected rate of appreciation of the domestic currency (alternated stated as: plus the expected rate of appreciation of the foreign ones).

- Investors in secure economies seem to possess strong home country preference, with the result that the portfolios held are overwhelming composed of domestic stocks and bonds. Consequently, the correlation between domestic saving and investment is extremely high, contrary to the implications of perfect capital flows resulting in IRP.

- Long-run analysis is based on the assumption that net exports are elastic. However, they may be inelastic in the impact period and the short term. Therefore, many economies experience a J curve following a depreciation of their currency. This results in overshooting of the depreciation from that required for the long run.

- While the original mandate of the IMF had been the promotion of fixed exchange rates except in cases of long-run imbalances in the balance of payments, its policies shifted in 1971 to the promotion of flexible exchange rates.

- In making loans to the member countries, the IMF often imposes conditions on the pursuit of monetary (low money supply growth rates) and fiscal policies (smaller fiscal deficits). In addition, there is also pressure toward increased liberalization of the economy of the borrowing country — that is, the reduction of restrictions (tariffs, quotas, and regulations) on commodity and capital flows.

REVIEW AND DISCUSSION QUESTIONS

1. [This question is partly based on material in Chapter 3.] Using your own experiences, provide some examples of the differences in the prices of seemingly identical goods among stores (a) in the city centre and the suburbs, (b) in different parts of the country, and (c) between countries. What factors account for these ostensible deviations from purchasing power parity? Are these factors likely to be stronger for (c) than for (a) and (b)?

2. [This question is partly based on material in Chapter 3.] How does relative purchasing power parity differ from (absolute) purchasing power parity between countries? Why might neither do well over the long term for a given pair of countries (say USA and Mexico or India)?

3. What are the determinants of the supply of the domestic currency (dollars) in the foreign exchange markets? Explain.

4. Identify two variables changes in which shift the demand curve in the foreign exchange market for our/domestic currency (dollars) to the right. Identify two variables changes in which shift the supply curve in the foreign exchange market for the domestic currency to the right.

5. What is the J curve? Why might countries experience a J curve following a depreciation of their currency?

6. Using the IRP hypothesis, discuss whether Canada or another country of your choice normally offers a premium over the corresponding interest rate in the USA, or vice versa. Discuss the reasons for this premium.

7. Explain the notion of the stability versus instability of the foreign exchange market. What does each imply for the movement in the exchange rate following an accidental decline?

8. Why are balances of payments deficits not always corrected or at least reduced by depreciation, and surpluses not corrected or at least reduced by an appreciation of the exchange rate?

9. In a two-country model, how would changes in the domestic economy be transmitted to the foreign one?

10. What is the IMF? What are its major functions nowadays?

11. What was the Bretton Woods system? Does this system still apply? If not, how has it been changed?

12. [Optional] What is meant by moral hazard as it applies to loans to countries (see Extended Analysis Box 12.2)? What implications does it have for risk taking by borrowing countries and the subsequent repayment of loans? What mechanism has been created by the IMF to limit moral hazard?

13. Why does globalization promote increases in the standard of living of countries that liberalize their trade in commodities and capital?

14. What is mercantilism? How does it modify globalization to its truncated form? Give at least two examples of this truncation.

ADVANCED AND TECHNICAL QUESTIONS

T1. You are given the following information:

$$P = 3, \quad P^{\mathrm{F}} = 2.$$

(a) If the central bank fixes the nominal exchange rate at 0.5, what is the real exchange rate?

(b) What does the absolute PPP imply for the nominal exchange rate?

T2. If $r^F = 0.25$, $P = 2$, $P^F = 4$, $\bar{\rho} = 4$ (that is, the exchange rate has been fixed by the central bank at this level), and the public expects it to remain at this level, what does (the benchmark) interest rate parity imply for the domestic interest rate?

T3. You are given the following information:

$$P = 110, \quad P^F = 220.$$

(a) What does absolute PPP imply for the nominal exchange rate?

(b) If the domestic rate of inflation is 5% and the foreign one is 20%, what does absolute PPP imply for the appreciation/depreciation of our (domestic currency's) *nominal* exchange rate?

(c) What does PPP imply for the change in the *real* exchange rate?

T4. Let the domestic currency be the dollar and the foreign one be the Japanese yen. Suppose that you are given the following information and questions:

Interest rate on dollar assets (i.e., assets denominated in dollars): 8% per annum; interest rate on yen assets (i.e., assets denominated in yen): 10%; current exchange rate: 100 yen per dollar; and actual exchange rate after one year: 120 yen.

(a) For a domestic resident, what is the actual rate of return on investing $5000 in yen assets?

(b) For a domestic resident, what is the actual rate of return on holding $5000 in dollar assets per year?

(c) *A priori*, what does (the benchmark) interest rate parity theory imply for the expected rate of change in the yen–dollar exchange rate? Is this different from the actual rate of change. If so, why?

CHAPTER 13
The Open Economy Under a Fixed Exchange Rate Regime

This chapter extends the macroeconomic analysis of the open economy to the fixed exchange rate case.
For a country with a fixed exchange rate, fiscal policies are likely to be more effective than monetary policies in changing aggregate demand in the economy.
Under a fixed exchange rate, since the exchange rate does not change to maintain equilibrium in the foreign exchange market, the pursuit of monetary and fiscal policies is more complicated than if the fixed exchange rate is floating.

This chapter presents the IS-LM model to derive aggregate demand for the small open economy that maintains a fixed exchange rate. As discussed in Chapter 5, the real interest rates are more relevant for the commodity sector and its IS curve, while the nominal rates are more relevant for international capital flows and the BP curve, which specifies the equilibrium points of the balance of payments. However, our use of the Fisher equation on interest rates and the assumption that the expected inflation rate π^e equals zero allows the simplification that $R = r$, so that R and r are used interchangeably for the interest rate in this chapter.

Chapter 6 with a flexible exchange rate derived the IS-LM framework for the open economy. Our arguments in this chapter show that for an economy that has a fixed exchange rate,

- We need to supplement the IS and LM curves with a balance of payments equilibrium curve (called the BP curve). The BP curve is upward sloping in the IS-LM diagram. The BP curve may be flatter or steeper than the LM curve.
- The IS curves between the fixed and flexible exchange rate cases have somewhat different properties.
- Balance of payments surpluses and deficits are likely under fixed exchange rates. These have the potential for changing the monetary base and the money supply. The central bank may allow this impact to occur or sterilize the balance of payments surpluses and deficits. The money market analysis and the LM curve are different under sterilization from that without sterilization.

13.1 The Balance of Payments (BP) Equilibrium Curve Under Fixed Exchange Rates

The equation for *equilibrium* in the balance of payments was derived in Chapters 3 and 12 as:

$$[X_c(\rho^r, y^F) - Z_c(\rho^r, y)] - [X_k(r, r^F) - Z_k(r, r^F)] + NR + NT = 0, \tag{1}$$

411

where:

  B = balance of payments,
  X_c = value of exports of commodities (goods and services),
  X_k = value of capital exports,
  Z_c = value of imports of commodities (goods and services),
  Z_k = value of capital imports,
NR = net interest and dividend inflows,
NT = net transfers from abroad,
  ρ = nominal exchange rate (£/$),
  ρ^r = real exchange rate $(= \rho P/P^F)$,
  P = domestic price level,
  P^F = foreign price level,
  r = domestic real interest rate,
  R = domestic nominal interest rate,
  r^F = foreign real interest rate,
  R^F = foreign real interest rate, and
  π^e = expected inflation rate.

To reiterate, an assumption made earlier in this chapter was that $\pi^e = 0$ for both the domestic and foreign economies, so that we have $R = r$ for both economies.

There are three endogenous variables (ρ^r, r, and y) and two exogenous variables (y^F and r^F) in the preceding equation. We can use this equation to plot a curve, called the BP curve, whose points indicate equilibrium in the balance of payments. The three potential forms of the BP curve relevant to the IS-LM framework are shown in Figures 13.1a, 13.1b, and 13.1c. Equilibrium in the balance of payments exists at each point of each of the BP curves in these figures.

In Figure 13.1a, start with the equilibrium point (r_0, y_0). Given the interest rate r_0, an increase in domestic income y beyond y_0 increases imports, leaving exports unchanged. For equilibrium in the balance of payments, this increase in imports has to be offset by an additional net capital inflow, which requires a rise in domestic interest rates. That is, an increase in national income y requires a rise in the interest rate r (with ρ^r held constant) to maintain equilibrium in the balance of payments, so that the BP curve between y and r has a positive slope.

There are also two *extreme* cases of the BP curve. One of these, illustrated in Figure 13.1b, occurs if there exists perfect capital mobility, implying interest rate parity. The second case, illustrated in Figure 13.1c, occurs if the capital flows are totally insensitive to interest rate changes. These are explained in the next section.

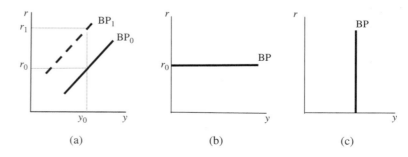

Figure 13.1

Note that the BP curve shifts if ρ^r changes. To illustrate, in Figure 13.1a, start with (r_0, y_0) on the curve BP_0. If P rises, ρ^r would increase, causing net exports at y_0 to decline, so that a larger net capital inflow induced through a higher interest rate than r_0 will be required to maintain equilibrium. Let this interest rate be r_1 and the BP curve through (r_1, y_0) be BP_1. Hence, the increase in the real exchange rate ρ^r shifts the BP curve upward from BP to BP_1. In Figure 13.1b, if ρ^r rises, the BP curve will also have to shift up. This cannot happen in Figure 13.1c: the capital flows have zero interest sensitivity.

13.2 The IS-LM Model for the Open Economy Under Fixed Exchange Rates

The IS-LM diagram for the fixed exchange rate case has four curves in the (y, r) space: a negatively sloping IS curve, positively sloping BP and LM curves and a vertical LRAS curve. Since both the LM and the BP curves have positive slopes, we need a hypothesis to determine their relative slopes.

13.2.1 The slope of the BP curve

On the slope of the BP curve, it was mentioned above that there are two *extreme* cases. These are:

1. Perfectly elastic capital flows. From Chapters 3 and 12, the IRP hypothesis under perfectly elastic capital flows is:

$$r = r^F - \rho''^e, \tag{2}^1$$

where ρ''^e is the expected change in the exchange rate. Assuming that the exchange rate is not only fixed but is also expected by the public to remain unchanged, $\rho''^e = 0$, so that IRP becomes:

$$r = r^F. \tag{3}$$

Hence, for a small open economy with a fixed exchange rate, the domestic interest rate is set by the foreign interest rate. In this case, the BP curve for any given exchange rate is horizontal, as shown in Figure 13.1b, at the interest rate r_0.

2. Capital flows are zero or completely insensitive to the domestic interest rate. In this case, the BP curve for any given exchange rate would be vertical, as shown in Figure 13.1c.

Economies with the financial markets well integrated into the global ones would have a BP curve closer to the horizontal form, while developing economies with virtually non-existing or isolated financial markets would tend toward the vertical BP curve.

13.2.2 The relative slopes of the LM and BP curves

We can, therefore, base further analysis on one of the extreme cases or on two slightly less extreme ones, one of which assumes that the BP curve is flatter than the LM curve, while the other assumes that it is steeper. The former is likely to be more applicable to the developed economies and is treated as the normal case for them.

---

[1]As the preceding chapter pointed out, this is an approximation.

It will be called the *interest-sensitive capital flows case*. The latter is likely to be more applicable to some of the developing economies and will be called the *interest-insensitive capital inflows case*.

Extended Analysis Box 13.1: Differences between the IS-LM Diagrams for the Flexible and Fixed Exchange Rates

There are two major differences between the IS-LM diagrams for the flexible and the fixed exchange cases.

First, if the nominal exchange rate is fixed, there would exist a BP curve showing the (y, r) combinations for equilibrium in the balance of payments. But if it is flexible and adjusts to yield continuous equilibrium in the balance of payments, the balance of payments equilibrium can exist at any (y, r) combination, so that there will not be a separate BP curve. Therefore, we have two quite different versions of the IS-LM diagram, one with a BP curve for the fixed exchange rate case and the other without a BP curve for the flexible one.

Second, any exogenous shift in the fixed exchange rate will shift the IS curve. But, for the flexible exchange rate case, a change in the exchange rate due to a change in the domestic interest rate will not shift the IS curve: the slope of the IS curve will incorporate within it any impact of this on net exports and thereby on income.[2]

Note also that the LM curve is identical between the flexible and fixed exchange analyses if the balance of payments flows are not allowed to influence the money supply under an active monetary policy. The short-run equilibrium analysis of the flexible exchange rate case assumes balance of payments equilibrium, so that there are no net inflows or outflows of foreign exchange. Therefore, the assumption of the sterilization of balance of payments surpluses and deficits is not needed for it. It is needed for the fixed exchange rate case.

13.2.3   General equilibrium under fixed exchange rates, a diagrammatic treatment

Figure 13.2a shows general equilibrium for the developed economy in the fixed exchange rate case. All the curves intersect at the general equilibrium point a. To reiterate, the steeper slope of the LM curve compared with the BP ones assumes that the international capital flows are more sensitive to interest rate changes than

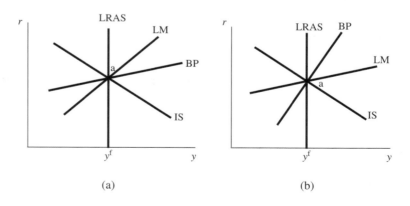

Figure 13.2

---

[2]However, as discussed earlier, changes in the domestic or foreign prices or foreign interest rates will shift the IS curve.

is the domestic money market,[3] so that an increase in y requires a larger increase in the interest rate to keep the monetary sector in equilibrium than that required to keep the balance of payments in equilibrium. Figure 13.2b shows what we referred to as the interest insensitive capital-inflows case. All the 'curves' are shown as straight lines.

In order to limit the number of cases that are investigated, we will henceforth mainly analyze the developed economy case, mostly without even referring to it as such. That is, the default assumption in the rest of this chapter is that the BP curve for any given exchange rate has a flatter slope than the LM curve. However, some analysis of the interest insensitive capital-inflows case — relevant to many LDCs — is also presented in the Extended Analysis Boxes 13.2 and 13.3.

To analyze the roles of monetary and fiscal policies in the open economy, remember that these are demand management policies. As such, the analysis of their role can be simplified by first focusing only on aggregate demand (AD) in the economy and only later studying the interaction between aggregate demand changes and supply responses.

13.3 Managing Aggregate Demand in the Open Economy: Monetary and Fiscal Policies Under Fixed Exchange Rates

The basic difference between the fiscal and the monetary policies in the macroeconomic static models arises because an expansionary fiscal policy raises the interest rate, while an expansionary monetary policy lowers them. A rise in the domestic interest rate increases net capital inflows, while a fall in this interest rate decreases such capital inflows. Therefore, if the balance of payments is initially in equilibrium, an expansionary fiscal policy creates a surplus ($\Delta R^F > 0$)[4] by raising interest rates. But an expansionary monetary policy creates a deficit ($\Delta R^F < 0$) in the balance of payments by lowering the rate of interest.

Assume that the economy has a fixed exchange rate, has a flatter BP curve relative to the LM one, and is initially in overall equilibrium, as shown in Figure 13.3a.

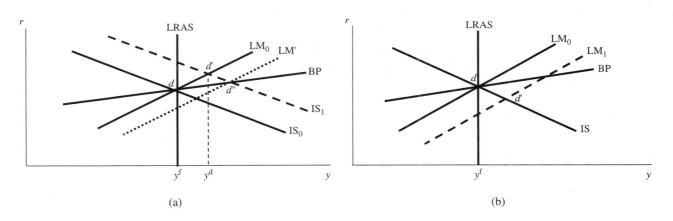

(a)   (b)

Figure 13.3

---

[3]The international and domestic bond markets are different in nature: the former represents an exchange of domestic for foreign bonds while the latter represents exchanges between money and bonds and requires equilibrium in the market for money.

[4]Note that R^F refers to foreign exchange reserves.

13.3.1 The impact of an expansionary fiscal policy on aggregate demand

In Figure 13.3a, an *expansionary fiscal policy* will shift the IS curve from IS_0 to IS_1. This would increase aggregate demand to d', at the intersection of the IS and LM curves. As shown in Figure 13.3a, this policy would raise the domestic interest rate and create a balance of payments surplus (since the interest rate at d' is higher than required for equilibrium in the balance of payments) while increasing domestic demand. The further effects are:

- If the balance of payments is *sterilized* under an active monetary policy, the money supply will not expand, but the domestic interest rate will stay above the foreign ones. The balance of payments surplus will continue, with a resultant continuing increase in foreign exchange reserves. Many countries consider this outcome to be quite desirable.
- If the balance of payments is *not sterilized*, as under a passive monetary policy, it will cause an expansion of the monetary base and hence of the money supply, thereby shifting the LM curve to the right from LM_0 to LM'. This will place downward pressure on interest rates, causing interest rates to fall toward their former level, while causing a further expansion of demand. Aggregate demand will eventually settle at d'' at the intersection of IS', BP, and LM', so that the fiscal expansion is supported by an induced expansion in the money supply.

13.3.2 The impact of an expansionary monetary policy on aggregate demand

Now consider the effects of an *expansionary monetary policy*. The increase in the money supply shifts the LM curve from LM_0 to LM_1 in Figure 13.3b, thereby increasing aggregate demand in the economy to d' while lowering the interest rate. The latter reduces net capital inflows and causes a deficit in the balance of payments. This deficit causes the money supply to fall unless this effect was offset by the monetary authorities through an active monetary policy. Hence, the two further scenarios are:

1. If the balance of payments is *sterilized*, the money supply would remain at its new enlarged level and its expansionary impact upon the economy would continue. But so would the external deficit, with the result that the country will run down its foreign exchange reserves by a corresponding amount. Such a policy clearly has a limit and can be pursued only up to the point where the reserves begin to fall to unacceptably low levels. The money supply will then have to be cut back to its initial level so that aggregate demand will also return to its initial level at d.
2. If the balance of payments deficit is *not sterilized*, the money supply will fall, shifting the LM curve to the left and thereby decreasing aggregate demand. This counteracts the initial monetary expansion. The balance of payments deficit will continue until the money supply has fallen to its initial amount and the LM curve has returned to its original position. Therefore, the restoration of general equilibrium will require a return to the point d in Figure 13.3b. Hence, the expansion in the money supply would be offset through outflows of funds from the economy.

Therefore, for the developed economies' case with fixed exchange rates, an expansionary monetary policy is clearly circumscribed by the availability of foreign reserves to finance deficits, while an expansionary fiscal policy is not thus circumscribed and can be pursued indefinitely. The latter is also reinforced by an induced expansion in the money supply in the case of a passive monetary policy. Hence, the pursuit of fiscal policy is preferable to that of monetary policy in the fixed exchange rate case.

Extended Analysis Box 13.2: Monetary and Fiscal Policies in the Case of Interest–Insensitive Capital Flows and Fixed Exchange Rates

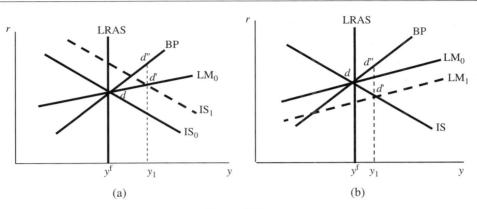

(a)   (b)

Figure 13.4.

If the net capital inflows are relatively insensitive to domestic interest rates, as in many LDCs, the BP curve could be steeper than the LM one. This case is shown in Figures 13.4a and 13.4b.

For the expansionary fiscal policy analysis in Figure 13.4a, the IS curve shifts from IS_0 to IS_1. At the new level of interest rates given by the point d', there would be a balance of payments deficit, which causes a loss of foreign reserves. If it is not sterilized, the money supply will fall, with a contractionary effect running counter to the expansionary objective of fiscal policy, so that the desired expansion of aggregate demand will not be achieved. But if it is sterilized, the balance of payments deficit will continue and foreign reserves will continue to fall.

For the expansionary monetary policy analysis in Figure 13.4b, the increase in the money supply shifts the LM curve from LM_0 to LM_1, increasing aggregate demand from d to d'. The point d' is associated with a balance of payments deficit, so that the earlier analysis based on Figure 13.3b continues to apply, though the deficit will be even greater in Figure 13.4b.[5] As before, this balance of payments deficit, in the case when it is not sterilized, will result in a continuing reduction in the money supply until the original money supply is restored. If it is sterilized, there will be a continuing loss of reserves.

Hence, with fixed exchange rates in the interest–insensitive capital flows case, both expansionary fiscal and monetary policies will cause balance of payments deficits and loss of foreign exchange reserves. Further, in the passive money supply case, the expansionary fiscal policy will be accompanied by an induced contractionary rather than expansionary money supply, so that the desired expansion will not occur. An expansionary monetary policy will also cause balance of payments deficits and loss of foreign exchange reserves. Neither type of policy can be pursued for long unless the country has foreign exchange reserves whose depletion through deficits can be tolerated by the authorities. Since LDCs tend to have interest–insensitive capital flows, their pursuit of expansionary monetary and fiscal policies tends to pose relatively greater problems in terms of balance of payments deficits and loss of foreign exchange reserves, leading to an eventual reversal of such policies.

---

[5]The size of the balance of payments deficit can be related to the interest gap between the one given by the intersection of the IS and LM curves and, for this level of aggregate demand, that given by the BP curve.

13.4 Bringing Aggregate Supply into the IS-LM Analysis with a Fixed Exchange Rate

For an economy with developed financial markets, we have shown that an expansionary fiscal policy is more effective in increasing aggregate demand than monetary policy. However, the benefits from this increase in demand depend upon the supply response of the economy. As in the closed economy analysis, there are three different types of supply responses. They are:

1. *Long-run analysis*: the economy maintains full employment. In this case, the increase in demand will merely increase the price level, without an increase in output. It will also decrease net exports and worsen the balance of payments, as we show in the next section. Therefore, the relative efficacy of fiscal policy in increasing demand becomes a disadvantage.
2. *Short-run analysis*: the increase in aggregate demand induces an increase in the equilibrium employment and output beyond their full-employment levels. Therefore, there is some advantage from pursuing an expansionary fiscal policy rather than an expansionary monetary one. However, this advantage is temporary since the economy will eventually move to its full-employment state.
3. *Disequilibrium analysis*: if the economy was experiencing deficient demand, the relative efficacy of fiscal policy in increasing aggregate demand becomes a major consideration in pursuing it rather than monetary policy.

13.5 Macroeconomic Equilibrium in the Small Open Economy with Full Employment and IRP

The modern classical approach assumes *continuous* full employment and perfect capital markets. The following specifies the open economy macroeconomic model for this approach.

Perfect capital mobility between the domestic and foreign capital markets implies interest rate parity (IRP), which is the condition that:

$$r = r^F - \rho''^e.$$

IRP should properly be stated in terms of nominal interest rates R rather than real interest rates r. However, we have used the Fisher equation, $R = r + \pi^e$, and the assumption that the expected inflation rate π^e is zero, to state IRP in real interest rates r. Further, assume that the exchange rates are fixed and that the public also expects them to remain unchanged.[6] In this case, $\rho''^e = 0$, so that IRP becomes:

$$r = r^F.$$

Hence, r is exogenously determined by r^F. In Figure 13.5, this condition is shown by the horizontal IRP curve, which is the form of the BP curve under the interest rate parity assumption.

Further, given continuous labor market clearance, there would be continuous full employment and output would remain at y^F. This is shown by the LRAS curve in Figure 13.5. Therefore, under the assumptions of IRP and full employment, the IS-LM figure would become that shown in Figure 13.5. The equilibrium interest rate would be at r^F and the equilibrium output will be at y^f.

---

[6]The second assumption is sometimes violated when the authorities have fixed the exchange rate but the public believes that this exchange rate cannot be maintained. Suppose that the public expects a devaluation. In such a case, there are usually speculative outflows of foreign exchange, which reduce the country's foreign exchange reserves and worsen the balance of payments, thereby putting pressure on the authorities to devalue in an attempt to stem the outflow of reserves.

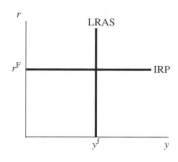

Figure 13.5

13.5.1 Fiscal policies under IRP and full employment

Fiscal policy cannot alter the equilibrium shown in Figure 13.5 since it cannot affect the exogenously determined interest rate or the full-employment output, and must accommodate itself to (r^F, y^f). Hence, expansionary fiscal policy cannot be used to increase domestic output and/or change the interest rate. The only impact of fiscal policy will be on net exports. This impact occurs through the IS equilibrium condition derived in its three-gaps version in Chapter 5. Under the assumptions of this section, this condition, with $r = r^F$ and $y = y^f$, can be written as:

$$\{x_c - (P^F/\rho P)z_c\} = -\{i(r^F) - s(y^f - t(y^f))\} - \{g - t(y^F)\}, \tag{4}$$

where the left side is net exports, so that:

$$\text{net exports} = -\{i(r^F) - s(y^f - t(y^f))\} - \{g - t(y^f)\}.$$

In this equation, investment i and saving s are determined by the interest rate given by r^F and national income at its full-employment level y^f, so that the only variable that can be affected by a fiscal deficit is net exports. Hence, from this equation, an increase in the fiscal deficit, by decreasing the right side, will decrease the equilibrium level of net exports and worsen the balance of payments on current account. Consequently, it will worsen the balance of payments and cause a fall in the country's foreign exchange reserves. Conversely, a contractionary fiscal policy will improve the balance of payments and build up foreign exchange reserves, without causing a fall in output or rise in the interest rate.

13.5.2 Monetary policy under IRP and full employment

Under the assumptions behind Figure 13.5, an expansion in the money supply also cannot change output or the interest rate: the interest rate is set by IRP at r^F and output is set at its full-employment level y^f by the assumption of long-run equilibrium. Hence, the position of the LM curve cannot change either r^F or y^f, so that we did not even bother to draw it in Figure 13.5.

In this context, the demand for real balances is specified by:

$$m^d = m^d(y^f, r^F). \tag{5}$$

With the demand for real balances determined by y^f and r^F, the equilibrium domestic supply of real balances must adjust to this amount. The process by which this result is achieved is as follows. An attempted expansion of the nominal money supply would lower the interest rate, which leads to an outflow of capital, a balance of payments deficit and an outflow of the domestic currency by enough to maintain the interest rate at r^F. Therefore, the equilibrium amount of the domestic money supply will adjust to the unchanged domestic demand for real balances, making domestic monetary policy completely ineffective. Hence, if the money supply is decreased, the interest rate will rise, leading to a balance of payments surplus, which will increase the money supply sufficiently, so that it equals the demand for money at (r^F, y^f). That is, the domestic money supply becomes *endogenous* to money demand at the fixed exchange rate, world interest rates, and full-employment output, only changing if these variables change.

Therefore, *with a fixed exchange rate, IRP and full employment*, there is no role in equilibrium for monetary or fiscal policies for changing output. In fact, with output already at its full-employment level, there is no scope or need for such policies. The only role of these policies is in inducing inflows or outflows of foreign exchange: contractionary monetary policies and expansionary fiscal ones will induce an inflow.

13.6 PPP, the World Rate of Inflation and the Convergence in National Inflation Rates

This section investigates the implications of PPP in the context of the *quantity equation*, which was presented in Chapter 2 and is an identity.

13.6.1 The world rate of inflation in the fixed exchange rate case

Assume that all the countries of the world have fixed exchange rates, so that we can treat the world as a single economy, with a world money supply defined by the weighted[7] sum of the money supplies of the individual countries.

From the quantity equation, we have:

$$\pi^w \equiv M^{w\prime\prime} + V^{w\prime\prime} - y^{w\prime\prime}, \tag{6}$$

where the superscript w stands for the world, V is the velocity of circulation and $\prime\prime$ again indicates the rate of growth. This equation implies that a general expansion of the money supplies among the countries will be a major source of world inflation. This occurred during the 1960s and 1970s when many countries simultaneously followed expansionary monetary policies in an attempt to increase their output and employment. The result was worldwide inflation. By the mid-1980s, most countries had abandoned such policies and were exercising much stricter controls on their money growth. As a consequence, the world rate of inflation in the 1990s fell drastically from its levels in the 1970s and 1980s.

If we also assume relative PPP, then the fixed exchange rate for the jth country implies that:

$$\pi_j = \pi^w - k^{\prime\prime}, \tag{7}$$

where π_j is the rate of inflation in country j and $k^{\prime\prime}$ is the change in its relative competitiveness. Assuming $k^{\prime\prime} = 0$, this condition implies that the individual country inflation rates will be identical with the world one — or at least converge to it. Since the domestic inflation rate is determined by the exogenously specified world one, the equilibrium money supply of each country must adjust to accommodate this inflation rate and the money supplies of the individual countries become *endogenous*. While money supply growth and the price level in each country would then be closely related, note that causation runs from the world inflation rate to the small economy's inflation rate, and then to its money supply, not from its money supply to its price level.[8]

---

[7]The weights would be the national exchange rates.
[8]However, at the world level, causation does run from the world money supply to the world price level.

Box 13.1: The impact of a *large* economy on smaller economies

The USA has the largest single economy in the world. Its economy cannot be assumed to be a 'small' one since its economic variables influence those in other countries. This influence on other countries occurs through commodity and capital flows. This influence can be seen in various ways:

- An increase in the interest rate in the USA puts upward pressure on the interest rates in other countries, since a reduction is the US interest rates leads to capital flows to other countries. These are significant enough for their smaller economies to cause a reduction in their interest rates. The reverse occurs if the USA raises its interest rates.
- A recession, with a decrease in the GDP, in the USA decreases other countries' exports to the USA. These are significant enough for their smaller economies to cause a reduction in their aggregate demand and output. The reverse occurs if the USA has a boom.
- A fall in the US price level (or a lower inflation rate) increases the US exports and the decreases the US imports. These reduce the net exports of the smaller economies and lower their aggregate demand and price level (or inflation rate).

Consequently, in empirical studies, since the US price levels and interest rates cause similar movements in those of the small open economies trading with the USA, the US price levels and the interest rates are often used as proxies for those of the world economy in the PPP and IRP equations for those economies. This causation is only one-way from the US economy to the smaller economies.

However, the emergence of the European Union as a single country and the rapid economic growth of Russia, China, and India in this century imply that the rest of the world as a whole, but not any single country, can be treated as a large economy for the study of the USA economy. That is, similar exogenous (to the USA) economic developments in these economies collectively can exert a powerful influence on the US economy.

13.7   Economic Blocs, Fixed Exchange Rates and the Convergence in Inflation Rates

The above analysis can be adapted to the case of a bloc of countries committed to a fixed exchange rate among its members. In the case of regional blocs such as the European Union with fixed exchange rates among its members, the member countries' inflation rates will converge to those of the bloc as a whole. This has been the experience of the European Union countries since the 1980s, as the European Union has increasingly limited the permissible range of exchange rate variations among its member countries. Its long-term objective of a European Monetary Union with a European currency and fixed exchange rates among its members' national currencies and the European one would effectively impose a common inflation rate on the member countries and limit their monetary independence.

13.8   Disequilibrium in the Domestic Economy and Stabilization through Monetary and Fiscal Policies: The Fixed Exchange Rate Case with Interest Sensitive Capital Flows

Figures 13.2a and 13.2b had shown the case of general equilibrium in the developed economy, with all the curves, including the long-run supply LRAS curve, intersecting at the same point a. Figure 13.6a shows

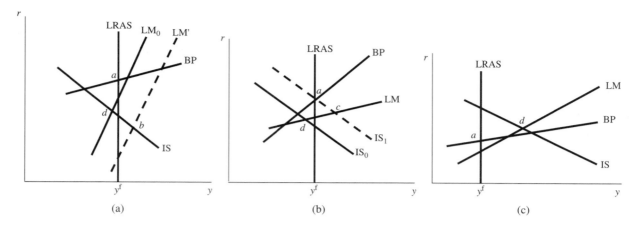

Figure 13.6

the case corresponding to Figure 13.2a, but for an economy with disequilibrium and therefore with several intersections. Assuming as before for analytical purposes that the commodity and the money markets adjust faster than the labor market and the balance of payments, the economy will be at the point *d* (intersection of the IS and LM curves) in Figure 13.6a. At this point, the economy has deficient demand, relative to output y^f. There is also a balance of payments deficit, measured from the point d to the BP curve: the interest rate at *d* is below that necessary to restore equilibrium in the balance of payments, so that the capital inflows are inadequate for equilibrium. The deficient demand at *d* forces prices to fall, so that the LM curve would shift down from LM$_0$ to LM' to go through the point *b*. While this movement will lower interest rates and worsen the balance of payments on capital account, the fall in prices will increase net exports. However, this increase need not be enough to ensure balance of payments equilibrium at full employment and is in any case going to be a long run rather than a short-term solution. In the meantime, the country will lose foreign exchange reserves. Since the exchange rate is fixed, appropriate monetary and fiscal policies will be needed to bring the economy into overall equilibrium. This could, for instance, be done in Figure 13.6a by an expansionary fiscal policy and a contractionary monetary policy [not shown in Figure 13.6a], so that the IS and LM curves shift to go through the point *a*. Such a procedure will also avoid the need for price adjustments, in addition to avoiding balance of payments problems.

A caveat

The preceding arguments have made the implicit assumption that the BP, IS, and LRAS curves do not shift as prices change. Our earlier arguments show that they do so. Thus, if we start again from the point *d* in Figures 13.6a and 13.6b, as prices fall, the IS curve shifts to the right, the BP curve shifts down and the LRAS curve shifts left (as in some of the Keynesian models). It is unlikely that there would exist any fall in prices so fortuitous as to make all the curves intersect at the same point, so that one or more policy tools will still be necessary to restore equilibrium.

> **Extended Analysis Box 13.3:** Disequilibrium in the Domestic Economy and Stabilization through Monetary and Fiscal Policies: The Fixed Exchange Rate Case with Interest Insensitive Capital Flows

> In the interest–insensitive capital-flows case depicted in Figure 13.6b, the initial equilibrium at the point *d* has deficient demand and balance of payments deficit. Let an expansionary fiscal policy shift the IS curve

from IS_0 to IS_1 so as to pass through the point *c*. The excess demand at *c* would raise prices and shift the LM curve up (not shown) toward the point *a*. While this price level increase might fortuitously reduce the *real* money supply by just enough to take the LM curve through the point *a*, its likelihood is not encouraging. Alternatively, an appropriate expansionary fiscal policy, combined with an appropriate contractionary monetary policy could (hopefully) ensure that all the curves intersect at the point *a*, thereby obviating the need for domestic price level changes and also eliminating the balance of payments deficit.

13.9 The Need for Monetary and FiscalPolicies under Fixed Exchange Rates

Suppose that the authorities are willing to pursue both monetary and fiscal policies to restore equilibrium in Figures 13.6a and 13.6b. An expansionary fiscal policy could shift the IS curve to pass through the point a; a deflationary monetary policy could shift the LM curve to also pass through this point. An expansionary fiscal policy and a deflationary monetary policy could, therefore, cure a deficient demand and a balance of payments deficit.

Now consider the case shown in Figure 13.6c. At the point *d*, there is excess aggregate demand relative to output y^f. There is also a balance of payments surplus. A contractionary fiscal policy could shift the IS curve to pass through the point *a*. A contractionary monetary policy could also shift the LM curve to pass through *a*. A contractionary fiscal policy and/or an expansionary monetary policy could thus cure a balance of payments surplus and excess demand in the context of Figure 13.6c.[9]

The analysis of the above cases shows that the achievement of overall equilibrium in the context of fixed exchange rates is likely to require the use of fiscal and/or monetary policies. Alternatively stated, the economy with fixed exchange rates does not possess enough mechanisms that would automatically bring the economy into equilibrium so that appropriate policy actions are essential for maintaining equilibrium. Such a situation arises because one of the equilibrating' price variables, the exchange rate, has been fixed, so that a policy adjustment has to compensate for its failure to adjust.

13.9.1 Internal versus external balance

Chapter 12 had defined the *internal balance* of an economy as the equality of its domestic aggregate demand and domestic full-employment output, while *external balance* was defined as the equality of the demand and supply of foreign exchange. Fixed exchange rates prevent changes in the exchange rate from maintaining the latter. This imbalance does not pose a serious problem if the external balance is such that there is a balance of payments surplus and the country is willing to let its foreign exchange rate reserves increase, while sterilizing their effect on the money supply. However, a balance of payments deficit implies an outflow of foreign exchange. The country could tackle this outflow through the sale of foreign exchange from its foreign

---

[9]These arguments involving shifts in several curves become quite complex when price changes are considered. The complexity arises basically from the dependence of the various sectors on domestic prices. It is, therefore, preferable to work directly with the equations derived earlier. If one wishes to stay with the diagrammatic form, it would be better to adapt the arguments to the (y, P) space while eliminating r as a variable through a combination of the expenditure and the monetary sectors and a combination of the foreign and the monetary sectors.

exchange reserves. Once these threaten to fall below their desired level, continuing balance of payments deficits will have to be eliminated. Fixed exchange rates prevent the use of the exchange rate from eliminating them, forcing the use of at least one policy tool to ensure the external balance of the economy. In principle, this tool could be either monetary or fiscal policy. In practice, fiscal policy is too inflexible a tool relative to the speed of movement in trade and capital flows, so that monetary policy has to be diverted to maintaining the external balance of the economy. If this is done, monetary policy cannot be employed for maintaining internal balance.

13.9.2 A note of caution on the use of monetary and fiscal policies

A mix of monetary and fiscal policies can restore equilibrium in the open economy with fixed exchange rates and obviates any need for adjustments in prices. However, a strong cautionary note on the pursuit of such policies must be added here. To pursue such a policy efficiently and with the confidence that the wrong policies are not pursued requires a great deal of knowledge about the inter-relationships among the sectors. This knowledge may not exist or there may be shifts in these relationships because of the public's response to the policies pursued, so that the pursuit of discretionary stabilization policies can be risky: their outcome may make the economy worse rather than better. The impact of the attempted policies on the expectations of — and, therefore, speculation by — both domestic and foreign investors about the ability of the government to maintain its exchange rate must also be taken into account, and adds to the difficulty in deciding on the appropriate policies.

13.10 The Effect of Relatively Different Improvements in Productivity at Home and Abroad under Fixed Exchange Rates

One of the big problems with fixed exchange rates occurs when the rate of productivity growth is lower in the domestic economy than abroad. This reduces the international competitiveness of domestic industries relative to foreign ones — unless the lower level of domestic productivity is accompanied by a proportionately lower real wage — and leads to a fall in exports and a rise in imports. This fall in net exports has to be financed by a capital inflow, which increases the indebtedness of the domestic economy to foreigners and raises interest payments for the future. If the domestic productivity continues to fall relative to the foreign one, the process of falling net exports accumulates foreign debt and increases interest payments to foreigners until the existing fixed exchange rate becomes unsustainable. The country is then forced to devalue or let its currency float, which immediately leads to its depreciation. If the accumulation of foreign debt and interest outflows has become quite large, the devaluation/depreciation may have to be by a fairly large percentage. It may also be accompanied by large capital outflows and have severe consequences on the economy in the form of a decline in output and employment and a rise in inflation.

In order to keep exports competitive, the alternative to these adjustments is for the domestic real wage to decline relative to the foreign one to match the relatively slower domestic productivity growth. This is likely to lead to migration to foreign countries, with warnings in the media about a brain drain.

Therefore, in the long run, a fixed exchange rate in a context of relatively lower productivity growth at home than abroad can pose severe problems. Conversely, in the long run, the domestic economy is likely to do quite well if it has higher productivity growth than abroad.

13.11 The Political Economy of Exchange Rates: The Choice between Fixed and Flexible Exchange Rate Regimes

This chapter and preceding one have considered some of the ways in which equilibrium in the balance of payments can be brought about or maintained in the face of disturbances. It could be done by market-determined changes in the exchange rate in a system of flexible exchange rates. But in a system of fixed exchange rates, equilibrium could only be maintained either by allowing induced changes in domestic income, prices, interest rates, etc. or by the appropriate use of the monetary and fiscal tools. It would, therefore, seem preferable for each country to allow its exchange rate to float rather than fix it, with all the constraints that the latter implies. However, there are several reasons why a country sometimes fixes its exchange rate against some or all foreign countries.

One reason for using a fixed exchange rate system is to avoid the possibility of instability in the foreign exchange markets, under the belief that flexible exchange rates promote such instability. The latter remains a moot point. Its likelihood is now minimized by many economists, especially those in the modern classical approach. Another reason for keeping a fixed exchange rate is that exporters and importers of both commodities and capital can make contracts without facing the uncertainty of exchange rate changes, which hinders international flows of both commodities and capital.

During the period from 1945 to the early 1970s, an often compelling reason for a country to have a fixed exchange rate was its membership of the International Monetary Fund (IMF), which had been set up in 1944. Most of the nations of the world are such members. A basic rule of the IMF from its inception to the early 1970s was that the member countries would fix their exchange rates and change them only in cases of a 'fundamental disequilibrium' in the balance of payments.[10] This rule was adopted to limit the uncertainties affecting international trade and thus to promote such trade. It was also designed as a way of preventing manipulations (devaluations) in the exchange rate by any one country as a way of improving its own balance of trade with others, with the possibility of retaliatory changes in the exchange rates by other countries whose balance of trade worsens. Such a retaliatory war of devaluations creates a great deal of uncertainty in international trade and is usually accompanied by other attempts by countries to curb their imports and promote their exports by other means such as tariffs, quotas, etc. The resulting reductions in exports and imports tend to substantially lower incomes and employment in the countries involved in such a 'war'.

A disadvantage of a country's adoption of a fixed exchange rate is that there sets in a great deal of reluctance for the country to change that rate even if a long-term disequilibrium emerges in the balance of payments. If the country has a surplus, which is sterilized and thus does not increase the money supply, it has no incentive to appreciate its currency since it could merely allow its reserves of foreign exchange to increase indefinitely. It might, however, face the jealousy of other nations and some international disapproval of its accumulation of reserves. In rare cases, it might even be faced with economic and political pressures from other countries to revalue. Thus, Germany and Japan, which had sizeable surpluses throughout the 1960s, came under strong pressures from 1971 to 1973 from the USA to revalue. Part of such pressure was a 10% (surcharge) duty imposed on imports into the USA with a promise that it would be abolished after the appropriate revaluations had been made. Both Japan and Germany were forced to revalue in 1971 and again in 1973 under such pressure from the USA. But such explicit pressure tactics tend to be rare are not always effective, and can be pursued by only a few powerful nations.

---

[10]A fundamental disequilibrium is to be thought of as a long-run disequilibrium rather than short-run — monthly or annual — disequilibrium.

A country with a fixed exchange rate and a persistent deficit in its balance of payments could eliminate this deficit by devaluation. But devaluations tend to be unpopular with the electorate. They are often interpreted as a 'cheapening of our money' and 'a loss of national face' and prestige. Further, devaluations represent a worsening of the terms of trade and increase the prices of imported goods. In some countries, often low-income ones, these price increases are resented by the public, which blames the government for them. Therefore, deficit countries, such as Britain and the USA in the 1960s, often let their reserves fall or used restrictive monetary or fiscal policies at home, rather than devalue. Such policies usually prove to be palliative rather than cures of the underlying disequilibrium. Thus, the USA, after resisting devaluation through the 1960s, finally succumbed to the market pressures, reinforced by speculation, in March 1973, and allowed its dollar to float.

13.12 Other Tools for Handling Balance of Payments Deficits

Countries also have at their disposal other tools to reduce deficits. These consist of direct measures to change exports and imports and capital flows. Imports can be hindered by the imposition of tariffs on their value or quantity, or by quota limitations on the quantity that can be imported, while exports can be encouraged by subsidies. These measures were formerly ruled out by the General Agreement on Tariffs and Trade (GATT) and now by the World Trade Organization (WTO), of which most nations are members. This is because such actions by one country hinder the exports of other countries and invite retaliation. Overall, such actions reduce the gains in efficiency and welfare that come from free trade. However, countries do often try to get around such rules, often in the form of explicit or hidden subsidies to exporters and home producers.

Controls on the flows of capital can similarly consist of a 'tax' on capital inflows or outflows, administrative barriers, or quota type limitations. A country trying to reduce its capital outflow could impose a 'tax' on such outflows.[11] A country trying to reduce its capital inflows could similarly impose a tax on the capital inflows or on the subsequent returns to them.[12] Quotas on the inflows of capital are commonly imposed by countries that are concerned about the foreign ownership of their real and financial assets.[13] Most LDCs have experimented with such controls. However, there was a marked worldwide trend during the decade of the 1990s toward the dismantling of such controls.

Extended Analysis Box 13.4: The Gold Standard and the Gold Exchange Standard

> The Gold Standard and its variation, the Gold Exchange Standard,[14] is a system under which countries maintain fixed rates of exchange of the national currencies against an ounce of gold. The Gold Standard is a system under which one or a few countries maintain fixed exchange rates of their national currencies — called 'key currencies' — against an ounce of gold, while other countries maintain fixed rates of exchange of their national currencies against a key currency. Both systems have very similar economic effects.

---

[11]The USA, for example, did so in 1964 when it imposed a 15% 'interest equalization tax' on interest and dividend payments from foreign stocks and bonds bought after 1964.

[12]Several European countries did so in 1973. An example of a quota on outflows of capital was the 'foreign credit restraint' program instituted by the USA in 1965 and designed to limit the growth of US investments abroad.

[13]Japan has had some such controls through most of the post-1945 period.

[14]The Gold Exchange Standard differs from the Gold Standard in that gold coins circulate in the latter but not in the former. In both, the central bank is willing to exchange its paper currency for gold bullion and vice versa.

Extended Analysis Box 13.4: (*Continued*)

Most countries of the world operated on the Gold Exchange Standard under the Bretton Woods System of the IMF from 1946 to about 1970, with the US dollar being the main key currency.

The Gold Standard was a major tenet of exchange rates regimes prior to World War II. Britain had set a fixed conversion rate between its currency — the pound — and gold, so that its currency was on a 'Gold Standard'. British colonies and dominions had fixed their exchange rates against the British pound, so that their currencies could also be converted into gold, if not directly, then through their conversion into pounds and then into gold. Canada was one of these countries. France and its colonies were also on the Gold Standard. These empires constituted trading blocs akin to customs unions, with trade among the member countries facilitated by fixed exchange rates and with gold flows serving to maintain these exchange rates.[15] While it was not obligatory for a country to be on the Gold Standard, most of the world's major trading nations were directly or indirectly on it.

From 1946 to the early 1970s, the US dollar was fixed against gold at $35 per ounce of gold. Most of the world's currencies maintained — directly or indirectly through other currencies — a fixed exchange rate against the US dollar, so that the world was said to be on the Gold Exchange Standard.[16]

Being on the Gold Standard limits the country's independence to create money, which limits its ability to pursue an independent discretionary monetary policy. When it is pursued fully, a balance of payments surplus for a country causes the inflow of gold to increase the money supply through exchanges of the gold inflow with the central bank for the local currency, while an outflow decreases the money supply. Consequently, aggregate demand and prices rise in the countries with balance of payments surpluses, thereby increasing their imports and decreasing their exports, so that their balance of payments would tend to equilibrium. Correspondingly, demand and prices fall in the countries with balance of payments deficits, thereby decreasing their imports and increasing their exports, so that their balance of payments also tends to equilibrium. When these changes are allowed by the individual countries to occur, the Gold Standard serves as a mechanism for equilibrating the balance of payments of the individual countries. It also prevents excessive creations of new money by national central banks.

The 19th and early 20th centuries were a period in which few countries had central banks and the monetary theories of inflation and output were poorly developed. The creation of currency was usually in the hands of private individuals and firms and subject to their private interests, so that there was little national control over the money supply in the economy. In these conditions, the Gold Standard provided countries with external restraints on their private institutions (usually banks) in creating currency, and in the aggregate over their national money supplies.

The Gold Standard has several defects. Among these are:

● The fixed exchange rate may not be the equilibrium one for the foreign exchange market. If the exchange rate for a national currency is set higher than the equilibrium, it will suffer a persistent balance of payments deficit. This would produce an outflow of gold and a decrease in its money supply. The consequent fall in aggregate demand would result in a fall in employment and output. This is likely until the exchange rate is lowered.

---

[15] In the modern period, the European Union has instituted fixed exchange rates among its member countries, though without having a fixed exchange rate between the euro and gold, so that it is not on the Gold Standard.

[16] Under the Gold Exchange Standard, gold coins did not circulate and private individuals in many countries were not permitted to hold or trade in gold (other than for jewelry) but countries could trade their currencies against gold.

- Even if the exchange rate is initially set at the equilibrium level, there exists the possibility that economic changes will render the national currency over- or under-valued. This can cause speculation about adjustments in the exchange rate and panic in the foreign exchange markets. Such bouts of intense speculation are especially troublesome in the modern period with the increasing international flows of capital.

- Countries may choose to adopt an independent monetary policy and try to sterilize the inflows and outflows of gold. This is especially likely for inflows of gold, since this would mean an increase in foreign exchange reserves, usually considered a desirable objective. This policy would hinder the automatic mechanism of the Gold Standard for correcting balance of payments disequilibria.

- The world supply of gold limits the world money supply, so that if it fails to grow proportionately with world trade and output, its lower growth rate will produce a persistent tendency toward inadequate world demand and recessions — which will hamper output and employment in national economies.

Starting in 1971, the Gold Standard was effectively abandoned by virtually all nations during the third and fourth quarters of the 20th century because of several developments. One of these was the setting up of the central banks, which wanted to maintain control over their money supply, as they thought appropriate for the national interest, rather than let it be determined by balance of payments flows. Accompanying this was the elimination of private note issues. Another was the increasing magnitude of capital flows, which can cause intense speculation against a currency leading to a crisis in its balance of payments. A third was the break-up of the large empires that had imposed fixed exchange rates on their colonies, dominions, and affiliated countries. While there are still some calls for the restoration of the Gold Standard, it is highly inadvisable in the modern age.

13.13 Summary of the Costs and Benefits of a Fixed Exchange Rate

The major benefit of a fixed exchange rate accrues from its elimination of exchange rate fluctuations. This reduces the risk from such fluctuations for importers and exporters and for investors, so that the volume of trade and investment would be larger. This allows the country to benefit more from specialization in the products in which it has a comparative advantage, and also to attract foreign investment.

Another advantage arises from the constraint that a fixed exchange rate imposes on the ability of the national central bank to expand the domestic money supply and cause inflation rates higher than in other countries. This becomes valuable if the central bank has a record of mismanagement in this respect. While this can provide the needed discipline for an otherwise irresponsible central bank, it does not necessarily do so if the central bank resorts to periodic devaluations to solve the problems caused by an excessive creation of the money supply.

The disadvantage of a fixed exchange rate is that monetary policy becomes constrained by the need to divert monetary policy (money supply and interest rates) to support of the level at which the exchange rate has been fixed. For example, if the interest rate is too low relative to ones abroad, the resulting net outflow of capital will soon exhaust the country's foreign exchange reserves, to be followed by either abandonment of the fixed exchange rate regime or tightening of monetary policy by raising interest rates. Further, under fixed exchange rates, monetary or confidence shocks are transmitted to the domestic economy unless the central bank rapidly moves domestic interest and inflation rates to compensate for such shocks.

By comparison, a floating exchange rate maintains equilibrium in the foreign exchange markets (i.e., *external balance*) so that monetary policy can concentrate on the objective of maintaining aggregate demand equal to the full-employment output (i.e., *internal balance*).

13.14 Dollarization

'Dollarization' means the adoption, by a country other than the USA, of the US dollar as its domestic currency, without a distinct national currency in existence at the same time. An example of this occurred in 1999 when Ecuador announced that it would adopt the US currency as its national currency.

Under dollarization, any fundamental deficit (surplus) in the balance of payments will have to be met by a fall (increase) in the domestic money supply, with a consequent fall (increase) in aggregate demand — ending up with a fall (increase) in domestic prices and output. For monetary purposes, the country adopting dollarization becomes in some ways an extension of the US economy. This promotes trade with the USA, and capital and technology flows. However, it does not necessarily attain the perfect flows of commodities, labor, capital, and technology that occur within the USA.

An increase in the monetary base represents a net increase in government revenues equal to the amount of the increase. This increase in revenues is called '*seigniorage*'. The retirement of a national currency in favor of the US dollar means that the seigniorage inherent in the existing monetary base and its future increases is lost by the domestic country while the USA gets this seigniorage. This is a very significant amount, so that the return by the USA of the seigniorage to the dollarizing country, or at least its division in some proportion, has to be negotiated and settled between the two countries.

Dollarization of a national currency has three consequences:

1. It represents the adoption of a fixed exchange rate (at one to one) between the national currency and the US dollar. This promotes international trade in commodities and increases capital flows.
2. It represents a commitment that this exchange rate will not, *and cannot*, be changed either by the policymakers (which they can do even under fixed exchange rates if there was a separate national currency) or even by the markets. This eliminates the possibility of speculative attacks on the currency in circulation, which has become the US dollar one.
3. The dollarizing country loses *seigniorage*[17] from the issue of the currency circulating within it. Unless there is an agreement to sharing this seigniorage, the USA will get the seigniorage from the adoption of its currency and its increased circulation in the economy.

Dollarization usually is an attempt to stabilize the value of the circulating medium of payments and to prevent speculation against its depreciation.

As shown in the analysis of monetary policy under a fixed exchange rate, the adoption of a fixed exchange rate through dollarization implies loss of control over the domestic money supply and, therefore, reduces the scope for monetary policy to address the ills (e.g., deficient aggregate demand) of the domestic economy.

---

[17]Seigniorage is the gain in revenue to the agency/country which issues the currency, since this currency costs very little to produce while it is used to buy bonds which pay interest or to buy commodities.

This is a potential cost of dollarization, as of a fixed exchange rate, which can become significant in demand-deficient recessions. But this limitation can also be of benefit to the economy if the national central bank has shown a lack of internal discipline on monetary policy and has itself been a significant source of inflation in the economy. This would have happened if the central bank itself had on its own volition created high money supply growth rates or had done so at the behest of the government. Such behavior has sometimes caused high rates of inflation, even hyperinflation in some countries in some periods, which significantly lowered output and employment. Therefore, whether the loss of national control over the money supply — and through it on domestic aggregate demand — is a cost or benefit depends on the public's trust in — and past experience with — the central bank's handling of its monetary policy instruments.

Having one's own currency with a flexible exchange rate allows an independent monetary policy, which can be used for counter-cyclical stabilization policies, as well as for reducing unemployment and increasing the output growth rate. However, the adoption by many central banks of price stability as the preferable goal itself imposes limits on the use of monetary policy, provided this goal is pursued with determination.

The importance of point (2) lies in dollarization preventing exchange rate speculation. Dollarization will prevent speculation not only against the local currency when there are (limited and transient) random fluctuations in the balance of payments — which occur under both fixed and flexible exchange rates — but also when there are fundamental shifts in the balance of payments. The latter scenario is the significant one for evaluating the merits of dollarization.

Why should one country adopt the currency of another country as its own, especially when it is likely to lose at least some of the seigniorage from issuing a national currency? Clearly, this should only be done when the net benefits from dollarization are positive. Often the expected benefit arises because the national central bank through substantial money supply increases had created very substantial inflation rates in the past and these have contributed to the collapse of production and employment in the economy in the recent past. Dollarization is meant to ensure a more stable currency and price level — and thereby to restore production and employment to their full employment levels. Another argument for dollarization arises if it is part of a package that includes free access to the US markets or a customs union (which has free flows of commodities among its member countries) with the USA.

Should the USA welcome dollarization by other countries? It earns seigniorage from the dollars floating in other countries, which benefits the US government and economy. However, it is likely that the country adopting dollarization would want to share in this seigniorage, so that a deal has to be struck on this division. Further, if the dollarizing economy is quite significant in size relative to the US one, the strength and stability of the US dollar in world markets will become partially dependent on the performance of the dollarizing economy. This represents a loss of control of the Fed over the internal and external value of the US dollar, which the Fed may be reluctant to accept.

For some countries, especially in Asia and Africa, the trade flows with Europe are more significant than with the USA. For them, appropriate dollarization would mean the adoption of the euro as their national currency.[18]

The forces in favor of dollarization recently have been:

- Globalization has meant lowering tariffs and quotas and increasing the levels of imports and exports relative to GDP, as well as increasing capital flows across countries (this topic was covered in Chapter 12).

---

[18]See A. Alesina and R. J. Barro, Dollarization, *American Economic Review*, **91**, May 2001, 381–385, for a compact discussion of this topic.

- The implementation of regional economic blocs or unification of several nations into one. The European Union provides a good example of the latter. Its currency, the euro, has replaced the national currencies of most of the countries in the European Union.

13.14.1 Dollarization and different productivity growth rates

The problems posed by a lower productivity growth at home than abroad were discussed above in the context of fixed exchange rates. Dollarization intensifies these problems. If the dollarizing economy has lower productivity growth than the USA, then its real wage must decline relative to that in the USA. This will cause migration — often a 'brain drain' of the best workers — from the domestic economy to the USA. If the free flow of labor is very limited or is not permitted at all, then the domestic economy is likely to maintain relatively high unemployment rates, as well as lower real wages and standard of living. It would become what is termed an 'economically depressed area'.

The Atlantic Provinces in Canada provide an example of this long-run phenomenon: these provinces share the Canadian dollar with the other Canadian provinces and so have 'Canadian dollar dollarization'. Canada's Atlantic Provinces have had slower productivity growth than some of the other Canadian provinces, such as Ontario, Alberta, and British Columbia, on a long-run basis. Consequently, over the 20th century, the former lost quite a bit of their population to these other provinces, but still had higher unemployment rates and lower real wages. By extension, if Canada was to adopt the US dollar as its currency but had slower productivity growth than the USA, Canada is likely to suffer a significant out-migration of its population to the USA, as well as experiencing higher unemployment rates and lower real wages.

Conversely, dollarization should be great for Canada if its productivity growth was higher than in the USA. It is then likely to experience increasing exports and favorable balance of payments, an inflow of population from the USA, lower unemployment rates and a higher standard of living.

Extended Analysis Box 13.5: A Dual Currency System: Dollarization Along with a Separate National Currency

---

Instead of complete dollarization with only the US dollar circulating as the sole medium of payments, a country may have two currencies functioning equally or almost equally efficiently as media of payments. Such cases are likely to involve a foreign currency, often the US dollar, in addition to a distinct domestic one. Such as case occurs in Lebanon, in which the US dollar and the Lebanese currency circulate interchangeably and payments, even in shops, are acceptable in either currency.

A country with two circulating media of payments can maintain a fixed exchange rate or a flexible one between the two currencies. A simple example of such a fixed rate case is the circulation of the cent, the five- and ten-cent coins, along with the dollar notes, within the USA. However, under a fixed exchange rate between the national currency and the US dollar, the central bank has to offset any shifts in their relative demands and supplies which threaten to change the pre-set exchange rate between them. This means that the central bank must have enough reserves of US dollars to meet any excess demand for them at the fixed exchange rate.

Alternatively, the country could allow a floating exchange rate between the currencies. In this case, changes in the demands and supplies of the two currencies will change the equilibrium/market exchange rate, so that the central bank does not need to buy or sell US dollars. However, the public must acquire continuous information even throughout the day on fluctuations in the exchange rate. This occurs on a continuous basis in Lebanon.

13.15 Currency Boards

A country, more so in the past but rarely nowadays, may have a currency board instead of an independent central bank.[19] With a currency board, the country maintains a fixed exchange rate against a designated foreign currency (often the US dollar), and the monetary base — a liability of the currency board — is backed fully by its foreign exchange reserves. As these reserves increase — e.g., through a balance of payments surplus — the currency board increases the monetary base and the money supply in the economy increases. Conversely, as foreign exchange reserves fall, the monetary base and the money supply are decreased. Other than this, the currency board does not have discretion to change the money supply or manage interest rates and, therefore, cannot pursue independent monetary policies for achieving domestic goals.

Currency boards were common in the colonies of imperial countries — e.g., the UK — during the first half of the 20th century. They were a means of linking the currency and the economies of the colonies to those of the imperial country. Further, if the imperial currency was under the gold standard — i.e., with its value fixed in terms of gold — the colonies also indirectly adhered to the gold standard. Such currency boards were usually replaced by central banks on independence. In other cases, countries, though independent, maintained currency boards with a strict adherence to the gold standard, implying a fixed value of the domestic currency in terms of gold.

The main reason for having a currency board, as under dollarization, is to impose discipline on the central bank, so that it cannot increase (or decrease) the domestic monetary base in an 'irresponsible' manner (e.g., such as to cause very high inflation rates). Under a currency board, changes in the domestic money supply are strictly determined by inflows and outflows of foreign exchange, just as under dollarization.

The disadvantage of having a currency board or dollarization is that the central bank does not have the discretion to pursue an independent monetary policy in the national interest, e.g., to stabilize aggregate demand at a level such as to ensure full employment in the economy or to reduce the impact of foreign shocks from on the domestic economy. In the modern context, countries prefer to have a central bank that can perform these roles, so that, with rare exceptions, they do not have a currency board.

13.16 Conclusions

- Fixed exchange rates continue to dominate at the intra-national and intra-bloc levels, with flexible exchange rates being the common rule between countries and between blocs of countries.
- One of the most remarkable changes in monetary arrangements in this respect in the world economy in recent decades has been the creation of a new currency called the euro, and the conversion of the national currencies of the European Union to a single one.
- Open economies impose considerable limitations on the successful pursuit of monetary and fiscal policies. The complexity of the interactions among the various sectors is greater for the open than for the closed economy, and greater under a fixed exchange rate than under floating ones.
- The requirements of the purchasing power parity and the interest rate parity operate as constraints on the policies that can be successfully pursued under fixed exchange rates. In the limiting case of the *continuous* clearing of the domestic labor markets at full employment and perfect capital flows, while monetary and fiscal policies could change aggregate demand in the domestic economy, they could have no impact on domestic real employment, output, and interest rates.

---

[19]As of 1998, currency boards exist in Hong Kong, Argentina, Estonia, Lithuania, and a few other countries.

- A major problem with maintaining fixed exchange rates arises when there are shifts in productivity among countries — especially if the domestic economy has a relatively low growth rate of productivity leading to a fall in net exports.
- If a country is unable to control its money supply growth and inflation rates, adoption of dollarization imposes a regimen for this control and tends to lower growth rates — at least in the early years. However, a relatively lower domestic growth rate of productivity or political instability will lead to a balance of payments crisis and either increased unemployment or the abandonment of dollarization.
- A dual currency system with dollarization and a national currency is usually not sustainable over time because of differences in relative productivity growth rates, etc.
- A given nation does use a single currency and, therefore, embodies dollarization among its various regions. However, this is supported by unhindered capital and labor flows, so that workers who become unemployed in regions with lower productivity growth tend to move to regions with higher productivity growth, thereby keeping unemployment lower and raising output. Such flows do not occur under the adoption of another country's currency, unless the latter allows free labor and capital mobility between the countries — which usually does not happen. A precondition or corequisite for successful dollarization over time is the free flow of labor, capital, and technology.

KEY CONCEPTS

Balance of payments curve
World inflation rate
Convergence of inflation rates under fixed exchange rates

Convergence of interest rates under fixed exchange rates
The Gold Standard and the Gold Exchange Standard
Seigniorage

Dollarization
A dual currency system with dollarization and a national currency, and
Currency board.

SUMMARY OF CRITICAL CONCLUSIONS

- Fiscal policy is more effective than monetary policy in changing aggregate demand if the exchange rate is fixed.
- Under a fixed exchange rate, with interest rate parity and continuous labor market clearance at full employment, there is no role for monetary and fiscal policies in changing output or employment or interest rates.
- Under a fixed exchange rate, with interest rate parity and continuous labor market clearance at full employment, an expansionary fiscal policy reduces net exports and worsens the trade balance. A contractionary fiscal policy increases net exports and improves the trade balance.
- Under purchasing power parity and a fixed exchange rate, the domestic price level is fully determined by the foreign one. The domestic inflation rates among countries will converge to the world inflation rate.
- Fixed exchange rates reduce the flexibility of the economy in adjusting to shocks and increase the difficulties, the uncertainty and the limitations on the successful pursuit of monetary and fiscal policies.
- Dollarization, in addition to the disadvantages of fixed exchange rates, involves loss of seigniorage and a risky economic strategy over time unless it is accompanied by unhindered flows of labor, capital and technology.

REVIEW AND DISCUSSION QUESTIONS

1. What are the main benefits to a country of maintaining a fixed exchange rate against other currencies?
2. Define the BP curve. Why is it essential to incorporate it into the analysis of the open economy with a fixed exchange rate?
3. Given a fixed exchange rate, what is the effect of an increase in (a) the foreign inflation rate and (b) exports, on the domestic money supply and price level? Base your analysis on the IS-LM framework for the open economy, making explicit your assumptions.
4. Given a small economy with a fixed exchange rate, why might the effects of fiscal policies differ for the developed economies with developed financial markets from those for the developing economies with under-developed financial markets? Base your analysis on the IS-LM-BP framework for the open economy.
5. Given a small open economy with a fixed exchange rate, what does interest rate parity imply for the determination of the domestic interest rate?
6. Under a fixed exchange rate regime, should the monetary authority try to manipulate the flows of commodities and capital to its own country? If so, what policies are appropriate for this purpose?
7. What are likely to be the advantages and disadvantages to the Canadian economy and the US economy of dollarization (replacement of the Canadian dollar by the US one)?
8. Why can dollarization be a threat to the maintenance of full employment and living standards in the dollarized country? What other policies are necessary to make it successful over time?
9. What is meant by the term "the Gold Standard"? Under the Gold Standard, what happened to an economy's money supply when it had a deficit or surplus? How did this restore equilibrium in the economy's balance of payments?
10. Why have most economies abandoned the Gold Standard? Should it be reinstituted for the modern economies? Discuss.
11. Discuss, from the perspective of (a) a small country and (b) the USA, the pros and cons of a free trade area with fixed exchange rates encompassing the Americas?
12. What is an exchange-rate crisis? What can cause it? What can a country undergoing an exchange rate crisis do to moderate it in (a) the short *term* and (b) the long *run*?

ADVANCED AND TECHNICAL QUESTIONS

T1. Can the same policies prescribed by the IMF for a developed economy and a developing economy, with both facing the same problem, benefit one economy but be detrimental to the other one. Discuss the relevant features of the two economies that bring about these results.
T2. Suppose controls on capital flows were imposed during an exchange rate crisis. What is likely to be the response of the investors to the imposition of such controls? Would this response improve or worsen the balance of payments situation?
T3. In the light of the European experience over the past decades on the evolution of the European Union and its single currency, the euro, discuss the following. What are the costs and benefits to Canada (or any other country of your choice) and the USA if they were to not become a single country but jointly (a) set their mutual exchange rate in a narrow band, (b) adopt a fixed exchange rate between their currencies, or

(c) adopt a single currency (with Canada adopting the US dollar)? What are the pros and cons of these options for (i) the country that you chose and (ii) the USA?

The Basic AD-AS Model for this Chapter

The commodity sector:

$$s = 0.2y_d$$
$$t = -100 + 0.2y$$
$$i = 1000 - 50r$$
$$g = 800$$
$$x_c = 100 - 0.5\rho^r$$
$$z_c = 500 + 0.1y_d + 0.2\rho^r$$

Additional information: $P = 2$, $P^F = 4$, $\bar{\rho} = 4$ (i.e., the exchange rate has been fixed by the central bank at this level). Further, assume that for the given price level, output is determined by the level of aggregate demand.

T4. Calculate the following.

   (a) Derive the IS equation.
   (b) Assuming that the central banks sets $r = 2$, what is the value of aggregate demand y^d [y_0^d]?
   (c) Assuming $r = 2$, if the government increases its expenditures to 1000, what is the value of y^d [y_1^d]?
   (d) What is the fiscal multiplier for aggregate demand?

T5. Given the basic model for the commodity market but with the interest rate set by the central bank at 0.25, what is the level of income? What becomes the level of income if autonomous investment i becomes 800? What is the investment multiplier in this case?

T6. Given the basic model for the commodity market, a perfect capital market and interest rate parity, as well as $r^F = 0.25$, $P = 2$, $P^F = 4$, $\bar{\rho} = 4$ (and with no change expected in this exchange rate):

   (a) What is the domestic interest rate?
   (b) Given this interest rate, what is the level of output (hint: use the commodity market equation for this derivation)?
   (c) Suppose the money demand function is $m^d = 0.25y - 60r$. Given the interest rate determined by the IRP condition, what is the money demanded equal to? What is the level of the money supply consistent with the above (i.e., derived in (a) and (b) above) levels of the interest rate and output?
   (d) Given the money demand function as $m^d = 0.25y - 60r$ and that the central bank maintains a constant money supply at 1,000, what will be the domestic interest rate (Hint: this is determined by the domestic commodity and money markets, i.e., IS and LM curves)?
   (e) If $r^F = 0.25$, $P = 2$, $P^F = 4$, and IRP holds, what will be the implied devaluation or revaluation of the exchange rate?

PART IV
Growth Economics

CHAPTER 14
Classical Growth Theory

The underlying model of growth analysis is known as the neoclassical, classical, or Solow growth model. It shows the impact of increases in physical capital and the labor force on the long-run growth rate of output and the standards of living. Among its distinguishing features are its assumptions of exogenous technical change and the absence of money. This chapter presents this analysis.

The next chapter extends the growth analysis of this chapter to encompass endogenous technical change and the relationship between the economy's output growth and its financial development.

This chapter studies the economic forces that increase the standard of living by examining the long-run determinants of the output growth rate. Improvements in living standards come about because of increases in output per worker. These increases are cumulative over time, so that even quite small (for instance, 1 to 4%) rates of increase, when compounded, can produce very large improvements in living standards over periods of 50 years or a century. For instance, over a century, a 4% growth rate leads to an output per capita that is seven times greater than what a 2% growth rate will produce. Since growth rates differ across countries, the underlying reason for the prosperity of some nations, while others are relatively poor, lie in the former having had higher growth rates over long periods in the past. Therefore, the study of the prosperity of nations is a study into the long-run growth of their output.

This chapter and the following one present the economic theories on the determination of the growth rate. The starting point of these theories is the 'classical or Solow growth model'. We have used this term for it because this model represents the basic growth theory element of the classical paradigm, as defined in Chapter 11. It was originally called the 'neoclassical growth model' and many expositions of it still continue to use this name. It is also known as the Solow model, since Robert Solow was the economist who proposed it in 1956.[1]

Fact Sheet 14.1: Long-Term Real GDP Growth in Selected Countries, 1960–2003

This Fact Sheet illustrates the variations in annual real GDP growth rates across countries and, for a given country, over time. For any given county, growth rates vary over the business cycle. 1980 and 1980 were recession years in most economies, so that the growth rates in these years were lower than in other years. Growth rates have been consistently lower in west European countries than in the north American ones. While India and China had lower growth rates than the USA in earlier years, China's and India's

---

[1] Solow, R. M. A contribution to the theory of economic growth. *Quarterly Journal of Economics*, **70**, February 1956, 65–94.

Fact Sheet 14.1: (*Continued*)

growth rates rose dramatically after 1990 when they started limited liberalization in production, foreign direct investment, foreign trade, etc.

	1960	1970	1980	1990	2000	2003
Total 29 Western Europe	6.43	4.44	1.57	1.21	3.78	1.08
Total Western Offshoots	2.57	0.59	0.24	1.60	3.70	2.71
Canada	3.11	2.58	1.34	0.25	5.25	1.99
The United States	2.49	0.17	0.05	1.75	3.66	2.70
Total 7 East European countries	6.20	3.52	0.52	−7.72	3.98	3.78
Total Former USSR	9.50	7.68	0.12	−2.42	8.45	7.67
Total Latin America	6.71	6.94	5.42	0.54	3.63	1.86
Total 29 East Asian countries	3.75	4.50	−0.57	2.39	4.64	6.75
China	−3.38	12.23	3.37	3.51	9.03	15.15
India	7.01	5.08	7.18	5.19	4.37	8.98
Japan	13.13	10.71	2.82	5.08	2.39	1.31
Thailand	12.13	6.55	4.61	11.17	4.75	6.87
Malaysia	7.26	6.09	8.32	9.55	8.55	5.20
Total 15 West Asian countries	6.39	8.46	−0.54	9.10	5.77	5.16
Total Asia	4.74	9.21	3.36	5.57	6.02	8.43
Total Africa	4.45	8.16	4.50	1.40	3.50	4.68
World Total	5.23	5.09	2.01	2.08	4.73	4.82

The very considerable variation in the growth rate of real GDP for a given country is illustrated in Fact Sheet 14.2 from data for the USA.

Fact Sheet 14.2: Real GDP Growth Rates in the USA

This Fact Sheet illustrates from the US data the very considerable variation in real GDP growth. A major reason for the variation in this growth rate is fluctuations in the rate of technical change, which is a major focus of this chapter. Other reasons for variation in this growth rate are fluctuations in aggregate demand and economic crises. Consequently, the variation in real GDP growth rates partly causes business cycles and is party caused by the other determinants of business cycles (see Chapter 16).

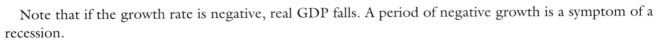

Fact Sheet 14.2: (*Continued*)

Note that if the growth rate is negative, real GDP falls. A period of negative growth is a symptom of a recession.

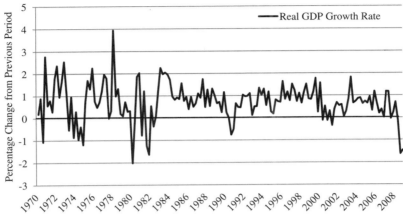

The assumptions of classical growth theory

Several fundamental assumptions distinguish the neoclassical/classical growth theory from the short-run macroeconomic models of the classical paradigm. For its growth model:

- The emphasis is on the evolution of the long-run equilibrium of the economy in response to changes in its three determinants of growth, which are the labor force, capital, and technology.
- All markets are assumed to be continuously in equilibrium. There is no uncertainty, so that the impact of errors in expectations is omitted. There are also no adjustment costs, whether of prices, employment, capital stock, or technology. Hence, the economy is always in long-run equilibrium at full employment, and the deviations from long-run growth path, along an SAS curve in the short-run analysis or due to disequilibrium, are omitted from the analysis.
- The economy is a closed one. It is also without a government sector. Further, the money and bond markets are omitted from the analysis.
- The physical capital stock is variable.
- The labor force is variable.
- Technology can change, so that the shifts in the production function are allowed. However, when technological change is incorporated in the standard classical growth models, the change in technology is assumed to be exogenously given.

These assumptions delineate the separate spheres of short-run models and growth theory. The raison d'être of short-run macroeconomic models is to examine the nature of the equilibrium in the different macroeconomic markets and the consequences of deviations from these. Growth theory, by assuming equilibrium in all markets, takes the full-employment state of the short-run models for granted. As a consequence, the main items of interest in the short-run macroeconomics models — such as the determination of prices, unemployment, deviation of output from its full-employment level, monetary and fiscal policy effects, etc., which are related to aggregate demand in the economy — are normally not considered in growth theory. The focus of the growth theories is on the impact of variations in capital, labor force, and technology on the evolution of full-employment output.

Classical growth theory studies the long-run equilibrium paths of the economy. A special state of such long-run growth paths is steady state (SS) paths along which the growth rates of designated variables, particularly the capital–labor ratio, do not change. Quite clearly, the actual economy of any country at any particular time may not even be in long-run equilibrium, let alone in an SS. However, most economists believe that, over long periods, economies tend toward the SS and that its study reveals the long-run tendencies of the economy. Given this belief, the usual focus of classical growth theory is on examining the existence and stability of SS output. But in practice, the public and the policymakers maintain a lively interest in the level of per capita output and its pre-SS (i.e., before the SS is reached) growth rates, so that we will also examine the long-run determinants of these variables.

Our interest in the growth theories will focus on three issues:

1. The SS level of output per capita, since this reflects the standard of living.
2. The SS growth rate of output per capita, since this reflects the growth of the standard of living.
3. The growth rate of the economy in the long-run equilibrium prior to or on the way to the SS one, i.e., the 'pre-SS growth rate'. This is an important and topical state to study since virtually no country at any point in time can be said to have reached the SS, but can be said to be on the way to one.

Exogenous shifts and policies that only change the level of per capita output are said to have level effects, while those which change its growth rate are said to have growth effects.

Basic mathematics of growth theory

For a variable Y (output), the change in Y over time has been compactly designated in this book as ΔY or Y' and its growth rate has been specified as $(\Delta Y/Y)$ or Y''. These are calculated for period t as:

$$Y'_t = (Y_{t+1} - Y_t)$$
$$Y''_t = Y'_t/Y_t = (Y_{t+1} - Y_t)/Y_t.$$

Since $Y = y \cdot L$, where y is output per worker and L is the labor force, we have $Y'' = y'' + L''$.[2] Therefore, for $y = Y/L$, we have $y'' = Y'' - L''$. Similarly, for $k = K/L$, we have $k'' = K'' - L''$.

If the growth rate of output Y is constant at the rate 4%, we will often write it as 0.04. In the latter version, $Y'' = 0.04 (= 4/100)$. If the growth rate is γ, we write $Y'' = \gamma$.[3] If Y does not change, its growth rate will be zero.

Extended Analysis Box 14.1: Setting the Boundaries of Macroeconomic Growth Theory

The boundaries of the standard treatments of classical growth theory analysis are set by:

- Classical growth theory focuses on output growth resulting from labor force growth, growth in the capital stock and change in technology. It ignores the growth in the stocks of money and bonds (including equities). In fact, many economists believe that the long-run growth of the economy is independent of

---

[2] $Y = y \cdot L$, $Y' = (y \cdot L') + L \cdot y'$, $Y'' = Y'/Y = y \cdot L'/Y + L \cdot y'/Y = y \cdot L'/yL + L \cdot y'/yL = L'/L + y'/y = L'' + y''$.

[3] If $Y'' = \gamma$, then the mathematical form for Y will be $Y = Y_0 e^{\gamma t}$, where Y_0 is the base period output and e is a mathematical symbol with the value 2.718. The natural log of e is 1. Therefore, we can also write output in logs as $\ln Y = \ln Y_0 + \gamma t$.

Extended Analysis Box 14.1: (*Continued*)

the money stock and even of its growth rate. Consequently, the inclusion of money in growth theory is left to the special topic of monetary growth theory.

- Most treatments of growth theory ignore the government sector — thereby ignoring government expenditures, taxation, and deficits.
- Most presentations of growth theory also ignore the external sector — thereby ignoring imports, exports, the terms of trade, the balance of trade, and the balance of payments.

The economy is always at full employment. Therefore, classical growth theory does not examine the determination of unemployment or changes in its rate in the short or even long run. Therefore, it does not see a need to differentiate between employment and the labor force. Further, it usually assumes that the labor force grows at the same rate as the population.

A critical assumption of short-run macroeconomic theory is that the saving and investment functions are distinct from each other. In reality, saving is done by households under utility maximization (subject to a budget constraint) while investment is done by firms based on profit maximization. Given a closed economy without a fiscal sector, short-run equilibrium requires the equality of saving and investment. Since growth theory starts by assuming such equilibrium, saving and investment have to be identical (always and not merely equal in equilibrium) in growth theory. While this identity could be defined in terms of an exogenous investment function and accommodative saving, classical growth theory assumes an exogenous saving function and accommodative investment.[4] That is, classical growth theory specifies the saving function from household behavior and assumes that investment always equals saving — which is determined independently from investment. Hence, an investment function independent of the saving one is not specified in classical growth theory. Further, since this theory assumes continuous full employment, saving is at its full-employment level, while investment is determined by — and always equal to — the full-employment saving.

14.1 The Classical (Solow's) Growth Model's Assumptions

This section sets out the benchmark classical growth theory. It was formulated by Solow in 1956 and is also known as the Solow model or the benchmark neoclassical growth model.[5]

Contrary to our earlier usage (in the short-run models) of capital symbols to designate the nominal values of the variables in the short-run models, we will use for growth theory capital symbols to designate the real values of the variables and the corresponding lower case symbols to designate their per capita values.

14.1.1 The technology of production

Assume a production function of the form:

$$Y = F(K, L) \qquad Y_K, Y_L > 0; \ Y_{KK}, Y_{LL} < 0, \ Y_{LK} > 0, \qquad (1)$$

---

[4]Some Keynesian theories assume exogenous investment and accommodative saving through changes in output.

[5]Solow, R. M. A contribution to the theory of economic growth. *Quarterly Journal of Economics*, **70**, February 1956, 65–94.

where:

$$
\begin{aligned}
Y &= \text{real output,}\\
K &= \text{physical capital stock,}\\
L &= \text{labor force,}\\
Y_K &= \text{marginal product of capital (MPK) } (= \partial Y/\partial K),\\
Y_{KK} < 0 &= \text{decreasing marginal product of capital (decreasing MPK),}\\
Y_L &= \text{marginal product of labor (MPL) } (= \partial Y/\partial L),\\
Y_{LL} < 0 &= \text{decreasing marginal product of labor (decreasing MPL), and}\\
Y_{LK} > 0 &= \text{increase in the marginal product of labor as capital is increased.}
\end{aligned}
$$

This production function is assumed to have constant returns to scale. This means that if both labor and capital are increased in the same proportion (say α), output will also increase in the same proportion (α). Hence:

$$\alpha Y = F(\alpha K, \alpha L), \tag{2}$$

where α can be any positive constant. If we set α equal to $1/L$, this equation implies that:

$$Y/L = F(K/L, 1),$$

which can be rewritten as:

$$y = f(k) \qquad y_k > 0, \quad y_{kk} < 0, \tag{3}$$

where:

$$
\begin{aligned}
y &= \text{output per worker}^6 \ (= Y/L),\\
k &= \text{capital per worker } (= K/L),\\
y_k &= \text{marginal increase in output per capita as capital per worker increases}\\
&\quad\ (= \text{MPk} = \text{MPK}),\\
y_{kk} &= \text{change in MPk as capital per worker increases,}\\
y_{kk} < 0 &= \text{diminishing MPk, and}\\
y_{kk} > 0 &= \text{increasing MPk.}
\end{aligned}
$$

This form of the production function asserts that, for the given technology, output per worker depends only on capital per worker.

14.1.2 Saving, investment and the change in the capital stock

The Solow model assumes that in the aggregate the average propensity to save (APS) is constant and always equal to the marginal propensity to save (MPS). Designate the value of the APS by σ (which is a Greek symbol, pronounced as 'sigma'). Since APS equals S/Y, we have $S/Y = \sigma$. Therefore, the economy's total saving S is given by:

$$S = \sigma Y.$$

Designate the per capita saving $(= S/L)$ by s. Therefore:

$$s = S/L = \sigma Y/L = \sigma y, \tag{4}$$

---

[6]We have made the assumption here and throughout our analysis of growth theory that the population and labor force can be taken to be identical for analytical purposes.

where:

S =   aggregate saving in the economy,

s =   saving per worker (per capita saving), and

σ =   average propensity to save (APS) out of output.[7]

The capital stock K changes by the amount of real investment I. Since there is continuous equilibrium in the commodity market in this closed economy without a government sector, investment (I) and the change in the capital stock (K') must equal saving S.[8] That is, designating the change in K as $K'(= \partial K/\partial t =$ change in K per period), we have:

$$K' = I = S,$$

so that,

$$K' = \sigma Y. \tag{5}$$

14.1.3 Labor force growth

The labor force growth rate is assumed to be constant at n. Using the convention that the growth rate of the labor force L is designated by L'', this assumption is:

$$L'' = \frac{1}{L}\frac{\partial L}{\partial t} = \frac{L'}{L} = n \tag{6}$$

where $L'(= \partial L/\partial t)$ is the change in L during the period and L'/L gives the growth rate of L.

14.2 The Analysis of the Solow Model

Equations (1) to (6) constitute the basic assumptions of the benchmark classical growth model. The analysis based on them is as follows.

First note that $k = K/L$, which implies that:

$$k'' = K'' - L''.$$

Since $k'' = k'/k$, $K'' = K'/K$, and $L'' = n$, we have:

$$k'/k = K'/K - n.$$

Multiplying each term in this equation by k gives:

$$k' = \{K' \cdot (k/K)\} - nk, \tag{7}$$

where $K' = S$ and, so that $\{K' \cdot (k/K)\}$ on the right-hand side of Equation (7) equals S/L. Hence:

$$k' = S/L - nk. \tag{8}$$

Since $S = \sigma Y$, S/L equals $\sigma Y/L$. Therefore:

$$k' = \sigma Y/L - nk.$$

Further, since $Y/L = f(k)$, we get:

$$k' = \sigma f(k) - nk. \tag{9}$$

The last equation has two components, $\sigma f(k)$ and nk, on the right-hand side. Of these, $\sigma f(k)$ is the increase in the capital stock per worker through saving and can be interpreted as 'the availability of new capital per

---

[7]σ is a Greek symbol and is being used as a parameter. It is pronounced as "sigma".

[8]An independent investment function is not being specified in this model. It is assumed that the interest rate adjusts instantly to determine the equilibrium level of investment by the amount of saving. In the short-run models, an independent investment function was specified so that the determination of the interest rate could be explicitly studied.

worker' (i.e., on average over all workers). Examining the second component, n is the number of new workers through population growth and k is the existing capital intensity (i.e., the capital per worker available to the existing workers), so that nk can be interpreted as 'the capital requirements of the new workers (at the existing capital intensity)'. Therefore, we have the intuitive interpretations:

$\sigma f(k) = (= S/L)$ the availability of new capital per worker and

$nk =$ the (per-capita) capital requirements of the new workers.

The value of k (designate it as k^*) at which the equality of these terms occurs is sometimes also referred to as the break-even capital-labor ratio, since the new capital then becoming available is just enough to equip new workers with the existing level of equipment per worker. Clearly, if $\sigma f(k)$ equals nk, the capital-labor ratio will not change, so that k^* is the SS value of k.

The SS of the Solow model without technical change is defined as the long-run equilibrium with a constant capital/labor ratio. That is, in the SS:

$$k' = 0,$$

so that, from Equation (9):

$$\sigma f(k) = nk. \tag{10}$$

This is the fundamental SS equation of the benchmark Solow model (without technical change). It determines the SS by the condition:

Availability of full-employment saving per worker = the capital requirements of new workers.   (11)

14.3 Diagrammatic Analysis of the Solow Model

Figure 14.1 graphs the fundamental equation of the SS for the Solow model with k on the horizontal axis. In this and similar figures later, we have designated the units of the vertical axis as output units. This axis[9] will be used to represent two different variables ($\sigma f(k)$ and nk) whose measurement units are output units. The concave curve representing $\sigma f(k)$ measures the per-capita availability of new capital (through saving), while the straight line marked nk measures the capital requirements of new workers at the existing capital–labor ratio.

In Figure 14.1, the curve marked $f(k)$ is output per capita. Since the MPL is positive but diminishing, this curve is concave. The curve marked $\sigma f(k)$ represents saving per capita. This curve is concave because $f(k)$ has a concave curve because of the diminishing marginal productivity of labor per capita. Since n is a constant, nk is represented by a straight line from the origin. The SS, with $\sigma f(k) = nk$, occurs at k_0^*. To the left of k_0^*, at k_1, saving (i.e., new capital) is greater than required to equip new workers with capital at the existing capital/labor ratio. Since all workers have to have the identical amount of capital per worker, the capital provided to all workers will increase, thereby causing a rightward movement toward k_0^*.

To the right of the point k_0^*, say at k_2, saving (i.e., new capital) is less than required to equip new workers with capital at the existing capital/labor ratio. Since all workers have to have the identical amount of capital per worker, the capital provided to all workers will decrease, prompting a leftward movement to k_0^*.[10] Therefore, if the economy is away from k_0^*, it will move back to k_0^*. That is, k_0^* is a stable SS capital–labor ratio.

---

[9]We will follow this pattern of not labeling the vertical axis for similar figures later in this and the next chapter.

[10]This incorporates an implicit assumption that capital is fungible and like putty, so that the adjustments to the implied capital/worker ratio can occur each period.

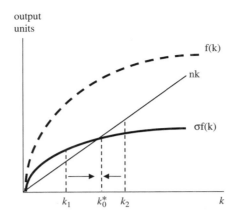

Figure 14.1

14.3.1 The SS growth rate of output

In Figure 14.1, in the SS at k_0^*, k (which equals K/L) is a constant at k_0^*. Substituting the SS value of k, designated as k_0^*, in the production function gives the SS level of y^* as:

$$y^* = f(k_0^*). \tag{12}$$

Since k_0^* is constant, y must also be a constant, say at y_0^*. Hence, in the steady state, y has a zero growth rate. That is:

$$y''(k_0^*) = 0. \tag{13}$$

Hence, the SS growth rate of output per capita is zero. Therefore, the standard of living becomes constant in the SS.

However, since $y = Y/L$ and $y'' = Y'' - L''$, in the SS:

$$y^{*''} = Y^{*''} - L'' = 0.$$

Hence,

$$Y^{*''} = n. \tag{14}$$

That is, the SS growth rate of output is determined by, and equals, the growth rate of the labor force.

We now derive the SS growth rate of capital. Since $k = K/L$, $k'' = K'' - L''$. Hence, in the SS, $k^{*''} = K^{*''} - L'' = 0$, so that $K^{*''} = n$. That is, the SS growth rate of capital, just as that of output, is determined by, and equals, the growth rate of the labor force.

Our conclusions for the SS of the Solow model without technical change are:

- The SS values of y and k are constant. Therefore, the standards of living and capital intensity (i.e., capital per worker) are constant in the SS.
- The SS growth rates of k and y are zero. That is, the standards of living do not change in the SS.
- The SS values of Y and K grow at the labor force growth rate. The lower the labor force growth rate, the lower the growth rate of output and capital in the SS.
- In the pre-SS stage, the growth rates of k and y are positive. Therefore, capital intensity and the standards of living increase as the economy goes to the SS.

Extended Analysis Box 14.2: Variability of the Saving Rate

The preceding model assumes that the saving rate will remain constant as the standards of living improve and the country approaches SS. In practice, poor countries with a static standard of living have a low marginal propensity to save (MPS), countries in the early stages of development and high growth rates often have high MPS but the MPS declines as the standard of living becomes quite high. The hypothesis of a constant saving rate in the preceding growth theory was, therefore, a simplifying device for the exposition. However, note that while this assumption may be suitable for static economies, it is not very realistic for economies during the process of development from the pre-industrial state to the industrial one.

Now suppose that the saving rate is endogenous and is a function of output per capita. Since the latter depends on capital intensity, the saving rate becomes a function of k. A plausible further assumption would be that the saving rate increases as the standard of living begins to rise above the low/subsistence levels (i.e., at low capital intensities) but declines at higher ones, eventually becoming a constant.[11] This hypothesis can be expressed as $\sigma = \sigma(y)$ or as:

$$\sigma = \sigma(k),$$

so that the SS condition becomes:

$$\sigma(k) f(k) = nk.$$

With this assumption for the saving propensity σ, $\sigma(k)$ first has a convex (increasing rate) segment, followed by a concave (decreasing rate) one. Such a curve is likely to cut the ray nk at three points, so that there would be three SS positions (not shown diagrammatically) for this curve.

14.3.2 The impact of shifts in the saving rate

Our conclusion from Solow's fundamental growth equation above was that the SS growth rates $Y^{*''}$ and $K^{*''}$ depend only on the growth rate of labor and not on the saving rate. Hence, a change in the saving propensity σ cannot change the growth rates of capital and output. This result can also be established diagrammatically, as shown in the following analysis.

An increase in the marginal propensity to save (MPS) from σ_0 to σ_1 shifts the $\sigma f(k)$ curve in Figure 14.2a upwards from $\sigma_0 f(k)$ to $\sigma_1 f(k)$ and establishes a new SS at k_1^*, with $k_1^* > k_0^*$. Since the capital per worker has increased to k_1^*, the output per worker — and therefore the standard of living — will be higher. However, the fundamental growth equation implies that the growth rate of output per worker in the new SS, as in the old one, will be zero, so that the growth rate of output per worker does not change from one SS to a new one. Therefore, in both the old and new SS, output will grow at the labor force growth rate n, so that the SS output growth rate is not changed by the increase in the saving rate. However, note that the output growth rate will rise above n during the transition from k_0^* to k_1^*: in Figure 14.2a, under the higher saving rate, the output growth rate is higher at k_2 (i.e., in the pre-SS) than at k_0^* and k_1^*.

Conversely, if there is a decrease in the saving rate, the Solow model implies a fall in investment and a reduction in both the growth rate and living standards in both the transition (which can take decades) to the new SS and the new SS itself — even though it does not change the SS growth rate of output per capita.

---

[11] The saving rate in normal times always tends to be positive because of the need to save for one's retirement age, and also because of precautionary saving against unexpected declines in income or increases in consumption needs.

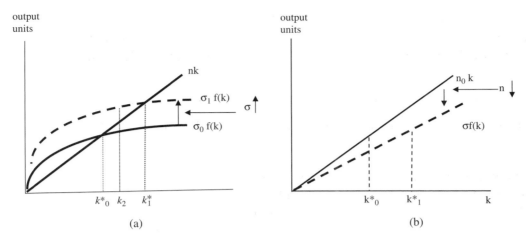

Figure 14.2

The Solow model's conclusions for the comparisons among countries that have different saving rates but are otherwise identical (the *ceteris paribus* assumption) are that:

- In the pre-SS stage, *ceteris paribus*, countries with higher saving rates will have higher growth rates of output and of output per worker, so that their standards of living will improve at a faster rate. However, their growth rate will fall over time to the SS one.
- In the SS, *ceteris paribus*, countries with higher saving rates will have the same growth rate (zero) of output per worker as those with lower saving rates.
- In the SS, *ceteris paribus*, countries with higher saving rates will have higher levels of output per worker and, therefore, higher standards of living.

To illustrate, many countries, including Canada and the USA, have low saving rates between 0% and 10%. These low saving rates are a cause for concern about their implications for the pre-SS growth rates of these countries. Conversely, the relatively high growth rates of certain developing countries, such as Japan during the 1960s and 1970s or Korea in the 1980s, were often attributed to their high saving rates. Note also that their high growth rates did eventually fall to the levels of the American and West European countries, as predicted by the Solow model.

Mathematical Box 14.1: Numerical Example A

Assume that a country has the production function:

$$y = 20k - 0.4k^2.$$

Also assume that the country also has the marginal and average propensity to consume (APC) identical at 0.9 and a labor force growth rate of 4%. That is, $\sigma = 0.1$ and $L'' = 0.04$.

Q: What are its SS capital–labor ratio and its output per worker?

The SS condition is: $\sigma f(k) = nk$. Therefore:

$$0.1(20k - 0.4k^2) = 0.04k.$$

Opening the bracket on the left side of the preceding equation, we can cancel k from both sides and solve the equation for the SS value of k. This yields $k^* = 49$. Substituting this value in the production function, we have:

$$y^* = 20k - 0.4k^2 = 20(49) - 0.4(49)^2 = 19.6.$$

For use in further numerical examples in Mathematical Boxes 14.1 and 14.2, designate these solutions as:

$$k_0^* = 49 \quad \text{and} \quad y_0^* = 19.6.$$

Q: What are the growth rates of output per worker and of output?

In the SS, since the SS capital–labor ratio $k^*(= 49)$ does not change, the SS output per worker $y^*(= 19.6)$ also does not change. Hence, $y^{*''} = 0$ and the SS output per worker remains at 19.6.

In the SS, $y'' = (Y/L)'' = Y'' - L'' = 0$ implies that $Y'' = L'' = 0.04$. Therefore, $Y'' = 0.04$. Hence, while output per worker remains constant at 19.6, output grows at 4%.

14.3.3 The impact of shifts in the labor force growth rate

Many countries of the world are currently experiencing decreases in their labor force growth rates. Therefore, the following analysis derives the effects of a decrease, rather than an increase, in the labor force growth rate. A decrease in the labor force growth rate from n_0 to n_1 will lower the nk curve in Figure 14.2b from n_0k to n_1k. This increases the SS values of k from k_0^* to k_1^* — that is, there is more capital to distribute among the smaller labor force. This higher value of the SS capital–labor ratio increases the SS output per worker, thereby improving the SS standard of living.

However, the growth rate of output per worker is zero in the SS. Therefore, the growth rate of output is n_0 at k_0^* while it is n_1 at k_1^*, with $n_1 < n_0$, so that the SS output growth rate falls as the labor force growth rate falls — though the output per worker has increased.

The Solow model's conclusions for comparisons among countries that have different labor force growth rates but are otherwise identical (the *ceteris paribus* assumption) are that:

- In the pre-SS stage, countries with lower labor force growth rates will have lower output growth rate but higher growth rate of output per worker, so that their standards of living will improve over time.
- In the SS, countries with lower labor force growth rates will have the same (zero) growth rate of output per worker but lower growth rates of output.
- In the SS, countries with lower labor force growth rates will have higher levels of both capital and output per worker and, therefore, higher standards of living.

Comparing the effects of increases in the APS σ and of the labor force growth rate n on output Y and output per worker y, the Solow model's conclusions are that:

- SS effects on y: increases in APS σ increase SS output per capita (y^*) but do not change its growth rate (y''^*, which remains at zero), while decreases in the labor force growth rate n increase the SS output per capita (y^*) but do not change its growth rate (y''^*, which remains at zero).

- SS effects on Y: increases in the APS σ raise the SS output level y^* but do not change its growth rate Y''^*. Decreases in the labor force growth rate n lower the growth rate Y''^*.
- In the pre-SS stage, the higher the saving rate and the lower the labor force growth rate, the faster the growth in capital and output per worker.

Mathematical Box 14.2: Numerical Example B

In Numerical Example A in Mathematical Box 14.1, the economy had the production function $y = 20k - 0.4k^2$ and $L'' = 0.04$. Now assume that the saving rate rises from 0.1 (in Example A) to 0.2. Hence, our information becomes:

$$y = 20k - 0.4k^2, \sigma = 0.2 \quad \text{and} \quad L'' = 0.04.$$

Q: What are the SS values of k and y?

The SS value of k is calculated from the SS fundamental equation, which gives:

$$0.2(20k - 0.4k^2) = 0.04k.$$

We can simplify this equation by canceling k in all the terms. This yields:

$$4 - 0.08k = 0.04,$$

so that $k^* = 49.5$.

Substituting this value of k in the production function gives:

$$y^* = 20k^* - 0.4k^{*2} = 20(49.5) - 0.4(49.5)^2 = 9.9.$$

Designating its solutions as k_1^* and y_1^*, we have $k_1^* = 49.5$ and $y_1^* = 9.9$. Comparing Examples A (in Mathematical Box 14.1) and B, the increase in the saving rate increased the SS capital–labor ratio (but lowered output per capita).

Note that while the capital–labor ratio increased, output per worker fell, which is a very unrealistic result.[12] This result is a consequence of the assumed quadratic production function, which is easy to work with but unrealistic. The more realistic result would be that the greater capital per worker increases output per worker. For such a result, a more appropriate production function would be one with an exponent less than two on the second term, but this would make the calculations much more difficult. Such a function is the Cobb–Douglas production function used in the Appendix [optional] to this chapter.

Q: What are the SS growth rates of k, y, K, and Y after the increase in the saving rate?

In the SS, since the SS capital–labor ratio $k^*(= 49.5)$ does not change, the SS output per worker $y^*(= 9.9)$ also does not change. Hence, $y^{*''} = 0$.

In the SS, $y'' = (Y/L)'' = Y'' - L'' = 0$ implies that $Y'' = L''$. Therefore, $Y'' = 0.04$. Hence, while output per worker remains constant at 9.9, output grows at 4%. Note that this SS growth rate is the same as in Numerical Example A in Mathematical Box 14.1. Therefore, the increase in the saving rate in B did not change the SS growth rate of output per capita (which was 0%) and the growth rate of output (which was 4%).

---

[12]This occurs in both Examples B and C when compared with Example A.

Mathematical Box 14.2: (*Continued*)

Numerical Example C

Now assume that the labor force growth rate decreases to 0.02. Hence, our information becomes:

$$y = 20k - 0.4k^2, \sigma = 0.2 \quad \text{and} \quad L'' = 0.02.$$

Its SS values are to be calculated from the SS fundamental equation, which gives:

$$0.2(20k - 0.4k^2) = 0.02k.$$

We can simplify this equation by canceling k in all the terms. This yields:

$$k^* = 49.75.$$

Substituting this value of k in the production function gives:

$$y^* = 20k^* - 0.4k^{*2} = 20(49.75) - 0.4(49.75)^2 = 4.975.$$

Designating these solutions as k_2^* and y_2^*, we have $k_2^* = 49.75$ and $y_2^* = 4.975$. Comparing Examples B and C, the decrease in the labor force growth rate increased the SS capital–labor ratio.[13]

Q: What are the SS growth rates of output per capita and of output?

In the SS, since the SS capital–labor ratio $k^*(= 49.75)$ does not change, the SS output per worker $y^*(= 4.975)$ also does not change. Hence, $y^{*''} = 0$.

In the SS, $y'' = (Y/L)'' = Y'' - L'' = 0$ implies that $Y'' = L''$. Therefore, $Y'' = 0.02$. Hence, comparing Examples B and C, the decrease in the labor force growth rate lowered the output growth rate from 4% to 2%.

14.4 The Growth Implications of a More General Production Function

A common form of the production function used in microeconomic analysis has a region of increasing MPK followed by one with diminishing MPK. We illustrate this case with an example. Suppose that the existing technology dictates a minimum functional type of a machine (computer) that can be useful. Below this size, if there are more workers than machines, there is forced and inefficient sharing of the machine among the available workers or some workers have to be left waiting or unemployed. Increases in capital are then likely to result in increasing marginal productivity. Once all the workers are equipped with the machines, further increases in the number of machines for the given number of workers results in decreasing marginal productivity. The analysis of this range yields the Solow diagram in Figure 14.3. In this figure, $\sigma f(k)$ is, as before, the saving done in the economy at the constant saving rate σ. The growth rate of the population is still assumed to be constant at n.

Figure 14.3 shows that the use of the more general production pattern generates two SS points k_1^* and k_2^*. Of these, if the economy is to the left of k_1^*, it does not generate enough new capital through its own savings to meet the capital requirement of new workers, so that it gradually decreases its capital per worker and therefore moves to lower standards of living. This movement continues until a new SS is reached. If the economy is to the right of k_1^*, it generates more new capital through its own saving than needed to meet the capital requirement of new workers, so that the economy gradually increases its capital per worker and

---

[13]It lowered output per capita but this is a result of the unrealism of the assumed production function.

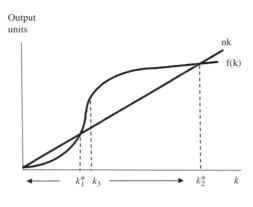

Figure 14.3

therefore moves to higher standards of living. Hence, k_1^* represents an unstable SS: the economy moves either to the left or to the right of k_1^*, but not toward it. k_1^* is called the *take-off capital–labor ratio*: to the right of it, the economy 'takes off' to self-sustaining growth leading to increasing higher standards of living.

k_2^* represents a stable SS point: once the economy is to the right of k_1^*, it moves towards k_2^*.

Hence, the more general production function produces an unstable SS at k_1^*, but a stable one at k_2^*. Economies which are to the left of the take-off ratio k_1^* will move to lower SS capital–labor ratios and will become increasingly poorer. Economies to the right of the take-off ratio k_1^* will progress to higher capital–labor ratios and will become increasingly richer. Over time, there occurs convergence in the living standards among the better-off countries (i.e., those to the right of k_1^*) while the standards of living of poorer countries (i.e., those to the left of k_1^*) diverge from those of the richer countries.

It is quite an oversimplification to fit the actual experience of countries to a single difference in the determinants of growth. Keeping this in mind, consider the growth experience of China in the context of a production function of the type shown in Figure 14.3. In recent decades, China drastically reduced its birth rate through a state-instituted one-child-per-family policy. This would have lowered its *nk* curve and reduced its take-off capital–labor ratio, as well as raised its pre-SS growth rate — thereby facilitating its entry onto a self-sustaining high growth path. Many sub-Saharan African countries have very low capital–labor ratios and high labor force growth rates, raising the possibility that they are below their take-off capital–labor ratios. Countries in this situation tend to remain poor and possess low growth rates unless some shift or shifts reduce their take-off capital ratios. Among these shifts would be increases in their capital growth rates (financed by increases in their own saving rates or through continuous inflows of foreign aid over time), or decreases in their labor force growth rates. A third possibility is a shift in technology. Certain forms of technical change can shift the $\sigma f(k)$ curve in such a way as to lower the take-off capital–labor ratio. However, other kinds of shifts could raise it. The role of technical change in growth theory is discussed later in this chapter and in Chapter 15.

14.5 Convergence Versus Divergence in Output per capita among Countries

We now return to the benchmark Solow model with diminishing MPK. This model implies that there is a tendency for all countries to move toward and converge to the same SS k and y ratios if they have:

- the same production function with a single technology possessing diminishing marginal productivity of capital,

- the same saving propensity, and
- the same population growth rate.

Even if countries have different production functions, saving propensities, and labor force growth rates, the Solow model implies that their capital per worker and output per worker would become constant in their respective SS, though at different levels.

The Solow model, assuming a given technology and saving rate, has several implications that are contrary to the general experience of growth. Among these are:

- All the countries converge to the same SS output per capita.[14] However, empirical studies do not show a general worldwide tendency toward the convergence of living standards among all countries of the world. In fact, the gap in the standard of living between the richest countries and the poorest ones seems to increase rather than decrease.
- The SS growth rate of output per worker for all economies will converge to the same (zero) growth rate. This is also contrary to the real-world experience since most countries continue to experience improving standards of living over long periods.[15]
- Countries with lower labor force growth will have lower output growth rates. This is often contradicted by experience, for example, between European and North American growth rates with those in Africa.
- For countries tending to the same SS but still in the pre-SS stage, countries with lower values of y and k will have higher growth rates of y than richer countries with higher values. While this is consistent with the experience of some countries, it is not always so.

Given these discrepancies between experience and the implications of the benchmark Solow model, we need to modify some of its assumptions. The most important modification to it is the introduction of technical change. This modification of the benchmark Solow growth model is based on another contribution of Solow (1957) to growth economics. This modification is presented in the next section.

14.6   Assessing the Importance of Technical Change in the Solow Model[16]

This section provides an empirical assessment of the importance of technical change. The following procedure is based on the contributions of Robert Solow.[17] For this purpose, modify the production function to:

$$Y = F(K, L, T), \tag{15}$$

where, taking technology to be a measurable variable, T is the 'technology index'. Solow (1957) offered a procedure for the estimation of technical change under the assumption that the production function takes the

---

[14]Note that the classical model does not necessarily imply convergence in the level of output per capita: it does not do so if the production functions are different, the saving propensities are different, or if the production function has segments with increasing MPK.

[15]Even if different countries have different production functions — though with diminishing MPK — and different saving rates, they would still converge to the same (zero) SS growth rate of output per worker. Such convergence has also not been observed in the real world.

[16]Solow, R. M. Technical change and the aggregate production function. *Review of Economics and Statistics*, **39**, August 1957, 312–320.

[17]*Ibid.*

specific form:

$$Y = A(T)g(L, K). \tag{16}$$

For this production function, output results from the joint contribution through $g(K, L)$ of labor and capital and the technology level, whose effect on production is captured in a multiplicative form by $A(T)$. The contribution of technology to output is assumed to be independent of the levels of the labor force and capital stock. T is measured by chronological years. Since the total contribution of the two factors of production, labor, and capital, to output/product is captured by $g(K, L)$, $g(K, L)$ is called the *total factor product*. Note that since labor is in man-hour units and physical capital is in terms of commodity units, they cannot just be added to arrive at an index of all the inputs, so that an index of inputs needs to be constructed.[18] This index can be constructed by using the function $g(K, L)$, which is the output that is produced at the technology level of a designated base year, with T normalized at unity for the base year. $A(T)$ is correspondingly called the *total factor productivity* (TFP) or *multifactor productivity*. The index for $A(T)$ can be constructed from:

$$A(T) = Y/[g(L, K)].$$

Intuitively, $A(T)$ is the ratio of real GDP to the (index of) total inputs and shows their productivity.

A major emphasis of growth analysis is on the 'growth rate of technology', which is measured by $A''(T)$. Intuitively, $A''(T)$ represents the growth rate of output that results from improvements in technology, with all inputs held constant. This assumed pattern of technical change shifts the production function and increases output year by year even if there are no changes in labor and capital inputs. Further, $A''(T)$ increases the marginal productivities of labor and capital in the same proportion, so that this form of technical change called *neutral technical change*.

Solow's contribution in 1957 — in addition to his contribution of 1956 on the growth theory model specified earlier — provided the following method of measuring this increase. The contribution of each unit of labor to output equals its marginal product.[19] Therefore, the contribution of labor as a whole to output equals $\text{MPL} \cdot L$ (note: not $\text{APL} \cdot L$), so that its contribution per unit of output Y is given by:

$$\alpha_L = (\text{MPL} \cdot L)/Y,$$

where MPL is the marginal productivity of labor. α_L is the elasticity of output with respect to labor, i.e., the percentage increase in output for an increase in labor. Under perfect competition, the profit maximizing firm employs labor up to the point where the MPL equals its real wage rate (i.e., $\text{MPL} = w$), so that:

$$\alpha_L = (w \cdot L)/Y,$$

where w is the real wage rate and wL is the total payment out of output to labor. This method of measuring α_L makes it the income share of labor (i.e., the share of labor in income) and provides a way of measuring α_L.

Similarly, the contribution of capital as a whole to output is captured by $(\text{MPK} \cdot K)$ and its contribution per unit of output Y is given by:

$$\alpha_K = (\text{MPK} \cdot K)/Y,$$

where α_K is the elasticity of output with respect to capital.

---

[18]This index can also be viewed as a composite index of all the inputs (factors of production) used in production, where each input is weighted by its income share in the base period and the weighted amounts of the inputs are summed.

[19]The assumptions for this procedure are constant returns to scale in production, perfect competition, profit maximization, and that technical change is independent of the quantities used of labor and capital. The procedure is explained in the appendix to this chapter.

The wage rate can be thought of as the rental or user cost per unit of labor per unit of time. Similarly, designating the rental or user cost of capital[20] under perfect competition by ρ_K, profit maximizing firms will use capital up to the point at which the MPK equals the rental cost ρ_K of capital, so that:

$$\alpha_K = (\rho_K K)/Y.$$

This provides the interpretation of α_K as the income share of capital and provides a way of measuring α_K.

Adding the contributions of labor and capital to output gives the total factor product (i.e., the weighted sum of the contributions of the factors of production to output) $g(K, L)$ as:

$$g(K, L) = \alpha_L \cdot L + \alpha_K \cdot K.$$

Measuring α_L and α_K at an initial level (i.e., in a given base year), the growth rate of total factor product $g(K, L)$ is specified by:

$$g'' = \alpha_L \cdot L'' + \alpha_K \cdot K''.$$

Therefore, the output growth rate can be decomposed into three components: the contribution of labor, the contribution of capital and a remainder, which is called the contribution of technical change to output. Since $Y = A(T) \cdot g(L, K)$, we have:

$$Y'' = A''(T) + g''(L, K),$$

where $g''(L, K) = \alpha_K K'' + \alpha_L L''$. Therefore:

$$Y'' = A''(T) + \alpha_K K'' + \alpha_L L''. \tag{17}$$

To reiterate:

$$
\begin{aligned}
A''(T) &= \text{growth rate of total factor productivity (TFP)}, \\
\alpha_K &= \text{share of capital in aggregate income/output, and} \\
\alpha_L &= \text{share of labor in aggregate income/output.[21]}
\end{aligned}
$$

For many industrialized countries, the estimated value of α_L (labor's share of national income) is about 0.7, while α_K (capital's share of national income) is about 0.3.

In the preceding equation, $(\alpha_K K'' + \alpha_L L'')$ is the share-weighted growth rate of output due to the growth of labor and capital. $A''(T)$ measures the growth rate of output that cannot be accounted for by factor growth and is the growth rate of TFP. It is usually attributed to the change in technology.

The preceding equation is known as the growth accounting equation since it 'accounts for' (separates) the output growth rate by the contributions of technology, capital and labor. Since $A''(T)$ is unobservable while all the other parameters and variables in the preceding equation are observable, rewrite the above equation as:

$$A''(T) = Y'' - \alpha_K K'' - \alpha_L L''. \tag{18}$$

All the terms on the right side of this equation are observable, so that the data on them can be used to calculate the technology growth rate.[22]

---

[20]The rental cost of a machine is what it would cost to rent it for one period. In perfect capital markets for both new and used machines, it equals the interest cost on the funds to buy it, plus depreciation and the decline in its market value (other than due to depreciation) during the period. This is often simplified to the interest cost alone by ignoring the last two components.

[21]The assumption of constant returns to scale implies that $(\alpha_L + \alpha_K) = 1$. That is, the shares of labor and capital in national income sum to unity.

[22]Equation (17) can be simplified further under the assumption of constant returns to scale, in which case $\alpha_L + \alpha_K = 1$, so that $\alpha_L = 1 - \alpha_K$. Substituting this in Equation (17) gives $A''(T) = Y'' - L'' - \alpha_K (K'' - L'')$. Since $y = Y/L$ and $k = K/L$, $y'' = Y'' - L''$ and $k'' = K'' - L''$, $A''(T) = y'' - \alpha_K k''$. That is, the growth of output due to technical change is the difference between the growth of output per worker and the weighted value of the growth of capital per worker.

14.6.1 Solow's estimates of the contribution of technical change to the improvement in living standards

Solow used the growth accounting formula to calculate $A''(T)$ and found that historically the main increase in per-capita output in the USA had been due to technical change rather than to increases in capital per worker, though there was considerable variation from year to year in the former. His conclusion for the period 1909–1949 for the USA was that while output per capita almost doubled, about 87.5% (i.e., 7/8) of this increase was due to technical change and only about 12.5% (i.e., 1/8) was due to more capital per worker. Another recent study for the USA indicates that between 1995 and 2000, output per hour grew annually by 2.79%.[23] Of this amount, the growth of multifactor productivity (i.e., $A''(T'')$) accounted for about 1.31% or 47% of the annual growth of output per hour of labor time.[24] Somewhat similar results indicating the importance of technical change in the growth of output per capita have been confirmed by many studies on other countries. Given this importance of technical change, we need to incorporate it explicitly into the formal growth models and study its determinants. The former is done later in this chapter. The latter is done in the next chapter.

Mathematical Box 14.3: Numerical Examples on Technical Change

To illustrate the calculation of the technology growth rate, suppose that the annual growth rate of labor is 2% and of capital is 3%, while output grows annually at 4%. With $\alpha_L = 0.7$ and $\alpha_K = 0.3$, we would have:

growth of output due to capital growth $= \alpha_K K'' = 0.3(0.03) = 0.009 = 0.9\%$,
growth of output due to labor force growth $= \alpha_L L'' = 0.7(0.02) = 0.014 = 1.4\%$, and
growth of output due to technical change $= A''(T) = 0.04 - 0.3(0.03) - 0.7(0.02) = 0.017 = 1.7\%$.

Hence, with total output growth at 4%, output grows by 1.7% each year as a result of the improvement in technology, while it grows by 0.9% because of the growth of capital and by 1.4% because of the increase in labor.

If we convert these results to the growth rate of output per capita (i.e., $y'' = Y'' - L''$), which represents the growth of the standard of living, we have:

growth of output per capita $= y'' = Y'' - L'' = 0.04 - 0.02 = 0.02 = 2\%$,
growth of output due to growth of K and $L = \alpha_L L'' + \alpha_K K'' = 0.7(0.02) + 0.3(0.03) = 0.023$,
growth of output per capita due to capital growth per capita $= \{(\alpha_L L'' + \alpha_K K'') - L''\}$[25]
$= \{0.7(0.02) + 0.3(0.03)\} - 0.02 = \{0.014 + 0.009\} - 0.02 = 0.023 - 0.02 = 0.003 = 0.3\%$, and
growth of output per capita due to technical change $= 0.02 - 0.003 = 0.017 = 1.7\%$.

Therefore, the total growth in living standards because of the growth of both labor and capital is only 0.3% per year. This figure of only 0.3% is very much smaller than the contribution to the growth of living standards due to technological change, which is 1.7%. While we can use other plausible numbers as calibration exercises for the growth accounting equation, they tend to show a similar point: the growth of total factor productivity (TFP) is the main cause of the improvements in living standards.

---

[23] Martin N. B. Distinguished lecture on economics in government: the new economy: post mortem or second wind? *Journal of Economic Perspectives*, **16**, Spring 2003, 2–22.

[24] This estimate is down from Solow's corresponding estimate of 87.5%. Most studies indicate that the rate of technical change decreased from 1973 to the mid-1990s, when it again picked up.

[25] This calculation subtracts 2% because we are dealing with output per worker and the labor force grows at 2%.

Mathematical Box 14.3: (*Continued*)

Now take the example of rapidly industrializing/growing economies, sometimes referred to as 'economic tigers' — a designation for a country with exceptionally high growth rates for many years. They tend to have a high output growth rate, a relatively high labor force growth rate and a relatively high capital growth rate. Suppose that their output growth rate is 10%, labor force growth is 3%, and capital growth is 8%. With $\alpha_L = 0.7$ and $\alpha_K = 1 - \alpha_L = 0.3$, these figures imply that:

$$A''(T) = 0.10 - 0.7(0.03) - 0.3(0.08) = 0.055 = 5.5\%.$$

Hence, the relative importance of technical change to the growth of output in this example increased dramatically over that in the first example: 5.5% per year as against only 1.7% per year. Therefore, the high growth rate of the economic tigers is likely to be largely due to their very rapid technical change.

14.6.2 The residual as the unexplained component of growth

The derived value of $A''(T)$ from the growth accounting equation is the residual (of the output growth rate) after deducting the contributions of labor and capital. It has been nicknamed the "Residual". Since Solow's growth theory does not explain the determinants of this residual, it represents a lack of knowledge, so that another nickname given to it has been 'The Measure of our Ignorance'. A continuing objective of growth studies has been to explain ever-larger percentages of the growth rate, so that the residual — or the unexplained measure of output growth — is gradually whittled down. One method of doing so is explained in Mathematical Box 14.4.

Mathematical Box 14.4: Detailed Estimation of the Contributions to Economic Growth

Estimating the returns to different educational levels

The growth accounting equation measures the return per period to labor by the wage rate. But labor is of many different kinds, usually differing in the amounts of human capital, and being paid different wage rates. We need a procedure for calculating the returns to different amounts of human capital. The following provides an illustration of the procedure used in growth accounting.

Assume that we have some workers (numbering X^{HS}) who have only a high school education while there are others (numbering X^{BA}) who have a BA degree. The economy provides data on the wages of these two types of workers, designated respectively as w^{HS} and w^{BA}. Assuming that the only difference between these two types is in their educational levels,[26] the difference $(w^{BA} - w^{HS})$ would measure the market return to the college education of the workers with the BA, while w^{HS} will be the return/wage of the workers with the high school education.[27] The income shares of all workers up to the completion of high school would be $[w^{HS}(X^{HS} + X^{BA})]$ while that of college education would be $[(w^{BA} - w^{HS})X^{BA}]$.

---

[26]This implicitly assumes that the two types of workers are otherwise identical, e.g., in their abilities, and there is perfect competition in the labor market.

[27]Under a perfectly competitive system, this provides the marginal productivities of the two inputs, high school graduates and college education resulting in the BA, respectively as $\rho^{HS}(= w^{HS})$ and $\rho^{BA}(= w^{BA} - w^{HS})$.

Mathematical Box 14.4: (*Continued*)

This procedure can be usually used to calculate the returns to a wide variety of inputs.

A general procedure for assessing the contribution of each input to output
For the general case of J inputs in the production function, we can calculate the contribution to output of the jth input as:

$$\text{Income of } j\text{th input} = (\text{MP}_j \cdot X_j) \qquad j = 1, 2, \ldots, J,$$

where MP_j is the marginal product of the jth input and X_j is the quantity of the jth input. Under the assumption that each unit of each input is paid the marginal product of the input, we can write the income share of the jth input (i.e., the share in national income Y) as:

$$\alpha_j = (\rho_j \cdot X_j)/Y \qquad j = 1, 2, \ldots, J,$$

where:

α_j	=	income share of jth input,
MP_j	=	marginal product of the jth input,
ρ_j	=	payment (rental/user cost) per period to the jth input, and
X_j	=	quantity of jth input used in production.

The general growth accounting equation
We can now generalize the growth accounting equation[28] to:

$$Y'' = A''(T) + \Sigma_j \alpha_j X_j'',$$

where X_j'' is the growth rate of the jth input. This equation provides a growth-accounting procedure according to which the contributions to the growth of output by technical change and the various inputs can be measured. Its empirical application requires the calculation of the income shares α_j, which equal $\rho_j X_j / Y$, so that we only need data on ρ_j (the rental cost per period), X_j (the input quantity), and total income Y.

The above procedure can be used to calculate the relative contribution to output for a wide variety of inputs. Edward Denison in an influential study in the early 1960s used this growth accounting procedure to derive the contribution of numerous factors to output growth in the USA. This procedure was adopted in many studies for many countries and continues to be used for evaluating the importance of the various inputs to output growth. Among the factors included in such growth accounting measures are the physical capital stock, number of hours worked, various educational levels, sex composition, and age, as well as factors that are more difficult to quantify. Among these are the workers' health, firms' competitiveness, the economy's openness to foreign trade, etc.

The residual of the growth rate from this procedure encompasses the contribution of all factors that are not explicitly incorporated in the growth accounting calculations. In general, the larger the number of factors taken into account, the smaller becomes the residual that needs to be attributed to the diffuse term 'technical change'.

---

[28] Remember its assumptions: constant returns to scale, perfect competition, and profit maximization.

Box 14.1: Deficiencies of the Growth Accounting Equation

The growth accounting procedure has several deficiencies, so that it can yield erroneous measurements of the contributions of the various inputs and the growth rate of technical change. These deficiencies/errors are related to:

(i) The measurement of the contributions of physical and human capitals. These are not only the inputs into production but also the carriers of technical change: without them, many forms of technical change will not occur. The above growth-accounting procedure ignores this carrier role of labor and capital, so that it underestimates their contribution to growth. Conversely, it overestimates the residual attributed to pure technical change.

(ii) Variations in work effort — without corresponding changes in wages — and in capital utilization over the business cycle: As Chapter 8 argued, the work effort of employees changes over the business cycle. In recessions, firms tend to hoard labor, so that its productivity falls. Further, the rate of capital utilization is decreased, so that even in the absence of technical change, output falls more than employment. Hence, total factor productivity falls. This fall is not a reflection of a negative growth rate of technology but only in the rates of utilization of labor and capital. However, if $A''(T)$ was actually equal to zero but labor productivity fell relative to wages in the recession, the growth accounting calculation would erroneously yield a negative value for it. As demand and output rise in the upturn, work effort and capital utilization increase, so that productivity rises more than wages. Hence, if $A''(T)$ was actually equal to zero, the growth accounting calculation would erroneously show a positive value for it in the upturns. Therefore, the calculated value of $A''(T)$ would be too low during recessions and too high during upturns.

(iii) The growth of intangible capital such as organizational and production skills and other skills acquired on the job. This type of capital is difficult to measure accurately. Further, the expenditures on such skills are usually treated as a current expense of firms rather than as an investment. Failure to include an accurate value of intangible human capital understates the amount of human capital in the economy, and so reduces the human capital's contribution in the growth accounting calculations.

(iv) Discrimination in the payments to factors of production. If the labour markets do not have perfect competition but are segmented in some way — e.g., by gender, race, color, etc. — the wages paid to workers need not equal their marginal productivity. In the presence of discrimination, wages would be greater than marginal productivity for the favored workers and less than marginal productivity for the discriminated-against workers. Further, some of the benefits of discrimination are likely to increase, as they normally do, the profits paid to capital beyond its marginal productivity. Therefore, measuring the contribution of the different types of inputs to the nation's output by their payments will overestimate the contribution of the favored workers, as well as of capital, and underestimate the contribution of the discriminated-against workers. It will also give erroneous estimates of technical change.

Other reasons for the deviation of the payments to the factors of production from their marginal productivity include monopoly, monopsony power, etc.

Table 14.1   Sources of output and productivity growth in the USA, % annual growth rates,[30] 1959–1998.

	1959–1998	1959–1973	1973–1990	1990–1995	1995–1998
Growth in output (Y'')	3.63	4.33	3.13	2.74	4.73
Growth in labour force in hours (L'')	1.59	1.38	1.69	1.37	2.36
Growth in output per man-hour (y'')	2.04	2.95	1.44	1.37	2.37
Due to more capital per worker	1.20	1.49	0.91	0.64	1.13
Due to higher labour quality	0.32	0.45	0.20	0.37	0.25
Due to growth of TFP	0.63	1.01	0.33	0.36	0.99

14.7   Some Empirical Findings on the Contributions to Growth

In Canada, total productivity growth was about 2% annually[29] over 1962–1973, after which it declined to about 0.45% over 1974–1992, but picked up sufficiently in the 1990s to become about 0.8% over 1974–1999. That is, there was a marked slowdown in technological growth after 1973. Similar patterns were observed for most western nations and Japan. Table 14.1 provides the findings of one study on US growth rates.

There are several points worth noting about the information in Table 14.1. The growth rates both of output and of output per hour worked decreased from 1959 to 1995 and then increased very significantly. This was also the case for the growth rates of capital per worker and of total factor product (TFP). This upsurge is a reflection of the benefits from the very extensive revolution in information technology (IT), based on the innovations of computers and the Internet, which started much earlier than 1995 but needed to reach sufficient maturity for their economic benefits to become apparent at the macroeconomic level.

The growth of TFP was a very significant reason for the growth of output per worker in every period. To illustrate, during 1995–1998, TFP growth (0.99) accounted for about 42% of the growth in output per worker (2.37). The growth of capital per worker (also called capital deepening) at 1.13 accounted for an even larger percentage (about 48%). Hence, the major source of increases in the standard of living came from more hours worked per worker, more capital per worker and higher TFP.

14.8   The Solow Growth Model with Exogenous Changes in the Quality of Labor

In view of the above results on the importance of technical change, we need to introduce technical change into the Solow growth model. While we can introduce neutral technical change of the type specified above into the

---

[29]This rate of productivity growth is quite large. It was partly due to a substantial expansion of the university system and the consequent increase in human capital per worker.

[30]Jorgensen, D. W. and Stiroh, K. J. Raising the speed limit: economic growth in the information age. *Brookings Papers on Economic Activity*, 2000 (1), 125–211; Stiroh, K. J. What drives productivity growth? *Federal Reserve Bank of New York Policy Review*, March 2001, 37–59.

growth model, the analysis is easier if technical change was assumed to be such that it increases the efficiency of each worker (i.e., the quality of labor) over time at a constant rate. To incorporate worker efficiency into the production function, write it as:

$$Y = F(K, E), \tag{19}^{31}$$

where E is the labor force measured in efficiency units.[32] Set $k^E = K/E$, and assuming constant returns to scale to proportionate increases in K and E, we can write:

$$Y/E = F(K/E, 1) = f(k^E). \tag{20}$$

Applying the Solow procedures presented above for this form of the production function modifies the equation for the change in the amount of capital per efficiency worker, i.e., in k^E, to:

$$k^{E'} = \sigma Y/E - E'' \cdot k^E. \tag{21}$$

In the steady state, $k^{E'} = 0$, so that the fundamental SS equation with technical change is:

$$\sigma Y/E = E'' \cdot k^E. \tag{22}$$

We now assume that the change in the efficiency of labor is caused by 'technical change'[33] T, so that we can specify E as:

$$E = B(T) \cdot L, \tag{23}$$

where B is a function of technology T. Therefore:

$$E'' = L'' + B'', \tag{24}$$

where B'' is the rate of growth of the average level of efficiency per worker, while L'' is the labor force growth in terms of the number of workers.[34] Assuming that B'' is a constant equal to η (which is a Greek letter pronounced 'eta'), we get:

$$E'' = n + \eta. \tag{25}$$

Substituting this into the above fundamental SS growth equation with technical change, we have:

$$\sigma \frac{Y}{E} = (n + \eta)k^E. \tag{26}$$

where η is the growth in labor efficiency. Equation (26) is Solow's fundamental SS growth equation when technical change increases the efficiency of labor.[35] This labor efficiency can be increased by increases in the average level of skills (e.g., by better or more education on average, more experience, etc.). The present model assumes that this increase is exogenous.

---

[31] This form of the production can also be written as $Y = F(K, E(L, T))$.

[32] For example, suppose we have two workers, one of whom produces 20 units per hour and the other produces 40 units per hour. Using the less productive worker as the base worker, the two workers in terms of efficiency together represent three (base level) efficiency workers. In this example, $L = 2$ and $E = 3$. Therefore, E would increase if L increases and/or its average efficiency level rises.

[33] Such 'technical change' could take the form of higher levels of education or more skills on average for the workers.

[34] That is, labor measured in constant efficiency units grows for two reasons: the growth of the number of 'raw' (i.e., at 'base level' productivity when $T = 1$) workers and the growth of efficiency per worker. The total growth rate of labor in constant efficiency units is $n + \eta$.

[35] Such technical change is of a different type from the neutral one used in the growth-accounting equation. This form of technical change is said to be *labor-augmenting technical change* — as against being capital-augmenting or being neutral between the capital and labor inputs — since it acts in the same way as an increase in the quantity of base-level workers.

The SS of the current model occurs when $k^{E'} = 0$ — i.e., when there is no change in k^E, which is the capital per efficiency worker. Since this amount is constant in the SS, the SS output per efficiency worker is also constant, so that there is no change in y^E and its growth rate is zero. That is, in the SS:

$$y^{E''} = 0.$$

Note that $y^E = Y/E$, so that $y^{E''} = Y'' - E'' = Y'' - (n + \eta)$. This equals zero in SS. That is, in the SS:

$$y^{E''} = Y'' - E'' = Y'' - (n + \eta) = 0.$$

Hence, in the SS:

$$Y'' = E'' = n + \eta. \tag{27}$$

Hence, SS output grows at the rate $(n + \eta)$. The growth rate of output per (base-level productivity) worker/capita, which specifies the standard of living, is given by:

$$y'' = Y'' - L'' = \eta. \tag{28}$$

Similar reasoning shows that $k'' = \eta$. Hence:

- Output per worker and capital per worker will continue to increase even in the SS at the growth rate of efficiency per worker.
- Countries that innovate and increase labor efficiency at a faster rate would have a higher rate of growth of output and output per worker.
- Birth rates per couple in Western countries have fallen in recent decades to less than 2, which is required for a constant population (i.e., $L'' = 0$). In some countries, it has become as low as 1.5. Barring an adequate immigration level, this would eventually lead to continuous declines in the labor force, so that L'' would become negative. However, what is required for the determination of the SS is the sum of L'' and the growth rate η of labor efficiency. Hence, for the SS, it is not necessary for L'' to be positive, as long as $(L'' + \eta)$ is positive.

14.8.1 Diagrammatic analysis

To incorporate changes in labor efficiency through labor-augmenting technical change into the diagrammatic analysis, Figure 14.1 is modified to Figure 14.4. The horizontal axis now measures k^E. The output growth rate equals $(n + \eta)$. Figure 14.4 assumes that n and η are both constant so that their sum is also a constant. Assume that this sum initially equals $(n_0 + \eta_0)$, so that $(n_0 + \eta_0)k^E$ specifies the capital requirements of new efficiency-workers (at the existing capital–labor ratio) and is represented by a straight line from the origin. The SS K/E ratio is k_0^{E*}. At this K/E ratio, Y/E becomes static but Y/L continues to increase at the rate η_0.

An increase in the technical change rate η from η_0 to η_1 raises the growth rate of labor in efficiency units to $(n_0 + \eta_1)$, which lowers the SS K/E ratio to k_1^{E*}.[36] Though this ratio falls, as does the Y/E ratio, there occurs an increase in the SS Y/L ratio, so that the workers' SS standards of living improve — and continue to improve over time.

Our conclusions on the effects of the increase in η (the efficiency level of workers) are that:

- It reduces the SS K/E ratio, so that less capital is used per unit of efficiency–labor. But the SS K/L ratio could rise (so that more capital is used per worker) or fall (so that less capital is used per worker). This would depend on the increase in the efficiency of labor and the fall in the K/E ratio.

---

[36]In this SS with technical change over time, each unit of output is produced by a smaller amount of raw labor, as well as a smaller amount of capital.

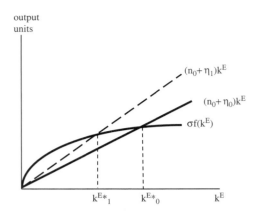

Figure 14.4

- Since the SS K/E ratio falls, so does the Y/E ratio. That is, output per unit of efficiency worker falls. However, our concern is with the growth rate of the Y/L ratio, which is the index for the standard of living. The SS standard of living increases over time at the efficiency growth rate η.

14.8.2 The role of human capital in changing the quality of labor

Labor-augmenting technical change in the above analysis can be viewed as a result of the increase in human capital, which represents the acquisition and use of skills relevant to production. The stock of human capital in the economy can increase in a variety of ways. Among these are:

- The allocation of labor and capital to impart the existing stock of knowledge in educational institutions. This is labeled as 'schooling'.
- The allocation of labor and capital to impart the existing stock of knowledge in firms through on-the-job training.
- Changes in the stock of knowledge.

The following distinctive aspects of this classification are worth noting.

- The mere duplication of human capital through schooling and on-the-job-training — as in the first two points of the above list — of new entrants to the labor force leaves the level of knowledge per capita (and E/L) unchanged.[37] Therefore, it does not change the average efficiency level of the workers so that the value of η does not change.
- An increase in human capital through more years of schooling on average for the population or a better quality of education increases the average efficiency of workers, which increases the value of η. This shifts the $(n + \eta)k^E$ curve upwards.
- New techniques of production — from innovations and inventions — constitute new knowledge, which raises the productivity of capital per efficiency worker and shifts the production function upwards. Therefore, they shift up the $\sigma f(k^E)$ curve.

The first two aspects of human capital have already been discussed in this chapter. The nature of the third element and how it comes about is presented in the next chapter.

---

[37] Using the analogy with physical capital, this process corresponds to equipping the workers with capital at the existing K/L ratio.

Extended Analysis Box 14.3: The Variability of the Labor Force Growth Rate

The historical experience of growth suggests that the labor growth rate is not a constant. It increases as standards of living rise from low levels, since this allows better food, greater access to medicine, better hygiene, etc. These reduce mortality rates, especially among infants, so that the population growth rate rises. At higher living standards, such effects on mortality become relatively insignificant, while control by families — given the availability and affordability of birth-control devices — on the number of children decreases the birth rate per woman. Consequently, the population growth rate increases at low values of y, but decreases at higher values. This has been the experience of many countries, including Canada, the USA, and Europe over several centuries. In these countries, during the early stages of industrialization in the 19th century, population growth rates rose dramatically as a result of the rise in their standards of living. They fell in the 20th century, especially after 1960 following the invention of the birth control pill, the increasing participation of women in the labor force and the cumulative rise in the standard of living. Other factors adduced for this decline are the feminist movement and the increasing costs of raising children, which includes the costs of providing them with an appropriate — as well as longer years of — education, the loss of income while the mother is out of the labor force, etc.

Some economists have interpreted the above historical evidence to suggest that the population growth rate is a function of the standard of living, i.e., of output per capita. Since the latter depends on capital per worker, this argument implies that:

$$L'' = L''(k).$$

The suggested form of this function implies that, over very long periods, L'' would be first positive and rising, then falling and becoming negative, so that population will first increase (at low capital–labor ratios), but eventually decline (at higher capital–labor ratios). It may or may not eventually stabilize. If it does so, its growth rate will eventually become zero.

In Canada, the fertility rate (number of children per woman) was about 3.7 in 1926, fell to about 2.7 in the 1930s — the period of the Great Depression, with exceptionally high unemployment — and then climbed to about 4.7 in the late 1950s. It started declining rapidly in the 1960s and continued declining until 1988 when it reached 1.4 children per woman. It recovered marginally in the 1990s to about 1.5 in 1997. The fertility rate for the USA is still above two, though marginally so. It is well below two for many west European countries, Japan, and Canada.

Family sizes in many of the richer countries of the world are now quite small, with an average of less than two children per couple. With births less than deaths on an annual basis, their population would decline unless there is adequate immigration. The Solow model without technical change poses problems for the analysis of a negative growth rate of the labor force.[38] Its exposition is more appropriate in the Solow model with technical change.

14.8.3 Technical change with falling or negative labor force growth rates

In the richer countries, the growth rate of the labor force has not been constant but has declined in recent decades. Many economists believe that as standards of living (output per worker) increase, L'' becomes smaller.

---

[38]This can be seen by its diagrammatic exposition for $n < 0$ and $\sigma > 0$, since the only intersection between the nk and the $\sigma f(k)$ curves would then be at zero. This SS will be unstable and there will be continuous growth of capita and output per worker.

Since output per worker is positively related to the increase in capital per worker, the hypothesis being advanced is that the labor force growth rate L'' is negatively related to k (i.e., capital per worker, not its growth rate). L'' may even become negative in some cases. Assume that it stabilizes at some value n_0, which could be negative.[39] Further, assume that the labor–efficiency growth rate η_0 is exogenous and constant. Under these assumptions, $(L'' + \eta_0)$ declines as k increases, eventually becoming constant at $(n_0 + \eta_0)$. Making the assumption that growth in labor efficiency more than offsets the decline in population, $(n_0 + \eta_0) > 0$. Under these assumptions, the Solow model implies that the economy's SS growth rates of capital and output would be $(n_0 + \eta_0)$. The SS standard of living will rise at the rate η_0, though population will be falling at a constant rate.

14.8.4 Shifts in participation rates

The participation rate is defined as the rate of participation of the population in the labor force. That is:

$$\text{Participation rate} = \frac{\text{labor force}}{\text{population}} = \frac{\text{male labor force} + \text{female labor force}}{\text{population}}$$

The labor force consists of workers who want a job for pay. The labor force participation rate of women — i.e., the ratio of women in the labor force to all women in the country — has increased very substantially since the 1960s. Some of the effects of this increase in the female participation rate have been offset by a decrease in the participation rate of males. Fact Sheet 14.3, also presented as Fact Sheet 10.1 in Chapter 10, presents the shifts in the female, male, and total participation rates for the USA since 1960.

Fact Sheet 14.3: Participation Rates in Canada and the USA, Male and Female, 1980–2008

The following table classifies participation rates in Canada and the USA as the fraction of the total working age population (over 15 years old) currently in the workforce.

	1960	1970	1980	1990	2000	2008
United States						
Male (%)	83.3	79.7	77.4	76.1	74.7	73
Female (%)	37.7	43.3	51.6	57.5	60.2	59.5
Total (%)	59.4	60.4	63.8	66.4	67.2	66
Canada						
Male (%)	82.8	77.8	78.3	76.1	72.4	72.9
Female (%)	30.1	38.3	50.6	58.5	58.9	62.8
Total (%)	56.2	57.8	64.3	67.1	65.8	67.8

Source: For 1960–1970 data, Sorrentino, C. International comparisons of labour force participation, 1960–81. *Monthly Labor Review*, February 1983, 23–36. For 1980–2008 Canada data, CANSIM V2062816. For 1980–2008 US data, US Bureau of Labour Statistics.

---

[39] Note that a negative value implies that population will fall.

Box 14.2: The Implications of Increases in the Labor Force Participation of Women

What would be the effects of the increasing labour force participation of women in the context of the Solow model?

To answer this question, we need to distinguish between the labor force and population, and between the output per worker (y) and the standard of living. The relevant proxy for the latter is output per person (i.e., per unit of the population, not per unit of the labor force). Assume that there is no technical change and that, in the initial state, the participation rate for the population was constant (so that $L = \beta \cdot$ population, where β is the population's labor-force participation rate) and that the growth rate of the population — and, therefore, of the labor force — was initially n_0. Let the increase in the participation rate occur in one step, so that the labor force growth rate jumps to $(n_0 + \alpha)$. After this step increase, the participation rate stabilizes at its new long-run level and the labor force growth returns to n_0. Further, assume that the skill levels of the new entrants are identical with those of the initial workers.

The Solow growth diagram implies that the increase in the participation rate will reduce the K/L ratio. If the economy was initially in the SS at k_0^*, it will move below this SS level, say to k_1, $k_1 < k_0^*$ (not shown diagrammatically, though the earlier Figure 14.1 can be used as a guide for the arguments here). Note that at k_1, as compared with that at k_0^*, output per worker (y) and the real wage rate (w) are lower, but the growth rate of y is higher. Since k_0^* is a stable SS, the economy will eventually return to k_0^*, at which time the economy will revert to its SS levels of y and w.

Since the participation rate has risen, the number of jobs (and pay-checks) per representative family would rise correspondingly. During the adjustment phase, family incomes would reflect two opposing changes: decrease in wages due to the lower k ratio and increase in the number of jobs per family. The net effect is likely to be an increase in family income. Since the rise in the number of jobs per family has its converse in the time left for non-job activities, i.e., for 'leisure and rest', the increase in family incomes comes at the cost of the decrease in its leisure and rest time.

Now add the assumption that the new entrants to the labor force have lower skills — due to lower educational levels and years of experience — than do the initial labor market participants.[40] This implies that their marginal productivity and wages will be lower than of the initial participants. Hence, the increase in the family income will be correspondingly less. As the new entrants accumulate experience and skills, their marginal product and wages would rise.

Hence, there are several stages in the likely effects.

1. The first stage incorporates the initial impact of an increased participation rate for the population and a lowering of the average skill level. These reduce the average real wage for two reasons: capital per worker falls and the average skill level falls. [However, note that it is likely that the income of the representative family (which now has a higher participation rate) rises. The increase in hours spent by the family in market jobs also reduces the average hours spent in home activities and time spent in the home on child rearing.]

2. The second stage occurs after this initial impact. In this stage, the economy starts recovering and moves toward its SS position. During this movement, both capital per worker and skills accumulate, which produces increases in real wages from the lower level of the first stage. A positive growth rate of output per worker occurs at the lower (pre-SS) level of the capital–labor ratio.

---

[40] The average wage of women in the last four decades of the 20th century was about 70% of male wages, so that their marginal product was assumed to be correspondingly lower. This was taken to reflect their lower skill levels.

Box 14.2: (*Continued*)

> 3. In the third stage, the economy has returned to the initial SS values of k, y, and wages, all of which have again become constant. Family incomes will have risen to their new SS level in proportion to the increase in the participation rate.
> 4. Note that the above findings were derived under the *ceteris paribus* assumptions that there was no technical change and no population growth. On the latter, we have already discussed the increase in the labor force participation rate of women in the last three decades of the 20th century. Associated with this trend was a decrease in the number of children per woman, which resulted in a decrease in the labor force growth rate some 20 years later.

14.9 SS Growth versus Level Effects of Exogenous Shifts

Comparing the impact of shifts in the various exogenous variables and parameters, the Solow growth model makes a distinction between those shifts that alter the SS growth rate (of output per capita) and those that only change its SS level. Exogenous shifts in the production function, the stock of schooling, the saving propensity, and population growth induce changes in the SS level, but not the SS growth rate of output per capita, while technical change also alters its SS growth rate.

Therefore, economies that want to grow faster in the SS must find ways of increasing the rate of technical change. However, this rate is exogenous to the Solow growth model and is not affected by the accumulation of capital, labor and other aspects of the model itself.[41] In recent decades, economists have become convinced that the rate of technical change is not invariant with respect to these variables. Allowing for such effects makes the rate of technical change endogenous to the model. The next chapter will examine some of the sources of endogenous growth and the possibility of increasing growth rates by policy measures.

14.10 The Implications of the Solow Analyses for Policy

The above exposition of the Solow model has the following implications for policy.

- In terms of the standard of living, countries are better off with a higher saving rate and a lower population growth rate. Therefore, policymakers desirous of a higher standard of living for the population should aim at a higher saving rate and a lower growth rate of the labor force.
- In the pre-SS stage, an increase in the saving rate will increase the growth rate of output per capita. This offers another justification for governmental policies that can raise the saving rate. Similarly, a decrease in the population growth rate will increase the growth rate of output per capita. However, a declining population is also an ageing population, with an increase in health costs and a decline in the working-age population. The adverse consequences of these are considered to be quite serious for economists not to generally advocate the use of governmental policies to reduce the country's population below its existing level.[42]

---

[41] Further, while it represents the minimum to which the economy's growth rate converges under a stable SS, actual economies often experience increasing rates of growth during some stages. The standard classical growth model does not cover this possibility.

[42] In conditions where the country's existing population has a negative growth rate, many economists tend to favor immigration to prevent the population from declining.

- However, variations in the saving rate and the labor force growth rate do not alter the SS growth rates of output per worker or capital per worker, which are both zero.[43] Therefore, if we were to focus only on the SS output per capita, governmental policies to change the saving rate or the population growth rate would not have a significant impact.
- In the SS, the growth in living standards occurs only due to technical change. Therefore, governments should try to promote R&D (research and development) expenditures in firms and universities, etc., and also promote entrepreneurship and investments to incorporate new technologies in the physical capital and the labor force.

Fact Sheet 14.4: Real GDP Per Capita, 2003 Population Growth Rates

This Fact Sheet provides a scatter graph of the relationship between real GDP per capita and population growth. The graph for the year 2003 shows a strong negative relationship between GDP per capita and population growth: countries with high GDP per capita tend to have lower population growth rates. This relationship is negative because, in the modern period, high-income families tend to have fewer children per couple than low-income families. However, Box 14.3 points out that earlier periods in history (especially the Malthusian stage and even the post-Malthusian (early industrial) one had a positive relationship between the standard of living and population growth because higher living standards increased the survival rates without a corresponding decrease in birth rates. Many developing countries still follow this pattern, especially in their poorer rural areas, which have a higher number of children per family than the middle class in the cities.

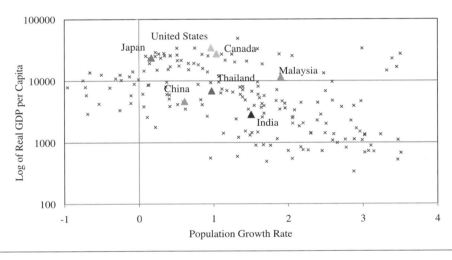

Box 14.3: Historical Growth Patterns, Labor force Growth, and Technology Shifts

To analyze the historical growth pattern of societies, we need to incorporate both technical change and changes in population/labor force growth rates into the Solow model. Doing so allows us to

---

[43]The former also does not alter the SS growth rate of output while a decrease in the population growth rate decreases the SS output growth rate.

Box 14.3: (*Continued*)

use growth theory to divide the historical economic experience of societies into the following stages/epochs:[44]

I. The Malthusian stage/'trap'

In this stage, technology does not change significantly and the long-run standard of living is virtually constant at or close to a (physical) subsistence level. Further, if increases in the standard of living do occur, population increases sufficiently in response to the higher living standards such as to cancel any improvement in them beyond the subsistence level.

II. The early industrial (post-Malthusian) stage

In this stage, technical change occurs and is greater than the population growth rate, so that output per capita rises. While population growth rate increases significantly through declines in the mortality rates, which occur in response to the improvements in the standard of living, output per worker, and living standards rise on a long-run basis.

III. The modern growth stage

In this stage, industrialization deepens and technology continues to improve, so that the standards of living continue to rise. A critical part of the technical change in this stage is the invention and widespread use of birth control technology. This reduces the number of births per family, even though mortality rates fall and longevity increases because of higher incomes and improvements in medical technology, sufficiently for the population growth rate to fall. It may eventually even become negative, in which case the average number of children per couple will become less than two, so that the country's population (ignoring immigration) will fall. The modern growth stage existed in most of the richer countries at the end of the 20th century. It has a falling, rather than constant, population growth rate and rising standards of living.

In the above classification of growth stages, the critical difference between the Malthusian stage and the post-Malthusian one is the acceleration in technical change while that between the post-Malthusian stage and the modern growth one is the demographic one: in these stages, population is endogenous and depends on the standard of living. Starting close to the physical subsistence level at the end of the Malthusian stage, population first expands in response to improvements in the standard of living. At high living standards and availability of birth control devices, it declines in response to further improvements in the standard of living.

IV. Globalization and the modern growth stage

Globalization (see Chapter 12) not only increases trade and capital flows but also accelerates the spread of technology, including the birth control one. The less-developed economies benefit from all of these, so that their time frame for moving through the various stages above is compressed from centuries to decades. Therefore, in recent decades, the developing economies tend to go from the historical Malthusian stage to the modern growth stage in a matter of decades rather than centuries.

---

[44]Our classification and its discussion are partly based on Galor, O. and Weil, D. N. Population, technology, and growth: From Malthusian stagnation to the demographic transition and beyond. *American Economic Review*, **90**, September 2000, 806–828.

Box 14.4: (*Continued*)

V. The post-modern growth stage

This stage is still somewhat speculative. It is based on the premise that while the average number of children per couple in the country will have fallen during the modern growth stage to less than two, (which is necessary to maintain population at a constant level, i.e., zero growth rate), this number will eventually stabilize by the end of the modern growth stage, so that the growth rate of population (ignoring immigration) will become constant, though with a negative value. This premise separates the post-modern growth stage from the modern growth stage (which had a falling, rather than constant, population growth rate). We will also assume that the rate of technical change will continue to be significant and have a positive value. For simplification so as to be able to use the Solow model, we will assume that the sum of the rate of technical change and of population growth rate will be positive. Hence, we deduce from the Solow model that, in the post-modern growth stage, SS output will growth at a rate equal to the sum of the rate of technical change and of population growth rate, while the standards of living will rise at the rate of technical change. Note that in this stage, the population will keep declining.

14.10.1 Malthus's theory of economic growth and the Malthusian stage

This theory was presented by Thomas R. Malthus in 1798. Its main assumptions were:

- The factors of production are labor and land. Of these, land is fixed in supply, so that the marginal productivity of labor, the only variable input in this theory, diminishes. Further, any expansion of the population reduces the land/population ratio.
- There is no effective birth control technology. Population is positively related to living standards and grows faster than productivity per worker in the economy. This occurs through rising live birth rates[45] and/or falling mortality rates due to improvements in living standards.
- Technology does not change. Innovations and inventions, when they do occur, are sporadic and with limited impact on the macroeconomy.

Malthus's theory was quite appropriate for the pre-industrial societies dominated by agriculture. In these societies, the capital/labor ratio was quite low and did not change much over long periods, so that the explicit treatment of capital was not necessary. The emphasis on land was justified since agriculture was the dominant economic activity. Standards of living were close to the physical subsistence levels (in terms of calories per day) for most of the population. Population increased rapidly in response to any improvements in the standard of living, through some increase in live birth rates, but more significantly through a fall in the mortality rates, especially among the very young.[46] In the absence of improvements in technology, population growth and the diminishing marginal productivity of labor caused the living standards to fall, which induced malnutrition, starvation, famines, and disease, as well as wars, so that births fell and deaths rose. The SS of this model was at the physical subsistence level.

---

[45]This occurs because improvements in living standards provide better nutrition to mothers and infants, thereby reducing their mortality. Conversely, a fall in living standards raises mortality rates, especially for the very young.

[46]This often happened after a major epidemic such as the Black Death in 13th century Europe, which reduced the population by about a third and led to a substantial increase in the living standards of the remaining population. The settlement of new lands (mainly Americas, Australia, and New Zealand) from the 17th to the 20th century by European settlers also raised living standards and led to a rise in labor force growth rates in West European countries until the twentieth century.

Malthus concluded for the pre-industrial societies that the long-run standard of living fluctuated around the subsistence level, with population growth rates adjusting to drive the economies to this SS.

14.10.2 The post-Malthusian stage

This stage differs from the Malthusian one because of the addition of the following assumptions:

- Technology improves very significantly over time and makes output per capita grow faster than the population, so that the standards of living rise.
- Population growth remains positively related to the improvement in the standard of living but is less than the technology-induced growth rate of output.
- A massive shift to industrial production occurs, which reduces the relative significance of agriculture and land while enhancing the importance of physical capital for the future growth of the economy.

The increase in the population growth rate occurs through a falling mortality rate as nutrition and private hygiene (for instance, by regular bathing and the use of soap) improve and public health measures (such as putting in flushing toilets, sewers, vaccinations, etc.) are undertaken. The number of births (especially live-births) per woman may also increase. The population growth rate offsets some of the increase in output per worker that would have occurred due to technical change but not fully, so that living standards rise. This is the SS of the Solow model modified to incorporate technical change and population growth positively related to standards of living.

14.10.3 The modern growth stage

This stage opens with living standards that are already substantially above the subsistence level. The analysis of this stage can also be based on the Solow model, with or without endogenous technical change, but with the addition of the assumption that the population growth rate is now negatively related to the (further) improvements in the standard of living. Mortality has already declined considerably prior to this stage and does not significantly fall further. But birth rates fall due to a decrease in the desired number of children per woman,[47] which can be implemented by an easily available birth control technology. The desired number of children per family falls partly because of the advancing technology, which raises the return to human capital and induces increased investment in the education of (fewer) children — which in turn stimulates the speed of technical change. Technological advances also reduce the labor time required for the home production of goods — such cooking, laundry, etc. — and the time required for ensuring the good health of children and other family members, over those in earlier times. These promote the increasing participation of women in the labor force, whose incomes and rising skill levels substantially increase the opportunity cost of having and raising children.[48] Other causes for the fall in the birth rate include changes in the social and cultural patterns affecting the socially desirable family size, which impacts on personal decisions on the desired number of children per family.

In the modern growth stage, the improvement in the standard of living occurs due to technical change and falling population growth rates — and the increase in the labor force participation rate.

---

[47]This stage requires the ability to control the number of births.
[48]The desire to build a career first tends to raise the mother's average desired age for the birth of the first child into the 30s (often the late 30s) and reduces the number of childbearing years.

For Europe and North America, this broad and rough classification places the centuries prior to the Industrial Revolution[49] in the Malthusian stage, the period from the Industrial Revolution to the 1960s in the post-Malthusian stage and the period after the 1960s in the modern growth stage.

Galor and Weil (2000)[50] summarize the historical evidence on standards of living as:

> For thousands of years, the standard of living was roughly constant and did not differ greatly across countries ... the growth rate of GDP per capita between 500 and 1500 was zero ... the real wage in England roughly the same in 1800 as it had been in 1300 ... real wages in China were lower at the end of the eighteenth century than they had been at the beginning of the first century ... even in the richest countries, the phenomenon of sustained growth in living standards is only a few centuries old. (p. 807)

> The growth rate of total output in Europe was 0 percent per year between 1500 and 1700, and 0.6 percent per year between 1700 and 1820 ... the growth of income per capita was only 0.1 percent per year in the earlier period and 0.2 percent per year in the later one .... Thus the initial effect of faster income growth in Europe was to increase population. (p. 808).

Their conclusion on population growth prior to the Industrial Revolution was:

> The rate of population growth in Europe between the years 500 and 1500 was 0.1 percent per year ... the growth rate of world population from the year 1 to 1750 was at 0.064 percent per year. (p. 807)

Galor and Weil also pointed out that:

> The prediction of the Malthusian model that differences in technology should be reflected in population density but not in standards of living is also borne out ... prior to 1800 differences in standards of living across countries were quite small by today's standards; yet there did exist wide differences in technology. China's sophisticated agricultural technologies, for example, allowed high per acre yields, but failed to raise the standard of living above subsistence. Similarly, in Ireland a new productive technology — the potato — allowed a large increase in population over the century prior to the Great Famine without any improvement in standards of living. (p. 807).

14.11 Conclusions

- The Solow growth model assumes constant returns to scale in labor and capital, diminishing returns to capital per worker, and exogenous technical change, as well as the absence of the government and financial markets in the economy. These assumptions imply that the growth rates of countries tend to the SS rate, in which per capita incomes grow at the rate of technical change.
- According to the Solow model, per capita incomes do not grow endlessly unless there is technical change.
- Assuming identical and static production technology across countries, the Solow model implies that the per capita growth rates of countries will converge to the same (zero) SS rate.
- The Solow model further implies that both the growth rate of the economy and the return to capital decrease as capital intensity increases. That is, the growth rates and the return to capital are higher in countries in which it is scarcer. In this model, while there is some impact of macroeconomic demand policies on growth, this impact is severely limited because the determinants of growth are exogenous. In the limiting case of the SS, there is no impact of policy on the per capita growth rate, which is determined by the exogenous rate of technical change.

---

[49] Britain was the first country to go through the Industrial Revolution in late 18th and early 19th centuries.

[50] Galor, O. and Weil, D. N. Population, technology, and growth: From Malthusian stagnation to the demographic transition and beyond. *American Economic Review*, **90**, September 2000, 806–828.

Some of these implications of the classical model seem to be contrary to the factual evidence. Among these are:

For example, Romer (1986) analysed the per capita growth rates for the USA and showed that these had a positive trend over the period 1800 to 1978, rather than the decline in the growth rate predicted by the traditional classical theory.

For at least some of the middle-income countries in the world in the last couple of decades, the rates of growth have been increasing rather than decreasing over some periods. Among such countries have been Korea, Taiwan, Singapore, Malaysia, Brazil, China and India.

Comparing the capital-intensive developed economies of North America and Europe with the least capital-intensive ones, mainly in Africa, the former economies have higher growth rates than the latter.

For pre-industrial societies, the Malthusian growth model is more appropriate than the Solow one.

KEY CONCEPTS

Constant returns to scale in production
Diminishing returns to capital per worker
Steady state output per capita
Steady state growth rate of output

Pre-steady state growth rate
Convergence and divergence of growth rates among countries
Exogenous technical change
Labor in efficiency units
Growth accounting

Total factor productivity
The Solow model
Malthus' growth model
The post-Malthusian growth stage, and
The modern growth stage.

SUMMARY OF CRITICAL CONCLUSIONS

- The Solow model implies that in the steady state without technical change, output per capita will be constant, so that the standards of living will become constant.
- In the Solow model, an increase in the saving rate does not alter the SS growth rate but will increase the SS output per capita.
- In the Solow model, countries with identical technology, saving rate and labor force growth rate, will converge to the same SS output per capita.
- The Solow model with exogenous technical change produces the SS growth rate of output per capita equal to the rate of technical change in labor productivity.
- Labor force growth rates have been falling in recent decades in most industrialized countries.
- Malthus' analysis of pre-industrial economies implied that the long-run standards of living would remain close to the subsistence level, as they did in many pre-industrial societies over centuries.
- Most economies have historically gone through several distinctive growth stages.

REVIEW AND DISCUSSION QUESTIONS

1. Present the benchmark Solow growth model (including its assumptions) without technical change and show diagrammatically its steady state position. Is this position stable? Explain your answer, using the appropriate diagram.

2. Is the economy always in the steady state? If not, assuming that there is no technical change, what are the differences in the growth rates of (a) output and (b) the standard of living, between the steady state position of the economy and the positions prior to reaching it?

3. It is often claimed that (a) the growth rate of output, (b) the level of the standard of living, and (c) the growth rate of the standard of living, are negatively related to the population growth rate. Using two different labor force growth rates for illustration in your analysis, show if each of the above relationships is implied by the Solow growth model without technical change or not. Give your answers for (i) the steady state and (ii) the pre-steady state.

4. It is often claimed that the economy's growth rate is independent of the saving rate of the economy. To investigate its implications in the Solow growth model without technical change, show the impact of increases and decreases in the saving rate on (i) the SS growth rate and (ii) the pre-SS growth rate.

5. It is sometimes claimed that while a war (on one's own land) destroys a great deal of the economy's capital, it also leads to very significant inventions and innovations that are incorporated into civilian production after the war. Assuming that the economy was in the steady state at the start of the war, present its diagrammatic analysis for the Solow-type economy, comparing the pre- and post-war SS output per capita. What happens in the 'recovery' period during which the capital stock is still below the pre-war SS level?

6. 'Countries (including the LDCs) in which governments pursued plans to increase their saving rates as a means of boosting their growth rates were misguided.' Discuss.

7. What is meant by 'convergence'? How does the Solow model explain convergence?

8. According to the Solow model, what factors determine the SS growth of output per capita? Can the long-run growth rate of output differ from the SS one? Can the short-run growth rate of output differ from the long-run and the SS ones? Explain your answers.

9. How does the growth accounting method calculate the contribution (to the host economy) of immigrants? What does the Solow model imply for the impact of a very significant rate of increase in immigration on the steady state?

10. Present the Malthusian theory of growth. What are its critical assumptions that cause long-run living standards to remain at the subsistence level? Are there countries for which this analysis is still applicable or at least indicative of their growth pattern?

11. Discuss the relationship (or different types of relationships) that seems to have occurred historically between population growth rates and living standards.

ADVANCED AND TECHNICAL QUESTIONS

T1. Assume that labor's and capital's shares of output are respectively 0.7 and 0.3, and that output is growing at 3% annually. There is no technical change. What is the growth rate of total factor productivity if:

(a) Both labor and capital are growing at 2%?
(b) Labor is stationary while capital is growing at 3%?

T2. Suppose that increases in the labor force participation rate occur over a particular decade, after which the participation rate stabilizes. Discuss its effects on the growth rate of output per capita over the decade relative to those before and after it. Specify any assumptions that you consider to be relevant to your analysis.

T3. What explanations have been offered for the falling population growth rates in the modern period? Can it be offset and how? Is there a limit to the fall in the population of (a) individual countries and (b) the world? Discuss.

T4. Assuming that all countries in the world have entered the 'modern growth stage' (as defined in this chapter), present the analysis of the long-run steady state for the world population and its standards of living under the modern growth theory with exogenous labor-saving technical change exogenous technical change.

Basic growth model for this chapter:

$$Y/L = 100(K/L) - 0.5(K/L)^2$$

$$\text{APC} = \text{MPC} = 0.8$$

$$L'' = 0.04.$$

T5. For the basic growth model of this chapter, calculate the marginal product of capital per worker (MPk). Is MPk constant in the steady state of the basic Solow model without technical change? Explain your answer.

T6. Using the basic growth model of this chapter:

(a) What is the SS value of k?

(b) What is the SS value of y?

(c) What are the SS levels of (a) consumption per capita and (b) saving per capita?

(d) If the MPC changes to 0.7, recalculate your answers to the previous questions.

(e) What was the change in the SS growth rates of output and capital for the two values of MPC?

Revised growth model A for this chapter, with labor-saving technical change:

$$y^E = 1000k^E - 2k^{E2}$$

$$\text{APC} = \text{MPC} = 0.8$$

$$L'' = n = 0.02 \quad \text{and} \quad \eta = 0.02,$$

where n is the growth rate of workers and η is the rate of growth of efficiency per worker.

T7. Using the Revised growth model A of this chapter:

(a) What are the SS growth rates of k^E and k?

(b) What are the SS growth rates of y^E and of y?

Revised growth model B for this chapter, with labor-saving technical change:

$$y^E = 2000k^E - 4k^{E2}$$

$$\text{APC} = \text{MPC} = 0.9$$

$$E'' = n + \eta$$

$$n = 0.005, \eta = 0.015.$$

T8. Using the Revised growth model B of this chapter:

(a) What is the SS value of k^E?

(b) What is the SS value of y^E?

(c) What is the growth rate of consumption per capita in the steady state?

Suppose that because of a low birth rate, aging population with rising numbers of retirees and inadequate immigration levels, the labor force growth rate falls to -0.01 while η remains at 0.015. Recalculate your answers to (a) to (c). Use a diagram to illustrate the general nature of your results for this part of the question.

[*General note*: in the presence of technical change, the information provided by models A and B (with technical change) above is inadequate to allow the calculation of the SS levels of variables such as y, k, c, and s, but allows the calculation of their SS growth rates.]

Mathematical Appendix

[OPTIONAL. For students who know differential calculus.]

A Mathematical Example of the Solow Model, Using the Cobb–Douglas Production Function
Assume a production function of the Cobb–Douglas form:

$$Y = AK^{\alpha'}L^{1-\alpha'} \qquad 0 < \alpha' < 1, \tag{29}$$

so that

$$y = Ak^{\alpha'}. \tag{30}$$

The return to capital

The return to capital equals its marginal product, which can be derived as Y_K or as y_k since they are identical. The MPK is given by:

$$y_k = Y_K = \alpha'Ak^{\alpha'-1} = \alpha'y/k \qquad 0 < \alpha' < 1. \tag{31}$$

Since $(\alpha' - 1) < 0$, $y_{kk} = \alpha'(1 - \alpha')Ak^{\alpha'-2} < 0$, so that the return to capital falls as k increases. In perfectly competitive markets, this return specifies the real interest rate in the economy, so that, as argued earlier, this model predicts a decline in the real rate of interest as k increases in the pre-SS stage.

The SS growth rate

The labor force growth rate is still assumed to be n. That is, $L'' = n$. As in the earlier arguments, the average propensity to save is assumed to be constant at σ, so that $K' = \sigma Y$, and:

$$K'' = \sigma Y/K = \sigma y/k.$$

From Equation (15):

$$Y' = Y_K K' + Y_L L',$$

so that:

$$Y'' = Y'/Y = (Y_K K/Y)K'' + (Y_L L/Y)L''$$
$$= \alpha'K'' + (1 - \alpha')L'', \tag{32}$$

which implies that:

$$y'' = \alpha'(K'' - L'')$$
$$= \alpha'\sigma y/k - \alpha'n$$
$$= \alpha'\sigma Ak^{\alpha'-1} - \alpha'n. \tag{33}$$

Hence:

$$\partial y''/\partial k = \alpha'(\alpha' - 1)\sigma Ak^{\alpha'-2}.$$

Since $(\alpha' - 1) < 0$, the growth rate of per capita output declines — and goes to zero[51] — as k increases. To derive the SS growth rate, rewrite Equation (33) as:

$$y'' = (\sigma y - kn)\alpha'k^{-1}. \tag{19}$$

In steady state, $\sigma y = kn$, so that the SS value $y''^* = 0$, where * indicates the SS value.

---

[51]As k approaches its SS value, our earlier analysis implied that the SS growth rate y'' will go to zero, so that in the steady state, output will grow at the same rate as the labor force.

Growth in the pre-SS stage

But, in the pre-SS stage, $\sigma y > kn$, so that $y'' > 0$. Further, with $\alpha' = y_k \cdot (K/Y)$:

$$y'' = y_k(\sigma - n(K/Y)), \tag{34}$$

so that, in the pre-SS stage, y'' depends positively on the saving rate and the marginal productivity of capital, but negatively on the labor force growth rate and the capital–output ratio.[52] Hence, countries with higher saving propensities (or better access to the savings of other countries) and a higher return to capital will have higher pre-SS growth rates of output and output per capita.

The impact on growth of a tax on the return to capital

Now, suppose that, for some reason, the rate of return on capital, Y_K, is reduced by τ_K. Such a reduction could be due to the imposition of tax on dividends and capital gains or due to the inefficiencies resulting from regulations imposed on the capital or financial markets. Let this reduction lower the return on capital from Y_K to $(1 - \tau)Y_K$. From Equation (34), this lowers the pre-SS growth rate of output per capita to:

$$y'' = (1 - \tau_K)Y_K(\sigma - n(K/Y)) \qquad 0 < \tau_K < 1. \tag{35}$$

Therefore, taxing the return to capital is inimical to the growth in the standards of living and in the capital–labor ratio. Further, the slower growth of the latter will increase the time taken to reach the steady state.

Diagrammatic Appendices: Sources of Economic Growth

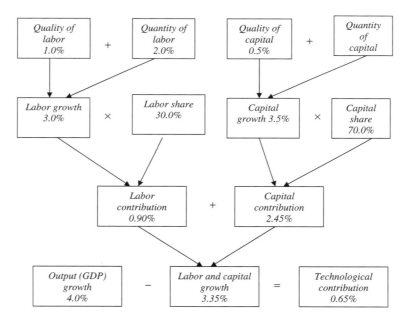

---

[52]However, note that $Y'' = \sigma y_K + (1 - \alpha')n$, so that the growth rate of output will also increase with n.

Calculation of Capital Input

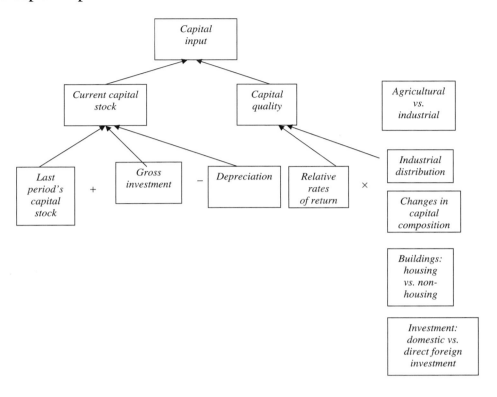

CHAPTER 15
Advanced Topics in Growth Theory

This chapter extends the theory of growth to include endogenous technical change, which is the outcome of decisions made by economic agents to change knowledge on the production technology. This knowledge can then be embodied in human or physical capital. Examples of such endogenous technical change are those resulting from the acquisition of new skills, research and development, investment in new or improved equipment, etc.

The second topic explored in this chapter is the relationship between inflation and growth, and that between the growth of the money supply and the growth of output. A somewhat distinct relationship from these is that between the development of the financial sector and output growth.

The classical growth model presented in the last chapter has several implications that run contrary to empirical evidence, at least for some countries. Among these were:

(i) If we focus only on the steady state, the Solow growth model without technical change implies that the standards of living would be constant. Common experience at least during the last two centuries of the Western economies suggests that the standards of living continue to increase over time, so that either the countries never achieve steady state, or it is continually shifting, or there is an important missing element from the theory.

We have already shown that the Solow model with exogenous technical change does imply rising living standards even in the steady state.

(ii) If we assume that all countries have the same production function, but different saving propensities and labor force growth rates, their SS output growth rate in the absence of technical change would be set by their labor force growth rate, which is exogenously given to the model. Hence, countries with higher population — and therefore higher labor force — growth rate should be observed to have higher output growth. This runs contrary to the general cross-country experience, since the industrialized countries with low population growth rates often have higher growth rates than developing countries with higher population growth rates.

One possible explanation that might be adduced for this contrary observation would be that the countries are not in steady state, but are scattered along the k (capital per worker) axis, with the industrialised countries having higher values of k and being closer to the steady state. However, starting from $k = 0$, as we move to higher values of k, the growth rate of output per capita (y'') should decline as the economy moves toward its steady state. This again does not appear to be consistent with the general growth experience across countries: countries with higher k ratios do not always have lower growth rates of output per worker.

A more satisfactory explanation for the higher growth rates of the richer and more industrialized economies seems to be that their technology and knowledge tend to increase continually while many of the poorer countries stay with a relatively static technology. This possibility is the focus of the first part of this chapter.

(iii) The real interest rate represents the real cost of borrowing funds with which firms buy physical capital. The marginal product of capital (MPK) is the return that they get from this capital. Therefore, profit maximizing firms will borrow and invest until their MPK equals the real interest rate. For the assumed production function, the MPK is diminishing. Since the real interest rate (excluding a risk premium) equals the MPK, the model implies that the economy's MPK and the real interest rate decline as it moves to higher capital/labor ratios and, therefore, higher output per worker. That is, countries with higher capital per worker and output per capita would have lower real rates of interest. Since investors prefer investing in countries with higher returns, capital would flow from the developed to the less developed countries. But, in reality, the poorest economies do not usually have higher real rates of return to capital than more developed economies and capital sometimes flows on a net basis from the former to the latter.

This suggests that we need to modify the theory to somehow eliminate the assumed decrease in the MPK as capital per worker rises, and replace it with either constant or increasing MPK at the economy's level. This is done by some of the endogenous technical change theories presented in this chapter.

15.1 Technology, Knowledge and Externalities

Technical change is a change in the methods of production and manifests itself as shifts in the production function, as well as shifts in the marginal productivities of labor and capital. Technical change is partly exogenous and partly endogenous. Of these, e*ndogenous technical change is that part of technical change that arises from the decisions of economic agents, often in response to economic incentives, to acquire new knowledge and embody it in workers or physical capital or both.* Examples of these decisions are research and development (R&D) expenditures, research in universities, etc. These improvements in technology may not require investment in human and/or physical capital, but usually do so. Endogenous technical change is often of a type that benefits its innovator in terms of higher profits and incomes. In many instances, it also benefits other economic agents — in the case of universities, the adoption by firms of the results of research conducted in the universities, and, in the case of firms, by the shifting of other firms' production functions and marginal productivities. The effects on economic agents other than the innovating one are known as *externalities*. Endogenous technical change may or may not have externalities.

15.1.1 The distinction between endogenous and exogenous technical change

The distinguishing features of endogenous technical change versus the exogenous technical change in the Solow model are:

(i) Endogenous technical change is the result of economic decisions to bring about a change in the technology of production and usually involves some cost. The theories that model these decisions are known as *endogenous growth theories.* By comparison, exogenous technical change does not require decisions by the economic agents and is usually postulated as occurring gratuitously; as such, economic reasoning is not used to explain it or derive its determinants.

(ii) Endogenous growth theories model technical change in such a way that, *at the macroeconomic level*, the *economy's* (also known as the *social) MPK* becomes constant or even incremental, even though the *private* MPK to the firm in question is diminishing. This implies that the economy does not reach a *stable steady state* but can continue to increase its output per worker (y) and capital per worker (k) beyond the steady state.

The modeling of endogenous technical change is still relatively new and imperfectly understood, so that there is no consensus around a single model. There are different ways of modeling endogenous technical change, leading to different versions of growth theory. The main rationale for the macroeconomic study of endogenous growth in recent years has been to use this concept to produce improvements in the standard of living even in the steady state. To achieve this, the endogenous growth theories have emphasized the externalities of the new knowledge. When this new knowledge occurs in a firm, it may arise costlessly from 'learning-by-doing' by workers or be a good produced through costly R&D expenditures. Its externality to other firms occurs because the knowledge thus created is not only utilized in the originating firm, but also becomes available to other firms and increases their productivity. This externality makes the *social return* to the creation of new knowledge greater than the private one.

Knowledge can be introduced into the analysis in two different ways:

(i) As a distinct input, which is itself produced, e.g., by firms through research.
(ii) Embodied in physical capital (such as in new types of machines) and/or human capital (such as in workers with more education and better skills).

15.1.2 The definition of capital in endogenous growth theories

Innovation and new knowledge often enter production through new forms of equipment or the knowledge and skills of the workers, so that physical capital and/or human capital often serve as the vehicles for endogenous technical change. The acquisition of both of these in endogenous growth theory occurs through economic decisions involving (physical and human) investments and both affect the economy's output and its growth rate. Given this similarity between the accumulation of physical and human capital, the endogenous technical change approach usually combines the two and defines the term *'capital' in the production function to consist not only of physical capital, but also to include human capital.* For this combined capital, the definitions of investment and saving are suitably modified to encompass those occurring in both physical and human capital. Among the latter are the amounts spent on formal education or otherwise on the acquisition of skills. Also note that the investment by governments, as in roads and other infrastructure, is part of this capital.

15.1.3 The externalities of new knowledge

The *generation* of new knowledge can be separated from its *dissemination* — i.e. *'spillover'* — to other firms. The former usually occurs within firms, universities, and research institutions. The latter is the process of its copying and adoption by other firms or by workers in other firms, and is an externality from the perspective of the firms and other units originating the new knowledge. The creation of new knowledge can therefore possess an externality. These externalities often occur because of the ability of firms to observe the types and quality of products, the methods of organisation and the technology employed by other firms and, if these are superior ones, to be able to replicate or adapt them to their own production.

Externalities in the economy can also arise in other ways, such as from the expansion of the industry and the economy. For example, as the output of some firms in an industry expands, the facilities for the transport of its raw materials, the training of workers appropriate to the industry and for the marketing of output, etc., tend to improve and lower the relevant costs for all firms in the industry.

Externalities of knowledge represent a *public good*,[1] which is available to all firms, even to those that do not contribute to its creation. Access to it does, however, usually require some action and investment in new physical capital by the firm. For example, new investment may be required to buy the machines embodying the economy's new knowledge of production techniques, so that new investment acts as the gateway to the firm's use of the increased knowledge. In some cases, the new machines may not require an increase in the firm's capital stock but rather require replacement, which could be covered through depreciation of the old machines.

New knowledge can have not only positive externalities but also negative ones for the economy. The incorporation of endogenous technical change into growth theory, in general, assumes that the net benefit from such change is positive; that is, there is an increase in output for given levels of labor and capital in the economy. We will continue with this assumption, but will later include some mention of the negative externalities.

Box 15.1: Inventions, Innovations, and Patents

Innovations versus inventions as forms of technical change
Looking from the perspective of economic history, we can take technical change to be characterized by

(a) *'Macro inventions'*. Inventions of this nature not only affect the particular industry in which they occur or first occur but sooner or later affect a wide range of industries in the economy — so that their affects are macroeconomic rather than being confined to a single industry. They are often technological breakthroughs. Illustrative of these are the inventions of the steam engine, blast furnace, cotton ginning, etc. during the Industrial Revolution in Great Britain during the 17th and 18th centuries, and the invention of the transistor, of the computer chip in the third quarter of the twentieth century, and of the Internet in the last quarter of the 20th century. Such breakthroughs are essentially unpredictable and occur unevenly over time. Since their nature and time of occurrence cannot be anticipated in advance, inventions are treated as being exogenous.

(b) *'Innovations'*. They consist of refinements of the existing technology and are largely confined in their effects to a single industry.[2] Therefore, innovations represent a cumulative process that builds on previous discoveries and previous innovations. This process can occur over very long periods following the macroinventions or other basic inventions. Among the hindrances particular to a country to the pace and extent of such innovations are the smallness of markets, the weakness of scientific education, the lack of economic incentives,[3] as well as the unwillingness of labor to adapt its ideas and skills, work habits, etc.

Since macroinventions are rarely continuous, their impact on the economy will eventually peter out so that they cannot be made the main vehicle in a theory of *continuing* technical change even in the steady state. Therefore, the main emphasis of endogenous growth theories for growth is usually placed

---

[1]A public good is a good in which other economic agents can share with others, without necessarily having to pay its full cost of production. Examples of public goods include defence of the country, and a monetary system. A pure public good is one in whose benefits each agent can share equally, even without paying any of its cost.

[2]Note that sometimes the innovations are themselves major improvements in technology and are therefore difficult to distinguish from inventions.

[3]Among such incentives are the protection of rights to the innovation through patents and copyright protection.

on innovations.[4] With the emphasis on innovations rather than inventions as the engine of *continuous* technical change, the ability of a nation to generate or improve on imported ideas, its propagation mechanisms for knowledge spillovers among its industries, and the learning capabilities of its workers become the main elements of its endogenous growth. Since government policies can affect these, the endogenous technical change theories imply that the long-run growth rate of the economy can be changed by such policies.

Further, it is not the occurrence of inventions that changes production and causes growth; rather, it is their adaptation and incorporation in production processes that does so. This process is essentially one of innovation and takes time, sometimes many years and even decades. Therefore, we should not expect an important invention and its early limited knowledge and implementation to have a significant impact on productivity at the macroeconomic level for quite some time. A potent example of this is the invention of the microchip and the Internet. While they were invented and in use long before 1990, their impact on productivity was not felt until after the mid-1990s: as Table 14.1 showed for US data, the slowdown in productivity growth continued through the 1980s and early 1990s, before picking up dramatically after 1995 (see also Table 15.1).

15.1.4 Patents and the protection of copyright, intellectual property and trade secrets

Intellectual property protection grants legal rights to the originator for written as well as oral inventions and innovations. Among such rights, *patents* grant legal rights to the innovator for the use of a new physical product or process. *Copyright* grants legal rights to the author for a new written or oral work, such as a book, or a song or software code.

Most countries have patent laws that confer on the inventor/innovator the exclusive ownership of the item or process that has been patented. To be granted a patent, the item or process must be original — and therefore, not known prior to the application for the patent — so that it represents new knowledge in the context of our earlier discussion. Copyright is the corresponding term for oral and written works, such as books. Both are encompassed in the concept of intellectual property rights. Owners of intellectual property rights get the exclusive right to market the goods and services arising from their creation of new knowledge for a limited period and within a specific jurisdiction.

The patented or copyright item or process can only be used with the owner's permission, which is usually not given without some financial compensation such as a fixed payment or through royalties, etc. Therefore, patents and copyright represent a way in which their owner can capture some or all of the positive externalities associated with new knowledge, so that the divergence between the private and social returns to new knowledge is reduced. Within a closed economy, *ceteris paribus*, patenting involves a redistribution of income to the owner of the patent from others who use it. Growth theory is not concerned with the redistribution of incomes but only with whether production increases or does not increase because of patenting.

Patents and copyright increase the returns and incentives to inventions and innovations, and therefore, provide incentives to the creation of new knowledge. But, during the life of the patent, they can also hinder or

---

[4]However, given the limitations on these and their long-run dependence on sporadic macroinventions, it cannot be taken for granted that they will always cause continual SS growth in any given economy or in all economies.

slow the dissemination of the patented knowledge, as well as hinder or reduce further innovation emanating from the patented knowledge.

At the international level, patenting confers a net economic advantage on the country in which the patent owners reside (since they get the profits from it) and in which the patent is put into production. But what of other countries, which get neither the profits from a patent nor have local production based on it? Their consumers can benefit from the imports of products based on the foreign patent. However, their production of the products displaced by the foreign patent will cease. Given the very limited immigration permitted by/among countries, workers thus displaced in a given country by foreign patents may be unable to flow to the jobs created in the foreign industries expanding on the basis of the patent. There could then be a net increase in unemployment and decrease in the standard of living in the former set of countries. The externalities of new knowledge controlled by patents can therefore have different effects from those when they are not thus controlled, and need not necessarily make countries better off when the patents and production are confined to other countries.

Patents create monopoly power for a specified duration. The period for which the patent is granted is relevant for endogenous growth. Lengthening the period increases the returns and incentives for the owner of the patent, but it also restricts usage of the patented product or process by others within the country and in other countries. Further, stronger patents discourage sequential research and follow-on inventions, especially by others. These constitute opposing effects of patents on the creation and use of new knowledge and imply that while some patent length is likely to be desirable, extremely long patent protection can stifle the growth of knowledge and reduce the long-term growth of the economy.

At the international level, longer patent protection periods work to the advantage of nations — such as the United States and the European Union — that generate more patents and to the disadvantage of nations that generate less.

Recent changes in patent protection

The United States in recent decades has strengthened patent protection. This has been done by extending patent protection to areas not previously covered — such as genetically engineered bacteria, plants and software — and by lengthening the life of the patents. Further, it has pushed for their stricter and more vigorous enforcement in other countries by using its influence in world bodies such as the World Trade Organisation (WTO). For example, countries such as China that did not at one time subscribe to the international patent and copyright protection laws, were persuaded to sign them and gradually to enforce them effectively.

15.2 The Production of New Knowledge

To evaluate the role of knowledge in production, assume that the firm (or different firms) produces two types of goods: '*commodities*' and '*new knowledge*'. Their respective production functions include *four* inputs:

- labor,
- capital,
- the firm's (existing) knowledge, and
- the economy's (existing) aggregate knowledge.

The production functions for both commodities and new knowledge have the usual assumptions made in the Solow growth model: constant returns to scale and the diminishing marginal productivity of each input, with all other inputs held constant. In deciding on the production levels of commodities and new knowledge, the firm maximizes profits by choosing its levels of capital and labor, while taking its existing knowledge and the economy's existing knowledge as given.

The firm's cost of production of the new knowledge can be labeled as its R&D expenditures. For the firm doing it, the production of knowledge through such expenditures is subject to diminishing returns to the variable inputs, which are labor and capital. Consequently, each profit-maximizing R&D firm (or the research done by the production firm) would produce only a limited amount of it since it[5] will only get its private (and not the social/macroeconomic) return to the new knowledge created by its R&D expenditures. However, this knowledge can be only partially kept secret or patented, so that the new knowledge, once created, also benefits other firms in the economy.[6] The output of new knowledge enters as an intermediate good in the production of (final) commodities.

From the economy's perspective, two distinct cases emerge for the production of final commodities. These are

a. *The new knowledge created in the economy and its externalities are not significant enough to create constant or increasing returns to the capital-labor[7] ratio at the macroeconomic level.* In this case, even after taking account of the externalities of new knowledge, the production function for the final commodities has diminishing returns to capital per worker, as in the preceding chapter, and the Solow growth analysis applies.

b. *The new knowledge and its externalities are strong enough to create constant or increasing returns to capital per worker in the production of final commodities for the macroeconomy.*[8] Assuming the case of increasing marginal productivity of capital for worker for the economy as a whole, the economy's production function has the convex (increasing MPK) shape shown in Figure 15.1. Note that this case requires not only a

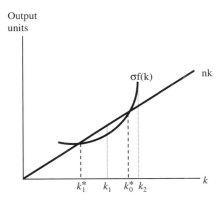

Figure 15.1

---

[5]The profit-maximizing amount is given by the equality of the marginal cost and marginal revenue of new knowledge, treating it as an output of the production process.

[6]While all firms could increase their profits if they were to collectively increase their research and therefore the economy's knowledge, such co-operation or collusion is ruled out by the usual incentives to shirk or cheat (i.e., not invest in R&D itself but take advantage of the results of R&D by other firms) in the presence of externalities.

[7]Note that capital includes both physical and human capital.

[8]A competitive equilibrium is ensured by assuming that the production and investment by a given *firm* are subject to diminishing private returns, even though their social/macroeconomic returns — i.e., private returns plus externalities — may be constant or increasing.

significant enough creation of new knowledge each year, but also its sufficiently extensive dissemination to the production of final commodities.

15.2.1 Diagrammatic analysis

The diagrammatic analysis for countries with increasing returns to capital intensity (i.e. capital per worker) was presented in Chapter 14. The increasing marginal productivity of capital per worker implies that the $\sigma f(k)$ curve would be convex rather than concave. Its diagram is repeated as Figure 15.1. This diagram shows two intersections between the $\sigma f(k)$ and nk curves and therefore, two SS values of k, k_0^* and k_1^*, at each of which $\sigma f(k) = nk$. Of these, k_1^* is stable but k_0^* is unstable. This is shown by the following arguments:

a. For $k > k_0^*$, saving per capita exceeds the capital requirement for new workers so that the capital–labor ratio k rises over time for all workers. The economy gradually moves further to the right of k_0^*.
b. For $k_1^* < k < k_0^*$, saving per capita is less than the capital requirement for new workers so that k decreases over time towards k_1^*.
c. For $k < k_1^*$, saving per capita exceeds the capital requirement for new workers so that k increases towards k_1^*.

Since any deviation from k_1^* brings the economy back to it, it is a stable SS value. But since a deviation of k from k_0^* leads the economy away from it, k_0^* is an unstable SS value. Even though k_0^* is unstable, it has the appealing empirical implication for economies with $k > k_0^*$ that the return to capital does not decrease as capital per worker increases nor do the growth rates of capital and output per capita go to zero, which seem to correspond to the experience of the developed economies. An objectionable implication of this case from the perspective of empirical validity is that the growth rate of the economy will continue to increase indefinitely, which is highly doubtful.

Consequently, the case of the increasing MPK was discounted by the growth theorists, at least for the developed economies, so that, for several decades following Solow's (1956) contribution, the profession mainly opted for the standard classical production function having diminishing MPK and implying a stable steady state. The endogenous growth theories allow only diminishing MPK at the *firm* (or individual's) level but, if all the firms collectively innovate enough, allow increasing MPK to physical and human capital — since they embody new knowledge with its externalities — for the macroeconomy.

In Figure 15.1, as shown above, the SS point at k_0^* is unstable, so that countries to the right of it (at k_2) will be on an ever-expanding path of output per worker. Countries (say, at k_1) with k less than k_0^* will be on a decreasing path of output per worker. Therefore, k_0^* represents a critical capital/labor ratio for the country and policy makers should ensure through their policies that their economy has a larger capital–labor ratio than this critical one. Such a critical ratio is called a *takeoff* or *threshold capital intensity*, and a '*growth trap*' occurs from k_1^* to k_0^*.

15.3 The Dissemination of Knowledge Across Countries

The preceding analysis can be extended for comparisons of growth across countries. As a simplification for the following discussion, we will adopt the country's existing capital–labor ($K/L = k$) ratio as the proxy for its existing knowledge as well as for its capacity to adopt new knowledge from other countries. For this purpose, 'capital' is defined as the sum of both physical and human capital.

For a country with the most advanced technology, there is no benefit from copying the inferior technology of other countries (with lower capital per worker).[9] But countries with less advanced technology have access to a large pool of knowledge, hitherto untapped by them, but available in other countries. But to take advantage of this pool requires:

(a) *Willingness to adapt and change in an appropriate manner.*
    This is likely to depend on social and cultural patterns and familiarity with foreign knowledge and practices. It may require cultural and social changes.
(b) *Adequate absorptive economic capacity.*
    This is likely to depend on the gap in the existing knowledge and skills and on the difference in the country's industrial structure from those of foreign countries.
(c) *Investment in human and physical capital.*
    Such investment is usually needed to access, adapt, and utilize the foreign knowledge hitherto not used in the domestic economy. In free enterprise economies, the amount of such investment is likely to depend on the incentives to the acquisition of new knowledge and the adoption of new technologies. In centralized economies, it will depend on the resources committed to this process.

Some countries may fulfil these conditions or do so at certain times or for certain types of changes. Others may not do so at all. It is often contended that open, free enterprise and capitalist economies give more scope to the creation and economy-wide use of new 'intellectual capital' by workers and firms than closed, traditional, or centralized and bureaucratic ones.[10] Further, countries with too low a capital (physical and/or human) intensity may not be able to effectively imitate the advanced technologies and, therefore, not be able to fully benefit from the knowledge already existing in developed countries. Still other countries may have an adequate base for understanding the new knowledge but not be sufficiently open to its acquisition or adaptation or be unwilling to invest sufficiently in its adoption. The reasons for this could lie in the nature of society and polity as well as in its economic structure.

The above arguments imply that:

(i) The prosperity and economic growth of countries depend in very important ways on the social, cultural, and political environment. These factors include the political system, the rule of law and protection of property and person, the capitalist ethic, ethnic and religious diversity, openness to new ideas and institutions, lack of corruption, level and distribution of income and of education, etc.
(ii) The growth rate is endogenous, so that it depends on the economy's capital intensity and its increase through investment and innovation.
(iii) The most technically advanced country, designated for simplification as the one with the highest value of k (with $k = k_{max}$), is already at the frontier of the world technology and benefits mainly from its own inventions and innovations. These increase its own — as well as worldwide — knowledge.

---

[9]We have assumed the simplification that this applies to all industries within each country. In reality, the technology (and capital intensity) of industries varies across countries at about the same stage of development, being more advanced (higher) for some industries in one country while being less advanced (lower) for other industries, so that there is always some scope for copying from other countries.

[10]This argument has been used in some explanations of the failure of centralized communist economies such as those of the Soviet Union and Eastern Europe prior to 1990 to generate economic growth rates comparable to those of the capitalist economies of North America and Western Europe, eventually leading to the collapse of communism in the former.

(iv) Other countries (with $k < k_{max}$) not only benefit from their own inventions and innovations, but also by copying techniques known to the more advanced countries. Hence, over a certain range, some *intermediate* set of developing economies (with lower existing values of k than k_{max}) can grow more rapidly through a faster change in their technology than more developed ones. This usually requires a faster accumulation of both physical and human capital.

(v) A country with extremely low technology and capital–labor ratio — and/or a rigid social and economic structure — may not be able to adopt other countries' techniques. If its own ability to innovate is also absent, it could continue with a relatively static technology, diminishing MPK, and low standard of living.

If there exist extensive *flows and adoption* of technical knowledge, we should expect standards of living among countries to converge. The European Union provides an example of such a tendency among its member countries. However, not all countries in the world have similarly high flows of technical knowledge, the capacity for the effective acquisition and use of others' knowledge, and the ability and willingness to invest in its adoption. Hence, some countries may continue to diverge over long periods from others in their standard of living: while the per capita incomes and growth rates of countries in the European Union in the coming decades are expected to converge, significant convergence need not occur between the European and some African countries during the next decade.

15.4 Diagrammatic Analysis

Figure 15.2 illustrates the general scenario. This diagram uses k as a proxy for the level of technology. Hence, k on the horizontal axis represents not only physical capital per worker but also the technology level, and movements along $f(k)$ incorporate technology shifts as k increases. The most advanced countries (with very high values of k) would have diminishing returns to capital intensity so that they would be on a concave segment of the curve $\sigma f(k)$ in the neighborhood of the stable SS ratio k_2^*. By comparison, countries in the intermediate range of the capital–labor ratio will benefit from the externalities of the knowledge of the more advanced economies. Some of these will have increasing growth rates and increasing returns to capital. Such countries will be in the region k_1^* to k_4. However, these higher-growth countries cannot increase or even maintain their higher growth rates indefinitely: their higher growth rates of output and saving per worker take them toward k_2^* and lower their growth rate. Eventually, their growth rates converge to those at k_2^*.

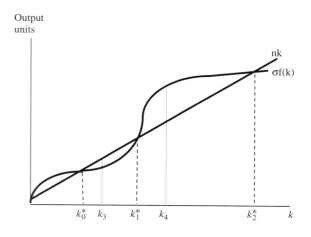

Figure 15.2

The poorest countries (with low capital–labor ratios to the left of k_0^*) can stagnate at low values of capital intensity and low growth rates. These countries are in a *growth trap* in the sense that even if they were somehow to advance above k_0^*, they will fall back to it — unless they manage to get to values of k higher than k_1^*, which will set them on a growth path of improvements in their standard of living. Further, being quite poor with limited savings, they have a limited capacity to invest in new knowledge, even in just taking advantage of the knowledge that already exists in the rest of the world. For them, the point k_1^* in Figure 15.2 represents a *threshold or take-off capital–labor ratio*, which they need to exceed if they are going to enter a path of increasing standards of living. Shocks (famines, civil, and other wars, diversion of the economy's output to consumption or wasteful expenditures rather than capital accumulation, etc.) and policies (e.g., those discriminating against capital accumulation) which shift the economy from the right of this threshold point to the left are highly undesirable, while those which do the reverse put the economy onto a path of ever-increasing standards of living. This danger is acute for an economy close to the point k_1^*.[11] Hence, it is very important for policy makers to push and position their economies appropriately along the k axis, and if they are LDCs with very low capital intensities, they must somehow exceed the threshold capital intensity.

Therefore, the countries with lower capital–labor ratios do not always have higher growth rates, though some of the countries with (intermediate) capital–labor ratios in the range k_1^* to k_2^* will have the highest growth rates and the highest return to capital. Furthermore, this figure implies both a divergence and a convergence: divergence between the countries moving toward k_0^* and those tending to k_2^*, while there is convergence of the poorest countries to k_0^* and the richest ones to k_2^*.

15.4.1 Growth rates and capital flows among countries

The preceding analysis implies that economies can be divided into three categories:

(a) The 'poorest' converging to k_0^* with very low values of k and y.
(b) The fast-growing (intermediate) countries ('the economic tigers') moving rapidly through high growth rates toward the k and y values of the most developed economies.
(c) The 'richest' industrialized countries converging to k_2^* with still higher values of k and y.

In this scenario, the growth rates are higher for the economic tigers than for the other economies. Further, since the MPK is highest for the economic tigers, capital flows from the poorest and the richest countries to the economic tigers. There is divergence of living standards between the poorest countries and those over the take-off point (k_1^*) — that is, the economic tigers and the richest countries — while there is bipolar convergence, with that of the poorest countries to k_0^* and its implied low output per capita, while the economic tigers and the developed economies converge to k_2^* and its implied high output per capita.

15.4.2 Convergence and divergence in living standards between countries

In the context of endogenous technical change, the convergence in living standards between countries occurs for two reasons: the movement toward roughly the same stable steady state as in the Solow model and the convergence of technologies through adoption of the more advanced technologies of other countries. Divergence can also occur for one or both of two reasons: an unstable steady state as in the Solow model and the divergence of technologies when there is an effective failure to adopt the more advanced technologies of other countries.

---

[11]This danger is minimal for the already developed economies, but can be acute for some developing economies.

15.4.3 Continuous growth in the advanced economies

Some studies in the endogenous growth literature suggest that advanced economies, including the country with the highest capital intensity (i.e., closest to k_2^*) and the most advanced technology, may escape for some time, diminishing returns to capital per worker if their creation of new knowledge is strong enough to produce constant returns or even increasing ones. If this were so, they would continue to have increasing output per worker and standards of living over time: the steady state capital/labor ratio rises continually rises because of endogenous technical change. However, this cannot be taken for granted: it may not happen and, when it does, it may cease after some time.

Box 15.2: Foreign Aid and Investment — and Capital Drain

Foreign aid is usually given to provide immediate relief from the misery caused by disasters such as droughts and earthquakes. It is often not enough to restore the prior standards of living of the recipients. It also often does not restore their prior levels of capital or saving. These disasters still reduce the amount of capital and investment — and consequently the growth rate.

Figure 15.2 provides a justification for aid and foreign investment from the context of growth theory. In Figure 15.2, increasing MPL occurs from k_3 to k_4. Countries that are between points k_3 to k_4 experience a rising growth rate — providing they can take advantage of it through adequate investment. Countries between k_1^* and k_4 do have adequate savings to raise their capital per worker and are on the path of rising growth rates. However, countries between k_0^* and k_1^* do not have adequate saving of their own to do so, so that over time their capital per worker and their growth rate falls. This provides one rationale for foreign investment and aid: if these, plus domestic saving, increase the capital/labor ratio, the growth rate rises. If these flows are maintained long enough to take the country beyond k_1^* — the self-sustaining take-off point — the country enters a high growth path sustained by its own saving.

Conversely, an outflow of domestic saving or human capital — a 'capital drain' — to foreign countries will lower the domestic growth rate. In an extreme scenario, such a capital drain could push the country below its take-off capital/labor ratio and send it on the path toward decreasing capital per worker and lower standards of living.

15.5 The Historical Experience of Growth

Romer (1986, p. 1008) pointed out that "Growth for a country that is not a leader will reflect at least in part the process of imitation and transmission of existing knowledge, where the growth rate of the leader gives some indication of growth at the frontier of knowledge."[12] He argued that the leader was Netherlands during 1700–1785 (with a growth rate of GDP per man-hour of −0.07%), the United Kingdom (UK) during 1785 to 1890 (with growth rates of 0.5% during 1785–1820 and 1.4% during 1820–1890) and the United States (USA) since 1890 (with a growth rate of 2.3%). This evidence suggests that the leader can change over time and that the growth rates of the leading country have been increasing over time.

Looking at the more recent experience with growth, the USA, Japan, Canada, and many western European countries are at or close to the frontiers of world knowledge. Their growth rates were fairly stable or declining

---

[12]Romer, P. M. Increasing returns and long-run growth. *Journal of Political Economy*, 94, October 1986, 1002–1037. See also Romer, P. M. Endogenous technical change. *Journal of Political Economy*, **98**, October 1990, S71–S102.

over several decades until the mid-1990s, when the benefits of the Information Technology (IT, including computers and the Internet) revolution eventually began to be realized.

The growth rates of Japan increased during its rapid development in the 1950s and 1960s, but decreased in the 1980s and 1990s. The growth rates of Korea, Taiwan, Thailand, Malaysia, and some other Asian countries increased in the 1980s and early 1990s as their pace of development picked up, though it remains to be seen if they will eventually also revert to slower growth rates.[13] This slowdown and convergence to a common growth rate are implied by the above model for countries as they approach the frontiers of world knowledge. Currently, China, India, Russia, and Brazil, along with some other countries, are going through a growth spurt.

The years since the mid-1990s have been especially exciting ones for the growth experience. Growth rates in many advanced economies increased rather than declined, contrary to the predictions of the Solow growth model. Proponents of endogenous growth theories have attributed this increase to the IT revolution, which had its beginnings in the 1980s but only seemed to make its macroeconomic impact in the late 1990s. The process consisted of the original major breakthroughs in knowledge, sporadic inventions, followed by decades of innovations and dissemination. Heavy investments in labor and capital had to be devoted to these. Countries that had the initial capacity to innovate and were willing to make the investments benefited the most in terms of higher growth and increases in the standard of living. Among these were Canada, the USA, and western European countries.

Box 15.3: Economic Globalization and Endogenous Technical Change

As discussed in Chapter 12 on globalization, the market system provides strong incentives in the form of larger profits for firms to increase the size of their market first within the nation and then across the nations. In the limiting case, this process leads to a single world market for individual products — i.e. globalization of the market. This expansion of the market requires a market-oriented system among countries, the dismantling of tariffs and quotas and reduction of communication and transport costs.

Economic liberalization:

- Increases the degree of competition, which acts as a stick for domestic industries to innovate so as to be able to compete with foreign firms.
- Increases the inflow of knowledge on more advanced production and management techniques.

Liberalization has, therefore, intensified the forces that promote endogenous growth among countries, especially among countries whose technology was not at the frontiers of knowledge and who are not successful in the creation of new knowledge.

Technology Clusters
In practice, it is not just one country that is at the frontiers of knowledge. Even for a given industry, many countries are often clustered at this level. There is both similarity and diversity of knowledge and production among these countries. Each is able to adapt the inventions and innovations originating in other countries. Consequently, there is considerable similarity in their standard of living and their growth rates.

---

[13]The long-run implications for growth of the crises in their exchange rates, stock markets, and economies generally during the latter half of the 1990s have yet to be determined. The short-term impact of these crises was to cut down their growth rates considerably.

Over time, some other countries initially outside the cluster at the frontiers of knowledge, begin to grow even more rapidly. Part of this growth comes from being able to share in the knowledge of the advanced cluster. Often, the countries that are best able to do so lie on the periphery — geographical, cultural, linguistic, etc. — of the advanced countries, so that development often proceeds in ever-expanding circles around an advanced country or countries. The formers eventually catch up with the cluster and join it. Subsequently, their growth tends to slow down to match those of the cluster. The invention of the Internet and the decrease in communication and transport costs have considerably reduced the effects of physical distance, so that physical distance has become relatively less important to the spread of innovations.

Globalization and Patents

The pressure for liberalization of the trade in commodities has often come from countries with an overall competitive edge over others. Since these are often the countries with greater innovations and innovations, they have also tended to espouse the strengthening and broadening of patent and copyright protections (in laws and implementations at the national level, at the regional bloc level and through international organizations such as the World Trade Organization) and lengthening the duration of the monopoly rights conferred by them. This increases the economic benefits from globalization to the countries whose firms obtain this power — and increases the national income and wealth of their countries — while reducing the benefits of globalization and liberalisation of external trade for other countries.

15.6 Human Capital

While human capital is often measured by the amount of schooling, the decision on the amount of schooling is like those on the amount of investment in physical capital. Increases in human capital improve output per capita, as we saw from the Solow growth model for increases in the saving and investment rate. For continuous growth in the SS standard of living, what is critical is not the schooling of children up to the existing levels of knowledge, but a continuous increase in the average knowledge of the population. One component of the latter is the generation of new knowledge. This depends on the ability and willingness to create new ideas or borrow and adapt them on an economy-wide basis, and on the incentives for doing so. It will ultimately depend on the economic decisions taken by the individuals, society, and government on the proportion of the human capital to be allocated to the creation of new human capital. Research-oriented universities and institutes are an important element in this creation, as are the R&D expenditures by firms.

Box 15.4: The Innovative Process and Its Creative Destruction

The pedagogical nature of classical, and even Keynesian, economics does not focus on the institutions and processes that lead to technical change in the economy. As against these schools, the *Austrian School* in economics, whose most famous exponent was Joseph Schumpeter, emphasizes the role of the institutional structure in the evolution of technology. According to it, self-interest in competitive markets constantly drives firms or entrepreneurs to improve their products and their technology in order to gain a competitive edge over others. This can be through invention or innovation. The successful firms create monopolistic rents by being the first to produce a new product or use a new process, so that such rents

Box 15.4: (*Continued*)

(which exceed normal profits under perfect competition) are the driving force for invention and innovation. Other firms try to reduce their losses by copying successful innovations and innovating on their own. Firms which do neither lose and are often forced out of production. Therefore, the production structure of the economy is in a continuing state of flux, with new firms coming into existence, some existing firms growing, while others become bankrupt or are taken over. This Austrian notion that the firms and the technology of an economy are constantly in flux clearly differs from the reliance on the mainly static (or with exogenous technical change) production function of the Solow growth model. The change in the economy is often compared to that in a forest, in which new trees are always coming into being and some are growing larger while others collapse. The introduction of endogenous technical change in growth theory in recent years is in some ways a movement toward modeling the Austrian view.

The above arguments suggest that the competitive capitalist economies possess an advantage in bringing about endogenous technical change since their firms are continually attempting to gain — by creating monopoly profits — from changing their products and/or techniques of production. By comparison, the centrally planned or highly regulated economies do not provide sufficient market incentives for their workers and production units to change and penalties for not keeping pace with competitors, with the result that such economies do not innovate as fast as the capitalist ones.

An aspect of the struggle among firms to gain an advantage over other firms through innovation and invention is that some of these will not prove successful in the market, so that the investment in them will be wasted. Another is that technical change not only has positive externalities, but also causes negative externalities. The process of innovation usually leads to what Joseph Schumpeter called '*creative destruction*', in which some firms lose their market share and may even close. Further, some of the existing machines embodying the older technology will become obsolete while some will need investments to update them. The benefits from the new technology in terms of output have to be offset by the losses in production resulting from the obsolescence of existing capital and the failure of firms which can no longer compete. The net social benefit is therefore reduced by these costs and may even become negative.

The innovative process also affects labor. The employees of firms that can no longer compete will be laid off and will need to find other jobs. Further, some of the workers even in the successful firms may be left with out-of-date skills and become unemployed. Such creative destruction by innovations thereby decreases some types of employment and by some firms, even while the innovations increase the average productivity of the employed workers and could increase employment in the economy.

Another source of the impact on employment arises from the substitution of capital for labor, or vice versa, in the shift from the old to the new technology. Whether this increases or decreases employment in the economy depends on the nature of technical change as being capital or labor intensive, the adaptability of labor to the new technology, and the increase in labor demand due to the shift in the production function. It is often suggested that the overall effect of innovations is to raise the unemployment rate in the short run but not necessarily in the long run. However, the effects are likely to differ for different types of technical change.

In the national context, the innovative process will lead to some industries expanding while others contract, and sometimes even disappear. Among the regions of a country, this process will cause output and employment in some regions to increase, while those in other regions decline. This usually translates into labor migration from the declining to the expanding regions and population shifts among the regions of the country.

Box 15.4: (*Continued*)

The negative impact of globalization and endogenous technical change

In the international context with free trade in commodities, if the innovating and expanding firms are abroad and the declining ones are domestic ones, the domestic economy would suffer a net decrease in employment and output from endogenous technical change. Therefore, worldwide increases in knowledge do not necessarily benefit all countries equally and may be detrimental on a net basis for some countries, especially those lagging in innovations. Since poorer countries have limited resources to allocate to the creation of new knowledge and less absorptive capacity for innovations occurring in other countries, they are likely to be the laggards — and, therefore, likely to be relative losers from the globalization of the trade in commodities and knowledge. Consider the computer and Internet revolution. The main innovating firms such as Microsoft were in the USA and earned monopoly profits on a worldwide basis. These benefited the Microsoft shareholders and workers, and the USA benefited from the inflow of royalties, etc. Other countries also benefited from the new technology but less so than the USA.

Since population flows across countries are controlled, population usually does not flow in adequate numbers from the losing countries to the expanding ones. Therefore, for the losing countries, the free flow of commodities but not of labor can produce declining standards of living and higher unemployment over long periods.

15.7 The Implications of Endogenous Growth Theories for Macroeconomic Policies

The Solow model assumes exogenous growth rates of labor and technical change, so that there is no scope for policy in influencing the SS output per capita and the SS growth rate. However, note that even in such a model, an increase in the saving rate would have increased the pre-SS growth rate, so that there was some scope for policy to increase the growth by increasing the saving rate in the economy. Since a particular economy may not reach its steady state for long numbers of years, the impact of increased saving rates on the growth rate would be observable over long periods even in the context of a strictly classical economy without endogenous technical change. Further, policy-induced changes in labor force growth rates will change the capital–labor and output–labor ratios.

The endogenous growth theories provide for effects of government policies on per capita output growth rate if they increase (or decrease) the growth rates of knowledge. Among such policies are those that promote research in universities, R&D expenditures by firms, and other creative processes. Any policies which lower the return to human or physical capital or reduce saving — and thereby reduce the growth rates of physical and human capital — reduce the growth rate of the standard of living. Among these policies are the imposition of taxes on profits and interest earnings, and policies detrimental to research, R&D, and innovation in general. Among other policies that could do so are excessive regulations, rampant corruption, hindrances to financial development, etc.

There can also be effects of short-run fiscal and monetary policies on the long-run growth rates. We illustrate these by considering the possible effects of recessions on growth. The Austrian school's notion of creative destruction from technical change implies that recessions weed out firms that are not sufficiently innovative in finding new markets and/or new processes. The ones that survive are more successful at doing at least one of these. Recessions, therefore, serve as a stick for staying competitive and for innovation and change. Stabilization policies that eliminate or moderate recessions could, therefore, lower the rate of endogenous technical change. So could rescuing ('bailing out') failing firms by providing huge government subsidies, as occurred in the USA and the UK in the financial and economic crisis of 2007–2010. Conversely, sharp and unexpected recessions which reduce demand beyond the capacity of firms to protect themselves by innovating would also eliminate some firms which, had they survived, would have innovated. However, the workers laid off in recessions do not acquire skills that occur by learning on the job and their previous skills may atrophy during the unemployment period. The resulting decrease in skills could, depending on the severity and duration of the recession, have a long-run detrimental impact on output. This is one type of *hysteresis effects*.[14]

To conclude, the endogenous technical change theories imply that governmental policies that affect the rate of technical change will affect output per capita over the long run, and not merely over the short run. Further, the former could prove to be much more significant for the long-run prosperity of the nation. Government policies are even more critical for countries close to an unstable SS equilibrium, where the policy effects can push the economy to either side of the threshold.

Extended Analysis Box 15.1: International Linkages and Growth

The recognition of the role of knowledge as a very important ingredient for the growth of economies enhances the role which international trade and capital flows play. The benefits of trade can be classified as:

(i) static, and
(ii) dynamic.

The *static benefits* can be defined as arising from the ability of the country to benefit from comparative advantage in relative factor intensities at its existing knowledge of production techniques. The *dynamic ones* can be defined as arising from the new knowledge acquired through trade and capital flows and other contacts. New knowledge can include knowledge of the goods produced — and processes used — in other countries but not yet in one's own, with some of this knowledge leading to innovations in the country's production techniques. The importation or imitation of existing techniques and products promotes — or reduces the cost of — the search for new ones.[15]

Education abroad, personal travel, and business contacts can contribute to increases in the country's knowledge of products and techniques. Direct investment by foreigners in the home country and agreements on the transfer of technology also contribute to the country's knowledge. Conversely, barriers to foreign education, travel, trade, and investment stem this flow of knowledge.

Therefore, from the perspective of economic growth, international flows, whether of products, capital or people, carry externalities in the form of knowledge flows. These knowledge flows are likely to be of greater benefit to those countries that lack the requisite knowledge than to those which already have it. They will also be of greater potential benefit for those that have the ability and production systems to use the knowledge of other countries than for those that cannot do so. Hence, developing economies are expected to be the greater beneficiaries of the international flows of knowledge, *provided* that they possess the openness, the absorptive capacity, and the environment — consisting of the political, social, and economic systems — to utilize them. The extent to which they actually benefit depends on their investment in this enterprise.

---

[14]Hysteresis occurs when a short-term deviation from the long-run position of the economy has effects on the subsequent course of the economy. In this case, the long-run position of the economy is not independent of short-run deviations from it.

Extended Analysis: Box 15.1: (*Continued*)

Historically, the openness of the economy and extensive international trade have been among the characteristics of rapidly growing economies. Also, economies on the 'periphery' (geographically, culturally and/or in terms of links and relationships) of the already industrialized economies tend to grow faster than more remote countries. Presumably, those on the periphery have greater scope for learning from the industrialized economies than those farther away, so that we would expect the former to grow faster than the latter, *ceteris paribus*. However, the invention of the Internet and reductions in travel, transport, and communications costs have virtually eliminated the notion of periphery in terms of geographical distances and made educational levels and cultural factors more important in its definition.

Our discussion of the endogenous technical change also implies that opening the domestic economy to the flow of foreign products and foreign firms is *often* very advantageous for the economy. But it need not *always* be to the home country's advantage. If the expansion of knowledge occurs mainly abroad while the destruction of productive capacity — through the inability or unwillingness of domestic firms to innovate at the rate attained by firms abroad — occurs at home, the domestic economy will end up with lower output. This is especially likely to occur in poorer countries with more limited resources for investments in R&D and in education. Whether this effect will be completely or more than offset by the inflows of investment and new knowledge is a moot point. Therefore, the endogenous growth theory does not imply that the liberalization of foreign trade will necessarily benefit all countries equally; in fact, some countries can be net losers — at least in the short term. For the poorer countries, even if they are not net losers, the gains may be insufficient for their standard of living to converge to those in the richer countries. To illustrate, the per capita incomes of most countries in sub-Saharan Africa relative to the world average income have declined in recent decades. Consequently, a considerable dispersion of per capita incomes across countries, and especially across continents, can continue to persist, even while there may be convergence in the standards of living of other countries.

15.8 The Importance of the Inflation Rate and the Quantity of Money for Growth

The relationship between the financial system and growth has two distinct aspects:

 (i) The effect of increases in the *quantity of money* and the *inflation rate* on the growth rate of output.
 (ii) The effect of the development of the *financial structure* on the growth rate of output.

The short-run macroeconomic models and growth theory entail the following two propositions for the relationship between money and growth, and inflation and growth:

 (i) The long-run growth of output is independent of money supply growth and the quantity of money.
 (ii) The long-run growth rate of output is independent of the rate of inflation.

---

[15] Such importation may involve the payment of royalties to other countries or loss of control of domestic firms to foreign corporations. Often, initially, imitation results in poor quality copies of foreign products, followed by quality improvements as production experience increases over time.

However, the short-run models and disequilibrium analysis (see Chapters 8 and 9) did show that higher money supply growth and inflation can in some cases and for some time lead to higher output. As against this, high inflation rates can be inimical to growth because they introduce distortions and inefficiencies in the economy.[16] Conversely, price stability enhances economic certainty and promotes investment, which is conducive to growth, so that growth rates can be negatively related to the inflation rate. Consequently, on balance, the net empirical effects of money growth and inflation on output growth need not deviate significantly from the above two propositions.

The effect of changes in the quantity of money on growth can be examined in one of two ways. It can be estimated directly by using the data on the money supply or indirectly by examining the effect of inflation on the growth rate of output. Among the empirical studies which report that the growth rate is independent of the rate of monetary growth and the inflation rate is Lucas (1996). Lucas plotted for 100 countries the relationship between 30-year averages of the output growth rate and the M2 growth rate. His finding was that the plots showed the former to be independent of the latter.[17] His conclusion was that, in the long run, money is neutral for the output growth rate. This has been confirmed by other studies. The exception to this sometimes occurs for low-inflation countries, such as the OECD countries, which show a positive, though weak, relationship between the growth rates of money (or the inflation rate) and output.

To conclude, the consensus in economics is that, in general, the *long-run* output growth is independent of the long-run inflation rate and the money growth rate. However, it is not independent of innovations in and the productivity of the financial sector.

Box 15.5: The Role of the Financial Sector in Growth: Some Conclusions from Economic History

One form of the evidence on the relationship between the financial sector and growth comes from the economic history of the early stages of Industrialization in countries noted for industrial innovation. Cameron's (1967) assessment on this was that "financial innovation, after all, is not so very different from technical innovation. The former is frequently necessary for realisation of the latter" (p. 12). This pattern occurred during the Industrial Revolution in Britain in the 19th century. The evolution and expansion of commercial banking was an essential concomitant of the Industrial Revolution. Further, "while it is rare for banks to finance directly a period of experimentation with a completely novel production technique by a new, inexperienced businessman or inventor … it is quite common for bankers to finance the expansion of firms that have already introduced successful innovations, and also to finance the adoption of the innovation by imitators." (Cameron, 1967, p. 13).

The assessment by Joseph Schumpeter, an early proponent of the importance of technological change (in current terminology, of endogenous technical change) to development, was: "The essential function of credit … consists in enabling the entrepreneur to withdraw the producer's goods which he needs from their previous employments, by exercising a demand for them, and thereby to force the economic system into new channels." (Schumpeter, 1933, p. 106).

These quotes point to the critical role of the financial sector in the innovation and restructuring processes which are elements of any technical change, including the endogenous one, and of economic development.[18]

---

[16]However, this effect is not considered to be large for stable rates of inflation in the single digit range.

[17]Lucas further shows that the correlation for 110 countries with 30-year averages of the data between the M2 growth and the rate of inflation is 0.95.

15.9 The Role of the Financial Sector in Growth: Recent Empirical Evidence

The financial system consists of retail banks (i.e., banks catering to customers through deposits) and other financial institutions (such as investment brokers and pension funds), bond and stock markets, and rules, regulations and accounting practices to ensure the accuracy of financial reports and prevention of fraud, etc. Firms use a combination of internal funds — from retained profits and personal capital — and external borrowing to finance their investment. Some industries, especially new innovative ones, tend to be short of internal funds and depend relatively more on external financing. This need for external financing varies among firms and industries and depends on factors such as the initial project scale, the gestation duration, internal generation through retained earnings and the amounts needed for further investment, etc. Financial development reduces the cost of external financing and, therefore, promotes the growth of existing firms and industries dependent on such financing. It also promotes the establishment of new firms and industries, which usually account for a large part of new ideas, innovations, and breakthroughs.[19] Financial development also reduces financial market imperfections, which usually favor the internal financing and the growth of existing firms relative to that of new firms.[20] Therefore, the lower cost and easier access to external finance provide a mechanism through which financial development influences the establishment and growth of innovating firms, and encourage the change and growth in the economy. Hence, endogenous technical change tends to occur faster in countries with more developed financial sectors.

As a major sector whose services are needed and used by all the other sectors in the economy but which, in turn, uses the inputs and knowledge originating in other sectors, there is a *symbiotic relationship* between an efficient and competitive financial sector and the rest of the economy. This makes it difficult to assign causality on the questions of whether the efficiency of the financial sector emanates from the other sectors of the economy versus the contribution that an efficient financial sector makes to the efficiency of the latter. It also creates considerable differences of opinion in the profession on the dynamic contribution that the expansion of an already efficient financial sector can make to the growth — especially in the steady state — of the economy. Empirical evidence indicates that financial development does contribute to higher per capita growth rates, more so through the external financing of firms and productivity growth than through just through facilitating capital accumulation.

In assessing the contribution of the financial system to the overall growth of the economy, the following points should be noted.

(i) The output of the financial sector is itself part of the GDP of the economy. Therefore, if the productivity of the financial sector grows at a faster rate, GDP will also grow at a faster rate.

(ii) We need to differentiate between the different components of the financial sector. Among these, commercial banks provide different services from those provided by investment banks, investment brokers and stock markets, so that each can have independent affects on economic growth. More broadly, the banking system is only a subset of a developed financial sector whose other segments are also vital to growth in the modern economy.

---

[18]As against these claims, a prominent contributor to growth theory has claimed that economists 'badly over-stress' the role of the financial system. Other economists have argued that the financial sector responds passively to growth in the production sector.

[19]In some cases, as much as two-thirds of the total growth of output in the economy comes from new firms, so that their number and development are major elements of growth. The effect of financial development on the growth rate of new firms is greater than that on existing firms.

[20]Financial development also promotes higher accounting standards, which reduce the costs of obtaining the external finance.

(iii) The contribution of the financial sector to growth rates is at least partly through the dynamics of the economy's industrial structure, especially in the external financing of new firms and new products. Adequate access to external financing is important for the financing of innovation by small firms and plays an important role in endogenous technical change.

(iv) Underdevelopment or breakdown of the credit structure of the financial sector reduces the flow of external funds to firms and reduces their production ability and the growth rate of the economy.

15.10 The Miracle of Economic Growth

Empirical studies indicate a large role for physical and human capital in explaining the growth. However, even taking account of these and other purely economic determinants of growth, there is still a very significant unexplained residual in such studies. This raises the possibility that there are also non-economic contributors to growth, such as the degree of openness of the economy, culture, ethnic divisions, political stability or the lack of it, natural resource endowments, chance and luck.

A word of caution is needed at this point. The precision of growth models conveys the erroneous impression that growth is a smooth process over time. In reality, it is highly uneven, even precarious. Part of this is due to the uneven pattern of advances in knowledge and their incorporation into production, which can be major sources of fluctuations in the macroeconomy. Further, the shift of a country to a successful development pattern — that is, going from relatively poor standards of living to long periods of high growth rates — has often come as a surprise and has enough fragility for the development process and its continuation to be considered by many economists a '*miracle*'. Growth experience indicates that few development miracles are sustained over very long periods, and definitely not without interruptions or crises.

15.10.1 The miracle of growth and financial crises in the economic tigers

Explosive growth and the rapid transformation of the economy through new technologies and new firms and industries require the rapid expansion of the sources of external financing (i.e., through loans, bonds, and equities). The unevenness, speculative nature and fragility of the process of invention and innovation, as well as of the nature of financial intermediation, make the economy prone to severe financial crises. The historical experience of the miracles of growth is littered with periodic financial crises followed by economic ones.

The major financial and economic crises of the 1990s afflicted the very nations that had been undergoing the growth miracle — the 'Asian tigers' such as Thailand, Korea, Malaysia, Indonesia, etc. The crises in the American and European stock markets in 2000–2002 affected most strongly the very firms that were at the forefront of the new Internet and telecommunications technologies. Most countries — though not all firms — do manage to come out of such crises after some years and resume their rapid growth.

15.10.2 The economic crisis of 2007–2010 in the USA

Major elements of the financial crisis in the USA during 2007–2009 were:

- Innovations of new financial products, such as derivatives, and new types of financial firms, such as hedge funds, in the late 1990s. These allowed layers of financial assets to be built on mortgage payments on houses, a real asset.
- Many mortgages had been given to persons who could not meet the mortgage payments out of their incomes but relied on rapidly rising house prices to justify the purchase.
- House prices rose rapidly during 200–2006, with a large positive bubble in them by 2006. They began to stabilize in 2006, and then dropped in 2007 as the bubble collapsed.

- The layering of financial assets, with asset-based corporate paper as one of the ultimate ones, 'hid' the real riskiness of the financial assets, which led to their being perceived as riskless assets. Given this perception, they came to be held by banks, investment banks, hedge funds, pension funds, and other investors.

Once the underlying house prices started to fall in 2007, there were extensive mortgage defaults, which implied that the promised returns on mortgage-based financial assets could not be met, leading to either defaults or a drastic decrease in the value of assets based on mortgage payments, which led to the insolvency of numerous financial institutions which had issued them or held them. This insolvency or near-insolvency led to a credit crisis in which banks drastically cut back on their lending to other banks and production firms. This, in turn, led to an economy-wide decrease in production and employment (a negative supply shock), as well as to loss of consumer and business confidence, which led to reductions in consumer and investment expenditures (a negative demand shock). The outcome of these negative shocks was a severe recession.

Since the USA is the world's largest economy, its financial and economic crises can easily spread to other countries and become worldwide, as happened with the spread of the crisis in the USA to the rest of the world.

Extended Analysis Box 15.2: The Economic, Social, and Political Environment for Growth: Markets, Competition, Capitalism, and Entrepreneurship

We have already emphasized that growth economics needs to go outside the narrow confines of growth modeling to examine the environments that propel and encourage growth. The hallmark of such environments has to be their fertilization of change: change in products, markets, machines, methods of organization, workers' knowledge and skills, etc. The base from which the change starts is important in determining the nature and extent of the change. Further, institutions and practices that encourage change are important, as are the incentives to profit from making changes. These need to promote experimentation, invention and innovation. These arguments make the nature of education, society, economy, and polity significant in explaining why some economies grow fast while others do not.

Adam Smith, one of the 'founders' of economics in the late 18th century, pointed out that the expansion of the size of the market, specialization, and competition were major forces for the expansion of production. A larger market permits specialization of labor and machines, which increases their marginal productivity and lowers the cost of production, resulting in more sales and more production. Markets, therefore, are a mechanism that encourages growth.

Some economists consider the market economy — and its dynamics — to be the core development that separates economies without significant growth from those with growth. However, this is an over-simplification. Markets can grow and specialization can proceed even under a virtually static technology, as occurred in many areas in many periods in history, without producing major technological breakthroughs and their manifestation in the industrial revolution. Adam Smith was writing against a background of technical change already occurring in Britain, but not yet in most other countries, so that its better technologies permitted lower costs, increased sales, and expansion into other markets. Both technical change and the growth of markets tended to occur more or less together over time, each promoting the other.

Technical change and the growth of markets have occurred concurrently over the last two centuries, so that GDP growth and the size of the market were closely correlated. This evidence raises several interesting questions. Did one produce the other? Which caused the other or were both caused by a third factor? A somewhat similar and topical question on the economic developments of the last two decades is whether the globalization of markets produced the Internet and its expansion or whether the Internet caused, or merely permitted, globalization to proceed as forcefully as it has done in the last decade.

Extended Analysis Box 15.2: (*continued*)

The importance of risk taking and incentives, and of the entrepreneurial spirit

Since invention and innovation by their nature require departures from past patterns of thought and production methods, as well as products, they tend to involve a high risk of failure and wasted effort and resources. Incentives in the form of profits provided by the capitalist system (especially if strengthened by patents and copyright protection) act as a reward for such risk taking and promote innovations and innovations.

However, some economists argue that the entrepreneurial spirit, especially the spirit that underlies the desire to set up new enterprises, is also essential to such activity. Societies and educational patterns that encourage such a spirit tend to do better at achieving higher rates of inventions and innovations over time. By comparison, traditional and conservative societies that encourage established patterns of behavior and pursuits and bureaucratic ones usually tend to do less well in this respect.

The entrepreneurial spirit is usually strongest in individuals and new small businesses than in old and very large firms. Some of these new small firms originate with a new idea, product or process, which is initially untried and untested in the market place, so that its owners find it difficult to raise external capital from banks and stock and bond markets. Their financing depends the owner's own resources and amounts borrowed from friends and relatives, followed, as they become somewhat better established, by loans from financial intermediaries providing venture capital. Failure is common among new small firms.

Education and corruption

Among the myriad issues that the environment of growth raises, two interesting issues for discussion relate to education and corruption. On education, should poor countries (with very limited budgets to devote to education) concentrate on providing a basic elementary level education to a high proportion of its citizens? Or, should they limit this proportion so as to devote some of their meagre resources to producing a cadre of highly educated persons, who possess the knowledge that will permit understanding and adoption of the newer technologies in the world? Which option will promote higher growth? Economics does not provide a definite answer to this question.

On corruption, incomes in many countries are low and corruption is rampant. Corruption can function as a lubricant for the economy by allowing the economic agents to get around regulations that bind and limit the economic activity and its expansion. But they also reduce the returns to private enterprise and channel the energy of entrepreneurs a nd the population into wasteful activities. Economists consider the latter very significant and believe that corruption is a major net retardant of growth.

15.11 Empirical Evidence on the Contributors to Growth

Our theoretical analysis of this and the last chapter on growth show that:

(i) The Solow growth model implies that the higher the standard of living — i.e., the higher the existing capital–labor ratio and output per worker — the lower its growth rate. Endogenous growth theories imply that this tendency could be offset by endogenous technical change. However, the richest countries at the frontiers of knowledge have more difficulty innovating than other countries. Barro (2001)[21] reported a

[21]Barro, RJ. Human capital and growth. *American Economic Review*, **91**, May 2001, 12–17.

positive effect of increasing GDP per capita on the *growth* rates of poor countries (with GDP per capita below US$580 in 1985 prices) but a significantly negative one for others. The effect was strongly negative for the richest countries. This supports the Solow model, without denying the importance of endogenous technical change to the growth of the standards of living.

(ii) The higher are the growth rates of physical and human capital, the higher is the growth rate of output per worker.

(iii) The greater is the amount of government consumption (i.e., excluding investment by the government), the lower is the growth rate. This can occur for two reasons: crowding out of private investment, which lowers the growth of physical capital, and the inefficiency of the government-owned enterprises.

(iv) For countries not at the forefront of technology, greater openness of the economy increases the growth rate.

(v) Higher population growth reduces the growth rate of output per capita. It does so by reducing the growth of capital per worker for two reasons: more children per family tend to reduce the saving and there are more workers among whom the capital has to be shared.

(vi) Both the growth of human capital and improvements in its quality contribute positively to growth of output per capita. Some studies have found that the quality of education — measured by scores on international examinations, pupil–teacher ratios, etc. — is more important for the growth of output per capita than its quantity (i.e., how many more students educated at the existing quality of education). Another empirical study found that the increasing superiority of the USA during the 20th century was due to the earlier and more rapid expansion of its high school system in the early 20th century, while high school education was much less common in other countries at the time or in the USA in the 19th century. This expansion and the pragmatic nature of schooling had produced by the middle of the 20th century a large difference between the educational stocks of the USA relative to other nations, including the European ones.[22]

(vii) The largest contributor to the growth of output is the growth of multifactor productivity.

(viii) Economic incentives provided by the capitalist system, risk-taking behavior and the entrepreneurial spirit are very important to continued high levels of inventions and innovations, and of new firms set up to bring them to the market. The extent of the entrepreneurial spirit and risk taking tends to be much higher among societies and economies based on the capitalist system versus those organized along centralized, bureaucratic ones. They can also depend on the educational system.

(ix) Patents and copyright protection increase the profits to be made from the protected item. Most economists maintain that they increase inventions and innovations over the amount that would have occurred in their absence, while some economists dispute this conclusion on the basis of empirical evidence.

15.11.1 Empirical evidence on growth in recent decades

The rate of economic growth differs among countries. However, the developed industrialized economies seemed to possess a common pattern of declining growth rates from the mid-1970s to the mid-1990s, followed by an increase in growth rates after the mid-1990s. This was discussed in Chapter 14 in the context of Table 14.1 for the USA. Table 15.1 below, from Baily (2003), presents another set of growth estimates[23] for the USA, and highlights the relative contributions to growth of the computer and Internet revolutions.

---

[22]Robert Barro's study using data for about 100 countries reported confirmation of most of these findings.

[23]These estimates use the growth-accounting method presented in Chapter 14.

Table 15.1   Growth accounting and the IT revolution.[24]

Period	1948–1973 (%)	1973–1995 (%)	1995–2000 (%)	Difference in % growth: 1995–2000 minus 1973–1995
Output per hour	2.9	1.4	2.79	1.39
Contributions from:				
Capital	0.8	0.7	1.14	0.44
Information technology capital	0.1	0.4	0.99	0.59
Other capital	0.7	0.3	0.15	−0.15
Labour quality	0.2	0.2	0.24	0.04
Multifactor productivity growth (MFP)	1.9	0.4	1.31	0.91
From R&D	0.2	0.2		
Computer sector MFP				0.18
Other MFP				0.72

This table shows that the annual rate of growth of output per hour was 2.9% during 1948–1973, 1.4% during 1973–1995 and 2.79% during 1995–2000.[25] The slowdown in growth during 1973–1995 relative to that during 1948–1973 was mainly due to the rate of decrease of multifactor productivity (MFP) growth, which decreased from 1.9% annually to 0.4%. The resurgence of growth after 1995 was also largely due to the recovery in the MFP growth, which was in turn mainly attributable to the development of the IT sector (including the computer one). This sector contributed to growth through contributions to capital's share and to MFP growth. It accounted for 0.4% of capital's contribution during 1973–1995, followed by an increase by 0.59% (to 0.99%) during 1995–2000. It also increased the rate of growth of MFP by 0.18%, so that the *increase* (as between 1973–1995 and 1995–2000) in annual output growth due to IT developments was 0.79%. This difference compares with labor's total contribution of 0.02% during 1973–1995 and 0.06% during 1995–2000. Clearly, the IT revolution has been the largest contributor to the growth of output per hour and hence to the growth of living standards during the past decade.

15.12   Conclusions

Conclusions from endogenous growth theory

- The political, social, geographical, and other factors are important determinates of a country's standard of living and its growth rate.
- The essential elements of endogenous technical theories are that technical change requires economic decisions on the acquisition of new knowledge and that new knowledge created by a firm has positive externalities. Positive externalities mean the return to a firm creating new knowledge is less than the social one. Therefore,

---

[24]This table is based on Tables 1 and 2 of Martin Neil Baily, "Distinguished Lecture on Economics in Government: The New Economy: Post mortem or second wind? *Journal of Economic Perspectives*, **16**, Spring 2003, 2–22. In combining the data from these two tables, the data used from Table 2 is that shown for the *Economic Report*. This table covers the non-farm business sector.

[25]Since growth rates are compounded over time, a small sustained increase in growth rates tends to represent large variations in output per capita after some years.

the invisible hand of competition does not produce the optimal rate of R&D expenditures or other investments leading to invention and innovation so that they will not yield the optimal long-run growth rate. Governmental policies that increase the acquisition and spread of new knowledge can increase this growth rate while inappropriate policies can lower it.

- Both human capital and physical capital are the carriers of knowledge. They are highly correlated with each other and with the country's growth rate.

- Solow's model with exogenous technical change implies that an increase in the saving rate can only increase the steady state output but not its SS growth rate. By comparison, the endogenous growth theory implies that the increase in the saving rate — and thus, investment and the rate of increase in capital intensity — can influence the pace of innovation and the steady state rate of growth of output. Hence, governmental policies that affect the saving rate and the rates of return to physical and human capital can have long-run growth effects.

- Inventions and innovations are normally a result of economic decisions and require investments. As such, both the readiness of firms to invest in these activities and of workers to invest in their education, and the governmental support for these activities, play important roles in endogenous growth theories. Macroeconomic policies that promote physical and human capital growth increase the growth rate, and some may do so even in the steady state.

- Patents and copyright protection increase the returns to inventions and innovations, and can enhance the latter.

- Policies that reduce the returns to the production of new knowledge slow technical change and the growth rate.

- In the case where there is an unstable steady state with a takeoff or threshold capital/labor ratio, policies that push the economy beyond this point become extremely important for the economic future of the country. Similarly, capital inflows would increase the domestic capital intensity and push up the country's growth rate.

- Patents and other exclusionary devices, which close off access or make access to the knowledge of production techniques more costly tend to lower the growth rates of the countries denied such access.

- Endogenous growth theories imply that, under certain (but not all) conditions, relatively less advanced countries can catch up to the standard of living of more advanced countries through higher growth rates. This catching up occurs partly through copying the knowledge of the more advanced countries. This ability to tap into the existing stock of knowledge in the world is a major determinant of the growth rates of developing countries. As they catch up to the lead countries, their growth slows, with eventual convergence in growth rates.

- However, there could also occur divergence of growth rates among countries: over time, the rich countries tend to get richer relative to some poorer countries. Part of this expanding gap stems from the relative inability of the poor countries to effectively tap into the world's stock of ever-expanding knowledge.

Conclusions on money, the financial sector, and growth

- Money allows specialization, trade, and expansion in the size of firms to an extent that can never occur under barter and in economies with rudimentary monetary systems. The usage of money is an essential element in the modern scale and complexity of production and exchange.

- In addition, an efficient financial sector allows the accumulation and more efficient allocation of savings to investment projects, and thereby promotes the growth of capital in the economy.

- The empirical evidence shows that there are none, or very limited, benefits for growth from inflation or the rapid growth of the money supply.
- The empirical evidence usually shows a significant positive relationship between the development of the financial sector and the economy's growth, though the direction of causality can go either way. Therefore, the implication of the empirical findings for monetary policy is that, from the long-run growth perspective, the central bank should support the greater efficiency, development, and stability of the financial sector.
- The efficiency of the financial sector is also dependent, as is of the other sectors, on regulations, technological change, and other aspects of the economic environment. Here again, the central bank can make important contributions.

KEY CONCEPTS

Exogenous technical change
Innovations and inventions
Endogenous technical change
Endogenous growth theory
Threshold capital–labor ratio
Human capital

Externalities generated by the creation of new knowledge
International flows of knowledge
Globalization
Patents and intellectual property protection

Creative destruction
Risk-taking and entrepreneurship, and
Financial development.

SUMMARY OF CRITICAL CONCLUSIONS

- The endogenous growth theories emphasize the roles of inventions and innovations and their production. They introduce knowledge, whether in the form of human capital or embodied in physical capital, as an additional input in the production of final goods. The production of new knowledge is itself subject to diminishing marginal productivity for the firm producing it, so that its profit maximizing production is limited. However, such knowledge, once created, has an externality so that the social/macroeconomic return to the production of new knowledge is greater than the private one.
- The new knowledge created by others requires absorptive capacity, investment, and effort, so that while some firms and countries benefit from it, others do not do so.
- The endogenous growth theories imply that the long-run differences in productivity among countries depend on their social, political and economic environment, as well on the incentives to innovate and invest. Government policies can make a difference to long-run growth, promoting, or hindering it.
- The endogenous growth theories can explain the convergence of the growth rates within groups of countries while allowing for the divergence of growth rates between groups of countries.
- Endogenous growth theories explain why the return to capital in the world economy need not decrease. They also provide a role for governmental policies in the promotion of long-run growth.
- The usage of money is an invention with remarkable externalities for the technology of commodity production and exchange: it increases the size of markets, promotes specialization and trade, allows the rise of large firms to take the advantage of economies of scale and shifts the commodity production frontier drastically. It also increases the supply of labor to firms.

- In the long run, the growth rate of the economy is independent of the rate of inflation and the growth rate of the quantity of money — that is, money is neutral in the long-run growth of countries.
- The monetary sector in the modern economy is merely one component of the financial sector. The appropriate focus of monetary growth theory should be on the efficiency and structure of the financial sector.
- Innovations in the financial sector contribute to the growth rate of output in the pre-SS stage and may also do so to the steady state rate.

REVIEW AND DISCUSSION QUESTIONS

1. What is meant by 'endogenous growth'?
2. Which is more significant (a) for SS growth and (b) for pre-SS growth: investment (without technical change) or innovation? Discuss.
3. What is meant by 'human capital'? Is it schooling or new knowledge or does it include both? What is the role of each one in growth? Discuss.
4. Discuss the relevance of capitalism versus totalitarianism (with a centralized economy) to growth.
5. What types of fiscal policies can promote growth? What types can hinder it? Give examples.
6. How do wars (a) reduce growth and (b) promote growth? Use diagrams to support your answer and give some examples.
7. What is meant by the globalization of international trade? Discuss its advantages and disadvantages for the less developed economies with agriculture as the dominant economic sector.
8. What is a patent? In what ways do patents encourage and in what ways do they discourage the growth and spread of new knowledge?
9. 'It is vital for understanding the contribution of money to growth that we distinguish between the quantity of money and the size and the efficiency of the financial sector.' Discuss.
10. LDCs have sometimes resorted to high money growth rates to finance their development efforts in an attempt to push up their growth rates. Why? Was it misguided in retrospect and, if so, why?
11. 'Banking inefficiency and the excessive regulation of the banking sector and interest rates in some of the LDCs have proved to be highly detrimental to their growth rates.' Discuss.
12. Define 'hyperinflation'. How might it hinder growth?
13. In explaining the growth rate of output per capita during the past 50 years for the USA, what factors explain its decrease from the mid-1970s to the mid-1990s, followed by its increase?

ADVANCED AND TECHNICAL QUESTIONS

T1. If the marginal product of physical capital is increasing for a given firm, it can indefinitely increase its profits by increasing its physical capital stock, so that (a) profit maximization under perfect competition implies that the firm would use increasingly larger and larger amounts of capital and (b) the firm would grow to meet the industry's total demand. This is clearly unrealistic. How does endogenous growth theory accommodate the increasing marginal productivity of capital for the economy while maintaining the assumption of competition among firms?

T2. Is there a link between rapid growth through invention and innovation and financial crises? Why? Discuss.

T3. 'Given that saving is positively related to the rate of interest and that an increase in the rate of inflation will increase the rate of interest, both the saving rate and the growth rate of the economy will be positively related to the inflation rate and the money growth rate.' Discuss. [Hint: modern classical economists believe that the saving rate depends on the real interest rate.]

CHAPTER 16

Business Cycles, Crises, and The International Transmission of Economic Activity

Business cycles are periodic fluctuations in economic activity. While the magnitudes of almost all economic variables fluctuate over time, the most significant variables for defining the business cycle are fluctuations in output and employment. The business cycle consists of a trough, upturn, peak, and downturn — followed by a trough and so on. In a growing economy, recessions tend to have a much shorter duration — usually of about six quarters to two years — than booms, which are often longer than six years.

Macroeconomics investigates the causes of business cycles and whether monetary and fiscal policies can eliminate or moderate business cycle fluctuations

Business cycles are periodic fluctuations in economic activity. To describe a typical business cycle, we can start with its phase when economic activity is increasing. This upturn/expansion in economic activity culminates in a peak. The peak is followed by a downturn/contraction in economic activity. The downturn reaches a bottom, which is called the trough. The trough is a turning point for economic activity, which then starts a new upturn, which becomes the beginning of a new cycle. Therefore, the business cycle has four phases: *upturn/expansion, peak, downturn/contraction*, and *trough*. Note that the description of the business cycle could have been given starting with any one of these phases. The peak and the trough are called the '*turning points*' of economic activity. The duration of a business cycle can be measured from one peak to the next one or from a trough to the next one.

Business cycles can be defined in two different ways:

1. They can be defined in terms of absolute movements in economic activity. To illustrate, under this definition, the downturn would be a decrease in output and employment.
2. For a growing economy, it can be defined as the movement around the trend level of economic activity. In this case, the downturn would be a decline in the growth rates of output and employment from their trend levels, even if there is no absolute decline in these variables.

Some economists choose the first one of these definitions, while others choose the second one, which seems to be more appropriate for a growing economy. Under this definition, the data would be detrended (i.e., the actual value of the variable less its trend value is used) to arrive at the cyclical changes in the variables.

Figure 16.1a illustrates the four *stylized* phases of a typical business cycle in a growing economy and Figure 16.1b illustrates the business cycle after the growth trend has been eliminated. Figures 16.1a and 16.1b use (real) output as the proxy for the economic activity and plot it on the vertical axis. Time is plotted on the horizontal axis. Figure 16.1a plots the value of output over time as *y*. Since output rises over time,

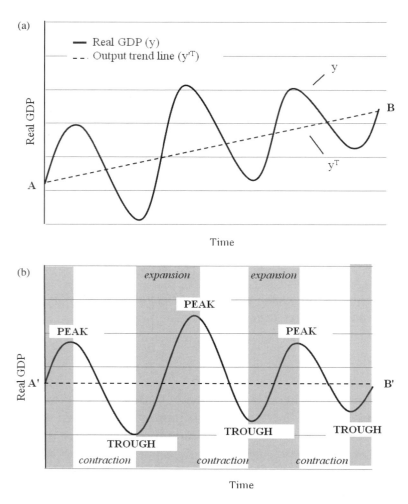

Figure 16.1

this figure shows an upward trend in y. While the plot for y shows that there are upward and downward deviations from this trend, the cyclical nature of these deviations is not fully clear. This nature becomes more readily apparent if the output data were detrended, i.e., the trend in output was eliminated, so that the output deviations were around the 'average' level of output.[1] This trend level of output, designated by y^T, is shown by the line AB in Figure 16.1a. If the trend output level were subtracted from the original data, we would get output deviations around the zero level. The detrended data, i.e., for $(y - y^T)$, is indicated in Figure 16.1b by the line $A'B'$ and shows the output levels if there had been no growth of output. $A'B'$ shows more clearly the four phases of the cycle in output.

Cyclical fluctuations occur in a large number of economic variables. Economists therefore usually construct an *index of economic activity,* which is a weighted composite of a select group of economic variables. The cycle in an established Index of Economic Activity — usually compiled and published by an economic agency — is

---

[1]This average could be taken separately over each cycle or over a longer period. The method of detrending the data and whether the period for averaging should be the cycle or longer are discussed later in this chapter.

referred to as the *reference cycle*. The most important components of this index are real GDP, employment, and the unemployment rate.

Though there are different ways of empirically defining the onset of upturns and downturns, an oft-used empirical guidepost of a downturn is when there occur two consecutive quarters of decline in the reference index of economic activity. Requiring two consecutive quarters of decline to signal, a downturn is to guard against the possibility that the decline over one quarter was due to random, rather than cyclical, factors. While this reduces the chance of misidentifying a random decline as a cyclical one, it introduces a two-quarter lag into the identification of when the downturn does, in fact, start. This recognition lag has the effect of delaying the pursuit of policies to counter the economy's recessionary tendencies to at least two quarters.

Business cycles are a symptom of industrial economies. While purely agricultural economies do experience fluctuations in economic activity, these are tied to the state of the harvest — which depends on the weather conditions, etc. — and are not necessarily cyclical.

Variables that increase in the upturn of the reference cycle and decline in the downturn are said to be *procyclical*. Those which fall during the upturn and rise during the downturn are said to be *countercyclical*. Of the main variables of interest, output and employment are procyclical, while the unemployment rate is countercyclical.

16.1 Recessions and Booms in Economic Activity

Descriptions of the business cycle frequently use the terms 'boom' and 'recession'. A *boom* describes the state of the economy when economic activity is close to or above the trend[2] level of output. The *recession* describes the state of the economy when economic activity is significantly below the trend level.

In a typical business cycle, the upturn eventually leads to the boom and the downturn leads into the recession. Note that, under these definitions, the terms 'boom' and 'upturn' are not synonymous; neither are 'recession' and 'downturn'. In fact, given the definition of a recession as occurring when output is below its trend level, the recession will usually include the later part of the downturn, the trough and the early part of the upturn. Correspondingly, the boom will include the later part of the upturn, the peak, and the early part of the downturn. The dividing line between the recession and the boom will be set by when the economy crosses the trend line for output.

In order to empirically specify the periods during which the boom and the recession occur, we need to know the trend level of real GDP. The procedure for deriving it is explained later.

16.1.1 The popular statistical designation of a recession

As explained above, a recession can be defined as a decrease in output below its full-employment level. If this level has a trend, one measure of the economy being in a recession is that output is below its trend line. A more commonly used measure requires a fall in output from its preceding level. Since output fluctuates due to random factors, which could cause a temporary decrease in output when there is no fundamental cause for the fall, a popular practical definition of the start of a recession is when real GDP falls for two quarters.

---

[2]Note that the term 'trend' in the definitions of booms and recessions is sometimes replaced by the term 'full employment'. The relationship between trend and full employment output is discussed later.

However, if we look beyond just GDP data, a recession is really a self-reinforcing decline in overall economic activity, with falling output, consumer expenditures, factory orders, industrial production, employment, and other major indices of the performance of the economy, though without a decline in them being due to purely random causes that are likely to be reversed sooner or later. Often, the various indices begin to signal a decline in the performance of the economy at different times: for example, output may have declined for two quarters while employment is still expanding, and some other indices indicate a static (rather than declining or improving) economy.[3] There are no standard methods of combining the movements in the relevant indices to arrive at a clear indication of a recession, so that whether the economy has really entered a recession or not becomes a judgment call, so that there can be a great deal of uncertainty, and disputes, about when and if the economy has entered a recession.

16.1.2 Monetary and fiscal policies to combat a recession

There are two broad approaches on the issue of whether or not to actively use monetary and fiscal policies to fight a recession or moderate a boom. One of these is proposed by strict adherents of the modern classical school (see Chapter 11) who view fluctuations in economic activity over the business cycle as an essential part of a well-functioning economy, with aggregate demand not having a significant impact on the real variables of the economy. This view is embodied in the real business cycle theory, presented later in this chapter. However, few central bankers, governments, and economists view it as presenting the acceptable approach to the pursuit of monetary and fiscal policies.

The alternative approach to business cycles rests on the view that declines in aggregate demand can cause a recession and increases in it can cause booms in economic activity. Further, even if the initial cause is not a change in aggregate demand, an aggregate demand deficiency usually emerges in a recession, which prolongs and worsens the recession, and excess demand emerges in a boom, which prolongs and intensifies the boom. This approach is usually accompanied by the view that serious recessions and booms impose costs on the economy, e.g., recessions cause output and wage losses while booms increase the inflation rate. Under this approach to business cycles, the appropriate policy response is to smooth out cyclical activity by pursuing expansionary monetary and fiscal policies in recessions and restrictive ones in booms. Most central bankers, governments, and economists adopt this view. However, both monetary and fiscal policies are rough tools for managing the economy, with variable degrees of impact, as well as variable lags (which for monetary policy in developed countries often range from six months to two years) for full impact, so that this approach does not advocate '*fine-tuning*' the economy to the extent of trying to eliminate all fluctuations in it. This is neither feasible nor necessarily desirable. The following analysis expands on this approach.

If a recession is due to a deficiency of aggregate demand or a demand deficiency emerges during the recession, the demand deficiency can be corrected by expansionary monetary and fiscal policies. An expansionary monetary policy requires a reduction in interest rates and an increase in the money supply, which increase aggregate demand (see Chapters 5 and 6). Since most recessions have a demand deficiency, central

---

[3] Real GDP data also exclude price movements, so that nominal GDP is divided by the price level to compute real GDP. This can give an erroneous picture about the performance of an economy that is heavily dependent on exports. For an example, suppose that exports prices rise while the amount exported falls but by a smaller percentage. While real GDP will show a decline in economic activity (production), the nominal income from exports would rise, which would raise consumer expenditures, so that GDP and consumer expenditures would give different signals on whether economic activity has declined.

banks usually pursue expansionary monetary policies to fight the recession, as they did in the economic recession of 2007–2010. Such an automatic response is built into the Taylor rule (see Chapter 5) for setting the interest rates. Under this rule, the central bank's interest rate depends positively on the output gap (i.e., current output less the full-employment one) and the deviation of inflation from the central bank's target inflation rate.

An expansionary fiscal policy is defined as an increase in the fiscal deficit, which increases aggregate demand. The fiscal deficit acts as an automatic demand-stabilizer if, without a change in tax rates and government's spending policies, it generates a deficit in recessions and a surplus in business cycle booms. Setting tax rates and spending policies to arrive at a balanced budget over the business cycle as a whole, while producing fiscal deficits in recessions and surpluses in booms, can achieve this result. Such a budgetary policy produces what is known as a *cyclically adjusted balanced budget*. With given tax rates, as incomes fall in a recession, tax revenues fall. Further, certain kinds of expenditures, such as for unemployment insurance benefits and minimum income support programs, increase in recessions. With tax revenues falling while fiscal expenditures rise, the budget automatically goes into a deficit in a recession, while generating a surplus in booms, so that its movement tends to boost aggregate demand in recessions and reduce it in booms. Hence, such an approach to budgetary policy makes the budget an *automatic stabilizer*.

Note that each recession and boom has its own distinctive aspects, so that following a set rule for all recessions and booms may not be the best policy. Therefore, the monetary and fiscal authorities might and often do deviate from *a priori* rules: for example, by pursuing a more vigorous fiscal policy by lowering its tax rates and increasing its expenditures during what they perceive as an exceptionally deeper and longer-lasting recession. The recession in 2007–2008 in the U.S. economy provides an example of such aggressive pursuit of monetary and fiscal policies. Mild recessions are likely to evoke moderate expansionary policies, and very mild ones may not elicit any explicit policy response.

It should also be noted that monetary and fiscal policies, whether pursued together or independently, are not likely to totally prevent a recession or avoid a boom for the following reasons.

i. Information on the actual course of the economy becomes available with a lag, so that policies may not be pursued in time.
ii. There are further lags in the impact of policies on the economy.
iii. Monetary and fiscal policies tools may be inappropriate, such as for a recession caused by a negative supply shock to the economy, which occurs when there is a rise in oil and other resource prices.

Therefore, the best hope for monetary and fiscal policies is that they moderate the business cycle, even if they cannot eliminate it.

Fact Sheet 16.1: Output Gap in the United States, 1980–2008

In the USA, over the past 30 years, real GDP has followed a more or less consistent pattern of growth, as indicated by its trend line, but not without periods of boom and bust where GDP surpasses or falls short of the trend level. The output gap, calculated as actual output minus trend output, serves to capture this cyclicality. During the recession of the early 1990s, the output gap was negative. This was followed by the economic upturn of the late 1990s and the dotcom bust of the early 2000s. Finally, although an above-trend level of GDP was experienced from 2003 to 2007 and was reflected in a decreasing output

Fact Sheet 16.1: (*Continued*)

gap, the financial and economic crisis starting in 2007 led to a fall in GDP in late 2008, which increased the output gap.

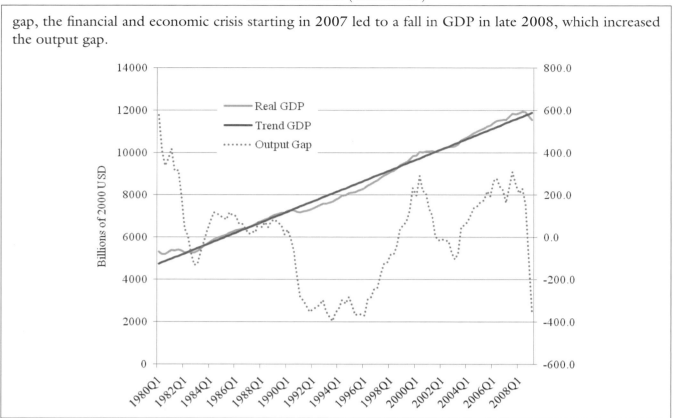

16.2 Business Cycles and the Growth Trend in Economic Activity

Virtually all economies go through periods of long-term growth in output and employment, so that there is a trend in economic activity. The shorter-term cyclical fluctuations in economic activity are superimposed on this trend. The pattern of cyclical fluctuations becomes clearer if the data are adjusted to eliminate its growth trend. Box 16.1 explains the procedures for detrending the data.

Box 16.1: Eliminating the Trend from the Data

Most time series of variables have a trend. Adjusting the original data on a variable to eliminate this trend clarifies the nature of the cyclical fluctuation in the variable. The first step in doing so requires calculation of the trend due to growth. The second step is to eliminate this trend from the data. The third step is to plot the adjusted data with time on the horizontal axis, and identify the four phases of the business cycle.

Deriving the trend rate of output

Economists use several different methods for calculating the trend level of output. One simple and fairly easy-to-use method is to use the simple average increase over a given number of quarters or over the cycle as the proxy for the trend. Doing so over the cycle means taking the difference between the amounts at two consecutive troughs (or peaks), dividing by the number of quarters between them, and then adding

Box 16.1: (*Continued*)

this amount quarter by quarter to the amount for the initial period.[4] The data thus derived can be used as the trend level of output. Subtracting the increases due to the trend from the original data gives the detrended (i.e., without a trend) output levels. Plotting this derived series would show the business cycle fluctuations around the average output level.

The unemployment rate as the proxy for the output gap

The variation of the unemployment rate around its trend can be used as a simple proxy for the output gap, which is the variation of output around its trend. Fact Sheet 10.4 in Chapter 10 has already shown both the trend unemployment rate for the USA and the variation around it, and can be reviewed at this point.

16.3 Stylized Facts of Business Cycles

The stylized facts (i.e., commonly observed patterns) on business cycles are

i. Business cycles are national — and in some cases, international — in scope.

ii. As mentioned above, there are four phases of the business cycle: boom, downturn, trough, and upturn.

iii. There is co-movement between pairs of variables, with some variables moving in the same direction while others move in an inverse one. To illustrate, output and employment usually move in the same direction over the business cycle, while output and unemployment tend to move in opposite directions.

iv. For a given variable, the general pattern of the movements is persistence since an increase is usually followed by a further increase (as happens during upturns) and a decline is usually followed by a further decline (as happens during downturns).[5] The exceptions to this pattern of persistence occur only at the two turning points (peaks and troughs). Persistence occurs during the downturns and the upturns.

v. Business cycles are recurrent (i.e., follow one another) but do not have an identical pattern over time. Different cycles tend to have different total durations, as well as different durations of upturns and downturns. Further, the amplitudes of the variables differ over different cycles. Therefore, each cycle is unique in some ways.

vi. Business cycles are different from seasonal fluctuations, which usually affect some industries but not all or most. The latter occur within a year. Business cycle movements are also different from short, erratic movements in variables in that the former span several years and are more widely diffused among the sectors of the economy.

vii. Downturns can be set off by a variety of causes, including negative demand (from a fall in investment, consumer expenditure, exports, decrease in the money supply, etc.) or supply shocks (a decrease in productivity, increase in prices of raw materials, decrease in the supply of credit, etc.).

viii. Compared with business cycles before 1939, cycles have become longer in duration, with longer expansions, though with shorter contractions. Before 1933, contractions were slightly shorter than expansions; after 1945, expansions have become about three times longer than contractions, which are on average now about one year. Recessions are now shorter and shallower than they used to be before 1933.

---

[4]Alternatively, the compound growth rate can be calculated over the given number of quarters and the data adjusted to remove this growth rate.

[5]Note that random fluctuations do not generally exhibit persistence in the above sense.

ix. Economic activity in agriculture, in terms of output and employment, is immune to business cycles, since it depends mainly on the weather. Most other industries participate in business cycle activity, with durable (consumer and producer) goods industries having much larger amplitudes than non-durable ones. Firms' inventories of finished goods rise in contractions and fall in upturns. Average labor productivity (i.e., output per hour of workers' time) rises in an upturn and declines in a downturn. This is explained by variations in the effort level of workers and labor hoarding by firms (see Okun's rule in Chapter 8).

x. Very severe and long-lasting recessions are called depressions. The Great Depression lasted from 1930 to 1939. It was truncated by the start of the World War II in 1939, but without the very large war expenditures would most probably have continued for many more years.

xi. Prior to 1950, prices often used to fall in contractions; since 1950, they rarely fall, but the rate of increase in prices (i.e., the inflation rate) tends to fall in downturns, so that there is often some disinflation without its becoming a fall in prices.

xii. Business cycle fluctuations in the USA, which is the largest economy in the world, are usually transmitted, often with a lag, to other countries through exports to the USA, which fall in contractions and rise in expansions. Cross-country effects also occur through international capital flows.

16.4 The Behavior of Variables Over the Business Cycle

16.4.1 Procyclical, acyclical, and countercyclical movements

Variables can be classified according to the direction of their movements. A variable is said to be *procyclical* if it increases in the upturns and declines in the downturns of the reference index of economic activity. Examples of procyclical variables are output, employment, interest rates, consumption, investment, stock market prices, etc. A given variable is said to be *countercyclical* if it decreases in the upturn and increases in the downturn of the index of economic activity. An example of a countercyclical variable is the unemployment rate. Certain other variables are *acyclical*, i.e., without a clear cyclical pattern. The real wage rate and the real interest rate tend to be acyclical over many business cycles.

16.4.2 Leading, lagging, and coincident variables

Variables can also be classified according to the timing of their changes. A variable is said to be *coincident* if the change in it occurs at the same time (whether pro-cyclically or counter-cyclically) as the change in the index of economic activity. Output, employment, unemployment, consumption, and investment are normally coincident. A variable is said to be *leading* if the change in it occurs somewhat earlier (whether pro-cyclically or counter-cyclically) than the change in the index of economic activity. Net exports, inventory investment, and stock market prices tend to be leading variables. Such variables are useful as indicators for predicting the future changes in the index of economic activity. In this role, they are known as *leading indicators*. A composite index based on such variables is the *Index of Leading Indicators*. This index turns down in advance of business cycle peaks and turns up before business cycle troughs, so that it is very useful for predicting the next turning point of economic activity in the economy. Finally, if the change in a variable occurs after the change in the index of economic activity, it is a *lagging variable*. The rate of inflation and the interest rate often fall into this category.

Consumer sentiment and business confidence, which reflect consumers' and firms' expectations of their future income and profitability, have a predominant leading pattern.

16.4.3 The volatility of variables over time

Variables can also be classified according to the degree of their volatility. Volatility is measured by the extent of their variance over time. Among the most volatile variables are inventory investment and the *rate of growth* of the money supply. Industrial production, net exports, unemployment, and interest rates are quite volatile but are not among the most volatile variables. Consumption, the productivity of labor and the inflation rate are even less volatile. To forecast the future course of the business cycle, economists pay close attention to changes in those variables that are both leading and highly volatile.

16.5 Business Cycles, the Full Employment Assumption and the Classical and Keynesian Paradigms

We have defined business cycles as fluctuations in economic activity (with output as the proxy) and, for empirical purposes, illustrated them by deviations around its trend level. What is the relationship between the trend level and the full-employment (long-run equilibrium) levels of economic activity? Macroeconomic theory provides three possibilities for this relationship. Using output or the unemployment rate as a shorthand measure of economic activity, these are:

1. The first approach to the relationship between the trend and full-employments level of output assumes that the actual level of output is *always* (and, therefore, in every period of time) the full-employment level. In this approach, the trend in output merely reflects (by assumption) the *time path of full-employment output*. Consequently, the deviations of actual output around its trend are not interpreted as deviations from the full-employment level, but rather as the deviation of full-employment output around its own trend. This case is shown in Figure 16.2a by the curve marked (y^f, y), since this approach assumes that y and y^f are identical.
2. The second approach to the relationship between the trend and full-employments level of output assumes that while the actual level of output does include deviations from the full employment level (so that y and y^f are not identical), full employment is maintained *on average over each* business cycle. Given the latter, the trend rate of output over *each* business cycle represents the growth of full-employment output.
3. The third approach to the relationship between the trend and full-employments level of output assumes that the full-employment is not necessarily maintained on average over each business cycle but *over a much longer period* (encompassing several business cycles) that approximates the duration of the analytical concept of the long run. In this case, the trend level of output over *each* business cycle does not represent the growth of full-employment output. In order to find the latter, the trend will need to be taken over the appropriate chronological period corresponding to the long run. Assuming that the total period shown in Figure 16.1a (presented earlier in this chapter) approximates the long run, the curve marked AB is the trend over the whole period and represents in this approach the path of full-employment output over time.

Figure 16.2b (also presented in Fact Sheet 10.4 of Chapter 10) uses unemployment (rather than output) as the proxy for economic activity and illustrates approaches 2 and 3 by actual data for the USA. Three business cycles are shown in this figure. Approach 2 to measuring full employment identifies its time path with the *trend line over each* business cycle, and is illustrated by the three dotted lines. Using this approach and comparing the three dotted lines, the full-employment rate of unemployment rose over the three successive cycles. Approach 3

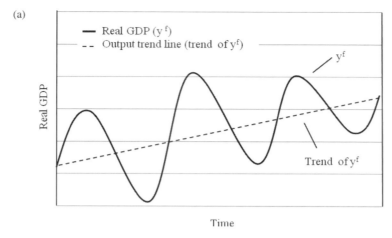

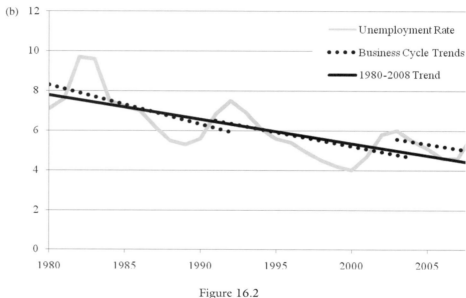

Figure 16.2

to measuring full employment identifies its time path with the *trend line over the whole period* (i.e., the long-run trend line), as illustrated by the darker solid line. Under this approach, actual unemployment was sometimes higher and sometimes lower than the long-run levels during the first two cycles but consistently higher in the third one.

To shed some factual light on this issue, let us consider the Great Depression through the 1930s. Unemployment throughout this decade in virtually all industrial economies was several times higher than in the preceding decade of the 1920s and the succeeding decades of the 1940s and 1950s. It is hard to believe that full employment existed on average over the 1930s or over any of its sub-periods, so that the trend line over the 1930s cannot plausibly be taken to represent the time path of full-employment output. But the economy of the 1950s and 1960s did well enough on average so as to be taken to have performed closer to the full-employment scenario, so that its trend line can more plausibly be taken to represent the time path of full-employment output. Consequently, we need to use intuition and general knowledge of the economy to decide which of the three approaches above is reasonable for the data period in question. Further, the trend of output over several business cycles and a really long period is more plausibly a better approximation to the time path of full-employment output than the trend over one business cycle. Hence, Approach 3 is the most plausible one in the light of actual experience.

The three approaches above lead to different theories of the business cycle. Approach 1 is the most consistent one with the real business cycle theory listed later in Section 16.7.1, which takes the view that business cycle fluctuations are fluctuations in full-employment output. Approach 3 is the most consistent one with the general business cycle $AD-AS$ theory listed in Section 16.6. Under this theory, actual output can differ from full-employment output, and the trend of output over any one business cycle is not necessarily the time path of long-run output. On the validity of the three approaches above and their related business cycle theories, our above indicated preference for Approach 3 on the basis of actual experience favors the general $AD-AS$ theory over the real business cycle theory.

Box 16.2: Business Cycles and The Assumption of Full Employment

The preceding discussion on the relationship between the trend of actual output and that of full-employment output raises several questions for theory and empirical analyses to answer. Among these are:

- Is full-employment output always reached in each period?
- If full employment does not exist in every period, is the trend in output (or economic activity) in the data *over a given business* cycle that of full-employment output?
- If full employment does not exist on average even over the business cycle, does it exist over a longer period?
- How is the full-employment level of output to be measured for actual economies? In what period or over what time span does it occur in an actual economy?
- Are the cyclical fluctuations ones in full-employment output or deviations from it?
- Are recessions really periods of output below its full-employment level? Are booms periods of output above its full-employment level?

Different answers to the above questions are given by different business cycle theories. These answers are not merely of academic interest. As will be shown later, they have strong implications for the pursuit of monetary and fiscal policies to moderate the business cycle fluctuations.

16.6 The General $AD-AS$ Theory of Business Cycles

The general $AD-AS$ theory claims that fluctuations in economic activity can occur through the economy's reactions to shocks initially coming from either the demand or the supply side of the economy, or both of them.

The impact of a positive demand shock raises the level of aggregate demand and shifts the AD curve to the right from AD_0 to AD_1, as shown in the $AD-AS$ Figure 16.3a. There are two distinct possibilities for the effects of this shift.

(i) The economy moves away from the $LRAS$ curve in the short run. To illustrate this case, suppose that, in response to the increase in demand, the economy moves from the point a to the point b along the $SRAS$ curve (see Chapter 8) in Figure 16.3a. In the short run, output increases, as does the price level. However, this is a temporary effect. In the long run, the economy reverts to the $LRAS$ curve, so that the economy goes from point b to the point c. Hence, output increases and then falls back to its initial level — thus exhibiting a cyclical pattern — while the price level continues to rise throughout.

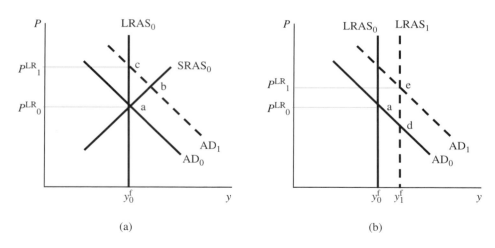

Figure 16.3

(ii) Even in the short run, the economy continuously retains full employment. In this case, as aggregate demand rises, the economy moves from point *a* along the vertical *LRAS* curve to point *c*, so that output does not change but only the price level rises (see Chapter 7).

The impact of a positive supply shock that raises the full-employment level of output and shifts the *LRAS* curve to the right from LAS_0 to LAS_1 is shown in the *AD–AS* Figure 16.3b. There are again two distinct possibilities.

(iii) Aggregate demand does not increase, so that the economy still maintains the AD_0 curve in Figure 16.3b. The economy moves from the point *a* on the old $LRAS_0$ and AD_0 curves to the point *d* on the new *LRAS* curve $LRAS_1$ and AD_0. Hence, output increases, while the price level falls.

(iv) The increase in aggregate supply, accompanied by an increase in aggregate employment and wages and a stock market boom, causes increases in investment and consumption (see Box 16.3). These result in an increase in aggregate demand, so that the economy shifts to a new AD_1 curve. In this case, the economy moves from the point a on the old $LRAS_0$ and AD_0 curves to the point *e* on the new curves $LRAS_1$ and AD_1. Hence, output increases, as does the price level. In the more general case, depending on the relative strengths of the supply and demand shifts, the price level may increase or may fall.

Therefore, in some cases, some kinds of positive demand shocks cause output to first rise and then to fall, while raising prices (cases [i] and [ii] above). Similarly, some kinds of negative demand shocks cause output to first fall and then to rise, while reducing the prices. This pattern is at least partly consistent with the positive relationship between output and prices/inflation over the business cycle. However, positive supply shocks cause output to rise consistently, while lowering prices/inflation (case [iii] above). Negative supply shocks cause output to fall, while raising prices/inflation. This pattern is not consistent with the positive comovement between output and prices/inflation over the business cycle, unless it is assumed that aggregate shocks cause aggregate demand shifts in the same direction (case [iv] above). This does occur in some cases of supply shocks (see Box 16.3 creating a stock market boom and increases in investment and consumption), but not necessarily in all cases.

In the general case, both supply and demand shocks are likely to hit the economy. Further, it is possible for a demand shock to create a supply shock, and vice versa. An illustration of this possibility is given in Box 16.3.

To conclude, the use of the *AD–AS* analysis indicates the possibility that economic fluctuations may be the result of supply shocks only, of demand shocks only or of a combination of demand and supply shocks. Further, the nature and intensity of the shocks of the different types, and of their mix, are likely to differ over different periods, so that each business cycle is likely to be unique in its causes, intensity and duration.

Note that the observed magnitudes of business cycles can be the cumulative effects of a series of small shocks with overlapping effects, so that a big shock is not needed for explaining the observed magnitudes of most business cycle fluctuations. Further, the economy adjusts slowly to shocks, so that the effects of shocks persist for some time, thereby accounting for the persistence of positive and negative movements in variables.

As against the preceding general *AD–AS* theory of business cycles, many economists favor a narrower view: some claim that only the shocks on the supply side of the economy are the relevant ones for explaining the business cycles, while others claim that only the shocks on the demand side of the economy are the relevant ones for explaining the business cycles. Their views are discussed in the following sections on the classical and Keynesian approaches to business cycles. Briefly, the proponents of the modern classical school tend to emphasize the supply shocks and shifts in the *LRAS* curve as the main cause of business cycles. Their views result in the real business cycle theory in Section 16.7.1. As against this supply-side approach, many Keynesians tend to emphasize the demand shocks and shifts in the *AD* curve as the main cause of business cycles. Their views are reflected in the multiplier-accelerator model of aggregate demand in Section 16.8.1.

Fact Sheet 16.2: The Structure of the *AD–AS* Model

The *AD–AS* model determines the interest rates and aggregate demand jointly by the interaction of the commodities and financial markets. The aggregate demand thus determined and the aggregate supply of commodities interact to determine the real income and output, and the price level.

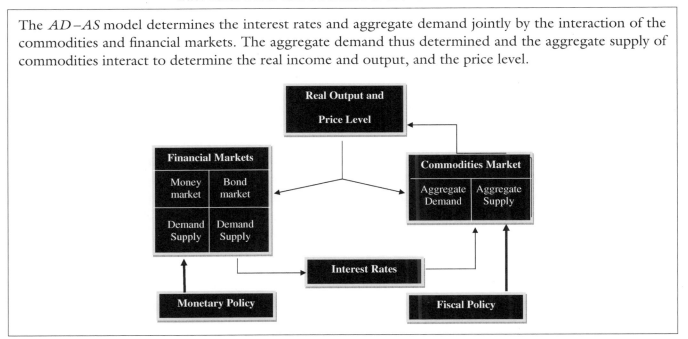

16.6.1 The propagation mechanism

The propagation mechanism is the name given to the manner in which shocks affect economic activity. To illustrate, an increase in investment by a given amount causes the nominal value of output to increase through the multiplier process, during which incomes and expenditures rise in a sequence. This process takes time, with the increase in nominal expenditures during a period followed by another, but smaller, increase in the next period. This pattern creates persistence, as in the cyclical upturn, of the change in expenditures, which, as was noted above, is a feature of business cycles. Further, the increases in expenditures diminish with each step of the multiplier, and eventually become insignificant. At some point during the multiplier process set off by the original positive shock to investment, other shocks also impact on aggregate expenditures. Some of these shocks have positive effects and buttress the ongoing increases in expenditures, while others have negative effects on expenditures. The cumulative effect of the numerous shocks may lengthen the duration of the increases in expenditures, thereby strengthening the persistence pattern, or, at some point, cause the expenditures to decline — thereby causing a downturn in expenditures. Because of the nature of the multiplier process, which embodies persistence, an initial rise (fall) in expenditures would be followed by a sequence of increases (declines) in expenditures, which are likely to cause persistent increases (declines) in output, i.e., a boom (downturn) in the economy.

Since the shocks tend to differ in magnitudes and sometimes in sign, the resulting pattern of economic activity will tend to differ among the cycles generated by them.

Box 16.3: An Illustration of Technical Change Creating Cycles through Aggregate Demand Shifts

Consider the innovations in the data processing and communications sectors in the 1980s and 1990s. These were clearly supply side shocks, which gradually moved the *LRAS* curve to the right.[6] But they also led to a mania in the stock markets, which multiplied the stocks of the companies in this field very many times, as well as leading to a general exuberance that lifted the stock prices of companies in many other fields. These stock market surges substantially increased the real wealth (i.e., nominal market values of assets divided by the price level of commodities) of households and led to increases in consumption. At the same time, they placed larger amounts of funds, through new stock offerings at grossly inflated prices, at the disposal of firms and created a substantial increase in investment expenditures.[7] These surges in investment and consumption expenditures translated into increases in aggregate demand. Thus, positive supply and demand increases became intertwined through the financial markets and were both essential to the proper explanation of the long upturn of the 1990s. In retrospect (from the perspective of 2003), for the study of the fluctuations in economic activity, it appears that while the technical innovations had initiated the shifts, the shift in aggregate supply was relatively much less significant than in aggregate demand. Once the euphoria over the profitability of the firms founded to implement the new technology started dissipating, the mania in their stocks collapsed in 2001, as did information technology investment, which led to a fall in aggregate demand. While innovations continued to occur after 1999, the fall in aggregate demand sent the economy into a downturn and then into the recession of 2001–2002. Therefore, somewhat surprisingly, the major impact of technology shocks on economic *fluctuations* seems to have occurred through aggregate demand fluctuations, rather than because of fluctuations in the rate of innovation and aggregate supply.

---

[6]They led to an upsurge in the rate of growth of total factor productivity, especially after 1995.

[7]Besides the heavy investment by the information technology corporations, which were the major beneficiaries of the stock market mania, there was also a widespread increase in information technology investment throughout the various sectors of the economy.

16.7 The Modern Classical Approach to Business Cycles

Two different approaches to business cycles emerge from the modern version of the classical paradigm, referred to as the modern classical approach in Chapter 11. These are:

i. The first approach to business cycles emanating from the classical paradigm uses the short-run macroeconomic model of Chapters 5 and 8, with the Friedman and Lucas supply rules to produce the impact of errors in price expectations on output. This approach allows the economy to move along the *SRAS* curve in the short run for *unanticipated* changes in aggregate demand or supply, while asserting the existence of full employment over the long run, whose length is taken to be the duration of the business cycle. This approach relies upon the Friedman and Lucas supply rules (see Chapter 8) to distinguish between the impact of anticipated and unanticipated changes in aggregate demand. The former do not cause deviations in output from the full-employment level. Unanticipated shifts in aggregate demand create errors in price expectations and cause deviations in output from the full-employment level. Similarly, unanticipated shifts in aggregate supply can create such deviations. These unanticipated shifts in either demand or supply set off deviations from the full-employment output level. However, since expectational errors are self-correcting, the deviations decrease over time and the economy reverts to the full-employment level.

ii. The second approach assumes that full employment is *continuously* maintained in the economy. That is, each period's output (level of economic activity) is the full-employment one.

For (ii), the classical approach is represented by the long-run equilibrium states of the *AD–AS* model. This representation ignores the transitory short-run states generated in response to errors in price expectations as being insignificant or not relevant, so that, in terms of the *AD–AS* diagram, the economy always operates on the vertical *LRAS* curve and never at other (non-*LRAS*) points on the positively sloping *SRAS* curve. Along the *LRAS* curve, the values of the real variables — such as output, employment, real interest rate, real wage rate, etc. — are independent of the level of aggregate demand (see Chapter 7). Therefore, the fluctuations or shocks to the demand-side variables (such as investment, consumption, money supply, etc.) do not cause cycles in real economic activity. Only shifts in the *LRAS* curve, i.e., in aggregate supply, can do so. A rightward shift of this curve creates an upturn, while a leftward shift creates a downturn.

The *LRAS* curve shifts in response to shifts in the supply structure of the economy. The two main sources of these shifts are those in labor supply and labor productivity. The latter occurs because of technical change (see Chapters 14 and 15) — which shifts the production function — and changes in the prices of raw materials (such as oil) and intermediate goods. Further, in this (second) classical approach to business cycles, since the economy continuously maintains full employment, shifts (whether anticipated or unanticipated) in aggregate demand do not make the economy change its level of output. Hence, according to this approach, the cyclical fluctuations in economic activity are to be solely explained by fluctuations of the *LRAS* curve, while shifts in the *AD* curve do not cause business cycle fluctuations.

The business cycle theory that embodies this (second) approach is called the real business cycle (RBC) theory, presented in the next section.

Note that under both of the classical approaches to business cycles, *anticipated* shifts in aggregate demand do not cause deviations of output from full employment,[8] so that they cannot be a source of business cycle fluctuations. The fundamental difference between these two business cycle approaches emanating from the

---

[8]See Chapter 8.

classical paradigm is whether the short-run deviations are significant or are so short-lived (until expectations adjust) that their importance can be discounted in explaining the recurrent cycles in economic activity. The first approach above allows a significant impact for a significant duration of time, while the second one denies such an impact. The policy implications of these two classical approaches are quite different. Under the second approach, there is no role — and, arguably, no need — for the demand-management monetary and fiscal policies, so that they should not be used in a futile attempt to moderate the business cycle. Under the first approach, there would be a role for such policies if the policy makers can anticipate the demand and supply shifts that the public cannot. That is, the monetary and fiscal policy makers can pursue policies to moderate the business cycle fluctuations if they possess 'superior information' (i.e., more than the public does), can act fast enough, and the policies have a fast enough impact.[9] If these conditions are not met, then the monetary and fiscal policies should not be pursued.

16.7.1 Real business cycle theory

The dominant classical approach to business cycles is the RBC model, which originated in the 1970s. It asserts that the economy operates continuously in long-run equilibrium — that is, along the vertical LRAS curve — and oscillates in response to real shocks. These shocks emanate from the production technology/function, the labor market or the commodity market,[10] but not from the money and bond markets.

The RBC theory attributes the most important cause of the real shocks to be shifts in the *production technology*, primarily due to the *uneven* (and *lumpy*) pace of technical change, or in the prices of critical ancillary inputs such as energy. These change labor productivity (i.e., the average product of labor). Most booms are due to positive productivity shocks, which shift the *LRAS* curve to the right and lead to higher output and employment. Recessions are usually due to unfavorable productivity shocks or increases in energy prices, which shift the *LRAS* curve to the left and reduce output and employment. Some presentations of the RBC models also include the effect of technological progress on investment and argue that since technological progress is uneven, it causes fluctuations in investment spending which cause fluctuations in aggregate demand. The shifts in technology increase labor productivity in the booms and reduce it in the recessions. Therefore, labor productivity is procyclical, as observed in the data.

Since real wages equal labor productivity, which rises in booms and falls in recessions, the RBC models also include the response of labor supply to the increase in real wages in booms and decline in recessions. Workers decide in recessions to cut back on their labor supply when real wages are lower and substitute more work for them during the following boom when real wages will be higher. As a consequence, unemployment rates will seem to be higher in recessions than in booms.

Some RBC models consider shifts in the *labor supply* curve between booms and recessions as another source of business fluctuations. Note that shifts in labor supply are also shifts in the real sector of the economy. An increase in the labor supply would produce a rightward shift of the *LRAS* curve and a decrease in labor supply would produce a leftward shift. Therefore, upturns can conceivably be explained as being due to a significant increase in workers' desire to work (i.e., a decrease in their demand for leisure). Conversely, a significant increase in the demand for leisure would cause a downturn. Therefore, economic cycles in employment and output would occur if there were significant fluctuations in workers' demand function for leisure. However, many economists doubt if there are significant cyclical fluctuations in the leisure demand function and discount the

---

[9]See Chapter 11 for this analysis.
[10]Including foreign trade.

empirical relevance of the actual shifts in labor supply as providing a satisfactory explanation of the observed magnitudes of the cycles in economic activity.

Real shocks can also arise in the commodity market, for instance, because of the volatility of investments and net exports, and changes in government expenditures and the fiscal deficit.[11] However, in the context of continuous long-run equilibrium, deficits and changes in investment and net exports cannot change the economy's output and employment,[12] which are major components of the index of economic activity. Further, shifts in monetary policy (i.e., in the money supply or central bank induced changes in the interest rate) only produce changes in prices and the nominal values of the variables, but do not change the output and other real variables.

Therefore, in the RBC theory, shifts in the *IS* curve and the *IRT* or *LM* curve due to exogenous shocks to the commodity,[13] money and bond markets are not considered to be relevant to the explanation of business cycle fluctuations. We have also discounted the empirical importance of shifts in the demand for leisure and, therefore, of the labor supply curve, as providing an adequate explanation of the observed business cycles. This leaves productivity shocks as the predominant exogenous source of the observed business cycle fluctuations in RBC theories.

The RBC theories explain especially well the following observed elements of business cycles in the economy.

i. Employment and its productivity are positively related and procyclical. In the RBC theories, both rise in response to positive productivity shocks and fall in response to negative ones.
ii. There is a high degree of positive correlation in the timing of the business cycle turning points, though with some leads and lags, among countries. In the RBC theory, productivity shocks are the main source of business cycles and tend to hit the industrialized countries at about the same time, thereby causing this correlation.
iii. The real wage rate is procyclical. Given profit maximization by firms, the wage is determined by the marginal productivity of labor. In the RBC theory, labor productivity is procyclical since cycles are caused by productivity shifts, and this produces the procyclical fluctuations in wages.

While the RBC theories can explain the above important characteristics of the observed business cycles, they do not satisfactorily explain several other characteristics. Among these are

i. The observed rate of inflation is procyclical: it increases in the booms and decreases in the recessions. According to the RBC theories, as the *LRAS* curve shifts to the right, output increases while the price level falls. Therefore, the prediction of the RBC theory is that the price level and the inflation rate would decrease as output rises in the booms, while the price level and inflation would increase in the recessions, in which output falls.[14] This is contrary to the observed pattern of inflation over business cycles.
ii. In recessions, unemployment rises due to a rise in layoffs while quits fall. This suggests that the number of jobs falls in the recession, with the result that some workers have been laid off by firms, even though they would have liked to stay employed. Further, the laid-off worker cannot find other jobs, since the number of jobs in the economy as a whole has fallen. Therefore, there exists involuntary unemployment

---

[11] Classical economists who believe in Ricardian equivalence (see Chapter 11) discount the importance of fiscal deficits in *shifting cycles in the shifts* of the IS curve and, therefore, creating fluctuations in real interest rates and other variables of the economy.
[12] As shown in Chapter 7, they only shift the interest rate in the long-run equilibrium but do not change output.
[13] The uneven changes in investment due to the uneven technological progress are endogenous, so that some RBC models encompass them.
[14] Note that under the *ceteris paribus* clause, the money supply is held constant.

in recessions.[15] But, according to the RBC theories, there is no involuntary unemployment at any time. The RBC theories explain the increase in unemployment in recessions as the result of an increase in the natural rate of unemployment: this rate rises because workers shift toward an increased preference for leisure or reflects a rise in voluntary unemployment at the lower marginal productivity and wage rates during the recession.[16] Many economists dispute this and instead claim that at least part of the observed unemployment in most recessions is involuntary unemployment, whether or not it occurs in other phases of the business cycle. The real business theories do not satisfactorily explain the rise in layoffs, the fall in quits, and the resulting increase in unemployment during recessions.

iii. Real business cycle theories fail to explain the recessions caused by a credit crisis or the bursting of a bubble in asset prices (see Chapter 2). They cannot explain the mid-1990s economic crises and recessions in many East Asian countries or that in the USA in 2007–2010. Clearly, no exogenous adverse shift in technology or in workers' preferences for work versus leisure occurred in these cases.

16.7.2 Policy implications of the RBC theories

Chapter 7 showed that monetary and fiscal policies could not change the real values of the variables in the long-run equilibrium of the *AD–AS* model. Since RBC theories assume that the economy always stays in long-run equilibrium (except possibly for very minor and transient departures), these theories imply that monetary and fiscal policies will not be effective in eliminating or moderating the cyclical fluctuations in the real variables such as output and employment. Therefore, according to the RBC theory, there is no justification for pursuing these policies to moderate the business cycles. Such policies could only change the inflation rate and the nominal, but not the real, values of the variables.

The underlying paradigm of the RBC theories is the classical one. As explained in Chapter 11, this paradigm asserts that the economy behaves optimally without interference by the government or the central bank. Consistent with this, the RBC theory claims that the economy handles disturbances in an optimal manner and does not recommend the pursuit of monetary and fiscal policies to moderate the business cycles. This is so even if unemployment rises substantially during a recession. However, few governments or the central banks are willing to following this policy recommendation during deep recessions. Nor did they do so in alleviating the worldwide recession that occurred in 2007–2010.

16.8 Keynesian Explanations of the Business Cycle

Keynesians tend to view the shifts in aggregate demand, rather than in aggregate supply, as the major initiator, though not the sole one, of business cycles. In fact, several components of aggregate demand are highly volatile. These include investment, exports, growth rates of money demand, supply, etc. Of these, investment depends on business confidence and the performance of stock markets, as does money demand. Even consumer expenditures are subject to volatility, since they depend on consumer confidence and household wealth (see Chapter 9), which includes financial assets such as bonds and stocks. The prices of these assets, determined

---

[15]A feature of such unemployment in recessions is that the layoffs of workers by firms rise, as do the number of workers on recall — and obviously willing to resume work as soon as the employer calls them back.

[16]If the increase in unemployment in recessions were due to an increase in voluntary unemployment only, then quits (by workers of jobs) should increase in the recessions. They do not do so. Rather, firms are reducing the number of jobs offered and lay off some workers.

in the bond and stock markets, are highly susceptible to rumours and bouts of confidence and pessimism.[17] Rapid surges in stock prices increase households' wealth, which increases consumer expenditures. Rapid falls in stock prices decrease consumer expenditures.

In the *AD–AS* diagram, since the economy does not respond to shocks in aggregate demand by instantly reverting to its long-run equilibrium, the volatility in the several major components of aggregate demand causes fluctuations in output.[18] The departures of output from its long-run full-employment level were explained in Chapter 8 as short-run (equilibrium) departures and in Chapter 9 as disequilibrium ones. Chapter 8 explained how fluctuations in aggregate demand produce short-run fluctuations in output and employment due to the possibility of errors in expectations (the Friedman and Lucas Supply rules), the costs of adjusting price (sticky price theory), and the costs of adjusting employment (implicit contract theory), Chapter 9 explained how fluctuations in aggregate demand produce fluctuations in output and employment due to the faster responses of firms and workers than markets to demand shifts, especially since they form expectations on sales and employment prospects.

When aggregate demand increases, the departures from full employment cause output to rise above its full-employment level, along with some rise in the price level or the inflation rate. When aggregate demand falls, output falls below this level, along with some fall in the price level or the inflation rate. Employment follows a similar pattern as output, while unemployment follows a contrary pattern. Further, since the economy will eventually adjust to its long-run equilibrium, the effects of any increase or decrease in demand will gradually peter out, thereby increasing the probability of a turning point.

If the shifts in the components of aggregate demand are themselves cyclical or if they are not cyclical but set off a cyclical response by the economy, the aggregate demand fluctuations will cause cycles in economic activity. In these cycles, output, employment, and inflation will be procyclical. Since inflation is procyclical in the observed business cycles, aggregate demand shifts offer a better explanation of the procyclicality of inflation than do aggregate supply shifts.

16.8.1   The multiplier-accelerator model of aggregate demand

While the initial shifts in aggregate demand can come from a variety of sources, some Keynesians choose to focus on the volatility of investment as the premier cause of these shifts. For this purpose, the changes in investment are modeled by replacing the static investment of the *IS* model of Chapters 4 to 6 by a dynamic one. The most favored dynamic investment equation is specified mathematically as

$$i_t = \kappa(y_{t+1} - y_t) \tag{16.1}$$

where *i* is the real investment,[19] *y* is the output, *t* refers to the current time period and κ (the Greek letter 'kappa') is a parameter. The justification for this investment function is that firms need an appropriate amount of capital to produce their desired output, which is determined by the expected future demand for their products. If the output needed to satisfy the future demand (i.e., in the following period *t* + 1) rises, firms have to invest

---

[17]John Maynard Keynes referred to these psychological factors as 'animal spirits'. Alan Greenspan, Chairman of the U.S. Federal Reserve System at the time of the stock (especially of dot.com companies) mania of the late 1990s, referred to the rapid multiple increases in the prices of Internet, computer, and other communication stocks, as 'irrational exuberance'.

[18]Remember that for the Keynesians, both anticipated and unanticipated increases in aggregate demand would increase output, and vice versa (see Chapter 11).

[19]This investment is in addition to that required for the maintenance of the existing capital stock.

in the current period in order to increase their capital.[20] In the above equation, κ represents the increase in investment (in addition to that needed to make up for depreciation of the existing capital stock) due to a unit increase in the desired output. The value of κ is positive and is less than one. This dynamic investment function is known as the 'accelerator'. Combined with the multiplier explained in Chapters 4 and 5, the resulting model is known as the multiplier–accelerator model of aggregate demand.

The general form of relationship between aggregate demand and investment was derived in Chapters 4 and 5 as:

$$y_t^d = \alpha \cdot i_t,$$

where α is the multiplier whose value depends on the marginal propensity to consume, the tax rate, and the marginal propensity to import (see Chapter 5). The value of α normally exceeds unity. This equation implies that

$$\Delta Y_t^d = \alpha \cdot \Delta I_t, \tag{16.2}$$

where we have switched to nominal values of aggregate demand and investment by multiplying both sides of the equation by the price level P, and stated the relationship in terms of changes in the variables. This equation states that the change in nominal aggregate demand equals the multiplier α times the change in nominal investment. Since ΔY_t^d equals $(Y_{t+1}^d - Y_t^d)$, the multiplier relationship becomes

$$Y_{t+1}^d - Y_t^d = \alpha \cdot \Delta I_t.$$

We can now see the link between the accelerator and the multiplier equations. If the desired output increases due to a shock or growth of the economy, the accelerator will induce firms to incur a positive level of net (i.e., in addition to that required to cover depreciation of the existing capital stock) investment. The multiplier will use this induced increase in investment to increase nominal aggregate demand, which increases the desired value of output, so that the accelerator further increases desired investment, and the process continues on.

To incorporate other sources of the volatility of expenditures, the preceding multiplier–accelerator model can be easily extended to include the sources of volatility of exports, consumption, and other components of aggregate demand. To see the simple intuitive working of the multiplier–accelerator model as specified above, we need to start with a shock to the desired level of output. This can come from a positive shock to one of the components (such as to investment, exports, consumption, money demand or supply, etc.) of aggregate demand or to an increase in the output (due to a fall in their cost of production) that firms wish to supply. To accommodate this increase in the desired output level, firms need to build up their capital stock, which causes an increase in their investment. For the given increase in the desired output, the increase in investment is determined by the accelerator function. This increase in investment will expand aggregate demand by a multiple, as specified by the multiplier.

16.8.2 Limitations of the validity of the multiplier–accelerator model

Note that the multiplier–accelerator model will give us the fluctuations in aggregate demand. They cannot become corresponding fluctuation in aggregate supply. Since the determination of actual output requires the behavior of both demand and supply factors, we need to specify an aggregate supply model in order to translate aggregate demand fluctuations into output fluctuations. The early expositions by Keynesians of the

---

[20]The interest rate can be introduced into this investment function, so that changes in the interest rate will modify the time path of investment.

multiplier–accelerator model unrealistically assumed an infinitely elastic supply of output such as might possibly exist when the economy is in a deep recession. However, any such assumption is not valid for most stages of the economy.

Therefore, we need to add at this point several considerations that are often left out of the simple multiplier–accelerator models.

- One of these considerations is that, in most stages of the economy, any increase in aggregate demand is likely to be split between some increase in output and some increase in the price level. The proportion by which each increases will depend on whether the economy is below or above its full-employment level, and how far away it is from this level.
- The second consideration relates to the functioning of the financial markets, which affect the financing of new investment, exports and imports, durable consumer goods, etc. Poorly developed financial markets, as in the developing economies, or investor pessimism, which sometimes occurs even in financially developed markets, do not allow borrowers to raise at a reasonable or acceptable cost the capital needed for new investment or other expenditures, and will reduce the value of the coefficient κ in the accelerator.
- A third consideration is the extent to which the investment is incurred on domestically produced versus imported capital equipment. For example, if all of the investment expenditure were on machines produced abroad, as happens in many developing economies, the accelerator would produce a quite limited impact on the domestic economy. Rather, its main impact would be on aggregate demand in foreign economies. A similar consideration applies to consumption expenditures. If these are mainly on imported goods, the multiplier would be smaller than if they were on domestically produced ones.

Extended Analysis Box 16.1: A Taxonomy of the General Reasons for the Occurrence of Business Cycles

Business cycles can be viewed as the result of interaction between the structure of the economy and shocks — that is, exogenous shifts — hitting the economy. Therefore, at a very general level, we need to understand the nature of the economy and the nature of the shocks.

In order to explain why the observed economic activity is cyclical, the relevant nature of the economy can be classified into three extreme types as follows.

(A) The economy generates cycles, even in the absence of shocks, by virtue of its internal structure. An example of this would be ocean waves, whose height changes whether a ship passes by or not. However, shocks (such as the passage of ships) can accentuate these fluctuations.

(B) The economy is stable on its own, but responds to shocks in a cyclical manner, with the intensity of its response gradually decreasing, so that if the shocks stop occurring, the economy would sooner or later stop having cycles. Therefore, continual shocks are needed to generate a continuing series of cycles, but the shocks themselves need not be cyclical in nature. An intuitive example of this is a drum whose surface — and the resulting sound — vibrates in response to a hand hitting it. However, the vibrations gradually decrease and the drum surface becomes static — until the drummer starts playing again.

(C) The economy responds to shocks but without fluctuations, i.e., a single shock produces a shift in the values of the variables but without cyclical fluctuations in them. In this case, for the observed movements in economic activity to be cyclical, the shocks themselves have to be cyclical in nature.

Extended Analysis Box 16.1 (*Continued*)

The nature of the shocks can be of two types:

 (i) The shocks are random, or at least not cyclical.
(ii) The shocks are cyclical in nature.

Given these possible variations in the nature of the economy and the shocks hitting it, we need to know the nature of the economy, the nature and origins of shocks and how the economy responds to them. The *IS–LM/AD–AS* model studied in earlier chapters essentially represents a stable economy, which needs shocks to produce fluctuations. Therefore, an economy with this model will only produce cycles if the shocks are themselves cyclical in nature. Hence, this case belongs to categories (C) and (ii) above. However, it is unlikely that the shocks have a cyclical nature.

Keynesians economists claim that the economy is of type (B), while the shocks may be cyclical or not. The theoretical innovation often proposed for achieving such a structure of the economies modifies the static investment function[21] used in the *IS–LM* model to the dynamic accelerator one explained above. This accelerator is part of some of the Keynesian approaches to business cycles.

The RBC theories belong to category (B), while the individual shocks may be cyclical or not. In this approach, the economy itself is a stable one, so that the productivity shocks have to be cyclical in nature in order to generate business cycles.

Note that a common element of virtually all business cycle models is that time lags are introduced in the various functions. This is done to produce persistence in the direction of movement.

16.9 International Linkages Among National Business Cycles

Business cycle fluctuations in the industrialized open economies tend to occur at about the same time, though with some leads and lags. The major reasons for this positive correlation between cyclical fluctuations among countries are:

  i. Exports and imports link the commodity markets of countries. As economic activity rises in an economy, its imports tend to rise. This increases the exports of its trading partners, so that their aggregate demand also rises.
 ii. Shifts in technology occur because of inventions and innovations. Knowledge of these is communicated across countries in a variety of ways. One of these is just by observing and learning from the practices of other countries. Another is by multinational corporations with plants in several countries, or through technology transfer agreements.
iii. Capital by firms is raised on international capital markets, and the stock and bond markets of countries, especially developed ones, are closely linked. This creates a positive correlation in the ability of firms in different countries to raise funds for investment and in the cost of these funds.
 iv. Households invest in international capital markets to a considerable extent and the cross-country returns on their investments are positively correlated. This globalization of investments and the impact of wealth on consumption create a positive correlation between consumption expenditures among countries.

---

[21] This function was that investment depends only on the interest rate.

v. There is a high correlation between the monetary and fiscal approaches used by the policy makers in different countries. This is partly a result of the evolution of economic theory and its dissemination across the countries. In the past, periods of expansionary monetary and fiscal policies have coincided among countries, as have periods in which the policy makers pursued the objective of price stability.

Clearly, cyclical changes in the larger economies tend to exert greater impact on other countries than those of smaller countries. Since the world's largest economy is that of the USA, it seems that 'if the U.S. economy sneezes, the world economy catches a cold'.

16.9.1 A world business cycle

Since a great many of the world's larger economies tend to move in a similar cyclical pattern, there is empirical evidence of a world business cycle, which reflects many worldwide economic occurrences, especially connecting the more open, developed market-oriented economies. For these countries, these occurrences include the steady growth of the 1960s, the recessions of the mid-1970s, early 1980s, early 1990s and early 2000s, and the world recession of 2008–2010. The link among economies occurs through exports and imports, capital flows and consumer and business pessimism and optimism, which tend to be contagious across countries. The impact of large economies, especially that of the USA, which is the world's largest, on other countries is larger than of smaller ones. This was illustrated quite clearly in the world recession of 2008–2010, which started with insolvency problems in U.S. housing and its financial sector, and spread to other countries since the recession in the USA significantly reduced other countries' exports to the USA.

In addition to such common international experiences of cyclical activity, individual countries will also have country-specific elements. Such country-specific elements will be more dominant for the less open economies. Less developed economies often fall into this category. Hence, the economies of the more open and more developed market economies tend to respond more to the world business cycle than those of the less open or less developed economies.

16.10 Crises in Economic Activity

The phrase 'crisis in economic activity' refers to a sudden precipitous decline in economic activity, rather than the gradual and more limited decreases that occur at the start of the downturn of most business cycles. Such a crisis occurred in 1930 at the start of the Great Depression and in 2008 in the USA. The economies of several East Asian countries also went through a crisis in the mid-1990s, as illustrated from data for Malaysia and Thailand in the following Fact Sheet. Common elements of such crises are often a financial crisis, with several bank failures, decreases in the money supply and especially in credit extended by the financial sectors to firms and households, and exchange rate depreciations.

Fact Sheet 16.3: The Asian Crisis of the Mid-1990s

Following a period of high economic growth, Thailand and Malaysia as well as several other East-Asian countries, entered into a deep financial crisis. When high, unsustainable asset prices fell and borrowers started defaulting on their debt payments, a mass pull-out of lenders occurred, which created a massive credit crunch. The massive withdrawal of foreign investments in the countries created large deficits in capital inflows and the balance of payments, and resulted in rapid exchange rate depreciations. To stimulate domestic investment and consumption, and through them, aggregate demand, countries lowered interest

Fact Sheet 16.3: (*Continued*)

rates, but, given the prevailing degree of pessimism, did not succeed fast enough in restoring the investment and aggregate demand to their former levels. To stop the precipitous depreciation of their currencies, Thailand took large IMF loans and Malaysia pegged its exchange rate. All countries affected underwent widespread restructuring. Most of the East-Asian countries, including Thailand and Malaysia, eventually succeeded in stabilizing their exchange rates and economies by 2001, though the latter ending up with lower GDP growth rates.

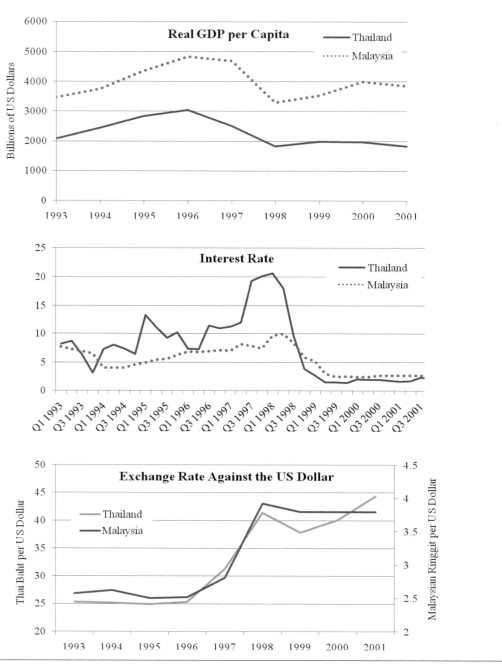

16.11 Long-Term Effects of Recessions and Booms

There is definitely a link from growth to business cycles. One of the major determinants of economic growth is technical change (see Chapters 14 and 15), whose variability over time is a major cause of the cyclical fluctuations in economic activity, as emphasized in the RBC theory. Conversely, the fluctuations over the business cycles can alter economic growth. This affect can occur for a variety of reasons, of which the most important are related to the accumulation of physical and human capital and their fixity. The impact of the shorter-term cyclical activity on the longer-term growth of the economy is an aspect of *hysteresis* — defined as the impact of short-term economic events on the long-term output levels. Some economists — especially among supporters of the classical paradigm — believe that such effects are insignificant enough to be ignored, while others — especially among the Keynesians — believe that drawn-out recessions and booms can affect the long-term output level and/or its growth rate. The factors that can cause hysteresis are discussed in the following.

16.11.1 The accumulation of human capital

Recessions are periods in which jobs are relatively scarce. There are two results of this scarcity: relatively more workers are unemployed and, of those who get jobs, many workers have to accept jobs that do not fully utilize their abilities and knowledge. The unemployed workers do not acquire the skills they would have acquired through on-the-job learning. Further, there is a deterioration of their prior skills through not getting the opportunity to use them. Among those who find jobs, the mismatched workers do not get to fully utilize their education and abilities, or learn the skills they would have acquired in more appropriate jobs. As a consequence, recessions leave behind relatively less human capital and some mismatch of workers and jobs. The mismatch of workers may not be fully corrected during the following boom because of the very long number of years in which workers usually stay in their jobs. If the recession was brief and mild, the subsequent correction is more likely to occur than if the recession was drawn out and deep. In the latter case, the future productivity of the affected workers would remain less because of the recession's reduction of human capital accumulation. However, note that this reduction may not significantly affect the future unemployment rate: as jobs increase after the end of the recession, the workers with the lessened skills do get employed, though in less skilled jobs than otherwise. Further, while the post-recession period will start with a smaller human capital base, the further growth of human capital (from this smaller base) need not be affected. This implies that while the smaller post-recession human capital will mean a lower post-recession starting base level for output per capita, the post-recession growth rate of output per capita need not be affected: the latter will depend upon technical change and capital accumulation in the post-recession period.

Long drawn-out booms in employment could have the opposite effect. Workers with somewhat inadequate skills or capabilities get employed and, through on-the-job learning and training, manage to acquire the skills they would otherwise not have had the opportunity to learn. Other workers get slotted into more skilled jobs than in the absence of the boom, and acquire higher levels of human capital. Therefore, the boom will leave behind higher skill levels in the economy and higher labor productivity. If this happens, the post-boom period will start with a higher base level of output per capita. However, this need not change the post-boom growth rate of output per capita.

Looking at the recessions and booms occurring in sequence, as they do, some of the affects of the recessions on the accumulation of human capital will be reversed by the following boom, and vice versa. But there may remain a net effect in either direction. The magnitude of this net effect is likely to depend on the severity and duration of the recession relative to the boom, and the adaptability of labor.

16.11.2 The accumulation of physical capital

Recessions reduce the level of investment and thereby reduce the accumulation of physical capital. Booms enhance the level of investment and thereby enhance the accumulation of physical capital. Therefore, comparing recessions with periods of normal economic activity, recessions leave behind comparatively lower physical capital per worker, so that output per worker is smaller than otherwise at the end of the recession. If, during the following boom, the firms do not make up for the recession's lower investment levels, the long-term capital/labor ratio will remain lower. If the firms do make up for the recession's lower investment levels, the effects of the recession on the capital/labor ratio will be eliminated. The latter scenario is the more likely one following most recessions,[22] so that, in general, the long-term ratio of physical capital to labor need not be reduced by recessions. Therefore, as far as the accumulation of physical capital is concerned, there should not, in general, be a long-term reduction in output per capita or in its growth rate.

Similar arguments apply to the impact of booms on investment, the capital/labor ratio and output per capita.

16.11.3 Technical change

Machines embody production techniques, just as workers embody human capital. However, there is an important difference between them. Firms acquire machines when needed. As firms build up their capital stock in the post-recession period, the new machines would embody the latest technology, which could be an improvement on the technology that would have been available in the preceding recession. Therefore, recessions do not cause less advanced technologies to be embodied in the capital carried over the long term.

As mentioned in Chapter 15, the early 20th century economist Joseph Schumpeter had taken a holistic, institutionalist approach to economic growth and business cycles. He had compared the evolution of firms over time to that of trees in a forest. He argued that recessions are periods in which the weakest firms — i.e., with older technology and less efficient — are driven out of business, thereby releasing their labor force. The boom brings in new and vigorous firms that possess a greater ability to innovate and adopt newer technology, and are able to use labor more efficiently. Therefore, the sequence of recessions and booms promotes technical change and the more efficient utilization of labor, and, therefore, brings about higher economic growth. Eliminating the recessions would eliminate the pruning of relatively inefficient firms from the economy, and would reduce economic growth.

16.11.4 The longer-term effects of cyclical fluctuations through aggregate demand

Now looking at the aggregate demand side, the recession would have reduced investment levels, which would have to correspondingly increase in the post-recession period. Therefore, the volatility of investment will be increased, as will be the amplitude of the fluctuations in aggregate demand. However, this effect will occur over the business cycle itself and need not carry over from one cycle to the next. Therefore, this is not a longer-term effect.

---

[22]The reason for this is that investment is the intended change in the desired capital stock. The desired capital stock depends on the expected demand for commodities. As this demand recovers in the post-recession period, the firms will increase the investment to build up their capital stock to its long-term desired level. However, this takes time, so that there would be some lingering effects until the capital stock reaches the desired level.

16.11.5 The longer-term impact of recessions and booms

The preceding arguments imply that there can be a longer-term impact of recessions and booms on labor productivity and the economy's output. This effect is likely to operate through the accumulation of human capital, rather than of physical capital or the technology embodied in physical capital. Further, this longer-term impact will be on the levels of labor productivity and the economy's output, rather than on their longer-term growth rates. While the unemployment rate will be temporarily higher (lower) than otherwise during the recession (boom), there may be no longer-term effects of the recession (boom) on the unemployment rate.

Empirical evidence does bear out these implications. According to one study,[23] on average, recessions shift the economy's output to a base level lower by as much as 75% of the decline in output during the recessions. However, the longer-term growth rate of output is not affected by the recessions.

16.11.6 The implications of hysteresis for policy

The above empirical findings provide a *prima facie* case for policy makers to attempt to moderate the recessions. However, the success of such attempts depends on the cause of the business cycles and the lags in the economy. Further, whether or not the policy makers choose to pursue any stabilization policies depends on whether they believe in the Keynesian or the classical paradigm.

If the business cycles are due to shocks to aggregate demand, the above empirical findings and Keynesian theoretical analysis provides, in the general case, support for the pursuit of monetary and fiscal policies to moderate recessions by stabilizing aggregate demand. Looking through the perspective of the classical paradigm, even if the business cycles were to be the result of shocks to aggregate demand, their pursuit would not be consistent with the general advocacy by the classical paradigm that the policy makers should leave the economy alone. Further, according to this paradigm, only unanticipated demand shocks can cause changes in real economic activity, and policy makers can only offset such shocks if they can anticipate these shocks but the public cannot. Furthermore, in the dominant classical approach to business cycles — the RBC theory — recessions are an appropriate and optimal response of the economy to productivity shocks and monetary and fiscal policies would not be effective in moderating the recessions. While Schumpeter's trees-in-a-forest approach to cycles is not a part of the classical paradigm, its emphasis is also on technical change. It implies that recessions, at least up to a certain duration and intensity, serve the useful purpose of getting rid of firms that are not efficient enough, and promote more rapid innovation in the economy. Eliminating the recessions would be detrimental to economic growth and should not be attempted. Therefore, the classical paradigm and Schumpeter's analysis would not, in general, advocate the pursuit of monetary and fiscal policies to moderate the recessions and booms.

Leaving aside the confines of the paradigms, the pragmatic conclusion on this issue has to be based on the proposition that policy makers should attempt to stabilize the aggregate demand if doing so would moderate business cycles, but not do so if it will not. This is more likely to occur if the recessions are due to an aggregate demand deficiency or if this deficiency emerges during the recession and makes it worse. Conversely, if the (negative) shifts in aggregate supply are the cause of the recession and/or if no demand deficiency emerges during the period, the conclusion has to be that monetary and fiscal policies would not be advisable.[24]

---

[23]Charles Nelson and Charles Plosser. "Trends and random walks in macroeconomic time series: some evidence and implications". *Journal of Monetary Economics*, September 1982.
[24]If they are pursued, there could be benefits but also costs, but the net benefit is more likely to be negative.

16.12 Money, Credit and Business Cycles

16.12.1 Money supply and business cycles

The relationship between monetary policy and the output of commodities has been extensively discussed in many of the earlier chapters, especially Chapters 5–9. Shifts in the money supply, either because of shocks or the pursuit of monetary policy, change aggregate demand in the same direction. The classical and Keynesian paradigms propose two quite different approaches to the impact of this change in demand on real output and other components of real economic activity. In the classical paradigm, only the unanticipated shifts in aggregate demand — and, therefore, only unanticipated shifts in the money supply — can alter real economic activity. Hence, unanticipated shifts in the money supply can conceivably produce cyclical real economic activity, while the anticipated shifts in the money supply cannot do so[25] (see Chapters 7 and 8). In the Keynesian paradigm, both anticipated and unanticipated shifts in the money supply can alter aggregate demand and real economic activity, so that both types of shifts can be a source of cycles in real economic activity.

Empirical evidence has not been able to reject definitely either of these views. Some cycles, or parts of them, produce clear evidence in support of the classical paradigm's views, while other cycles provide clear evidence in support of the Keynesian views. However, empirical studies do show (though not always) that over many business cycles:

- There is a positive relationship between the monetary aggregate and economic activity. Further, changes in the monetary aggregates in general precede changes in economic activity (employment, both nominal and real output, etc.), so that the former appear to have caused the latter.[26]
- The relationship between the monetary aggregates and nominal output is one of the more stable ones among macroeconomic variables.
- The shifts in money supply — or money demand — can and sometimes do occur independently of prior changes in real economic activity.

These empirical observations support the Keynesian contention that the monetary sector has been a major initiator and contributor to the observed business cycles. But the contention between the Keynesian and the classical schools remains on the question of whether it is all of the change in the money supply or only its unanticipated part that causes the subsequent change in real economic activity.

16.12.2 Credit and business cycles

Firms need funds to finance their purchases of factors of production, such as physical, capital, and labor. Some of these funds come from their own savings and retained earnings (undistributed profits out of past profits) and the rest from external sources. The latter include share issues, bond issues, and loans. Financial markets and institutions are a major source of the funds obtained through these channels. Some of the funds are long term, e.g., when they are raised through shares and long term bonds, and some are short term, as and when they are raised through short-term bonds and loans. Firms especially rely on short-term sources of funds for the working capital needed to pay their workers and finance their holdings of inventories. While funds thus

---

[25]In the classical paradigm, anticipated money supply changes are 'neutral' in their impact on the long-run equilibrium values of the real variables. This proposition was discussed in Chapters 8 and 11 under the concept of the neutrality of money.

[26]Conversely, this implies that the changes in output and employment are not the cause of *all* of the changes in the monetary aggregates.

obtained are short term, there is continuous replenishment of such funds through reissues of short-term bonds or renewal of loans in normal conditions in the financial markets. Firms can economise on their need for short-term working capital to some extent by arranging trade credit, e.g., 30- to 90-day loans from manufacturers to wholesalers and from wholesalers to retailers. The short-term sources of funds, including trade credit, are grouped in one category as 'credit'.

Well-functioning financial and economic systems in normal times allow continuous roll-over of short-term bonds and loans, so that firms' production plans do not have to be cut back because of a shortage of credit. A credit crisis is said to occur if firms cannot obtain their usual amounts of credit due to a shortage of funds or deterioration in their ability to repay the funds. On the side of the providers of funds, a credit crisis could be due to a failure of commercial banks, since they are the major source of loans to firms, and of investment banks, which hold large amounts of short-term bonds. These reduce the availability of credit in the economy. On the side of the borrowers of funds, a deterioration in economic conditions and a fall in the demand for firms' products reduces firms' sales revenues and profits, thereby reducing their ability to re-pay the funds in due time. This makes it more risky to lend to firms, so that lenders reduce the amount of credit provided to firms. The resulting decreases in the amount of working capital forces firms to cut back production, by reducing their orders for inventories, their employment, and even long-term investment. Similarly, cutbacks in credit to households, e.g., for purchases of houses through mortgages, cars and household appliances, etc., reduce the households' expenditures on durable goods and reduce overall consumption expenditures.

Hence, there are two effects of a crisis in credit markets. One is from the aggregate demand side of the economy: decreases (through the relevant multipliers) as a result of cutbacks in investment and consumption expenditures (see Chapters 4 and 5). Therefore, a credit crisis decreases aggregate demand in the economy which shifts the *AD* curve to the left in the *AD*–*AS* diagram. The other effect is directly on aggregate supply, which falls through the reduction in working capital and firms' employment of labor and other inputs. This shifts the actual (not the long-run one) aggregate supply curve *AS* to the left in the *AD*–*AS* diagram. The overall impact on output and employment is thus greater than if there was only a decline in aggregate demand (the case analyzed in Chapter 5) or in aggregate supply only (in Chapters 7–9).

A credit crisis also has an impact on the money supply. Banks hold the major part of the monetary base. Banks receive demand deposits from the public and, under the fractional reserve system that operates in virtually all countries, re-lend (though loans or purchases of short-term bonds) most of the deposited amount, which is re-deposited by the public in the banking system. This process creates demand deposits. The amount of demand deposits and therefore of the money supply (of which demand deposits are the main part of M1) created by the banks per dollar of the monetary base depends on what proportion of the deposits is re-lent as credit to the economy. The smaller the amount re-lent, the smaller is the money supply for a given monetary base. A credit crisis increases the riskiness of credit and also raises banks' degree of risk aversion (i.e., dislike of taking on risk), so that it reduces the amount re-lent for a given monetary base and reduces the money supply. Hence, all other things (especially the monetary base) being the same, a credit crisis brings about a very significant decline in the money supply, which, in turn, reduces the aggregate demand (see Chapter 6).

A credit crisis is associated with an increase in risk in lending. It also increases the risk in holding financial assets, which include equities, so that the demand for them tends to fall, and share prices to decline. The more severe instances of this appear as stock market crises. This reduces the wealth of households, which tends to produce the declines in consumption. A stock market crisis also makes it more difficult to raise new funds for investment in stock markets through the sale of new shares, and reduces firms' investment. The reductions in consumption and investment further reduce aggregate demand and economic activity.

The credit crisis, the money supply crisis, and the stock market crisis are elements of most financial crises, all of them collectively producing a much greater decline in economic activity than a single one of them would.

Therefore, the impact of a financial crisis on the economy occurs through many directions: decrease in investment and consumption, decrease in the money supply, and decrease in financial wealth. These together cause a decline in aggregate demand. The credit crisis also produces a decrease in aggregate supply. Hence, the impact of a financial crisis is likely to be quite severe. Consequently, the more severe economic crises, appearing as deep recessions or depressions, incorporate a deep financial crisis.

16.12.3 Economic crises

Economic crises occur periodically as an aspect of capitalism and free-market economies. A few of their common elements are

- Rapid increases in asset (shares, houses, etc.) in the period preceding the crisis, so that there is clearly a price bubble (i.e., price levels far above those justified by fundamental economic factors) in such prices. Herd mentality builds up expectations of further increases, thereby fuelling further increases in the demand for assets and their prices.
- Rapid increases in credit in the economy, often with the assets with bubbles in their prices being used as collateral for loans. These fuel investment, production, and consumption increases.
- Accommodative monetary policy with low interest rates and high growth rates of the monetary base and the money supply.
- The eventual bursting of the price bubble in asset prices. The fall in asset prices causes a banking and credit crisis, with reductions in credit, investment, consumption, production, and employment. There may also be a money supply decrease, which can occurs since banks increase the ratio of their reserves to loans and demand deposits, possibly augmented by some bank failures.
- Transmission of crises to other countries occurs internationally through reductions in imports and capital flows, as well as decreases in investor, business, and consumer confidence. The extent and speed of such transmission are greater from larger economies to their smaller trading countries, than the other way around.

16.12.4 Some instances of financial crises

We have discussed the East-Asian Crises of the late 1990s earlier in Fact Sheet 16.3. Hallmarks of these crises were a severe fall in asset prices, a credit squeeze, decreases in investment and aggregate demand causing a fall in output and rise in unemployment, and a foreign exchange crises (i.e., drastic decrease in the foreign exchange rates) as foreign capital left the countries. These features were shared by the financial and economic crisis in the USA in 2007–2010, except that the USA did not experience a foreign exchange crisis.

The financial crisis starting in the USA in 2007 started as a fall in asset (especially housing) prices, became a crisis of the financial system, which led to a credit crisis. It also included elements of a money supply crisis, in which banks' reluctance to provide credit meant that, while the central banks of many developed economies especially that of the USA, increased the monetary base very considerably (called quantitative easing), the private banks mainly increased their reserves. The result was a financial crisis, with a credit and a money supply crisis as elements. This crisis, through its impact on aggregate demand and supply, reduced output and employment, and sent the world economies into an economic recession, which started in 2008.

Financial crises are an inherent aspect of the private capitalist financial system based on trust among borrowers and lenders, and on the stability of the economy. Such crises have occurred numerous times in numerous countries. Besides the crisis of 2007–2010, originating in the USA and spreading to many other countries, examples of some other crises are Spain, starting in 1977; Norway, starting in 1987; Finland, starting in 1991; Sweden, starting in 1991; Japan, starting in 1992; United Kingdom, starting in 1974, 1991, 1995; USA, starting in 1984; and in several East-Asian countries in the mid-1990s.

16.13 The Relevance of Monetary and Fiscal Policies to Business Cycles

Can monetary policy be used to moderate the fluctuations in real economic activity? The answer to this question depends on whether the classical or the Keynesian theories are relevant to the actual situation in the economy. The different answers have already been discussed in a number of chapters, especially Chapters 10 and 11. Briefly, if the Keynesian views are relevant — as in a cycle due to aggregate demand shifts — monetary policies can moderate the cycle and should be pursued to stabilize the aggregate demand.

However, if the classical views are relevant *and* if the cycle is due to unanticipated shifts in aggregate demand, monetary policies can only successfully moderate the cycle, but under certain difficult-to-meet conditions, such as the central bank's superiority of information relative to that of the private sector, and sufficiently rapid and predictable impact of monetary policies, etc. If these conditions are not met, unanticipated changes induced by the central bank in the money supply could accentuate changes in economic activity in an undesired direction. Note that if the classical views are the relevant ones *and* if the cycle is due to the volatility of technology shifts or shifts in the prices of resources, then monetary policy would not be effective in moderating the cycle.

Hence, whether monetary policies should be pursued or not depends on the source of the particular cyclical fluctuation, the information at the disposal of the central bank and the public, and the relative speed of the impact of monetary policy — as knowledge of the economic theory that is really valid for the economy and the period in question. Further, whether it is actually pursued or not depends on the economic philosophy and beliefs of the monetary authorities.

Note also that most central banks often use changes in their discount/bank rate as their preferred instrument of monetary policy. These changes induce changes in both the economy's interest rates and in its monetary aggregates. All these changes collectively affect economic activity, so that the changes in the discount/bank rate become the central bank's instrument for its attempt to limit the business cycle fluctuations. Chapter 5 is the relevant one for further discussion of interest rates as the monetary policy instrument.

Fiscal policy and its effects on the economy were extensively discussed in Chapters 5–11. Briefly, the case for the pursuit of fiscal policy is very similar to that for the pursuit of monetary policy. However, there are some differences between the case for monetary policy and that for fiscal policy. One of these is related to the Ricardian equivalence hypothesis, which was briefly discussed in Chapter 11. Ricardian equivalence implies that private saving increases by the amount of the fiscal deficit, so that national saving and aggregate demand do not change as a result of the deficit. Therefore, if this hypothesis holds, fiscal policy cannot function as an instrument for stabilizing the business cycle fluctuations, even if monetary policy is effective in this role. Another difference between fiscal and monetary policies is related to their relative speeds of implementation and impact. The lag from the recognition of the need for policy and the implementation of the appropriate fiscal policy depends upon the political and administrative structures of the government of the country in question. This lag is usually much longer for the USA, with its strong division between the President and Congress but with joint control over the government's budget, than it is for most parliamentary systems, as in the UK and Canada. As a result, fiscal policy is usually not the policy instrument of choice for business cycle stabilization in the USA. Monetary policy has to play that role to a greater extent than in the parliamentary systems. The second lag that differs between fiscal and monetary policies is the impact one. This lag is likely to be shorter for fiscal deficits than for changes in the monetary aggregates since fiscal deficits directly increase the aggregate expenditures while the expansionary monetary policy has to first increase investment, which would then increase the aggregate expenditures.

Box 16.4: Anatomy of the Financial and Economic Crisis of 2007–2010 in the World Economy

The crisis of 2007–2010 starting in 2007 has already been discussed earlier in Section 16.12.1. Given its importance to the world economy, this box further elaborates on the information there. This crisis had two distinct phases. One of these was the initial period of financial crisis, starting in August 2007 and mainly confined in its early stage up to October 2008 to the U.S. financial sector. This crisis followed:

- A remarkable period of financial innovation, including new types of marketed credit instruments, leading to strong credit growth.
- Rapidly rising house prices. This increase was at least partly fuelled by remarkably easy access to mortgages, sometimes with mortgages exceeding the purchase price of the house and/or obtained by borrowers who did not have the income flows to meet the mortgage payments and relied on rapidly rising house prices to create positive equity value in the house. Such mortgages have a high risk of default and are called 'subprime'. Financial intermediaries securitized/bundled mortgages and sold short-term bonds (called structured mortgage instruments), interest on which was paid from the mortgage payments. The funds obtained from their sale allowed the issuers to increase the availability of mortgage funds, so that additional mortgages could be issued. This process and its repetition resulted in a substantial increase in credit in financial markets. Since the mortgaged-backed bonds were issued by extremely large financial institutions and were short term, they were viewed as riskless by the buyers. Since they offered a slightly yield than Treasury bills, they were bought by other financial institutions, pension funds, private individuals, and numerous other types of investors, both in the USA and in foreign countries, as a means of increasing the yield on their portfolios.
- The pre-2007 period was also characterized by financial euphoria or exuberance during which investors, including large financial firms themselves, did not look closely at the riskiness of their investments or chose to ignore the risk. There was therefore a speculative boom not only in houses but also in shares.
- Average house prices in the USA began to stabilize in 2006 and then fell in 2007. This led to many mortgagees defaulting on their mortgages payments, especially if the mortgage was sub-prime and beyond the income availability of the mortgagee to meet the mortgage payments. The rising defaults hurt the ability of the financial firms that had issued short-term mortgage-backed bonds to meet the interest payments on the bonds, putting the defaulting ones in danger of insolvency and bankruptcy. The number of investments firms thus affected included some of the largest and oldest ones in the USA, and put the USA financial system as a whole in crisis.
- The banking crisis led to a sharp decline in share prices on stock markets, both in the USA and other countries, leading to a major decrease in the net worth of households and firms.
- The policy response of the U.S. government to the potential or actual collapse of major financial firms was for the U.S. government and the Fed to rescue (bail out) some, though not all, of the investment houses in risk of bankruptcy by lending close to a trillion dollars to such institutions.
- By late 2008, the crisis in the financial system had led to the affected, as well as other, financial institutions to suspend or drastically reduce their credit to other financial firms, as well as to firms engaged in production and households. It also became difficult for firms to raise funds by the issue of bonds in the bond markets. Therefore, the financial crisis had created a credit crisis or crunch by the last quarter of 2008.

Box 16.4: (*Continued*)

- Firms use short-term credit in the form of loans, issue of short-term bonds and trade credit to finance their short-term working capital needs. The credit crisis drastically decreased the supply of credit and led firms to cut down their employment, and production and investment. It also led consumers to cut down their spending. These led to decreases in both aggregate demand and aggregate supply. The result was the evolution of the financial crisis into a broad-based economic one by late 2008. The U.S. economy and that of many other industrial economies entered a recession, with falling output and rising unemployment rates in the last quarter of 2008. Growth rates fell in late 2008 and continued to be negative through 2009 and early 2010 in most Western countries. While those of China and India remained positive, they declined significantly from the growth rates preceding 2007. While some countries began to experience increases in their GDP in 2009, many aspects of the worldwide recession continued into 2010.

The policy responses

- The fiscal policy response of the U.S. government was to increase its spending and deficits to an unprecedented extent, as well as to call on the governments of other countries to do so.
- The monetary policy response of the Fed was to reduce the Federal Funds discount rate in a series of steps until this rate was between 0% and 0.25%. The Fed also injected large increases in the monetary base through open market operations and also by encouraging commercial banks to borrow from it.
- Another policy action of the Fed and the government acting in concert was to rescue individual financial firms and provide loans or equity capital to other firms, such as General Motors.
- With the high degree of globalization of capital markets in the preceding decades, the financial crisis in the USA precipitated a financial crisis in many other countries, especially European ones. Further, with the increased globalization of international trade and production in the preceding decades, the U.S. economic crisis spread to other countries through cutbacks in imports by the USA and became a worldwide economic recession. There was a push by the USA and other countries for concerted international action by the major trading nations on rescuing the financial sectors and stimulating world aggregate demand.
- It was recognized that regulatory and market failures had led to the financial crisis. The overhaul of the regulatory framework of financial institutions is being planned and will inevitably lead to increased surveillance and regulation by the Fed, as by central banks in many other countries. It is quite likely that new regulations will require higher ratios of capital to liabilities, as well as limit risk-taking by financial intermediaries.

16.14 Inflation and Unemployment

Some booms produce relatively low unemployment and high inflation rates. This especially occurs during booms based on the expansion of aggregate demand due to money supply increases beyond the full capacity of the economy. If the inflation rate reaches undesirable levels, the public begins to demand its reduction. But, doing this through drastic reductions in the money supply has often forced the economy into a downturn and raised unemployment rates. Therefore, it is often asked whether the reduction in the inflation rate though contractionary policies, especially monetary ones, will necessarily cause a recession, with an increase in the unemployment rate.

The underlying analyses of the relationships between money supply reductions, inflation, and unemployment have been presented in several of the earlier chapters, with Chapter 10 being the most relevant one. Chapter 10 had presented the relevant analyses in general and in the context of the Phillips' curve (*PC*) and the Expectations Augmented Phillips' curve (*EAPC*).

The *EAPC* is based on the deviation of the actual unemployment rate from the natural rate due to errors in price expectations.[27] Its equation was

$$u_t^* = u_t^n + \alpha\left(\pi_t - \pi_t^e\right) \quad \alpha > 0, \tag{16.3}$$

where u^* is the short-run (*SR*) unemployment rate, u^n is the natural one (i.e., the long-run equilibrium one), π is the actual inflation rate and π^e is the expected one for the period. Starting from a situation in which the expected and actual inflation rates were identical, as were the actual and natural unemployment rates, the *EAPC* implies the following.

(a) If the policy-induced decrease in inflation is anticipated, the economy will continue to maintain the natural unemployment rate. Therefore, unemployment will not increase.

(b) If the policy-induced decrease in inflation is not anticipated, so that the actual inflation rate falls below the expected one, unemployment will rise above its natural rate in the short term (i.e., until expectations adjust). But only the unanticipated part of the decline in inflation will cause a rise in the inflation rate. Therefore, the best anti-inflationary policy will be one in which the central bank manages to convince the public of its lowered inflation targets. This implication has led some economists to claim that the resulting increase in the unemployment rate is really due to the failure of the central bank to adequately inform and convince the public of its lowered inflation targets.

(c) Stabilizing the inflation rate at the existing level, when inflation was expected to accelerate, would raise the unemployment rate.

(d) According to the *EAPC*, there is no cost in terms of output and unemployment of maintaining a high inflation rate as long as the actual and expected inflation rates are identical. However, Chapter 10 had pointed out that there would nevertheless be other costs, so that central banks often choose not to leave the economy with continuously high inflation rates.

Most economists believe that expectations adjust only gradually to a decline in the actual inflation rates, in which case the *EAPC's* implication is that unemployment will rise during the deflationary adjustment period.

Keynesians do not fully subscribe to the *EAPC*, which is based on the assumption of short-run equilibrium and errors in price expectations. In the Keynesian paradigm, reductions of the money supply and therefore, of aggregate demand, would send the economy into disequilibrium (see Chapter 9) and raise unemployment, irrespective of the relationship between the actual and expected inflation rates. This increase in unemployment is again a short-term one and occurs while the economy takes its time to reach the new long-run equilibrium.

Empirical experience has generally been that policy-induced reductions in the money supply, sufficient enough to significantly reduce the aggregate demand, do lower the economy's real output and raise its unemployment rate in the short term, but not necessarily in the long term. This has happened in countries with high credibility of the central bank's targets, as well as in countries where this credibility was low. It has especially happened in countries where there was a fast reduction in the money supply, though it has also tended to occur in countries that adopted gradual reductions. Therefore, reducing the inflation rate should normally be

---

[27] Its two forms were the Friedman and the Lucas supply rules.

expected to raise the unemployment rate in the short term. Stated differently, the reduction in the inflation rate will come at the cost of higher unemployment and lower levels of real economic activity in the short term. Hence, the policy makers have to make their decision after an evaluation of the relative costs and benefits of lower inflation and higher unemployment.

16.15 Conclusions

- Business cycles are periodic fluctuations in economic activity and are empirically measured by the movement of a composite index of economic activity. Business cycles are endemic to industrial economies.
- A cycle consists of a peak, downturn, trough, and an upturn. A recession is the part of the cycle when economic activity is below its trend level. A boom is the part when economic activity is above its trend level.
- Business cycles can result from the response of the economy to shocks to aggregate demand and/or to aggregate supply.
- The classical paradigm explains business cycles as representing the response of the economy in the short run to unanticipated demand shocks or to supply shocks. It emphasizes shocks to the real sectors of the economy as the main source of business cycles.
- The RBC theory focuses on fluctuations in labor productivity due to the variation over time in the occurrence of technical change as the major source of business cycle fluctuations.
- The Keynesian paradigm explains business cycles by aggregate demand shocks, including anticipated ones, and supply shocks, but emphasizes aggregate demand volatility as the dominant cause of business cycle fluctuations.
- The accelerator–multiplier model generates cyclical fluctuations in aggregate demand.
- Cyclical fluctuations in economic activity in open, industrialized economies are interrelated.
- Long and deep recessions have the potential of reducing the base level of output per capita for the future, while long booms have the potential of raising the base level of output per capita for the future.
- Economic crises are an inherent feature of capitalist free-market economies. They usually include or may originate with financial and credit crises.
- Deep and long-lasting recessions are called depressions.
- In a crisis, monetary and fiscal policies can be used to bolster aggregate demand and the availability of credit. The increasing integration (through exports and capital flows) of the economies of industrialized countries in the globalization process has speeded up and increasingly coordinated the transmission of crises and business cycles among the countries.

KEY CONCEPTS

Trend level of output versus
   full-employment output
   level
Peak, downturn, trough, upturn
Recession, boom

Procyclical and countercyclical
   variables
Index of economic activity
Index of leading indicators
Shocks

Credit crisis
Propagation mechanism
Real business cycle theory, and
Multiplier–accelerator model.

SUMMARY OF CRITICAL CONCLUSIONS

- In principle, the cyclical fluctuations in economic activity can be due to shocks to the demand side or the supply side of the economy. The shocks to aggregate demand can come from shocks to the commodity, money, or bond markets.
- Classical economists emphasize the shocks to the supply side from shifts in productivity or labor supply, or the short-run response of the supply structure, through the *SRAS* curve, to unanticipated shifts in aggregate demand.
- The RBC is part of the classical paradigm and emphasizes shifts in labor productivity coming from changes in technology as the predominant cause of the observed business cycles.
- Keynesian economists allow both shifts in aggregate supply and demand to initiate the cyclical fluctuations, but consider the latter to be dominant source of the observed business cycles. Further, both anticipated and unanticipated shocks to aggregate demand can initiate business cycles.
- Technology, capital markets, and trade links create positive comovements in cyclical activity among countries, though with some leads and lags.
- Recessions (booms) have the potential for leaving long-term reductions (increases) in the post-recession (boom) level of output per capita, but are less likely to affect its growth rate.
- A credit crisis can cause a reduction in both aggregate demand and aggregate supply, thereby resulting in a severe economic crisis.
- Globalization has speeded up and coordinated the transmission of crises and business cycle across countries.

REVIEW AND DISCUSSION QUESTIONS

1. Specify the four phases of business cycles and describe them.
2. What can cause business cycles in the *full-employment* (i.e., the long-run equilibrium) output level? Can cycles occur in the growth rate of output?
3. Show, using the *AD–AS* diagram, how changes in (a) the money supply (b) investment, might cause cycles in real output.
4. Show, using the *AD–AS* diagram, how changes in (a) the technology of production, (b) the demand for leisure, might cause changes in real output.
5. Explain the real business cycle theory and its policy implications for preventing or moderating the business cycles.
6. Explain the Keynesian approach to business cycles and its policy implications for preventing or moderating the business cycles.
7. Why do many economists believe that the real business cycle theory fails to adequately explain the recessions? What seems to be the main reason for this failure?
8. Explain the multiplier–accelerator model and show how shocks to investment can cause business cycles.
9. What causes the positive relationship in cyclical economic activity among countries?
10. Can recessions leave long-term economic effects? How, and of what kind? What is the name given to such effects? Define this term.

11. Discuss the role, if any, of monetary and fiscal policies in moderating the business cycles. If this is possible, should they do so?

12. What is a credit crisis and how can it cause an economic crisis?

ADVANCED AND TECHNICAL QUESTIONS

T1. 'Governments and central banks should not do anything to alleviate the rise in unemployment during recessions.' Discuss the alternative answers that different economic theories provide to this statement.

T2. 'Even if firms fail on a large scale due to a fall in aggregate demand during recessions, such failure is the mechanism by which the competitive functioning of the economy weeds out inefficient firms. The failing firms do not deserve to be bailed out. Productivity will be higher if such firms close down'. Discuss.

T3. Should large firms (e.g., General Motors and Chrysler in the automobile industry; AIG, Citigroup, Lehman Brothers, etc., in the financial industry of the USA) faced with heavy losses due to a drastic shift away in the demand for their particular models/products, poor management, management's failure to anticipate demand shifts, and/or excessive risk-taking, etc., be bailed out by massive government grants/aid/subsidies? Discuss.

T4. Discuss the role of innovations and inventions in increasing aggregate demand and causing stock market booms and crises. Are the latter an essential result of the former? If so, why?

Index